# Fifth Workshop on Arabic Natural Language Processing (WANLP 2020)

Held online due to COVID-19

Barcelona, Spain
12 December 2020

ISBN: 978-1-7138-2843-3

COLING 2020

# The Fifth Arabic Natural Language Processing Workshop
# WANLP 2020

## Proceedings of the Workshop

December 12, 2020
Barcelona, Spain (Online)

# Preface

Assalamu 3alaykum, e-greetings! Welcome to The Fifth Arabic Natural Language Processing Workshop (WANLP 2020) held jointly with COLING 2020 online.

This workshop aims at providing opportunities for researchers and engineers working on Arabic NLP to share and discuss their ongoing work. Similar to COLING 2020, we will not be traveling to Barcelona, Spain to attend the workshop. The location for this year is different than in the past; WANLP 2020 would be hosted online, a shift due to the unprecedented challenges caused by the COVID-19 virus. We want this workshop to offer a sign of inclusion for everyone around the globe to come share their knowledge and learn from each other, in a safe and welcoming environment. We will be attending online from anywhere in the world, including my living room. This is our first time having WANLP as a virtual workshop. This workshop is the fifth in a series, following the First workshop on Arabic NLP held at EMNLP 2014 in Doha, Qatar; the Second workshop on Arabic NLP held at ACL 2015 in Beijing, China; the Third workshop on Arabic NLP held at EACL 2017 in Valencia, Spain; and the Fourth workshop on Arabic NLP held at ACL 2019 in Florence, Italy.

We received 44 main workshop submissions, out of which 20 were accepted. Papers submitted to the main workshop were reviewed by at least three reviewers. This workshop also includes a shared task on Nuanced Arabic Dialect (NADI). NADI is the first shared task to target naturally-occurring fine-grained dialectal text at the sub-country level, as opposed to previous shared tasks that focused on regional level dialect labeling. The shared task is a success with 18 teams participating. The shared task system descriptions papers were reviewed by two reviewers each. They are included in the proceedings and will be presented during the workshop. A long paper describing the shared task is accepted as part of the main workshop. The selection process was competitive and we believe it resulted in a balanced and diverse program that is appealing to the audience. We observed a high quality of contributions that resulted in an acceptance rate of 45% in the main workshop. The higher number of submissions to the main workshop relative to previous instances and the success of the shared task are strong indicators that provide compelling evidence for the continued need for a dedicated Arabic NLP workshop.

We would like to thank everyone who submitted a paper to the workshop. We would also like to express our gratitude to the members of the Program Committee, who worked very hard to provide reviews supporting a tight schedule. Organizing WANLP 2020 is a team effort.

Imed Zitouni, General Chair, on behalf of the workshop organizers.


Website of the workshop: http://wanlp2020.arabic-nlp.net/

# Workshop Organizers

**General Chair:**

Imed Zitouni, Google, USA

**Program Chairs:**

Muhammad Abdul-Mageed, UBC, Canada
Houda Bouamor, Carnegie Mellon University in Qatar
Fethi Bougares, University of Le Mans, France
Mahmoud El-Haj, Lancaster University, England

**Publication Chair:**

Nadi Tomeh, LIPN, Université Sorbonne Paris Nord

**Publicity Chair:**

Wajdi Zaghouani, Hamad Bin Khalifa University, Qatar

**Advisory Committee:**

Muhammad Abdul-Mageed, UBC, Canada
Ahmed Ali, Qatar Computing Research Institute, Qatar
Hend Alkhalifa, King Saud University, Saudi Arabia
Houda Bouamor, Carnegie Mellon University in Qatar
Fethi Bougares, Le Mans University, France
Khalid Choukri, ELDA, European Language Resource Association, France
Kareem Darwish, Qatar Computing Research Institute, Qatar
Mona Diab, George Washington University, USA
Mahmoud El-Haj, Lancaster University, UK
Samhaa El-Beltagy, Nile University, Egypt
Wassim El-Hajj, American University of Beirut, Lebanon
Nizar Habash, New York University Abu Dhabi, UAE
Lamia Hadrich Belguith, University of Sfax, Tunisia
Hazem Hajj, American University of Beirut, Lebanon
Walid Magdy, University of Edinburgh, Scotland
Khaled Shaalan, The British University in Dubai, UAE
Kamel Smaili, University of Lorraine, France
Nadi Tomeh, Université Sorbonne Paris Nord, France
Wajdi Zaghouani, Hamad Bin Khalifa University, Qatar
Imed Zitouni, Google, USA

**Program Committee:**

Mourad Abbas, CRSTDLA, Algeria
Ahmed Abdelali, Qatar Computing Research Institute, HBKU, Qatar
Muhammad Abdul-Mageed, The University of British Columbia, Canada
Bayan Abu Shawar, Al Ain University, UAE

Wafia Adouane, University of Gothenburg, Sweden
Haithem Afli, Cork Institute of Technology, Ireland
Hussein Al-Natsheh, Mawdoo3 Limited, Jordan
Almoataz Al-Said, Cairo University, Egypt
Bashar Alhafni, New York University Abu Dhabi, UAE
Ahmed Ali, Qatar Computing Research Institute, HBKU, Qatar
Hend Alkhalifa, King Saud University, KSA
Chafik Aloulou, Univeristé de Sfax, Tunisia
Areeb Alowisheq, Imam University, KSA
Mohammed Attia, George Washington University
Gilbert Badaro, American University of Beirut, Lebanon
Riadh Belkebir, New York University Abu Dhabi, UAE
Houda Bouamor, Carnegie Mellon University in Qatar
Karim Bouzoubaa, Mohammad V University, Morocco
Shammur Chowdhury, Qatar Computing Research Institute, HBKU, Qatar
Kareem Darwish, Qatar Computing Research Institute, HBKU, Qatar
Mahmoud El Haj, Lancaster University, UK
Wassim El-Hajj, American University of Beirut, Lebanon
Shady Elbassuoni, American University of Beirut, Lebanon
Mariem Ellouze, University of Sfax, Tunisia
Tamer Elsayed, Qatar University, Qatar
Sahar Ghannay, LIUM Laboratory, France
Nada Ghneim, Higher Institute for Applied Sciences and Technology, Syria
Nizar Habash, New York University Abu Dhabi, UAE
Bassam Haddad, University of Petra, Jordan
Lamia Hadrich Belguith, University of Sfax, Tunisia
Hazem Hajj, American University of Beirut, Lebanon
Salima Harrat, École Normale Supérieure (Bouzaréah), Algeria
Maram Hasanain, Qatar University, Qatar
Go Inoue, New York University Abu Dhabi, UAE
Mustafa Jarrar, Bir Zeit University, Palestine
Ganesh Jawahar, The University of British Columbia, Canada
Salam Khalifa , New York University Abu Dhabi, UAE
Walid Magdy, University of Edinburgh, Scotland
Azzeddine Mazroui, University Mohamed I, Morocco
Seif Mechti, University of Sfax, Tunisia
Salima Medhaffar, Le Mans University, France
Karima Meftouh, Badji Mokhtar University, Algeria
Hamdy Mubarak, Qatar Computing Research Institute, HBKU, Qatar
El Moatez Billah Nagoudi, The University of British Columbia, Canada
Preslav Nakov, Qatar Computing Research Institute, HBKU, Qatar
Alexis Nasr, University of Marseille, France
Joshi Praveen, Cork Institute of Technology, Ireland
Younes Samih, Heinrich Heine Universität Düsseldorf, Germany
Khaled Shaalan, The British University in Dubai, UAE
Khaled Shaban, Qatar University, Qatar
Peter Sullivan Sullivan, The University of British Columbia, Canada
Reem Suwaileh, Qatar University, Qatar.
Nadi Tomeh, Université Sorbonne Paris Nord, France
Omar Trigui, University of Sousse, Tunisia

Wajdi Zaghouani, Hamad Bin Khalifa University, Qatar
Nasser Zalmout, Amazon Inc., USA
Taha Zerrouki, University of Bouira, Algeria
Chiyu Zhang, The University of British Columbia, Canada

**Invited Speaker:**

Perslav Nakov, Qatar Computing Research Institute, HBKU, Doha, Qatar

# Table of Contents


*German-Arabic Speech-to-Speech Translation for Psychiatric Diagnosis*
Juan Hussain, Mohammed Mediani, Moritz Behr, M. Amin Cheragui, Sebastian Stüker and Alexander Waibel . . . . . . . . . . . . . . . . . . . . . . . . . . . . . . . . . . . . . . . . . . . . . . . . . . . . . . . . . . . . . . . . . . . . . . . . . . 1

*Hate Speech Detection in Saudi Twittersphere: A Deep Learning Approach*
Raghad Alshaalan and Hend Al-Khalifa . . . . . . . . . . . . . . . . . . . . . . . . . . . . . . . . . . . . . . . . . . . 12

*Is it Great or Terrible? Preserving Sentiment in Neural Machine Translation of Arabic Reviews*
Hadeel Saadany and Constantin Orasan . . . . . . . . . . . . . . . . . . . . . . . . . . . . . . . . . . . . . . . . . . 24

*Deep Diacritization: Efficient Hierarchical Recurrence for Improved Arabic Diacritization*
Badr AlKhamissi, Muhammad ElNokrashy and Mohamed Gabr . . . . . . . . . . . . . . . . . . . . . . . . 38

*A Semi-Supervised BERT Approach for Arabic Named Entity Recognition*
Chadi Helwe, Ghassan Dib, Mohsen Shamas and Shady Elbassuoni . . . . . . . . . . . . . . . . . . . . 49

*Empathy-driven Arabic Conversational Chatbot*
Tarek Naous, Christian Hokayem and Hazem Hajj . . . . . . . . . . . . . . . . . . . . . . . . . . . . . . . . . 58

*Machine Generation and Detection of Arabic Manipulated and Fake News*
El Moatez Billah Nagoudi, AbdelRahim Elmadany, Muhammad Abdul-Mageed and Tariq Alhindi
69

*Transliteration of Judeo-Arabic Texts into Arabic Script Using Recurrent Neural Networks*
Ori Terner, Kfir Bar and Nachum Dershowitz . . . . . . . . . . . . . . . . . . . . . . . . . . . . . . . . . . . . . 85

*NADI 2020: The First Nuanced Arabic Dialect Identification Shared Task*
Muhammad Abdul-Mageed, Chiyu Zhang, Houda Bouamor and Nizar Habash . . . . . . . . . . . . . . 97

*Multi-dialect Arabic BERT for Country-level Dialect Identification*
Bashar Talafha, Mohammad Ali, Muhy Eddin Za'ter, Haitham Seelawi, Ibraheem Tuffaha, Mostafa Samir, Wael Farhan and Hussein Al-Natsheh . . . . . . . . . . . . . . . . . . . . . . . . . . . . . . . . . . . . . . . 111

*On the Importance of Tokenization in Arabic Embedding Models*
Mohamed Alkaoud and Mairaj Syed . . . . . . . . . . . . . . . . . . . . . . . . . . . . . . . . . . . . . . . . . . . 119

*Tracing Traditions: Automatic Extraction of Isnads from Classical Arabic Texts*
Ryan Muther and David Smith . . . . . . . . . . . . . . . . . . . . . . . . . . . . . . . . . . . . . . . . . . . . . . . . 130

*Embed More Ignore Less (EMIL): Exploiting Enriched Representations for Arabic NLP*
ahmed younes and Julie Weeds . . . . . . . . . . . . . . . . . . . . . . . . . . . . . . . . . . . . . . . . . . . . . . . 139

*MANorm: A Normalization Dictionary for Moroccan Arabic Dialect Written in Latin Script*
Randa Zarnoufi, Hamid Jaafar, Walid Bachri and Mounia Abik . . . . . . . . . . . . . . . . . . . . . . . 155

*A Unified Model for Arabizi Detection and Transliteration using Sequence-to-Sequence Models*
Ali Shazal, Aiza Usman and Nizar Habash . . . . . . . . . . . . . . . . . . . . . . . . . . . . . . . . . . . . . . 167

*Multi-Task Sequence Prediction For Tunisian Arabizi Multi-Level Annotation*
elisa gugliotta, Marco Dinarelli and Olivier Kraif . . . . . . . . . . . . . . . . . . . . . . . . . . . . . . . . . 178

*AraWEAT: Multidimensional Analysis of Biases in Arabic Word Embeddings*
Anne Lauscher, Rafik Takieddin, Simone Paolo Ponzetto and Goran Glavaš . . . . . . . . . . . . . . 192

*Parallel resources for Tunisian Arabic Dialect Translation*
Saméh Kchaou, Rahma Boujelbane and Lamia Hadrich-Belguith . . . . . . . . . . . . . . . . . . . . . . . . . . . . . . . . 200

*Bert Transformer model for Detecting Arabic GPT2 Auto-Generated Tweets*
Fouzi Harrag, Maria Dabbah, Kareem Darwish and Ahmed Abdelali . . . . . . . . . . . . . . . . . . . . . . . . . 207

*Contextual Embeddings for Arabic-English Code-Switched Data*
Caroline Sabty, Mohamed Islam and Slim Abdennadher . . . . . . . . . . . . . . . . . . . . . . . . . . . . . . . . . . . . 215

*Improving Arabic Text Categorization Using Transformer Training Diversification*
Shammur Absar Chowdhury, Ahmed Abdelali, Kareem Darwish, Jung Soon-Gyo, Joni Salminen
and Bernard J. Jansen . . . . . . . . . . . . . . . . . . . . . . . . . . . . . . . . . . . . . . . . . . . . . . . . . . . . . . . . . . . . . . . . . 226

*Team Alexa at NADI Shared Task*
mutaz younes, Nour Al-khdour and Mohammad AL-Smadi . . . . . . . . . . . . . . . . . . . . . . . . . . . . . . . 237

*Comparison between Voting Classifier and Deep Learning methods for Arabic Dialect Identification*
GHOUL dhaou and Gaël Lejeune . . . . . . . . . . . . . . . . . . . . . . . . . . . . . . . . . . . . . . . . . . . . . . . . . . . . . 243

*Simple vs Oversampling-based Classification Methods for Fine Grained Arabic Dialect Identification in
Twitter*
Mohamed Lichouri and Mourad Abbas . . . . . . . . . . . . . . . . . . . . . . . . . . . . . . . . . . . . . . . . . . . . . . . . . 250

*Semi-supervised Fine-grained Approach for Arabic dialect detection task*
Nitin Nikamanth Appiah Balaji and Bharathi B . . . . . . . . . . . . . . . . . . . . . . . . . . . . . . . . . . . . . . . . . . 257

*Arabic Dialect Identification Using BERT-Based Domain Adaptation*
Ahmad Beltagy, Abdelrahman Abouelenin and Omar ElSherief . . . . . . . . . . . . . . . . . . . . . . . . . . . 262

*Weighted combination of BERT and N-GRAM features for Nuanced Arabic Dialect Identification*
Abdellah El Mekki, Ahmed Alami, Hamza Alami, Ahmed Khoumsi and Ismail Berrada . . . . . . 268

*Arabic dialect identification: An Arabic-BERT model with data augmentation and ensembling strategy*
Kamel Gaanoun and Imade Benelallam . . . . . . . . . . . . . . . . . . . . . . . . . . . . . . . . . . . . . . . . . . . . . . . . 275

*Faheem at NADI shared task: Identifying the dialect of Arabic tweet*
Nouf AlShenaifi and Aqil Azmi . . . . . . . . . . . . . . . . . . . . . . . . . . . . . . . . . . . . . . . . . . . . . . . . . . . . . . . 282

*Identifying Nuanced Dialect for Arabic Tweets with Deep Learning and Reverse Translation Corpus
Extension System*
Rawan Tahssin, Youssef Kishk and Marwan Torki . . . . . . . . . . . . . . . . . . . . . . . . . . . . . . . . . . . . . . . 288

*The QMUL/HRBDT contribution to the NADI Arabic Dialect Identification Shared Task*
Abdulrahman Aloraini, Massimo Poesio and Ayman Alhelbawy . . . . . . . . . . . . . . . . . . . . . . . . . . . 295

*Arabic Dialects Identification for All Arabic countries*
Ahmed aliwy, Hawraa Taher and Zena AboAltaheen . . . . . . . . . . . . . . . . . . . . . . . . . . . . . . . . . . . . 302

*Arabic Dialect Identification Using BERT Fine-Tuning*
Moataz Mansour, Moustafa Tohamy, Zeyad Ezzat and Marwan Torki . . . . . . . . . . . . . . . . . . . . . 308

*LTG-ST at NADI Shared Task 1: Arabic Dialect Identification using a Stacking Classifier*
Samia Touileb . . . . . . . . . . . . . . . . . . . . . . . . . . . . . . . . . . . . . . . . . . . . . . . . . . . . . . . . . . . . . . . . . . . . . 313

# Conference Program

**Saturday December 12, 2020 - Time zone · Central European Time (CET)**

14:00–14:10    *Opening Remarks*
Imed Zitouni

14:10–15:00    *Keynote Speaker*
Perslav Nakov

**15:00–15:20**    ***Discussion: Arabic Language Technology Association***

**15:20–15:25**    ***Short Break***

**15:25–17:45**    **Session 1: Main Workshop Papers**

15:25–15:40    *German-Arabic Speech-to-Speech Translation for Psychiatric Diagnosis*
Juan Hussain, Mohammed Mediani, Moritz Behr, M. Amin Cheragui, Sebastian Stüker and Alexander Waibel

15:40–15:55    *Hate Speech Detection in Saudi Twittersphere: A Deep Learning Approach*
Raghad Alshaalan and Hend Al-Khalifa

15:55–16:10    *Is it Great or Terrible? Preserving Sentiment in Neural Machine Translation of Arabic Reviews*
Hadeel Saadany and Constantin Orasan

16:10–16:25    *Deep Diacritization: Efficient Hierarchical Recurrence for Improved Arabic Diacritization*
Badr AlKhamissi, Muhammad ElNokrashy and Mohamed Gabr

**16:25–16:45**    ***Break***

16:45–17:00    *A Semi-Supervised BERT Approach for Arabic Named Entity Recognition*
Chadi Helwe, Ghassan Dib, Mohsen Shamas and Shady Elbassuoni

17:00–17:15    *Empathy-driven Arabic Conversational Chatbot*
Tarek Naous, Christian Hokayem and Hazem Hajj

17:15–17:30    *Machine Generation and Detection of Arabic Manipulated and Fake News*
El Moatez Billah Nagoudi, AbdelRahim Elmadany, Muhammad Abdul-Mageed and
Tariq Alhindi

17:30–17:45    *Transliteration of Judeo-Arabic Texts into Arabic Script Using Recurrent Neural
Networks*
Ori Terner, Kfir Bar and Nachum Dershowitz

**17:45–18:15    Session 2: NADI Shared Task: Summary and Winner**

17:45–18:00    *NADI 2020: The First Nuanced Arabic Dialect Identification Shared Task*
Muhammad Abdul-Mageed, Chiyu Zhang, Houda Bouamor and Nizar Habash

18:00–18:15    *Multi-dialect Arabic BERT for Country-level Dialect Identification*
Bashar Talafha, Mohammad Ali, Muhy Eddin Za'ter, Haitham Seelawi, Ibraheem
Tuffaha, Mostafa Samir, Wael Farhan and Hussein Al-Natsheh

**18:15–18:20    *Short Break***

**18:20–18:53    Session 3: Main Workshop Poster Boasters**

18:20–18:23    *On the Importance of Tokenization in Arabic Embedding Models*
Mohamed Alkaoud and Mairaj Syed

18:23–18:26    *Tracing Traditions: Automatic Extraction of Isnads from Classical Arabic Texts*
Ryan Muther and David Smith

18:26–18:29    *Embed More Ignore Less (EMIL): Exploiting Enriched Representations for Arabic
NLP*
ahmed younes and Julie Weeds

18:29–18:32    *MANorm: A Normalization Dictionary for Moroccan Arabic Dialect Written in
Latin Script*
Randa Zarnoufi, Hamid Jaafar, Walid Bachri and Mounia Abik

18:32–18:35    *A Unified Model for Arabizi Detection and Transliteration using Sequence-to-
Sequence Models*
Ali Shazal, Aiza Usman and Nizar Habash

18:35–18:38     *Multi-Task Sequence Prediction For Tunisian Arabizi Multi-Level Annotation*
elisa gugliotta, Marco Dinarelli and Olivier Kraif

18:38–18:41     *AraWEAT: Multidimensional Analysis of Biases in Arabic Word Embeddings*
Anne Lauscher, Rafik Takieddin, Simone Paolo Ponzetto and Goran Glavaš

18:41–18:44     *Parallel resources for Tunisian Arabic Dialect Translation*
Saméh Kchaou, Rahma Boujelbane and Lamia Hadrich-Belguith

18:44–18:47     *Bert Transformer model for Detecting Arabic GPT2 Auto-Generated Tweets*
Fouzi Harrag, Maria Dabbah, Kareem Darwish and Ahmed Abdelali

18:47–18:50     *Contextual Embeddings for Arabic-English Code-Switched Data*
Caroline Sabty, Mohamed Islam and Slim Abdennadher

18:50–18:53     *Improving Arabic Text Categorization Using Transformer Training Diversification*
Shammur Absar Chowdhury, Ahmed Abdelali, Kareem Darwish, Jung Soon-Gyo,
Joni Salminen and Bernard J. Jansen

18:53–19:00     *Concluding Remakrs (Underline)*
Imed Zitouni


19:00–20:00     **Session 4: Main Workshop Posters and NADI Shared Task Papers**

        *Team Alexa at NADI Shared Task*
mutaz younes, Nour Al-khdour and Mohammad AL-Smadi

        *Comparison between Voting Classifier and Deep Learning methods for Arabic Dialect Identification*
GHOUL dhaou and Gaël Lejeune

        *Simple vs Oversampling-based Classification Methods for Fine Grained Arabic Dialect Identification in Twitter*
Mohamed Lichouri and Mourad Abbas

        *Semi-supervised Fine-grained Approach for Arabic dialect detection task*
Nitin Nikamanth Appiah Balaji and Bharathi B

*Arabic Dialect Identification Using BERT-Based Domain Adaptation*
Ahmad Beltagy, Abdelrahman Abouelenin and Omar ElSherief

*Weighted combination of BERT and N-GRAM features for Nuanced Arabic Dialect Identification*
Abdellah El Mekki, Ahmed Alami, Hamza Alami, Ahmed Khoumsi and Ismail Berrada

*Arabic dialect identification: An Arabic-BERT model with data augmentation and ensembling strategy*
Kamel Gaanoun and Imade Benelallam

*Faheem at NADI shared task: Identifying the dialect of Arabic tweet*
Nouf AlShenaifi and Aqil Azmi

*Identifying Nuanced Dialect for Arabic Tweets with Deep Learning and Reverse Translation Corpus Extension System*
Rawan Tahssin, Youssef Kishk and Marwan Torki

*The QMUL/HRBDT contribution to the NADI Arabic Dialect Identification Shared Task*
Abdulrahman Aloraini, Massimo Poesio and Ayman Alhelbawy

*Arabic Dialects Identification for All Arabic countries*
Ahmed aliwy, Hawraa Taher and Zena AboAltaheen

*Arabic Dialect Identification Using BERT Fine-Tuning*
Moataz Mansour, Moustafa Tohamy, Zeyad Ezzat and Marwan Torki

*LTG-ST at NADI Shared Task 1: Arabic Dialect Identification using a Stacking Classifier*
Samia Touileb

**20:00–21:00**  **Panel Discussion (Zoom)**

# German-Arabic Speech-to-Speech Translation for Psychiatric Diagnosis

**Juan Hussain, Mohammed Mediani, †Moritz Behr, Sebastian Stüker**
KIT - Karlsruhe Institute of Technology
`firstname.lastname@kit.edu`
`†uceul@student.kit.edu`

**M. Amin Cheragui**
University of Adrar
`m_cheragui@yahoo.fr`

**Alexander Waibel**
Carnegie Mellon University
`alexander.waibel@cmu.edu`

## Abstract

In this paper we present the Arabic related natural language processing components of our German–Arabic speech-to-speech translation system which is being deployed in the context of interpretation during psychiatric, diagnostic interviews. For this purpose we have built a pipe-lined speech-to-speech translation system consisting of automatic speech recognition, machine translation, text post-processing, and speech synthesis systems. We have implemented two pipelines, from German to Arabic and vice versa, to conduct interpreted two-way dialogues between psychiatrists and potential patients. All systems in our pipeline have been realized as all-neural end-to-end systems, using different architectures suitable for the different components. The speech recognition systems use an encoder/decoder + attention architecture, the machine translation system is based on the Transformer architecture, the post-processing for Arabic employs a sequence-tagger for diacritization, and for the speech synthesis systems we use Tacotron 2 for generating spectrograms and WaveGlow as a vocoder. The speech translation is deployed in a server-based speech translation application that implements a turn-based translation between a German-speaking psychiatrist administrating the Mini-International Neuropsychiatric Interview (M.I.N.I.) and an Arabic speaking person answering the interview. As this is a very specific domain, in addition to the linguistic challenges posed by translating between Arabic and German, we also focus in this paper on the methods we implemented for adapting our speech to speech translation system to the domain of this psychiatric interview.

## 1 Introduction

In psychiatry the Mini-International Neuropsychiatric Interview (M.I.N.I.) is a short structured diagnostic interview for psychiatric disorders (Sheehan et al., 1998). In Germany it is, among others, used for diagnosing Arabic speaking refugees. Here, the language barrier is an obvious one, that is normally overcome with the help of human interpreters. However, human interpreters are scarce, expensive and very often not readily available when an urgent diagnosis is needed. In the project *Removing language barriers in treating refugees—RELATER* we are therefore building a speech-to-speech translation (S2ST) system for interpreting between a German speaking psychiatrist and an Arabic speaker taking the M.I.N.I. interview.

The natural language processing (NLP) technology for this scenario faces two challenges: a) the general linguistic challenges when translating between German and Arabic and b) the specific domain of the interview for which only very little adaptation data is available.

In this paper, we describe the Arabic related NLP components with which we implemented the speech to speech translation between German and Arabic for the interview. These components are part of a server-based application, where the client application is capable of running on mobile platforms; whereas the components themselves run on remote powerful computation servers. The application realizes a turn-based interpretation system between the psychiatrist and the potential patient.

While end-to-end S2ST translation systems are the latest trend in research, for our system we opted for pipe-lined systems, because a) pipe-lined systems still outperform end-to-end systems (Ansari et al.,

---





*Proceedings of the Fifth Arabic Natural Language Processing Workshop*, pages 1–11
Barcelona, Spain (Online), December 12, 2020"""

2020), and b) to the best of our knowledge no suitable corpus for training German–Arabic end-to-end S2ST systems exists, for any domain.

All systems in our pipeline have been realized as all-neural end-to-end systems, using different architectures suitable for the different components. The speech recognition system uses an encoder/decoder + attention architecture (Nguyen et al., 2020b), the text segmentation component, and the machine translation are based on the Transformer architecture (Vaswani et al., 2017a), and for the speech synthesis we use Tacotron 2[1] (Shen et al., 2018) for generating spectrograms and WaveGlow as vocoder (Prenger et al., 2019).

The rest of the paper is structured as follows: Section 2 describes the Arabic speech recognition system in the pipeline, while section 3 describes the machine translation component and section 4 the Arabic speech synthesis system. As the the topic of diacritization is very prominent for Arabic NLP, we discuss the specific issues we faced in our S2ST system in section 5. In section 6, we study the real-time aspect of our pipeline system which is essential for the deployment.

## 2  Automatic Speech Recognition

For Automatic Speech Recognition (ASR), we employ an LSTM-based sequence to sequence (S2S) model with encoder/decoder + attention architecture. This model yields better performance compared to the self-attention S2S model with a comparable parameter size. Before the LSTM layers in the encoder, we place a two-layer Convolutional Neural Network (CNN) with 32 channels and a time stride of two to down-sample the input spectrogram by a factor of four. In the decoder, we adopt two layers of uni-directional LSTMs and the approach of Scaled Dot-Product (SDP) Attention to generate context vectors from the hidden states. More details about the models can be found in (Nguyen et al., 2020b). In section 2.1, we list the data used for the training, testing, and domain adaptation. For the latter, we use primary methods described in section 2.2. We report some implementation details and experimental results in section 2.3.

### 2.1  Data

We use the following data sets. For each data set we give a short name and the duration in hour (h) or in minutes (m):

- **Alj.1200h**: We use this set for the training or bootstrapping of our model. It consists of 1200 hours of broadcast videos recorded during 2005–2015 from the Aljazeera Arabic TV channel as described in (Ali et al., 2016). As reported, 70% of this set is in Modern Standard Arabic (MSA) and the rest is Dialectal Arabic (DA), such as Egyptian (EGY), Gulf (GLF), Levantine (LEV), and North African (NOR). The categories of the speech range from conversation (63%), interview (19%), to report (18%).

- **Alj.MSA+dialect.10h**: A test set of 10 hours described in (Ali et al., 2016) as well. It includes non-overlapped speech from Aljazeera, which was prepared according to (Ali et al., 2016) for an Arabic multi-dialect broadcast media recognition challenge. We use the set as it is without normalizing Alif, Hamza or any other characters.

- **Alj.MSA.2h**: This is a subset from Alj.MSA+dialect.10h where we cut only MSA utterances free from dialects from the beginning of the set until we reached the duration of 2 hours.

- **mini.que.ans.3.34h**: This dataset consists of 915 utterances and 3.34 hours of reading M.I.N.I questions (Sheehan et al., 1998) and free answers from two speakers. We transcribed the answers with our ASR system and then corrected them manually with our desktop application DaC-ToR (Hussain et al., 2020) which we used to correct the automatic transcription. For the recording we employed our online application TEQST[2] which allows the user to read texts and record with their own mobile devices.

---

[1] https://github.com/NVIDIA/tacotron2
[2] https://github.com/TEQST/TEQST

- **`mini-ans.42m`**: A test set that has been processed similarly to `mini.que.ans.3.34h`. It consists of 224 free answers on M.I.N.I questions with a duration of 42 minutes by one speaker.

- **`mini.ques.50m`**: 225 M.I.N.I questions by the same speaker as from `mini-ans.42m` with a duration of 50 minutes.

### 2.2 Domain Adaptation for ASR

As we will see in section 2.3, we obtain extremely poor performance on our target domain (psychiatric interview). Therefore, we are investigating many approaches to adapt our speech recognition system to the target domain. In this paper, we report about two experiments: the mixed-fine-tuning and the fine-tuning experiment (Chu et al., 2017). For mixed-fine-tuning, we begin with the pre-trained model on `Alj.1200h` data as a baseline and mixed-fine-tune it on the data resulting from mixing `Alj.1200h` with the domain data `mini.que.ans.3.34h`. For mixed-fine-tune or fine-tuning the decoder, we freeze the encoder, and train only the decoder. For fine-tuning, we don't mix the data. Instead we use only `mini.que.ans.3.34h` set. For mixed-fine-tuning and fine-tuning, We use the learning rates (0.0009) and (0.00001) respectively. We report the result in section 2.3.

### 2.3 Experimental Results

We experimented with the LSTM-based encoder-decoder + attention using 40 log-Mel features, two-layer Convolutional Neural Network (CNN) with 32 channels, 6 encoder-layers, 2 decoder-layers. For data augmentation, we use *dynamic time stretching* and *specAugument* as described in (Nguyen et al., 2020b).

For the output, we employed a sub-word tokenization method, byte-pair encoding (BPE) (Sennrich et al., 2015), (Gage, 1994). Empirical experiments indicated that 4k tokens yielded the best performance. The tokenizer is trained on MSA texts since we aim to have a well-performing system on MSA. For this reason, we obtain on the first test set MSA+dialect.10h, which contains dialect besides MSA, Word Error Rate (WER) of 18.8% (see Table 1). While, On the second test set MSA.2h with only MSA data, we reach a WER of 12.6%. We employ the beam-search algorithm for the output sequence prediction, where the beam-size of 4 yields the best WER. This low beam-size is considered very efficient for the real-time capability of the system.

For **Domain adaption**, the results of the main model on both test sets `mini-ans.42m` and `mini.ques.50m` of the target domain have a very high WER: 40% and 30.4% respectively. Our speech recognition model is S2S without an additional language model scoring or a dictionary. The decoder learns the language model from the training data directly. The out-of-vocabulary (OOV) rate between the test sets and the training data `Alj.1200h` is 3%. Hence, The main reason of the high WER is not the OOV but the domain mismatch since the training data is from broadcast videos and the domain of both test sets is psychiatric interviews. The results in the next section gives evidence for this hypothesis, since tuning only the decoder yields a considerable improvement.

By mixed-fine-tuning the whole model with the same architecture, we reach an improvement on both domains, where the WER is reduced by 0.7% on both `Alj.MSA+dialect.10h` and `Alj.MSA.2h`. Besides, on `mini-ans.42m` and `mini.ques.50m` we obtain a WER reduction of about 22%. By mixed-fine-tuning only the encoder we obtain comparable results. On the other hand, although fine-tuning the decoder only causes the forgetting of the out-of-domain (i.e. `Alj.MSA+dialect.10h` and `Alj.MSA+dialect.10h`) by increasing their WER by about 8%, it improves the in-domain (i.e. `mini.ques.50m`) to 6.2%. This is likely due to the questions being identical in the training and test set, however by different speakers. The reason of forgetting is that the fine-tuning does not use the whole training but only the in-domain data.

## 3 Machine Translation

It is a known fact that translating between structurally or morphologically different languages is a very difficult task. Two well-known examples of these hard language pairs are English–German and English–Arabic. In this work, we are associating the worst of these two worlds: Arabic and German. An example

| test set | baseline | mixed-FT | Dec mixed-FT | Dec FT |
|---|---|---|---|---|
| Alj.MSA+dialect.10h | 18.8 | 18.1 | 18.6 | 25.7 |
| Alj.MSA.2h | 12.6 | 11.8 | 12.3 | 20.5 |
| mini-ans.42m | 40.0 | 16.4 | 18.4 | 14.8 |
| mini.ques.50m | 30.4 | 8.6 | 10.3 | 6.2 |

Table 1: ASR results, where FT stands for fine-tuning and dec for Decoder. The values are the Word Error Rate (WER) ↓ in percent

of the unmistakable differences between these two languages is that both of them are morphologically rich: Arabic is highly inflectional ((Farghaly and Shaalan, 2009)) and German possesses word compounding. At the syntactic level, word order is a substantial difference between the two languages. Arabic is much more flexible in this respect.

In this work, we face two major challenges: data scarcity caused by the understudied language pair and the specificity of the domain of application. Indeed, the language pair under consideration here has been out of the focus of the international machine translation campaigns. Such campaigns (such as WMT[3] and IWSLT[4]) are organized on a yearly basis, and have boosted considerably both the performance and the available resources for the language pairs they consider. The data scarcity problem becomes even more severe when we know that the resulting system is to be involved in the communication between psychiatrists and their patients. The genre of the language used therein is quite different from that used in the news. This latter makes most of the available training data.

In the following, we explain the steps we followed to overcome these limitations and to produce a reasonable translation system. Then, we show the developed systems in action through empirical evaluations.

## 3.1 Data

Although the language pair under consideration is not commonly studied, a reasonable training set could be gathered, thanks to the different data sources publicly exposed on the Internet. In Part A of Table 2, we give a summary about the exploited data sets and some of their important attributes.

The TED corpus[6] is our first source of data. This corpus is collected by (Cettolo et al., 2012) from the translations generated by volunteers for the TED talks, over the course of several years. By looking at the data, we think that TED is cleaner and more suitable for speech translation. Therefore, we always start by a baseline trained on TED data only, and then we gradually introduce more data from other sources.

Another extremely important source is the OPUS[7] repository. OPUS is a large depot where parallel data is collected from different sources and sometimes also preprocessed for a very large number of language pairs. It turned out that not all of the data available in this repository is in a good shape. Therefore, we manually examined those corresponding to our language pair, and discarded those of which we were convinced that they include very large amounts of noise. A good example of this noisy data is the OpenSubtitle corpus. After this manual filtering, the corpora used from OPUS are: Multi UN, News Commentary, Global Voices, and Tatoeba.

The Wikipedia corpus is generated from German–English and Arabic–English corpora by pivoting over their English side. Although OPUS repository offers these two corpora for download, it does not offer the direct version Arabic–German. We use strict string matching of the English sides to find the Arabic–German translations (i.e. Finding sentence pairs from the two corpora where the English sentences are exactly equal in both pairs).

The QED corpus is a multilingual corpus for the educational domain produced by QCRI in Qatar

---

| Corpus | Sent. Pairs ($\times 10^3$) | Words ($\times 10^6$) | | Vocab ($\times 10^3$) | |
|---|---|---|---|---|---|
| | | Ar | De | Ar | De |
| **A: Training Data** | | | | | |
| TED | 199 | 2.800 | 3.200 | 278.0 | 214.0 |
| Multi UN | 165 | 4.700 | 4.800 | 165.0 | 121.0 |
| News Commentary | 208.783 | 7.565 | 6.396 | 226.779 | 228.481 |
| Wikipedia | 9.833 | 0.146 | 0.142 | 33.308 | 32.448 |
| QED | 18.537 | 0.124 | 0.146 | 24.796 | 20.184 |
| JW300 | 358.501 | 5.805 | 5.479 | 215.926 | 255.981 |
| GlobalVoices | 9 | 0.150 | 0.170 | 43.0 | 35.0 |
| Tatoeba | 1 | 0.004 | 0.003 | 2.2 | 1.9 |
| Q+A-TRAIN[5] | 0.257 | 0.004 | 0.005 | 1.899 | 1.657 |
| **Total** | **954.408** | **21.383** | **20.348** | - | - |
| **B: Test Data** | | | | | |
| TED-TEST | 1.717 | 0.021 | 0.025 | 8.572 | 6.897 |
| JW-TEST | 1.974 | 0.031 | 0.029 | 10.455 | 9.245 |
| Q+A-TEST[5] | 0.129 | 0.002 | 0.002 | 1.209 | 1.060 |

Table 2: Summary of the translation data sets

(Abdelali et al., 2014). Similar to TED talks, this corpus consists of the transcription and translation of educational lectures. In this work, we use the version 1.4 of this corpus.[8]

Finally, the `JW300` corpus was crawled from the Jehovah's Witnesses website[9] by (Agić and Vulić, 2019). The contents are of religious nature and are available in a large number of language pairs. This corpus is also made available on the OPUS repository. However, unlike the other corpora, this one comes unaligned on the sentence level. Consequently, we perform sentence alignment on the raw downloaded data. The process was held by the `hunalign`[10] tool. However, this tool requires a dictionary for the language pair; we automatically created one from the other aligned corpora. We used the `fast_align`[11] tool to align the corpora at the word level in two directions. Afterwards, We restricted our dictionary to word pairs appearing 5 times or more in the two directions.

The last row in Part A of Table 2 shows a part of our in-domain data. The other small part is used for testing (Last row, `Q+A-TEST` in Part B of the same Table). This consists of the translations of the M.I.N.I questions. Added to them are manual translations of the transcribed answers by some patients. These latter correspond to the `mini.que.ans.3.34h` data set (mentioned in speech data stes in Section 2.1).

In addition to the training data, we use three test sets to evaluate the performance of our systems on different kinds of data. Some details about these test sets are given in Part B of Table 2 (`JW-TEST`, `TED-TEST`, `Q+A-TEST`). The first two of these sets are considered as general domain and used to measure the model's performance on out-of-domain tasks. While these two sets are both out-of-domain for our purpose, they still represent different domains. The `JW-TEST` is a random subset drawn from the `JW300`, while ensuring that the test and the training sets remain disjoint. The `TED-TEST` set is the test set used in IWSLT evaluation in 2012 (IWSLT2012). The last test set (`Q+A-TEST`), as mentioned in the previous paragraph, consists of what was held out from the in-domain data to evaluate the system's performance on in-domain tasks. This latter test set, as well as its training counter-part (`Q+A-TRAIN`), is work in progress and will be extended in the future.

---

[8] `http://alt.qcri.org/resources/qedcorpus/`
[9] `https://www.jw.org/en/`
[10] `http://mokk.bme.hu/resources/hunalign/`
[11] `https://github.com/clab/fast_align`

## 3.2 Domain Adaptation for Machine Translation

The similarity between training and test data is a common assumption in machine learning (See e.g. (Daumé and Marcu, 2006) for an elaborate description of this issue). In most cases however, this assumption is violated in the field. This issue is usually resolved by performing in-domain adaptation. That is tweaking a model trained on large quantities of out-of-domain data using only the very few available examples from the domain under consideration. As a result, the similarity between probability distributions of the model and the domain is augmented.

The tasks we perform in this work are no exception to the aforementioned problem. In order to adapt the general system to the domain under consideration, some few in-domain examples are mandatory. In our work, these examples are the Q+A sets shown in the last rows of Parts A and B of Table 2. It is noteworthy however, that these sets are being actively extended, since the manual data creation is time-consuming.

So far, we explored two approaches to the adaptation: fine-tuning and data selection. Fine-tuning is accomplished by resuming the training for very few additional epochs using only the in-domain data. Data selection provides us with more in-domain data. This is achieved by choosing a special subset of training examples from the general domain training set. This subset consists of general domain examples, which are the most similar to the in-domain examples. The selection process is carried out using (Moore and Lewis, 2010) with more careful out-of-domain language model selection as proposed by (Mediani et al., 2014). The language models used in this procedure are 4-gram language models with Witten-Bell smoothing. We perform the selection for both languages (i.e. once for Arabic and once for German). Then, we take the intersection of the two selected subsets.[12]

## 3.3 Experimental Results

The input data is preprocessed using the `sentence_piece`[13] algorithm. For Arabic the vocabulary size is set to 4000 and for German to 16000. Lines longer than 80 words are discarded. The model's architecture is transformer encoder-decoder model (Vaswani et al., 2017b). Both the encoder and decoder are 8-layers. Each layer is of size 512. The inner size of the feed-forward network inside each layer is 2048. The attention block consists of 8 heads. The dropout is set to 0.2. All trainings are run for 100 epochs. While the number of epochs used for fine-tuning is taken to be 10. We use the Adam scheduling with a learning rate initially set to 1 and with 2048 warming steps. The results are summarized in Table 3.

| System | JW-TEST | TED-TEST | Q+A-TEST |
|---|---|---|---|
| **A: German → Arabic** | | | |
| TED only | 5.06 | 12.44 | 7.99 |
| TED+Extra data | 23.90 | 14.62 | 8.19 |
| Fine-tuned | 5.34 | 12.94 | 12.18 |
| Fine-tune-select | 23.18 | 14.35 | 19.16 |
| **B: Arabic → German** | | | |
| TED+Extra data | 17.17 | 9.67 | 6.18 |
| Fine-tune-select | 16.60 | 9.06 | 15.96 |

Table 3: Summary of the translation experiments (results are expressed as BLEU (↑) scores)

The scores in Table 3 are BLEU scores (Papineni et al., 2002). The table is subdivided into two panels, one for each translation direction. We report all tested combinations for the German → Arabic direction. For the reverse direction we report results only for the most promising configurations. The configurations shown here are as follows:

---

[12] Other ways of combining selections from the two sides of the parallel corpus were not explored in this work. Our choice (i.e. the intersection) is motivated by our aim for higher precision.

[13] `https://github.com/google/sentencepiece`

- TED only The training is performed on TED corpus only.

- TED+Extra data the system is trained on all data.

- Fine-tune The fine-tuning is done with the very small in-domain `Q+A-train` only.

- Fine-tune-select where the fine-tuning is accomplished using the set consisting of the merge between `Q+A-train` and the 20K more sentences selected from the training corpora.

As the table shows, using all the available data is helpful for all test sets. However, the `JW-TEST` is the one which benefits the most. This is to be expected as an important part from the training data comes from the `JW300` corpus. That corpus was originally in the same set with `JW-TEST`. The fine tuning on the tiny `Q+A-train` data set was not a good help to all test sets. While it introduces small improvement on the in-domain test, it was very harmful to the other sets. It causes the system to quickly overfit; most likely due to its small size and very restricted type of sentences. This is where the data selection comes in handy to fix these problems of the in-domain data set. This is demonstrated on the last row of the two panels of the table. The selection was able to bring a large improvement for the in-domain test set, without harming the other test sets from different domains.

## 4  Speech Synthesis

For speech synthesis or Text-To-Speech (TTS), we use the state-of-the-art model, namely Tacotron 2[14] (Shen et al., 2018) which is a recurrent S2S network with attention that predicts a sequence of Mel spectrogram frames for a given text sequence. For generating time-domain waveform samples conditioned on the predicted Mel spectrogram frames, we chose WaveGlow (Prenger et al., 2019) where the authors claim that it has a faster inference than WaveNet (Oord et al., 2016) used with Tacotron 2 in (Shen et al., 2018).

### 4.1  Experiments

We trained Tacotron 2 and used a pre-trained WaveGlow model found on the Github page of WaveGlow. We also kept most of the default parameters from the implementation except for the sampling rate where we use 16kHz for the audio. As input to the Tacotron 2, we used Arabic character sequences with diacritics in Buckwalter format[15].

The corpus used for the training (Halabi, 2016) contains 1813 utterances with a duration of 3.8 hours. We first experimented with Arabic characters without diacritics to synthesize the audio directly from the MT output. Unfortunately, the model did not converge since even the same word in a different context is diacritized differently. Employing BPE used for ASR (section 2) without diacritics did not work either even with pretraining with over 400 hours of the data set `Alj.1200h`. For this reason we developed the diacritization component (section 5) to our pipeline.

The resulting speech sounds natural (see section 4.2), however, when synthesizing for only one word, the model does not terminate and reaches the maximum decoding steps. As a solution, we implemented data augmentation by both splitting and merging utterances. We apply splitting on 708 out of the total 1813 utterances which are in form of spoken separate words separated by silence, for instance:

`"ta>aa~wSawa~ra - wata>aa~wSara - watu&a~wSa - taSa>aa~w"`

with an automatic approach. The algorithm simply finds positions with values under a threshold. These are simple to find since the corpus is recorded using a professional studio. Besides, we merge randomly 2 and 3 utterances with the probabilities 0.2 and 0.1 respectively if the duration stays under 30 seconds. This approach solved the one words synthesizing. However, another issue appeared, the synthesis contained short silence where it is not supposed to. This is due to the silence between the concatenated utterances which we solved by adding the symbol for silence "-" used already in the corpus between to concatenated utterances. It is worth to mention that this method solved an issue of the German synthesis for long sentences.

---

[14]The source code is available at `https://github.com/NVIDIA/tacotron2`
[15]Buckwalter transliteration can be found here: `http://www.qamus.org/transliteration.htm`

## 4.2   Results

For the evaluation of the naturalness of the resulting speech, we constructed an online form including 10 synthesized speech from the first 10 utterances of the test set `Alj.MSA.2h` (section 2.1) after diacritizing them manually. Besides, we added 3 real speech samples from the training data to judge the seriousness of the evaluators and whether the task has been properly understood by the participants. The scale we use is 1 if the speaker is a robot, 2 near to a robot sound, 3 no difference, 4 near to human sound, and 5 the sound is from a human. From the 18 participations we received, we deleted the whole evaluation of participants who evaluated one or more of the 3 real audio samples with 2 or below. It remains 11 valid votes with an average of 4.05 as a Mean Of Opinion (MOP ↑). For the whole 18 participations without deleting any invalid votes we obtain a MOP of 3.82. This means that the synthesized speech is of very good quality, in most cases judged as very close to human speech.

## 5   Diacritization

As mentioned earlier (Section 4), the dicritization was introduced to make the TTS understandable. We were, indeed, unable to synthesize good Arabic speech without these short vowels. The synthesis, then, consists of incomprehensible mumbles as the system tends to insert the vowels arbitrarily.

Diactritics have a crucial role in giving the Arabic text a phonetics (Abbad and Xiong, 2020). Moreover, they allow for better comprehension by reducing the level of ambiguity inherent in the Arabic transcription system. Having that said, most modern written Arabic resources omit these diacritics and rely on the ability of the native speakers to guess them from the context. In particular, all the parallel data used to train our translation systems has no diacritics.

We employ a sequence-tagger trained using the Flair-framework (Akbik et al., 2018), which is a BiLSTM-CRF proposed by (Huang et al., 2015). besides (Akbik et al., 2018) introduces Contextual String Embeddings. Thereby, sentences are passed as sequences of characters into a character-level Language Model (LM) to form word-level embeddings. This is done by concatenating the output hidden state after the last character in the word from the forward LM and the output hidden state before the word's first character from the backward LM. These two language models result from utilizing the hidden states of the forward-backward recurrent neural network (see (Akbik et al., 2018) for more details about the approach).

### 5.1   Data

Fortunately, some available Arabic resources are diacritized. Al-Shamela corpus (Belinkov et al., 2016) is a large-scale, historical corpus of Arabic of about 1 billion words from diverse periods of time. It is important to specify that the corpus in its initial state will not be exploitable in our resolution process, for this reason, a series of operations will be carried out, as follows:

- Delete empty lines and lines with a single character and keep only lines with a high amount of vowels ($> 40\%$ of characters are short vowels)

- Split words to obtain pairs consisting of (letter, Diacritic Mark).

Applying these steps to the Al-Shamela corpus gives an amount of around 5 million lines of training data. We used only a part of this large corpus ($\approx 1.5$ million lines). Some other parts of this corpus were held out for validation and testing (1300 validation set and 8000 lines for testing).

### 5.2   Results

We use the sequence to sequence biLSTM provided by the Flair framework. We kept the configuration as simple as possible. The embeddings are obtained by stacking forward and backward embeddings of size 512 each. They were computed while training a one layer language model. The network consists of an RNN encoder of 1 layer and 128 hidden states and a CRF decoder. With such a configuration, an accuracy of 95.34% was achieved on the held out test set.

## 6 Real-Time Aspects

All components of the pipeline reside on only one GPU of type `TITAN RTX` with 24 GB memory. The number of components is 7 where there are 3 for each S2ST direction plus the diacritization component for Arabic side.

We measured the latency of the system components by using 5 Arabic sentences from the test set `Alj.MSA.2h` consisting of 16, 9, 8, 12 and 9 words, hence 54 words in total. For ASR, we use the synthesis of this sentences which has the total duration of 47.85 seconds. The ratio of the total duration of processing the 5 sentences by the whole pipeline system to the total input speech duration is $\frac{7.95}{47.85} = 0.17$. This means that the processing time is about 6 times faster than the input speech duration. Hence, the system is real-time capable and Long sentences can be chunked into smaller parts in a stream-like output (see (Nguyen et al., 2020a) as an example of using The LSTM-based model for ASR to process a stream). Table 4 shows the time duration in total for the 5 sentences, the average time per sentence, per word, and the model size on the GPU.

| component | total time | avg. per sentence | per word | GPU model size (GB) |
|---|---|---|---|---|
| ASR | 1.06 | 0.212 | 0.020 | 1.4 |
| MT | 1.90 | 0.381 | 0.035 | 0.9 |
| Diacritization | 0.68 | 0.136 | 0.014 | 0.8 |
| TTS | 4.31 | 0,861 | 0.080 | 1.7 |

Table 4: The measurement of the latency for each component of the pipeline. Times are in seconds($\downarrow$). The measurements are for 5 sentences with (16,9,8,12,9) words, i.e 54 words in total

It can also be noted from the Table that the TTS is the slowest component in the pipeline.

## 7 Conclusion

In this work, we presented the different components of our German–Arabic speech-to-speech translation system which is being deployed in the context of interpretation during psychiatric, diagnostic interviews. For this purpose, we have built a pipe-lined speech-to-speech translation system consisting of automatic speech recognition, machine translation, text post-processing, and speech synthesis systems. We also described the problems we faced while building these components and how we proceeded to overcome them.

The speech recognition system uses an LSTM-based encoder/decoder + attention architecture, the machine translation component is based on the Transformer architecture, the post-processing for Arabic employs a sequence-tagger for diacritization, and for the speech synthesis systems we use Tacotron 2 for generating spectrograms and WaveGlow as a vocoder.

For domain adaptation, we used fine-tuning and mixed-fine-tuning on hand-created in-domain data. We achieved thereby considerable improvements despite the scarce collected domain data. This result confirms the already well established fact about the extreme importance of in-domain data. Therefore, collecting more of this domain-related data is on the top of our priorities in the near future. Certainly, this data collection process will not prevent us from trying more ways to exploit the data we already have. For instance, more efforts will be put into exploring other adaptation techniques. Additionally, we are investigating the exploitation of the large quantities of monolingual data in the translation components.

## Acknowledgements

The work in this paper was funded by the German Ministry of Education and Science within the project *Removing language barriers in treating refugees—RELATER*, no. 01EF1803B.

# References


Hamza Abbad and Shengwu Xiong. 2020. Multi-components system for automatic arabic diacritization. In *European Conference on Information Retrieval*, pages 341–355. Springer.

Ahmed Abdelali, Francisco Guzman, Hassan Sajjad, and Stephan Vogel. 2014. The amara corpus: Building parallel language resources for the educational domain. In Nicoletta Calzolari (Conference Chair), Khalid Choukri, Thierry Declerck, Hrafn Loftsson, Bente Maegaard, Joseph Mariani, Asuncion Moreno, Jan Odijk, and Stelios Piperidis, editors, *Proceedings of the Ninth International Conference on Language Resources and Evaluation (LREC'14)*, Reykjavik, Iceland, may. European Language Resources Association (ELRA).

Željko Agić and Ivan Vulić. 2019. JW300: A wide-coverage parallel corpus for low-resource languages. In *Proceedings of the 57th Annual Meeting of the Association for Computational Linguistics*, pages 3204–3210, Florence, Italy, July. Association for Computational Linguistics.

Alan Akbik, Duncan Blythe, and Roland Vollgraf. 2018. Contextual string embeddings for sequence labeling. In *COLING 2018, 27th International Conference on Computational Linguistics*, pages 1638–1649.

Ahmed Ali, Peter Bell, James Glass, Yacine Messaoui, Hamdy Mubarak, Steve Renals, and Yifan Zhang. 2016. The mgb-2 challenge: Arabic multi-dialect broadcast media recognition. In *2016 IEEE Spoken Language Technology Workshop (SLT)*, pages 279–284. IEEE.

Ebrahim Ansari, Amittai Axelrod, Nguyen Bach, Ondřej Bojar, Roldano Cattoni, Fahim Dalvi, Nadir Durrani, Marcello Federico, Christian Federmann, Jiatao Gu, Fei Huang, Kevin Knight, Xutai Ma, Ajay Nagesh, Matteo Negri, Jan Niehues, Juan Pino, Elizabeth Salesky, Xing Shi, Sebastian Stüker, Marco Turchi, Alexander Waibel, and Changhan Wang. 2020. FINDINGS OF THE IWSLT 2020 EVALUATION CAMPAIGN. In *Proceedings of the 17th International Conference on Spoken Language Translation*, pages 1–34, Online, July. Association for Computational Linguistics.

Yonatan Belinkov, Alexander Magidow, Maxim Romanov, Avi Shmidman, and Moshe Koppel. 2016. Shamela: A large-scale historical arabic corpus. *arXiv preprint arXiv:1612.08989*.

Mauro Cettolo, Christian Girardi, and Marcello Federico. 2012. Wit$^3$: Web inventory of transcribed and translated talks. In *Proceedings of the $16^{th}$ Conference of the European Association for Machine Translation (EAMT)*, pages 261–268, Trento, Italy, May.

Chenhui Chu, Raj Dabre, and Sadao Kurohashi. 2017. An empirical comparison of domain adaptation methods for neural machine translation. In *Proceedings of the 55th Annual Meeting of the Association for Computational Linguistics (Volume 2: Short Papers)*, pages 385–391.

III Hal Daumé and Daniel Marcu. 2006. Domain Adaptation for Statistical Classifiers. *J. Artif. Int. Res.*, 26(1):101–126, May.

Ali Farghaly and Khaled Shaalan. 2009. Arabic natural language processing: Challenges and solutions. *ACM Transactions on Asian Language Information Processing*, 8(4), December.

Philip Gage. 1994. A new algorithm for data compression. *C Users Journal*, 12(2):23–38.

Nawar Halabi. 2016. *Modern standard arabic phonetics for speech synthesis*. Ph.D. thesis, University of Southampton.

Zhiheng Huang, Wei Xu, and Kai Yu. 2015. Bidirectional lstm-crf models for sequence tagging. *arXiv preprint arXiv:1508.01991*.

Juan Hussain, Oussama Zenkri, Sebastian Stüker, and Alex Waibel. 2020. Dactor: A data collection tool for the relater project. In *Proceedings of The 12th Language Resources and Evaluation Conference*, pages 6627–6632.

Mohammed Mediani, Joshua Winebarger, and Alexander Waibel. 2014. Improving In-Domain Data Selection for Small In-Domain Sets.

Robert C. Moore and William D. Lewis. 2010. Intelligent Selection of Language Model Training Data. In *ACL (Short Papers)*, pages 220–224.

Thai-Son Nguyen, Ngoc-Quan Pham, Sebastian Stueker, and Alex Waibel. 2020a. High performance sequence-to-sequence model for streaming speech recognition. *arXiv preprint arXiv:2003.10022*.

Thai-Son Nguyen, Sebastian Stüker, Jan Niehues, and Alex Waibel. 2020b. Improving sequence-to-sequence speech recognition training with on-the-fly data augmentation. In *ICASSP 2020-2020 IEEE International Conference on Acoustics, Speech and Signal Processing (ICASSP)*, pages 7689–7693. IEEE.

Aaron van den Oord, Sander Dieleman, Heiga Zen, Karen Simonyan, Oriol Vinyals, Alex Graves, Nal Kalchbrenner, Andrew Senior, and Koray Kavukcuoglu. 2016. Wavenet: A generative model for raw audio. *arXiv preprint arXiv:1609.03499*.

Kishore Papineni, Salim Roukos, Todd Ward, and Wei-Jing Zhu. 2002. Bleu: a method for automatic evaluation of machine translation. In *Proceedings of the 40th Annual Meeting of the Association for Computational Linguistics*, pages 311–318, Philadelphia, Pennsylvania, USA, July. Association for Computational Linguistics.

Ryan Prenger, Rafael Valle, and Bryan Catanzaro. 2019. Waveglow: A flow-based generative network for speech synthesis. In *ICASSP 2019-2019 IEEE International Conference on Acoustics, Speech and Signal Processing (ICASSP)*, pages 3617–3621. IEEE.

Rico Sennrich, Barry Haddow, and Alexandra Birch. 2015. Neural machine translation of rare words with subword units. *arXiv preprint arXiv:1508.07909*.

David V. Sheehan, Yves Lecrubier, K. Harnett Sheehan, Patricia Amorim, Juris Janavs, Emmanuelle Weiller, Thierry Hergueta, Roxy Baker, and Geoffrey C. Dunbar. 1998. The mini-international neuropsychiatric interview (m.i.n.i.): The development and validation of a structured diagnostic psychiatric interview for dsm-iv and icd-10. *The Journal of Clinical Psychiatry*, 59(20):22–33.

Jonathan Shen, Ruoming Pang, Ron J Weiss, Mike Schuster, Navdeep Jaitly, Zongheng Yang, Zhifeng Chen, Yu Zhang, Yuxuan Wang, Rj Skerrv-Ryan, et al. 2018. Natural tts synthesis by conditioning wavenet on mel spectrogram predictions. In *2018 IEEE International Conference on Acoustics, Speech and Signal Processing (ICASSP)*, pages 4779–4783. IEEE.

Ashish Vaswani, Noam Shazeer, Niki Parmar, Jakob Uszkoreit, Llion Jones, Aidan N Gomez, Ł ukasz Kaiser, and Illia Polosukhin. 2017a. Attention is all you need. In I. Guyon, U. V. Luxburg, S. Bengio, H. Wallach, R. Fergus, S. Vishwanathan, and R. Garnett, editors, *Advances in Neural Information Processing Systems 30*, pages 5998–6008. Curran Associates, Inc.

Ashish Vaswani, Noam Shazeer, Niki Parmar, Jakob Uszkoreit, Llion Jones, Aidan N Gomez, Ł ukasz Kaiser, and Illia Polosukhin. 2017b. Attention is all you need. In I. Guyon, U. V. Luxburg, S. Bengio, H. Wallach, R. Fergus, S. Vishwanathan, and R. Garnett, editors, *Advances in Neural Information Processing Systems 30*, pages 5998–6008. Curran Associates, Inc.

# Hate Speech Detection in Saudi Twittersphere:
# A Deep Learning Approach


**Raghad Alshalan**
King Saud University & Imam
Abdulrahman bin Faisal University,
Saudi Arabia
Rsalshaalan@iau.edu.sa

**Hend Al-Khalifa**
King Saud University, College of
Computer and Information Sciences,
Saudi Arabia
hendk@ksu.edu.sa


## Abstract


With the rise of hate speech phenomena in Twittersphere, significant research efforts have been undertaken to provide automatic solutions for detecting hate speech, varying from simple machine learning models to more complex deep neural network models. Despite that, research works investigating hate speech problem in Arabic are still limited. This paper, therefore, aims to investigate several neural network models based on Convolutional Neural Network (CNN) and Recurrent Neural Networks (RNN) to detect hate speech in Arabic tweets. It also evaluates the recent language representation model BERT on the task of Arabic hate speech detection. To conduct our experiments, we firstly built a new hate speech dataset that contains 9,316 annotated tweets. Then, we conducted a set of experiments on two datasets to evaluate four models: CNN, GRU, CNN+GRU and BERT. Our experimental results on our dataset and an out-domain dataset show that CNN model gives the best performance with an F1-score of 0.79 and AUROC of 0.89.


## 1   Introduction

In the Arab region, Twitter is considered as one of the most popular platforms used by Arabic speaking users and it has indeed revolutionized the way people communicate and share opinions, ideas and information. However, due to the dynamic, democratic and unrestricted nature of Twitter platform, it has been increasingly exploited for the dissemination of aggressive and hateful content. While there is no formal definition of hate speech, there is a general agreement among scholars and service providers to define it as any language that attack a person or a group based on some characteristic such as race, color, ethnicity, gender, religion, or other characteristic (Schmidt & Wiegand, 2017).

The pressing need for effective automatic solutions for hate speech detection has attracted significant research efforts recently. Several studies relied on traditional machine learning approaches and leveraged surface features such as bag of words, word and character n-grams which have been shown to be very effective for hate speech detection (Davidson et al., 2017; Fortuna & Nunes, 2018; Jaki & De Smedt, 2018; Waseem & Hovy, 2016). Recently, there has been a clear trend towards the adoption of deep learning methods, which indeed showed better performance over classic methods in hate speech detection task (Badjatiya et al., 2017; Gambäck & Sikdar, 2017; Park & Fung, 2017; Pitsilis et al., 2018; Zhang et al., 2018). However, there is a very limited work that employed deep learning approaches to address the problem in Arabic language (Al-Hassan & Al-Dossari, 2019). To the best of our knowledge, Albadi et al. (2018) work is the only Arabic study published in the area, and it examined GRU architecture, focusing mainly on religious hate speech.

While different deep learning models have been investigated in this area, we are more interested to explore these methods for Arabic language. We believe that the special nature of Arabic languages and its richness and complexity at morphological, lexical and orthographical levels (Darwish et al., 2012) pose some unique challenges that could complicate the task of detecting hate speech. Moreover, the high variety of dialectal Arabic used by Arabic users on social media makes the problem even more complex. In fact, dialects of Arabic are manifold, varying not only from country to country but also within the same country, resulting in many similarly spelled words to have different meanings across different dialects and regions.






*Proceedings of the Fifth Arabic Natural Language Processing Workshop*, pages 12–23
Barcelona, Spain (Online), December 12, 2020

Recently, Devlin et al. (2019) introduced BERT (Bidirectional Encoder Representations from Transformers.), a new language representation model that has been successfully applied to numerous NLP tasks, achieving the state-of-the-art results for eleven NLP tasks including sentiment analysis, question-answering and textual entailment. However, works examining BERT effectiveness for hate speech detection, specifically in Arabic are very limited.

To that end, this paper presents a set of experiments to investigate the merit of using different neural networks including Recurrent Neural Networks (RNNs) and Convolutional Neural Networks (CNNs) and their variants for hate speech detection in Arabic. We also evaluated BERT on our downstream classification task by using the pre-trained BERT model, adding a simple task-specific layer and then fine-tuning the entire model on the hate speech detection task. Given the fact that Arabic is considered as a low-resourced language, this paper also described our approach for creating a hate speech dataset for Arabic, covering racist, religious and ideological hate speech. Following this approach, we created a new dataset containing a total of 9,316 tweets labeled as normal, abusive or hateful as well as a new annotation guideline.

The main contributions of this work are three-folds:
1) Constructing a public dataset of 9,316 tweets labelled as hateful, abusive and normal.
2) Comparing the performances of three neural network models CNN, GRU, CNN+GRU for Arabic hate speech detection task.
3) Evaluating the recent language representation model BERT for Arabic hate speech detection task.

The remaining of the paper is organized as follows. Section 2 reviews work related to hate speech detection. Section 3 describes the data construction process. Section 4 describes our methods, including a detailed description of the investigated models' architectures and the preprocessing steps. Section 0 and 6 discuss the experiments and the results, respectively. Finally, Section 7 concludes our work and discusses future directions.

## 2   Related work

Abusive language in social media is a complex phenomenon with a wide spectrum of overlapping forms and targets. Hate speech, offensive language, and cyberbullying are examples of abusiveness and several works in the literatures have been conducted to detect and locate such types of languages.

Recently, researchers have shown an increased interest in automatic hate speech detection in social media. Most of the existing studies in the literature have primarily modeled the problem as a supervised classification task whether using classical machine learning approaches or deep neural network approaches (Fortuna & Nunes, 2018; Schmidt & Wiegand, 2017).

As for classical machine learning approaches, there were several studies that leveraged simple surface and linguistic features such as bag of words (BOW), n-grams, and POS as fundamental features. Schmidt and Wiegand (2017) presented a review of the various features that were used for the task in the literature. One of the earliest studies that addressed the problem of hate speech detection was presented by Warner & Hirschberg (2012), which focused on detecting anti-Semitic language as the specific type of hate speech. Kwok & Wang (2013) proposed a supervised machine learning model to detect racist hate speech against black people in Twittersphere and they suggested to improve the model by considering other features such as sentiment features and bigrams. Waseem and Hovey (2016) presented a study to detect hate speech in Twitter platform and specifically targeted two types of hate: racism and sexism. They also built and published a dataset of 16K annotated tweets which has become a well-known benchmarking dataset for following studies. Word embeddings as features were also investigated by Djuric et al. (Djuric et al., 2015) and the experimental results on Yahoo! Finance user comments showed that paragraph2vec representation performed better in term of Area Under the Curve (AUC). Following this study, Nobata et al. (2016) incorporated various features such as n-grams, linguistic and syntactic features and distributional semantics to detect abusive language in online user comments. The results showed that combining all features led to outperform the prior art in term of AUC. Davidson et al. (2017) trained a multi-class classifier to distinguish between offensive and hate language in tweets. They also built and published a dataset of tweets labelled for three categories: hate speech, offensive language, or neither, resulted into 24,802 labelled tweets.

In recent years, attention has shifted toward deep learning approaches to tackle the problem of hate speech detection. Most of the works have employed various architectures of Convolutional Neural Network (CNN) and Recurrent Neural Networks (RNN). Park & Fung (2017) proposed a two-step classification approach by combining two classifiers: one to classify the text to abusive or not, and another to classify the text into a specific type of abusive language (sexist or racist) given that the text is abusive. Gambäck and Sikdar (2017) proposed the use of CNN-classifier with word2vec word vectors and their results outperformed the prior art. Pitsilis et al. (2018) built an ensemble of LSTM-based classifiers to detect hate speech content in Twitter. The results showed that the proposed approach achieved better results compared to the state-of-the-art approaches. Zhang et al. (2018) showed that a CNN+GRU neural network model has improved the performance of hate speech detection. Badjatiya et al. (2017) investigated three different neural models for hate speech detection and the results showed that embeddings learned from LSTM model when combined with GBDT led to the best accuracy result. Recently, some works showed that incorporating BERT-based models to learn the representations for noisy text (Dai et al., 2020) and capturing hateful context (Mozafari et al., 2020) can enhance the offensive and hate speech detection systems.

There are several works that tackle the problem of hate speech and offensive language in non-English languages such as German (Jaki & De Smedt, 2018), Greek (Pitenis et al., n.d.), Danish (Sigurbergsson & Derczynski, n.d.), and Turkish (Çöltekin, 2020) corpora. Arabic studies that address the problem of hate speech detection are still limited, however, there are several studies that address some related problems such as detecting ISIS support messages (Magdy et al., 2015) and identifying vulgar, obscene, offensive or flaming language (Alakrot et al., 2018; Mubarak et al., 2020, 2017). A recent dataset for Levantine hate speech and abusive detection has been published by Mulki et al. (2019). This dataset contains 5,846 tweets labeled as Hate, Abusive or Normal, collected from Twitter using terms of potential entities that are usually targeted by abusive/hate speech. Albadi et al. (2018) proposed an RNN architecture with Gated Recurrent Units (GRU) and pre-trained word embeddings to detect religious hate speech in Arabic tweets. For evaluation, they created a dataset containing 6,000 Arabic tweets, 1,000 for each of the six religious' groups (Muslims, Jews, Christians, Atheists, Sunnis and Shia). The tweets were annotated as hate or not-hate tweet. The results showed that the GRU-based RNN model outperformed other traditional classifiers with respect to all evaluation. They also published their dataset as the first and the only available hate speech dataset for Arabic language.

## 3   Dataset construction

In this work, we built a new dataset that covers different types of hate speech, e.g., racist, religious and ideological hate speech, focusing mainly on Saudi Twittersphere. We used the standard Twitter search/streaming API with tweepy[2] python library to collect our data. The data was collected in span of 6 months, from March 2018 to August 2018 using a keyword-based and thread-based search. In keyword-based approach, we included in the search query a total of 164 impartial unique terms (excluding the various morphological variations of the same term) that refer to groups, or to people belonging to groups that are likely to be targeted by hate speech. For example, we used terms that refer to people who belong to different tribes (such as "Otaibi"," عتيبي " ) and different regions ("Hijaz"," حجازي ") to collect tweets related to tribal and regional hate speech, respectively. For the thread-based search, we included in the search query different hashtag that discusses controversial topics which are considered to be strong indicators of hate speech. We monitored twitter trends during the period of the data collection, and we ended up with a total of 10 hashtags used for data retrieving. Examples of the used terms and hashtags are illustrated in Table 1.

| Hate speech type | Example of Terms/hashtags |
| --- | --- |
| Racist | عرب الشمال, هوية_الحجاز |
| Regional | نجدي، قصيمي ،حجازي |
| Tribal | عتيبي، زهراني، قحطاني |
| Inter-religious | الوهابية، الشيعة، الأشاعرة |
| Ideological | ليبرالية، يسارية، نسوية |

Table 1. Examples of terms used for data retrieving

Since hateful tweets are generally less common than natural tweets, we further boost our dataset and improve the representation of the hate class by using the top-scored terms in the lexicon of religious hate terms released by Albadi et al. (2018). For all queries, we collected only original and Arabic tweets, excluding retweets and non-Arabic tweets from the search. In total, we retrieved 54 million tweets, from

---

[2] https://www.tweepy.org/

which we sampled 10,000 tweets for annotation. To obtain the annotations for the dataset, Figure Eight[3] crowdsourcing platform was utilized to recruit both crowed and internal workers (volunteers and freelancers). Before submitting the task to the annotators, we generated an annotation guideline for hate speech annotation with the help of experts in interreligious dialogue, Islamic jurisprudence and media studies. The guideline is available online on GitHub[4]. The entire annotation process was completed in a course of three weeks, starting from 1 to 23 September 2019. The dataset was submitted to the annotators in different batches. The first batch (1,000 tweets) was annotated by crowed workers. The second batch (4,000 tweets) was annotated by 15 different Saudi annotators. The third and final batch (5,000 tweets) was annotated by three freelancers who are familiar with Saudi dialect. The annotated dataset is available online on GitHub[5]

## 4    Methods

In this section, we present the main components of our proposed approach to detect Arabic hate speech. As a first step, the tweets pass through various preprocessing steps to clean and prepare the data for the training phase. Then, several classification models for detecting hate speech in Arabic texts are investigated. In this work, we evaluated three neural network architectures: CNN-based classifier, GRU-based classifier, and finally, a classifier that combines both CNN and GRU. Moreover, we evaluated BERT (Devlin et al., 2019), a recent language representation models, on the task of hate speech detection. In the next subsections we discuss more these steps.

### 4.1    Data preprocessing

Before feeding the tweets as an input to the classification models, we applied several preprocessing steps:

- **Hashtags removal**: to avoid any bias toward certain classes, we dropped any hashtag used as a keyword search while collecting the data from the tweets.
- **Spam filtering:** in this step, we implemented the rule-based algorithm and lexicon proposed in (Al-Humoud et al., 2016) to filter spams with some additional terms and hashtags that we found to be highly associated with spam tweets.
- **Stop words removal:** In this step we used a list of 356 stop words that were made publicly available by (Albadi et al., 2018) on GitHub[6].
- **Emojis description:** Motivated by (Singh et al., 2019) work, we used demoji[7], a python library that provide utilities to replace emojis with their description. This library utilized readily available lists of emojis and their textual descriptions in English[8]. For our task, we translated the list into Arabic by Google translator API[9]. Then, the produced translations were manually revised and updated. The translated list was used with demoji to replace emojis in tweets with their Arabic textual description.
- **Cleaning:** In this step, punctuations, additional whitespaces, diacritics, non-Arabic characters are removed.
- **Normalization:** The goal of this step is to reduce orthographical variations observed in tweets as well as normalizing Twitter specific tokens. The normalization steps are as follows:
  - Different forms of "ا " (" إ ,"أ " and "آ") were replaced by "ا", "ى" is replaced by "ي" and "ة" is replaced by "ه"
  - Links and mentions are replaced by "URL" and "mention", respectively.
- **Lemmatization.** We applied this step using the Farasa stemmer (Abdelali et al., 2016). We selected Farasa based on a study by El Mahdaouy et al. (2018) which showed that Farasa outperformed other tools such as MADAMIRA.

### 4.2    Neural network models

In this section, we first briefly describe the feature representation for the evaluated neural networks, then we describe the architectures of each model (CNN, GRU, and CNN+GRU).


[3] https://www.figure-eight.com/
[4] https://github.com/raghadsh/Arabic-Hate-speech/blob/master/Annotation%20Guidlines.pdf
[5] https://github.com/raghadsh/Arabic-Hate-speech
[6] https://github.com/nuhaalbadi/Arabic_hatespeech
[7] https://pypi.org/project/demoji/
[8] http://unicode.org/Public/emoji/12.0/emoji-test.txt
[9] https://cloud.google.com/translate/docs/

**Features representation:** the first layer of all proposed architectures is an embedding layer that maps each tweet, represented as a sequence of integer indexes, to a 300-dimension vector space using a pretrained word2vec model (Mikolov et al., 2013). We trained our own word2vec model using the Continuous Bag of Words (CBOW) training algorithm. We used a subset of our collected data as training collection. The collection has a total of 17.6 million tweets and 536K tokens. Before training, all tweets were preprocessed following the same preprocessing steps described earlier. As for the model's hyperparameters, we selected a window of size 3, since the length of tweets is generally small. We set the vector dimensions to 300 and the other hyper-parameters to their defaults.

**CNN architecture:** The first model we evaluated is a CNN model inspired by Kim's work (Kim, 2014) for text classification. Our CNN architecture, as illustrated in Figure 1, contains five layers: input layer (embedding layer), a convolution layer, which basically consists of 3 parallel convolution layers with different kernel sizes (2,3 and 4), pooling layer, hidden dense layer, and finally the output layer.

**GRU architecture:** Currently, GRU is the state-of-the-art model for Arabic hate speech detection. In this experiment, we employed a GRU-based network similar to the one applied in (Albadi et al., 2018). Our network architecture, as illustrated in Figure 2 contains 4 layers: input layer (embedding layer), GRU layer, hidden dense layer, and finally the output layer.

**CNN+GRU architecture:** The third experimented architecture is combination of both CNN and GRU, as illustrated in Figure 3. In this architecture, CNN is used as a feature extractor that passes the 'extracted feature' to a GRU layer which treats the generated feature dimension as timesteps. CNN+GRU architecture contains 6 layers: input layer (embedding layer), convolution layer with 100 filters and a kernel size of 4, max pooling layer, GRU layer, another max pooling layer, and finally the output layer.

**BERT model:** BERT (Devlin et al., 2019) was released in multilingual versions, pre-trained on monolingual corpora (Wikipedia) in 104 languages including Arabic. In this experiment, we fine-tuned the cased version of the multilingual pre-trained model by adding a simple classification layer that performs a binary classification to classify the tweets into hate or not hate. To prepare our data for BERT, we examined two different preprocessing procedures. The first one followed the same steps described in Section 4.1. The second one is a lite version of the first one in which stop words, punctuations and non-Arabic words are kept. The lite preprocessing showed a better result in term of F1 score on 5-fold cross validation on training set.

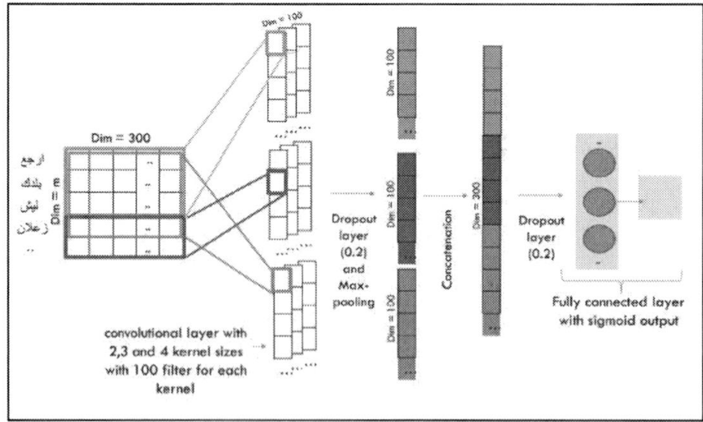

Figure 1. Neural network models architecture

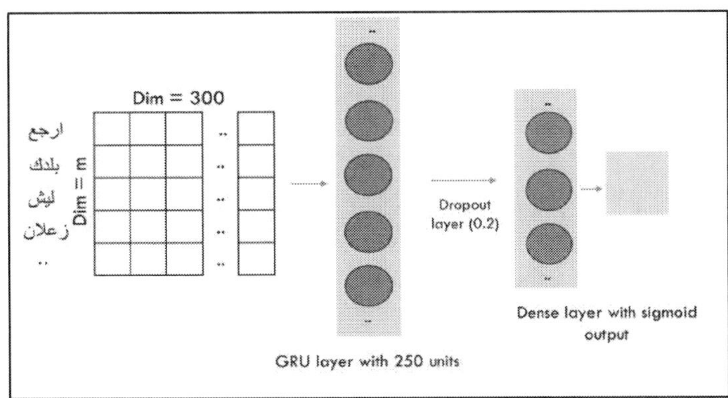


Figure 2. GRU architecture

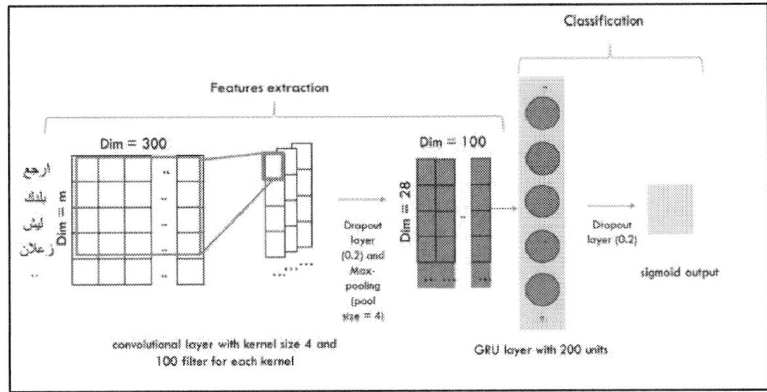


Figure 3. CNN +GRU architecture

## 5 Experiments

We conducted a set of experiments to evaluate the proposed models for Arabic hate speech detection tasks (CNN, GRU, CNN+GRU and BERT). In all experiments, we performed a binary classification task in which tweets are classified to hate or non-hate classes. In this section we describe the datasets used in our experiments and the experiment setup including the models' implementation, hyperparameters tuning, baselines and evaluation metrics.

### 5.1 Datasets

In all experiments, we used our created dataset (as described earlier in this paper) to train the proposed models for hate speech detection. The dataset contains a total of 9,316 tweets classified as hateful, abusive or normal (not hateful or abusive). Since our task is to perform a binary classification to classify the tweet into hate or non-hate speech, we only kept tweets annotated as hateful or normal. This left us with 8,964 tweets, split into 75%–25% for training (6425 instances) and testing (2539 instances). We used the 75% for training and hyperparameter-tuning through cross-validation and then we tested the optimized models on the 25% held-out data. Hereinafter, we refer to this dataset as general hate speech dataset (GHSD).

|  | GHSD | RHSD (testing) |
|---|---|---|
| # Tweets | 8,964 | 600 |
| # Hate instances | 2539 | 250 |
| # Non-hate instances | 6425 | 350 |

Table 2. Statistics of datasets used in the experiments

To investigate to what extent the models trained on our dataset generalize to other datasets that focused on different/specific types of hate speech, we used Albadi et al. (2018) religious hate speech dataset (referred as Religious hate speech dataset (RHSD) hereinafter) to test our models. Particularly, we trained our proposed models using the whole GHSD dataset and use the testing set of RHSD, which contains 600 tweets to test the models. Statistics of the used datasets are shown in Table 2.

## 5.2 Experimental settings

**Implementation.** We implemented all neural network models using Keras library with a TensorFlow as a backend[10] while we implemented BERT using huggingface Pytorch library[11]. We run the experiments on Google Collaboratory[12], which provides a free Jupyter notebook environment with GRU accelerator.

**Hyperparameters tuning.** In all experimented models, we employed a grid search using 5-fold cross-validation on the training set to find the optimal training-specific and model-specific hyperparameters. All proposed network architectures were experimented with binary cross entropy as a loss  function and "Adam" as an optimizer. We modified the loss function to incorporate class weights during evaluation, since our dataset is relatively imbalanced, and we are particularly interested in increasing the recall of the positive class (hate class). Then, we evaluated all network architectures with and without incorporating class weights. When fine-tuning BERT model, all hyperparameters were kept the same as in pretraining except batch size, learning rate, and number of training epochs. For batch size and number of epochs, we searched according to the suggested ranges in (Devlin et al., 2019). For the learning rate, we found that the suggested range produce poor results, so we extended the searched range to be {0.2e-5, 0.3e-5 ... 3e-5, 5e-5}.

**Baselines and evaluation metrics.** For our baselines, we used SVM (support vector machine) and LR (logistic regression) classifiers because they have shown to be effective in previous studies (Chen et al., 2018; Davidson et al., 2017; Waseem & Hovy, 2016). For features, we found that character n-gram features (n = 1-4) yielded the highest F1 score. We used Python scikit-learn library[13] to implement both models. We used macro-averaged Precision (P), Recall (R), accuracy, F1-measures and Area Under the Receiver Operating Characteristic curve (AUROC) for evaluation. Moreover, since our hate speech data collection is relatively imbalanced and given the serious consequences of failing to detect a hateful content, we also reported our results using positive class recall.

## 6    Experiments results

In this section we discuss the results of two set of experiments. The first one is the in-domain experiments, where all models were trained on the training set of our created dataset (GHSD) and tested on its testing set. We also performed a set of out-domain experiments to assess how well our models, when trained on one dataset generalize to work on different datasets. For that purpose, we trained all the models on the whole GHSD dataset, then we used Albadi et al. (2018) test set (RHSD) for testing.

| Model | GHSD (in-domain) | | | | | | RHSD (out-domain) | | | | | |
|---|---|---|---|---|---|---|---|---|---|---|---|---|
| | Precision | Recall | F1 | Accuracy | Hate class recall | AUROC | Precision | Recall | F1 | Accuracy | Hate class recall | AUROC |
| SVM (char n-grams) | 0.74 | 0.74 | 0.74 | 0.78 | 0.63 | 0.85 | 0.70 | 0.66 | 0.66 | 0.68 | 0.46 | 0.73 |
| LR (char n-grams) | 0.75 | 0.74 | 0.75 | 0.79 | 0.63 | 0.84 | 0.68 | 0.66 | 0.65 | 0.68 | 0.47 | 0.72 |
| CNN | **0.81** | **0.78** | **0.79** | **0.83** | **0.67** | **0.89** | 0.72 | **0.69** | **0.69** | **0.70** | **0.56** | **0.79** |
| GRU | 0.80 | 0.77 | 0.78 | 0.82 | 0.63 | 0.87 | 0.70 | 0.65 | 0.64 | 0.68 | 0.43 | 0.76 |
| CNN+GRU | 0.80 | 0.76 | 0.77 | 0.82 | 0.62 | 0.88 | **0.74** | 0.67 | 0.67 | **0.70** | 0.44 | 0.77 |
| BERT | 0.76 | 0.76 | 0.76 | 0.80 | 0.65 | 0.76 | 0.63 | 0.60 | 0.59 | 0.63 | 0.38 | 0.6 |

Table 3. Evaluation results of the experimented models. Best result for each metric is boldfaced.

---

[10] https://keras.io/
[11] https://github.com/huggingface/transformers
[12] https://colab.research.google.com
[13] https://scikit-learn.org/

### 6.1    Results and discussion

Table 3 summarizes the best results achieved by our evaluated models: CNN, GRU, CNN+GRU and BERT in terms of precision, recall, F1-score, accuracy, hate class recall and AUROC. The left part of the table shows the results of the in-domain experiments. The right part of the table illustrates the out-domain experiments results.

Since neural networks are stochastic in nature, we expect some variations in models' performance at every different run. Therefore, we performed 10 runs for each experiment and reported the average of all metrics (we limited the number of runs to 10 given the time constraint on the project).

**Baselines performance**. Results in all metrics show that SVM and LR classifiers achieved almost the same performance on both datasets (GHDS and RHSD). We can also notice that both classifiers achieved a considerably high AUROC scores, suggesting that they were highly capable of distinguishing between the two classes.

**Neural models performance on GHDS**. As Table 3 shows, we experimented with three neural models, namely CNN, GRU and CNN+GRU and compared their performance against our baselines. Generally, the results show that all models outperformed the baselines by approximately 3-5% in all metrics. The only exception was the hate class recall for both GRU and CNN+GRU, in which they achieved similar and 1% lower results than the baselines, respectively. It can be noticed that CNN model achieved the best results among the three neural network models. It showed a consistent improvement in all metrics with a high AUROC score. It also achieved the highest hate class recall compared to other models. The performance improvement achieved by CNN can be attributed to its ability at extracting local and position-invariant features such as surrounding words and word orders. These features can work very well on tasks like hate speech, since hate speech, much similar to sentiment can be determined by some terms and multi-word phrases. GRU also showed very similar results to those achieved by CNN, with a minor decrease (only 1%) in the performance with respect to all metrics except for the hate class recall. While not expected, stacking GRU layer on the top of the CNN architecture led to a slight drop in CNN performance. We suspect that the reason of the performance decline is the complexity of the CNN+GRU architecture, which may not be able to work very well on relatively small datasets. As a final note, neural network models showed to be more effective in the task of hate speech detection, and it can be attributed to their abilities to capture more contextual information and long-term dependencies and hence, a deeper understanding of the texts. However, it is worthwhile to mention that our baselines were also able to achieve a very competitive results, specifically in terms of AUROC and hate class recall. This confirms previous studies that show that character n-grams can be highly predictive feature in hate speech detection.

**BERT performance on GHDS**. We fine-tuned BERT model for the binary text classification task by adding a simple classification layer. From Table 3, we can notice that BERT offers a slight performance improvement over the baselines with respect to almost all metrics. However, it showed a large drop (approximately 10%) in terms of AUROC compared to the baselines. Compared against our neural network models, BERT failed to provide any improvement in the classification performance. This was not expected, since BERT model has been proved to be very powerful, achieving the state-of-the-art results in many NLP tasks such as sentiment analysis, question-answering, textual entailment [94]. The poor performance of BERT can be attributed to the fact, as stated by Al-Twairesh & Al-Negheimish (2019), that BERT was trained on different dataset genre (Wikipedia).

**Out-Domain experiments**. The right part of Table 3 shows the results of the out-domain experiments. Not surprisingly, all models' performance, including the baselines, is always lower on the out-domain dataset. While being always lower, results of the out-domain experiments are very consistent with the results obtained in the in-domain experiments. Specifically, CNN in both set of experiments achieved the best results compared to the baselines and other models in almost all metrics. Moreover, GRU and CNN+GRU showed comparative results. However, in out-domain experiments, BERT failed to beat the baselines with respect to all metrics. There are many reasons that could cause the consistent drop in the classification performance of all experimented methods on the RHSD dataset. Firstly, RHSD focuses on different type of hate speech, namely a religious hate speech. This type of hate speech was not directly considered while collecting the GHSD dataset (used for training), which focus on wider range of hate speech types including racism, ideological, and inter-religious. In fact, this could cause the two datasets to have different types of swear/abusive/offensive terms and also different targets names. This can greatly impact the lexical distribution of the two datasets, and hence, will impact how/what the models learn as predictive features. To investigate this, we firstly generated two lexicons from our dataset (GHSD) following two corpus statistical-based approach: chi-square ($x^2$) and Pointwise Mutual

Information (PMI), which leverage the labeled corpus in order to learn a domain-specific lexicon and measures the association strength between a term and a class (hate or non-hate classes, in our case). More details on how $x^2$ and PMI values are calculated can be found in (Kaji & Kitsuregawa, 2007). Then, we examined the lexicons generated from RHSD by Albadi et al. (2018) and from GHSD and analyzed the terms with high positive scores (strongly associated with hate class). We found that some of the highly scored terms in RHSD have a very low score (nearly zero) in GHSD. Examples of these words are the religious affiliations such as *"Christian/نصراني"* and *''polytheist /مشرك''*. Beside the lexicon differences, we notice that tweets in RHSD testing set were mostly written in MSA, while tweets in GHSD dataset were mostly written in Saudi dialect. The differences of the linguistic characteristics between MSA and dialects could also affect the ability of our in-domain models to generalize well. In the next section, we attempt to analyze the error produced by our evaluated models to gain deeper understanding of the limitation and the challenges of the hate speech detection task.

## 6.2    Error analysis

To understand the challenges of this task, we carry out further analysis of the errors made by our models, including the baselines. We identified the hateful tweets that all evaluated models on both datasets predicted incorrectly (misclassified as non-hate). We ended up with a total of 151 tweets for GHSD and 51 tweets for RHSD. We further qualitatively analyzed these tweets and we found that nearly 90% of the misclassified tweets do not have offensive/abusive terms, this could confuse the classifiers and cause its performance to be degraded.

We also found that many tweets would be even difficult for human to classify as hate without being provided with the full context of the tweet. For example, some of the tweets contain comments on images or videos, which will be very tricky to interpret without seeing the associated media. The lack of the context problem also appeared with tweets that refer to external links or quoted tweet. For example, this tweet quoted another tweet and with this comment *"This is serious, this means that those people will be back to work in secret so that no one will pay attention to them"*. This tweet was written by an extremely patriotic user who uses "those" to refer to foreigners working in Saudi Arabia, indicating they have some agenda to call for separation of Hijaz region from the rest of the country. This tweet is difficult to be interpreted correctly without knowing what it quoted exactly. Mentions also have the same problem, some mentions contain only few natural words, but it should be classified as hate when we take into the account the original tweet that it replied to. For example, this tweet *"@user Qahtani freshman"* replied to an offensive tweet that negatively stereotypes a particular tribe's members, but the classifiers incorrectly classified it as non-hate. Finally, we found that some tweets were indirect, implicit or sarcastic, which make it difficult of automatic solutions to detect correctly. For example, this sarcastic tweet *"Be hold for now we present a play called 'Freemen with #Mohammad_Bin_Salman in #Saudi_The_Great'"* was misclassed as non-hate, but it was written by non-Saudi user against a Saudi user as a part of hateful conversation between them.

We also performed further analysis to understand the cases in which the classifiers misclassified non-hate tweets as hateful. We ended up with 33 misclassified non-hate tweets in GHSD and 20 tweets in RHSD. Mostly all of these tweets include one or more religious, national or ideological affiliations terms, which are highly associated with hate class (according to our generated lexicons). Examples: *"Hahaha... Fear Allah brother, first of all Khurasan scholars are not related to the Persians Magians! Second Arab was and still the head of knowledge"* and *"Hahaha... you blended with our Hadarms[14] ladies so that's why they consider you one of them; that's the way our parents raised us even if you're Saudi"*. These tweets may cause some confusion that leads the classifiers to classify them as hateful. We also found that some of misclassified tweets are debatable and could be hard to decide whether to consider it hate or non-hate even for human annotators, such as this tweet: *"Most of them moved from one radicalism to another; and what we got here in this world are people called the new Arab liberals and you can see what's on their shoulders (different Ideas that contradict the simplest principles of liberalism)"*.

---

[14] From/of Hadramaut; Hadramauti.

All these factors led us to conclude that hate speech is still a difficult phenomenon. It is highly dependent on the context and, in fact can be conveyed in a very polite and genuine form (without using any offensive words or being aggressive).

## 7    Conclusion and future work

Hate speech in Arabic Twittersphere has become a notable problem, resulted in a pressing need for effective automatic solution for hate speech detection. In this work, we constructed a public dataset of 9,316 tweets labeled as hateful, abusive, and normal. We evaluated and compared four different models: CNN, GRU, CNN+GRU and BERT. The obtained results from our experiments were promising, showing the effectiveness of the proposed models in the detection task. The results showed that CNN successfully outperformed other models, with an F1-score of 0.79 and AUROC of 0.89. Our results also showed that BERT failed to improve over the baselines and the other evaluated models. This could be attributed to the fact that BERT was trained on different dataset genre (Wikipedia).

We believe that there are several ways to extend and improve this study in the future. The dataset can be extended to capture more writing styles, patterns and topics. The dataset can also be annotated with multi-labels to enhance the results of the detection task beyond the binary classification. For example, annotating the target of the hate speech and the aggressive level (week/strong) could introduce new direction for future works and applications.

We also think that the conducted experiments could be enhanced in different ways. First, we aim to extend our out-domain experiments and evaluate the proposed models on other abusive/offensive language datasets such as those found in (Alakrot et al., 2018; Mubarak et al., 2017). This could help us to understand how to distinguish between hate speech and abusive/offensive language. Moreover, different embeddings methods could be investigated beside Word2Vec such as ELMo (Peters et al., 2018), BERT, FastText (Joulin et al., 2016), and the Universal Sentence Encoder (USE) (Cer et al., 2018). Other features can be also incorporated with word embeddings such as the user's gender, age and location. Moreover, to alleviate the lack of the context problem we found when we analyzed the errors made by our models, we aim to incorporate tweets' context (e.g. the original tweet of the replies, quoted tweets, text from the external links) into the feature space and investigate if this could boost the performance of the classifiers.

## References


Abdelali, A., Darwish, K., Durrani, N., & Mubarak, H. (2016). Farasa: A Fast and Furious Segmenter for Arabic. *Proceedings of the 2016 Conference of the North American Chapter of the Association for Computational Linguistics: Demonstrations*, 11–16

Alakrot, A., Murray, L., & Nikolov, N. S. (2018). Towards Accurate Detection of Offensive Language in Online Communication in Arabic. *Procedia Computer Science*, *142*, 315–320. https://doi.org/10.1016/j.procs.2018.10.491

Albadi, N., Kurdi, M., & Mishra, S. (2018). Are they Our Brothers? Analysis and Detection of Religious Hate Speech in the Arabic Twittersphere. *2018 IEEE/ACM International Conference on Advances in Social Networks Analysis and Mining (ASONAM)*, 69–76. https://doi.org/10.1109/ASONAM.2018.8508247

Al-Hassan, A., & Al-Dossari, H. (2019). DETECTION OF HATE SPEECH IN SOCIAL NETWORKS: A SURVEY ON MULTILINGUAL CORPUS. *Computer Science & Information Technology(CS & IT)*, 83–100. https://doi.org/10.5121/csit.2019.90208

Al-Humoud, S., Al-Twairesh, N., Altuwaijri, M., & Almoammar, A. (2016). *Arabic Spam Detection in Twitter*.

Al-Twairesh, N., & Al-Negheimish, H. (2019). Surface and Deep Features Ensemble for Sentiment Analysis of Arabic Tweets. *IEEE Access*, *7*, 84122–84131. https://doi.org/10.1109/ACCESS.2019.2924314

Badjatiya, P., Gupta, S., Gupta, M., & Varma, V. (2017). Deep Learning for Hate Speech Detection in Tweets. *Proceedings of the 26th International Conference on World Wide Web Companion*, 759–760. https://doi.org/10.1145/3041021.3054223

Cer, D., Yang, Y., Kong, S., Hua, N., Limtiaco, N., John, R. S., Constant, N., Guajardo-Cespedes, M., Yuan, S., Tar, C., Sung, Y.-H., Strope, B., & Kurzweil, R. (2018). Universal Sentence Encoder. *ArXiv:1803.11175 [Cs]*. http://arxiv.org/abs/1803.11175

Chen, H., McKeever, S., & Delany, S. J. (2018). A Comparison of Classical Versus Deep Learning Techniques for Abusive Content Detection on Social Media Sites. In S. Staab, O. Koltsova, & D. I. Ignatov (Eds.), *Social Informatics* (pp. 117–133). Springer International Publishing.

Çöltekin, Ç. (2020). A Corpus of Turkish Offensive Language on Social Media. *Proceedings of The 12th Language Resources and Evaluation Conference. 2020.*, 6174–6184. https://www.aclweb.org/anthology/2020.lrec-1.758

Dai, W., Yu, T., Liu, Z., & Fung, P. (2020). Kungfupanda at SemEval-2020 Task 12: BERT-Based Multi-Task Learning for Offensive Language Detection. *ArXiv:2004.13432 [Cs]*. http://arxiv.org/abs/2004.13432

Darwish, K., Magdy, W., & Mourad, A. (2012). Language processing for arabic microblog retrieval. *Proceedings of the 21st ACM International Conference on Information and Knowledge Management*, 2427–2430.

Davidson, T., Warmsley, D., Macy, M., & Weber, I. (2017). Automated Hate Speech Detection and the Problem of Offensive Language. *ArXiv:1703.04009 [Cs]*. http://arxiv.org/abs/1703.04009

Devlin, J., Chang, M.-W., Lee, K., & Toutanova, K. (2019). BERT: Pre-training of Deep Bidirectional Transformers for Language Understanding. *ArXiv:1810.04805 [Cs]*. http://arxiv.org/abs/1810.04805

Djuric, N., Zhou, J., Morris, R., Grbovic, M., Radosavljevic, V., & Bhamidipati, N. (2015). Hate Speech Detection with Comment Embeddings. *Proceedings of the 24th International Conference on World Wide Web - WWW '15 Companion*, 29–30. https://doi.org/10.1145/2740908.2742760

El Mahdaouy, A., El Alaoui, S. O., & Gaussier, E. (2018). Word-embedding-based pseudo-relevance feedback for Arabic information retrieval. *Journal of Information Science*, 016555151879221. https://doi.org/10.1177/0165551518792210

Fortuna, P., & Nunes, S. (2018). A Survey on Automatic Detection of Hate Speech in Text. *ACM Comput. Surv.*, *51*(4), 85:1–85:30. https://doi.org/10.1145/3232676

Gambäck, B., & Sikdar, U. K. (2017). Using Convolutional Neural Networks to Classify Hate-Speech. *Proceedings of the First Workshop on Abusive Language Online*, 85–90. https://doi.org/10.18653/v1/W17-3013

Jaki, S., & De Smedt, T. (2018). Right-wing German hate speech on Twitter: Analysis and automatic detection. *Manuscript Submitted.*

Joulin, A., Grave, E., Bojanowski, P., & Mikolov, T. (2016). Bag of Tricks for Efficient Text Classification. *ArXiv:1607.01759 [Cs]*. http://arxiv.org/abs/1607.01759

Kaji, N., & Kitsuregawa, M. (2007). Building Lexicon for Sentiment Analysis from Massive Collection of HTML Documents. *Proceedings of the 2007 Joint Conference on Empirical Methods in Natural Language Processing and Computational Natural Language Learning (EMNLP-CoNLL.*

Kim, Y. (2014). Convolutional Neural Networks for Sentence Classification. *Proceedings of the 2014 Conference on Empirical Methods in Natural Language Processing (EMNLP)*, 1746–1751. http://www.aclweb.org/anthology/D14-1181

Kwok, I., & Wang, Y. (2013). Locate the hate: Detecting tweets against blacks. *Twenty-Seventh AAAI Conference on Artificial Intelligence.*

Magdy, W., Darwish, K., & Weber, I. (2015). #FailedRevolutions: Using Twitter to Study the Antecedents of ISIS Support. *ArXiv:1503.02401 [Physics]*. http://arxiv.org/abs/1503.02401

Mikolov, T., Chen, K., Corrado, G., & Dean, J. (2013). Efficient Estimation of Word Representations in Vector Space. *ArXiv:1301.3781 [Cs]*. http://arxiv.org/abs/1301.3781

Mozafari, M., Farahbakhsh, R., & Crespi, N. (2020). A BERT-Based Transfer Learning Approach for Hate Speech Detection in Online Social Media. In H. Cherifi, S. Gaito, J. F. Mendes, E. Moro, & L. M. Rocha (Eds.), *Complex Networks and Their Applications VIII* (pp. 928–940). Springer International Publishing. https://doi.org/10.1007/978-3-030-36687-2_77

Mubarak, H., Darwish, K., & Magdy, W. (2017). Abusive Language Detection on Arabic Social Media. *Proceedings of the First Workshop on Abusive Language Online*, 52–56. http://www.aclweb.org/anthology/W17-3008

Mubarak, H., Rashed, A., Darwish, K., Samih, Y., & Abdelali, A. (2020). Arabic Offensive Language on Twitter: Analysis and Experiments. *ArXiv:2004.02192 [Cs]*. http://arxiv.org/abs/2004.02192

Mulki, H., Haddad, H., Bechikh Ali, C., & Alshabani, H. (2019). L-HSAB: A Levantine Twitter Dataset for Hate Speech and Abusive Language. *Proceedings of the Third Workshop on Abusive Language Online*, 111–118. https://doi.org/10.18653/v1/W19-3512

Nobata, C., Tetreault, J., Thomas, A., Mehdad, Y., & Chang, Y. (2016). Abusive Language Detection in Online User Content. *Proceedings of the 25th International Conference on World Wide Web - WWW '16*, 145–153. https://doi.org/10.1145/2872427.2883062

Park, J. H., & Fung, P. (2017). One-step and Two-step Classification for Abusive Language Detection on Twitter. *Proceedings of the First Workshop on Abusive Language Online*, 41–45. https://doi.org/10.18653/v1/W17-3006

Peters, M. E., Neumann, M., Iyyer, M., Gardner, M., Clark, C., Lee, K., & Zettlemoyer, L. (2018). Deep contextualized word representations. *ArXiv Preprint ArXiv:1802.05365.*

Pitenis, Z., Zampieri, M., & Ranasinghe, T. (n.d.). *Offensive Language Identification in Greek.* 7.

Pitsilis, G. K., Ramampiaro, H., & Langseth, H. (2018). Effective hate-speech detection in Twitter data using recurrent neural networks. *Applied Intelligence, 48*(12), 4730–4742. https://doi.org/10.1007/s10489-018-1242-y

Schmidt, A., & Wiegand, M. (2017). A Survey on Hate Speech Detection using Natural Language Processing. *Proceedings of the Fifth International Workshop on Natural Language Processing for Social Media,* 1–10. http://www.aclweb.org/anthology/W17-1101

Sigurbergsson, G. I., & Derczynski, L. (n.d.). Offensive Language and Hate Speech Detection for Danish. *Proceedings of The 12th Language Resources and Evaluation Conference,* 3498--3508.

Singh, A., Blanco, E., & Jin, W. (2019). Incorporating Emoji Descriptions Improves Tweet Classification. *Proceedings of the 2019 Conference of the North American Chapter of the Association for Computational Linguistics: Human Language Technologies, Volume 1 (Long and Short Papers),* 2096–2101. https://doi.org/10.18653/v1/N19-1214

Warner, W., & Hirschberg, J. (2012). Detecting Hate Speech on the World Wide Web. *Proceedings of the Second Workshop on Language in Social Media,* 19–26. http://dl.acm.org/citation.cfm?id=2390374.2390377

Waseem, Z., & Hovy, D. (2016). Hateful Symbols or Hateful People? Predictive Features for Hate Speech Detection on Twitter. *Proceedings of the NAACL Student Research Workshop,* 88–93. https://doi.org/10.18653/v1/N16-2013

Zhang, Z., Robinson, D., & Tepper, J. (2018). Detecting Hate Speech on Twitter Using a Convolution-GRU Based Deep Neural Network. In A. Gangemi, R. Navigli, M.-E. Vidal, P. Hitzler, R. Troncy, L. Hollink, A. Tordai, & M. Alam (Eds.), *The Semantic Web* (pp. 745–760). Springer International Publishing.

# Is it Great or Terrible? Preserving Sentiment in Neural Machine Translation of Arabic Reviews


**Hadeel Saadany**
Centre for Translation Studies
University of Surrey, UK
hadil.saadany@gmail.com

**Constantin Orăsan**
Centre for Translation Studies
University of Surrey, UK
C.Orasan@surrey.ac.uk


## Abstract


Since the advent of Neural Machine Translation (NMT) approaches there has been a tremendous improvement in the quality of automatic translation. However, NMT output still lacks accuracy in some low-resource languages and sometimes makes major errors that need extensive post-editing. This is particularly noticeable with texts that do not follow common lexico-grammatical standards, such as user generated content (UGC). In this paper we investigate the challenges involved in translating book reviews from Arabic into English, with particular focus on the errors that lead to incorrect translation of sentiment polarity. Our study points to the special characteristics of Arabic UGC, examines the sentiment transfer errors made by Google Translate of Arabic UGC to English, analyzes why the problem occurs, and proposes an error typology specific of the translation of Arabic UGC. Our analysis shows that the output of online translation tools of Arabic UGC can either fail to transfer the sentiment at all by producing a neutral target text, or completely flips the sentiment polarity of the target word or phrase and hence delivers a wrong affect message. We address this problem by fine-tuning an NMT model with respect to sentiment polarity showing that this approach can significantly help with correcting sentiment errors detected in the online translation of Arabic UGC.


## 1 Introduction

Translation of user generated content (UGC) such as user reviews is becoming common on multilingual websites which sell products and services such as amazon.com or booking.com. In this context, sentiment preservation in automatic machine translation (these days usually neural machine translation (NMT) output) is of great importance because many decisions about purchasing a product or service are based on the comments made by others. There have been different studies which explored the transfer of sentiment in MT, but most of these studies assess how far automatic sentiment classification systems can capture sentiment information from the translations (Afli et al., 2017; Araujo et al., 2016; Shalunts et al., 2016). The objective of most research in this area is from a sentiment classification perspective rather than a translation accuracy perspective. Hence, it measures how far automatic translation of a language into English can help with the sentiment classification of that language by applying the available English sentiment resources on the target text (Demirtas and Pechenizkiy, 2013; Barhoumi et al., 2018; Mohammad et al., 2016; Abdalla and Hirst, 2017).

This study is concerned with NMT accuracy of sentiment transfer at the word/phrase level and shows that inaccurate translation can transfer a completely opposite affect message. Moreover, the translation of UGC such as product reviews constitutes a significant challenge for NMT online tools in general and for Arabic UGC in particular. The reason is that Arabic UGC is usually a mix of Dialectical Arabic (DA) and Modern Standard Arabic (MSA) which differ significantly on the lexico-grammatical level. The same word or phrase can have opposite sentiment polarities in the two versions of the Arabic language, which often leads to a mistranslation of the sentiment message. If the NMT engine is robust enough to handle this type of code-switching, it can become more reliable not only in downstream NLP tasks such






*Proceedings of the Fifth Arabic Natural Language Processing Workshop*, pages 24–37
Barcelona, Spain (Online), December 12, 2020

as cross-lingual information retrieval, but also in real-life scenarios when Internet users resort to online translation tools to check the reviews of a particular product of interest. In this study, we assess the degree to which the NMT online tools transfer sentiment accurately at the word/phrase level and suggest methods for improving the accuracy of the translation of sentiment in Arabic UGC. We aim to answer the following questions:

1. What type of errors in the output of NMT of Arabic UGC cause problems in sentiment preservation?

2. How can a sentiment sensitive input for an NMT model help with a more accurate sentiment polarity transfer of Arabic UGC?

3. How can sentiment preservation in the target language be measured and whether the BLEU score is the most appropriate metric for evaluating translation of sentiment?

To answer the above research questions, this paper is divided as follows: section 2 presents related work on sentiment transfer in MT. Section 3 analyzes sentiment translation errors of NMT online tools of Arabic reviews and provides a qualitative typology of most frequent error types. In section 4, we present different methodological approaches for correcting the NMT online sentiment transfer errors. Section 5 provides task-specific evaluation metrics for assessing the sentiment accuracy improvement by the proposed methods. Section 6 presents a conclusion on the different experiments as well as limitations of the present study.

## 2   Related Work

Research on the translation of sentiment in MT has focused on the idea that despite significant errors in sentiment transfer, automatic sentiment classification systems are still able to capture sentiment information from the translations (Demirtas and Pechenizkiy, 2013; Shalunts et al., 2016; Mohammad et al., 2016; Barhoumi et al., 2018). Salameh et al. (2015) showed that although certain attributes of automatically translated text 'may mislead humans' with regards to the true sentiment of the source text, they do not seem to affect the automatic sentiment analysis systems (Salameh et al., 2015). The rationale behind these studies is that if we have a good machine translation model, it will eliminate the necessity to develop sentiment analysis resources specific of the source language (Afli et al., 2017). Given the proliferation of English sentiment analysis tools, we can always make use of them by conducting sentiment analysis on the English translation of the source text, even if the translation is not of high quality (Abdalla and Hirst, 2017; Araujo et al., 2016). Studies also show that developed MT models, as well as online translation tools such as Google Translate and Microsoft Translate, can be relied upon to perform sentiment classification of the target text despite any accuracy errors (Shalunts et al., 2016). This is because sentiment classification systems can learn an appropriate model even from mistranslated text — especially when automatic translation makes consistent errors (Salameh et al., 2015). Moreover, statistically, studies of sentiment translation have shown that automatic translation leads to only about 60% match with manually annotated sentiment labels. Yet, automatic sentiment classifiers can still perform well despite these errors which can markedly impact human perception of sentiment in the source tweet/review (Salameh et al., 2015; Mohammad et al., 2016).

Recently, MT studies started to tackle how sentiment can be preserved in the translation of UGC from a translation accuracy perspective. Bérard et al. (2019) show that back translation of restaurant reviews can provide significant improvement over existing online systems particularly in preserving sentiment of translated UGC. They translate a large corpus of reviews from the target language into English and then use it in model training. They use domain tags at the training stage to distinguish user-generated source text. Their results prove that both synthetic data and domain tags can achieve good results in preserving the affect polarity on the sentence level. While their model is promising, they still point to serious errors in the translation of UGC such as missing negations, hallucinations, unrecognized named entities and insensitivity to context. They suggest that this task is far from solved (Bérard et al., 2019).

Lohar et al. (2018) makes an attempt to improve the sentiment transfer of translated tweets. They show that freely available translation tools often cause the sentiment encoded in the original tweet to be altered. As a consequence, they build separate negative, neutral and positive sentiment SMT models to improve sentiment preservation in the target language. They show that a translation model specific of each sentiment pole provides much better results over a single baseline model trained on the whole twitter data, regardless of the sentiment class. They attempt to strike a balance between improving sentiment transfer and preserving translation accuracy as measured by evaluative metrics such as BLEU and METEOR (Lohar et al., 2018). A similar technique is used by Si et al. (2019) as they build a valence sensitive NMT model for the translation of ambiguous words that can have different polarities in different contexts. Each input sentence is annotated with a positive or negative label to indicate its polarity. They show that adding this tag to the source sentence at the training time and creating dual polarity embedding vectors for ambiguous words can improve sentiment transfer at the word level (Si et al., 2019).

There has also been some research on finding alternative means for assessing the transfer of sentiment in MT other than the typical accuracy metrics. Bérard et al. (2019) show that automatic evaluation metrics such as BLEU and METEOR tend to neglect sentiment discrepancies between source and target output. They suggest assessing the accuracy of sentiment preservation by targeted metrics that measure how well polysemous words are translated, or how well sentiments expressed in the original text can be recovered from its translation (Bérard et al., 2019). To assess sentiment preservation in MT, Lohar et al. (2017) use a sentiment lexicon-based measure in combination with regular evaluation metrics such as the BLEU score. Several studies also resort to human evaluation to measure how far a model improves sentiment transfer at the word/phrase level (Si et al., 2019; Mohammad et al., 2016).

In this study, we evaluate the preservation of sentiment in translation not as a sentiment classification task, but from a translation accuracy perspective. We show that translation inaccuracies at the word/phrase level can seriously impact the transfer of sentiment in Arabic UGC, which can lead to problems for users of the MT tools in real-life situations. Several commercial global platforms rely on publicly available MT engines to translate product reviews into the customers own language to facilitate communication between partners and customers[1]. Inaccurate translation of reviewers' sentiment would defeat the purpose of using such tools. Moreover, in commercial situations, companies may want to find out what their users think of particular products so the accuracy of each translation review counts. Broadly speaking, online tools such as Google Translate, are commonly utilized as an off-the-shelf solution for the translation of UGC in Arabic as well as in other languages. Error-analysis of sentiment translation by online tools, however, has proved that the true sentiment of Arabic reviews can be either missed or flipped to its exact opposite pole.

## 3 Error Analysis

In order to measure how accurately NMT online tools transfer sentiment of Arabic UGC, we chose a dataset of book reviews scraped from Goodreads[2] (Aly and Atiya, 2013). Each review has a rating between 1-5 assigned by its author. The language of the reviews is a mix of MSA and DA, with the largest majority of DA reviews in the Egyptian dialect. Reviews in the dataset are of varying lengths, but a large number of them have over than 100 tokens. Long reviews were split to a maximum of 20 tokens per review. After splitting, the data amounted to about 230,000 sentences. This dataset was translated into English using the Google Translate API and was analysed using both manual and automatic error analysis, focusing on mistranslation of sentiment. Automatic sentiment analysis tools were utilized to detect sentiment errors in the dataset and subsequently select a sample for manual error analysis.

Since the main objective is to assess the accuracy of sentiment translation at the word level, we used an automated lexicon-based sentiment measure on the Google Translate output. We applied the cloud-based Microsoft Azure Text Analytics tools for sentiment analysis [3] on around 13,000 target sentences. The Azure's Sentiment Analysis API generates sentiment scores using classification features such as n-gram sentiment scores, part-of-speech tags and word embeddings. It evaluates text and returns a label (positive, neutral, negative) for each sentence as well as numeric confidence scores that range from 0 to 1

---

[1]For example, Booking.com uses Google API to translate reviews on hotels for customers on the fly.
[2]https://www.goodreads.com
[3]Microsoft Azure Text Analytics

for each sentiment category. Scores closer to 1 indicate a higher confidence in the label's classification, while lower scores indicate lower confidence. For each sentence, the predicted scores associated with the labels (positive, negative and neutral) add up to 1. Following traditional methods in sentiment classification (Pang et al., 2002), we used the rating of the book review as indicative of its sentiment polarity and compared it to the confidence scores generated by the Azure Sentiment Analysis API. Accordingly, reviews were categorized based on discrepancies between the ratings and the confidence scores. A positive review that had a rating of 4 or above and an English negative sentiment score of 0.5 and above was extracted as an example of potential wrong negative polarity in the target text. Similarly, reviews with negative ratings of 2 and below and a positive English sentiment score of 0.5 and above were extracted as instances of potential wrong positive polarity in the target text. This amounted to a total of around 4,000 potentially negative sentiment errors and around 2,000 of potentially positive sentiment errors.

A sample of reviews of 1000 parallel sentences from the dataset that had discrepancies between the automatic sentiment score and the review rating were manually analyzed to detect reasons for these discrepancies. By analyzing the causes of mistranslation of sentiment in this sample, the mistakes were categorized into a five group typology. The typology of sentiment translation errors are summarized in the following sections. One or two examples for each type of errors will be mentioned in the following sections. The table in appendix A gives more examples of each type.

## 3.1 Contronyms

Manual analysis of the data revealed that the first type of errors which distorts the reviewer's affect message is mistranslations of contronyms. These are words used both in DA and MSA which can have the exact opposite sentiment polarity in each of the two language varieties or in the same variety but in different contexts. For example, the word 'رهيبه' means 'terrible' in MSA, but in DA it often means 'great'. This word was frequently mistranslated as 'terrible' in the reviews dataset, causing a distortion of the sentiment of the source text. For example, the review ' الروايه رهيبه عيبها الوحيد الجزء الاخير' is translated as "The narration is terrible, its only flaw is the last part". The correct translation, however, is 'The novel is great, its only flaw is the last part'. Even when the infrequent positive use of the contronym is used in Arabic MSA context it is flipped to a negative pole in the translation. For example, in the review ' ثم قال هذه الكلمه الرهيبه اقرأ' (then he said this magnificent word: Read) the word 'رهيبه' is used positively to mean 'great' or 'magnificent'. The automatic translation, however, flips it to the more common negative sense by translating the review as 'then he said this terrible word: Read'. Similarly, the negation of these contronyms is often mistranslated and hence alters the sentiment message of the source text. For example, the low-rated review ' أدب الكاتب مش الفظيع' (the writer's literature is not that great) has the negated contronym ' الفظيع' which can either mean 'not terrible' or 'not great' in MSA and DA respectively. The review was mistranslated as 'the writer's literature is not terrible' which had a positive sentiment score whereas the original review had a low rating.

Another example is the word 'جامد'. In DA, it means 'great' or 'awesome,' whilst in MSA it refers to its literal meaning, i.e. 'rigid'. Reviews stating ' كتاب جامد جدا' (a very good book) were constantly mistranslated as 'a very rigid book' which incorrectly reflected a negative sentiment score. A list of contronyms that caused sentiment inconsistencies between source and target text was identified by the manual analysis of the sample dataset and extracted from the larger dataset of the Goodreads reviews (see appendix A for more examples of this type of error).

## 3.2 Diacritic Errors

The vowels in the Arabic language are realized by diacritics which indicate the pronunciation of the word. The same word can have different meanings based on the diacritic marks assigned, since a change in a diacritic is a change of a vowel sound. Arabic UGC is usually lacking diacritics since Arabic native speakers can easily guess which diacritic mark is intended based on the context of the word. Automatic translation, however, often fails to realize the different meanings of words if diacritics are missing and this can lead to a wrong sentiment polarity. For example, 'من اظرف ما قرأت' (One of the nicest things I've read) is translated as 'The envelope of what I read'. This is because the word 'اظرف' can either mean 'the nicest' or 'most entertaining' if it has a 'fatha' (a short /a/) on the third letter or 'envelopes' if it has 'Damma' (a short /u/ as in "you") on the same letter. Moreover, absence of diacritics causes a confusion between the transitive and intransitive use of sentiment adjectives. For example, the adjective 'متعبه' can either mean 'tired' if the diacritic 'fatha' (a short /a/) is on the third letter or it can mean 'tiring' if the diacritic 'kasrah' (short /i/) is on the same letter. Thus, for example, a book review with a positive rating starting with 'متعبه هذه الروايه' is mistranslated as 'Tired of this narration'. The correct translation of the adjective is 'This novel is tiring' where the reviewer is referring to the intellectual depth of the novel. Diacritic errors as such cause a misinterpretation of reviewer's sentiment stance. More examples are given in Appendix A.

### 3.3 Idiomatic Expressions

Idiomatic expressions both in MSA and DA are consistently mistranslated in the dataset which leads to a complete miss of the sentiment message in the review. For example, the MSA phrase 'خفيف الظل' is an idiom used to describe a 'funny' animate or inanimate noun. The idiom in the positive review 'كتاب خفيف الظل' (a funny book) is mistranslated as 'a light-shaded book'. The target text incorrectly reflects a neutral sentiment rather than the correct positive one. This idiom's counterpart in DA 'دمه خفيف' (funny) is also constantly mistranslated in the dataset. The review 'كتاب دمه خفيف جدا' ( the book is very funny) is mistranslated as 'his blood book is very light'. The manual analysis of the dataset set showed that, generally speaking, idioms, either in MSA or DA, constituted a challenge to the online automatic translation tool. A large number of idioms were literally translated which did not only affect the sentiment preservation of the source text, but often produced nonsensical target text. For example, the MSA phrase 'وهل يخفى القمر' is an idiom used to describe something that is unquestionably commended by the speaker. If the idiom is used in reference to a book, a good human translation would be: 'It really shines through'. The Google Translate gives a literal translation – ' Is the moon hidden?'– which flips the sentiment polarity of the review from highly positive to neutral. (See Appendix A for more examples).

### 3.4 Dialectical Expressions

Research studies have shown that dialectical Arabic presents several challenges to MT in general (Zbib et al., 2012). It was also observed from the manual analysis of the sample data that dialectical expressions constituted a special challenge for the preservation of sentiment in the source text. Arabic UGC is acceptably written in DA or MSA or a mix of both in the same text. A large number of DA sentiment expressions were either completely missed in the translation or mistranslated. For example, positive adjectives such as 'هايل' (great), or negative adjectives such as 'عبيط' (silly) were mostly mistaken for proper nouns and transliterated into non-English words (Hayel, Abit). In some instances, the translation was a complete opposite of the intended affect message (e.g. 'من الجمل العبيطه المنتشره' (one of the widespread silly sentences) was translated as 'one of the popular sentences spread ' (see more example in Appendix A).

### 3.5 Negation

Another type of sentiment errors that is also associated with the use of DA in Arabic UGC is the mistranslation of DA negation markers. Different Arabic dialects often treat negative particles as clitics, and hence a letter is added to the stem of the word to change it to negative (Mohamed et al., 2012). The majority of DA in the dataset belongs to the Egyptian dialect where negation is realized by the morpheme 'مش' (mish) which is either placed in front of the verb or preposition, or wrapped around it (Soltan, 2017). From the analysis, it was found out that the translation frequently either misses the negation and hence flips the phrase to the opposite sentiment pole or mistranslates the negated phrase all together. For example, in the review 'معجبنيش ان بطل الروايه ضعيف الشخصيه' (I didn't like that the

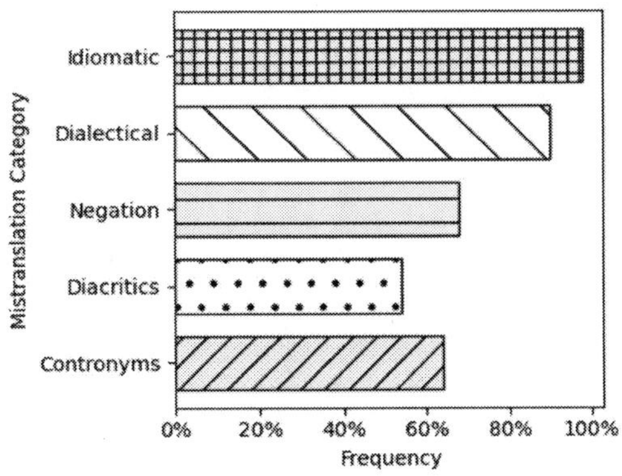

Figure 1: Frequency of Error Types

protagonist of the novel has a weak character) the negation is missed and hence the online translation output is 'I admire that the protagonist of the novel is weak in character'. There are several similar instances where the mistranslations of the DA negative structure switches the sentiment to its opposite pole (see more examples in appendix A).

## 4 Notes on Error Typology

In order to get an indication of the frequency of each type of errors in the whole dataset, words/phrases belonging to each group were extracted based on their frequency in the corpus then the frequency of their mistranslation in the dataset was manually calculated. Figure 1 shows the frequency of the mistranslation instances in the total reviews dataset of the extracted words as representative of each type of errors. As can be seen almost all the instances of the most frequent idiomatic and dialectical expressions are mistranslated. Moreover, around 65% of the time the positive meaning of contronyms was flipped to negative. Consequently, there were sentimentally incongruous terms where a positive noun was described with a highly improbable negative adjective (e.g. horrible achievement, terrible masterpiece, terrible happiness, and so on).

Our error typology showed that more than one type of errors is due to code-switching between DA and MSA in Arabic UGC. There have been several approaches to tackle the challenges of translating Arabic DA such as paraphrasing source text in MSA before translation (Salloum and Habash, 2013). Other studies have also proved that concatenating small amount of Arabic dialectical data can significantly improve the translation quality (Zbib et al., 2012). However, our error analysis has shown that even in MSA context the sentiment of words/phrases can be mistranslated. Pivoting on MSA can solve straightforward problems such as dialectical phrases and dialectical idioms. However, preserving the sentiment of the source text would require addressing the polarity of words with opposite meanings such as contronyms. Since it is beyond the scope of this paper to tackle all the error types, an attempt was made to address the problem of contronyms in Arabic UGC. In this paper we propose a sentiment-sensitive NMT model that is robust to the opposite sentiment polarities of Arabic contronyms either due to code-switching between DA and MSA or to contextual variations in Arabic UGC. Details of the experiment are explained in the following sections.

## 5 Sentiment Oriented NMT System

In order to improve the translation of contronyms in Arabic UGC, we propose two transformer (NMT) models infused with sentiment information at the encoding stage. We show that training on a sentiment oriented small-sized data can provide high performance results in preserving the sentiment of challenging contronyms in Arabic UGC. Details of data preprocessing and model architectures are explained in the following sections.

29

## 5.1 Parallel Data Preparation and Preprocessing

It is worth mentioning here that the available authentic parallel English/Arabic data is mostly English to Arabic data (e.g. UN parallel corpora, TEDx scripts, and Tatoeba project (Alotaibi, 2017; Ho and Simon, 2016)). The greatest part of this data is in Arabic MSA and is not sentiment-oriented. Authentic Arabic(DA)-English parallel data in general and authentic Arabic(UGC)-English parallel data in particular is very scarce. Recently, the use of synthetic corpora in NMT led to promising results especially when authentic parallel data is scarce (Chinea-Rios et al., 2017; Cheng et al., 2020). Moreover, infusing contextual cues in the input layer has proved successful in improving the robustness of the NMT models for different translation tasks even with relatively small-sized datasets (Johnson et al., 2017; Pal et al., 2014; Si et al., 2019). Accordingly, in order to identify the correct sentiment polarity of contronyms in Arabic UGC, we opted for using the synthetic parallel data of the Goodreads reviews dataset ($\approx 230,000$ sentences) for model training but with three main modifications. First, all the mistranslation instances of the chosen list of contronyms were manually post-edited (see appendix C for a list of most frequent contronyms used in the dataset). Second, the Arabic script underwent a number of preprocessing operations such as the normalization of orthographic letter forms, deletion of elongation and extra spaces. This has significantly reduced the number of out-of-vocabulary words. Third, we manually tagged all the contronyms in the source text with the right sentiment polarity according to its context. We experimented with both the tagged and the untagged post-edited source text. Details of the model architectures are in the following section.

## 5.2 NMT System Setup

In order to explore how we can improve the translation quality, we constructed three NMT models. The first is a baseline model that takes an untagged post-edited source text as input. The baseline is a seq2seq model with an LSTM of 200 hidden states for the encoder and decoder models trained with global attention. The other two models are sentiment sensitive models that take a tagged source text as input. For the two sentiment sensitive models, we mimicked the Google Translate setup (Vaswani et al., 2017) by using a transformer for both the encoding and decoding layers with 8 heads of self-attention and with an inner feed-forward layer of size 2048, but reduced the number of training steps from 200k to 100k. We used the Adam optimizer with $\beta1 = 0.9$, $\beta2 = 0.98$ and $\epsilon = 10^9$ and the Google set up special learning rate as described by Vaswani et al. (2017). The first of the two sentiment sensitive models was initialized with random input vectors. For the second model, we created a vector space model (VSM) of the tagged source dataset where each contronym was given two distinct vectors according to its tagged sentiment polarity. A bag of words Word2Vec model was used to create the pretrained vectors of the source text (Řehůřek and Sojka, 2010). It was trained with a hierarchical softmax and a window size of 5 tokens. The pretrained word embeddings were used to initialize the second transformer model with the same parameters used for the first. All experiments were run using OpenNMT (Klein et al., 2017).

## 5.3 Evaluation results

The evaluation of the proposed models was conducted on two test sets. The first was a held-out set from the Goodreads reviews ($\approx 47,000$ parallel sentences). The second was a hand-crafted test set of 140 sentences where we used the list of extracted contronyms with their positive and negative sentiment connotations in an equal number of sentences and code-switched between Arabic (MSA) and Arabic (DA) either in the same sentence or among different sentences. A reference translation was created by manually translating the hand-crafted set by a native speaker. In order to adequately evaluate the performance of the models in preserving the polarity of contronyms in the source text, we conducted two types of sentiment evaluations, at the word level and at the sentence level on the held-out test set and the hand-crafted test set respectively. We compared the quality measures on both the sentence and word levels of the proposed models with the Google Translate output for the test set and the hand-crafted test set. The BLEU score was also used as a metric to assess how far the quality of the translation is balanced with the preservation of sentiment by our proposed models. Details of the experiment evaluations are explained in the next sections.

| | Sentence Level | | Word Level | | | BLEU | | |
| | Hand-Crafted Set | | Test Set | | | Test Set | Hand-Crafted Set | |
| Model | Positive | Negative | Precision | Recall | F1 | | Positive | Negative |
|---|---|---|---|---|---|---|---|---|
| Seq2seq (no tagging) | .24 | .44 | 0.60 | 0.52 | 0.55 | 33.9 | 31.48 | 36.94 |
| Transformer 1 (tagging) | .14 | .21 | 0.74 | 0.65 | 0.69 | **38.77** | 37.56 | **44.83** |
| Transformer 2 (tagging and pre-trained) | **.06** | **.14** | **0.85** | **0.79** | **0.81** | 37.14 | **38.82** | 42.06 |
| Google Translate | .71 | .15 | 0.80 | .06 | .12 | | | |

Table 1: Results of Three Evaluation Metrics for Assessing Sentiment Preservation in Translation

### 5.3.1 Quality level

The first evaluation metric conducted on the two datasets was based on the BLEU score. We used the metric-internal multi-detokenized BLEU (Sennrich et al., 2015). The BLEU score was used to check that the quality of the translation is not distorted while fine-tuning the models for sentiment preservation. Results in table 1 show that both transformer models with tagged source text outperform the baseline on the two datasets. The first transformer model with tagged input, but without pretrained vectors, achieves the highest BLEU score on the test set and the negative hand-crafted test set with scores 38.77 and 44.83 respectively. The second transformer model trained on tagged source and pre-trained sentiment-oriented vectors achieves the best BLEU score on the positive hand-crafted test set (38.77). Results indicate that the overall translation quality as measured by BLEU has not been impaired with the sentiment-preservation approaches of the proposed transformer models.

### 5.3.2 Word-level Sentiment Evaluation

The BLEU score can reflect the translation quality of the NMT output, but for the present study it would not be appropriate to capture how the opposite sentiments of contronyms are correctly translated. This is because the BLEU score does not give a penalty to a mistranslated sentiment lexicon that is adequately proportional to the distortion of the sentiment message. The translation of the right sentiment polarity of a contronym can be pivotal in transferring the affect message of the source text. For example, the positive use of the contronym 'رهيبه' in the low-rated book review 'ليست تحفه ابداعيه رهيبه' (not a great creative masterpiece) is mistranslated as 'not a terrible creative masterpiece' by the baseline model. The mistranslation of the contronym completely distorts the sentiment message of the review, however, the BLEU score for this mistranslation is around 76.

Accordingly, we measured the precision, recall and F1 score of the different models to assess their ability to correctly predict the true positive and true negative polarity of the contronyms in the test dataset. Table 1 shows that the baseline model was not able to detect the correct sentiment orientation of a contronym with high accuracy, as compared to the two transformer models, despite the post-editing of the training dataset. Feeding in correct instances was not sufficient to improve the sentiment preservation of Arabic contronyms. Infusing linguistic information at the training stage, however, improved sentiment accuracy. Moreover, the low F1 score of the Google Translate (.12) was due to the fact that it was able to translate correctly instances of contronyms when used with negative sentiment, but failed to translate those where their positive meaning is used. Such positive cases constituted around 40% of the instances of contronyms in the dataset. This is because the negative meaning of contronyms is more frequent in Arabic MSA, whereas the positive is used more in Arabic DA context. As explained by the error typology, Google Translate performs far better with MSA than DA. On the other hand, the second transformer model which is trained on sentiment-sensitive pretrained vectors and tagged source text achieved best performance in depicting the true sentiment at the word level with an F1 score of .81 and a precision score of .85. The sentiment-sensitive pretrained vectors of contronyms and their polarity tagging with the second transformer model significantly helped in translating the correct sentiment at the word-level.

### 5.3.3 Sentence-level Sentiment Evaluation

The second metric for evaluating the translation of sentiment in Arabic UGC was carried out on the hand-crafted test set. In order to assess how the correct or incorrect translation of contronyms affects the total sentiment message of the source sentence, we propose a sentiment-score based metric. We compute the distance between the sentiment score of the reference sentence and the model output to measure not only how far the model preserves the sentiment of a contronym, but also the effect of translation on the sentiment context. We use the sentiment scoring methods used for error analysis, i.e. Microsoft Azure Sentiment Analysis scoring. We measure a translation cost as the mean square distance to the reference score:

$$\mu_C = \frac{1}{N} \sum_{i=1}^{N} (s_t - s_r)^2 \tag{1}$$

where $s_t$ is the score of the target sentence, $s_r$ is the score of the reference translation, and $N$ is the number of sentences.

As seen from table 1 the second transformer model trained on tagged contronyms and pretrained word vectors performed best (i.e. with the lowest cost) for both the positive and negative reviews (.06, .14 respectively). It was not only more sensitive to different polarities of contronyms due to the code-switching between MSA and DA, but produced the lowest sentiment discrepancy with the sentiment scores of the reference sentence. It is also worth noting that Google Translate performed much better with the negative sense of contronyms than the positive sense. This is in line with the findings presented in the previous section. With negative contronyms, Google Translate and the second transformer model had the lowest costs of .15 and .14, respectively. However, Google Translate produced the highest discrepancy with the positive instances (.71). Moreover, it was observed that the cost score was highest with short sentences. For instance, the positive sense of the contronym 'رهيبه' (awesome, great) in the short reference sentence 'رهيبه بكل المقاييس' (By all means awesome) is translated by Google Translate as 'Terrible by all accounts'. In such cases, the sentiment cost was maximum. It is evident that if a similar distortion of sentiment messages occurs in real-life situations, it would have adverse effects on the reviewers judgement. Examples of the output of the second transformer model (Trans2) as compared to the reference translation (Ref) and Google Translate is given in Appendix B.

## 6 Conclusion

This study has shown that Arabic UGC has peculiar qualities which constitute a challenge to automatic translation tools especially in its ability to preserve the sentiment message. An error typology was derived after analysing the data. This typology has highlighted how sentiment errors can impair the translation of sentiment-oriented Arabic UGC such as product reviews. Since automatic online translation tools are heavily relied upon by users and commercial platforms to translate reviews, it is of essential importance to fine-tune NMT models to the correct sentiment message in the source text. Moreover, it has been common practice for NMT training to use big parallel data which involves very high computational power and requires availability of large authentic data. The proposed NMT models in this study, however, showed that infusing contextual cues at the training stage of a relatively small data can improve the translation of sentiment in Arabic UGC both on the word and sentence level. This approach can help in providing greener training and make it feasible to construct competitive NMT tools for low-resource domains such as Arabic UGC. Moreover, we showed that translation quality metrics of sentiment-oriented Arabic UGC needs to be supplemented with other metrics that assess the preservation of sentiment. We proposed lexicon-based metrics that take into account the sentiment score of single words as well as their context. Finally, this study has tackled one of several challenges in the translation of sentiment in Arabic UGC. Future research will address the whole spectrum of challenges to improve the accuracy of sentiment preservation which is of vital importance in the translation of Arabic UGC.

# References


Mohamed Abdalla and Graeme Hirst. 2017. Cross-lingual sentiment analysis without (good) translation. *arXiv preprint arXiv:1707.01626.*

Haithem Afli, Sorcha Maguire, and Andy Way. 2017. Sentiment translation for low resourced languages: Experiments on Irish general election tweets. In *18th International Conference on Computational Linguistics and Intelligent Text Processing, Budapest, Hungry*, pages 17–21.

Hind M Alotaibi. 2017. Arabic-English parallel corpus: a new resource for translation training and language teaching. *Arab World English Journal (AWEJ) Volume*, 8.

Mohamed Aly and Amir Atiya. 2013. Labr: A large scale Arabic book reviews dataset. In *Proceedings of the 51st Annual Meeting of the Association for Computational Linguistics (Volume 2: Short Papers)*, pages 494–498.

Matheus Araujo, Julio Reis, Adriano Pereira, and Fabricio Benevenuto. 2016. An evaluation of machine translation for multilingual sentence-level sentiment analysis. In *Proceedings of the 31st Annual ACM Symposium on Applied Computing*, pages 1140–1145.

Amira Barhoumi, Chafik Aloulou, Nathalie Camelin, Yannick Estève, and Lamia Belguith. 2018. Arabic sentiment analysis: an empirical study of machine translation's impact. In *Proceedings of the second Conference on Language Processing and Knowledge Management Kerkennah (Sfax), Tunisia*.

Alexandre Bérard, Ioan Calapodescu, Marc Dymetman, Claude Roux, Jean-Luc Meunier, and Vassilina Nikoulina. 2019. Machine translation of restaurant reviews: New corpus for domain adaptation and robustness. *arXiv preprint arXiv:1910.14589.*

Shanbo Cheng, Shaohui Kuang, Rongxiang Weng, Heng Yu, Changfeng Zhu, and Weihua Luo. 2020. Auto-repair the synthetic data for neural machine translation. *arXiv preprint arXiv:2004.02196.*

Mara Chinea-Rios, Alvaro Peris, and Francisco Casacuberta. 2017. Adapting neural machine translation with parallel synthetic data. In *Proceedings of the Second Conference on Machine Translation*, pages 138–147.

Erkin Demirtas and Mykola Pechenizkiy. 2013. Cross-lingual polarity detection with machine translation. In *Proceedings of the Second International Workshop on Issues of Sentiment Discovery and Opinion Mining*, pages 1–8.

Trang Ho and Allan Simon. 2016. Tatoeba: Collection of sentences and translations. http://www.manythings.org/anki/.

Melvin Johnson, Mike Schuster, Quoc V Le, Maxim Krikun, Yonghui Wu, Zhifeng Chen, Nikhil Thorat, Fernanda Viégas, Martin Wattenberg, Greg Corrado, et al. 2017. Google's multilingual neural machine translation system: Enabling zero-shot translation. *Transactions of the Association for Computational Linguistics*, 5:339–351.

Guillaume Klein, Yoon Kim, Yuntian Deng, Jean Senellart, and Alexander M. Rush. 2017. OpenNMT: Open-Source Toolkit for Neural Machine Translation. In *Proc. ACL*.

Pintu Lohar, Haithem Afli, and Andy Way. 2017. Maintaining sentiment polarity in translation of user-generated content. *The Prague Bulletin of Mathematical Linguistics*, 108(1):73–84.

Pintu Lohar, Haithem Afli, and Andy Way. 2018. Balancing translation quality and sentiment preservation (non-archival extended abstract). In *Proceedings of the 13th Conference of the Association for Machine Translation in the Americas (Volume 1: Research Papers)*, pages 81–88.

Emad Mohamed, Behrang Mohit, and Kemal Oflazer. 2012. Transforming standard Arabic to colloquial Arabic. In *Proceedings of the 50th Annual Meeting of the Association for Computational Linguistics (Volume 2: Short Papers)*, pages 176–180.

Saif M Mohammad, Mohammad Salameh, and Svetlana Kiritchenko. 2016. How translation alters sentiment. *Journal of Artificial Intelligence Research*, 55:95–130.

Santanu Pal, Braja Gopal Patra, Dipankar Das, Sudip Kumar Naskar, Sivaji Bandyopadhyay, and Josef van Genabith. 2014. How sentiment analysis can help machine translation. In *Proceedings of the 11th International Conference on Natural Language Processing*, pages 89–94.

Bo Pang, Lillian Lee, and Shivakumar Vaithyanathan. 2002. Thumbs up? sentiment classification using machine learning techniques. *arXiv preprint cs/0205070.*

Radim Řehůřek and Petr Sojka. 2010. Software Framework for Topic Modelling with Large Corpora. In *Proceedings of the LREC 2010 Workshop on New Challenges for NLP Frameworks*, pages 45–50, Valletta, Malta, May. ELRA. http://is.muni.cz/publication/884893/en.

Mohammad Salameh, Saif Mohammad, and Svetlana Kiritchenko. 2015. Sentiment after translation: A case-study on Arabic social media posts. In *Proceedings of the 2015 conference of the North American chapter of the association for computational linguistics: Human language technologies*, pages 767–777.

Wael Salloum and Nizar Habash. 2013. Dialectal Arabic to English machine translation: Pivoting through modern standard Arabic. In *Proceedings of the 2013 Conference of the North American Chapter of the Association for Computational Linguistics: Human Language Technologies*, pages 348–358.

Rico Sennrich, Barry Haddow, and Alexandra Birch. 2015. Neural machine translation of rare words with subword units. *arXiv preprint arXiv:1508.07909*.

Gayane Shalunts, Gerhard Backfried, and Nicolas Commeignes. 2016. The impact of machine translation on sentiment analysis. *Data Analytics*, 63:51–56.

Chenglei Si, Kui Wu, Aiti Aw, and Min-Yen Kan. 2019. Sentiment aware neural machine translation. In *Proceedings of the 6th Workshop on Asian Translation*, pages 200–206.

Usama Soltan. 2017. The fine structure of the Neg-domain: evidence from Cairene Egyptian Arabic sentential negation. *Florida Linguistics Papers*, 4(3).

Ashish Vaswani, Noam Shazeer, Niki Parmar, Jakob Uszkoreit, Llion Jones, Aidan N Gomez, Łukasz Kaiser, and Illia Polosukhin. 2017. Attention is all you need. In *Advances in neural information processing systems*, pages 5998–6008.

Rabih Zbib, Erika Malchiodi, Jacob Devlin, David Stallard, Spyros Matsoukas, Richard Schwartz, John Makhoul, Omar Zaidan, and Chris Callison-Burch. 2012. Machine translation of Arabic dialects. In *Proceedings of the 2012 conference of the north american chapter of the association for computational linguistics: Human language technologies*, pages 49–59.

# Appendix A    Examples of the Error Typology for Sentiment Translation of Arabic UGC

| Error Category | Arabic Source | Google API | Correct Translation |
| --- | --- | --- | --- |
| Contronyms | لو ان هناك اكثر من الخمسه نجوم لاعطيتها لهذه الروايه الرهيبه | If there were more than five stars, I would have given it to this terrible narration | If there were more than five stars, I would have given it to this great novel |
| | جامد جدا | Very rigid | Excellent |
| | روايه رائعه واسلوبه جامد | Wonderful narration and rigid style | Wonderful novel and excellent style |
| | رائع بل وفظيع | Wonderful, even terrible | Wonderful, even magnificent |
| | الروايه فظيعه انصح الكل بقراءتها | The novel is horrible, I advise everyone to read it | The novel is magnificent, I advise everyone to read it. |
| | أدب الكاتب مش الفظيع | the writer's literature is not terrible | The writer's literature is not that great |
| Diacritic | من اظرف ما قرات | The envelope of what I read | One of the most entertaining things I read |
| | كم انت متعبه ياغاده في رومانسيتك | How tired you are Ghada in your romance | How tiring you are Ghada with your romance |
| | متعبه هذه الروايه | Tired of this narration | This narration is tiring |
| Idiomatic | كتاب دمه خفيف | The book of his blood is light | The book is funny |
| | اسلوب الكتاب خفيف الظل | The book's style is light in shade | The book's style is funny |
| | اسلوبه السهل الممتنع | His easy, reflexive style | His inimitably simple style |
| Dialectical | وحسيت انها قصه عبيطه | and I felt that it was a sweet story | And I felt it was a silly story |
| | روايه هايله | Haila narration | Excellent novel |
| Negation | محبتهاش | I love it | I didn't like it |
| | الشيء الوحيد الي معجبنيش استخدامه للالفاظ البذئنه | The only thing you like is that you use obscene words | The only thing I didn't like is the use of obscene words |
| | معجبنيش ان بطل الروايه ضعيف الشخصيه | I admire that the protagonist of the novel is weak in character | I didn't like that the protagonist of the novel has a weak character |

# Appendix B    Examples of Translation Models Output

| Arabic | Ref | Trans2 | Google |
|---|---|---|---|
| كتاب جامد  فعلا روايه رهيبه | A <u>great</u> book really an <u>awesome</u> novel | A really <u>good</u> book, a <u>great</u> narration | A <u>rigid</u> book really a <u>terrible</u> novel |
| روايه رهيبه كانت الظروف تمنعنى من البدء فيها | A <u>great</u> novel the circumstances were preventing me from starting it | A <u>great</u> narration the circumstances prevented me from starting it | A <u>horrible</u> novel the circumstances were preventing me from starting it |
| لو ان هناك اكثر من الخمسه نجوم لاعطيتها لهذه الروايه الرهيبه | If there were more than five stars, I would give it to this <u>awesome</u> novel | If there were more than five stars, I would have given it to this <u>great</u> novel | If there were more than five stars, I would give her for this <u>horrible</u> novel |
| رهيبه ملهاش حل بجد | <u>Amazingly great</u> | Awesome, <u>absolutely great</u> | <u>Terrible</u> you can't solve really hard |
| جامد  جدا لدرجه انى خلصته فى يومين | It is so <u>good</u> that I finished it in two days | <u>Very good</u> to the point that I concluded it in two days | <u>Too rigid</u> to the point that I finished it in two days |
| الروايه ساحره بطريقه فظيعه | The novel is charming in a <u>terrific</u> way | The novel is charming in an <u>awesome</u> way | The novel is <u>terribly</u> charming |
| بغض النظر عن الاخطاء الاملائيه الفظيعه | Despite the <u>terrible</u> spelling mistakes | Regardless of the <u>terrible</u> spelling mistakes | Regardless of the <u>horrible</u> misspellings |
| كتاب و روايه جامده لا تشويق فيها | A <u>rigid</u> book and a novel that has no suspense | A book and a <u>rigid</u> novel with no suspense | A book and a <u>static</u> novel with no suspense |
| تحفه فظيعه | A <u>great</u> masterpiece | <u>Awesome</u> masterpiece | A <u>terrible</u> masterpiece |

# Appendix C    List of Most Frequent Contronyms

| Contronyms | Negative Meaning | Positive Meaning |
| --- | --- | --- |
| جامد | Rigid | Good |
| جامده | Rigid | Good |
| الجامد | The rigid | The Good |
| الجامده | The rigid | The Good |
| رهيب | Terrible | Great |
| رهيبه | Terrible | Great |
| الرهيب | The terrible | The Great |
| الرهيبه | The terrible | The Great |
| فظيع | Horrible | Terrific |
| فظيعه | Horrible | Terrific |
| الفظيع | The horrible | The Terrific |
| الفظيعه | The horrible | The Terrific |
| خرافي | Mythical | Fabulous |
| خرافيه | Fairy | Fabulous |
| الخرافي | The mythical | The fabulous |
| الخرافيه | The fairy | The fabulous |
| يجنن | Drives one crazy | Amazing |
| تجنن | Drives one crazy | Amazing |
| لاتشبع | You cannot have enough | Insatiable |
| يشد | Attracts | Tightens |
| تشد | Attracts | Tightens |
| اعجزت | Mesmerized | Crippled |

# Deep Diacritization: Efficient Hierarchical Recurrence for Improved Arabic Diacritization


Badr AlKhamissi[1], Muhammad N. ElNokrashy[1,2], and Mohamed Gabr[2]

badr@khamissi.com, muhammad.nael@gmail.com, mohamed.gabr@hotmail.com

[1]*The American University in Cairo (AUC)*
[2]*Microsoft Egypt Development Center (EGDC)*


## Abstract


We propose a novel architecture for labelling character sequences that achieves state-of-the-art results on the Tashkeela Arabic diacritization benchmark. The core is a two-level recurrence hierarchy that operates on the word and character levels separately—enabling faster training and inference than comparable traditional models. A cross-level attention module further connects the two, and opens the door for network interpretability. The task module is a softmax classifier that enumerates valid combinations of diacritics. This architecture can be extended with a recurrent decoder that optionally accepts priors from partially diacritized text, which improves results. We employ extra tricks such as sentence dropout and majority voting to further boost the final result. Our best model achieves a WER of 5.34%, outperforming the previous state-of-the-art with a 30.56% relative error reduction.


## 1 Introduction

The Arabic script (and similarly Hebrew, Aramaic, Pahlavi...) is an impure abjad. These writing systems represent short consonants and long vowels using full letter graphemes, but generally omit short vowels and consonant length from writing. This leaves the task of inferring the missing phonemes to the reader by using context from neighbouring words and knowledge of the language structure to determine the correct pronunciation and disambiguate the meaning of the text. Those sounds are represented by diacritical marks—small graphemes that appear usually above or below a basic letter in the abjad. Table 2 shows the diacritics considered in this work. Diacritics are usually utilized in specific domains where it is important to explicitly clear up ambiguities or where inferring the correct forms might be difficult for non-experts, such as religious texts, some literary works such as poetry, and language teaching books as novice readers have yet to build up the intuition for reading undiacritized text.

We focus in this work on diacritization of Arabic texts. However, our proposed architecture has no explicitly language-dependent components and should be adaptable for other character sequence labelling tasks. Although it is the first language of several million people, and is spoken in some of the fastest growing markets (Tinsley and Board, 2013), the Arabic language, like many others, lacks attention from the NLP community compared to established test bed languages such as English or Chinese, which both enjoy higher momentum and an abundance of established resources and techniques. The automatic restoration of diacritics to Arabic text is arguably one of the most important NLP tasks for the Arabic language. Besides direct applications like facilitating learning, diacritics are used to enhance language modeling, acoustic modeling for speech recognition, morphological analysis, machine translation, and text-to-speech systems (which need to restore the lost phonemes to render words properly) (Zitouni and Sarikaya, 2009; Azmi, 2013).




Affiliation emails: [1]{balkhamissi, m.n.elnokrashy}@aucegypt.edu
[2]{muelnokr, mogabr}@microsoft.com
* This work is not sponsored by the affiliated institutions of the authors.
** This work was accepted at the Fifth Arabic Natural Language Processing Workshop (WANLP 2020).





*Proceedings of the Fifth Arabic Natural Language Processing Workshop*, pages 38–48
Barcelona, Spain (Online), December 12, 2020

To illustrate this further, Table 1 shows the Arabic word *Elm*[1] in different diacritized forms with their corresponding English translations, showcasing the importance of diacritics in resolving ambiguity. Note that the MADA (Habash et al., 2009) morphological analyzer produces at least 13 different forms for this undiacritized word (Belinkov and Glass, 2015).

| Arabic (diacritized) | Transliteration | English Translation |
|---|---|---|
| عَلِمَ | *Ealima* | He knew |
| عُلِمَ | *Eulima* | It was known |
| عَلَّمَ | *Eal∼ama* | He taught |
| عِلْمُ | *Eilomu* | Knowledge |
| عَلَمُ | *Ealamu* | Flag |

Table 1: Subset of possible diacritized forms for *Elm* adapted from (Belinkov and Glass, 2015)

Table 2 shows the different diacritics commonly used in Arabic texts along with their phonemic symbols. They fit roughly into four kinds. (1) Ḥarakāt are diacritics for short vowels; we have three: fatḥah, kasrah, dammah. The symbols for those vowels have another form (usually a visual doubling) used at the end of a word to form a (2) tanwīn, or nunation, which is a VC sound of the ḥarakah's vowel followed by the consonant "n" ($\{a, i, u\}n$). (3) The shaddah is the gemination symbol used to indicate consonant doubling. It can be combined with one of the ḥarakāt or tanwīn on the same character. Finally, (4) the sukūn is used to indicate that the current consonant is not followed by a vowel and instead forms a cluster with the next consonant. Diacritics which appear at the end of a word are referred to as case-endings (CE); most of which are specified by the syntactic role of the word. They are harder to infer than the core-word diacritics (CW) that specify lexical selection and appear on the rest of the word (Mubarak et al., 2019).

| Symbol | Name | Type | Transliteration | IPA phoneme |
|---|---|---|---|---|
| ُ | dammah | ḥarakāt | *u* | /u/ |
| َ | fathah | ḥarakāt | *a* | /a/ |
| ِ | kasrah | ḥarakāt | *i* | /i/ |
| ٌ | dammatain | tanwīn | *N* | /un/ |
| ً | fathatain | tanwīn | *F* | /an/ |
| ٍ | kasratain | tanwīn | *K* | /in/ |
| ّ | shaddah | shaddah | ∼ | /h:/ Gemination. |
| ْ | sukūn | sukūn | *o* | No vowel. |

Table 2: Primary Arabic diacritics on letter ه

The paper is structured as follows: First we cover some of the approaches used in related works on restoring Arabic diacritics. Then we introduce our system and support it by comparing experimental results on an adapted version of the Tashkeela corpus (Zerrouki and Balla, 2017) proposed by (Fadel et al., 2019a) as a standard benchmark for Arabic diacritization systems. Each design decision will then be motivated by an ablation study. We analyze the learned attention model then discuss existing limitations in an error analysis. Finally, we offer directions for future work.

---

[1]This paper uses Buckwalter transliteration.

## 2   Related Work

The literature surrounding the automatic diacritization of Arabic text provides methods in two categories: classical rule-based solutions, and statistical modeling-based methods. Early approaches have worked on constructing a large set of language specific rules to restore the lost diacritics (Habash et al., 2009; Zitouni et al., 2006; Pasha et al., 2014; Darwish et al., 2017). Researchers have then shifted to rely more on learning-based methods that do not require extra expert systems such as morphological analyzers and part-of-speech taggers. (Belinkov and Glass, 2015) have shown that recurrent neural networks are suitable candidate models for learning the task entirely from data and can be easily extended to other languages and dialects without the use of manually engineered features. Other methods such as hidden Markov models (HMMs) (Elshafei et al., 2006), conditional random fields (CRFs) (Darwish et al., 2017), maximum-entropy models (Zitouni et al., 2006) and finite-state transducers (Nelken and Shieber, 2005) have similarly been employed. However, more recent works have started to use deep (neural-based) architectures such as sequence-to-sequence transformers and recurrent cell-based models inspired by work in Neural Machine Translation (Mubarak et al., 2019). Solutions combining both rule-based and deep learning methods appear in recently published work (Abbad and Xiong, 2020). (Zalmout and Habash, 2020) have shown that the diacritization task benefits from jointly modelling lexicalized and non-lexicalized morphological features instead of targeting only the diacritization task.

## 3   Approach

### 3.1   Datasets

We report on the cleaned version of the Tashkeela corpus (Fadel et al., 2019a)—a high quality, publicly available dataset. It is split into train (2,449k tokens), dev (119k tokens), and test (125k tokens) sets.

### 3.2   Architecture

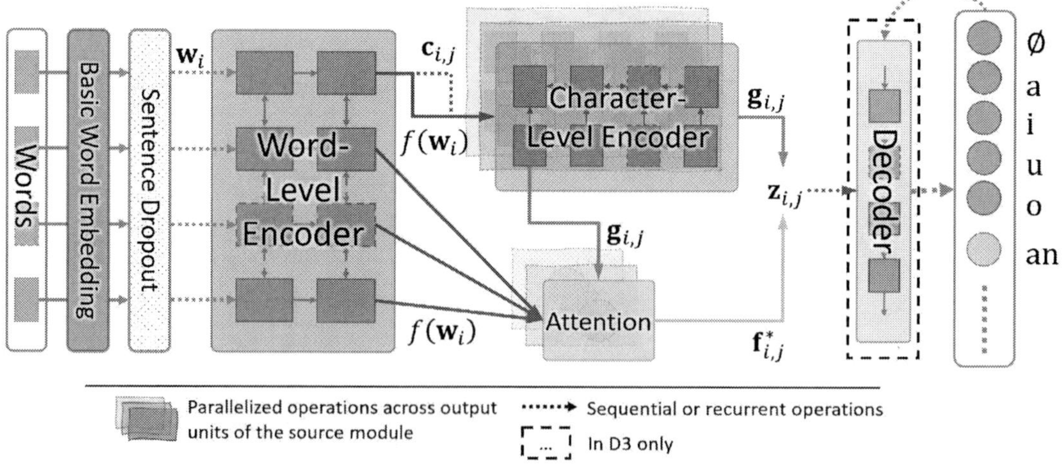


Figure 1: D3 Architecture

In this work, we propose two models: The Two-Level Diacritizer (D2) and the Two-Level Diactritizer with Decoder (D3). D3 extends D2 by allowing partially diacritized text to be taken as input—a much needed feature for neural diacritizers (Fadel et al., 2019a). D2 outperforms fully character-based models in both task and runtime performance measures.

### 3.2.1   Two-Level (Hierarchical) Model

Restoring diacritics can be seen as a character sequence labeling task. Each label depends on word- and character-level context. This structure motivates the hierarchy in our two-level encoder architecture— the first encoder sees the sequence of words (where words are atoms) and provides word-level context for the second, character-level encoder. The character-level encoder is evaluated independently for each word in the sentence, enabling much faster training and inference compared to character-level recurrent cell-based models of similar structure to previous works (Belinkov and Glass, 2015; Mubarak et al., 2019; Zalmout and Habash, 2020; Fadel et al., 2019b). Let $T_s$ be the maximum number of words allowed in a sentence and $T_w$ the maximum number of characters allowed in a word. Then the overall character sequence length that a model in prior works would see is in the order of $(T_s \cdot T_w)$. In contrast, our approach operates on a maximum sequence length of $T_s$ at the word level and $T_w$ at the character level. Because character-level recurrence is independent of characters outside the current word, the serial bottleneck complexity goes from $O\left(\sum_{w \in s} |w|\right) \approx O(T_s \cdot T_w)$ down to $O\left(|s| + \max_{w \in s}\{|w|\}\right) \approx O(T_s + T_w)$, assuming adequate parallelization across word units. See Table 4 for a speed comparison.

Let $s = \{w_i\}_{i=1}^{T_s}$ denote a sequence of words. $\mathbf{w} = \{\mathbf{w}_i\}_{i=1}^{T_s}$ are the corresponding fastText features pretrained on CommonCrawl Arabic data (Bojanowski et al., 2017). Let $w_i = \{c_{i,j}\}_{j=1}^{T_w}$ denote the sequence of characters for the word at index $i$ in sentence $s$. Each character is assigned a 32-dimensional learned embedding $\mathbf{c}_{i,j}$. Let $f(\mathbf{w})_i$ denote the feature vector from the word-level encoder which maps each word in $s$ to a contextual word representation. Let $g(\cdot)_{i,j}$ denote the character-level recurrence that outputs a contextual encoding of the character relative to its parent word and sentence. See Figure 1 for an overview. Formally, the contextual embedding $\mathbf{z}_{i,j}$ of $c_{i,j}$ is

$$\mathbf{g}_{i,j} = g\left([\mathbf{c}_{i,j} ; f(\mathbf{w})_i]\right) \tag{1}$$

$$\mathbf{z}_{i,j} = \left[\mathbf{g}_{i,j} ; \mathbf{f}_{i,j}^*\right] \tag{2}$$

Where $\mathbf{f}_{i,j}^*$ is the attention view. Both $f(\cdot)$ and $g(\cdot)$ use Bidirectional LSTM (Bi-LSTM) layers (Graves et al., 2005) trained with backpropagation through time. We note that any similar sequence modelling architecture would be applicable (Chung et al., 2014; Vaswani et al., 2017) but leave that to future work.

### 3.2.2 Cross-level Attention Module

This module attends over the word-level encodings $f(\mathbf{w})$ based on the character encodings $g(\cdot)$ of each character in a word. In other words, it uses the initial contextualization of the characters ($\mathbf{g}_{i,j}$) to attend to all words in the sentence (except the current) to refine the character's representation. We use the attention formulation from (Vaswani et al., 2017). For each character $c_{i,j}$, we calculate

$$\mathbf{f}_{i,j}^* = \text{AttendReduce}\left(\mathbf{u} = \mathbf{g}_{i,j} ; \mathbf{X} = \{...f(\mathbf{w})_{0:i-1}, f(\mathbf{w})_{i+1:T_s}...\}\right) \tag{3}$$

where

$$\text{AttendReduce}\left(\mathbf{u}; \mathbf{X}\right) = W^O \left(\underset{t}{\text{Softmax}} \left(\frac{W^Q(\mathbf{u}) \cdot W^K(\mathbf{X})_t^\top}{\sqrt{d_K}}\right) \cdot W^V(\mathbf{X})\right) \tag{4}$$

where in eq. (4), $W^Q$, $W^K$, $W^V$, and $W^O$ are independent linear layers. We tried to remove $W^O$ but faced lower performance.

### 3.2.3 Decoder

Used in D3, this component is a forward-only LSTM that takes as input a concatenation of the basic contextual character embedding $\mathbf{z}_{i,j}$ and a one-hot representation of the output of the previous character from the classifier module. Formally: $[\mathbf{z}_{i,j}; \hat{\mathbf{y}}_{i,j-1}]$. The $\hat{\mathbf{y}}_{i,j-1}$ signal passed to the decoder also encodes the Beginning-of-Word in addition to the previous-character diacritics. This allows the model to accept partially diacritized sentences such that the ground truth diacritic is injected in place of $\hat{\mathbf{y}}_{i,j-1}$ during inference. This feature is important as many Arabic texts contain sparse diacritics that act as hints to assist readers. Having this clean signal yields improvements as shown in Figure 2.

### 3.2.4 Task Objective

The final classifier optimizes a Softmax objective over an enumeration of all valid diacritic combinations. Combined, we have 3 ḥarakāt in 4 variants (with tanwīn, shadda, tanwīn and shadda, and neither), the sukūn, and the plain shadda. Thus 15 classes including the None (no diacritic) class.

### 3.3 Experimental Setup

#### 3.3.1 Parameters, Hyper-parameters, and Regularization

**Optimization**  We use the Adam optimizer (Kingma and Ba, 2014) with an initial learning rate of 0.002. The model is left to converge until the validation loss does not improve for 3 consecutive epochs where each epoch enumerates a randomly shuffled version of the training segments exactly once. The learning rate is reduced by half when the validation loss does not improve for one epoch. We train with a mini-batch size of 128 segments.

**Encoders and Decoder**  The word and character level encoders are *each* a 2-layer stacked Bi-LSTM with 256 and 512 hidden units, respectively. We apply feature-level dropout (Srivastava et al., 2014) with probability 0.2 to the input of the character level encoder. The decoder in D3 is a one-layer forward-only LSTM with 1024 hidden units. All recurrent cells use a vertical and recurrent dropout of 0.25 each. The recurrent dropout used is untied between time-steps, in contrast to (Gal and Ghahramani, 2016).

**Context Window and Voting**  Similar to (Mubarak et al., 2019), we use a sliding context window of size $T_s$ on each sentence. A given sentence is split into several overlapping segments each of which is given separately to the model during training. This works well as the local context is often sufficient for correct inference. During inference, the same sequence of characters may appear in different contexts (different segments from one sentence) and potentially lead to different diacritized forms. To choose the final diacritic, we use a popularity voting mechanism and, in the case of a tie, choose one of the outputs at random. The values chosen for $T_s$, $T_w$ and the *stride* are: $T_s = 10$ with *stride* $= 1$ for training and validation (a small $T_s$ was observed to stabilize training and improve results); $T_s = 20$ with *stride* $= 2$ for evaluation/testing; and $T_w = 13$ for both training and evaluation.

**Sentence Dropout**  We randomly dropout 20% of the words given to the word-level encoder during training. The positions of the dropped out words are preserved, and their embedding vectors $\mathbf{w}_i$ are replaced with zeros. This was observed to lead to better generalization in some cases.

#### 3.3.2 D3 Training

This model is not trained from scratch, but uses the weights of the encoders and character embeddings learned from D2. Those weights are kept frozen and only the decoder and classifier are trained.

**Ramp-up of Teacher-forcing Signal**  We pass the ground truth of $p\%$ of the previous-character diacritics as input to the decoder at the current time-step. This value is ramped up from $p = 0\%$ (all characters receive previous diacritics as zeros; i.e. no signal) to $p = 100\%$ (all characters receive ground truth of previous diacritic as signal). This is done over a period of $n = 10$ epochs in increments of 10%. Then the model is left to converge using the same stopping criteria as in D2. We found this to be the best approach as otherwise the model overfits early on the teacher forcing signal given from the previous time-step.

#### 3.3.3 Source Code

The code is made open source and is available on GitHub[2]. We also provide an accompanying web application to demo the proposed models which can be found at this web address[3]. The system uses PyTorch for implementing the neural training and inference components (Paszke et al., 2019). The PyTorch LSTM cell implementation used is due to (ElNokrashy, 2020).

### 3.4 Results

We use the script provided by (Fadel et al., 2019a) to evaluate our results. To be consistent with prior work, we report our results in terms of both word error-rate (WER) and diacritic error-rate (DER), with and without case-endings, as well as including and excluding characters with no diacritics. Table 3 shows our results on the Tashkeela benchmark in comparison with the more recent works. We outperform state-of-the-art by 30.56% relative (2.35% absolute) error reduction on "WER with case-ending".

---

[2]https://github.com/bkhmsi/deep-diacritization
[3]https://deep-diacritization.herokuapp.com
[4]Results from (Fadel et al., 2019a).

| DER/WER | Including 'no diacritic' | | Excluding 'no diacritic' | |
|---|---|---|---|---|
| | w/ case ending | w/o case ending | w/ case ending | w/o case ending |
| (Barqawi, 2017)[4] | 3.73% / 11.19% | 2.88% / 6.53% | 4.36% / 10.89% | 3.33% / 6.37% |
| (Fadel et al., 2019b) | 2.60% / 7.69% | 2.11% / 4.57% | 3.00% / 7.39% | 2.42% / 4.44% |
| (Abbad and Xiong, 2020) | 3.39% / 9.94% | 2.61% / 5.83% | 3.34% / 7.98% | 2.43% / 3.98% |
| D2 (Ours) | 1.85% / 5.53% | 1.49% / 3.27% | 2.11% / 5.26% | 1.71% / 3.15% |
| D3 (Ours) (@0% hints) | **1.83% / 5.34%** | **1.48% / 3.11%** | **2.09% / 5.08%** | **1.69% / 3.00%** |

Table 3: Results on the Tashkeela benchmark

| Method | #Params | T/epoch | Convergence | Inference | Full DER/WER |
|---|---|---|---|---|---|
| **D2 – {Attn}** | 13.369M | **28 mins** | 17 epochs | **34,996 wps** | **1.94% / 5.80%** |
| **Flat** | **13.304M** | 121 mins | **13 epochs** | 2,466 wps | 2.20% / 6.39% |

Table 4: Speed Comparison[5]

Table 4 compares our plain 2-level hierarchy design (without Attention) with a "Flat" model in task and runtime performance. The Flat model comprises a 4-layer stacked Bi-LSTM with similar implementation details as described in 3.3.1 for D2, including Sentence Dropout and the Voting mechanism. The Flat model sees each sentence as one sequence of characters.

**Partially Diacritized Text**  Figure 2 shows the results of DER including 'no diacritic' with and without case ending when the model is supplied with partially diacritized text as input. For each character in the sentence, with some probability, we may replace the predicted output of the previous time-step with the ground truth as input to the decoder in the current step. The reported output of the previous time-step is masked to force the provided hint to be the model's "prediction" even if the inferred were different (see Figure 2b)—in contrast to Figure 2a where the final predictions are the model's unmodified outputs. The results are averaged across five runs with different seeds (i.e. injecting the ground truth signal at different characters in the sentence). Error bars represent standard deviation. Many Arabic texts already come with some hints that can improve model performance. Here we show how a neural model could be trained to leverage that.

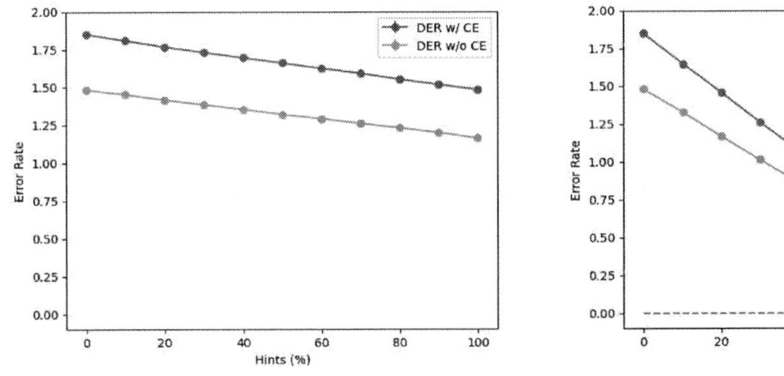
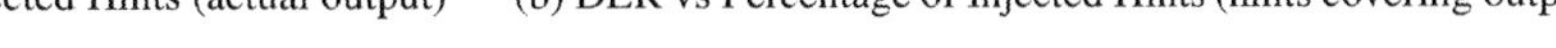

(a) DER vs Percentage of Injected Hints (actual output)  (b) DER vs Percentage of Injected Hints (hints covering output)

Figure 2: Error Rate of Partially Diacritized Text

[5]All models use the same custom LSTM implementation and are run on a single Nvidia GeForce RTX 2080 Ti.

## 4  Discussion

### 4.1  Ablation Study

We conduct an ablation study to measure the effect of components proposed for the final model. We train and evaluate the D2 model previously detailed but with the component(s) specified removed. Table 5 shows the results after removing the sentence dropout and cross-level attention module.

| DER/WER | Including 'no-diacritic' | | Excluding 'no-diacritic' | |
|---|---|---|---|---|
| | w/ case ending | w/o case ending | w/ case ending | w/o case ending |
| (Fadel et al., 2019b) | 2.60% / 7.69% | 2.11% / 4.57% | 3.00% / 7.39% | 2.42% / 4.44% |
| D3 (@0% hints) | **1.83% / 5.34%** | **1.48% / 3.11%** | **2.09% / 5.08%** | **1.69% / 3.00%** |
| D2 | 1.85% / 5.53% | 1.49% / 3.27% | 2.11% / 5.26% | 1.71% / 3.15% |
| D2 − {Attention 3.2.2} | 1.94% / 5.80% | 1.58% / 3.44% | 2.23% / 5.52% | 1.80% / 3.31% |
| D2 − {SDO 3.3.1} | 1.91% / 5.71% | 1.54% / 3.36% | 2.18% / 5.43% | 1.75% / 3.23% |
| D2 − {Attn, SDO} | 1.93% / 5.78% | 1.57% / 3.45% | 2.21% / 5.49% | 1.79% / 3.32% |

Table 5: Ablation Study

### 4.2  Attention Analysis

The cross-level attention module allows us to gauge the contribution of each word to each output diacritic. Here we examine some examples to see whether the model was able to learn such Arabic grammar rules as a human expert would use when annotating case endings. The examples presented in this section reflect patterns we have found repeated during our analysis.

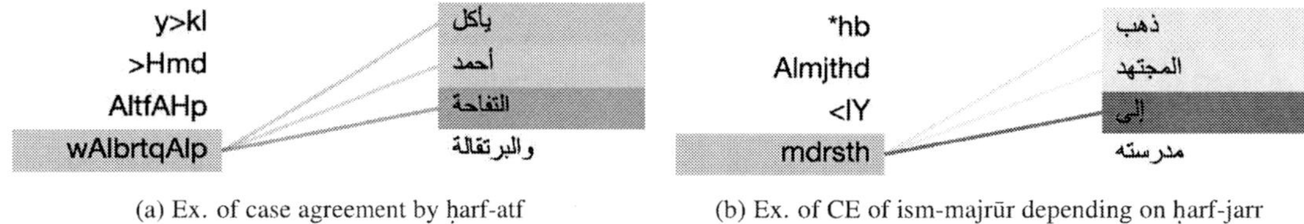

(a) Ex. of case agreement by ḥarf-atf

(b) Ex. of CE of ism-majrūr depending on ḥarf-jarr

Figure 3: Attention visualization of words correctly attending to grammatical parents.

The pattern in Figure 3a is related to the ḥarf-atf[6] rule (generally prepositions), which states that the word coming after it gets the same case as the main word of the phrase it is related to—the grammatical parent. We see indeed that the word coming after the ("w") ḥarf-atf attends the most on the word that comes before it. This is similar to what an expert would do; look at the main word in the phrase preceding the "w" in order to determine the case and case-ending of what follows.

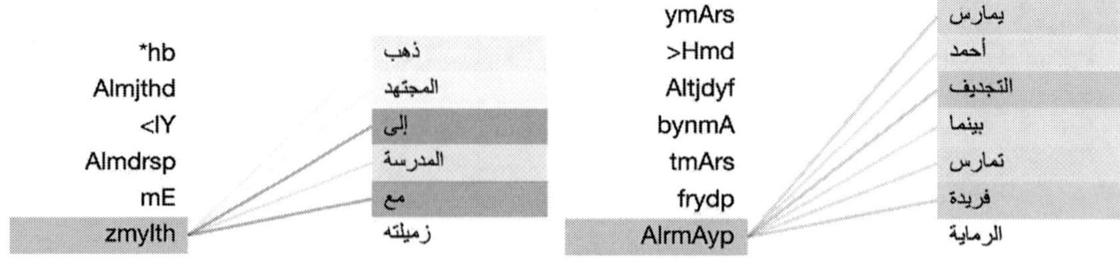

(a) *Self* attends on a local word with similar *effect* on *Self*

(b) *Self* attends on a local word with similar *role* to *Self*

Figure 4: Attention visualization of confusion of grammatical parents.

---

حرف عطف[6]

Figure 3b shows another prevalent example where the word in question attends the most on the ḥarf-jarr[7] preceding it. However, in other cases where the same rule appears twice in a segment, we found that the model may choose to attend equally or more on the components of the first occurrence rather than the occurrence the current word is actually affected by—the grammatical parent. Figure 4a shows one example of this where the word ("zmylth") attends equally to two words that would affect it the same ("<lY" and "mE"), but only the second should be affecting it. In Figure 4b we see that the second maf'ool-bih[8] (roughly an object of a verb) ("AlrmAyp") attends heavily on the first occurrence of a mf'ool-bih in the segment ("Altjdyf"), rather than the verb that should be affecting it ("tmArs"). This behavior of attending on a previous word with a similar role suggests that the attention mechanism is aware of grammatical rules; it is able to group words with the same role together.

Generally, we found that not all sentences yield interpretable attention weights. We leave the task of comprehensively studying the extent of agreement of the learned weights with Arabic grammatical rules to future work.

### 4.3   Error Analysis

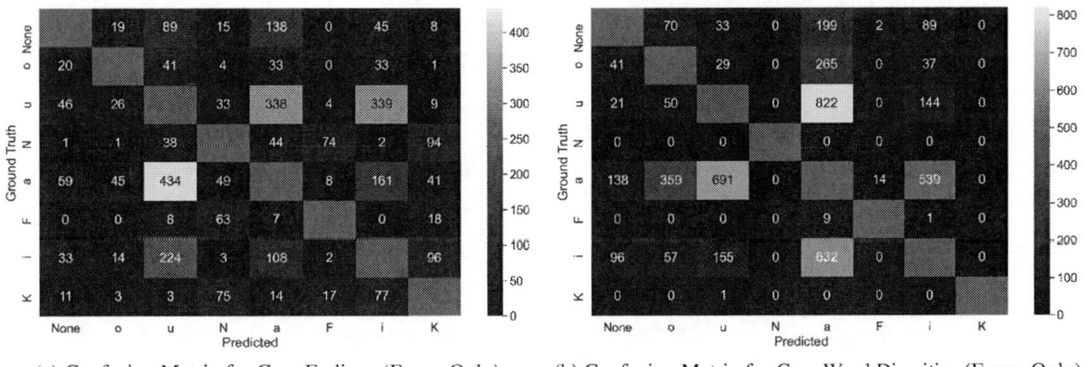

(a) Confusion Matrix for Case Endings (Errors Only)    (b) Confusion Matrix for Core Word Diacritics (Errors Only)

Figure 5: Error Confusion Matrix for CE and Core Diacritics

Figures 5a and 5b show the the confusion matrices (for visualization clarity we show errors only) of case ending and core words diacritics respectively. Many confusions are between the dammah and kasrah, and between dammah and fatḥah, and the confusion goes both ways. We analyze the errors between kasrah and dammah for case endings and try to correlate them with grammar rules.

The first error example is related to the start of a new sentence in Arabic grammar. The word "wa" composed of one letter can either mark a conjunction (e.g. in an enumeration), or mark the start of a new sentence, based on context. An example with such confusion is in the following sentence, with the ground truth: "wa yarud~u Ealayohi >an~a faAqida AlT~ahuwrayoni wa naHowahu layosa lahu SalaApN <l~aA <*aA DaAqa Alowaqotu" [9] . We see one confusion example where "wa naHowah" was predicted as "wa naHowih". Grammatically, the "wa" relates the next word to a "sentence starter" word ("faAqida") in a case that would make **a** the correct diacritic. Instead, we observe it follows the word immediately before the "wa" ("AlT~ahuw**r**ayoni"), which is indeed in a grammatical case that would make **i** the correct diacritic for "naHow{a/i}h", were it the correct grammatical parent of this "wa".

The second example is related to the use of punctuation marks that signal an abrupt start of a new sentence or an end of one with unique context that may not be easily learnt. In the following sentence with the ground truth: "kaqaA}ilK : AloHar~u >awo Alobarod**u** Al$~adiyd**u**" [10] was predicted as

حَرْف جَرّ [7]

مفعول به [8]

وَيَرُدُّ عَلَيْهِ أَنَّ فَاقِدَ الطَّهُورَيْنِ وَنَحْوَهُ لَيْسَ لَهُ صَلَاةٌ إِلَّا إِذَا ضَاقَ الْوَقْتُ [9]

كَقَائِل: الْحَرُّ أَوِ الْبَرْدُ الشَّدِيدُ... [10]

"kaqaA}ilK : AloHar~i >awo Alobarodi Al$~adiydi...". The mark ":" here denotes the start of a new sentence, by convention, as we start a quotation. In speech, this would manifest as a brief pause or change in tone. Without ":", the word would be an ism-majrūr that takes the kasrah ḥarakah (**i**) in this position, which the model mistakenly outputs. But because it starts a new sentence, the correct diacritic is a dammah ḥarakah (**u**). Further, the predictions for the words following ">awo" behave grammatically by following the case of the parent word ("AloHar~**i**") (according to "wa"), but are incorrect because the error has propagated.

One other type of errors is related to inconsistencies in the corpus—the same word with the same role in the sentence is not diacritized the same way across the dataset. For instance, the word "<lY", which is the second top word that causes a core word error as shown in Table 6, appears multiple times in different forms: "<ilY", "<lY", and "<ilaY"—all correct. There are other examples that show the need to clean the dataset (at least the test set) to evaluate the published models properly.

| Top words / Rank | 1 | 2 | 3 | 4 | 5 | 6 | 7 | 8 | 9 | 10 |
|---|---|---|---|---|---|---|---|---|---|---|
| With wrong CE diacritics | غير | عن | كل | بن | قلت | مثل | ثم | يوم | و | من |
| With wrong core diacritics | الله | إلى | ذكر | من | إلا | علم | إن | قبل | وسلّم | قوله |

Table 6: Top 10 Words with CE and Core Word Errors

Looking at the top words that yield confusions in both core words and case ending diacritics, we find a notable intersection between Table 6 and the most frequent tokens in the Tashkeela corpus with an average max-normalized frequency of 0.24 (0.24 as frequent as the most frequent word).

## 5 Conclusion

In this work, we presented a novel architecture that outperforms previously published results on the Tashkeela Arabic diacritization benchmark. Future work may include:

- Replacing the word- and character- level Bi-LSTM encoders with transformer-based encoders.
- Using byte-pair-encoding (BPE) (Sennrich et al., 2016) to better handle suffixes and prefixes as Arabic is a moderately fusional language.
- Investigating more efficient use of injected hints to improve performance.
- Training/Evaluating this design/model on Modern Standard Arabic and dialectical benchmarks.
- Cleaning the testset of Tashkeela to remove any inconsistencies as described in the error analysis.
- Finally, achieving more interpretable attention weights through multi-task training, training on larger datasets, or otherwise.

## Acknowledgements

We offer special thanks to *Khaled Essam*, as well as *Mohamed Afify* and *Ahmed Tawfik* of *Microsoft EGDC*, for many helpful discussions, suggestions and comments on the paper.

## References

Hamza Abbad and Shengwu Xiong. 2020. Multi-components system for automatic arabic diacritization. In Joemon M. Jose, Emine Yilmaz, João Magalhães, Pablo Castells, Nicola Ferro, Mário J. Silva, and Flávio Martins, editors, *Advances in Information Retrieval*, pages 341–355, Cham. Springer International Publishing.

Aqil Azmi. 2013. A survey of automatic arabic diacritization techniques. *Natural Language Engineering*, 21, 10.

Zerrouki Barqawi. 2017. Shakkala, Arabic text vocalization. https://github.com/Barqawiz/Shakkala.

Yonatan Belinkov and James Glass. 2015. Arabic diacritization with recurrent neural networks. In *Proceedings of the 2015 Conference on Empirical Methods in Natural Language Processing*, pages 2281–2285, Lisbon, Portugal, September. Association for Computational Linguistics.

Piotr Bojanowski, Edouard Grave, Armand Joulin, and Tomas Mikolov. 2017. Enriching word vectors with subword information. *Transactions of the Association for Computational Linguistics*, 5:135–146.

Junyoung Chung, Çaglar Gülçehre, KyungHyun Cho, and Yoshua Bengio. 2014. Empirical evaluation of gated recurrent neural networks on sequence modeling. *CoRR*, abs/1412.3555.

Kareem Darwish, Hamdy Mubarak, and Ahmed Abdelali. 2017. Arabic diacritization: Stats, rules, and hacks. In *Proceedings of the Third Arabic Natural Language Processing Workshop*, pages 9–17, Valencia, Spain, April. Association for Computational Linguistics.

Muhammad N. ElNokrashy. 2020. Extensible RNN cells for PyTorch. https://github.com/munael/pt-rnn.

Moustafa Elshafei, Husni Al-Muhtaseb, and Mansour Alghamdi. 2006. Statistical methods for automatic diacritization of arabic text. *The Saudi 18th National Computer Conference. Riyadh*, 18:301–306, 01.

Ali Fadel, Ibraheem Tuffaha, Bara' Al-Jawarneh, and Mahmoud Al-Ayyoub. 2019a. Arabic text diacritization using deep neural networks. In *2019 2nd International Conference on Computer Applications Information Security (ICCAIS)*, pages 1–7, May.

Ali Fadel, Ibraheem Tuffaha, Bara' Al-Jawarneh, and Mahmoud Al-Ayyoub. 2019b. Neural Arabic text diacritization: State of the art results and a novel approach for machine translation. In *Proceedings of the 6th Workshop on Asian Translation*, pages 215–225, Hong Kong, China, November. Association for Computational Linguistics.

Yarin Gal and Zoubin Ghahramani. 2016. A theoretically grounded application of dropout in recurrent neural networks. In D. D. Lee, M. Sugiyama, U. V. Luxburg, I. Guyon, and R. Garnett, editors, *Advances in Neural Information Processing Systems 29*, pages 1019–1027. Curran Associates, Inc.

Alex Graves, Santiago Fernández, and Jürgen Schmidhuber. 2005. Bidirectional LSTM Networks for Improved Phoneme Classification and Recognition. In Włodzisław Duch, Janusz Kacprzyk, Erkki Oja, and Sławomir Zadrożny, editors, *Artificial Neural Networks: Formal Models and Their Applications – ICANN 2005*, pages 799–804, Berlin, Heidelberg. Springer Berlin Heidelberg.

Nizar Habash, Owen Rambow, and Ryan Roth. 2009. MADA+TOKAN: A toolkit for Arabic tokenization, diacritization, morphological disambiguation, POS tagging, stemming and lemmatization. *Proceedings of the 2nd International Conference on Arabic Language Resources and Tools (MEDAR)*, 01.

Diederik P. Kingma and Jimmy Ba. 2014. Adam: A method for stochastic optimization. cite arxiv:1412.6980Comment: Published as a conference paper at the 3rd International Conference for Learning Representations, San Diego, 2015.

Hamdy Mubarak, Ahmed Abdelali, Hassan Sajjad, Younes Samih, and Kareem Darwish. 2019. Highly effective Arabic diacritization using sequence to sequence modeling. In *Proceedings of the 2019 Conference of the North American Chapter of the Association for Computational Linguistics: Human Language Technologies, Volume 1 (Long and Short Papers)*, pages 2390–2395, Minneapolis, Minnesota, June. Association for Computational Linguistics.

Rani Nelken and Stuart M. Shieber. 2005. Arabic diacritization using weighted finite-state transducers. In *Proceedings of the ACL Workshop on Computational Approaches to Semitic Languages*, pages 79–86, Ann Arbor, Michigan, June. Association for Computational Linguistics.

Arfath Pasha, Mohamed Al-Badrashiny, Mona Diab, Ahmed El Kholy, Ramy Eskander, Nizar Habash, Manoj Pooleery, Owen Rambow, and Ryan Roth. 2014. MADAMIRA: A fast, comprehensive tool for morphological analysis and disambiguation of Arabic. In *Proceedings of the Ninth International Conference on Language Resources and Evaluation (LREC'14)*, pages 1094–1101, Reykjavik, Iceland, May. European Language Resources Association (ELRA).

Adam Paszke, Sam Gross, Francisco Massa, Adam Lerer, James Bradbury, Gregory Chanan, Trevor Killeen, Zeming Lin, Natalia Gimelshein, Luca Antiga, Alban Desmaison, Andreas Kopf, Edward Yang, Zachary DeVito, Martin Raison, Alykhan Tejani, Sasank Chilamkurthy, Benoit Steiner, Lu Fang, Junjie Bai, and Soumith Chintala. 2019. Pytorch: An imperative style, high-performance deep learning library. In H. Wallach, H. Larochelle, A. Beygelzimer, F. d'Alché-Buc, E. Fox, and R. Garnett, editors, *Advances in Neural Information Processing Systems 32*, pages 8024–8035. Curran Associates, Inc.

Rico Sennrich, Barry Haddow, and Alexandra Birch. 2016. Neural machine translation of rare words with subword units. In *Proceedings of the 54th Annual Meeting of the Association for Computational Linguistics (Volume 1: Long Papers)*, pages 1715–1725, Berlin, Germany, August. Association for Computational Linguistics.

Nitish Srivastava, Geoffrey Hinton, Alex Krizhevsky, Ilya Sutskever, and Ruslan Salakhutdinov. 2014. Dropout: A simple way to prevent neural networks from overfitting. *Journal of Machine Learning Research*, 15(56):1929–1958.

Teresa Tinsley and Kathryn Board. 2013. *Languages for the Future*. British Council.

Ashish Vaswani, Noam Shazeer, Niki Parmar, Jakob Uszkoreit, Llion Jones, Aidan N. Gomez, Lukasz Kaiser, and Illia Polosukhin. 2017. Attention is all you need. *CoRR*, abs/1706.03762.

Nasser Zalmout and Nizar Habash. 2020. Joint diacritization, lemmatization, normalization, and fine-grained morphological tagging. In *Proceedings of the 58th Annual Meeting of the Association for Computational Linguistics*, pages 8297–8307, Online, July. Association for Computational Linguistics.

Taha Zerrouki and Amar Balla. 2017. Tashkeela: Novel corpus of arabic vocalized texts, data for auto-diacritization systems. *Data in Brief*, 11:147 – 151.

Imed Zitouni and Ruhi Sarikaya. 2009. Arabic diacritic restoration approach based on maximum entropy models. *Computer Speech & Language*, 23:257–276, 07.

Imed Zitouni, Jeffrey S. Sorensen, and Ruhi Sarikaya. 2006. Maximum entropy based restoration of Arabic diacritics. In *Proceedings of the 21st International Conference on Computational Linguistics and 44th Annual Meeting of the Association for Computational Linguistics*, pages 577–584, Sydney, Australia, July. Association for Computational Linguistics.

# A Semi-Supervised BERT Approach for Arabic Named Entity Recognition

**Chadi Helwe**[1]**, Ghassan Dib**[2]**, Mohsen Shamas**[2]**, Shady Elbassuoni**[2]
[1]Télécom Paris, Institut Polytechnique de Paris
[2]Department of Computer Science, American University of Beirut
`chadi.helwe@telecom-paris.fr`
`{gid01, mys12, se58}@aub.edu.lb`


## Abstract


Named entity recognition (NER) plays a significant role in many applications such as information extraction, information retrieval, question answering, and even machine translation. Most of the work on NER using deep learning was done for non-Arabic languages like English and French, and only few studies focused on Arabic. This paper proposes a semi-supervised learning approach to train a BERT-based NER model using labeled and semi-labeled datasets. We compared our approach against various baselines, and state-of-the-art Arabic NER tools on three datasets: AQMAR, NEWS, and TWEETS. We report a significant improvement in F-measure for the AQMAR and the NEWS datasets, which are written in Modern Standard Arabic (MSA), and competitive results for the TWEETS dataset, which contains tweets that are mostly in the Egyptian dialect and contain many mistakes or misspellings.


## 1 Introduction

In recent years, researchers have become increasingly interested in developing deep learning solutions for Arabic Natural Language Processing applications. Arabic is considered one of the most spoken languages in the world. However, compared to any non-Arabic language such as English, it is considered a much more challenging language because of its high ambiguity and rich morphology.

In this paper, we tackle the problem of Arabic Named Entity Recognition (NER) using a semi-supervised learning approach. NER is the task of extracting, locating, and classifying named entities in a given piece of text. The named entity can be a proper noun, a numerical expression representing type unit or monetary value, or a temporal value that represents time. In this work, we focus on recognizing proper nouns only and classifying them into one of three classes: a person, a location, or an organization in a BIO (beginning, inside, outside) format.

NER is a particularly difficult task for Arabic. First, there is no capitalization in the Arabic script, commonly used in non-Arabic languages such as English to detect named entities. Second, Arabic can be ambiguous; for instance, a lot of named entities are also used as common nouns and adjectives. Arabic is also known for its rich morphology. Finally, one major issue that hinders Arabic NLP research, including NER, is the lack of sufficient resources. Such resources include Arabic corpora and gazetteers that can be leveraged to perform the NLP tasks. Even if some of these resources are present, they are usually limited in scope or not publicly available.

To overcome the aforementioned challenges related to Arabic NLP, we propose a semi-supervised deep learning approach for Arabic NER inspired by the work of Yalniz et al. (Yalniz et al., 2019). The idea is to train two BERT-based models: a teacher model and a student model. BERT stands for Bidirectional Encoder Representations from Transformers. The BERT teacher model is trained on a small labeled data set and then applied on a huge semi-labeled dataset to predict the classes of its unlabeled tokens. The output is then used to train a student model with the same architecture as the teacher model, and then the student model is fine-tuned using the small labeled dataset used to train the teacher model.






*Proceedings of the Fifth Arabic Natural Language Processing Workshop*, pages 49–57
Barcelona, Spain (Online), December 12, 2020

To evaluate our approach, we used three different Arabic NER benchmarks, namely AQMAR (Mohit et al., 2012), NEWS (Darwish, 2013) and TWEETS (Darwish, 2013). We compared our approach to various baselines and state-of-the-art NER tools and we outperformed all of them in the case of AQMAR and NEWS datasets and achieved comparable performance in the case of the TWEETs dataset.

The paper is organized as follows. In Section 2, we review the related work. Section 3 describes our semi-supervised learning approach. In Section 4, we evaluate our proposed approach on different datasets. Finally, we conclude and present future directions in Section 5.

## 2   Related Work

Many approaches have been proposed in the literature to perform Arabic NER. These approaches can be categorized into three main categories: machine-learning-based approaches, rule-based approaches, and hybrid approaches.

In a survey on Arabic NLP (Shaalan, 2014), the authors reviewed a set of machine-learning-based Arabic NER approaches. Some approaches utilized conditional random fields (CRF) (Abdul-Hamid and Darwish, 2010; Benajiba and Rosso, 2007; Benajiba et al., 2007), while others relied on support-vector machines (SVM) (Abdelali et al., 2016; Benajiba et al., 2008b; Koulali and Meziane, 2012; Pasha et al., 2014). Other approaches relied on meta-classifiers (AbdelRahman et al., 2010; Benajiba et al., 2008a; Benajiba et al., 2010). All these approaches utilized different combinations of features such as lexical, contextual, morphological, gazetteer, syntactic and POS features. To date, there are a few works that studied deep learning for the task of Arabic NER. Gridach (Gridach, 2016) utilized character-level neural networks and conditional random fields, in a fully-supervised fashion. However, this approach was trained and tested using only one dataset and was not evaluated on multiple datasets as in our case to assess its generalization capabilities. Helwe and Elbassuoni (Helwe and Elbassuoni, 2019) proposed a semi-supervised learning approach based on an algorithm called co-training, which was adapted to the context of deep learning for the task of Arabic NER. Their method makes use of a small amount of labeled data, which is augmented with partially labeled data that is automatically generated from Wikipedia. Their model is based on an ensemble of two BI-LSTMs. We used the same training, validation, and testing datasets from (Helwe and Elbassuoni, 2019) to evaluate our approach. Antoun et al. (Antoun et al., 2020) pre-trained a BERT model for Arabic called AraBERT, which was evaluated on different tasks such as sentiment analysis and NER. In our approach, we used their pre-trained model and re-trained it in a semi-supervised fashion for the task of Arabic NER.

Many rule-based approaches have been proposed for Arabic NER. Most of these approaches relied on different combinations of features including lexical triggers (Abuleil, 2004; Al-Shalabi et al., 2009), morphological analyzers (Elsebai et al., 2009; Maloney and Niv, 1998; Mesfar, 2007), regular expressions and gazetteers (Shaalan and Raza, 2007), and transliteration (Samy et al., 2005). Most of these reviewed methods however were trained and tested using very limited data, typically less than a hundred documents, thus it is not clear how well they can generalize to other datasets. Moreover, none of these approaches were evaluated on any established benchmarks for the task of Arabic NER. The only exceptions are the approaches by Shaalan and Raza (Shaalan and Raza, 2007), which were trained and tested on the Automatic Content Extraction (ACE) (Doddington et al., 2004) and the Treebank Arabic datasets, and the approach by Elsebai et al. (Elsebai et al., 2009), which was trained and tested using more than 500 news articles.

Another type of approaches commonly used for NER is the hybrid approaches, which combines machine-learning-based and rule-based techniques such as (Abdallah et al., 2012; Oudah and Shaalan, 2012; Shaalan and Raza, 2009). The advantage of our approach over the above mentioned approaches is that we build a more robust machine-learning-based model by training a BERT neural network in a semi-supervised fashion using fully labeled and semi-labeled datasets. We compared our approach to the state-of-the-art approaches (i.e,. those with the highest reported performance from the list above, namely MADAMIRA (Pasha et al., 2014), FARASA (Abdelali et al., 2016) and Deep Co-learning (Helwe and Elbassuoni, 2019)) and outperformed them on two different MSA datasets.

# 3  Approach

To train a robust model for Arabic NER using deep learning, a sufficiently large training data is needed. Given the lack of such data in the case of Arabic, we propose a semi-supervised learning approach. Our approach is based on a teacher-student learning mechanism inspired by (Yalniz et al., 2019). It relies on two datasets for training: a fully labeled dataset and a partially labeled dataset. Each instance of these datasets is a sentence composed of word tokens and their labels (person, organization, location or other) if they exist. Figure 1 shows an example instance of the fully labeled dataset. As can be seen from the figure, every token is associated with a label. Figure 2 shows an example instance of the partially labeled dataset, where some of the tokens are labeled and some are not.

The core model in our approach is a pre-trained Arabic BERT model called AraBERT. In brief, our semi-supervised approach works as follows: a BERT teacher model is trained on the fully labeled training dataset to classify the non-labeled tokens of the partially labeled dataset. The best instances from these weakly labeled sentences are then chosen to train a BERT student model, which will be later fine-tuned using the fully labeled training dataset. In the remaining of this section, we first describe the pre-trained AraBERT model. We then describe our proposed semi-supervised learning approach for Arabic NER.

Figure 1: Instance of the Fully Labeled Dataset    Figure 2: Instance of the Partially labeled Dataset

## 3.1  AraBERT Model

AraBERT is a pretrained Arabic language model developed by Antoun et al. (Antoun et al., 2020) based on a transformer architecture called BERT. The BERT model consists of a stack of transformer blocks which was pre-trained on two tasks: Masked Language Modeling (MLM) and Next Sentence Prediction (NSP).

The task of MLM consists of training the model to predict a masked word given the other words in a sentence. The task's dataset is constructed by choosing 15% of its tokens to be masked by replacing: 80% with the [MASK] token, 10% with a random token, and 10% with the original token. While the task of NSP consists of training the model to learn the relationship between two sentences by taking as input two sentences A and B and predicting if sentence B follows sentence A.

The AraBERT model was pre-trained on a large dataset of 70M Arabic sentences with 3B words. The training data was collected from different publicly available corpora such as the Arabic Wikidumps, the 1.5B words Arabic Corpus, the OSIAN Corpus, and a corpus of Assafir news articles. In addition to the publicly available datasets, the authors augmented the dataset by manually crawling news websites such as Al-Akhbar, Annahar, AL-Ahram, and AL-Wafd.

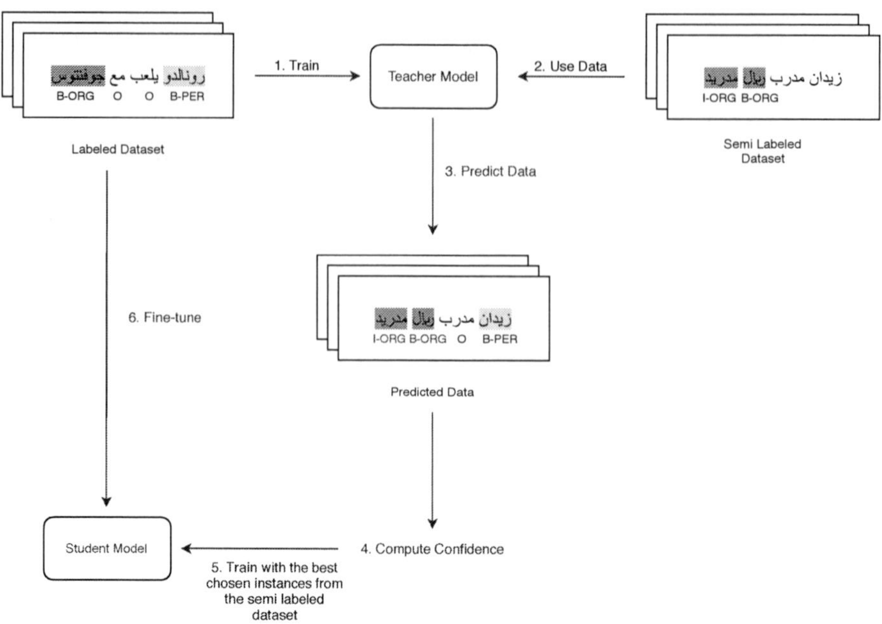


Figure 3: Semi-Supervised Learning Approach

## 3.2 Semi-Supervised Learning Model for Arabic NER

---

**Algorithm 1** Semi-Supervised Learning Model for Arabic NER

---

**Require:** Labeled Data $D^l$
**Require:** Semi Labeled Data $D^{sl}$
**Require:** Confidence Threshold $\tau$
1: Train BERT teacher model $BERT_{teacher}$ with $D^l$
2: $pred\_D^{sl} \leftarrow$ Predict the non-labeled tokens from the semi labeled data $D^{sl}$ with $BERT_{teacher}$
3: **for** sentence i of $pred\_D^{sl}$ **do**
4:    $confidence \leftarrow$ Compute the confidence of $pred\_D^{sl}[i]$
5:    **if** $confidence >= \tau$ **then**
6:       $chosen\_D^{sl} \leftarrow$ Save $D^{sl}[i]$
7:    **end if**
8: **end for**
9: Train BERT student model $BERT_{student}$ with $chosen\_D^{sl}$
10: Fine-tune student BERT model $BERT_{student}$ with $D^l$
11: **return** $BERT_{student}$

---

Our semi-supervised learning approach is shown in Figure 3 and summarized in Algorithm 1. In our approach, we make use of two different datasets, one that is fully labeled but limited in size and one that is large but partially labeled by an automatic technique. First, we train a BERT teacher model $BERT_{teacher}$ with the labeled dataset $D_l$. Second, we predict the labels of the non-labeled tokens of the semi-labeled (i.e., partially labeled) dataset $D_{sl}$ using our trained BERT teacher model $BERT_{teacher}$ and then save them into $pred\_D_{sl}$. Third, we compute the average confidence score of the predicted labels of each instance (sentence) of $pred\_D_{sl}$, and we check if it is higher than a predefined threshold $\tau$. If the condition is met, we pick the instances from $pred\_D_{sl}$ and save them into $chosen\_D_{sl}$. This condition is required to choose the best instances from the data annotated by the teacher model. The average confidence score for each sentence $i$ is computed as follows:

$$s_i = \frac{1}{n} \sum_{j=1}^{n} \arg \max_{0<=l<=6} tok_j^l$$

where $n$ is the number of unlabeled tokens in a sentence $i$, $tok_j^l$ is the probability of the unlabeled token $tok_j$ in sentence $i$ belonging to label $l \in \{$B-PER, I-PER, B-ORG, I-ORG, B-LOC, I-LOC, O$\}$. That is, the average confidence score $s_i$ is computed using only the non-labeled tokens. For example, in Figure 3, only "Real" and "Madrid" are labeled while the others are not. To label the remaining tokens, we use the teacher model which labels "Zidane" as B-PER and "trainer" as O. The newly labeled tokens are used to compute the average confidence score to check if this instance should be added or not into the chosen dataset $chosen\_D_{sl}$. We then train another BERT model $BERT_{student}$, called the student model that has the same architecture of the teacher model, with the chosen instances $chosen\_D_{sl}$. Finally, we fine-tune the student model using the labeled dataset $D_l$.

## 4 Evaluation

### 4.1 Datasets

In this paper, the datasets used for training, validation, and testing are the same as those used by Helwe and Elbassuoni (Helwe and Elbassuoni, 2019). We adopted six different datasets such that one set is used for training, one set is used for validation, three sets are used for testing and one set which is partially annotated is used to train our semi-supervised model described in the previous section. First, there is the training dataset (ANERCorp dataset (ANE, 2007)), which consists of 114,926 labeled tokens (about 10,880 articles), and it was used to train the teacher model and fine-tune the student model. Then there is the validation data, the NewsFANE_Gold corpus (Alotaibi and Lee, 2014), which consists of 71,067 labeled sentences (about 1,360 articles), and we used it for validation to fine-tune the hyperparameters of the model. Our approach was then tested on three different Arabic NER benchmarks. The first dataset we evaluated our model on is the AQMAR dataset, an annotated corpus for the task of ArabicNER. AQMAR by Mohit et al. (Mohit et al., 2012) consists of 2,456 sentences from 28 articles from Arabic Wikipedia. The articles belong to four domains, particularly history, science, sports, and technology. The second dataset is the NEWS dataset, which is also an annotated corpus for the task of Arabic NER constructed by Darwish (Darwish, 2013). The NEWS dataset consists of 292 sentences retrieved from the RSS feed of the Arabic (Egypt) version of news.google.com from October 6, 2012. The corpus contains news from different sources and covers international and local news related to politics, finance, health, sports, entertainment, and technology. The third and final dataset we used for evaluation is the TWEETS dataset, also constructed by Darwish (Darwish, 2013). The TWEETS dataset consists of 982 tweets randomly selected from tweets posted between November 23, 2011 and November 27, 2011. The tweets were retrieved from Twitter API using the query lang: ar (language=Arabic). Finally, we used a semi-labeled dataset in order to train our semi-supervised model. The semi-labeled data consists of 1,617,184 labeled and unlabeled tokens. Each line contains a set of tokens and their labels if they exist. This dataset was automatically generated by annotating all the entities in randomly selected Wikipedia articles using an LSTM neural network model (Helwe and Elbassuoni, 2019). This model takes as input the summary of the entity's Wikipedia article and classifies it into one of four classes: person, location, organization, or other.

### 4.2 Experiment

In this section, we evaluate our semi-supervised approach for the task of Arabic NER. We tested our approach described in Section 3 on three different datasets and compared it with various approaches. More precisely, we compared our approach to both FARASA (Abdelali et al., 2016) and MADAMIRA (Pasha et al., 2014), which are well-known Arabic NER tools as based on recent evaluations. In addition, we compared our approach to the deep co-learning approach from (Helwe and Elbassuoni, 2019) and a fully supervised AraBERT model. The fully supervised AraBERT model was trained solely using the

ANERCorp dataset and validated using the NewsFANE Gold corpus. This allows us to evaluate the benefit of training an AraBERT model in a semi-supervised fashion using the semi-labeled dataset. The fully supervised AraBERT model was trained for 20 epochs with a batch size of 32, a dropout of 0.2 with early stopping, and we used ADAM as the optimization algorithm. All the hyperparameters were tuned based on the validation set. In order to experiment with our proposed semi-supervised learning BERT approach, we used the fully supervised AraBERT model as the teacher model. We applied the latter model, called the teacher model, on the semi-labeled dataset to predict the non-labeled tokens. We set the threshold $\tau$ to a value of 0.95. This threshold is a parameter that was tuned based on the validation set. To choose the instances that satisfy the threshold condition, we computed each instance's average confidence score. We then trained a student model with an architecture similar to the teacher model with the chosen instances of the semi-labeled dataset. Then we fine-tuned the pre-trained student model with the training set, which is the ANERCorp dataset in our case. We realize that fine-tuning the student model on a clean labeled dataset is significant to achieve a better performance after being pre-trained on a large semi-labeled dataset. The training configuration used in the semi-supervised learning approach is similar to the fully supervised AraBERT models' training configuration. All experiments were run on an Ubuntu machine with a 24 GB RAM, a CPU Intel Core I7 and a GPU NVIDIA GeForce GTX 1080 TI 11GB.

## 4.3  Results

In this section, we evaluate our AraBERT semi-supervised model for the task of Arabic NER. We tested our approach, as mentioned above, on three different datasets and compared the results against different Arabic NER tools and approaches. To calculate all the F-measures reported in this section, we used the CoNLL evaluation script (Tjong Kim Sang and De Meulder, 2003).

### 4.3.1  AQMAR Dataset

The first dataset we evaluated our model on is the AQMAR dataset. As can be seen from Table 1, MADAMIRA and FARASA, which are machine learning tools that use feature engineering, have very low F-measure than the deep learning approaches. The Deep Co-learning approach scores a slightly higher F-measure than the AraBERT Fully Supervised since it is a semi-supervised learning method that used the semi-labeled dataset during training. Our approach scores an F-measure of 65.5, which is the highest.

| Model | LOC | ORG | PER | Avg |
|---|---|---|---|---|
| MADAMIRA | 39.4 | 15.1 | 22.3 | 29.2 |
| FARASA | 60.1 | 30.6 | 52.5 | 52.9 |
| Deep Co-learning | 67.0 | 38.2 | 65.1 | 61.8 |
| AraBERT Fully Supervised | 63.6 | 31.0 | 70.9 | 61.5 |
| AraBERT Semi-Supervised | 68.4 | 34.6 | 74.4 | **65.5** |

Table 1: The F-measure of the various models and the Arabic NER tools on AQMAR

### 4.3.2  NEWS Dataset

The second dataset is the NEWS dataset. As shown in Table 2, the results of the different approaches and tools are similar to the AQMAR dataset results. The MADAMIRA and FARASA have low scores compared to the deep learning approaches. The Deep Co-learning has a higher F-measure than the AraBERT model trained in a fully supervised fashion, while our approach outperforms all the different approaches and tools, with an F-measure of 78.6.

|            Model            | LOC  | ORG  | PER  | Avg      |
|-----------------------------|------|------|------|----------|
| MADAMIRA                    | 39.4 | 15.1 | 22.3 | 29.2     |
| FARASA                      | 73.1 | 42.1 | 69.5 | 63.9     |
| Deep Co-learning            | 81.6 | 52.7 | 82.4 | 74.1     |
| AraBERT Fully Supervised    | 74.2 | 54.2 | 85.1 | 73.2     |
| AraBERT Semi-Supervised     | 80.5 | 60.8 | 89.5 | **78.6** |

Table 2: The F-measure of the various models and the Arabic NER tools on NEWS

### 4.3.3 TWEETS Dataset

The third and final dataset we used for evaluation is the TWEETS dataset. As can be seen from Table 3, the MADAMIRA and FARASA tools performed poorly compared to the deep learning approaches with an F-measure of 24.6 and 39.9, respectively. Only in this dataset, the Deep Co-learning approach has the highest score, which is better than the AraBERT trained in a fully supervised fashion and to the AraBERT trained in a semi-supervised fashion with an F-measure of 59.2. The reason behind this result is that the AraBERT model was pre-trained on MSA corpora, which highly differ in nature from tweets that are mostly in the Egyptian dialect and contain mistakes or misspellings.

|            Model            | LOC  | ORG  | PER  | Avg      |
|-----------------------------|------|------|------|----------|
| MADAMIRA                    | 40.3 | 8.9  | 18.4 | 24.6     |
| FARASA                      | 47.5 | 24.7 | 39.8 | 39.9     |
| Deep Co-learning            | 65.3 | 39.7 | 61.3 | **59.2** |
| AraBERT Fully Supervised    | 57.9 | 30.7 | 60.9 | 54.0     |
| AraBERT Semi-Supervised     | 63.3 | 42.1 | 59.4 | 57.3     |

Table 3: The F-measure of the various models and the Arabic NER tools on TWEETS

We conclude that our semi-supervised approach is making a significant improvement in the performance of the Arabic NER task when the texts are written in MSA. To have better results on other types of Arabic texts like tweets, we need to study the performance of our approach when pre-trained on this type of Arabic texts.

## 5   Conclusion

This paper presented a new approach to detect and classify named entities in any Arabic text. Our approach consists of training an already pre-trained BERT model for Arabic NER in a semi-supervised fashion. We made use of two datasets. The first dataset was fully labeled, while the second dataset was partially labeled. We evaluated our approach on three datasets. It outperforms all other Arabic NER tools and approaches on two testing datasets, namely NEWS and AQMAR datasets. For the TWEETS dataset, Helwe and Elbassuoni's deep co-learning approach (Helwe and Elbassuoni, 2019) scores a higher F-measure than our method because the BERT model was pre-trained and trained on mainly MSA corpora that do not contain mistakes and misspellings.

In future work, we plan to pre-train the BERT model on tweets to make it more suitable for text that could contain misspellings and mistakes and which is not necessarily written in MSA. We believe that this will result in an improved performance of our approach on the TWEETS datasets. Finally, we plan to apply our semi-supervised BERT-based learning approach to other NLP tasks such as part-of-speech tagging and dependency parsing.

## References

Sherief Abdallah, Khaled Shaalan, and Muhammad Shoaib. 2012. Integrating rule-based system with classification for arabic named entity recognition. In *International Conference on Intelligent Text Processing and Computational Linguistics*, pages 311–322. Springer.

Ahmed Abdelali, Kareem Darwish, Nadir Durrani, and Hamdy Mubarak. 2016. Farasa: A fast and furious segmenter for arabic. In *Proceedings of the 2016 Conference of the North American Chapter of the Association for Computational Linguistics: Demonstrations*, pages 11–16. Association for Computational Linguistics, San Diego, California.

Samir AbdelRahman, Mohamed Elarnaoty, Marwa Magdy, and Aly Fahmy. 2010. Integrated machine learning techniques for arabic named entity recognition. *IJCSI*, 7:27–36.

Ahmed Abdul-Hamid and Kareem Darwish. 2010. Simplified feature set for arabic named entity recognition. In *Proceedings of the 2010 Named Entities Workshop*, pages 110–115. Association for Computational Linguistics.

Saleem Abuleil. 2004. Extracting names from arabic text for question-answering systems. In *Coupling approaches, coupling media and coupling languages for information retrieval*, pages 638–647. LE CENTRE DE HAUTES ETUDES INTERNATIONALES D'INFORMATIQUE DOCUMENTAIRE.

Riyad Al-Shalabi, Ghassan Kanaan, Bashar Al-Sarayreh, Khalid Khanfar, Ali Al-Ghonmein, Hamed Talhouni, and Salem Al-Azazmeh. 2009. Proper noun extracting algorithm for arabic language. In *International conference on IT, Thailand*.

Fahd Alotaibi and Mark G Lee. 2014. A hybrid approach to features representation for fine-grained arabic named entity recognition. In *COLING*, pages 984–995.

2007. Anercorp. http://www1.ccls.columbia.edu/ ybenajiba/downloads.html.

Wissam Antoun, Fady Baly, and Hazem Hajj. 2020. Arabert: Transformer-based model for arabic language understanding. *arXiv preprint arXiv:2003.00104*.

Yassine Benajiba and Paolo Rosso. 2007. Anersys 2.0: Conquering the ner task for the arabic language by combining the maximum entropy with pos-tag information. In *IICAI*, pages 1814–1823.

Yassine Benajiba, Paolo Rosso, and José Miguel Benedíruiz. 2007. Anersys: An arabic named entity recognition system based on maximum entropy. In *International Conference on Intelligent Text Processing and Computational Linguistics*, pages 143–153. Springer.

Yassine Benajiba, Mona Diab, and Paolo Rosso. 2008a. Arabic named entity recognition using optimized feature sets. In *Proceedings of the Conference on Empirical Methods in Natural Language Processing*, pages 284–293. Association for Computational Linguistics.

Yassine Benajiba, Mona Diab, Paolo Rosso, et al. 2008b. Arabic named entity recognition: An svm-based approach. In *Proceedings of 2008 Arab International Conference on Information Technology (ACIT)*, pages 16–18.

Yassine Benajiba, Imed Zitouni, Mona Diab, and Paolo Rosso. 2010. Arabic named entity recognition: using features extracted from noisy data. In *Proceedings of the ACL 2010 conference short papers*, pages 281–285. Association for Computational Linguistics.

Kareem Darwish. 2013. Named entity recognition using cross-lingual resources: Arabic as an example. In *ACL (1)*, pages 1558–1567.

George R Doddington, Alexis Mitchell, Mark A Przybocki, Lance A Ramshaw, Stephanie Strassel, and Ralph M Weischedel. 2004. The automatic content extraction (ace) program-tasks, data, and evaluation. In *LREC*, volume 2, page 1.

Ali Elsebai, Farid Meziane, and Fatma Zohra Belkredim. 2009. A rule based persons names arabic extraction system. *Communications of the IBIMA*, 11(6):53–59.

Mourad Gridach. 2016. Character-aware neural networks for arabic named entity recognition for social media. In *Proceedings of the 6th Workshop on South and Southeast Asian Natural Language Processing (WSSANLP2016)*, pages 23–32.

Chadi Helwe and Shady Elbassuoni. 2019. Arabic named entity recognition via deep co-learning. *Artificial Intelligence Review*, 52(1):197–215.

Rim Koulali and Abdelouafi Meziane. 2012. A contribution to arabic named entity recognition. In *ICT and Knowledge Engineering (ICT & Knowledge Engineering), 2012 10th International Conference on*, pages 46–52. IEEE.

John Maloney and Michael Niv. 1998. Tagarab: a fast, accurate arabic name recognizer using high-precision morphological analysis. In *Proceedings of the Workshop on Computational Approaches to Semitic Languages*, pages 8–15. Association for Computational Linguistics.

Slim Mesfar. 2007. Named entity recognition for arabic using syntactic grammars. In *Natural Language Processing and Information Systems*, pages 305–316. Springer.

Behrang Mohit, Nathan Schneider, Rishav Bhowmick, Kemal Oflazer, and Noah A Smith. 2012. Recall-oriented learning of named entities in arabic wikipedia. In *Proceedings of the 13th Conference of the European Chapter of the Association for Computational Linguistics*, pages 162–173. Association for Computational Linguistics.

Mai Oudah and Khaled F Shaalan. 2012. A pipeline arabic named entity recognition using a hybrid approach. In *COLING*, pages 2159–2176.

Arfath Pasha, Mohamed Al-Badrashiny, Mona T Diab, Ahmed El Kholy, Ramy Eskander, Nizar Habash, Manoj Pooleery, Owen Rambow, and Ryan Roth. 2014. Madamira: A fast, comprehensive tool for morphological analysis and disambiguation of arabic. In *LREC*, volume 14, pages 1094–1101.

Doaa Samy, Antonio Moreno, and Jose M Guirao. 2005. A proposal for an arabic named entity tagger leveraging a parallel corpus. In *International Conference RANLP, Borovets, Bulgaria*, pages 459–465.

Khaled Shaalan and Hafsa Raza. 2007. Person name entity recognition for arabic. In *Proceedings of the 2007 Workshop on Computational Approaches to Semitic Languages: Common Issues and Resources*, pages 17–24. Association for Computational Linguistics.

Khaled Shaalan and Hafsa Raza. 2009. Nera: Named entity recognition for arabic. *Journal of the American Society for Information Science and Technology*, 60(8):1652–1663.

Khaled Shaalan. 2014. A survey of arabic named entity recognition and classification. *Computational Linguistics*, 40(2):469–510.

Erik F Tjong Kim Sang and Fien De Meulder. 2003. Introduction to the conll-2003 shared task: Language-independent named entity recognition. In *Proceedings of the seventh conference on Natural language learning at HLT-NAACL 2003-Volume 4*, pages 142–147. Association for Computational Linguistics.

I Zeki Yalniz, Hervé Jégou, Kan Chen, Manohar Paluri, and Dhruv Mahajan. 2019. Billion-scale semi-supervised learning for image classification. *arXiv preprint arXiv:1905.00546*.

# Empathy-driven Arabic Conversational Chatbot


**Tarek Naous, Christian Hokayem, and Hazem Hajj**
Department of Electrical and Computer Engineering
American University of Beirut
Beirut, Lebanon
{tnn11,cph04,hh63}@aub.edu.lb



## Abstract

Conversational models have witnessed a significant research interest in the last few years with the advancements in sequence generation models. A challenging aspect in developing human-like conversational models is enabling the sense of empathy in bots, making them infer emotions from the person they are interacting with. By learning to develop empathy, chatbot models are able to provide human-like, empathetic responses, thus making the human-machine interaction close to human-human interaction. Recent advances in English use complex encoder-decoder language models that require large amounts of empathetic conversational data. However, research has not produced empathetic bots for Arabic. Furthermore, there is a lack of Arabic conversational data labeled with empathy. To address these challenges, we create an Arabic conversational dataset that comprises empathetic responses. However, the dataset is not large enough to develop very complex encoder-decoder models. To address the limitation of data scale, we propose a special encoder-decoder composed of a Long Short-Term Memory (LSTM) Sequence-to-Sequence (Seq2Seq) with Attention. The experiments showed success of our proposed empathy-driven Arabic chatbot in generating empathetic responses with a perplexity of 38.6, an empathy score of 3.7, and a fluency score of 3.92.


## 1 Introduction

Empathy is described as the ability of recognizing others' state of mind and making sense of their feelings. Empathetic behavior is provoked after being exposed to others' emotional states (Yalçın, 2020). Empathy is an innate capacity in most human beings, and is also described as a responsive and spontaneous act of copying of an implied feeling. Empathy in humans triggers a sense of concern for others, leading to appropriate emotional reactions that impose a positive effect on interacting individuals. For instance, empathetic behavior is applicable to situations such as acknowledging others' pain, showing interest, gratitude, being supportive, or providing encouragement.

Building chatbots that can exhibit empathetic behavior becomes a necessary step towards building emotionally intelligent conversational systems (Yalçın and DiPaola, 2018). Such a trait allows conversational systems to be perceived as genuine and warm by users, rather than oblivious and boorish. This characteristic is highly desirable since it could boost user satisfaction in various chatbot applications. Hence, the objective of this work is to develop an empathetic chatbot for the Arabic language. An example of the desired chatbot with empathetic behavior is illustrated in Fig. 1 that shows the difference between empathetic and unempathetic responses. For instance, in Fig 1a the chatbot infers a feeling of sadness in the user's text and provides an empathetic response to comfort the user, while in Fig 1b the chatbot infers a feeling of pride in the user's statement and thus congratulates them.

Recent advances in Artificial Intelligence (AI) and Natural Language Processing (NLP) have made the development of such systems possible. Specifically, the introduction of Sequence-to-Sequence (Seq2Seq) models and Transformer networks have improved performance significantly. Empathetic chatbots have grabbed interest in recent years with many sequence architectures proposed to generate






*Proceedings of the Fifth Arabic Natural Language Processing Workshop*, pages 58–68
Barcelona, Spain (Online), December 12, 2020

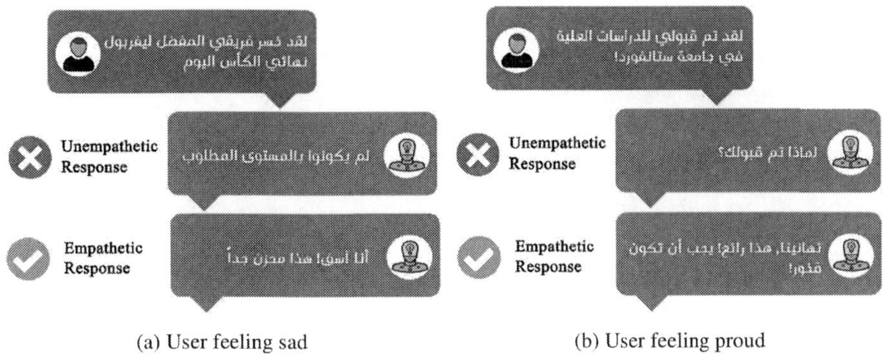


(a) User feeling sad

(b) User feeling proud

Figure 1: Examples for Empathetic Responding

empathetic responses given a user's emotional statement (Zhong et al., 2020; Zhou et al., 2020). The recent attempts in building empathetic chatbots for English have focused on training sequence generation models on a dataset of empathetic conversations (Rashkin et al., 2018), where models are trained on input/output sequences of speaker statements and their corresponding empathetic responses. The dataset used for English is based on empathetic conversations between a speaker and a listener. The speaker describes a situation he previously experienced, while the listener infers the emotional state of the speaker and provides a suitable empathetic response. Hence, by training the model on such samples of speaker statements and listener empathetic responses, the chatbot learns to develop a sense of empathy and provides suitable responses to any given context.

Despite the various works presented in the literature on empathetic chatbots for English (Shin et al., 2019; Ghandeharioun et al., 2019; Asghar et al., 2020), no work has previously addressed the problem of building such a model for the Arabic language. This is mainly due to the difficulties that arise when dealing with a morphologically rich language such as Arabic. Another important reason is the scarcity of resources available for Arabic compared with the English language, including corpora, tools, and pre-trained models. To address these challenges, we propose a neural sequence generation model based on Seq2Seq with LSTM units combined with Attention. We select this model over state-of-the-art transformer models due to their low computational cost and suitability for smaller datasets that are more feasible for Arabic. Additionally, we create a corpus for empathetic conversations in Arabic by translating datasets available for English. The developed model successfully exhibited empathetic behavior and provided emotional responses to the input of users in Arabic.

The rest of this paper is organized as follows: Section 2 summarizes the recent literature on empathetic chatbots. Section 3 describes the Arabic dataset created for empathetic chatbots and presents the proposed Seq2Seq model. Experiments and results are presented in Section 4. Concluding remarks and future directions follow in Section 5.

## 2 Related Work

In this section, we start by reviewing the recent literature on empathetic chatbots for the English language, including datasets and models used. We then review the current state of Arabic chatbots and highlight the existing gaps.

### 2.1 Empathetic English Chatbots

English empathetic chatbots have been of interest over the last few years. Recently, the first dataset for empathetic conversations dubbed EmpatheticDialogues was introduced by Rashkin et al. (2018). In their work, the authors gathered the dataset through the use of Amazon Turk Workers and then implemented retrieval-based and generative-based models. Overall, they observed higher levels of empathy in the chatbot's responses compared with models trained on conventional non-empathetic datasets. The same dataset would later be used as the main benchmark for assessing empathetic models. For instance, Lin et al. (2020) proposed an improved model which employed a Generative Pre-trained Transformer (GPT). This model was pre-trained on the BooksCorpus dataset (Zhu et al., 2015) that contains over 7000 unpublished books, thus improving the Natural Language Understanding (NLU) ability of the transformer. They also pre-trained on the PersonaChat dataset (Zhang et al., 2018) to give the chatbot a certain persona and enhance its engagingness. Following this pre-training procedure, the model was fine-tuned on EmpatheticDialogues with results showing significant improvements in the empathetic responding capability of the model. In a different approach, Shin et al. (2020) modeled empathetic responding as a reinforcement learning problem where they defined a reward function for a Seq2Seq model based on Gated Recurrent Units (GRU) and attention. Their approach named "Sentiment Look-ahead" is also shown to be effective in generating empathetic responses when tested on the EmpatheticDialogues dataset. Asghar et al. (2020) approached the problem from a different perspective, splitting it into an emotion recognition and a response generation problem. Inspired by Affect Control Theory, they map every user sentence to an EPA (Evaluation Potency Activity) vector using a BiLSTM network with attention and then prescribe a corresponding EPA response vector which they use for conditioning the response generation. Both Conditional Variable Auto Encoders and Seq2Seq models are considered for the generation. They are seen to yield similar results. Zhou et al. (2020) also make use of a Seq2Seq model for their chatbot's general chitchat. They represent empathy through the use of two empathy vectors, one which represents the user (including sentiment, opinion, and contextual information) and one which represents the chatbot (including its opinion and personality). They condition the decoder on these empathy vectors and learn the best replies for each situation using data from interactions with over 660 million users.

## 2.2 Arabic Chatbots

Arabic is a complex language and thus the development of Arabic chatbots has been a great challenge to the research community. To date, only a handful of works have attempted to build Arabic chatbots. One such work is ArabChat: a rule-based chatbot capable of pattern matching and providing suitable answers to queries by the users (Hijjawi et al., 2014). Another work is BOTTA, a retrieval-based model supporting specifically the Egyptian dialect (Ali and Habash, 2016). For the medical domain, Ollobot is another rule-based chatbot which presents health tracking and support (Fadhil and AbuRa'ed, 2019). Overall, in a survey conducted by AlHumoud et al. (2018), it was seen that Arabic chatbots are still in their infancy. Their development being mainly hindered by a lack of available datasets. Some works have managed to break through this limitation by leveraging translation tools: an example is the question answering system developed by Mozannar et al. (2019), another one is the Arabic language model developed by Antoun et al. (2020). The success of these works, as well as the work of ElJundi et al. (2019) demonstrate the potential of neural models in understanding the Arabic language and motivates us to look into neural solutions for the open challenge of Arabic empathetic response generation.

## 3 Proposed Method

In this section, we present the proposed model for Arabic empathy-driven conversational bots and the dataset we created. We start by describing the details of the proposed encoder-decoder model in Subsection 3.1. We then present the dataset created for Arabic empathetic chatbots in Subsection 3.2, which we used to train our proposed model.

### 3.1 Proposed Arabic Encoder-Decoder Model

The purpose of the model is to infer an emotional state in an input sequence, that is the user's statement, and generate a sequence in Arabic representing the empathetic response that the chatbot needs to reply with. The proposed model, illustrated in Fig. 2, is a Seq2Seq model with LSTM units combined with Attention. The components and parameters of the proposed model were obtained following a process of hyperparameter tuning that determined the combination of choices that will deliver the best performance on the validation set. The hyperparameters tuned were the number of encoder/decoder layers (1, 2, or 3 layers), unit type (LSTM or GRU), embedding dimensions (100, 200, or 300), and choice of optimization algorithm (Stochastic Gradient Descent (SGD), Adam, or Adagrad). After trying all combinations and comparing performance on the validation set, the resulting choices of hyperparameters were two layers for each the encoder and decoder, LSTM units, an embedding dimension of 500, and SGD as the optimizer during training and validation. A dropout probability of 0.3 was chosen after each layer to avoid over-fitting.

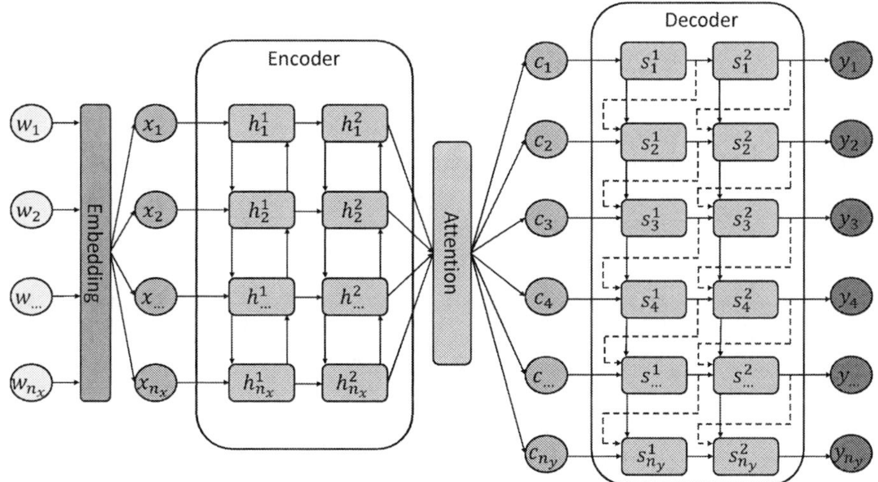


Figure 2: Architecture of the proposed Seq2Seq model with Attention

We consider the empathetic conversations to be alternating sequences between the user and the chatbot. Let $w = [w_1, w_2, \ldots, w_{n_x}]$ be the input one-hot representations of a sequence of $n_x$ words, corresponding to the utterance said by the user. We use the Farasa (Abdelali et al., 2016) Arabic text processing toolkit for pre-processing and tokenizing Arabic sentences. The obtained tokens are then fed into an embedding matrix $E \in \mathbb{R}^{d \times V}$ where $d$ is the dimension of the embedding vector, and $V$ is the vocabulary size. We set $d$ to be 500 and obtain a vocabulary size $V$ of 12900. The output of the embedding layer results in $x = [x_1, x_2, \ldots, x_{n_x}]$ where $x_i$ is the embedding vector of the $i$-th word $w_i$. The target output sequence is the sentence containing an empathetic response by the chatbot and which we represent by $y = [y_1, y_2, \ldots, y_{n_y}]$.

The encoder consists of two bidirectional layers with LSTM units for better extraction of complicated features. Each unit computes a hidden state $h_i^l$ where $l$ is the layer index. To avoid the problem of fixed-length vectors in encoder-decoder models (Bahdanau et al., 2014), we used an attention mechanism which generates a context vector $c = [c_1, c_2, \ldots, c_{n_y}]$ given the hidden states $h_i^2$ from the second layer of the encoder. The context vector $c$ is then fed as input to the decoder that consists of two layers with LSTM units. Each unit computes the hidden state $s_i^l$. The sequence $y$ representing the empathetic response can then be generated by the second layer of the decoder, where a decoding strategy is used such as beam search or random sampling. The mathematical details of the model are provided here for completeness.

### 3.1.1 Encoder

The encoder is formed by two stacked layers of bidirectional LSTM units (BiLSTM) that compute the encoder hidden states denoted by $h_i^l$ where $l$ is the layer index. The first layer reads the input embeddings $x$ and computes the hidden state $h_i^1 = [\overrightarrow{h^1}_i; \overleftarrow{h^1}_i]$ in both directions as follows:

$$
\begin{aligned}
\overrightarrow{h^1}_i &= \text{LSTM}(\overrightarrow{h^1}_{i-1}, x_i) \\
\overleftarrow{h^1}_i &= \text{LSTM}(\overleftarrow{h^1}_{i+1}, x_i)
\end{aligned}
\tag{1}
$$

The obtained hidden states of the first layer are then fed as input to the second layer to compute $h_i^2 = [\overrightarrow{h^2}_i; \overleftarrow{h^2}_i]$ as follows:

$$\overrightarrow{h^2}_i = \text{LSTM}(\overrightarrow{h^2}_{i-1}, \overrightarrow{h^1}_{i-1})$$
$$\overleftarrow{h^2}_i = \text{LSTM}(\overleftarrow{h^2}_{i+1}, \overleftarrow{h^1}_{i+1}) \tag{2}$$

### 3.1.2 Attention

We employ the attention mechanism where attention weights $\alpha_{ji}$ are assigned to each hidden state $h_i^2$ obtained by the encoder. These weights are computed by:

$$\alpha_{ji} = \frac{\exp(e_{ji})}{\sum_k^{n_x} \exp(e_{ki})} \tag{3}$$

where the energy $e_{ji}$ associated with each weight $\alpha_{ji}$ determines how significant an encoder state $h_i$ is to a decoder state $s_{j-1}$ in generating the next state $s_j$. The energy is computed using the alignment model given by:

$$e_{ji} = f_{NN}(s_{j-1}, h_i) \tag{4}$$

where $f_{NN}$ denotes a regular feed-forward neural network that is trained simultaneously with the rest of the system. The context vector $c_j$ can now be computed by the weighted sum of $\alpha_{ji}$ and $h_i$ for $j = 1, \ldots, n_x$ as follows:

$$c_j = \sum_{j=1}^{n_x} \alpha_{ji} h_i \tag{5}$$

### 3.1.3 Decoder

The decoder consists of two stacked layers of LSTM units that compute the decoder states $s_j^l$ as follows:

$$s_j^1 = \text{LSTM}(c_j, s_{j-1}^1, s_{j-1}^2)$$
$$s_j^2 = \text{LSTM}(s_j^1, s_{j-1}^2, y_{j-1}) \tag{6}$$

Hence, the next word in the generated empathetic response $y_j$ can be predicted given the previously predicted words $y_1, y_2, \ldots, y_{j-1}$ and the context vector $c$.

$$p(\mathbf{y}) = \prod_{j=1}^{n_y} p(y_j / y_1, y_2, \ldots, y_{j-1}, c) \tag{7}$$

where $\mathbf{y} = y_1, y_2, \ldots, y_{n_y}$.

## 3.2 Arabic Dataset for Empathetic Chatbots

The proposed model requires training on a dataset of empathetic conversations. A sample input in this dataset would be a statement of a speaker describing personal experience in which they felt a specific emotion. The corresponding output would be the empathetic response of a listener, which infers the emotional state of the speaker and provides an appropriate reply. The proposed model needs to be trained on these input-output pairs so that it could generate human-like empathetic responses.

Since no such dataset is available in the Arabic language, we translated the EmpatheticDialogues dataset (Rashkin et al., 2018), which is the only available dataset in English for building empathetic chatbots. EmpatheticDialogues consists of 24,850 English conversations obtained via crowd-sourcing. These conversations are between a speaker that describes a certain situation they went through and a listener who infers the emotional state of the speaker and provides a suitable emotional response, thus creating an empathetic dialogue. We make use of the Googletrans[1] API to perform the translations from

---

[1] https://pypi.org/project/googletrans/

English to Arabic. A sample conversation is provided in Table 1, showing the original English sentences and their Arabic translations.

| |
| --- |
| Hello |
| مرحبا |
| Hello! I am in such a good mood since I got my new home |
| مرحبا! أنا في مزاج جيد منذ أن حصلت على منزلي الجديد |
| Funny - we just built a house where we used to go camping when I was a kid |
| مضحك ـ قمنا ببناء منزل حيث كنّا نذهب للتخييم عندما كنت طفلا |
| I have a ton of backyard space that we have plans for. Camping would be a fun one |
| لدي الكثير من مساحة الفناء الخلفي التي نخطط لها. التخييم سيكون ممتعا |
| That's wonderful! Do you have any plans to have a fire? |
| هذا رائع. هل لديك خطط لإشعال النّار؟ |
| I want to look in to getting a nice fire pit for the house |
| أريد أن أنظر للحصول على حفرة نار جميلة |

Table 1: Sample conversation from the created dataset.

To evaluate the quality of the dataset[2], we chose 100 random translated samples and compared them with the original English samples to assess the quality of the translation. Our interest in the dataset is not to obtain accurate translations, but rather to create dialogues that are meaningful even if they were not perfect translations. As a result, our evaluation of the dataset focused on checking whether the translated conversation makes sense in Arabic. The results indicated that only 6 of the 100 randomly chosen samples were found to be unreasonable while the rest of the samples were deemed reasonable. Therefore, we considered the dataset to be of high quality for the purpose of training the proposed empathetic conversational model. A few unreasonable samples are shown in Table 2. Such poor translations are mainly due to idioms of the English language, where the individual words do not represent the literal meaning. For instance, by looking at the sample "Planning out my new home has turned out to be a blast!" the word "blast", in the context of the sentence, means "exciting" while its literal meaning is "explosion". Another reason for unreasonable translations are slang words, which are commonly found in informal conversations. These types of errors are rare in the generated conversation dataset and the translation system was thus deemed to be sufficiently accurate (94%) for the purpose of model development.

| |
| --- |
| Planning out my new home has turned out to be a blast! |
| ! تبيّن أن التخطيط لمنزلي الجديد كان إنفجارا |
| I suppose you do have a point there |
| أعتقد أن لديك نقطة هناك |

Table 2: Examples of unreasonable translations.

## 4  Experiments and Results

In this section, we start by defining the experimental setup in Subsection 4.1, including how the dataset is split and what model configurations is trained. We analyze the results in Subsection 4.2. We then present the results of the human evaluations in Subsection 4.3 and provide a discussion on the strengths and shortcoming of the proposed model.

---

[2]https://github.com/aub-mind/Arabic-Empathetic-Chatbot

## 4.1  Experimental Setup

The created dataset contains around 35K samples which are split into 80% for training, 10% for validation, and 10% for testing. We train the proposed Seq2Seq model, presented earlier in Section 3 for three
different embedding dimensions ($d$) of 100, 300, and 500, to explore how this dimension will influence
the performance of the model given the vocabulary size we have. SGD was chosen as the optimization
algorithm during training. Additionally, we applied a dropout probability of 0.3 after each layer. The
models were developed using the OpenNMT (Klein et al., 2017) toolkit which is commonly used for
neural sequence learning.

## 4.2  Model Training and Evaluation

During the training and validation process, the models are evaluated using the Perplexity (PPL) automated metric. The curves in Fig. 3 show the variation of the validation PPL over 8000 training steps,
for the three choices of $d$. As observed in Fig. 3, the model with $d = 500$ achieved the best value for
the PPL on the validation set, reaching nearly 30, while the models with $d = 100$ and $d = 300$ showed
a validation PPL around 50. The summary performance of these models is reported on the test set in
Table 3, where beam search is used at inference time. We use the BLEU score as an additional metric
for evaluation. The model with an $d = 500$ outperforms the rest of the models by achieving the highest
BLEU score of 0.5 and lowest PPL of 38.6 on the test set. Given these obtained values for the PPL and
the BLEU score, the model delivered state of the art performances for Arabic. The state of the art models
for English reached a PPL level close to 10. However, the achieved results for Arabic are considered as
very good given the relatively small size of the dataset used and the more complex nature of the Arabic
language. Reaching even better PPL and BLEU score levels would require more data samples to learn
from. A possible solution could be pre-training on larger conversational datasets in Arabic, that would
contain hundreds of thousands of samples, and fine-tuning on the empathetic conversations dataset.

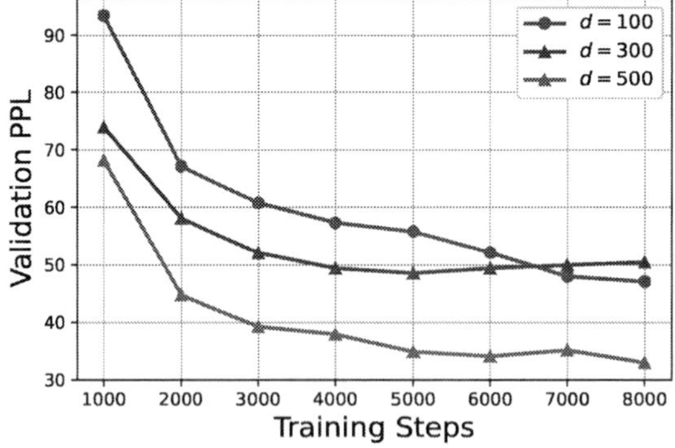



Figure 3: Validation PPL curves for several word embedding dimensions $d$

| Embedding Dimension $d$ | PPL | BLEU |
|---|---|---|
| 100 | 53.5 | 0.11 |
| 300 | 48.7 | 0.32 |
| 500 | **38.6** | **0.50** |

Table 3: Performance of the models on the test set in terms of PPL and BLEU score.

## 4.3  Evaluation by Human Annotators

Automated metrics such as PPL and BLEU score do not capture all aspects of performance of models
in sequence generation and cannot be used alone to judge the quality of the responses generated since

they don't always correlate with human judgment. This problem is especially applicable to empathetic chatbots, where no metric exists to evaluate how empathetic the response generated is. Thus, human ratings are an important part of the overall evaluation. To this end, we collected ratings from 50 speakers of the Arabic language. The raters were given samples from each model and were asked to rate them in terms of Empathy, Relevance, and Fluency, by answering the following questions:

- Empathy: Did the response show an ability of inferring the emotions in the given context?
- Relevance: How relevant was the generated response to the given input context?
- Fluency: How understandable was the generated response from a language perspective?

The raters were asked to rate responses on a scale from 0 to 5, where 0 conveys terrible performance and 5 conveys excellent performance. The average of the obtained human ratings are reported in Table 4 for each model. We experimented with two decoding strategies at inference time, which are namely beam search and random sampling. The model with $d = 500$ and which uses beam search in sequence generation achieved the highest ratings in all of the specified metrics. These ratings suggest that the model exhibits state of the art performance for Arabic with average levels of Empathy and Fluency reaching of 3.7 and 3.92 respectively. However, the Relevance metric was at 3.16 reflecting that the model did not always stay on topic while generating responses. Hence, it can be deduced that the model provides fluent and empathetic responses, but could go off topic in some cases and respond with irrelevant statements.

| Decoding Strategy | Embedding Dimension $d$ | Empathy | Relevance | Fluency |
|---|---|---|---|---|
| | 100 | 2.24 | 1.96 | 3.08 |
| Beam Search | 300 | 2.5 | 2.26 | 3.03 |
| | 500 | **3.70** | **3.16** | **3.92** |
| | 100 | 2.04 | 1.68 | 2.44 |
| Random Sampling | 300 | 2.03 | 1.69 | 2.57 |
| | 500 | 2.40 | 1.92 | 2.80 |

Table 4: Average of human ratings collected for several embedding dimensions and decoding strategies.

| Generated Response | | Context |
|---|---|---|
| **Random Sampling** | **Beam Search** | |
| هذا أمر محزن<br>هل أنت متوتر للذهاب إلى مكان ما ؟ | كنت سعيدا جدا في ذلك اليوم | مرحبا كيف ، حالك ، ؟ |
| هذا أمر محزن للغاية<br>آمل أن يكون لديك الكثير من المرح | نعم، لقد كان الوقت متأخرا جدا | هل زرت لاس فيجاس من قبل ؟ |
| و لكن علي أن يتعافى مرة أخرى | كنت خائفة من السير إلى المنزل | ماذا تفعل ؟ |
| لا يزال أتذكرني فقط من قبل | ماذا حدث ؟ | اليوم يوم سيئ جدا |
| هذا لطيف جدا لهم<br>ما الذي جعلك تعمل بسرعة ؟ | هذا مثير للإعجاب، ماذا فعلت ؟ | أنا سعيد جدا |
| هل فكرت في نفسها ؟ | يا للروعة، يجب أن تكون فخورا جدا | لقد ربحت مباراة كرة القدم اليوم |
| هذا فظيع، نفس الشعور | يا للروعة، هذا يبدو مثير للإعجاب | خلال عيد الميلاد قبل بضع سنوات<br>لم أحصل على أي هدايا |
| هذا يبدو رائع<br>يجب أن تكون فخورا حقا بنفسك | يا للروعة، يجب أن تكون فخورا جدا | لقد تلقيت ترقية في عملي اليوم |

Table 5: Sample generated responses by the proposed model. Generated responses are shown using both beam search and random sampling decoding strategies at inference.

For further analysis of the model's performance, we show in Table 5 examples of generated responses by the model on a set of context sentences that were not included in the training dataset. We also compare these generated responses for the same model using the random sampling decoding strategy. Several points can be deduced by analyzing the generated responses in Table 5. We notice that even though beam search provides fluent and empathetic responses, the responses from beam search are limited to a few choices. For instance, we observed that the tokens (يا للروعة) were repeated several times for different contexts. Sometimes, a full sequence is repeated such as (يا للروعة، يجب أن تكون فخور جدا). This repetitive behavior makes the model seem limited by only a few sequences to choose from and gives the impression that it is not capable of generating more general sequences. In few cases, the response did not make perfect sense or the response went totally off-topic. This issue is commonly encountered when using beam search even for English models. Another drawback of beam search is the heavy computational load it imposes since it needs to perform exhaustive search.

With random sampling, the next token in the sequence is generated based on the probability distribution obtained by the softmax function. This approach, as seen in Table 5, generated lengthy sequences and avoided being too generic as in beam search, and thus offered more richness in the response choices. However, the human ratings for the random sampling approach dropped significantly compared with the models using beam search. This is because in random sampling, many unlikely tokens had an increased probability of being generated, and much more training data would be needed to learn from for the performance to improve.

Additionally, it is noticed from Table 5 that when the context is a simple question that infers no emotions in the speaker such as (ماذا تفعل؟) or (مرحبا كيف حالك؟), the model still provided a response with an unnecessary emotional state. This incapability of the model to generate regular chit-chat responses is observed when using either of the decoding strategies, and is mainly due to it being trained merely on a dataset of empathetic conversations. Hence, it will always opt to generate an empathetic response to any context it receives. Pre-training the model on standard Arabic conversational datasets, and then fine-tuning on our proposed Arabic empathetic dialogues dataset should help alleviate this problem.


## 5  Conclusion

In this paper, we proposed the first model for Arabic empathetic conversational bots and a dataset of empathetic conversations in Arabic. Our proposed model is a Seq2Seq model with LSTM units combined with attention. The dataset created was translated from the EmpatheticDialogues dataset available in English and showed an accuracy of 96% on a sample of the data, which was deemed as sufficient for the purpose of training conversational bots. Upon experimenting with several model configurations, the proposed model with an embedding dimension of 500 reached state of the art performance for Arabic with a PPL of 38.6 and a BLEU score of 0.5. Human evaluation of the generated responses also validated the success of the proposed model, which reached an average Empathy score of 3.7 and an average Fluency score of 3.92. Our results were promising and showed the ability of the proposed model in inferring speaker emotions and generating empathetic responses. However, the model showed average score in Relevance indicating that the response may sometimes go off topic. The limitations of this model are mainly due to the small size of the dataset created. Therefore, our future directions include creating a large conversational dataset for the Arabic language. The larger dataset will also enable the exploration of complex sequence generation models such as Transformers and pre-trained models.


## Acknowledgement

This work has been funded by the American University of Beirut (AUB) University Research Board (URB).

## References

Ahmed Abdelali, Kareem Darwish, Nadir Durrani, and Hamdy Mubarak. 2016. Farasa: A fast and furious segmenter for arabic. In *Proceedings of the 2016 conference of the North American chapter of the association for computational linguistics: Demonstrations*, pages 11–16.

Sarah AlHumoud, Asma Al Wazrah, and Wafa Aldamegh. 2018. Arabic chatbots: A survey. *International Journal of Advanced Computer Science and Applications*, 9(8):535–541.

Dana Abu Ali and Nizar Habash. 2016. Botta: An arabic dialect chatbot. In *Proceedings of COLING 2016, the 26th International Conference on Computational Linguistics: System Demonstrations*, pages 208–212.

Wissam Antoun, Fady Baly, and Hazem Hajj. 2020. AraBERT: Transformer-based model for Arabic language understanding. In *Proceedings of the 4th Workshop on Open-Source Arabic Corpora and Processing Tools, with a Shared Task on Offensive Language Detection*, pages 9–15, Marseille, France, May. European Language Resource Association.

Nabiha Asghar, Ivan Kobyzev, Jesse Hoey, Pascal Poupart, and Muhammad Bilal Sheikh. 2020. Generating emotionally aligned responses in dialogues using affect control theory. *arXiv preprint arXiv:2003.03645*.

Dzmitry Bahdanau, Kyunghyun Cho, and Yoshua Bengio. 2014. Neural machine translation by jointly learning to align and translate. *arXiv preprint arXiv:1409.0473*.

Obeida ElJundi, Wissam Antoun, Nour El Droubi, Hazem Hajj, Wassim El-Hajj, and Khaled Shaban. 2019. hULMonA: The universal language model in Arabic. In *Proceedings of the Fourth Arabic Natural Language Processing Workshop*, pages 68–77, Florence, Italy, August. Association for Computational Linguistics.

Ahmed Fadhil and Ahmed AbuRa'ed. 2019. OlloBot - towards a text-based Arabic health conversational agent: Evaluation and results. In *Proceedings of the International Conference on Recent Advances in Natural Language Processing (RANLP 2019)*, pages 295–303, Varna, Bulgaria, September. INCOMA Ltd.

Asma Ghandeharioun, Daniel McDuff, Mary Czerwinski, and Kael Rowan. 2019. Emma: An emotion-aware wellbeing chatbot. In *2019 8th International Conference on Affective Computing and Intelligent Interaction (ACII)*, pages 1–7. IEEE.

Mohammad Hijjawi, Zuhair Bandar, Keeley Crockett, and David Mclean. 2014. ArabChat: an arabic conversational agent. In *2014 6th International Conference on Computer Science and Information Technology (CSIT)*, pages 227–237. IEEE.

Guillaume Klein, Yoon Kim, Yuntian Deng, Jean Senellart, and Alexander M Rush. 2017. OpenNMT: Open-source toolkit for neural machine translation. *arXiv preprint arXiv:1701.02810*.

Zhaojiang Lin, Peng Xu, Genta Indra Winata, Farhad Bin Siddique, Zihan Liu, Jamin Shin, and Pascale Fung. 2020. CAiRE: an end-to-end empathetic chatbot. In *AAAI*, pages 13622–13623.

Hussein Mozannar, Karl El Hajal, Elie Maamary, and Hazem Hajj. 2019. Neural arabic question answering. *arXiv preprint arXiv:1906.05394*.

Hannah Rashkin, Eric Michael Smith, Margaret Li, and Y-Lan Boureau. 2018. Towards empathetic open-domain conversation models: A new benchmark and dataset. *arXiv preprint arXiv:1811.00207*.

Jamin Shin, Peng Xu, Andrea Madotto, and Pascale Fung. 2019. Happybot: Generating empathetic dialogue responses by improving user experience look-ahead. *arXiv preprint arXiv:1906.08487*.

Jamin Shin, Peng Xu, Andrea Madotto, and Pascale Fung. 2020. Generating empathetic responses by looking ahead the user's sentiment. In *ICASSP 2020-2020 IEEE International Conference on Acoustics, Speech and Signal Processing (ICASSP)*, pages 7989–7993. IEEE.

Özge Nilay Yalçın and Steve DiPaola. 2018. A computational model of empathy for interactive agents. *Biologically Inspired Cognitive Architectures*, 26:20–25.

Özge Nilay Yalçın. 2020. Empathy framework for embodied conversational agents. *Cognitive Systems Research*, 59:123–132.

Saizheng Zhang, Emily Dinan, Jack Urbanek, Arthur Szlam, Douwe Kiela, and Jason Weston. 2018. Personalizing dialogue agents: I have a dog, do you have pets too? *arXiv preprint arXiv:1801.07243*.

Peixiang Zhong, Yan Zhu, Yong Liu, Chen Zhang, Hao Wang, Zaiqing Nie, and Chunyan Miao. 2020. Endowing empathetic conversational models with personas. *arXiv preprint arXiv:2004.12316*.

Li Zhou, Jianfeng Gao, Di Li, and Heung-Yeung Shum. 2020. The design and implementation of XiaoIce, an empathetic social chatbot. *Computational Linguistics*, 46(1):53–93.

Yukun Zhu, Ryan Kiros, Rich Zemel, Ruslan Salakhutdinov, Raquel Urtasun, Antonio Torralba, and Sanja Fidler. 2015. Aligning books and movies: Towards story-like visual explanations by watching movies and reading books. In *Proceedings of the IEEE International Conference on Computer Vision*, pages 19–27.

# Machine Generation and Detection of Arabic Manipulated and Fake News

**El Moatez Billah Nagoudi[1], AbdelRahim Elmadany[1], Muhammad Abdul-Mageed[1],**
**Tariq Alhindi[2], Hasan Cavusoglu [3]**
[1] Natural Language Processing Lab,
[1,3] The University of British Columbia
[2] Department of Computer Science, Columbia University
[1] {moatez.nagoudi,a.elmadany,muhammad.mageed}@ubc.ca,
[2] tariq@cs.columbia.edu, [3] cavusoglu@sauder.ubc.ca

## Abstract

Fake news and deceptive machine-generated text are serious problems threatening modern societies, including in the Arab world. This motivates work on detecting false and manipulated stories online. However, a bottleneck for this research is lack of sufficient data to train detection models. We present a novel method for automatically generating Arabic manipulated (and potentially fake) news stories. Our method is simple and only depends on availability of true stories, which are abundant online, and a part of speech tagger (POS). To facilitate future work, we dispense with both of these requirements altogether by providing AraNews, a novel and large POS-tagged news dataset that can be used off-the-shelf. Using stories generated based on AraNews, we carry out a human annotation study that casts light on the effects of machine manipulation on text veracity. The study also measures human ability to detect Arabic machine manipulated text generated by our method. Finally, we develop the first models for detecting manipulated Arabic news and achieve state-of-the-art results on Arabic fake news detection (macro $F_1 = 70.06$). Our models and data are publicly available.

## 1 Introduction

The last few years witnessed a striking rise in creation and dissemination of fake news (Egelhofer and Lecheler, 2019; Allcott et al., 2019). Such fake stories are propagated not only by individuals, but also by groups or even nation states (Allcott et al., 2019). For example, Allcott and Gentzkow (2017) discuss the role fake news have played in the 2016 U.S. presidential election, arguing that Donald Trump's voters have been more influenced to believe fake stories. More recently, concerns have also been raised about possible abuse of machine-generated text such as by GPT3 (Brown et al., 2020) for deceiving readers.

In the Arab context, Arab countries have had their share of misinformation. This is especially the case due to the sweeping waves of uprisings and popular protests

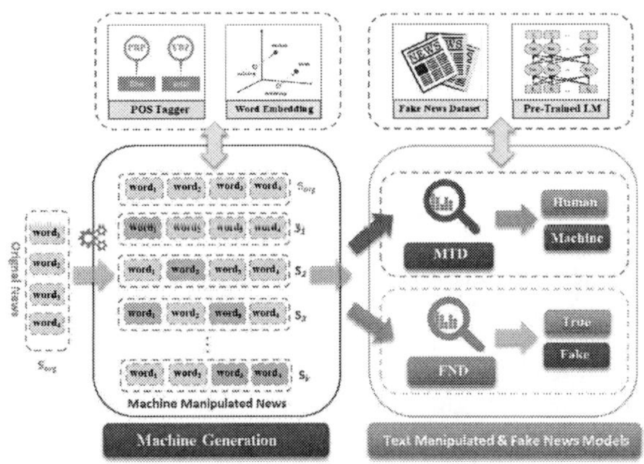

Figure 1: Our proposed methods. **Left:** Machine generation of manipulated text. **Top Right:** manipulated text detection model (MTD). **Bottom Right:** fake news detection model (FND). **word**$_i$: original word. **word**$_j$: substituted word.

(Torres et al., 2018; Helwe et al., 2019). Although there has been considerable research investigating the

---





*Proceedings of the Fifth Arabic Natural Language Processing Workshop*, pages 69–84
Barcelona, Spain (Online), December 12, 2020

legitimacy, or lack thereof, of news in many languages (Conroy et al., 2015; Kim et al., 2018; Bondielli and Marcelloni, 2019), work on the Arabic language is still lagging behind.

In this paper, we first report an approach to automatically generate manipulated (and possibly fake) stories in Arabic. Our approach is simple: Given a dataset of legitimate news, a part-of-speech (POS) tagger, and a word embedding model, we are able to automatically generate significant amounts of news stories. Since these generated stories are machine manipulated such that original words (e.g., named entities, factual information such as numbers and time stamps) are substituted, some of these stories can be used as training data for fakes news detection models.

To illustrate our method, we provide the following scenario: Given a human-authored sentence, we output a manipulated version of the original. The veracity of the manipulated version can either: (1) **Stay Intact.** For instance when changing an adjective with its synonym, e.g., أفضل ("top") with أحسن ("best") in أفضل هاتف ذكي هو الأيفون ("The best smartphone is the iPhone") or (2) **Change.** For example, when substituting a named entity with another that does not necessarily communicate the meaning of the original as closely. For example, changing the named entity أرامكو ("Aramco") with أمازون ("Amazon") in أرامكو تحقق هذه السنة أعلى أرباح ("Aramco achieved the highest profit this year").

As such, we emphasize that changing a certain POS does not automatically flip the sentence veracity. For example changing مصر ("Egypt") with المحروسة ("Almahrousa") does not alter the sentence veracity. We manually validate the claim that our method of text manipulation can generate fake stories via a human annotation study (Section 5). We then use our generated data to create models that can detect manipulated stories from our method and empirically show the impact of exploiting our generated stories on the fake news detection task on a manually-crafted external dataset (Section 6). We make our models and data publicly available.[1]

We make the following contributions: (1) We introduce AraNews, a new large-scale POS-tagged news dataset covering a wide range of topics from diverse sources. (2) We propose a simple, yet effective, method for automatic manipulation of Arabic news texts. Applying this methods on AraNews, we create and release the first dataset of manipulated Arabic news dataset to accelerate future research. (3) We perform a human annotation study to measure the ability of native speakers of Arabic to detect (a) machine manipulated and (b) fake news stories without resorting to external resources such as fact checking websites. The annotation study aims at gauging the extent to which a human can fall prey to deceptive news in a semi-real situation (i.e., where an average reader do not check third party sources when reading through a news story). (4) We develop effective models for detecting manipulated news stories, and then test the utility of our generated data for improving fake news detection on an external dataset.

The rest of the paper is organized as follows: Section 2 provides an overview of related work. In Section 3, we describe the two *true*[2] news datasets used in this work. Section 4 is about our methods for generating manipulated text (and potentially fake news stories). Section 5 describes our human annotation study. In Section 6, we present our detection models. We conclude in Section 7.

## 2   Related Work

**Knowledge-Based Fact Checking.** Recent work on developing automatic methods for fake news detection has mainly followed two lines of research as categorized in the literature (Thorne and Vlachos, 2018; Potthast et al., 2018). First, work that compares a claim against an evidence from (trusted) collections of factual information whether the evidence is a sentence (i.e. fact-checking modeled as textual entailment) or a full document (i.e. stance detection between a claim-document pair). This includes work that created synthetic claims verified against Wikipedia (Thorne et al., 2018), and naturally occurring claims verified against news articles (Ferreira and Vlachos, 2016; Pomerleau and Rao, 2017), discussion forums (Joty et al., 2018), or debate websites (Chen et al., 2019). These datasets are labeled using 2 tags (*true, false*) (Alhindi et al., 2018) 3 tags (*supported, refuted, not-enough-information*) (Thorne et al., 2018), or 4 tags (*agree, disagree, discuss, unrelated*) (Pomerleau and Rao, 2017). They vary in size from 300 claims (Fer-

---

[1]Models and data are at: `https://github.com/UBC-NLP/wanlp2020_arabic_fake_news_detection`.
[2]We use the terms "true" and "legitimate" interchangeably to refer to stories that are not "fake".

reira and Vlachos, 2016) to 185,000 claims (Thorne et al., 2018). Approaches on developing models to predict claim veracity using these datasets include hierarchical attention networks (Ma et al., 2019), pointer networks (Hidey et al., 2020), graph-based reasoning (Zhou et al., 2019; Zhong et al., 2019), and (similar to our methods) fine-tuning of pre-trained transformers (Hidey et al., 2020; Zhong et al., 2019).

**Style-Based Detection.** The second line of research focuses on analyzing the linguistic features of a claim to determine its veracity without considering external factual information. This approach is based on investigating linguistic characteristics of fake content in comparison to true content. In news and various fact-checked political claims, Rashkin et al. (2017) found that first and second person pronouns, superlatives, modal adverbs, and hedging are more prevalent in fake content, while concrete and comparative figures, and assertive words are more widespread in truthful content. Other work found the properties of deceptive language to differ between domains (Pérez-Rosas et al., 2018). Misleading content itself has been classified into sub-categories such as (a) the 3 types of fake (serious fabrication, hoaxes, and satire) (Rubin et al., 2015), (b) propaganda and its different techniques (Da San Martino et al., 2019), and (c) misinformation and disinformation (Ireton and Posetti, 2018). The differences between these different categories depend on many factors such as genre and domain, targeted audience, and deceptive intent (Rubin et al., 2015; Rashkin et al., 2017). In addition to categories, truth was classified to more than two *levels*. For example, Politifact.com introduced 6 levels: pants-on-fire, false, mostly-false, half-true, mostly-true and true. These different levels have been exploited in previous work, with a goal to automate this more challenging six-way classification task (Rashkin et al., 2017; Wang, 2017; Alhindi et al., 2018).

**Automatic Generation of Data.** The development of automatic fake news detection models was possible as the afore-mentioned datasets became available. More related to our work, previous work has focused on developing methods to automatically generate more robust, and large-scale, fake news datasets. Thorne et al. (2019) showed that current fact-checking systems are vulnerable to adversarial attacks by doing simple alteration to the training data. To increase robustness of such systems, previous work has extended available fake news datasets both manually and automatically using lexical substitution (Alzantot et al., 2018), rule-based alterations (Ribeiro et al., 2018), phrasal addition and temporal reasoning (Hidey et al., 2020), or using transformer models such as GPT-2 (Radford et al., 2019) and Grover (Zellers et al., 2019) for claim and news article generation (Niewinski et al., 2019; Zellers et al., 2019). As a way to increase our understanding and trust in fact-checking systems, Atanasova et al. (2020) developed a transformer-based model for generating fact-checking textual explanations along with the prediction of claim veracity.

**Arabic Work.** All of the datasets described above, however, are in English with limited availability of similar ones in other languages such as Arabic. Available Arabic datasets cover tasks such as determining claim check-worthiness of tweets (Barrón-Cedeño et al., 2020), news and claims from fact-checking websites (Elsayed et al., 2019), and translated political claims from English (Nakov et al., 2018). In addition, there are datasets for stance and factuality prediction of claims from news or social media with or without the evidence retrieval task  (Baly et al., 2018; Khouja, 2020; Elsayed et al., 2019; Alkhair et al., 2019; Darwish et al., 2017). These corpora are created by either using credibility of publishers as proxy for veracity (*true/false*) then manually annotating the stance between a claim-document pair (*agree, disagree, discuss, unrelated*) (Baly et al., 2018) or by manual alteration of true claims to generate fake ones about the same topic (Khouja, 2020)–all requiring a manual, slow, and labor-intensive process. We alleviate this by introducing our simple and scalable approach for automatic generation of Arabic manipulated text, including potential fake stories, using the abundant legitimate online news data as seeds for the generation model. We also introduce a large-scale dataset in true and manipulated form for detection work. We now introduce our datasets.

## 3 Datasets

### 3.1 ATB: Arabic TreeBank

We exploit a number of Arabic Treebank datasets from the Linguistic Data Consortium (LDC). Namely, we use 4 LDC resources comprising Arabic news stories in Modern Standard Arabic (MSA). These are: Arabic Treebank (ATB) Part 1 v4.1 (LDC2010T13), Part 2 v3.1 (LDC2011T09), Part 3 v3.2 (LDC2010T08) and Broadcast News v1.0 (LDC2012T07), the latter being a collection of Arabic news stories built as part of of the DARPA TIDES project.[3] These 4 parts contain over $2,000$ news stories produced by a handful of Arabic news services with a total of 1.5M tokens. Moreover, we use the Arabic Treebank Weblog (LDC2016T02), which contains 13K Arabic news and a total of 308K tokens. We refer to all the 5 LDC resources collectively as **ATB**. For each token in ATB, there is a Latin-based transliteration, a unique identifier (lemma ID), a breakdown of the constituent morphemes (prefixes, stem, and suffixes), POS tag(s), and the corresponding English gloss(es).

### 3.2 AraNews: A New Large-Scale Arabic News Dataset

In order to study misinformation in Arabic news, we develop, **AraNews**, a large-scale, multi-topic, and multi-country Arabic news dataset. To create the dataset, we start by manually collecting a list of 50 newspapers belonging to 15 Arab countries, the United States of America (USA), and the United Kingdom (UK). Then, we scrape the news articles from this list of newspapers. Ultimately, we collected a total of $5,187,957$ news articles. The map in Figure 2 shows the geographic distribution of AraNews.

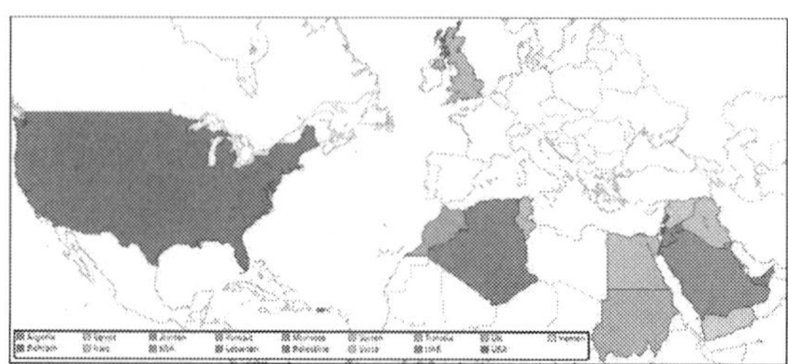

Figure 2: Geographical distribution of AraNews.

We assign each article in AraNews a thematic category as follows: We first consider the category assigned on each newspaper website to the article. We identify a total of 118 unique categories, which we manually map to only 17 categories using the dictionary illustrated in Table A2 in Appendix A.2. The 17 categories are in the set {*Politics, History, Society, Media, Entertainments, Weather, Sports, Social Media, Heath, Culture and Art, Economy, Religion, Education, Technology, Fashion, Local News, International News*}. For each article in the AraNews collection, we document several types of information. These include: (1) name of the newspaper in Arabic and English, (2) newspaper origin country, (3) newspaper link, (4) title, (5) content, (6) summary (if available), (7) author (if available), (8) URL, (9) date, and (10) topic. More details about AraNews are in Table A1 in Appendix A.1. AraNews is available for research.[4]

## 4   Methods

To generate a large scale manipulated news dataset, we exploit ATB (see Section 3.1) and 1M news articles extracted from AraNews (Section 3.2). In the following, we describe our data splits and methodology for automatically generating manipulated text from these two 'legitimate' sources.[5]

### 4.1   Data Splits

We split both ATB and AraNews at the article level into TRAIN, DEV, and TEST. Table 1 provides the related statistics at both the article and sentence levels across the different data sources for all three splits.

### 4.2   POS Tagging

The first step in our approach is to perform POS tagging of the news articles. ATB is already POS tagged. Thus, we use MADAMIRA (Pasha et al., 2014), a morphological analysis and disambiguation tool for Arabic, to POS-tag AraNews.[6]

---

[3]https://www.ldc.upenn.edu/collaborations/past-projects.

[4]https://github.com/UBC-NLP/wanlp2020_arabic_fake_news_detection.

[5]We do not check the veracity of stories in these two sources, but we have no reason to think they may have fake stories. As such, we make the assumption they consist of "true" stories.

[6]MADAMIRA was trained on the training sets of Penn Arabic Treebank corpus (parts 1, 2 and 3) (Maamouri et al., 2004) and the Egyptian Arabic Treebanks (Maamouri et al., 2014).

| Data | TRAIN (80%) | | | DEV (10%) | | | TEST (10%) | | |
|---|---|---|---|---|---|---|---|---|---|
| | Artic. | Sent. | Tokens | Artic. | Sent. | Tokens | Artic. | Sent. | Tokens |
| **ATB Weblog** | 1.9K | 8.6K | 154.8K | 235 | 1K | 17.9K | 235 | 1.2K | 19.5K |
| **ATB Part 1** | 587 | 4.7K | 117.3K | 73 | 580 | 14.9K | 74 | 536 | 13.3K |
| **ATB Part 2** | 400 | 3.4K | 117.6K | 50 | 387 | 13.9K | 51 | 382 | 12.7K |
| **ATB Part 3** | 479 | 10.5K | 268.5K | 60 | 1.5K | 36.5K | 60 | 1.4K | 34.7K |
| **ATB BN** | 96 | 21.5K | 334.3K | 12 | 3.1K | 47.7K | 12 | 2.4K | 40K |
| **AraNews** | 800K | 3.3M | 1.1B | 100K | 55.1K | 209.9M | 100K | 61.6K | 197.2M |

Table 1: Statistics of ATB and AraNews (only 1M articles) datasets across the data splits.

### 4.3 News Word Embedding Model

The second component needed in our model is a word vector model. We train a fastText model (Joulin et al., 2016) on a concatenation of MSA data sources (Wikipedia Arabic,[7] Arabic Gigaword Corpus (Parker et al., 2009), and ATBP1V3 [8]). We perform light pre-processing involving removing punctuation marks, non-letters, URLs, emojis, and emoticons. We also convert elongated words back to their original form by reducing consecutive repetitions of the same character as suggested in (Lachraf et al., 2019). For example : استفساااااالر (*inquiries*) and الجزائــــــر (*Algeria*) are converted to استفسار and الجزائر. We then train our model using the Python Gensim library (Řehřek and Sojka, 2011). We set the vector size to 300, minimum word frequency at 100, and a window size of 5 words. We call this model **AraNewsEmb**. We then use this model to retrieve the most similar tokens of a given token in the original text using cosine similarity. Next, we use one of the set of relevant tokens to replace the original token, focusing only on tokens corresponding to the following POS tags: proper nouns (N_PROP), cardinal numbers (N_NUM), common adjective (ADJ), comparative adjective (ADJ_COMP), ordinal numbers (ADJ_NUM), and negative particles (NEG_PART). In theory, substitution of these words should have no syntactically harmful effect on the sentence. However, changes can happen if the gold or predicted POS tag is wrong.

### 4.4 Automatic Text Manipulation

To generate a machine manipulated story, we substitute the selected words (ones matching the listed POS tags) by a chosen one from the $k$ most similar ($k$-closest) words in our AraNewsEmb model as described in (Nagoudi and Schwab, 2017). We remove negation from the sentence, using the negative particle (NEG_PART) POS as a guide, and substitute the cardinal number related to (N_NUM) with a random number. For tokens related to the rest of POS tags, we needed to identify a reasonable *character-level* similarity threshold between the original token and the retrieved most-similar token to ensure the two belong to different lemmas. [9]

| POS Label | Count | Avg | Median |
|---|---|---|---|
| ADJ | 99, 538 | 3.79 | 3.00 |
| ADJ_COMP | 4, 513 | 2.81 | 2.00 |
| ADJ_NUM | 5, 752 | 3.06 | 3.00 |
| N_NUM | 60, 615 | 0.55 | 0.00 |
| N_PROP | 75, 771 | 2.93 | 2.00 |

Table 2: Descriptive statistics of $k-$closest words excluded in each POS class. We simply remove the negation token corresponding to **NEG_PART** from the sentence, and so the embedding model is not used in this case.

We performed a manual analysis based on $5,000$ random substitution examples from AraNewsEmb and identify a similarity *ratio* of 50%. This threshold gave us new words in 100% of the cases. For instance, if we want to substitute the word لبنان (Lebanon), we exclude three words: بلبنان, لبنانيا, ولبنان, before considering the $4^{th}$-closest word which is سوريا (Syria). Other examples for the substitution process are illustrated in Table 3. We also provide in Table 2 the average number of $k$-closest words excluded in each POS class. The results of this step are two new machine manipulated datasets. We refer to these datasets as **ATB$^+$** and **AraNews$^+$**. More details about these two datasets are in Table A3 in Appendix A.3. We now provide an example illustrating how our text manipulation method works.

---

[7] https://archive.org/details/arwiki-20190201.

[8] https://catalog.ldc.upenn.edu/LDC2010T08

[9] We use the following formula to compute the character-level similarity ratio between two tokens: $ratio = 2 * M/T$, where $M$ is matching characters and $T$ is total of characters.

| Word | Translation | POS | $k$-closet (ratio similarity%) | Token rank |
|---|---|---|---|---|
| قصير | Short | ADJ | طويل (25%) | 0 |
| أكثر | More | ADJ_COMP | واكثر (89%), أقل (28%) | 1 |
| باكستان | Pakistan | N_PROP | لباكستان (93%), اوزباكستان (82%), بنغلاديش (26%) | 2 |
| الثالث | The third | ADJ_NUM | والثالث (92%), الثاني (67%), الاول (72%), الرابع (49%) | 4 |
| وسبعة | And seven | N_NUM | وسبع (89%), وسبعه (80%), وسبعون (73%), وثلاثون (17%) | 4 |

Table 3: Illustration of substitution process based on the word embeddings model. **Token rank:** refers to rank of chosen word in the returned word embedding list (from AraNewsEmb) after applying our char-based cosine similarity threshold. **Light red:** excluded word. **Light green:** selected word. <u>Under lined</u> words represent the false negative of the selection process (i.e., words based on a different lemma and hence could work but were ignored by the algorithm).

## 4.5 Illustrative Example

We present a typical example illustrating the automatic text manipulation process by our method. Consider the following sports news sentence: محرز ينتقل الى برشلونة مقابل 120 مليون دولار ("Mahrez moves to Barcelona for \$ 120 million"). The method proceeds in the following steps:

**Step 1: Identify POS tags.** The sentence can be POS-tagged as shown in Table 4.

**Step 2: POS and Token Selection.** In this step, tokens corresponding to one or more POS tags must be chosen for substitution. For our illustrative example, we will select and substitute only the *proper noun* and *digit* tokens. The sentence has two proper nouns, برشلونة and محرز and one digit (120).

**Step 3: Sentence Manipulation.** If we select only the noun proper: برشلونة (Barcelona), we can retrieve the 5-closest words from AraNewsEmb. In this case, we obtain: مدريد (Madrid), ميلان (Milan), باريس (Paris), فالنسيا (Valencia), and مانشستر (Manchester). Indeed, we can generate 5 fake sentences from the original sentence. However, if we select two proper nouns محرز, برشلونة and the digit token 120, we can generate 75 ($3 * 5 * 5$) manipulated sentences from the single human sentence. Both scenarios are presented in Table 5.

| Words | | POS Tags |
|---|---|---|
| محرز | → | N_PROP |
| ينتقل | → | VERB |
| الى | → | PREP |
| برشلونة | → | N_PROP |
| مقابل | → | NOUN |
| 120 | → | NUM |
| مليون | → | NOUN |
| دولار | → | NOUN |

Table 4: POS tags of our example

| Subs. with 5-closest of برشلونة | Subs. with 5-closest of برشلونة , محرز and 120 |
|---|---|
| محرز ينتقل الى مدريد مقابل 120 مليون دولار | صلاح ينتقل الى ليدز مقابل 350 مليون دولار |
| محرز ينتقل الى باريس مقابل 120 مليون دولار | ميسي ينتقل الى مدريد مقابل 450 مليون دولار |
| محرز ينتقل الى فالنسيا مقابل 120 مليون دولار | رونالدو ينتقل الى باريس مقابل 155 مليون دولار |
| محرز ينتقل الى ميلان مقابل 120 مليون دولار | ماني ينتقل الى فالنسيا مقابل 280 مليون دولار |
| محرز ينتقل الى مانشستر مقابل 120 مليون دولار | اغويرو ينتقل الى مرسيليا مقابل 70 مليون دولار |

Table 5: Illustrative output example from our text manipulation method. Given a sentence and a target POS tag, we substitute the word corresponding to the POS tag with the word closest to it (based on cosine similarity) in the AraNewsEmb model. **Left:** Substitution of word برشلونة (*Barcelona*) with its 5-closets words. **Right:** Substitution of محرز, برشلونة and *120* (*Barcelona, Mehrez* [name of a soccer player], and 120) each with 5-closest words.

# 5  Human Annotation Study

## 5.1  Annotation Data

We perform a human annotation study in order to identify (1) the ability of humans to detect machine manipulated text using our method, and (2) the extent to which text identified as machine manipulated can be *fake*. For this purpose, we randomly select 300 samples from the ATB development set (see Table 1), among which 145 sentences are from the original ATB sentences and the rest (i.e., 155 samples) are machine manipulated.

## 5.2  Annotation Procedures

For annotation, we follow two stages: The first stage is for **manipulated text detection**. We shuffle the samples and ask the annotators to label each sentence as either original/produced by humans (*human*) or generated by machine (*machine*). The second stage is for detecting **veracity of manipulated text**. This stage is applied only on the 155 machine manipulated sentences generated from ATB. Note that here we provide annotators with a sentence *pair* including the machine generated sentence itself and its human counterpart (original sentence in ATB). Annotators are then asked to compare

|        |          | | Annotators Agreement (%) | | |
|--------|----------|--------|----------|-----------|--------|
|        |          | #Sent. | Hum/Mach | True/Fake | %Fake  |
| **Hum**  |              | 145 | 97.93 | N/A   | N/A   |
|        | **ADJ**      | 27  | 96.30 | 74.07 | 48.15 |
|        | **ADJ_COMP** | 24  | 100   | 91.67 | 58.33 |
|        | **ADJ_NUM**  | 26  | 76.92 | 73.08 | 78.85 |
| **Mach** | **NEG_PART** | 32  | 87.50 | 90.63 | 76.56 |
|        | **N_NUM**    | 19  | 100   | 73.68 | 76.32 |
|        | **N_PROP**   | 27  | 92.59 | 74.07 | 83.33 |
|        | **Overall**  | 155 | 94.67 | 80    | 70.32 |

Table 6: Percentages of inter-annotator agreement on a random sample of 300 sentences (original and manipulated).

the manipulated sentence to its original and assign the label *fake* if the manipulated sentence differs in meaningful ways (e.g., provides contradictory information) from the original, but a *true* label otherwise. That is, a *true* tag is assigned if difference between the sentence pair is only grammatical such as cases where the machine sentence is a paraphrase. Each sample is annotated by two experts, both of whom is native speakers of Arabic with a Ph.D. degree. Inter-annotator agreement in term of Kappa ($\kappa$) scores is 79.46% for *human* vs. *machine* and 81.07% for *fake* vs. *true*. As shown in Table 6, the substitution of tokens with the POS tags ADJ_NUM, NEG_PART, N_NUM, and N_PROP changes between 76.32% and 83.33% of sentence veracity. Meanwhile, changing tokens whose POS tags are ADJ or ADJ_COMP changes the veracity of the sentence less than 50% of the time. The reason is that the selected $k-$closets tokens in the second scenario is more or less of a paraphrase. Table 7 provides examples where annotators disagree on either or both tasks, and Table 8 illustrates cases where annotators agree.

| Annotator 2 | | Annotator 1 | | POS | Gold | Sentence |
|------|------|------|------|-----|------|----------|
| T/F  | M/H  | T/F  | M/H  |     |      |          |
| True | Mach | Fake | Mach | N_PROP | Hum  | ذخائر القديسه تريز **المراهق** يسوع في القبيات واحتفالات دينيه تكريما لها حتي الخميس |
|      |      |      |      |        | Mach | ذخائر القديسه تريز **الطفل** يسوع في القبيات واحتفالات دينيه تكريما لها حتي الخميس |
| True | Mach | Fake | Hum  | N_PROP | Hum  | هذه المؤامره تستهدف احباط العمليه السياسيه وارجاع **العراق** الي اه حكم اه العصابه البعثيه |
|      |      |      |      |        | Mach | هذه المؤامره تستهدف احباط العمليه السياسيه وارجاع **الاردن** الي اه حكم اه العصابه البعثيه |
| Fake | Hum  | True | Mach | ADJ    | Hum  | وتابع ان التوجه الاعلامي الجديد **مرفوض** والحكومه تطلب منا المستحيل |
|      |      |      |      |        | Mach | وتابع ان التوجه الاعلامي الجديد **مضلل** والحكومه تطلب منا المستحيل |
| Fake | Hum  | Fake | Mach | NEG_PART | Hum  | واوضح ان مقعدين **لم** يتم البت بهما بعد في الاسكندريه وان ذلك عائد الي قرار قضائي |
|      |      |      |      |          | Mach | واوضح ان مقعدين يتم البت بهما بعد في الاسكندريه وان ذلك عائد الي قرار قضائي |
| Fake | Hum  | True | Mach | ADJ_NUM  | Hum  | ابيكم تعطوني سعر هالقطعه هذي ووين تركب حقت اي بندق **ثانية** من نفس الصناعه |
|      |      |      |      |          | Mach | ابيكم تعطوني سعر هالقطعه هذي ووين تركب حقت اي بندق **رابع** من نفس الصناعه |

Table 7: Examples of disagreement between annotators on either one or the two tasks.

| Sentence | Gold | POS | Task Labels | |
|---|---|---|---|---|
| | | | H/M | T/F |
| وصدر بيان عن اتحاد علماء المسلمين في **العراق** جاء فيه | Hum | N_PROP | Hum | Fake |
| وصدر بيان عن اتحاد علماء المسلمين في **الاردن** جاء فيه | Mach | | | |
| حياك **الله** اخي الغالي | Hum | N_PROP | Hum | True |
| حياك **الرحمن** اخي الغالي | Mach | | | |
| هذه الصور اعادت الي اذهان مشاهد مقتل نحو واحد **وعشرين** ألف شخص | Hum | N_NUM | Hum | Fake |
| هذه الصور اعادت الي اذهان مشاهد مقتل نحو واحد **وثلاثين** ألف شخص | Mach | | | |
| احتل الهولندي كارستن المركز الاول في المرحله الثامنة من دوره فرنسا ال ٨١ للدراجات | Hum | N_NUM | Hum | Fake |
| احتل الهولندي كارستن المركز الاول في المرحله الثامنة من دوره فرنسا ال ٨٩ للدراجات | Mach | | | |
| يلف الغموض **العديد** من المشكلات في اداء الجيش الاسرائيلي | Hum | ADJ | Hum | True |
| يلف الغموض **الكثير** من المشكلات في اداء الجيش الاسرائيلي | Mach | | | |
| احترم نفسك **احسن** لك والا ساشن حمله لمقاطعه مدونتك ابداها بتوقيعات الزملاء السعوديين | Hum | ADJ | Hum | True |
| احترم نفسك **افضل** لك والا ساشن حمله لمقاطعه مدونتك ابداها بتوقيعات الزملاء السعوديين | Mach | | | |
| الصابونجي : الهجره المسيحيه **لا** تتصل بموضوع ديني | Hum | NEG_Part | Hum | Fake |
| الصابونجي : الهجره المسيحيه تتصل بموضوع ديني | Mach | | | |
| واضاف كورماك ان واشنطن تفكر في الخضوع في المستقبل في حال **لم** تنجح الضغوط السياسيه | Hum | NEG_Part | Hum | Fake |
| واضاف كورماك ان واشنطن تفكر في الخضوع في المستقبل في حال تنجح الضغوط السياسيه | Mach | | | |

Table 8: Example labels from one annotator on a sample of our data.

## 6 Manipulated Text and Fake News Detection

### 6.1 Manipulated Text Detection (MTD)

**Approach.** We use the ATB[+] and AraNews[+] datasets for training deep learning models for detecting manipulated text. From each of these datasets, we select 61K human and 61K machine manipulated sentences (total $\sim$ 122K) and split them into 80% training (TRAIN), 10% development (DEV), and 10% test (TEST) as shown in Table 9.

| # Split | Human | Machine Manipulated | | | | | | |
|---|---|---|---|---|---|---|---|---|
| | # Sent. | ADJ | ADJ_COMP | ADJ_NUM | N_NUM | N_PROP | NEG_PART | Total |
| **TRAIN** | $48,727$ | $9,600$ | $4,513$ | $5,752$ | $9,600$ | $9,600$ | $9,600$ | $48,665$ |
| **DEV** | $6,573$ | $1,300$ | $638$ | $844$ | $1,300$ | $1,300$ | $1,300$ | $6,682$ |
| **TEST** | $5,895$ | $1,200$ | $592$ | $665$ | $1,200$ | $1,200$ | $1,200$ | $6,057$ |

Table 9: The TRAIN, DEV, and TEST splits form ATB[+] (with a similar split from AraNews[+]) for developing our manipulated news detection models. The same amount of data from the different POS categories is extracted from each of the two datasets.

**Models.** For the purpose of training our manipulated text detectors, we exploit 4 large pre-trained masked language models (MLM): mBERT (Devlin et al., 2018), AraBERT (Antoun et al., 2020), XLM-R$_{\text{Base}}$, and XLM-R$_{\text{Large}}$ (Conneau et al., 2020). [10]

**Training Data & Hyper-Parameters.** We fine-tuned all these models on the TRAIN split of (1) ATB[+], and (2) AraNews[+], independently. For each model, we run for 25 epochs with a batch size of 32, maximum sequence length of 128 tokens, and a learning rate of $1e^{-5}$.

---

[10]Each of the mBERT, AraBERT, and XLM-R$_{\text{Base}}$ models has 12 layers each with 12 attention heads, and 768 hidden units. The XLM-R$_{\text{Large}}$ model has 24 layers each with 16 attention heads, and $1,024$ hidden units.

**Evaluation Data.** We evaluate each of the two models on its respective DEV and TEST splits (i.e., from either ATB$^+$ or AraNews$^+$). Although the data in the two classes are reasonably balanced, we use *both* accuracy and macro $F_1$ for evaluation. Table 10 shows the results on the two datasets.

**Results & Discussion.** As Table 10 shows, the best performance on ATB$^+$ is at 83.20 $F_1$ (acquired with XLM-R$_{Base}$). For AraNews$^+$, the best model is at 89.25 $F_1$ (acquired with AraBERT). These results show that it is harder to detect manipulated text exploiting ATB$^+$ than that exploiting AraNews$^+$. This could be due to two reasons: (a) ATB$^+$ contains news stories that are diachronically different from the data the language models are trained on, which is less true for the case of AraNews (since the latter dataset is crawled in late 2019 and early while most ATB data were acquired prior to 2004), (b) ATB$^+$ is POS tagged manually, which makes generations based on it less error-prone.

| Data | Models | Dev | | Test | |
|---|---|---|---|---|---|
| | | Acc. | F1 | Acc. | F1 |
| ATB$^+$ | mBERT | 77.16 | 77.08 | 77.42 | 77.36 |
| | XLM-R$_{Base}$ | 81.72 | 81.72 | **83.22** | **83.20** |
| | XLM-R$_{Large}$ | 82.41 | 82.38 | 81.38 | 81.36 |
| | AraBERT | **83.19** | **83.17** | 82.63 | 82.62 |
| AraNews$^+$ | mBERT | 79.39 | 79.38 | 83.51 | 83.52 |
| | XLM-R$_{Base}$ | 82.77 | 82.56 | 86.09 | 86.08 |
| | XLM-R$_{Large}$ | 82.12 | 82.10 | 86.35 | 86.35 |
| | AraBERT | **87.21** | **87.21** | **89.23** | **89.25** |

Table 10: Performance results of our the MTD models on the dev and test split of ATB$^+$ and AraNews$^+$.

## 6.2 Fake News Detection (FND)

**Approach.** Evaluating on an external human-crafted fake news dataset, we also develop a host of models for detecting fake news. The dataset is developed by Khouja (2020) by sampling a subset of news titles from the Arabic News Texts corpus (Chouigui et al., 2017), a collection of Arabic news from multiple news media sources in the Middle East. Crowd-sourcing is used to generate true and false claims starting from a news title. Khouja (2020) asks annotators to modify each news title into a new claim by: (1) paraphrasing the original title via changing wording and syntax while maintaining the same meaning, thus producing a legit (or *true*) sentence, and (2) modifying the meaning of the original title such that a sentence that contradicts that title is acquired (constituting a false, or *fake*, claim). We refer to this dataset from (Khouja, 2020) as **Khouja**. It comprises $3,072$ *true* sentences and $1,475$ *fake* sentences. We now describe our various fake news detection models.

**Models.** As explained, our primary goal is to test how data generated by our methods will fare on the problem of fake news detection, as evaluated on a human-created fake news dataset (i.e., Khouja). For this reason, we only test models reported in this section on the DEV and TEST splits of Khouja. We have the following modeling settings:

1. **Fine-Tuning on Khouja (Baseline).** Here, we fine-tune all MLMs (i.e., models from Section 6.1) on the train split of Khouja.

2. **Zero-Shot Detection.** Based on our human annotation study (Section 5), we hypothesize that our machine-manipulated sentences will be closer to the *fake* class than the *true* class in the fake news context. To test this hypothesis, we fine-tune our MLMs *only* on our generated data (and hence naming this setting *zero-shot*, i.e., since we do not train on Khouja TRAIN at all). We have the following configurations pertaining the parts of our data we fine-tune on: (a) ATB$^+$ TRAIN, (b) AraNews$^+$ TRAIN, and (c) double the size the TRAIN of AraNews$^+$.

3. **Data augmentation.** We augment the Khouja TRAIN split with the 3 training configurations from our data listed in the zero-shot setting above (i.e., a, b, and c), each time fine-tuning on Khouja and one of these 3 splits.

**Evaluation Data & Hyper-Parameters.** For the current experiments, as explained earlier, we use the original split of Khouja (2020) (i.e., 80% TRAIN, 10% DEV, and 10% for TEST). We evaluate all the

FND models on the DEV and TEST splits of Khouja and use the same hyper-parameters as in Section 6.1.

**Results & Discussion.** As Table 11 shows, best performance when training on *Khouja TRAIN (gold, our baseline)* is 67.21 $F_1$ (acquired with XLM-R$_{Large}$). This is already 2.91% points higher than the best system reported by Khouja (2020) (64.30 $F_1$, not shown in Table 11).

For our *zero-shot experiments*, our best model is at 52.71 $F_1$ when training on AraNews$^+$ base setting (i.e., setting **a** in Table 11, with TRAIN data $= 48,655$ sentences). This result shows that use of data generated by our method is effective on the fake news detection task, even without access to gold training data. In particular, the 52.71 $F_1$ we acquire is higher than the baseline majority class in Khouja (2020) (40.20 $F_1$) and close to their 53.10 $F_1$ character-level LSTM model trained on gold data.

Our *data augmentation experiments* show that using double-sized generated data from AraNews (Train$= 97,310$ sentences, our setting **c**) is most effective and results in 70.06 $F_1$. *This is the best model we report in this paper. It is $\sim 2.85$ $F_1$ higher than our own baseline, and 5.76 $F_1$ better than Khouja (2020)'s best model. Overall, our results clearly demonstrate the positive impact of our manipulated data on the fake news detection task, thereby lending value to our novel machine generation method.*

| Setting | TRAIN Split | Model | DEV | | TEST | |
|---|---|---|---|---|---|---|
| | | | Acc. | F1 | Acc. | F1 |
| Baseline | KH | mBERT | **73.40** | 64.74 | 70.39 | 61.93 |
| | | XLM-R$_{Base}$ | 72.74 | 64.27 | 72.15 | 64.92 |
| | | XLM-R$_{Large}$ | 71.52 | **65.60** | 72.15 | **67.21** |
| | | AraBERT | 73.07 | 67.10 | 72.59 | 67.05 |
| Zero-Shot | (a) | mBERT | 61.92 | 48.14 | 60.96 | 49.12 |
| | | XLM-R$_{Base}$ | 61.81 | 47.42 | 60.53 | 47.37 |
| | | XLM-R$_{Large}$ | **62.36** | 49.52 | 62.28 | 50.28 |
| | | AraBERT | 62.03 | 47.72 | 61.62 | 49.27 |
| | (b) | mBERT | 53.09 | 49.12 | 53.73 | 50.70 |
| | | XLM-R$_{Base}$ | 58.28 | 47.66 | 57.89 | 48.59 |
| | | XLM-R$_{Large}$ | 58.06 | 46.99 | 61.18 | **52.71** |
| | | AraBERT | 54.42 | **49.94** | 53.29 | 50.12 |
| | (c) | mBERT | 55.41 | 48.87 | 54.61 | 49.18 |
| | | XLM-R$_{Base}$ | 55.85 | 48.21 | 56.58 | 48.77 |
| | | XLM-R$_{Large}$ | 56.62 | 48.75 | 57.89 | 50.33 |
| | | AraBERT | 54.86 | 48.65 | 57.24 | 51.49 |
| Data Augmentation | KH+(a) | mBERT | 71.96 | 65.51 | 68.20 | 60.72 |
| | | XLM-R$_{Base}$ | 70.86 | 62.39 | 69.96 | 62.71 |
| | | XLM-R$_{Large}$ | 65.89 | 61.40 | 66.67 | 62.86 |
| | | AraBERT | 72.63 | 67.15 | 70.83 | 65.38 |
| | KH+(b) | mBERT | 70.20 | 64.68 | 69.74 | 64.58 |
| | | XLM-R$_{Base}$ | 72.52 | 67.05 | 72.37 | 67.40 |
| | | XLM-R$_{Large}$ | **73.29** | 65.71 | 72.37 | 65.79 |
| | | AraBERT | 72.96 | 62.94 | 73.90 | 66.44 |
| | KH+(c) | mBERT | 69.54 | 64.79 | 68.42 | 64.11 |
| | | XLM-R$_{Base}$ | 69.65 | 64.65 | 72.15 | 66.94 |
| | | XLM-R$_{Large}$ | 71.85 | **67.15** | **74.12** | **70.06** |
| | | AraBERT | 70.20 | 65.38 | 73.03 | 69.90 |

Table 11: Performance results of our the MTD models on the DEV and TEST splits of Khouja. **KH**: refer to Khouja TRAIN split. **(a)** ATB$^+$, **(b)** AraNews$^+$, and **(c)** 2x AraNews$^+$.

## 7 Conclusion

We presented a novel, simple method for automatic generation of Arabic manipulated text for the news domain. To enable off-the-shelf use with our method, we also collected and released a new POS-tagged Arabic news dataset. Exploiting our dataset, we developed and released the first Arabic model for detecting manipulated news text. We performed a human annotation study shedding light on the impact of our text manipulation approach on news veracity. Finally, we leveraged our generated data for augmenting gold fake news data from an external source and report a new SOTA on the task of fake news detection.

In the future, we plan to explore applying our method to languages other than Arabic. This should be straightforward, since the method itself is language-agnostic and only needs a POS tagger and a dataset from a given language. We also plan to investigate more sophisticated text manipulation methods, exploiting data from different domains. We will also study the impact of these methods on detection of machine generated text as well as fake news detection.

## Acknowledgements

MAM gratefully acknowledges support from the Natural Sciences and Engineering Research Council of Canada, the Social Sciences Research Council of Canada, Compute Canada (www.computecanada.ca), and UBC ARC–Sockeye (https://doi.org/10.14288/SOCKEYE).

# References

Tariq Alhindi, Savvas Petridis, and Smaranda Muresan. 2018. Where is your evidence: Improving fact-checking by justification modeling. In *Proceedings of the First Workshop on Fact Extraction and VERification (FEVER)*, pages 85–90, Brussels, Belgium, November. Association for Computational Linguistics.

Maysoon Alkhair, Karima Meftouh, Kamel Smaïli, and Nouha Othman. 2019. An arabic corpus of fake news: Collection, analysis and classification. In *International Conference on Arabic Language Processing*, pages 292–302. Springer.

Hunt Allcott and Matthew Gentzkow. 2017. Social media and fake news in the 2016 election. *Journal of economic perspectives*, 31(2):211–36.

Hunt Allcott, Matthew Gentzkow, and Chuan Yu. 2019. Trends in the diffusion of misinformation on social media. *Research & Politics*, 6(2):2053168019848554.

Moustafa Alzantot, Yash Sharma, Ahmed Elgohary, Bo-Jhang Ho, Mani Srivastava, and Kai-Wei Chang. 2018. Generating natural language adversarial examples. In *Proceedings of the 2018 Conference on Empirical Methods in Natural Language Processing*, pages 2890–2896.

Wissam Antoun, Fady Baly, and Hazem Hajj. 2020. Arabert: Transformer-based model for arabic language understanding. *arXiv preprint arXiv:2003.00104*.

Pepa Atanasova, Jakob Grue Simonsen, Christina Lioma, and Isabelle Augenstein. 2020. Generating fact checking explanations. In *Proceedings of the 58th Annual Meeting of the Association for Computational Linguistics*, pages 7352–7364, Online, July. Association for Computational Linguistics.

Ramy Baly, Mitra Mohtarami, James Glass, Lluís Màrquez, Alessandro Moschitti, and Preslav Nakov. 2018. Integrating stance detection and fact checking in a unified corpus. In *Proceedings of the 2018 Conference of the North American Chapter of the Association for Computational Linguistics: Human Language Technologies, Volume 2 (Short Papers)*, pages 21–27.

Alberto Barrón-Cedeño, Tamer Elsayed, Preslav Nakov, Giovanni Da San Martino, Maram Hasanain, Reem Suwaileh, and Fatima Haouari. 2020. Checkthat! at clef 2020: Enabling the automatic identification and verification of claims in social media. In *European Conference on Information Retrieval*, pages 499–507. Springer.

Alessandro Bondielli and Francesco Marcelloni. 2019. A survey on fake news and rumour detection techniques. *Information Sciences*, 497:38–55.

Tom B Brown, Benjamin Mann, Nick Ryder, Melanie Subbiah, Jared Kaplan, Prafulla Dhariwal, Arvind Neelakantan, Pranav Shyam, Girish Sastry, Amanda Askell, et al. 2020. Language models are few-shot learners. *arXiv preprint arXiv:2005.14165*.

Sihao Chen, Daniel Khashabi, Wenpeng Yin, Chris Callison-Burch, and Dan Roth. 2019. Seeing things from a different angle: Discovering diverse perspectives about claims. In *Proceedings of the 2019 Conference of the North American Chapter of the Association for Computational Linguistics: Human Language Technologies, Volume 1 (Long and Short Papers)*, pages 542–557.

Amina Chouigui, Oussama Ben Khiroun, and Bilel Elayeb. 2017. Ant corpus: an arabic news text collection for textual classification. In *2017 IEEE/ACS 14th International Conference on Computer Systems and Applications (AICCSA)*, pages 135–142. IEEE.

Alexis Conneau, Kartikay Khandelwal, Naman Goyal, Vishrav Chaudhary, Guillaume Wenzek, Francisco Guzmán, Edouard Grave, Myle Ott, Luke Zettlemoyer, and Veselin Stoyanov. 2020. Unsupervised cross-lingual representation learning at scale. In *Proceedings of the 58th Annual Meeting of the Association for Computational Linguistics*, pages 8440–8451, Online, July. Association for Computational Linguistics.

Niall J Conroy, Victoria L Rubin, and Yimin Chen. 2015. Automatic deception detection: Methods for finding fake news. *Proceedings of the Association for Information Science and Technology*, 52(1):1–4.

Giovanni Da San Martino, Seunghak Yu, Alberto Barrón-Cedeno, Rostislav Petrov, and Preslav Nakov. 2019. Fine-grained analysis of propaganda in news article. In *Proceedings of the 2019 Conference on Empirical Methods in Natural Language Processing and the 9th International Joint Conference on Natural Language Processing (EMNLP-IJCNLP)*, pages 5640–5650.

Kareem Darwish, Walid Magdy, and Tahar Zanouda. 2017. Improved stance prediction in a user similarity feature space. In *Proceedings of the 2017 IEEE/ACM international conference on advances in social networks analysis and mining 2017*, pages 145–148.

Jacob Devlin, Ming-Wei Chang, Kenton Lee, and Kristina Toutanova. 2018. Bert: Pre-training of deep bidirectional transformers for language understanding. *arXiv preprint arXiv:1810.04805*.

Jana Laura Egelhofer and Sophie Lecheler. 2019. Fake news as a two-dimensional phenomenon: a framework and research agenda. *Annals of the International Communication Association*, 43(2):97–116.

Tamer Elsayed, Preslav Nakov, Alberto Barrón-Cedeno, Maram Hasanain, Reem Suwaileh, Giovanni Da San Martino, and Pepa Atanasova. 2019. Overview of the clef-2019 checkthat! lab: automatic identification and verification of claims. In *International Conference of the Cross-Language Evaluation Forum for European Languages*, pages 301–321. Springer.

William Ferreira and Andreas Vlachos. 2016. Emergent: a novel data-set for stance classification. In *Proceedings of the 2016 conference of the North American chapter of the association for computational linguistics: Human language technologies*, pages 1163–1168.

Chadi Helwe, Shady Elbassuoni, Ayman Al Zaatari, and Wassim El-Hajj. 2019. Assessing arabic weblog credibility via deep co-learning. In *Proceedings of the Fourth Arabic Natural Language Processing Workshop*, pages 130–136.

Christopher Hidey, Tuhin Chakrabarty, Tariq Alhindi, Siddharth Varia, Kriste Krstovski, Mona Diab, and Smaranda Muresan. 2020. DeSePtion: Dual sequence prediction and adversarial examples for improved fact-checking. In *Proceedings of the 58th Annual Meeting of the Association for Computational Linguistics*, pages 8593–8606, Online, July. Association for Computational Linguistics.

Cherilyn Ireton and Julie Posetti. 2018. *Journalism, fake news & disinformation: handbook for journalism education and training*. UNESCO Publishing.

Shafiq Joty, Lluís Màrquez, and Preslav Nakov. 2018. Joint multitask learning for community question answering using task-specific embeddings. In *Proceedings of the 2018 Conference on Empirical Methods in Natural Language Processing*, pages 4196–4207.

Armand Joulin, Edouard Grave, Piotr Bojanowski, Matthijs Douze, Hérve Jégou, and Tomas Mikolov. 2016. Fasttext. zip: Compressing text classification models. *arXiv preprint arXiv:1612.03651*.

Jude Khouja. 2020. Stance prediction and claim verification: An Arabic perspective. In *Proceedings of the Third Workshop on Fact Extraction and VERification (FEVER)*, pages 8–17, Online, July. Association for Computational Linguistics.

Jooyeon Kim, Behzad Tabibian, Alice Oh, Bernhard Schölkopf, and Manuel Gomez-Rodriguez. 2018. Leveraging the crowd to detect and reduce the spread of fake news and misinformation. In *Proceedings of the Eleventh ACM International Conference on Web Search and Data Mining*, pages 324–332. ACM.

Raki Lachraf, El Moatez Billah Nagoudi, Youcef Ayachi, Ahmed Abdelali, and Didier Schwab. 2019. ArbEngVec : Arabic-English cross-lingual word embedding model. In *Proceedings of the Fourth Arabic Natural Language Processing Workshop*, pages 40–48, Florence, Italy, August. Association for Computational Linguistics.

Jing Ma, Wei Gao, Shafiq Joty, and Kam-Fai Wong. 2019. Sentence-level evidence embedding for claim verification with hierarchical attention networks. In *Proceedings of the 57th Annual Meeting of the Association for Computational Linguistics*, pages 2561–2571.

Mohamed Maamouri, Ann Bies, Tim Buckwalter, and Wigdan Mekki. 2004. The penn arabic treebank: Building a large-scale annotated arabic corpus. 27:466–467.

Mohamed Maamouri, Ann Bies, Seth Kulick, Michael Ciul, Nizar Habash, and Ramy Eskander. 2014. Developing an Egyptian Arabic treebank: Impact of dialectal morphology on annotation and tool development. In *Proceedings of the Ninth International Conference on Language Resources and Evaluation (LREC'14)*, pages 2348–2354, Reykjavik, Iceland, May. European Language Resources Association (ELRA).

El Moatez Billah Nagoudi and Didier Schwab. 2017. Semantic similarity of Arabic sentences with word embeddings. In *Proceedings of the Third Arabic Natural Language Processing Workshop*, pages 18–24, Valencia, Spain, April. Association for Computational Linguistics.

Preslav Nakov, Alberto Barrón-Cedeno, Tamer Elsayed, Reem Suwaileh, Lluís Màrquez, Wajdi Zaghouani, Pepa Atanasova, Spas Kyuchukov, and Giovanni Da San Martino. 2018. Overview of the clef-2018 checkthat! lab on automatic identification and verification of political claims. In *International Conference of the Cross-Language Evaluation Forum for European Languages*, pages 372–387. Springer.

Piotr Niewinski, Maria Pszona, and Maria Janicka. 2019. Gem: Generative enhanced model for adversarial attacks. In *Proceedings of the Second Workshop on Fact Extraction and VERification (FEVER)*, pages 20–26.

Robert Parker, David Graff, Ke Chen, Junbo Kong, and Kazuaki Maeda. 2009. Arabic gigaword.

Arfath Pasha, Mohamed Al-Badrashiny, Mona T Diab, Ahmed El Kholy, Ramy Eskander, Nizar Habash, Manoj Pooleery, Owen Rambow, and Ryan Roth. 2014. Madamira: A fast, comprehensive tool for morphological analysis and disambiguation of arabic. In *LREC*, volume 14, pages 1094–1101.

Verónica Pérez-Rosas, Bennett Kleinberg, Alexandra Lefevre, and Rada Mihalcea. 2018. Automatic detection of fake news. In *Proceedings of the 27th International Conference on Computational Linguistics*, pages 3391–3401.

Dean Pomerleau and Delip Rao. 2017. The fake news challenge: Exploring how artificial intelligence technologies could be leveraged to combat fake news. *Fake News Challenge*.

Martin Potthast, Johannes Kiesel, Kevin Reinartz, Janek Bevendorff, and Benno Stein. 2018. A stylometric inquiry into hyperpartisan and fake news. In *ACL (1)*.

Alec Radford, Jeffrey Wu, Rewon Child, David Luan, Dario Amodei, and Ilya Sutskever. 2019. Language models are unsupervised multitask learners. *OpenAI Blog*, 1(8):9.

Hannah Rashkin, Eunsol Choi, Jin Yea Jang, Svitlana Volkova, and Yejin Choi. 2017. Truth of varying shades: Analyzing language in fake news and political fact-checking. In *Proceedings of the 2017 conference on empirical methods in natural language processing*, pages 2931–2937.

Radim Řehřek and Petr Sojka. 2011. Gensim—statistical semantics in python. *statistical semantics; gensim; Python; LDA; SVD*.

Marco Tulio Ribeiro, Sameer Singh, and Carlos Guestrin. 2018. Semantically equivalent adversarial rules for debugging nlp models. In *Proceedings of the 56th Annual Meeting of the Association for Computational Linguistics (Volume 1: Long Papers)*, pages 856–865.

Victoria L Rubin, Yimin Chen, and Nadia K Conroy. 2015. Deception detection for news: three types of fakes. *Proceedings of the Association for Information Science and Technology*, 52(1):1–4.

James Thorne and Andreas Vlachos. 2018. Automated fact checking: Task formulations, methods and future directions. In *Proceedings of the 27th International Conference on Computational Linguistics*, pages 3346–3359.

James Thorne, Andreas Vlachos, Christos Christodoulopoulos, and Arpit Mittal. 2018. Fever: a large-scale dataset for fact extraction and verification. In *Proceedings of the 2018 Conference of the North American Chapter of the Association for Computational Linguistics: Human Language Technologies, Volume 1 (Long Papers)*, pages 809–819.

James Thorne, Andreas Vlachos, Christos Christodoulopoulos, and Arpit Mittal. 2019. Evaluating adversarial attacks against multiple fact verification systems. In *Proceedings of the 2019 Conference on Empirical Methods in Natural Language Processing and the 9th International Joint Conference on Natural Language Processing (EMNLP-IJCNLP)*, pages 2937–2946.

Russell Torres, Natalie Gerhart, and Arash Negahban. 2018. Epistemology in the era of fake news: An exploration of information verification behaviors among social networking site users. *ACM SIGMIS Database: the DATABASE for Advances in Information Systems*, 49(3):78–97.

William Yang Wang. 2017. "liar, liar pants on fire": A new benchmark dataset for fake news detection. In *Proceedings of the 55th Annual Meeting of the Association for Computational Linguistics (Volume 2: Short Papers)*, pages 422–426.

Rowan Zellers, Ari Holtzman, Hannah Rashkin, Yonatan Bisk, Ali Farhadi, Franziska Roesner, and Yejin Choi. 2019. Defending against neural fake news. In *Advances in Neural Information Processing Systems*, pages 9054–9065.

Wanjun Zhong, Jingjing Xu, Duyu Tang, Zenan Xu, Nan Duan, Ming Zhou, Jiahai Wang, and Jian Yin. 2019. Reasoning over semantic-level graph for fact checking. *arXiv preprint arXiv:1909.03745*.

Jie Zhou, Xu Han, Cheng Yang, Zhiyuan Liu, Lifeng Wang, Changcheng Li, and Maosong Sun. 2019. GEAR: Graph-based evidence aggregating and reasoning for fact verification. In *Proceedings of the 57th Annual Meeting of the Association for Computational Linguistics*, pages 892–901, Florence, Italy, July. Association for Computational Linguistics.

# Appendices

## A AraNews Data

### A.1 AraNews: Country, Domain, and Statistics

| Country | # Newspaper | Newspaper Name | | #News/Newspaper | #News/Country |
|---|---|---|---|---|---|
| Morocco | 7 | الشارع ٢٠ | Rue20 | 36, 556 | 178, 911 |
| | | خبر المغرب | Khabarmaroc | 2, 196 | |
| | | يا بلادي | Yabiladi | 28, 760 | |
| | | البيضاوي | Albidaoui | 14, 019 | |
| | | الأسد | Assdae | 18, 600 | |
| | | الصباح | Assabah | 68, 564 | |
| | | الأخبار | Alakhbarpressma | 1, 021 | |
| Algeria | 6 | الشروق | Echoroukonline | 187, 936 | 520, 162 |
| | | الخبر | Elkhabar | 121, 441 | |
| | | الشعب | Ech chaab | 147, 960 | |
| | | المساء | el-massa | 59, 917 | |
| | | الجديد اليومي | Eljadidelyawmi | 2, 556 | |
| | | الامة | Alomah | 352 | |
| Tunisia | 5 | الجريدة | Aljaridah | 44, 354 | 451, 278 |
| | | الصريح | Assarih | 99, 468 | |
| | | المغرب | Lemaghreb | 76, 550 | |
| | | حقائق اونلاين | Hakaekonline | 128, 553 | |
| | | الشروق | Alchourouk | 102, 353 | |
| Egypt | 5 | اليوم | Elyom | 22, 993 | 3, 021, 352 |
| | | الأهالي | Alahalygate | 25, 235 | |
| | | طريق الاخبار | Akhbarway | 80, 561 | |
| | | صوت الامة | Soutalomma | 133, 128 | |
| | | اليوم ٧ | Youm7 | 2, 759, 435 | |
| Saudi | 5 | أنحاء | An7a | 70, 985 | 304, 899 |
| | | الرياض | Alriyadh | 212, 666 | |
| | | أم القرى | Uqngovsa | 20, 994 | |
| | | الحدث | Alhadath | 220 | |
| | | الجزيرة | Aljazeera | 34 | |
| Syria | 3 | صدى الشام | Sadaalshaamnet | 12, 994 | 47, 058 |
| | | الوطن | Alwatansy | 104, 68 | |
| | | الأيام السورية | Ayyamsyrianet | 23, 578 | |
| Sudan | 3 | السوداني نيوز | Alsudaninews | 11, 153 | 113, 121 |
| | | السودان اليوم | Alsudanalyoum | 10, 1924 | |
| | | ألوان السودانية | Alwandaily | 44 | |
| Yemen | 3 | الشارع نيوز | Alsharaeanews | 1, 261 | 83, 802 |
| | | الصمود | Alsomoud | 94, 86 | |
| | | الثورة | Althawrah | 73, 055 | |
| USA | 2 | بيروت تايمز | Beiruttimes | 9, 629 | 99, 080 |
| | | صدى الوطن | Sadaalwatan | 11, 091 | |
| | | وطن سرب | Watanserb | 78, 360 | |
| UK | 2 | ميدل ايست اونلاين | Middleeastonline | 295, 190 | 295, 566 |
| | | بي بي سي | BBC | 376 | |
| UAE | 2 | الأيام | Alayam | 5471 | 63897 |
| | | البيان | Elbyan | 58426 | |
| Bahrian | 1 | البحرين | Bahrian | 7, 612 | 7, 612 |
| Iraq | 1 | الزمان | Azzaman | 120, 311 | 120, 311 |
| Kuwait | 1 | صحيفة الوسط | Alwasat | 31, 354 | 31, 354 |
| Jordan | 1 | الدستور | Addustour | 689, 444 | 689, 444 |
| Lebanon | 1 | أخبار الأرز | Cedarnews | 42, 388 | 42, 388 |
| Palestine | 1 | عرب ٤٨ | Arab48 | 35, 286 | 35, 286 |

Table A1: Descriptive statistics of our ArNews dataset.

## A.2  AraNews: Domain Normalization

| Sub-Categories | | Category |
|---|---|---|
| ثقافة قرأنية ,الاسلامي ,اسلاميات ,الدين والحياة | → | الدين Religion |
| التربية و التعليم ,تربية ,تربية وتعليم ,الصباح التربوي | → | تعليم Education |
| ثقافية ,الثقافة و الفن ,فن وثقافة ,منوعات و فنون ,ثقافة وفنون ,الثقافة ,ثقافي | → | ثقافة Culture |
| علوم وتكنولوجيا ,تكنولوجيا ,علوم تكنولوجية ,علوم وتك ,علوم ,اخبار التكنولوجيا | → | تكنولوجيا Technology |
| مال و اعمال ,أخبار الاقتصاد ,اقتصاد وسياحة ,الاخبار الاقتصادية ,اسواق ,اقتصاد وبورصة | → | اقتصاد Economy |
| سياسة ,نقابات ,برلمان ,الاحزاب ,مجلس النواب ,قرارات وزارية ,مراسيم ملكية ,مجلس الوزراء | → | سياسة Politics |
| رياضة ,رياضة محلية ,رياضة وطنية ,رياضة دولية ,أخبار الرياضة ,رياضة عالمية ,مواقف رياضية | → | رياضة Sport |
| صحة ,أخبار الصحة والطب ,صحة وطب ,فايروس كورونا ,الصحة ,طبّ و صحّة ,العلم والصحة | → | صحة Health |

Table A2:  Story sub-categories and main categories to which we map in AraNews.

## A.3  ATB$^+$ and AraNews$^+$ Data Splits

| Data | # Split | Human | Machine Manipulated | | | | | |
|---|---|---|---|---|---|---|---|---|
| | | # Sent. | ADJ | ADJ_COMP | ADJ_NUM | N_NUM | N_PROP | NEG_PART |
| ATB$^+$ | TRAIN | 48.7$K$ | 99.5$K$ | 4.5$K$ | 5.8$K$ | 60.6$K$ | 75.8$K$ | 43.6$K$ |
| | DEV | 6.6$K$ | 13.4$K$ | 638 | 844 | 7.1$K$ | 10.6$K$ | 5.6$K$ |
| | TEST | 5.9$K$ | 11.9$K$ | 592 | 665 | 8.1$K$ | 9.5$K$ | 5$K$ |
| AraNews$^+$ | TRAIN | 3.27$M$ | 6.2$M$ | 251.4$K$ | 298.5$K$ | 1.4$M$ | 2.3$M$ | 387.6$K$ |
| | DEV | 5.51$K$ | 7.8$M$ | 290.6$K$ | 293.7$K$ | 1.4$M$ | 3.6$M$ | 704.7$K$ |
| | TEST | 6.16$K$ | 64$M$ | 343.6$K$ | 303.4$K$ | 1.3$M$ | 5.8$M$ | 496.9$K$ |

Table A3: Data splits and distribution of POS tags in our machine manipulated datasets : ATB$^+$ and AraNews$^+$

# Transliteration of Judeo-Arabic Texts into Arabic Script
# Using Recurrent Neural Networks


**Ori Terner**
School of Computer Science
Tel Aviv University
Ramat Aviv, Israel
oriterner@gmail.com

**Kfir Bar**
School of Computer Science
College of Management
Academic Studies
Rishon LeZion, Israel
kfirb@colman.ac.il

**Nachum Dershowitz**
School of Computer Science
Tel Aviv University
Ramat Aviv, Israel
nachum@tau.ac.il



## Abstract

We trained a model to automatically transliterate Judeo-Arabic texts into Arabic script, enabling Arabic readers to access those writings. We employ a recurrent neural network (RNN), combined with the connectionist temporal classification (CTC) loss to deal with unequal input/output lengths. This obligates adjustments in the training data to avoid input sequences that are shorter than their corresponding outputs. We also utilize a pretraining stage with a different loss function to improve network converge. Since only a single source of parallel text was available for training, we take advantage of the possibility of generating data synthetically. We train a model that has the capability to memorize words in the output language, and that also utilizes context for distinguishing ambiguities in the transliteration. We obtain an improvement over the baseline 9.5% character error, achieving 2% error with our best configuration. To measure the contribution of context to learning, we also tested word-shuffled data, for which the error rises to 2.5%.


## 1 Introduction

Many great Jewish literary works of the Middle Ages were written in Judeo-Arabic, a Jewish dialect of the Arabic language family that adopts the Hebrew script as its writing system. Prominent authors include Maimonides (12th c.), Judah Halevi (11th–12th c.), and Saadia Gaon (10th c.). In this work, we develop an automatic transliteration system that converts Hebrew-letter Judeo-Arabic into readable Arabic text.

Generally speaking, given a text, transliteration is a process of converting the original graphemes to a sequence of graphemes in a target script. Specifically, transliterating a Judeo-Arabic text into the Arabic script almost invariably results in a text that has a similar number of letters. Yet, the correspondence between the letters in the transliteration is not one to one. Judeo-Arabic Hebrew script includes matres lectionis (e.g. ‏ا، و، ي‎) to mark some of the vowels but it typically does not include nunation – *tanween* in Arabic (e.g. ‏اً‎). Additionally, the *hamza* letter (‏ء‎), a relative latecomer to the Arabic writing system (Shaddel, 2018), is missing in the Judeo-Arabic script when it is placed "on the line" and not as a decoration for one of the matres lectionis.

Some other challenges are: (1) Authors of Judeo-Arabic texts sometimes use different mappings between Hebrew and Arabic letters. Some authors use the Hebrew letter ‏ג‎ to transliterate the Arabic letter ‏ج‎, and others will use it to transliterate the Arabic letter ‏غ‎. (2) Diacritic marks (small dots placed either above or below letters) are often omitted in the Hebrew script, another source of ambiguity. For example, the Arabic letters ‏د‎ and ‏ذ‎ are sometimes represented by the same letter in Hebrew. When the diacritic marks are maintained in the original Hebrew script, usually they are used in an inconsistent way. Even if they are used in the original manuscript, in many cases those marks appear differently or are completely missing in digital editions (such as those we used in this work). Figure 1 shows a few examples of this problem. The *apostrophe* is the only diacritic mark that is used in the digital texts we used. One important diacritic mark that is often missing from digital versions is *shadda* (gemination), which may be used






*Proceedings of the Fifth Arabic Natural Language Processing Workshop*, pages 85–96
Barcelona, Spain (Online), December 12, 2020

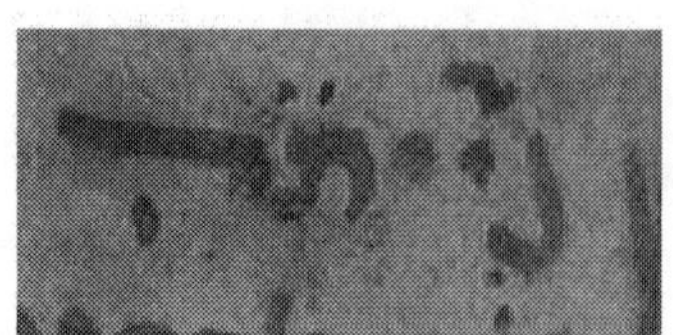

(a) Left: manuscript, right: printed edition, but digital-text reads: ניתא (missing *shadda* diacritic)

(b) Left: manuscript, right: printed edition, but digital-text reads: נאקצא (missing *tanwin* diacritic)

Figure 1: Information missing from the digital text and present in the manuscript and critical edition.

to easily resolve some lexical ambiguities. For example, the word درس ("he studied") has a different meaning when it appears with a *shadda* on the second consonant درّس ("he taught"). (3) There are several Arabic letters that do not have a one-to-one mapping with a Hebrew letter. For example, the Hebrew letter י typically refers either to ي or ى when appearing at the end of a word. (4) Judeo-Arabic is heavily affected by Hebrew and Aramaic; therefore, Judeo-Arabic texts are typically enriched with Hebrew and Aramaic citations, as well as with borrowed words and expressions from the two languages. Those citations and borrowings should not be blithely transliterated into Arabic, but rather need to be either left in the original script, semantically translated into Arabic, or otherwise annotated. Sometimes those borrowed words get inflected as if they were original Arabic words. For example, the word אלשכינה, composed of the Hebrew שכינה (*shkhina*, "divine spirit") and Arabic definite article אל (in Arabic ال); see (Bar et al., 2015).

The Friedberg Jewish Manuscript Society (`https://fjms.genizah.org`) has recently released a collection of hundreds of Judeo-Arabic works from different periods of time, formatted digitally as plain text and decorated with HTML tags. Hebrew and Aramaic citations and borrowings are annotated in those texts by domain experts. In the present work, we use texts from this collection. We noticed that some common borrowings were missed by the annotators; therefore, in this work we focus on the task of the transliteration of Judeo-Arabic words that originated in Arabic words only. Detecting the boundaries between Arabic-origin words and borrowings from other languages, a task that is known as "code switching", is left for future improvements. Since in our approach we consider the context of a word that needs to be transliterated, mostly to resolve lexical ambiguity, we masked those citation and borrowings, allowing the model to handle a continuous sequence of characters.

This Judeo-Arabic-to-Arabic transliteration problem has been addressed in one previous work (Bar et al., 2015). We elaborate on this and some other relevant previous works in the next section. In this work, we propose an end-to-end model to handle the transliteration task, by training a flavor of a recurrent neural network (RNN) on relatively short parallel texts, augmented with some synthetically generated data. Our model was designed with the capability of memorizing words in the output language. Section 3 describes the texts at our disposal. It is followed by a description of the baseline algorithm, and then our RNN solution.

## 2   Related Work

The only previous effort dealing with the transliteration of Judeo-Arabic texts (Bar et al., 2015) employed a method inspired by statistical machine translation, which was state of the art before deep neural nets took over. It consisted of a log linear model where the main component is a phrase table that counts the number of occurrences in the training data. As in (Rosca and Breuel, 2016), they also regarded transliteration as translation at the character level, that is, imagining single letters to be words. They improved their results by reranking their model's top predictions using a word-level language model. This is expected to be beneficial since using a character-level mechanism would incur the danger of generating non-words and nonsensical sequences of letters. A word-level language model that is rich enough to avoid high unknown rates would screen those results out.

Proper noun transliteration is a related task, which has been addressed previously in many works. The input term is usually provided without context, and the task is to rewrite the name in the target script, maintaining the way the name is pronounced. A direct phrase-based statistical approach to transliterating proper nouns from English to Arabic script is described in (AbdulJaleel and Larkey, 2002). It was preceded by largely handcrafted methods for romanization from Arabic to English such as (Arbabi et al., 1994; Stalls and Knight, 1998). A deep-belief approach for proper names was taken in (Deselaers et al., 2009). An attention-based method for transliteration from Arabic named entities to English and vice-versa is taken in (Hadj Ameur et al., 2017).

In Rosca and Breuel (2016), a transliteration system of names that employs a recurrent neural network (RNN), in two different ways, was described. In one way, they developed a sequence-to-sequence model that elegantly handles the different lengths of the input and output, with CTC alignment (see Section 5.1). A minor difference is their use of "epsilon insertion" to deal with input sequences that are shorter than the matching output, which CTC cannot handle. We instead use a similar solution of letter doubling discussed later. The second approach is a model inspired by recent work in the field of machine translation applying an encoder-decoder architecture with an attention mechanism. They report on improved results using RNN compared to previous methods, as is usually the case when employing deep learning techniques with problem previously solved by other means.

Another closely related problem is the transcription of *Arabizi*, which is a romanized transcription of Arabic that emerged naturally as a means for writing Arabic in chats, especially in the days of limited keyboards. Transcription into Arabic graphemes was studied by (Bies et al., 2014). Except for the different dialects and code switches from colloquial Arabic of different dialects to modern standard Arabic (MSA), they also had to handle changes in the language induced by the platform it appears in, including *emoticons* and deliberate manipulation of words, such as repetition of a single letter for emphasis common with internet social media. The same problem was addressed in (Al-Badrashiny et al., 2014), which maps Roman letters to Arabic scripts to produce a set of possibilities and chooses from them using a language model.

In another related task, the goal was to translate written text to the International Phonetic Alphabet (IPA), capturing the pronunciation of the written text. The work in (Rao et al., 2015) tried different RNN models, handling unequal sized input-output pairs by epsilon post-padding. They experimented with time delays, that is, postponing the output by a few timestamps (by pre-padding the output while post-padding the input accordingly). This allows the network to catch more of the input before deciding on the output. They also compared this with a bidirectional long-short-term-memory (LSTM) network that is able to see the entire context backward and forward. They combined the bidirectional LSTM with a CTC layer, handling the longer-output-than-input issue with epsilon post-padding (we used doubling). They reported, as expected, that greater contextual information contributes to performance. The bidirectional LSTM performs better than the unidirectional one even when the full context (whole word) is fed to the network before it starts its prediction. The best performance was obtained using the bidirectional LSTM, combined with an n-gram (non-RNN) model.

This transcription from a written language to IPA can potentially be used as a mediator to transcribe between any two languages were we to have an encoder from IPA to the source language and a decoder from IPA for the target script. Another potential use for this ability of transliteration to IPA would be for improved spell checking and correction (for those who only have basic knowledge of the sounds of the letters). A model could predict the utterances from the graphemes and recognize the word by similarity in the sound domain, to arrive at the correct spelling. For example: *neyber → neɪber → neighbor*.

## 3   Data

*Kuzari.* To train and evaluate our RNN model, we needed a considerable amount of parallel text in Judeo-Arabic along with its Arabic transliteration. Thankfully, the *Kuzari* (*Kitab al Khazari*), a medieval philosophical treatise composed by Judah Halevi in Andalusia around 1140, was recast in Arabic by Nabih Bashir (Halevi, 2012). We use this Arabic version and the original Judeo-Arabic as a parallel resource for training. The original Judeo-Arabic text of the Kuzari is taken from the Friedberg repository, and is derived from the critical edition edited by David H. Baneth. It was based on several manuscripts and comprises 47,348 word tokens (15,532 unique types), about 11% of which are Hebrew and Aramaic insertions. It is important to mention that Bashir's book provides translations for those insertions, and that there is no distinction in his edition between the *transliterated* and *translated* words. As mentioned before, we postpone handling the Hebrew and Aramaic citation and borrowings in our work, and we use the annotations provided by the Friedberg's experts in the Judeo-Arabic text, to mask out all words that are not originated in Arabic.

After cleaning the data from translation comments, section numbering and other elements irrelevant for transliteration, we needed to align the Arabic translation with the Judeo-Arabic source, on the word level. Aligning the texts is necessary because Bashir's translation does not perfectly match the Judeo-Arabic text, there being some word insertions, deletions and edits. To do that, we begin by breaking the two texts into words, and then iterating the two sequences of words. At each iteration we choose between skipping a word from the source (Judeo-Arabic) text, skipping a word from the target (Arabic) text, or adding both as an aligned source/target pair. The decision is the choice that minimizes the total edit distance of the alignment. To calculate edit distance between strings of different scripts, we applied the simple map to the Arabic source to get a basic transliteration into Hebrew letters. (The details of the algorithm are given in (Terner, 2020, Appendix).) After this alignment process we only keep pairs of words in the alignment that are close enough edit-distance wise. We set the threshold for edit-distance similarity heuristically, after normalizing the edit distance result by the maximum length of the two words that were compared, to the value of 0.5. This left us with a total of 47,083 word pairs, of which 20% were chosen randomly as test data, and the rest left for training. We are aware of the generalization problem of training and testing on data from the same source.

Words that do not align well according to the predefined threshold, such as Hebrew insertions, are removed and replaced by a fixed symbol (H) both in the source and target texts. We do the same for Hebrew insertions that are annotated as such by Friedberg's annotators. We do this to preserve the sentence structure since we suspect that this information is of value to the model for making better predictions.

We see punctuation as an important feature of the language and we want to keep this information for the model to train with. Where there are disagreements (e.g. comma vs. period) in the source and target languages, we favor the source language.

Additionaly, we removed from the Arabic text the *harakat* marks (short vowel marks): *fathah*, *kasrah*, *dammah* and *sukun*. They appear rarely in written Arabic (except for text intended for children or in religious texts) and are usually considered "noise" for language-related algorithms due to their scarcity (Habash, 2010). In the Judeo-Arabic text, the equivalent to these diacritics is the Hebrew *niqqud* signs. They appear only for Hebrew insertions; hence they are removed incidentally by the replacement of Hebrew insertions. Sometimes we even make use of those marks to identify Hebrew insertions missed by Friedberg's experts. Note that the *tanwīn* symbols when combined with *alif* were standardised to the modern style, so the diacritic symbol appears on top of the *alif* and not on the letter preceding it.

***Beliefs and Opinions.*** We identified an additional parallel text, namely Sa'adiah Gaon's *The Book of Beliefs and Opinions* (*Kitāb al-Amānāt wa l-I'tiqādāt*). It contains roughly the same quantity of data and was also transliterated by Bashir. We did not use it as training data; rather, we extracted 20% of it as additional test data, for evaluating how well the model performs on unseen text.

**Synthetic data.** Although we have a considerable amount of parallel data, since we use only one text source for training, we faced the problem of the model fitting to the specific writing style of the training data, but generalizing poorly to other texts. To improve the model and make it more robust, we generated synthetic data, using a simple technique, again leveraging the fact that the opposite direction of transliteration, that is, from Arabic to Hebrew, has almost no ambiguities (at least in the sources that we worked with in this study).

We found some additional texts online that correspond to the same era in which our texts were written. We used a simple mapping to produce a pseudo-transliteration from Arabic to Judeo-Arabic for them (Table 2 in Appendix). For instance, for the first two words in the text of *Ilāhiyyāt*, كتاب الشفا،, a pseudo-Judeo-Arabic transliteration is generated: כתאב אלשפא. The generated Judeo-Arabic text along with its Arabic counterpart are added to the parallel data for training the model.

| سُئِلْتُ | סילת |
|---|---|
| إِسْرَائِيل | אסראיל |

Table 1: Different transliterations of ـى. In the first row it matches Hebrew י, while in the second row it matches א. The unusual transliteration might stem from the spelling of the translation.

This gave us parallel data that are genuine on the Arabic side but fictitious on the Judeo-Arabic side. Thus, it might include words written in a different way than an original Judeo-Arabic author might have written them. The use of such training data is justified partly by the fact that we are likewise only interested in the accuracy of our model's predictions on the target (Arabic) side. Therefore, we are less concerned about providing the model with noisy examples. This synthetic data significantly enlarged the quantity available for training.

## 4  Baseline Algorithm

The evaluation metric that we use is simply the average edit distance over all examples in the test dataset. The edit distance (ED) that we use is the Levenshtein distance, which is calculated between the predicted characters and the ground truth. It is then normalized by the length of the ground truth. The formula for *label error rate (LER)* is $\frac{1}{|S|}\sum_{(x,z)\in S} ED(h(x),z)/|z|$ for model $h$ on test data $S \subseteq X \times Z$, where $X$ are the inputs, $z$ is ground truth and $|z|$ is the length of $z$. This is a natural measure for a model where the aim is to produce a correct label sequence (Graves et al., 2006).

To evaluate results, we start by creating a baseline transliteration on the test data that translate each Hebrew letter to the most common letter according to the predefined mapping mentioned earlier (Table 2 in Appendix). We produced the list manually according to a modern convention for transliterating Arabic into Hebrew. This simple mapping achieves a relatively high accuracy (LER 9.51%) and demonstrates the nature of this Judeo-Arabic transliteration problem. Though it is easy to achieve high accuracy, to produce readable text and to be able to confront ambiguities in the text, some language ability is desirable. The baseline results still do not guarantee fluent reading of the generated target text.

**Common baseline mistakes.** The baseline errors arise mainly from ambiguous letters that have more than a single mapping. In what follows, we enumerate the most prominent ambiguities.

**Transliteration of Hebrew *alef*.** The letter *alef* (א) most commonly should be transliterated as the Arabic letter *alif* (ا). This Arabic grapheme usually indicates an elongated /a/ vowel attached to the preceding consonant. However, it can also sometimes indicate a glottal stop, that is an *alif with hamza on top* (أ). As (Habash, 2010) mentions, Arabic writers often ignore writing the *hamza* (especially with stem-initial *alifs*) and it is "de-facto optional". This will also lead to false negatives for the test data, deciding that the transliteration is an error while in fact it would be accepted by a human reader, unjustifiably increasing LER; see (Rosca and Breuel, 2016, Section 2.3). A more complex model could hopefully predict the places were *hamza* is required for disambiguation (for instance words with stem-*non*-initial *alifs*). Alternatively, such a model would hopefully have a rich enough memory of the Arabic words it has seen, attaching the *hamza* sign for words it has seen in the training data. If indeed there are two legitimate forms, this model will also know to disambiguate according to the context, as we train on sequences, that is, words in context.

Rarer cases for transliteration of א are as follows: *hamza* on the line (ء) even though it is usually not transcribed in Hebrew. Also it can mean an *alif maqsura* (ى) at the end of a word, but *alif maqsura* is usually mapped to the letter *yod* (י). For instance, the 3-letter word גוא is transliterated as the 4-letter جاءو. Here it is not clear whether the letter א corresponds to the *hamza* or to the long vowel *alif* that precedes it, in which case the *hamza* is missing from the transliteration. In the baseline algorithm, we map א to the most common transliteration, that is, a non-*hamza alif*. Thus we miss all the other variations.

**Transliteration of Hebrew *yod*.** The two most common uses of the *yod* (י) are for the Arabic letter

| באלרוחאאניאת ואן יוצף | בالروحانيات وان يوصف | بالروحانيات وان يوصف | 0.0500 |
| מכ'אטבה' אללה לה פיקפון | مخاطبة الله له فيقفون | مخاطبة الله له فيقفون | 0.0000 |
| יר פיהא את'ר אלאהי מע | ير فيها اثر إلهيَ مع | ير فيها اثر الاهي مع | 0.2000 |
| קאבל מע אלשראיט אלשרעיה | لها قابل مع الشرائط الشرعية | لها قابل مع الشرايط الشرعيه | 0.0741 |
| אלי אלנבוה כל מן אסתעד | إلى النبوّة كلّ من استعد | الي النبوه كل من استعد | 0.2400 |

Figure 2: Baseline results. Columns, right to left: Judeo-Arabic text, ground truth, baseline prediction, error rate. Errors are marked in blue. Observe, for instance, the 4th word in row 3, missing a *shadda* in the prediction and with an extra א in the source sentence.

*ya* (ي) and for *alif maqsura* (ى), a dotless *ya* appearing always at the end of a word. Less frequently it can also be a transliteration of *ya hamza* (ئـ). But there are variations. For instance, in the first of the examples in Table 1, the *ya hamza* is transliterated as *yod* (י), while in the second when followed by a regular *ya*, it can be seen as either transliterated to a Hebrew *alef* (א) or dropped. In this example, the variation can be due to the spelling in Hebrew of the translation that uses א: "ישראל" (Israel in Hebrew).

In Egypt, but not necessarily in other Arabic countries, a final *ya* is often written dotless, that is, as an *alif maqsura* (Habash, 2010). This seems to be the case in the transliteration of Maimonides' book, *The Guide for the Perplexed* (*Dalālat al-ḥā'irīn*; http://sepehr.mohamadi.name/download/ DelalatolHaerin.pdf), as transliterated by Hussein Attai (e.g. p. 45). Unfortunately, the book is not available as a digital text. (A page of the *Guide*, with human and machine transliterations, is shown in Figure 6 in Appendix.) In the baseline algorithm, we map *yod* invariably to a regular *ya*.

**Arabic *shadda* (gemination).** Another critical issue is the *shadda* diacritic (e.g. بّ). The shadda is not present in the Judeo-Arabic text, or was omitted in the digitized version of the text as described above. Unfortunately, we could not figure out a simple rule of thumb to handle the presence or absence of shadda that could be adopted for the baseline algorithm.

**Baseline results.** As mentioned above, the baseline algorithm fully disregards *shadda*, *hamza*, *alif maqsura*, *tanwin* and a few other marks. Nonetheless the error on the test data does not increase (LER 9.5%). Some results of the baseline algorithm are shown in Figure 2.

## 5 Method and Results

### 5.1 Training using CTC Loss with Letter Doubling

The connectionist temporal classification (CTC) loss is a method introduced in (Graves et al., 2006) that enables a tagging recurrent neural network (RNN) to learn to predict discrete labels from a continuous signal without requiring the training data to be aligned input to output. Instead, the model produces a distribution over all alignments of all possible labels while facilitating an extra character (the *blank* symbol) added to its softmax layer in order to produce the alignment. Thus, the probability of any label conditioned on the input can be calculated as the sum over all possible alignments of the given label. CTC is appropriate for our mission because the Judeo-Arabic inputs and Arabic outputs are not always of equal length. Also, there is no available alignment of the two texts at the character level.

Applying CTC loss is a convenient solution for handling this problem. However, the CTC loss is only defined when the input sequence is longer than the output sequence, which is not always the case for us. Actually, since there are diacritic signs in the Arabic transliteration included in the character count that do not appear in the Judeo-Arabic source—this is a prevalent situation. This will require an adaptation of the dataset below.

It should be noted that, as (Chan et al., 2016) describes, the CTC mechanism implicitly assumes independence of characters over time. By using the multiplicative rule between probabilities over time, it disregards the dependencies between timestamps. In spite of this strong assumption, CTC achieves a substantial improvement in performance for various sequential tasks, such as speech recognition (Graves et al., 2006), OCR (Shi et al., 2017) and handwriting recognition (Graves et al., 2007).

**Doubling.** This technique of dealing with shorter input than output sequences that we use is similar to that used by (Rosca and Breuel, 2016). But instead of using a special character (epsilon) inserted between each timestamps a constant number of times, known as *epsilon insertions*, we filled the extra spaces by repetition of the previous timestamp label. For instance, the sequence עלי מא שהד וג'א פי would become עעללי ממאא ששההדד ווגג"אא פפיי. Note the doubling of the apostrophe sign, which is performed separately from the letter ג that it decorates.

Aesthetically speaking, this brings the usage of CTC closer to its original usage of transcribing a continuous signal to discrete labeling (as in speech recognition) in the sense that the input text obtains the appearance of a continuous signal, whereas epsilon insertions break the succession. Further work is required to examine the impact on performance of these two alternatives.

## 5.2 Training the RNN

We use for our model GRU (Cho et al., 2014) cells, stacked in four layers, followed by a linear layer activated by softmax for the CTC loss. Each layer is bidirectional (meaning the cells observed the input both backwards and forwards), and contains 1,024 units. We use letter embedding for the input of dimension 8. The model is implemented with TensorFlow, and optimized with RMSprop. The text is divided into short 20 characters sequences (according to the lengths in the input side). The sequences contain complete words. If the 20th character happens to be midword, the rest of the word was included in the sequence. The batch size is 128.

## 5.3 Pretraining on Single Letters

A method that was beneficial for speeding up convergence of the network was to pretrain the network with single letters according to the simple letter mapping between the Hebrew and Arabic alphabet. This is as if "to set the model in the right direction". This is intuitively reasonable if you think of the way children learn how to read. First they learn to identify the individual letters and then to assemble them into words. We use for this training step the *sparse cross entropy loss* trained on generated random parallel character sequences of length 10. As we show, this makes it feasible to train deeper networks. It might also be helpful, for instance in the task of speech recognition, to pretrain the network first on single time samples from a certain phoneme to teach the network to map to the correct grapheme, before training on continuous speech with CTC loss, which is more complex, and with which it is less obvious for the network how to start to optimize than with the simpler cross entropy loss.

**Intermediate results.** With pretraining with the cross entropy loss, the network converges quite fast to reach error rate of 2% on the test data. On the other hand, without pretraining, it gets stuck at a local minimum, transliterating each character in the input to the most prevalent character in the target data, which is a space character, producing as output strings of repeating spaces. Figure 3 shows the losses and accuracy measures. In the remainder of the experiments, we include this pretrain stage.

Running this model against the additional text of *Emunoth ve-Deoth* yields a higher error rate of 3.24%. In other words, we see a decrease in performance for unseen texts. We continue with an exploration of ways for improving prediction for unseen texts.

## 5.4 Training with Synthetic Data

As described in Section 3, we propose a technique to augment the training data by generating pseudo-parallel texts using Arabic writings of roughly the same era in which our Judeo-Arabic texts were written.

The texts we used for this purpose in the current experiments are: (1) Avicenna's *Ilāhiyyāt*, (2) Al-Farabi's *Kitab Rilasa al-Huruf*, (3) Al-Farabi's *Kitab Tahsil al-Saida* and (4) Averroes's *Al-Darurī fī Isul al-Fiqh*. To all that we add the original "real" dataset of the *Kuzari*. By doing this, we significantly enlarge the amount of data that we have for training.

**Results.** With the synthetic data, the accuracy on the original text data *decreased*, as expected, to 2.48%. On the additional data the accuracy also *decreased* but to a lesser extent, to 3.37%. This drop in performance might indicate that the Arabic texts that we chose for generating the synthetic data are not perfectly suitable for Judeo-Arabic. Perhaps there are other sources to consider that are more suitable.

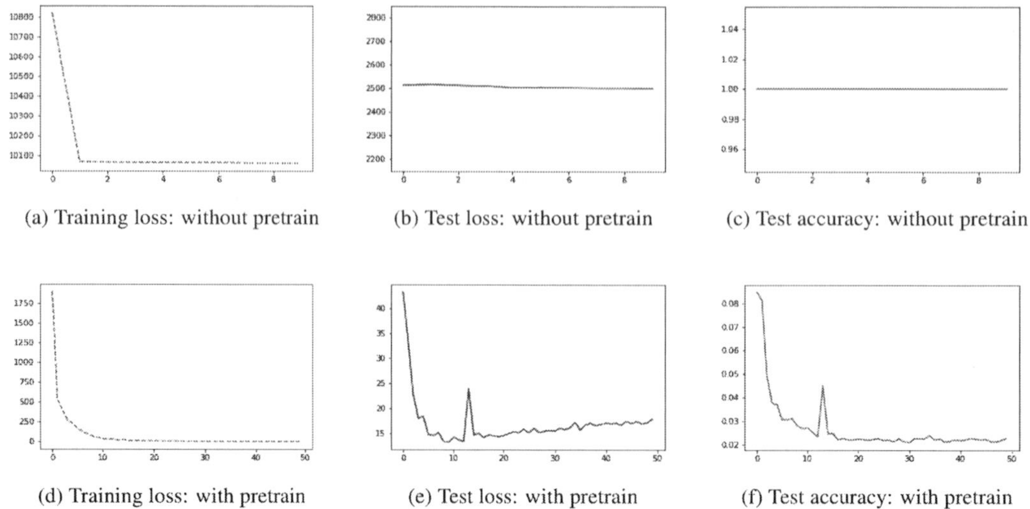

(a) Training loss: without pretrain     (b) Test loss: without pretrain     (c) Test accuracy: without pretrain

(d) Training loss: with pretrain     (e) Test loss: with pretrain     (f) Test accuracy: with pretrain

Figure 3: Comparing results with pretraining with single graphemes with CE loss (bottom) and without (top). Beware of the differences in scales.

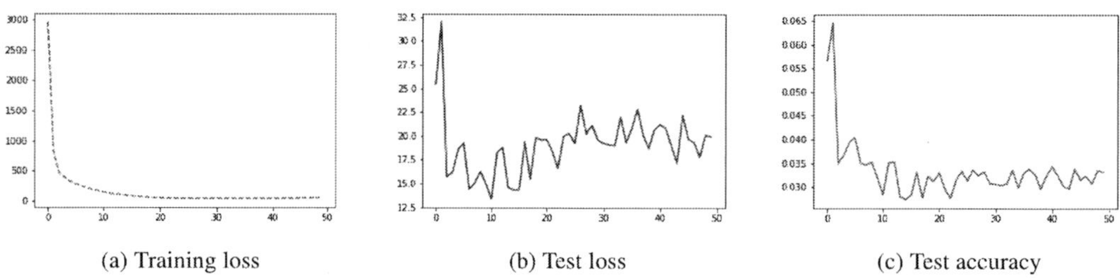

(a) Training loss     (b) Test loss     (c) Test accuracy

Figure 4: Results of training with added synthetic data.

Note that the degree of fluctuation in the learning curve on the test is greater. This might be because the synthetic data is shuffled between epochs. The results are presented in Figure 4.

## 5.5 Dropout

We are mainly interested in making the network to remember what would make sensible Arabic outputs, relying on the letter mapping, but allowing some flexibility. It should be able to output Arabic words that were seen during training even though the input sequence is not the exact one seen during training. Experimenting with a small model showed the plausibility of this direction of thinking. An immediate implication was to use *dropout* on the input sequence to make the network more robust to noise in the Judeo-Arabic input. We achieved this by randomly setting a percentile of the nonspace symbols in the input sequence (before doubling the letters) to the *blank* symbol.

**Results.** With dropout rate of 15% of the nonspace symbols that was performed on the synthetic data, the test results for the original test of the *Kuzari* is set at 2.26%, which is worse than the accuracy without synthetic data and without dropout but better than the results when trained on the synthetic data without the dropout. On the other hand, for the additional text of *Emunot*, a marked improvement is achieved, yielding an error rate of 3.14% (a 0.1 percent improvement).

92

**(a)** 0.0000 | بكتاب , في قصور الملوك | بكتاب , في قصور الملوك | פי קצור אלמלוכ , בכתאב

**(b)** 0.0870 | H . وفي صدور أهل الرينا | H . وفي صدور أهل الرياء | H . ופי צדור אהל אלריא

**(c)** 0.0000 | على فعل ما شاء متى شاء | على فعل ما شاء متى شاء | עלי פעל מא שא מתי שא

**(d)** 0.1364 | بعضهم لولده موصى عند | بعضهم لولده موصياً عند | בעצ'הם לולדה מוצי ענד

**(e)** 0.0400 | الله تابوتاً , وأقام عليها | الله تابوتاً , وأقام عليه | אללה תאבותא , ואקאם עליהא

**(f)** 0.1667 | وبإيمات من تعجب وسؤال | وبإيماءات من تعجب وسؤال | ובאימאאת מן תעג'ב וסאול

**(g)** 0.0000 | بأفراد كانوا لباباً | H | بأفراد كانوا لباباً | H | H באפראד כאנוא לבאבא

**(h)** 0.0000 | تشكّلت السماوات والأرض | تشكّلت السماوات والأرض | תשכלת אלסמאואת ואלארצ'

**(i)** 0.0800 | : إنّا خالق العالم وخالقكم | : أنا خالق العالم وخالقكم | : אנא כ'אלק אלעאלם וכ'אלקכם

**(j)** 0.0000 | المتكرّر عليه , بأن يطلب | المتكرّر عليه , بأن يطلب | אלמתכרר עליה , באן יטלב

Figure 5: Example transliteration results for proposed model. Right to left: Judeo-Arabic, ground truth, baseline prediction, error rate. In (b), for the last word the network misses the ground truth. Notice the correct positioning of the *Alif Hamza*. In (d) the mistake is partly due to noise in the data since the ground truth form موصياً is a conjugation of the noun موصي (meaning "recommender"), which the Judeo-Arabic מוצי form resembles more. The form that the network finally produced also exists. Example (i) shows a mistake in distinguishing between word senses since both diacritizations of انا produce legitimate words.

## 6 Discussion

We designed a model for automatic transliteration of Judeo-Arabic texts into Arabic scripts. Endeavoring to overcome the problem of ambiguous mappings in the transliteration, we trained an RNN model using the CTC loss that has enabled us to cope with unequal length input/output sequences due to the addition of diacritics in the target (Arabic) side of the data. As mentioned, we wanted to create a network that will have memory, along with some language capability in the output side that will enable it to distinguish between different word senses and overcome small variations in the transliteration.

The results demonstrate a substantial decrease in error compared to the baseline, from 9.5% to 2% LER, showing that the network is capable of attaching correct diacritics to the Arabic. On unseen text, the network incurs a 3.24% error rate. This is important since Judeo-Arabic texts vary according to the writer, time period, and region. Examples and some remaining problems are included in Figure 5.

We experimented with several methods to enhance training. First, we exercised pre-training of the network with cross-entropy loss to teach the network the simple mapping used in the baseline transliteration. This can enlarge and deepen the network and still guarantee convergence. Without this pretraining stage, the network failed to discover this mapping by itself. Since we only train on parallel text from a single source, and we are interested in making the model generalize better to unseen texts, we augment the training dataset by generating parallel texts out of available medieval Arabic texts. This had a slight adverse affect on accuracy and might depend on the choice of Arab texts that were used for the synthetic data. Dropout was considered and implemented on the synthetic data with the desired affect. While accuracy on the first test data, taken from the same source as the original training data decreased as expected, accuracy for the additional test data improved. We suspect that the network assimilates more language skills due to the dropout on the training data.

Examining the top 5 results of the CTC-decode beam search, instead of only the top one, reveals that sometimes the correct transliteration, at least the one that was chosen by the human transliterator, is among those five. Therefore, running a pure Arabic language model should enhance model accuracy.

One question that arises is how much of the language the network catches. To examine this, we perform a forward pass on the shuffled test data. Shuffling is done at word level. This generates a parallel dataset of words that lack context, sharing the same word distribution as the real test data. Indeed as expected, on the shuffled test data the error increases by ~0.5% on average.

## References

Nasreen AbdulJaleel and Leah Larkey. 2002. English to Arabic transliteration for information retrieval: A statistical approach. Technical Report IR-261, Center for Intelligent Information Retrieval Computer Science, University of Massachusetts.

Mohamed Al-Badrashiny, Ramy Eskander, Nizar Habash, and Owen Rambow. 2014. Automatic transliteration of romanized dialectal Arabic. In *Proceedings of the Eighteenth Conference on Computational Natural Language Learning (CoNLL-2014)*, pages 30–38, June.

Mansur Arbabi, Scott M. Fischthal, Vincent C. Cheng, and Elizabeth Bar. 1994. Algorithms for Arabic name transliteration. *IBM Journal of Research and Development*, 38(2):183–193.

Kfir Bar, Nachum Dershowitz, Lior Wolf, Yackov Lubarsky, and Yaacov Choueka. 2015. Processing Judeo-Arabic texts. In *Proceedings of the First International Conference on Arabic Computational Linguistics (ACLing '15, Cairo)*, pages 138–144, April.

Ann Bies, Zhiyi Song, Mohamed Maamouri, Stephen Grimes, Haejoong Lee, Jonathan Wright, Stephanie Strassel, Nizar Habash, Ramy Eskander, and Owen Rambow. 2014. Transliteration of Arabizi into Arabic orthography: Developing a parallel annotated Arabizi-Arabic script SMS/chat corpus. In *Proceedings of the EMNLP 2014 Workshop on Arabic Natural Language Processing (ANLP)*, pages 93–103.

William Chan, Navdeep Jaitly, Quoc V. Le, and Oriol Vinyals. 2016. Listen, attend and spell: A neural network for large vocabulary conversational speech recognition. In *2016 IEEE International Conference on Acoustics, Speech and Signal Processing (ICASSP)*, pages 4960–4964.

Kyunghyun Cho, Bart van Merriënboer, Caglar Gulcehre, Dzmitry Bahdanau, Fethi Bougares, Holger Schwenk, and Yoshua Bengio. 2014. Learning phrase representations using RNN encoder–decoder for statistical machine translation. In *Proceedings of the 2014 Conference on Empirical Methods in Natural Language Processing (EMNLP)*, pages 1724–1734, Doha, Qatar, October. Association for Computational Linguistics.

Thomas Deselaers, Saša Hasan, Oliver Bender, and Hermann Ney. 2009. A deep learning approach to machine transliteration. In *Proceedings of the Fourth Workshop on Statistical Machine Translation*, StatMT '09, pages 233–241. Association for Computational Linguistics.

Alex Graves, Santiago Fernández, Faustino Gomez, and Jürgen Schmidhuber. 2006. Connectionist temporal classification: Labelling unsegmented sequence data with recurrent neural networks. In *Proceedings of the 23rd International Conference on Machine Learning*, pages 369–376. ACM.

Alex Graves, Santiago Fernández, Marcus Liwicki, Horst Bunke, and Jürgen Schmidhuber. 2007. Unconstrained on-line handwriting recognition with recurrent neural networks. In J. C. Platt, D. Koller, Y. Singer, and S. T. Roweis, editors, *Advances in Neural Information Processing Systems 20 (NIPS 2007)*, volume 20, pages 577–584, January.

Nizar Y. Habash. 2010. *Arabic Natural Language Processing*. Synthesis Digital Library of Engineering and Computer Science. Morgan & Claypool Publishers.

Mohamed Seghir Hadj Ameur, Farid Meziane, and Ahmed Guessoum. 2017. Arabic machine transliteration using an attention-based encoder-decoder model. In *Third International Conference On Arabic Computational Linguistics (ACLING 2017, November 2017, Dubai, United Arab Emirates)*, volume 117 of *Procedia Computer Science*, pages 287–297, November.

Yehuda Halevi. 2012. *The Kuzari – In Defense of the Despised Faith*. Al-Kamel Verlag, Beirut. Transliterated, translated into Arabic and annotated by Nabih Bashir.

Kanishka Rao, Fuchun Peng, Haşim Sak, and Françoise Beaufays. 2015. Grapheme-to-phoneme conversion using long short-term memory recurrent neural networks. In *IEEE International Conference on Acoustics, Speech and Signal Processing (ICASSP)*, pages 4225–4229.

Mihaela Rosca and Thomas Breuel. 2016. Sequence-to-sequence neural network models for transliteration. *CoRR*, abs/1610.09565.

Mehdy Shaddel. 2018. Traces of the hamza in the early Arabic script: The inscriptions of Zuhayr, Qays the Scribe, and "Yazd the King". *Arabian Epigraphic Notes*, 4:35–52.

Baoguang Shi, Xiang Bai, and Cong Yao. 2017. An end-to-end trainable neural network for image-based sequence recognition and its application to scene text recognition. *IEEE Transactions on Pattern Analysis & Machine Intelligence*, 39(11):2298–2304, November.

Bonnie Glover Stalls and Kevin Knight. 1998. Translating names and technical terms in Arabic text. In *Proceedings of the COLING/ACL Workshop on Computational Approaches to Semitic Languages (Semitic '98)*, pages 34–41, August.

Ori Terner. 2020. Transliteration of Judeo-Arabic texts to Arabic using RNN. M.Sc. thesis, School of Computer Science, Tel Aviv University.

## Appendix: Figures and Tables

(a) Original Judeo-Arabic orthography.

(b) Transliteration by Hussein Attai.

(c) Our model transliteration.

Figure 6: First page of Maimonides' *The Guide for the Perplexed*.

| Judeo-Arabic | Arabic | Judeo-Arabic | Arabic |
| --- | --- | --- | --- |
| א | ا | כ | ك |
| ב | ب | כ' | خ |
| ג' | ج | ל | ل |
| ג | ع | מ | م |
| ד | د | נ | ن |
| ד | ذ | ס | س |
| ה | ه | ע | ع |
| ה' | ة | פ | ف |
| ו | و | צ | ص |
| ז | ز | צ' | ض |
| ח | ح | ק | ق |
| ט | ط | ר | ر |
| ט' | ظ | ש | ش |
| י | ي | ת | ت |
|  |  | ת' | ث |

Table 2: Simple mapping rules for baseline transliteration.

# NADI 2020: The First Nuanced Arabic Dialect Identification Shared Task

**Muhammad Abdul-Mageed, Chiyu Zhang, Houda Bouamor,[†] Nizar Habash[‡]**
The University of British Columbia, Vancouver, Canada
[†]Carnegie Mellon University in Qatar, Qatar
[‡]New York University Abu Dhabi, UAE
`muhammad.mageed@ubc.ca`      `chiyuzh@mail.ubc.ca`
`hbouamor@cmu.edu`      `nizar.habash@nyu.edu`

## Abstract

We present the results and findings of the First Nuanced Arabic Dialect Identification Shared Task (NADI). This Shared Task includes two subtasks: country-level dialect identification (Subtask 1) and province-level sub-dialect identification (Subtask 2). The data for the shared task covers a total of 100 provinces from 21 Arab countries and are collected from the Twitter domain. As such, NADI is the first shared task to target naturally-occurring fine-grained dialectal text at the sub-country level. A total of 61 teams from 25 countries registered to participate in the tasks, thus reflecting the interest of the community in this area. We received 47 submissions for Subtask 1 from 18 teams and 9 submissions for Subtask 2 from 9 teams.

## 1   Introduction

The Arab world is an extensive geographical region across Africa and Asia, with a population of $\sim$ 400 million people whose native tongue is Arabic. Arabic could be classified into three major types: (1) Classical Arabic (CA), the language of the Qur'an and early literature, (2) Modern Standard Arabic (MSA), the medium used in education and formal and pan-Arab media, and (3) dialectal Arabic (DA), a host of geographically and politically defined variants. Modern day Arabic is also usually described as a *diglossic* language with a so-called 'High' variety that is used in formal settings (MSA), and a 'Low' variety that is the medium of everyday communication (DA). The presumably 'Low variety' is in reality a collection of variants. One axis of variation for Arabic is geography where people from various sub-regions, countries, or even provinces within the same country, may be using language differently.

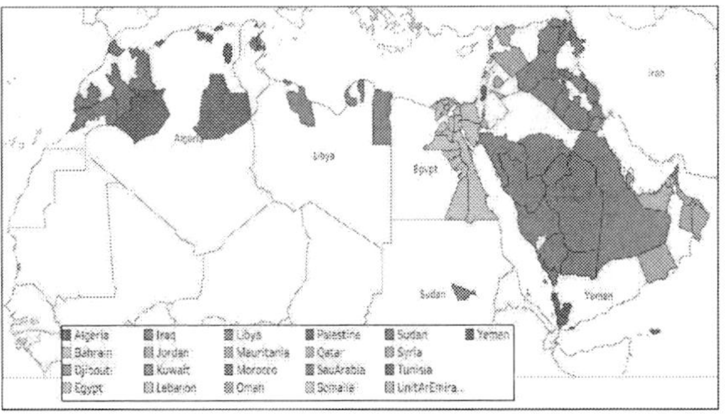


Figure 1: A map of the Arab World showing countries and provinces in the NADI dataset. Each of the 21 countries is represented in a color different from that of a neighboring country. Provinces are marked with lines inside each country.

The goal of the First Nuanced Arabic Dialect Identification (NADI) Shared Task is to provide resources and encourage efforts to investigate questions focused on dialectal variation within the collection of Arabic variants. The NADI shared task targets 21 Arab countries and a total of 100 provinces across these countries. The shared task consists of two subtasks: *country-level* dialect identification (Subtask 1) and *province-level* detection (Subtask 2). We provide participants with a new Twitter labeled dataset that we collected exclusively for the purpose of the shared task. The dataset is publicly available for research.[1] A total of 52 teams registered for the shard task, of whom 18 teams ended up submitting their systems for scoring. We then received 15 papers, of which we accepted 14.



[1]The dataset is accessible at the shared task page: `http://nadi2020.arabic-nlp.net`.



*Proceedings of the Fifth Arabic Natural Language Processing Workshop*, pages 97–110
Barcelona, Spain (Online), December 12, 2020

This paper is organized as follows. We provide a brief overview of the computational linguistic literature on Arabic dialects in Section 2. We describe the two subtasks and dataset in Sections 3 and Section 4, respectively. And finally, we introduce participating teams, shared task results, and a high-level description of submitted systems in Section 5.

## 2   Related Work

As we explained in Section 1, Arabic could be viewed as comprised of 3 main types: CA, MSA, and DA. While CA and MSA have been studied and taught extensively, DA has only received more attention relatively recently (Harrell, 1962; Cowell, 1964; Badawi, 1973; Brustad, 2000; Holes, 2004).

A majority of DA computational efforts have targeted creating resources for country or regionally specific dialects (Gadalla et al., 1997; Diab et al., 2010; Al-Sabbagh and Girju, 2012; Sadat et al., 2014; Smaïli et al., 2014; Jarrar et al., 2016; Khalifa et al., 2016; Al-Twairesh et al., 2018; El-Haj, 2020). The expansion into multi-dialectal data sets and models to identify them was initially done at the regional level (Zaidan and Callison-Burch, 2011; Elfardy et al., 2014; Bouamor et al., 2014; Meftouh et al., 2015). A number of Arabic dialect identification shared tasks were organized as part of the VarDial workshop. These focused on regional varieties such as Egyptian, Gulf, Levantine, and North African based on speech broadcast transcriptions (Malmasi et al., 2016) but also acoustic features (Zampieri et al., 2017) and phonetic features (Zampieri et al., 2018) extracted from raw audio. Althobaiti (2020) presents a recent survey of computational work on Arabic dialects.

An early effort for creating finer grained parallel dialectal corpus and lexicon was done under the Multi Arabic Dialects Application and Resources (MADAR) project  (Bouamor et al., 2018). The parallel data was created by commission under controlled settings to maximize its use for cross-dialectal comparisons and machine translation. Their data was also used for dialectal identification at the city level (Salameh et al., 2018; Obeid et al., 2019) of 25 Arab cities. One issue with the MADAR data in the context of identification is that it was commissioned and not naturally occurring. Concurrently, larger Twitter-based datasets covering 10-21 countries were also introduced (Mubarak and Darwish, 2014; Abdul-Mageed et al., 2018; Zaghouani and Charfi, 2018). Researchers are also starting to introduce DA datasets labeled for socio-pragmatics, e.g., (Abbes et al., 2020; Mubarak et al., 2020). The MADAR shared task (Bouamor et al., 2019) comprised two subtasks, one focusing on 21 Arab countries exploiting Twitter data manually labeled at the user level, and another on 25 Arab cities mentioned above. During the same time as NADI, Abdul-Mageed et al. (2020) describe data and models at country, province, and city levels.

The NADI shared task follows these pioneering works by availing data to the (Arabic) NLP community, and encouraging work on Arabic dialects. Similar to the MADAR shared task, we include a country-level dialect identification task (Subtask 1), and a sub-country dialect identification task (Subtask 2). However, our sub-country task is a province-level identification task with a much larger label set than MADAR's city-level task, and is based on naturally occurring data. We hope that our work will be setting the stage for exploring variation in geographical regions that have not been studied before.

## 3   Task Description

The NADI shared task consists of two subtasks for country-level and province-level classification.

### 3.1   Subtask 1: Country-level Classification

The goal of Subtask 1 is to identify country-level dialects from short written sentences (tweets). NADI Subtask 1 is similar to previous works that have also taken country as their target (Mubarak and Darwish, 2014; Abdul-Mageed et al., 2018; Zaghouani and Charfi, 2018; Bouamor et al., 2019). Labeled data was provided to NADI participants with specific TRAIN and development (DEV) splits. Each of the 21 labels corresponding to the 21 countries is represented in both TRAIN and DEV. Teams could score their models through an online system on the DEV set before the deadline. Our TEST set of unlabeled tweets was released shortly before the system submission deadline. Participants were invited to submit their predictions to the online scoring system that housed the gold TEST set labels. We provide the distribution of the TRAIN, DEV, and TEST splits across countries in Table 1.

| Country | # of | # of Tweets | | | | |
|---|---|---|---|---|---|---|
| Name | Provinces | Train | Dev | Test | Total | % |
| Algeria | 7 | 1,491 | 359 | 364 | 2,214 | 7.15 |
| Bahrain | 1 | 210 | 8 | 20 | 238 | 0.77 |
| Djibouti | 1 | 210 | 10 | 51 | 271 | 0.88 |
| Egypt | 21 | 4,473 | 1,070 | 1,092 | 6,635 | 21.43 |
| Iraq | 12 | 2,556 | 636 | 624 | 3,816 | 12.33 |
| Jordan | 2 | 426 | 104 | 104 | 634 | 2.05 |
| Kuwait | 2 | 420 | 70 | 102 | 592 | 1.91 |
| Lebanon | 3 | 639 | 110 | 156 | 905 | 2.92 |
| Libya | 5 | 1,070 | 265 | 265 | 1,600 | 5.17 |
| Mauritania | 1 | 210 | 40 | 5 | 255 | 0.82 |
| Morocco | 5 | 1,070 | 249 | 260 | 1,579 | 5.10 |
| Oman | 6 | 1,098 | 249 | 268 | 1,615 | 5.22 |
| Palestine | 2 | 420 | 102 | 102 | 624 | 2.02 |
| Qatar | 2 | 234 | 104 | 61 | 399 | 1.29 |
| Saudi Arabia | 10 | 2,312 | 579 | 564 | 3,455 | 11.16 |
| Somalia | 1 | 210 | 51 | 51 | 312 | 1.01 |
| Sudan | 1 | 210 | 51 | 51 | 312 | 1.01 |
| Syria | 5 | 1,070 | 265 | 260 | 1,595 | 5.15 |
| Tunisia | 4 | 750 | 164 | 208 | 1,122 | 3.62 |
| UAE | 5 | 1,070 | 265 | 213 | 1,548 | 5.00 |
| Yemen | 4 | 851 | 206 | 179 | 1,236 | 3.99 |
| **Total** | **100** | **21,000** | **4,957** | **5,000** | **30,957** | **100.00** |

Table 1: Distribution of country-level dialect identification data for Subtask 1 across our data splits.

## 3.2 Subtask 2: Province-level Classification

The goal of Subtask 2 is to identify the specific state or province (henceforth, *province*) from a list of 100 provinces. The provinces are unequally distributed among the list of 21 countries. While efforts on city-level and country-level prediction were the topic of a previous shared task (Bouamor et al., 2019), to the best of our knowledge, the target of automatic dialect prediction at a small geographical region such as a province has not been previously investigated, thus lending novelty to this subtask. We acknowledge that this subtask has some affinity to work focused on predicting geolocation based on tweets. Nevertheless, geolocation prediction is performed at the level of users not tweets and hence is different. There are also differences between our work here and geolocation as to how the data was collected. We further explain this nuance in Section 4. The distribution of the classes across the 100 provinces in our data splits is presented in Table A1 in Appendix A.

For both Subtask 1 and Subtask 2, tweets in the TRAIN, DEV and TEST splits come from distinct sets of *users*, such that no user had their tweets in any two of the TRAIN, DEV, and TEST splits.

## 3.3 Restrictions and Evaluation Metrics

To ensure fair comparisons and common experimental conditions, we provided participating teams with a set of restrictions that apply to the two subtasks, and clear evaluation metrics. Our method of distributing the data as well as our evaluation setup through the CodaLab online platform also facilitated the competition management, enhanced timeliness of acquiring results upon system submission, and guaranteed ultimate transparency.[2]

We directly provided participants with the actual tweets posted to the Twitter platform, rather than tweet IDs. This enabled comparison between systems exploiting identical data. Since we shared actual tweets, we did not share tweet IDs with participants. This made it harder to collect data from the same

---

[2] https://codalab.org/

| Country | Province | Tweet |
| --- | --- | --- |
| Algeria | Bordj-Bou-Arreridj | وانتم سيد الفاظل ملائكة اكبر مصائبنا منكم والعربان دمرتوا كل شيء جميل الله المستعان |
| | Jijel | ابراهيم غدوة تبلا فيه مليح |
| Egypt | Asyut | يا اقرع انت واخوك إبراهيم اللي زرع شعره واكيد الكل عارف جاب الشعر منين في جسمه وحطه في رأسه انت نسيت نفسك ولا ايه الزمالك هو اللي لك من الشارع بعد ما صالح سليم طردك زي الكلب نسيت وانت مدرب ماحدش طلعك السما غير الزمالك ورجل شيكابالا الزمالك سيدك يا اقرع #ادعم _باسم _مرسي |
| | Suez | يبقى حد يوريني نفسه بقي انا قولت حلووو غلط |
| KSA | Ar-Riyad | فيه كثير أمور عني ما تعرفونها ياليت ان الأمر بالسهولة وياليتني مرتاحه فعلا ومستقله بشكل كامل ما كان لقيتيني اشتكي ولا اقول هالكلام راح ابعد عنهم كثير ان شاء الله واهاجر وما ارجع لهالبقعة الجغرافية ابد واترك كل شي شين وراي وابدأ حياة حقيقية من أول وجديد الله يعدي الأيام بسرعه بس |
| | Najran | #يسعد _مساكم حمودي يسمي عليكم ويقول رايح يشتري ثوب #العيد #عيدكم _مبارك _وعساكم _من _عواده |
| Morocco | Marrakech-Tensift-Al-Haouz | السيادة في الدنيا والسعادة في العقبى لا يوصل إليها إلا على جسر من المتاعب. #ابن _القيم |
| | Tanger-Tetouan | #اليابان _كولومبيا المبارة مانجا ولا فيلر |
| Oman | Muscat | بصراحة... غريبين هدول الثورجية يلي بيجلسوا ينظروا من برا و بخبروك انو هنن تركوا شغلهم واموالهم وبيتهم وهلأ عايشين برات البلاد بسبب الظلم على قولهم... طيب بالأول ما حدا طلب منك تترك البلاد... ثانيا... ليش عم تحرض الناس يلي موجود بالبلد وهي يلي لازم تتبهدل وتعتقل وحضرتك برا البلاد. |
| | Ad-Dakhiliyah | الحين بتبدي الشماته |
| Sudan | Khartoum | نحن نبقى عليها والله شنطة زاتو ما دايرة ارح امفكو ساي |
| UAE | Abu-Dhabi | ولو بالغلط يعني . #اليوم _العالمي _للرسائل |
| | Ras-Al-Khaymah | عليك أغار و أكتم هالشعور أخاف غيرتي بالحيل تزعجك. |

Table 2: Randomly picked examples from select provinces and corresponding countries.

user from which a tweet comes. For the two subtasks, we asked to only and exclusively use our distributed data. In other words, we provided instructions not to use any external data nor search or depend on any additional user-level information such as geolocation. In addition to our labeled TRAIN and DEV splits, we provided tweet IDs for 10M tweets and a simple script that can be used to collect the tweets. We did not provide any labels for this additional 10M tweet set, and encouraged participants to use it in developing their models in any way they deemed useful.

For both subtasks, the official metric is macro-averaged $F_1$ score obtained on blind test sets. We also report performance in terms of macro-averaged precision, macro-averaged recall and accuracy for systems submitted to each of the two subtasks. Each participating team was allowed to submit up to five runs for each subtask, and only the highest scoring run was kept as representing the team. Although official results are based only on a blind TEST set, we also asked participants to report their results on the DEV set in their papers. We setup two CodaLab competitions for scoring participant systems.[3,4]

[3]The CodaLab competition for Subtask 1 is accessible at: https://competitions.codalab.org/competitions/24001.

[4]The CodaLab competition for Subtask 2 is accessible at: https://competitions.codalab.org/competitions/24002.

We will keep the Codalab competition for each task live post competition, for researchers who would be interested in training models and evaluating their systems using the shared task TEST set.

## 4   Shared Task Datasets

We distributed a single dataset with two sets of labels, one for Subtask 1 and another for Subtask 2. In other words, the same tweet occurs in each of the two subtasks but with different subtask-specific labels. Additionally, we made available an unlabeled dataset for optional use in any of the two subtasks. We now provide more details about both the labeled and unlabeled data.

### 4.1   Data Collection

We used the Twitter API to crawl data from 100 provinces belonging to 21 Arab countries for 10 months (Jan. to Oct., 2019).[5] Next, we identified users who consistently and *exclusively* tweeted from a single province during the whole 10 month period. We crawled up to 3,200 tweets from each of these users.

### 4.2   Data Sets

**Subtask 1 and Subtask 2 Data**   We labeled tweets from each user with the country and province from which the user posted for the whole of the 10 months period, thus exploiting user consistent posting *location* as a proxy for *dialect labels*. Note that this labeling method can still have issues as we explain in Section 4.3. We randomly sampled 30,957 tweets of length 5 words or more from the collection and split them into TRAIN (n=21,000), DEV (n=4,957), and TEST (n=5,000). Although the task is at the tweet level, we sampled the data for each of the TRAIN, DEV, and TEST from a unique set of users (i.e., users are not shared across the 3 splits). We distribute data for the two subtasks directly to participants in the form of actual tweet text (i.e., hydrated content). Tables 1 and A1 show the distribution of tweets across the data splits for both Subtask 1 and Subtask 2, respectively.

**Unlabeled 10M**   We also crawled 10 million posts from Arabic Twitter during 2019. We call this dataset UNLABELED 10M and distribute it in the form of tweet IDs along with a script that can be used to crawl the actual tweets. We put no restrictions on using UNLABELED 10M for system development for either of the two subtasks.[6] Next, we discuss a number of nuances and issues found in the data.

### 4.3   Data Issues

**Location as proxy for dialect.**   Our method of using consistent location (i.e., posting from the same location for at least 10 months) as a proxy for assigning dialect labels is useful, but not ideal. Even though this method allows us to collect provably relevant data, as manually verified in a small random sample of users (n=30), it can be error prone since a user with a dialect of one country can be posting from a different country during this whole period of 10 months.

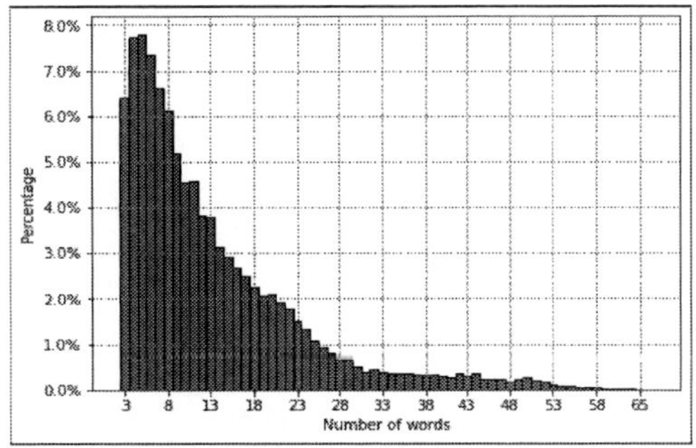

Figure 2: Distribution of tweet length in words in NADI labeled data.

**MSA vs. Dialect.**   As we explained in Section 1, Arabic is usually characterized as a diaglossic language with MSA being the 'High' variety and DA as the 'Low' variety. Arabic users also switch between these two varieties. Most relevant to our work, communication in DA over social media is not devoid of MSA even at a level as short as that of a tweet. This can vary from one dialect to another, but also

---

[5]Although we tried, we could not collect data from Comoros to cover all 22 Arab countries.

[6]Subtask 1, Subtask 2, and UNLABELED 10M data is available at `http://nadi2020.arabic-nlp.net`. More information about the data format can be found in the accompanying README file.

depending on a range of other factors including the user educational background, career, and the actual goal of the post itself. To illustrate, based on our intuition and occasional observation, users with training in language sciences (education), those in careers such as media or higher education (job), or those trying to reach out to especially older generations or project religious or cultural authority (goal or pragmatic function) will likely use more MSA. Due to the co-existence of MSA and DA in the same tweet, we opted for using all the data we collected from the users for the competition. Alternatively, we could have identified MSA tweets either manually or automatically and removed these. We did not take that step in order to keep the task more challenging since a classifier would need to learn about patterns of MSA-DA mixing to perform well. A model would also need to acquire skills enabling it to tease apart tweets that may be overly or exclusively MSA. To explore the extent of MSA in the dataset, we run an in-house neural MSA-DA model ($acc = 89.1\%$, $F_1 = 88.6\%$) on it. The model predicts the percentages of MSA data as follows: 49.5% for TRAIN, 46.6%for DEV, and 49.7% for TEST. This distribution needs to be couched with caution, however, since dialectal features can be subtle and mixed with MSA to varying degrees. Upon manual inspection of a random sample of tweets the model labeled as MSA, we identify examples that are fully and verifiably MSA such as #1 below. In addition, we observe sequences that carry dialectal features. For example #2 and #3 below have dialectal words (highlighted in  orange ):

1. ‏الحمد لله رب العالمين على نعمه التي لا تعد ولا تحصى ولم يغفل عن رزق كل خلقه.

2. ‏البيض الفاسد يتدردب على بعضه يا صاحبي . قاتلهم الله

3. ‏ما أبي اخذك منهم ، أبيك انت تبديني عليهم

We also observe that the more confident the MSA-DA model is (based on softmax value), the more likely its decision is correct. This suggests we can use a thresholding approach to filter out MSA tweets, should we desire to reduce MSA in the data. We leave further investigation of this issue to the future.

**Non-Arabic Text.**    Despite efforts to exclusively keep Arabic content, our dataset had a small percentage (2.52%) of Farsi. While collecting the data, we only kept tweets assigned an Arabic language tag by the Twitter API. However, the API is error prone and hence some non-Arabic was not filtered out. To circumvent this, we only kept tweets that have at least three word written in Arabic script after running an internal normalizer that removes diacritics and reduced repetitions of consecutive characters of $> 2$ to only 2, replaced URLs and usernames with the generic strings $URL$ and $@USR$. Even after this step, some Farsi leaked to our data. The reason is that Farsi is written in the same script as Arabic, with only a few differences. Aliwy et al. (2020) manually inspected the NADI TRAIN set and provided a distribution of Farsi tweets over the different countries. We share this distribution in Table 3.

## 5   Shared Task Teams & Results

### 5.1   Our Baseline Systems

We have two baseline classifier, Baseline I and Baseline II. **Baseline I** is based on the majority class in the TRAIN data for each subtask. It scores at $accuracy = 21.84\%$ and $F_1 = 1.71\%$ for Subtask 1 and $accuracy = 1.92\%$ and $F_1 = 0.04\%$ for Subtask 2. For **Baseline II**, we initially train two classifiers for these two sub-tasks individually. For each task, we fine-tune on Google's pre-trained multi-lingual BERT-Base (mBERT).[7] We set the maximum length of sequences in our model to 50 tokens, and employ batch training with a batch size of 8 for this model. We run the network for 20 epochs and save the model at the end of each epoch, choosing the model that performs highest on DEV as our best model. For country-level identification (Subtask 1), our best result is acquired with 16 epochs. Our best result is obtained with 20 epochs on province-level task (Subtask 2). Our mBERT model obtains $accuracy = 32.38\%$ and $F_1 = 13.32\%$ on country-level classification and $accuracy = 3.32\%$ and $F_1 = 2.13\%$ for province-level classification.

---

[7]https://github.com/google-research/bert

| Country | # tweet | # Farsi | % Farsi |
|---|---|---|---|
| **Algeria** | 1,491 | 5 | 0.34 |
| **Egypt** | 4,473 | 2 | 0.04 |
| **Iraq** | 2,556 | 382 | 14.95 |
| **Morocco** | 1,070 | 1 | 0.09 |
| **Oman** | 1,098 | 26 | 2.37 |
| **Saudi Arabia** | 2,312 | 6 | 0.26 |
| **Syria** | 1,070 | 3 | 0.28 |
| **Tunisia** | 750 | 2 | 0.27 |
| **UAE** | 1,070 | 7 | 0.65 |
| **Yemen** | 851 | 70 | 8.23 |
| **Total** | 21,000 | 504 | 2.40 |

Table 3: Distribution of tweets manually labeled as Farsi in TRAIN. We only provide countries with Farsi tweets, and remove the rest of 21 countries in NADI.

| Team | Affiliation | Tasks |
|---|---|---|
| **Mawdoo3 AI** (Talafha et al., 2020) | Mawdoo3 AI, Jordan | 1 |
| **BERT_NGRAMS** (El Mekki et al., 2020) | Mohammed VI Polytechnic University, Morocco | 1,2 |
| **ArabicProcessors** (Gaanoun and Benelallam, 2020) | Institut National de Statistique et d'Economie, Morocco | 1,2 |
| **Tri-directional** (Beltagy et al., 2020) | Faculty of Engineering, Alexandria University, Egypt | 1 |
| **MMZ** (Mansour et al., 2020) | Faculty of Engineering, Alexandria University, Egypt | 1 |
| **QMUL Team** (Aloraini et al., 2020) | Queen Mary University of London, United Kingdom | 1 |
| **Code Lyoko** (Tahssin et al., 2020) | Faculty of Engineering, Alexandria University, Egypt | 1 |
| **TRY_NLP** (Balaji and Bharathi, 2020) | SSN College of Engineering, India | 1,2 |
| **Sorbonne** (Ghoul and Lejeune, 2020) | Sorbonne Université, France | 1 |
| **Speech Translation** (Lichouri and Abbas, 2020) | CRSTDLA Research Center, Algeria | 1 |
| **LTG-ST** (Touileb, 2020) | University of Oslo, Norway | 1 |
| **Alexa** (Bni Younes et al., 2020) | Jordan University of Science and Technology, Jordan | 1 |
| **Alpha** (AlShenaifi and Azmi, 2020) | King Saud University, Saudi Arabia | 1 |
| **IRAQ** (Aliwy et al., 2020) | University of Kufa, Iraq | 1 |

Table 4: List of the 14 teams that participated in Subtasks 1 and 2 *and* submitted description papers.

## 5.2 Participating Teams

We received a total of 61 unique team registrations, among which 7 teams registered to participate in Subtask 1 only, 1 team registered to participate in Subtask 2 only, and 53 teams registered to participate in both subtasks. After evaluation phase, we received 47 submissions for Subtask 1 from 18 teams and 9 submissions for subtask 2 from 4 teams. Of participating teams, a total of 15 teams submitted description papers all of which except one were accepted for publication. Table 5.2 lists the 14 teams whose papers were accepted.

## 5.3 Shared Task Results

Table 5 presents the best TEST results for all 18 teams who submitted systems for Subtask 1, regardless of whether they have submitted a paper. Based on the official metric, $macro - F_1$, Mawdoo3-AI obtained the best performance with 26.78% $F_1$ score. Table 6 presents the best TEST results of each of the 4 teams who submitted systems to Subtask 2. Team BERT-NGRAMS achieved the best $F_1$ score that is 6.39%. [8]

## 5.4 General Description of Submitted Systems

In Table 7, we provide a high-level description of the systems submitted to each subtask. For each team, we list the overall number of submissions per subtask, their overall best score, the features employed, the methods adopted/developed, and whether they have used the 10M unlabeled tweet dataset we provided

---

[8]The full sets of results for Subtask 1 and Subtask 2 are in Tables A2 and A3, respectively, in Appendix A.

| Team | F1 | Accuracy | Precision | Recall |
|---|---|---|---|---|
| **Mawdoo3 AI** | **26.78 (1)** | **42.86 (1)** | **32.52 (1)** | **25.19 (1)** |
| **BERT_NGRAMS** | 25.99 (2) | 39.66 (2) | 30.26 (2) | 24.85 (2) |
| **Arabic Processors** | 23.26 (3) | 38.34 (3) | 27.17 (4) | 22.43 (5) |
| **Tri-directional** | 23.09 (4) | 37.70 (5) | 26.40 (5) | 23.04 (4) |
| **MMZ** | 22.58 (5) | 38.28 (4) | 24.28 (8) | 23.36 (3) |
| **QMUL Team** | 20.77 (6) | 34.32 (11) | 21.62 (13) | 21.09 (6) |
| **Code Lyoko** | 20.34 (7) | 36.26 (8) | 27.83 (3) | 20.56 (8) |
| **TRY_NLP** | 20.04 (8) | 33.66 (15) | 20.07 (14) | 21.07 (7) |
| **Sorbonne** | 18.80 (9) | 36.54 (7) | 24.87 (7) | 18.05 (12) |
| **Iktishaf** | 18.63 (10) | 33.98 (14) | 20.21 (15) | 18.76 (9) |
| **Speech Translation** | 18.27 (11) | 36.68 (6) | 23.75 (10) | 18.06 (11) |
| **LTG-ST** | 17.71 (12) | 36.22 (9) | 24.93 (6) | 17.21 (13) |
| **Alexa** | 17.29 (13) | 34.16 (12) | 22.09 (12) | 16.81 (15) |
| **NAYEL** | 16.84 (14) | 30.98 (18) | 17.88 (16) | 18.20 (10) |
| **DNLP** | 16.50 (15) | 31.28 (17) | 17.84 (17) | 17.04 (14) |
| **NLPRL** | 15.77 (16) | 35.06 (10) | 23.96 (9) | 15.92 (16) |
| **Alpha** | 15.10 (17) | 34.02 (13) | 22.34 (11) | 14.71 (17) |
| **Our Baseline II** | 13.32 | 32.38 | 14.57 | 14.69 |
| **IRAQ** | 12.45 (18) | 31.60 (16) | 16.39 (18) | 12.67 (18) |
| **Our Baseline I** | 1.71 | 21.84 | 1.04 | 4.76 |

Table 5: Results for Subtask 1. The numbers in parentheses are the ranks. The table is sorted on the $macro - F1$ score, the official metric. Some teams did not submit description papers.

| Team | F1 | Accuracy | Precision | Recall |
|---|---|---|---|---|
| **BERT_NGRAMS** | **6.39 (1)** | 6.50 (2) | **7.84 (1)** | 6.54 (2) |
| **Arabic Processors** | 5.75 (2) | **6.80 (1)** | 6.78 (2) | **6.74 (1)** |
| **NAYEL** | 4.99 (3) | 5.22 (3) | 5.52 (3) | 5.17 (3) |
| **TRY_NLP** | 4.03 (4) | 4.86 (4) | 3.74 (4) | 4.68 (4) |
| **Our Baseline II** | 2.13 | 3.32 | 4.04 | 3.22 |
| **Our Baseline I** | 0.03 | 1.92 | 0.02 | 1.00 |

Table 6: Results for Subtask 2. The numbers in parentheses are the ranks. Table is sorted on the $macro - F1$ score, the official metric. Team NAYEL does not have a description paper.

to all teams. As can be seen from the table, the majority of the top teams have (1) used Transformers, (2) exploited the unlabeled data for further pre-training, and/or (3) have used self-training to enhance their models. The rest of participating teams have either used a type of neural networks other than Transformers or resorted to linear machine learning models, usually with some form of ensembling.

## 6  Conclusion and Future Work

We presented an overview of the NADI 2020 shared task. We described the dataset and identified areas of improvement especially related to its collection. We also provided a high-level description of participating teams. The number of submissions to the shared task reflects an interest in the community and calls for further work in the area of Arabic dialect detection, but also more generally Arabic dialect processing.

In the future, we plan to host a second iteration of the NADI shared task that will use new datasets and pursue a number of novel questions inspired by the issues discovered in this year's task. For example, in addition to DA classification, we will propose *MSA regional use classification* as a subtask. Since MSA is shared across the Arab world, we hypothesize this will be a more challenging task than DA classification. We will also encourage teams to experiment with studying the interaction between MSA and DA in

| Team | # Submissions | $F_1$ | Features | | | | | Methods | | | | | Uses Unlabelled 10M | | |
|---|---|---|---|---|---|---|---|---|---|---|---|---|---|---|---|
| | | | N-grams | TF-IDF | Word Embed. | Topic Models | Sampling | Classical ML | Neural Nets | Transformer | Ensemble | Hierarchical | Pre-Training | Data Augment. | Self-Training |
| **SUBTASK 1** | | | | | | | | | | | | | | | |
| **Mawdoo3 AI** | 3 | 26.78 | ✓ | ✓ | ✓ | | ✓ | ✓ | ✓ | ✓ | ✓ | | ✓ | | |
| **BERT_NGRAMS** | 4 | 25.99 | ✓ | ✓ | | | | ✓ | | ✓ | ✓ | | | ✓ | |
| **Arabic Processors** | 3 | 23.26 | ✓ | ✓ | | | | ✓ | | ✓ | ✓ | | | | ✓ |
| **Tri-directional** | 1 | 23.09 | | | | | ✓ | ✓ | | ✓ | | ✓ | ✓ | | |
| **MMZ** | 2 | 22.58 | ✓ | ✓ | | | | ✓ | | ✓ | ✓ | | ✓ | | |
| **QMUL Team** | 2 | 20.77 | ✓ | ✓ | ✓ | ✓ | | | ✓ | | | | ✓ | | |
| **Code Lyoko** | 2 | 20.34 | ✓ | ✓ | ✓ | | | ✓ | ✓ | ✓ | | | ✓ | | |
| **TRY_NLP** | 3 | 20.04 | ✓ | ✓ | ✓ | | | | ✓ | ✓ | | | | | ✓ |
| **Sorbonne** | 3 | 18.80 | ✓ | ✓ | ✓ | | | ✓ | ✓ | | ✓ | | ✓ | | |
| **Speech Translation** | 3 | 18.27 | ✓ | ✓ | | | ✓ | ✓ | | | ✓ | | | | |
| **LTG-ST** | 2 | 17.71 | ✓ | ✓ | | | | ✓ | | | ✓ | | | | |
| **Alexa** | 3 | 17.29 | ✓ | ✓ | | | | ✓ | | | ✓ | | | | |
| **Alpha** | 5 | 15.10 | ✓ | ✓ | | | | ✓ | | | | | | | |
| **IRAQ** | 3 | 12.45 | ✓ | ✓ | | | | ✓ | | | ✓ | | | | |
| **SUBTASK 2** | | | | | | | | | | | | | | | | |
| **BERT_NGRAMS** | 3 | 6.39 | ✓ | ✓ | | | | ✓ | ✓ | ✓ | ✓ | ✓ | | ✓ | |
| **Arabic Processors** | 1 | 5.75 | ✓ | ✓ | | | | ✓ | ✓ | ✓ | | | | | ✓ |
| **TRY_NLP** | 2 | 4.03 | ✓ | ✓ | ✓ | | | | ✓ | ✓ | | | | | ✓ |

Table 7: Summary of approaches used by participating teams in Subtasks 1 and 2. Classical ML refers to any non-neural machine learning methods such as naive Bayes and support vector machines. The term "neural nets" refers to any model based on neural networks (e.g., RNN, CNN) except Transformer models. Transformer refers to neural networks based on a Transformer architecture such as BERT. The table is sorted by official metric , $macro - F_1$. We only list teams that submitted a description paper.

novel ways. For example, questions as to the utility of using DA data to improve MSA regional use classification systems and vice versa can be investigated exploiting various machine learning methods.

## Acknowledgments

We gratefully acknowledge the support of the Natural Sciences and Engineering Research Council of Canada (NSERC), the Social Sciences Research Council of Canada (SSHRC), and Compute Canada (`www.computecanada.ca`). We thank AbdelRahim Elmadany for assisting with dataset preparation, setting up the Codalab for the shared task, and providing the map in Figure 2.

## References

Ines Abbes, Wajdi Zaghouani, Omaima El-Hardlo, and Faten Ashour. 2020. Daict: A dialectal Arabic irony corpus extracted from twitter. In *Proceedings of The 12th Language Resources and Evaluation Conference*, pages 6265–6271.

Muhammad Abdul-Mageed, Hassan Alhuzali, and Mohamed Elaraby. 2018. You tweet what you speak: A city-level dataset of Arabic dialects. In *Proceedings of the Language Resources and Evaluation Conference (LREC)*, Miyazaki, Japan.

Muhammad Abdul-Mageed, Chiyu Zhang, AbdelRahim Elmadany, and Lyle Ungar. 2020. Toward micro-dialect identification in diaglossic and code-switched environments. *arXiv preprint arXiv:2010.04900*.

Rania Al-Sabbagh and Roxana Girju. 2012. YADAC: Yet another Dialectal Arabic Corpus. In *Proceedings of the Eighth International Conference on Language Resources and Evaluation (LREC-2012)*, pages 2882–2889.

Nora Al-Twairesh, Rawan Al-Matham, Nora Madi, Nada Almugren, Al-Hanouf Al-Aljmi, Shahad Alshalan, Raghad Alshalan, Nafla Alrumayyan, Shams Al-Manea, Sumayah Bawazeer, Nourah Al-Mutlaq, Nada Al-manea, Waad Bin Huwaymil, Dalal Alqusair, Reem Alotaibi, Suha Al-Senaydi, and Abeer Alfutamani. 2018. SUAR: Towards building a corpus for the Saudi dialect. In *Proceedings of the International Conference on Arabic Computational Linguistics (ACLing)*.

Ahmed Aliwy, Hawraa Taher, and Zena AboAltaheen. 2020. Arabic Dialects Identification for All Arabic countries. In *Proceedings of the Fifth Arabic Natural Language Processing Workshop (WANLP 2020)*, Barcelona, Spain.

Abdulrahman Aloraini, Ayman Alhelbawy, and Massimo Poesio. 2020. The QMUL/HRBDT contribution to the NADI Arabic Dialect Identification Shared Task. In *Proceedings of the Fifth Arabic Natural Language Processing Workshop (WANLP 2020)*, Barcelona, Spain.

Nouf AlShenaifi and Aqil Azmi. 2020. Faheem at NADI shared task: Identifying the dialect of Arabic tweet. In *Proceedings of the Fifth Arabic Natural Language Processing Workshop (WANLP 2020)*, Barcelona, Spain.

Maha J Althobaiti. 2020. Automatic Arabic dialect identification systems for written texts: A survey. *arXiv preprint arXiv:2009.12622*.

MS Badawi. 1973. Levels of contemporary Arabic in Egypt. *Cairo: Dâr al Ma'ârif*.

Nitin Balaji and B. Bharathi. 2020. Semi-supervised Fine-grained Approach for Arabic Dialect Detection . In *Proceedings of the Fifth Arabic Natural Language Processing Workshop (WANLP 2020)*, Barcelona, Spain.

Ahmad Beltagy, Abdelrahman Abouelenin, and Omar ElSherief. 2020. Arabic Dialect Identification Using BERT-Based Domain Adaptation. In *Proceedings of the Fifth Arabic Natural Language Processing Workshop (WANLP 2020)*, Barcelona, Spain.

Mutaz Bni Younes, Nour Al-Khdour, and Mohammad AL-Smadi. 2020. Team Alexa at NADI Shared Task. In *Proceedings of the Fifth Arabic Natural Language Processing Workshop (WANLP 2020)*, Barcelona, Spain.

Houda Bouamor, Nizar Habash, and Kemal Oflazer. 2014. A multidialectal parallel corpus of Arabic. In *Proceedings of the Language Resources and Evaluation Conference (LREC)*, Reykjavik, Iceland.

Houda Bouamor, Nizar Habash, Mohammad Salameh, Wajdi Zaghouani, Owen Rambow, Dana Abdulrahim, Ossama Obeid, Salam Khalifa, Fadhl Eryani, Alexander Erdmann, and Kemal Oflazer. 2018. The MADAR Arabic Dialect Corpus and Lexicon. In *Proceedings of the Language Resources and Evaluation Conference (LREC)*, Miyazaki, Japan.

Houda Bouamor, Sabit Hassan, and Nizar Habash. 2019. The MADAR shared task on Arabic fine-grained dialect identification. In *Proceedings of the Fourth Arabic Natural Language Processing Workshop*, pages 199–207.

Kristen Brustad. 2000. *The Syntax of Spoken Arabic: A Comparative Study of Moroccan, Egyptian, Syrian, and Kuwaiti Dialects*. Georgetown University Press.

Mark W. Cowell. 1964. *A Reference Grammar of Syrian Arabic*. Georgetown University Press, Washington, D.C.

Mona Diab, Nizar Habash, Owen Rambow, Mohamed Altantawy, and Yassine Benajiba. 2010. COLABA: Arabic dialect annotation and processing. In *LREC workshop on Semitic language processing*, pages 66–74.

Mahmoud El-Haj. 2020. Habibi - a multi dialect multi national Arabic song lyrics corpus. In *Proceedings of the 12th Language Resources and Evaluation Conference*, pages 1318–1326, Marseille, France, May.

Abdellah El Mekki, Ahmed Alami, Hamza Alami, Ahmed Khoumsi, and Ismail Berrada. 2020. Weighted combination of BERT and N-GRAM features for Nuanced Arabic Dialect Identification. In *Proceedings of the Fifth Arabic Natural Language Processing Workshop (WANLP 2020)*, Barcelona, Spain.

Heba Elfardy, Mohamed Al-Badrashiny, and Mona Diab. 2014. Aida: Identifying code switching in informal Arabic text. In *Proceedings of the Conference on Empirical Methods in Natural Language Processing (EMNLP)*, pages 94–101, Doha, Qatar.

Kamel Gaanoun and Imade Benelallam. 2020. Arabic dialect identification: An Arabic-BERT model with data augmentation and ensembling strategy. In *Proceedings of the Fifth Arabic Natural Language Processing Workshop (WANLP 2020)*, Barcelona, Spain.

Hassan Gadalla, Hanaa Kilany, Howaida Arram, Ashraf Yacoub, Alaa El-Habashi, Amr Shalaby, Krisjanis Karins, Everett Rowson, Robert MacIntyre, Paul Kingsbury, David Graff, and Cynthia McLemore. 1997. CALLHOME Egyptian Arabic transcripts LDC97T19. Web Download. Philadelphia: Linguistic Data Consortium.

Dhaou Ghoul and Gael Lejeune. 2020. Comparison between Voting Classifier and Deep Learning methods for Arabic Dialect Identification. In *Proceedings of the Fifth Arabic Natural Language Processing Workshop (WANLP 2020)*, Barcelona, Spain.

R.S. Harrell. 1962. *A Short Reference Grammar of Moroccan Arabic: With Audio CD*. Georgetown classics in Arabic language and linguistics. Georgetown University Press.

Clive Holes. 2004. *Modern Arabic: Structures, Functions, and Varieties*. Georgetown Classics in Arabic Language and Linguistics. Georgetown University Press.

Mustafa Jarrar, Nizar Habash, Faeq Alrimawi, Diyam Akra, and Nasser Zalmout. 2016. Curras: an annotated corpus for the Palestinian Arabic dialect. *Language Resources and Evaluation*, pages 1–31.

Salam Khalifa, Nizar Habash, Dana Abdulrahim, and Sara Hassan. 2016. A Large Scale Corpus of Gulf Arabic. In *Proceedings of the Language Resources and Evaluation Conference (LREC)*, Portorož, Slovenia.

Mohamed Lichouri and Mourad Abbas. 2020. Simple vs Oversampling-based Classification Methods for Fine Grained Arabic Dialect Identification in Twitter. In *Proceedings of the Fifth Arabic Natural Language Processing Workshop (WANLP 2020)*, Barcelona, Spain.

Shervin Malmasi, Marcos Zampieri, Nikola Ljubešić, Preslav Nakov, Ahmed Ali, and Jörg Tiedemann. 2016. Discriminating between similar languages and arabic dialect identification: A report on the third dsl shared task. In *Proceedings of the third workshop on NLP for similar languages, varieties and dialects (VarDial3)*, pages 1–14.

Moataz Mansour, Moustafa Tohamy, Zeyad Ezzat, and Marwan Torki. 2020. Arabic Dialect Identification Using BERT Fine-Tuning. In *Proceedings of the Fifth Arabic Natural Language Processing Workshop (WANLP 2020)*, Barcelona, Spain.

Karima Meftouh, Salima Harrat, Salma Jamoussi, Mourad Abbas, and Kamel Smaili. 2015. Machine translation experiments on padic: A parallel Arabic dialect corpus. In *Proceedings of the Pacific Asia Conference on Language, Information and Computation*.

Hamdy Mubarak and Kareem Darwish. 2014. Using Twitter to collect a multi-dialectal corpus of Arabic. In *Proceedings of the Workshop for Arabic Natural Language Processing (WANLP)*, Doha, Qatar.

Hamdy Mubarak, Kareem Darwish, Walid Magdy, Tamer Elsayed, and Hend Al-Khalifa. 2020. Overview of osact4 Arabic offensive language detection shared task. In *Proceedings of the 4th Workshop on Open-Source Arabic Corpora and Processing Tools, with a Shared Task on Offensive Language Detection*, pages 48–52.

Ossama Obeid, Mohammad Salameh, Houda Bouamor, and Nizar Habash. 2019. ADIDA: Automatic dialect identification for Arabic. In *Proceedings of the 2019 Conference of the North American Chapter of the Association for Computational Linguistics (Demonstrations)*, pages 6–11, Minneapolis, Minnesota, June. Association for Computational Linguistics.

Fatiha Sadat, Farnazeh Kazemi, and Atefeh Farzindar. 2014. Automatic identification of Arabic language varieties and dialects in social media. *Proceedings of SocialNLP*, page 22.

Mohammad Salameh, Houda Bouamor, and Nizar Habash. 2018. Fine-grained Arabic dialect identification. In *Proceedings of the International Conference on Computational Linguistics (COLING)*, pages 1332–1344, Santa Fe, New Mexico, USA.

Kamel Smaïli, Mourad Abbas, Karima Meftouh, and Salima Harrat. 2014. Building resources for Algerian Arabic dialects. In *Proceedings of the Conference of the International Speech Communication Association (Interspeech)*.

Rawan Tahssin, Youssef Kishk, and Marwan Torki. 2020. Identifying Nuanced Dialect for Arabic Tweets with Deep Learning and Reverse Translation Corpus Extension System. In *Proceedings of the Fifth Arabic Natural Language Processing Workshop (WANLP 2020)*, Barcelona, Spain.

Bashar Talafha, Mohamed Ali, Muhy Eddin Za'ter, Haitham Seelawi, Ibraheem Tuffaha, Mostafa Samir, Wael Farhan, and Hussein T. AL-NATSHEH. 2020. Multi-dialect Arabic BERT for Country-level Dialect Identification. In *Proceedings of the Fifth Arabic Natural Language Processing Workshop (WANLP 2020)*, Barcelona, Spain.

Samia Touileb. 2020. LTG-ST at NADI Shared Task 1: Arabic Dialect Identification using a Stacking Classifier. In *Proceedings of the Fifth Arabic Natural Language Processing Workshop (WANLP 2020)*, Barcelona, Spain.

Wajdi Zaghouani and Anis Charfi. 2018. ArapTweet: A Large Multi-Dialect Twitter Corpus for Gender, Age and Language Variety Identification. In *Proceedings of the Language Resources and Evaluation Conference (LREC)*, Miyazaki, Japan.

Omar F Zaidan and Chris Callison-Burch. 2011. The Arabic online commentary dataset: an annotated dataset of informal Arabic with high dialectal content. In *Proceedings of the 49th Annual Meeting of the Association for Computational Linguistics: Human Language Technologies: short papers-Volume 2, Organization = Association for Computational Linguistics*, pages 37–41.

Marcos Zampieri, Shervin Malmasi, Nikola Ljubešić, Preslav Nakov, Ahmed Ali, Jörg Tiedemann, Yves Scherrer, and Noëmi Aepli. 2017. Findings of the vardial evaluation campaign 2017.

Marcos Zampieri, Shervin Malmasi, Preslav Nakov, Ahmed Ali, Suwon Shon, James Glass, Yves Scherrer, Tanja Samardzic, Nikola Ljubešić, Jörg Tiedemann, et al. 2018. Language identification and morphosyntactic tagging: The second vardial evaluation campaign. In *Proceedings of the Fifth Workshop on NLP for Similar Languages, Varieties and Dialects (VarDial 2018)*, pages 1–17.

# Appendices

## A  Appendix

| Province Name | # of Tweets | | | Province Name | # of Tweets | | |
|---|---|---|---|---|---|---|---|
| | train | dev | test | | train | dev | test |
| Damascus City | 214 | 53 | 52 | Minya | 213 | 53 | 52 |
| Ariana | 212 | 52 | 52 | BBordj Bou Arreridj | 213 | 53 | 52 |
| Asyut | 213 | 53 | 52 | Hawalli | 210 | 51 | 51 |
| Marrakech-Tensift-Al Haouz | 214 | 53 | 52 | Al Butnan | 214 | 53 | 53 |
| Bouira | 213 | 53 | 52 | Abu Dhabi | 214 | 53 | 52 |
| Ash Sharqiyah | 32 | 10 | 8 | Kairouan | 114 | 8 | 52 |
| Khenchela | 213 | 53 | 52 | Banaadir | 210 | 51 | 51 |
| As-Sulaymaniyah | 213 | 53 | 52 | Ar Riyad | 213 | 54 | 52 |
| Ad Dakhiliyah | 213 | 53 | 52 | Baghdad | 213 | 53 | 52 |
| Fujairah | 214 | 53 | 52 | Djibouti | 210 | 10 | 51 |
| An-Najaf | 213 | 53 | 52 | Musandam | 213 | 27 | 52 |
| Oriental | 214 | 37 | 52 | Muscat | 213 | 53 | 52 |
| Ibb | 213 | 50 | 52 | Doha | 24 | 52 | 10 |
| Al Quassim | 213 | 53 | 52 | Khartoum | 210 | 51 | 51 |
| Qena | 213 | 53 | 52 | Aswan | 213 | 53 | 52 |
| Sousse | 212 | 52 | 52 | North Sinai | 213 | 53 | 52 |
| As-Suwayda | 214 | 53 | 52 | Ash Sharqiyah | 395 | 97 | 96 |
| Ha'il | 213 | 54 | 52 | Beni Suef | 213 | 53 | 52 |
| Jizan | 213 | 53 | 52 | Tabuk | 213 | 53 | 52 |
| Jijel | 213 | 53 | 52 | Tripoli | 214 | 53 | 53 |
| Mahdia | 212 | 52 | 52 | Béchar | 213 | 41 | 52 |
| Ismailia | 213 | 53 | 52 | Najran | 213 | 53 | 52 |
| Meknes-Tafilalet | 214 | 53 | 52 | West Bank | 210 | 51 | 51 |
| Wasit | 213 | 53 | 52 | Alexandria | 213 | 53 | 52 |
| Gaza Strip | 210 | 51 | 51 | Dhofar | 213 | 53 | 52 |
| Kafr el-Sheikh | 213 | 53 | 52 | Capital | 210 | 8 | 20 |
| Nouakchott | 210 | 40 | 5 | Misrata | 214 | 53 | 53 |
| Gharbia | 213 | 53 | 52 | Aqaba | 213 | 52 | 52 |
| Al Anbar | 213 | 53 | 52 | Cairo | 213 | 10 | 52 |
| Arbil | 213 | 53 | 52 | North Lebanon | 213 | 52 | 52 |
| Akkar | 213 | 6 | 52 | South Lebanon | 213 | 52 | 52 |
| Makkah | 213 | 54 | 52 | Faiyum | 213 | 53 | 52 |
| Hims | 214 | 53 | 52 | Souss-Massa-Draa | 214 | 53 | 52 |
| Benghazi | 214 | 53 | 53 | Beheira | 213 | 53 | 52 |
| Lattakia | 214 | 53 | 52 | Al Jabal al Akhdar | 214 | 53 | 53 |
| Port Said | 213 | 53 | 52 | Ouargla | 213 | 53 | 52 |
| Oran | 213 | 53 | 52 | Monufia | 213 | 53 | 52 |
| Aden | 213 | 52 | 52 | Sohag | 213 | 53 | 52 |
| Al Madinah | 213 | 54 | 52 | Al Batnah | 214 | 53 | 52 |
| Red Sea | 213 | 53 | 52 | Dubai | 214 | 53 | 52 |
| Karbala | 213 | 53 | 52 | Maysan | 213 | 53 | 52 |
| Zarqa | 213 | 52 | 52 | Ninawa | 213 | 53 | 52 |
| Basra | 213 | 53 | 52 | Al Hudaydah | 213 | 52 | 52 |
| Suez | 213 | 53 | 52 | Jahra | 210 | 19 | 51 |
| Dakahlia | 213 | 53 | 52 | Al-Muthannia | 213 | 53 | 52 |
| South Sinai | 213 | 53 | 52 | Ras Al Khaymah | 214 | 53 | 52 |
| Umm Al Qaywayn | 214 | 53 | 5 | Dihok | 213 | 53 | 52 |
| Aleppo | 214 | 53 | 52 | Ar Rayyan | 210 | 52 | 51 |
| Tanger-Tetouan | 214 | 53 | 52 | Luxor | 213 | 53 | 52 |
| Asir | 213 | 54 | 52 | Dhamar | 212 | 52 | 23 |

Table A1: Distribution of the NADI data over provinces, by country, across our TRAIN, DEV, and TEST splits.

| Team Name | F1 | Accuracy | Precision | Recall |
|---|---|---|---|---|
| Mawdoo3 AI | **26.78 (1)** | 42.86 (2) | **32.52 (1)** | 25.19 (2) |
| Mawdoo3 AI | 26.77 (2) | 42.56 (3) | 31.51 (4) | **25.45 (1)** |
| Mawdoo3 AI | 26.47 (3) | **43.18 (1)** | 31.59 (3) | 25.12 (3) |
| BERT_NGRAMS | 25.99 (4) | 39.66 (5) | 30.26 (6) | 24.85 (4) |
| BERT_NGRAMS | 25.99 (4) | 39.66 (5) | 30.26 (6) | 24.85 (4) |
| BERT_NGRAMS | 25.02 (5) | 38.92 (6) | 30.92 (5) | 23.81 (5) |
| BERT_NGRAMS | 23.83 (6) | 40.88 (4) | 32.50 (2) | 23.36 (7) |
| Arabic Processors | 23.26 (7) | 38.34 (8) | 27.17 (9) | 22.43 (9) |
| Tri-directional | 23.09 (8) | 37.70 (10) | 26.40 (11) | 23.04 (8) |
| Arabic Processors | 23.03 (9) | 38.42 (7) | 27.40 (8) | 22.40 (10) |
| MMZ | 22.58 (10) | 38.28 (9) | 24.28 (15) | 23.36 (6) |
| MMZ | 22.58 (10) | 38.28 (9) | 24.28 (15) | 23.36 (6) |
| Arabic Processors | 22.52 (11) | 38.28 (9) | 26.70 (10) | 22.12 (11) |
| QMUL team | 20.77 (12) | 34.32 (22) | 21.62 (28) | 21.09 (12) |
| Code Lyoko | 20.34 (13) | 36.26 (13) | 27.83 (7) | 20.56 (15) |
| TRY_NLP | 20.04 (14) | 33.66 (27) | 20.70 (29) | 21.07 (13) |
| TRY_NLP | 20.01 (15) | 33.58 (28) | 20.66 (30) | 21.03 (14) |
| TRY_NLP | 19.84 (16) | 34.80 (20) | 20.54 (31) | 20.17 (16) |
| QMUL team | 19.45 (17) | 33.74 (26) | 20.40 (33) | 19.84 (17) |
| Sorbonne | 18.80 (18) | 36.54 (12) | 24.87 (14) | 18.05 (21) |
| Iktishaf | 18.63 (19) | 33.98 (25) | 20.21 (34) | 18.76 (18) |
| Speech Translation | 18.27 (20) | 36.68 (11) | 23.75 (20) | 18.06 (20) |
| Speech Translation | 17.90 (21) | 35.68 (16) | 22.40 (23) | 17.64 (23) |
| Iktishaf | 17.84 (22) | 33.48 (29) | 19.07 (36) | 17.98 (22) |
| Sorbonne | 17.77 (23) | 35.44 (18) | 23.79 (19) | 17.15 (26) |
| LTG-ST | 17.71 (24) | 36.22 (15) | 24.93 (13) | 17.21 (25) |
| Speech Translation | 17.69 (25) | 36.24 (14) | 22.17 (25) | 17.41 (24) |
| Alexa | 17.29 (26) | 34.16 (23) | 22.09 (26) | 16.81 (29) |
| Alexa | 17.20 (27) | 35.64 (17) | 23.53 (21) | 16.86 (28) |
| NAYEL | 16.84 (28) | 30.98 (41) | 17.88 (38) | 18.20 (19) |
| LTG-ST | 16.81 (29) | 34.78 (21) | 23.90 (18) | 16.46 (31) |
| DNLP | 16.50 (30) | 31.28 (39) | 17.84 (39) | 17.04 (27) |
| DNLP | 16.27 (31) | 31.24 (40) | 17.66 (40) | 16.77 (30) |
| Sorbonne | 16.06 (32) | 31.90 (36) | 22.00 (27) | 15.90 (34) |
| NAYEL | 15.81 (33) | 32.22 (35) | 17.91 (37) | 16.01 (32) |
| NLPRL | 15.77 (34) | 35.06 (19) | 23.96 (17) | 15.92 (33) |
| Alpha | 15.10 (35) | 34.02 (24) | 22.34 (24) | 14.71 (39) |
| Alexa | 15.09 (36) | 34.78 (21) | 23.00 (22) | 15.68 (35) |
| Alpha | 14.91 (37) | 32.80 (32) | 25.43 (12) | 14.30 (42) |
| Alpha | 14.72 (38) | 33.00 (30) | 20.44 (32) | 14.61 (40) |
| Alpha | 14.61 (39) | 32.24 (34) | 17.30 (41) | 14.81 (37) |
| NAYEL | 14.37 (40) | 29.42 (42) | 15.32 (45) | 14.90 (36) |
| Alpha | 14.27 (41) | 32.84 (31) | 24.15 (16) | 14.33 (41) |
| Sorbonne | 14.21 (42) | 32.38 (33) | 19.13 (35) | 14.25 (43) |
| Code Lyoko | 13.57 (43) | 31.70 (37) | 15.32 (44) | 14.74 (38) |
| IRAQ | 12.45 (44) | 31.60 (38) | 16.39 (42) | 12.67 (44) |
| IRAQ | 12.20 (45) | 31.28 (39) | 15.76 (43) | 12.45 (45) |

Table A2: Full results for Subtask 1. The numbers in parentheses are the ranks. The table is sorted on the $macro\ F_1$ score, the official metric.

| Team Name | F1 | Accuracy | Precision | Recall |
|---|---|---|---|---|
| BERT_NGRAMS | **6.39 (1)** | 6.50 (2) | 7.84 (2) | 6.54 (2) |
| BERT_NGRAMS | 6.08 (2) | 6.16 (3) | 7.78 (3) | 6.03 (3) |
| Arabic Processors | 5.75 (3) | **6.80 (1)** | 6.78 (4) | **6.74 (1)** |
| BERT_NGRAMS | 5.42 (4) | 5.32 (4) | **8.00 (1)** | 5.24 (4) |
| NAYEL | 4.99 (5) | 5.22 (5) | 5.52 (5) | 5.17 (5) |
| NAYEL | 4.28 (6) | 4.48 (8) | 4.34 (6) | 4.69 (6) |
| TRY_NLP | 4.03 (7) | 4.86 (6) | 3.74 (9) | 4.68 (7) |
| TRY_NLP | 3.94 (8) | 4.54 (7) | 3.86 (7) | 4.45 (8) |
| NAYEL | 3.60 (9) | 3.84 (9) | 3.83 (8) | 3.85 (9) |

Table A3: Full results for Subtask 2. The numbers in parentheses are the ranks. The table is sorted on the $macro\ F_1$ score, the official metric.

# Multi-Dialect Arabic BERT
## for Country-Level Dialect Identification


**Bashar Talafha**[*]  **Mohammad Ali**[*]  **Muhy Eddin Za'ter**  **Haitham Seelawi**
**Ibraheem Tuffaha**  **Mostafa Samir**  **Wael Farhan**  **Hussein T. Al-Natsheh**

Mawdoo3 Ltd, Amman, Jordan
`{bashar.talafha,mohammad.ali,muhy.zater,haitham.selawi,`
`ibraheem.tuffaha,mostafa.samir,wael.farhan,h.natsheh}`
`@mawdoo3.com`


## Abstract


Arabic dialect identification is a complex problem for a number of inherent properties of the language itself. In this paper, we present the experiments conducted, and the models developed by our competing team, Mawdoo3 AI, along the way to achieving our winning solution to subtask 1 of the Nuanced Arabic Dialect Identification (NADI) shared task. The dialect identification subtask provides 21,000 country-level labeled tweets covering all 21 Arab countries. An unlabeled corpus of 10M tweets from the same domain is also presented by the competition organizers for optional use. Our winning solution itself came in the form of an ensemble of different training iterations of our pre-trained BERT model, which achieved a micro-averaged F1-score of 26.78% on the subtask at hand. We publicly release the pre-trained language model component of our winning solution under the name of Multi-dialect-Arabic-BERT model, for any interested researcher out there.


## 1 Introduction

The term Arabic language is better thought of as an umbrella term, under which it is possible to list hundreds of varieties of the language, some of which are not even mutually comprehensible. Nonetheless, such varieties can be grouped together with varying levels of granularity, all of which correspond to the various ways the geographical extent of the Arab world can be divided, albeit loosely. Despite such diversity, up until recently, such varieties were strictly confined to the spoken domains, with Modern Standard Arabic (MSA) dominating the written forms of communication all over the Arab world. However, with the advent of social media, an explosion of written content in said varieties have flooded the internet, attracting the attention and interest of the wide Arabic NLP research community in the process. This is evident in the number of held workshops dedicated to the topic in the last few years.

In this paper we present and discuss the strategies and experiments we conducted to achieve the first place in the Nuanced Arabic Dialect Identification (NADI) Shared Task 1 (Abdul-Mageed et al., 2020), which is dedicated to dialect identification at the country level. In section 2 we discuss related work. This is followed by section 3 in which we discuss the data used to develop our model. Section 4 discusses the most significant models we tested and tried in our experiments. The details and results of said experiments can be found in section 5. The analysis and discussion of the results can be obtained in section 6 followed by our conclusions in section 7.

## 2 Related Work

The task of Arabic dialect identification is challenging. This can be attributed to a number of reasons, including: a paucity of corpora dedicated to the topic, the lack of a standard orthography between and across the various dialects, and the nature of the language itself (e.g. its morphological richness among other peculiarities). To tackle these challenges, the Arabic NLP community has come up with a number of responses. One response was the development of annotated corpora that focus primarily on dialectical

---






*Proceedings of the Fifth Arabic Natural Language Processing Workshop*, pages 111–118
Barcelona, Spain (Online), December 12, 2020

data, such as the Arabic On-line Commentary dataset (Zaidan and Callison-Burch, 2014), the MADAR Arabic dialect corpus and lexicon (Bouamor et al., 2018), the Arap-Tweet corpus (Zaghouani and Charfi, 2018), in addition to a city-level dataset of Arabic dialects that was curated by (Abdul-Mageed et al., 2018). Another popular form of response is the organization of NLP workshops and shared tasks, which are solely dedicated to developing approaches and models that can detect and classify the use of Arabic dialects in written text. One example is the MADAR shared task (Bouamor et al., 2019), which focuses on dialect detection at the level of Arab countries and cities.

The aforementioned efforts by the Arabic NLP community, have resulted in a number of publications that explore the application of a variety of Machine Learning (ML) tools to the problem of dialect identification, with varying emphasis on feature engineering, ensemble methods, and the level of supervision involved (Salameh et al., 2018; Elfardy and Diab, 2013; Huang, 2015; Talafha et al., 2019b).

The past few years have also witnessed a number of published papers that explore the potential of Deep Learning (DL) models for dialect detection, starting with (Elaraby and Abdul-Mageed, 2018; Ali, 2018), who show the enhanced performance that can be brought about through the use of LSTMs and CNNs, all the way to (Zhang and Abdul-Mageed, 2019), who highlight the potential of pre-trained language models to achieve state of the art performance on the task of dialect detection.

## 3   Dataset

The novel dataset of NADI shared task consists of around 31,000 labeled tweets covering the entirety of the 21 Arab countries. Additionally, the task presents an unlabeled corpus of 10M tweets. The labeled dataset is split into 21,000 examples for training, with the rest of the tweets, i.e., 10,000, distributed equally between the development and test sets. Each tweet is annotated with a single country only. In Figure 1 we can see the distribution of tweets per country in which *Egypt* and *Bahrain* has the highest and lowest tweet frequencies, respectively. We also note that the ratio of the development to train examples is generally similar across the various dialects, except for the ones with lowest frequencies.

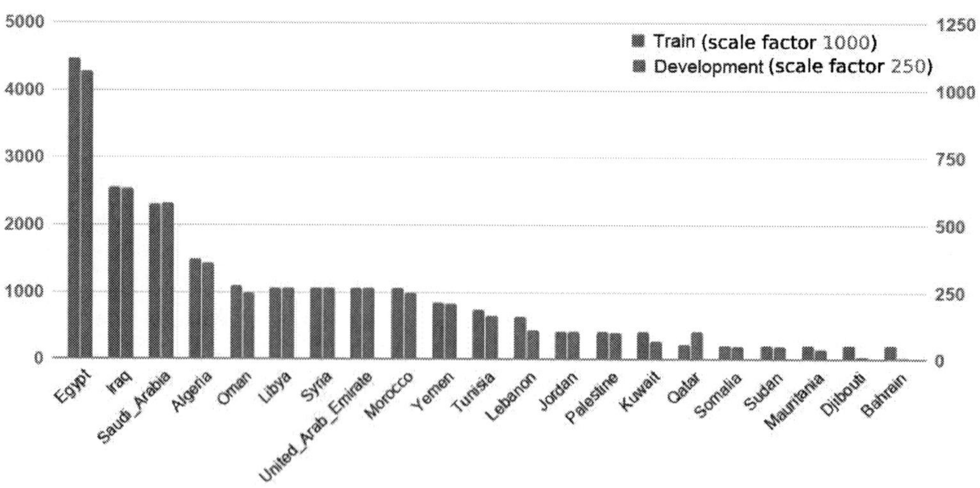


Figure 1: Classes distribution for both Train and Development sets

The unlabeled dataset is provided in the form a twitter crawling script, and the IDs of 10M tweets, which in combination can be used to retrieve the text of these tweets. We are able to retrieve 97.7% of them, as the rest seem to be unavailable (possibly deleted since then or made private). This dataset can be beneficial in multiple ways, including building embedding models (e.g., Word2Vec, FastText) (Mikolov et al., 2013; Bojanowski et al., 2017), pre-training language models, or in semi-supervised learning and data augmentation techniques. This dataset can also be used to further pre-train an already existing language model, which can positively affect its performance on tasks derived from a domain similar to that of the 10M tweets, as we show in our results in Section 6.

## 4 System Description

In this section, we present the various approaches employed in our experiments, starting with the winning approach of our Multi-dialect-Arabic-BERT model, followed by the rest of them. The results of our experiments are presented in Table 1.

### 4.1 Multi-dialect-Arabic-BERT

Our top performing approach, which achieved the number one place on the NADI task 1, is based on a Bidirectional Encoder Representations from Transformers (BERT) architecture (Devlin et al., 2018). BERT uses the encoder part of a Transformer (Vaswani et al., 2017), and is trained using a masked language model (MLM) objective. This involves training the model to predict corrupted tokens, which is achieved using a special mask token that replaces the original ones. This is typically done on a huge corpus of unlabeled text. The resultant model can then produce contextual vector representations for tokens that capture various linguistics signals, which in turn can be beneficial for downstream tasks.

We started with the *ArabicBERT* (Safaya et al., 2020), which is a publicly released BERT model trained on around 93 GB of Arabic content crawled from around the internet. This model is then fine-tuned on the NADI task 1, by retrieving the output of a special token [CLS], placed at the beginning of a given tweet. The retrieved vector is in turn fed into a shallow feed-forward neural classifier that consists of a dropout layer, a dense layer, and a softmax activation output function, which produces the final predicated class out of the original 21. It is worth mentioning that during the fine-tuning process, the loss is propagated back across the entire network, including the BERT encoder.

We then were able to significantly improve the results obtained from the model above, by further pre-training *ArabicBERT* on the 10M tweets released by the NADI organizers, for 3 epochs. We refer to this final resultant model as the *Multi-dialect-Arabic-BERT*.

In order to squeeze out more performance from our model, we ended up using ensemble techniques. The best ensemble results came from the voting of 4 models that were trained with different maximum sequence lengths (i.e., 80, 90, 100 and 250). The voting step was accomplished by taking the element-wise average of the predicted probabilities per class for each of these models. The class with the highest value is then outputed as the predicted label.

All of our models were trained using an Adam optimizer (Kingma and Ba, 2014) with a learning rate of $3.75 \times 10^{-5}$ and a batch size of 16 for 3 epochs. No preprocessing was applied to the data except for the processing done by ArabicBERT tokenizer. The vocabulary size for ArabicBert is 32000 and sentencepiece (Kudo and Richardson, 2018) is used as a tokenizer.

We publicly release the Multi-dialect-Arabic-BERT[1] on GitHub to make it available for use by all researchers for any task including reproducing this paper's results.

### 4.2 Other Traditional Machine and Deep Learning Models

In addition to our winning solution, we experimented with a number of other approaches, none of which has exceeded an F1-score of 21, but which we list here for the sake of completeness anyway.

- *MADAR-Mawdoo3 Model*
  Originally proposed by Ragab et al. (2019), three models (i.e., a Multinomial Naive Bayes (MNB), logistic regression, and weak dummy classifier) are trained separately on the data to obtain their dialect probability distributions, which then, in conjunction with TF–IDF vectors, make up the feature space. These features are then fed into an ensamble of five other models (i.e., MNB with one-vs-rest strategy, a Support Vector Machine model (SVM), a Bernoulli Naive Bayes classifier, a K-nearest-neighbours classifier with one-vs rest strategy, and finally a weak dummy classifier). The final predicted classes are obtained using a hard voting approach.

- *MADAR-Safina Model*
  This model follows Safina model proposed in (Bouamor et al., 2019). The model is an ensemble

---

[1] https://github.com/mawdoo3/Multi-dialect-Arabic-BERT

| Model | Dev Set Results | | Test Set Results | |
|---|---|---|---|---|
| | Accuracy | F1-Score | Accuracy | F1-Score |
| MADAR-Safina | 33.35 | 10.1 | - | - |
| Logistic-Regression | 35.65 | 16.57 | - | - |
| MADAR-1 Mawdoo3 | 33.45 | 12.24 | - | - |
| MADAR-1 JUST | 30.3 | 17.07 | - | - |
| FastText-embeddings | 34.28 | 19.74 | - | - |
| Aravec fully connected | 35.67 | 20.86 | - | - |
| Arabic-BERT-Single | 40.85 | 24.45 | - | - |
| Arabic-BERT-Ensemble-Diff-Len | 41.48 | 24.92 | - | - |
| Multi-dialect-Arabic-BERT | 43.7 | 26 | - | - |
| Multi-dialect-Arabic-BERT-Ensemble-Diff-Len | 44.95 | 27.58 | **42.86** | **26.78** |
| Multi-dialect-Arabic-BERT-Ensemble-Diff-Len with rules | **45.07** | **29.03** | 42.55 | 26.77 |

Table 1: Final results on NADI development and testing set

of 3 classifiers: Language model classifier based on 5-char n-gram features (Heafield et al., 2013), Naive Bayes classifier based on 4-to-6 char n-gram features, Naive Bayes classifier based on 1-word n-gram features. The only pre-processing step used is to duplicate every single word for the language model and the char n-gram classifiers. The purpose of duplicating every single word is to detect circumfix n-gram patterns.

- *MADAR-JUST Model*
  In this model, we applied the approach proposed by Talafha et al. (2019a). In order to balance the training data, a data augmentation technique based on random shuffling was performed to enlarge and balance the training data. After that, for each sentence, a vector of size 21 that represents a language model probability for each country was extracted and concatenated to a word and character level TF–IDF vectors. An MNB classifier is then applied with the One-vs-the-rest strategy.

- *FastText Model*
  FastText (Bojanowski et al., 2017) was originally implemented to help obtain enhanced word representations over simpler methods such as Word2Vec (Mikolov et al., 2013). In our experiments, we pool the fastText vectors of each token in a given sentence, to obtain a fixed-size dense representation of the sentence at hand. This is in turn fed into a multinomial logistic regression for classification (Zolotov and Kung, 2017; Joulin et al., 2016).

- *AraVec fully connected Model*
  AraVec is an Arabic based Word2Vec model, trained and published by (Soliman et al., 2017). Similar to our FastText model above, we pool the AraVec vectors of the constituent tokens of a sentence to obtain its fixed-size vector representation. However, instead of a conventional ML algorithm, we feed these representations into a feed forward classifier, which is trained to obtain the final predictions (Ashi et al., 2018).

## 5   Experiments and Results

As mentioned above, multiple approaches have been investigated in the experiments we conducted, starting with traditional ML techniques then moving to DL approaches, before finally settling on our winning BERT based model. For our traditional ML experiments, we tried various models such as SVM, Logistic Regression (LR) and Naive Bayes (NB), along with features such as TF–IDF. We also tried other ML models that performed well on previous similar tasks such as MADAR Mawdoo3-AI and MADAR Safina models. However, all of these models came short when compared to the BERT models as can be seen in Table 1, with the best Macro-Averaged F1-score achieved using traditional ML approaches being

| Model | Results | |
|---|---|---|
| | Accuracy | Macro-Averaged F1-Score |
| ArabicProcessors | 38.34 | 23.26 |
| BERT-NGRAMS | 39.66 | 25.99 |
| Mawdoo3-ai | **42.86** | **26.78** |

Table 2: Final results on NADI testing dataset for the 3 top performing participating teams

17.06%. We then experimented with a number DL models, along with pre-trained word embedding features, such as fastText and Word2Vec. These models easily surpassed the performance of their traditional ML counterparts, with a maximum macro-averaged F1 score of 20.86%.

As alluded to above, the best results were achieved by our BERT models. Using the standalone ArabicBERT (Safaya et al., 2020) we were able to achieve 24.45% Macro-Averaged F1-score on the development dataset. This score was further increased to 26.46% using ensemble techniques. This motivated us to further pre-train it on the 10 million unlabelled tweets to form the Multi-dialect-Arabic-BERT model. Using this setup, we were able to achieve a Macro-Averaged Macro-Averaged F1 score of 26%. Here again, we used the ensemble trick to obtain a 27.58% Macro-Averaged F1-score on the development set and 26.78% on the test set, thus winning the competition. We note that applying lexicon-based prediction rules to the best model mentioned above boosted the results of development set to 29.03 F1-score. However, these rules slightly decreased the test set results to 26.77 F1-score, concluding that such rules cause the system to suffer from over-fitting the development set.

## 6 Discussion and Analysis

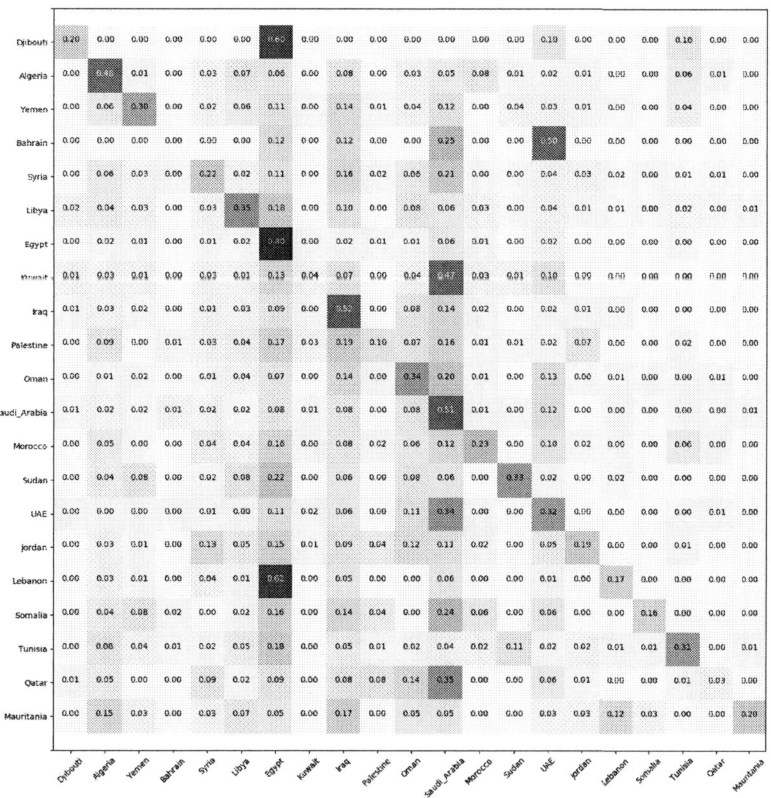

Figure 2: The confusion matrix of our best model on NADI development set

To aid us with the analysis of the strengths and weaknesses of our winning model, we provide the confusion matrix for its performance on the NADI development set in Figure 2. The matrix highlights a number of issues stemming from the training dataset itself. For instance, it can be clearly seen that the model is biased to the countries with more training data such as Egypt, Iraq and Saudi Arabia; for these countries, the model achieves better results, while achieving much worse F1-scores for the ones with the least training data available. It can also be seen that the model suffers when trying to differentiate between geographically nearby countries. For example, 50% of the development samples from Bahrain are labeled as UAE and 22% from Sudan are labeled as Egypt. This is expected, given the similarities in dialects between neighbouring countries. Some of the results shown in the confusion matrix have also led us to further investigate the datasets themselves. This resulted in finding that our model does in fact predict the correct class for certain tweets, which were somehow originally mislabeled. Some of these examples can be seen in Table 3.

| Tweet | Label | Predicton | Actual |
|---|---|---|---|
| اللهم ارحمه واغفرله | Mauritania | Egypt | MSA |
| احنا ناس تافهة ملناش في الكلام ده | Lebanon | Egypt | Egypt |
| راسلني على الخاص | Algeria | Saudi_Arabia | MSA |
| وش اسويلك طيب؟؟؟ | Syria | Saudi_Arabia | Saudi_Arabia |
| اللهم صل على محمد وال محمد | Palestine | Iraq | MSA |
| إي ديربالچ من قراراتي أبدا مو ثابتة | Morocco | Iraq | Iraq |

Table 3: Examples of mislabeled and confusing tweets.

## 7 Conclusion

In this paper we describe our first place solution for the NADI competition, task 1. This was achieved via three stages: firstly, we further pre-trained a publicly released BERT model (i.e., Arabic-BERT) on the 10 millions tweets supplied by the NADI competition organizers. Secondly, we trained the resultant model on the NADI labelled data for task 1, multiple times, independently, with each of these iterations using a different mixture of maximum sentence length and learning rate. Thirdly, we selected the 4 best performing iterations (based on their performance on the development dataset), and aggregated their softmax predictions via a simple element wise averaging function, to produce the final prediction for a given tweet. For future work, we would like to investigate other advanced pre-training methods, such as XLNET (Yang et al., 2019), and ELECTRA (Clark et al., 2020), which we believe might hold the key to better performance on this task.

## References


Muhammad Abdul-Mageed, Hassan Alhuzali, and Mohamed Elaraby. 2018. You tweet what you speak: A city-level dataset of arabic dialects. In *Proceedings of the Eleventh International Conference on Language Resources and Evaluation (LREC 2018)*.

Muhammad Abdul-Mageed, Chiyu Zhang, Houda Bouamor, and Nizar Habash. 2020. NADI 2020: The First Nuanced Arabic Dialect Identification Shared Task. In *Proceedings of the Fifth Arabic Natural Language Processing Workshop (WANLP 2020)*, Barcelona, Spain.

Mohamed Ali. 2018. Character level convolutional neural network for arabic dialect identification. In *Proceedings of the Fifth Workshop on NLP for Similar Languages, Varieties and Dialects (VarDial 2018)*, pages 122–127.

Mohammed Matuq Ashi, Muazzam Ahmed Siddiqui, and Farrukh Nadeem. 2018. Pre-trained word embeddings for arabic aspect-based sentiment analysis of airline tweets. In *International Conference on Advanced Intelligent Systems and Informatics*, pages 241–251. Springer.

Piotr Bojanowski, Edouard Grave, Armand Joulin, and Tomas Mikolov. 2017. Enriching word vectors with subword information. *Transactions of the Association for Computational Linguistics*, 5:135–146.

Houda Bouamor, Nizar Habash, Mohammad Salameh, Wajdi Zaghouani, Owen Rambow, Dana Abdulrahim, Ossama Obeid, Salam Khalifa, Fadhl Eryani, Alexander Erdmann, et al. 2018. The madar arabic dialect corpus and lexicon. In *Proceedings of the Eleventh International Conference on Language Resources and Evaluation (LREC 2018)*.

Houda Bouamor, Sabit Hassan, and Nizar Habash. 2019. The madar shared task on arabic fine-grained dialect identification. In *Proceedings of the Fourth Arabic Natural Language Processing Workshop*, pages 199–207.

Kevin Clark, Minh-Thang Luong, Quoc V Le, and Christopher D Manning. 2020. Electra: Pre-training text encoders as discriminators rather than generators. *arXiv preprint arXiv:2003.10555*.

Jacob Devlin, Ming-Wei Chang, Kenton Lee, and Kristina Toutanova. 2018. Bert: Pre-training of deep bidirectional transformers for language understanding. *arXiv preprint arXiv:1810.04805*.

Mohamed Elaraby and Muhammad Abdul-Mageed. 2018. Deep models for arabic dialect identification on benchmarked data. In *Proceedings of the Fifth Workshop on NLP for Similar Languages, Varieties and Dialects (VarDial 2018)*, pages 263–274.

Heba Elfardy and Mona Diab. 2013. Sentence level dialect identification in arabic. In *Proceedings of the 51st Annual Meeting of the Association for Computational Linguistics (Volume 2: Short Papers)*, pages 456–461.

Kenneth Heafield, Ivan Pouzyrevsky, Jonathan H. Clark, and Philipp Koehn. 2013. Scalable modified Kneser-Ney language model estimation. In *Proceedings of the 51st Annual Meeting of the Association for Computational Linguistics (Volume 2: Short Papers)*, pages 690–696, Sofia, Bulgaria, August. Association for Computational Linguistics.

Fei Huang. 2015. Improved arabic dialect classification with social media data. In *Proceedings of the 2015 Conference on Empirical Methods in Natural Language Processing*, pages 2118–2126.

Armand Joulin, Edouard Grave, Piotr Bojanowski, and Tomas Mikolov. 2016. Bag of tricks for efficient text classification. *arXiv preprint arXiv:1607.01759*.

Diederik P Kingma and Jimmy Ba. 2014. Adam: A method for stochastic optimization. *arXiv preprint arXiv:1412.6980*.

Taku Kudo and John Richardson. 2018. Sentencepiece: A simple and language independent subword tokenizer and detokenizer for neural text processing. *arXiv preprint arXiv:1808.06226*.

Tomas Mikolov, Kai Chen, Greg Corrado, and Jeffrey Dean. 2013. Efficient estimation of word representations in vector space. *arXiv preprint arXiv:1301.3781*.

Ahmad Ragab, Haitham Seelawi, Mostafa Samir, Abdelrahman Mattar, Hesham Al-Bataineh, Mohammad Zaghloul, Ahmad Mustafa, Bashar Talafha, Abed Alhakim Freihat, and Hussein Al-Natsheh. 2019. Mawdoo3 ai at madar shared task: Arabic fine-grained dialect identification with ensemble learning. In *Proceedings of the Fourth Arabic Natural Language Processing Workshop*, pages 244–248.

Ali Safaya, Moutasem Abdullatif, and Deniz Yuret. 2020. Kuisail at semeval-2020 task 12: Bert-cnn for offensive speech identification in social media. In *Proceedings of the International Workshop on Semantic Evaluation (SemEval)*.

Mohammad Salameh, Houda Bouamor, and Nizar Habash. 2018. Fine-grained arabic dialect identification. In *Proceedings of the 27th International Conference on Computational Linguistics*, pages 1332–1344.

Abu Bakr Soliman, Kareem Eissa, and Samhaa R El-Beltagy. 2017. Aravec: A set of arabic word embedding models for use in arabic nlp. *Procedia Computer Science*, 117:256–265.

Bashar Talafha, Ali Fadel, Mahmoud Al-Ayyoub, Yaser Jararweh, AL-Smadi Mohammad, and Patrick Juola. 2019a. Team just at the madar shared task on arabic fine-grained dialect identification. In *Proceedings of the Fourth Arabic Natural Language Processing Workshop*, pages 285–289.

Bashar Talafha, Wael Farhan, Ahmed Altakrouri, and Hussein Al-Natsheh. 2019b. Mawdoo3 ai at madar shared task: Arabic tweet dialect identification. In *Proceedings of the Fourth Arabic Natural Language Processing Workshop*, pages 239–243.

Ashish Vaswani, Noam Shazeer, Niki Parmar, Jakob Uszkoreit, Llion Jones, Aidan N Gomez, Łukasz Kaiser, and Illia Polosukhin. 2017. Attention is all you need. In *Advances in neural information processing systems*, pages 5998–6008.

Zhilin Yang, Zihang Dai, Yiming Yang, Jaime Carbonell, Russ R Salakhutdinov, and Quoc V Le. 2019. Xlnet: Generalized autoregressive pretraining for language understanding. In *Advances in neural information processing systems*, pages 5753–5763.

Wajdi Zaghouani and Anis Charfi. 2018. Arap-tweet: A large multi-dialect twitter corpus for gender, age and language variety identification. *arXiv preprint arXiv:1808.07674*.

Omar F Zaidan and Chris Callison-Burch. 2014. Arabic dialect identification. *Computational Linguistics*, 40(1):171–202.

Chiyu Zhang and Muhammad Abdul-Mageed. 2019. No army, no navy: Bert semi-supervised learning of arabic dialects. In *Proceedings of the Fourth Arabic Natural Language Processing Workshop*, pages 279–284.

Vladimir Zolotov and David Kung. 2017. Analysis and optimization of fasttext linear text classifier. *arXiv preprint arXiv:1702.05531*.

# On the Importance of Tokenization in Arabic Embedding Models


**Mohamed Alkaoud**
University of California, Davis
One Shields Ave
Davis, CA 95616
United States
maalkaoud@ucdavis.edu

**Mairaj Syed**
University of California, Davis
One Shields Ave
Davis, CA 95616
United States
msyed@ucdavis.edu


## Abstract


Arabic, like other highly inflected languages, encodes a large amount of information in its morphology and word structure. In this work, we propose two embedding strategies that modify the tokenization phase of traditional word embedding models (Word2Vec) and contextual word embedding models (BERT) to take into account Arabic's relatively complex morphology. In Word2Vec, we segment words into subwords during training time and then compose word-level representations from the subwords during test time. We train our embeddings on Arabic Wikipedia and show that they perform better than a Word2Vec model on multiple Arabic natural language processing datasets while being approximately 60% smaller in size. Moreover, we showcase our embeddings' ability to produce accurate representations of some out-of-vocabulary words that were not encountered before. In BERT, we modify the tokenization layer of Google's pretrained multilingual BERT model by incorporating information on morphology. By doing so, we achieve state of the art performance on two Arabic NLP datasets without pretraining.


## 1 Introduction

Word embeddings are one of the main building blocks of most natural language processing tasks. Many word embedding techniques have been proposed (Mikolov et al., 2013b; Pennington et al., 2014; Bojanowski et al., 2016) that try to capture better word representations. Although most of the approaches are language agnostic, they were historically designed to be used with English. Nonetheless, it was shown that these techniques work well in other languages (Grave et al., 2018; Soliman et al., 2017).

One feature that is unique to Arabic, and other highly inflected languages, is the expressiveness of its words. The fact that Arabic encodes a large amount of information in its word structure leads to potential problems in learning embeddings due to the large number of forms for each word, the more likely chances of out-of-vocabulary (OOV) instances, and the increase in model size.

In this work, we propose two embedding strategies for Arabic that take into consideration its rich morphology by modifying the tokenization phase. The first technique concerns traditional embedding models and the second a contextual one. Our experiments are done on Word2Vec (Mikolov et al., 2013a) and BERT (Devlin et al., 2018) since they are the most popular traditional and contextual embedding techniques, respectively. Nonetheless, the approaches we propose are embedding-agnostic and can be applied to other embedding techniques. Figure 1 summarizes our two approaches and illustrates what happens in the training and inferences stages of each approach.

In traditional embeddings, we analyze the effect of tokenizing words into subwords by splitting their suffixes and prefixes before training an embedding model and then combining these subwords using an algorithm we propose. We show that by doing so we get:

1. Better performance: our model outperforms Word2Vec in multiple tasks.

2. Smaller size: our model is 59.6% smaller than a Word2Vec model trained on the same corpus.






*Proceedings of the Fifth Arabic Natural Language Processing Workshop*, pages 119–129
Barcelona, Spain (Online), December 12, 2020

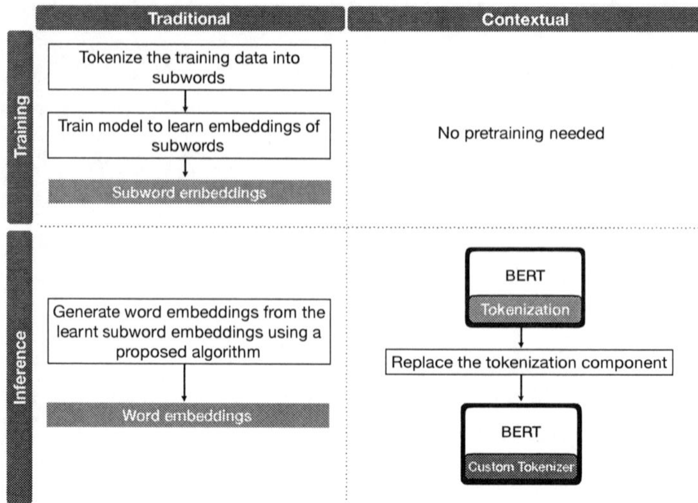



Figure 1: The training and inference stages of our two proposed strategies.

3. Superior out-of-vocabulary handling: our model is able to handle some OOV instances unlike Word2Vec.

In contextual embeddings, we investigate different tokenization schemes when using BERT without needing any pretraining, in contrast to previous approaches such as Antoun et al. (2020). We simply modify the tokenization part of Google's pretrained multilingual BERT model (Devlin et al., 2018) resulting in models that:

1. Achieve state of the art results on two Arabic NLP datasets.

2. Do not require pretraining and can work on top of existing models.

The rest of the paper is structured as follows: Section 2 introduces the background and explains some of the fundamental ideas of word embeddings; Section 3 defines the process of gathering and cleaning our data; Section 4 highlights the embedding approaches we are proposing; Section 5 details the experiments and the results; Section 6 discusses related work; and Section 7 concludes by summarizing our findings and pointing to potential directions for future work.

## 2 Background

Word embedding techniques rely on the distributional hypothesis (Harris, 1954) which suggests that words that appear in similar contexts tend to have similar meanings. Mikolov et al. (2013a) popularized word embeddings when they introduced Word2Vec and showed that it produces representations that capture not only syntax but also words' semantics. Many related techniques have been produced after that (Mikolov et al., 2013b; Pennington et al., 2014; Bojanowski et al., 2016; Joulin et al., 2016). The word vectors produced by such techniques capture interesting semantics; one popular example is how the the vectors capture relationships between them. For example, if we subtract the vector for 'man' from the vector of 'king', and then add the vector of 'woman' we get very close to the vector of 'queen'.

Contextual word embeddings were proposed (Devlin et al., 2018; Peters et al., 2018; Liu et al., 2019) to tackle the issues that arise from words have multiple senses and meanings. In traditional embeddings such as Word2Vec, each word is encoded in a vector, which is a fixed representation. This may cause problems with homographs and words that have multiple senses depending on the context. For example the wear 'bear' means two very different things in the following sentences: "The right of the people to keep and *bear* arms shall not be infringed." and "A wild *bear* was seen in the city." Yet, traditional embeddings will only capture one fixed representation. Contextual word embeddings aim to solve this issue by modeling embeddings where the context of the word will affect its generated representation.

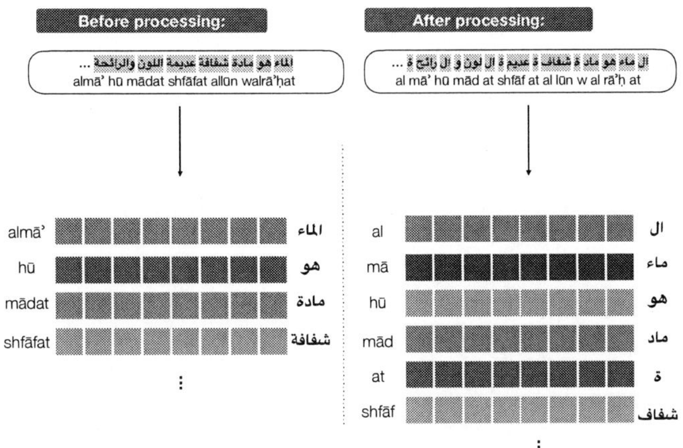



Figure 2: The effect of word segmentation on the resulting vectors. In the top we have representations of words and in the bottom we have representations of subwords.

| Verb | Forms |
|------|-------|
| go | go, went, going, gone, goes |
| ذهب | ذهب، يذهب، سيذهب، ذهبا، يذهبا، سيذهبا، ذهبوا، يذهبوا، سيذهبوا، ذهبنا، نذهب، سنذهب، ذهبت، تذهب، ستذهب، ذهبتا، تذهبا، ... |

Table 1: Verb forms in English and Arabic.

## 3   Data

In this section, we describe the process of gathering and preparing the data used for training the embeddings. We do not require any training data for contextual embeddings since we do not require pretraining: we use Google's multilingual BERT model (Devlin et al., 2018), which supports 104 languages (including Arabic) and was trained on their respective Wikipedia dumps. For traditional embeddings, we use Arabic Wikipedia as a corpus. We downloaded the Wikipedia dump from January 2018 and then cleaned it by using WikiExtractor[1], which is a utility that generates plain text from an XML formatted Wikipedia dump. We then use a custom set of regexes to filter out all non-Arabic words, such as English words and numbers, and remove all diacritics and kashidas resulting in over 86 million tokens.

## 4   Approach

One example of Arabic's morphological complexity is in the number of verb forms it possesses which is much higher than in English as we can see in Table 1. While traditionally, this aspect of Arabic has been challenging to the natural language processing and computational linguistics communities (Farghaly and Shaalan, 2009; Al-Ayyoub et al., 2018), we asked whether we may benefit from this characteristic. Can we tokenize text differently for Arabic than we do for English, and would that result in better performance on NLP tasks? We experimented with two approaches; one applied to traditional embedding models (Word2Vec) and the other on contextual models (BERT).

### 4.1   Traditional Embedding Models

Traditional word embedding models are trained on a large corpus of text. The main difference in our approach is that we preprocess the text before feeding it into the embedding algorithm by splitting every word into subwords, which are its prefix(es), stem, and suffix(es) using Farasa, an Arabic segmenter,

---

[1]https://github.com/attardi/wikiextractor

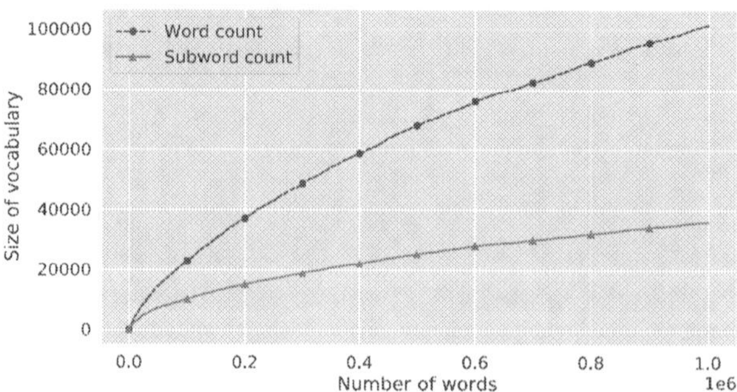


Figure 3: The increase in the size of the vocabulary when using words and subwords. The $x$-axis shows the number of words processed in the Arabic Wikipedia. The $y$-axis indicates the size of the vocabulary.

(Abdelali et al., 2016). The effect of using the Farasa segmenter can be seen in Figure 2[2], where each row of squares represents a vector. Then we train the resulting corpus using Word2Vec, though we note that our approach is embedding agnostic and may be used with any embedding model. Notice that our vocabulary, and the resulting vectors, will be completely different now as shown in Figure 2. It may seem at first glance that our vocabulary is increasing, but in fact it decreases as we keep adding more words as shown in Figure 3, which depicts the sizes of the vocabularies in the first million words in Arabic Wikipedia.

One question that comes to mind is how do we generate embeddings for words that were split into subwords because in most cases we want embeddings at the word level and not at the subword level. We propose the following technique for getting the embeddings of all types of words, including those with multiple subwords. For words with only one component, we just return the embeddings learnt by the model. For words with multiple components (subwords), we get the embedding of the longest subword, and the average of the embeddings of the remaining subwords. We then take a weighted average of the two values which results in our embedding as Equations 1 and 2 show.

$$l = \arg\max_{x \in S}(|x|) \tag{1}$$

$$v = \alpha * (M[l]) + (1 - \alpha) * \left( \sum_{x \in S \setminus \{l\}} \frac{M[x]}{n - 1} \right) \tag{2}$$

where $S$ is the set containing all the subwords contained in the word, $M$ is the learnt model that contains embeddings for all subwords, and $\alpha$ is a parameter that decides the weights between the longest subword and the other subwords. Algorithm 1 illustrates the algorithm used in determining embeddings for all cases.

This method not only allows us to generate embeddings for all words in the original corpus, but also increases its capacity to deal with out-of-vocabulary (OOV) words that the model has never seen before as shown in Figure 4. For example, in Figure 4, we see how our model can produce a representation of 'and their iPhone' which is one word in Arabic. A traditional model trained on the Arabic Wikipedia will fail to produce a representation of the word 'and their iPhone' because that word never appeared in Wikipedia. In fact, since there are many forms for each word, no matter how large the training corpus is, it is almost impossible for it to have seen occurrences of all possible forms of all words in it. Our model can tackle this problem because it operates on a subword level and has seen all the three components that make up the word: 'and', 'their' and 'iPhone' as shown in Figure 4. This procedure allows one to expand a model's vocabulary without retraining or requiring numerous examples of a given word. Of

---

[2]All transliterations in the paper follow the International Journal of Middle East Studies (IJMES) transliteration system.

---

**Algorithm 1** Generating embeddings of words from subwords

---

**function** GETEMBEDDING($word, \alpha, model$)
    **if** $word \in model$ **then**
        **return** $model[word]$
    **else**
        $S = \text{get\_components}(word)$
        **for** $s \in S$ **do**
            **if** $s \notin model$ **then**
                **return** $error$
        $l = argmax_{s \in S}(|x|)$
        $S = S - l$
        **return** $\alpha * (model[l]) + (1 - \alpha) * (sum([model[s] \text{ for } s \in S]) \div |S|)$

---

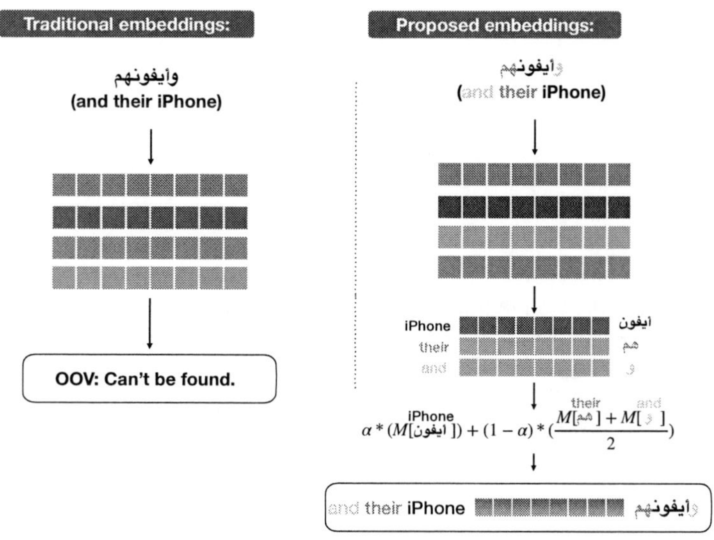


Figure 4: Dealing with out-of-vocabulary words in both the traditional models and our proposed model.

course, not all out-of-vocabulary words will be found this way. Nonetheless, it's a cheap way to generate representations of new words that is not possible in classical approaches.

## 4.2 Contextual Embedding Models

Transformer-based (Vaswani et al., 2017) contextual embedding models, such as BERT (Devlin et al., 2018), often require a tokenization step that solves problems such as the out-of-vocabulary issue. Byte-pair encoding (BPE) (Sennrich et al., 2015; Gage, 1994), one of the most popular tokenization methods relies on segmenting each word into the most frequent subwords. Shapiro and Duh (2018a) have shown that byte-pair encoding does not perform well for Arabic compared to other languages. One possible explanation of this is that byte-pair encoding does not include information derived from a given language's morphology. We did some experiments using BERT's pretrained tokenizer and found instances where the produced segments generated erroneous meanings. For example, the word *mal'ab* in most cases is a noun that refers to a stadium or field. BERT tokenizes *mal'ab* by segmenting it to *mal* (milliliter) and *'ab* (gulp or fill up), instead of the correct segmentation: *ma* (a prefix used to create nouns of place) and *l'ab* (play). BERT's segmentation seems to indicate that the word *mal'ab* is related to liquids and water (milliliter/gulp/fill up). Keep in mind that both *ma* and *l'ab* are in BERT's subword vocabulary.

We propose two methods that aim to incorporate a language's structure via better segmentations, which

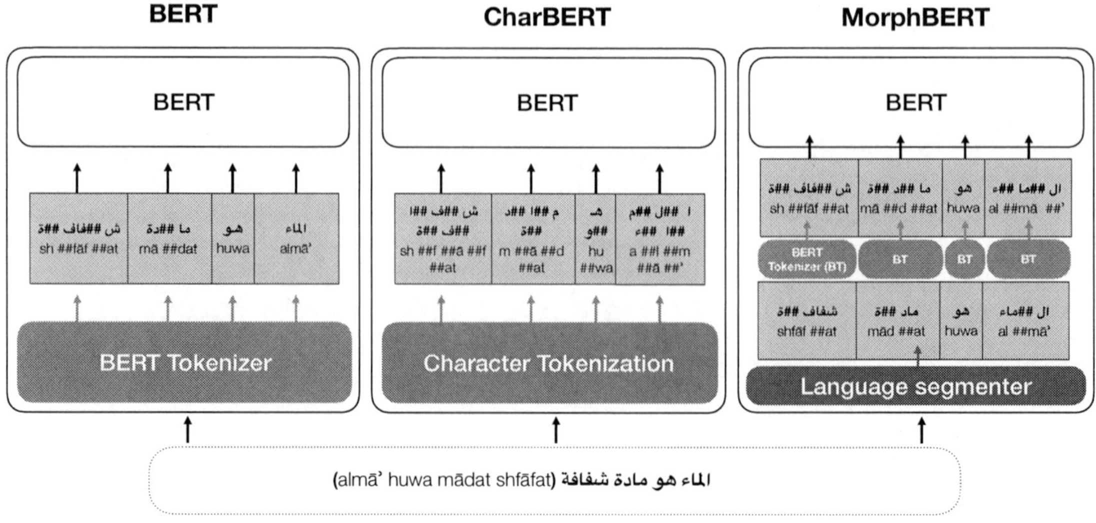


Figure 5: The different segmentation approaches: BERT (default tokenizer), CharBERT, and MorphBERT.

we call MorphBERT (Morphology BERT) and CharBERT (Character BERT). In MorphBERT, a custom tokenizer is used to replace the default tokenizer layer as seen in Figure 5. That custom tokenizer will use a language specific segmenter, Farasa (Abdelali et al., 2016) in our case, to segment each word before processing it. We then pass each word, after segmentation, to the original model's tokenizer to make sure that the produced segments are in the model's vocabulary. Keep in mind that MorphBERT differs from AraBERTv1 (Antoun et al., 2020), an Arabic BERT model that also utilizes Farasa, in that it does not require pretraining. In addition to that, Antoun et al. (2020) preprocess the training corpus by segmenting it using Farasa before training AraBERTv1 which is not the case with MorphBERT.

In CharBERT, we segment everything to characters as shown in Figure 5. The main idea behind CharBERT is to let the network learn these language structures on its own. Both of these models do not require training and can be used with any pretrained model as we see in Figure 5. This is important due to the expensive — money-wise, time-wise, and environment-wise — process of training BERT and other state of the art models. We believe that developing simpler, more sustainable, and more efficient NLP models is of an utmost importance due to the many problems that arise from computationally heavy models, (Strubell et al., 2019) which can take weeks to train on many TPUs/GPUs. Moreover, most people, especially in less developed countries, do not have the resources to train these models, which limits accessibility.

## 5 Experiments and Results

In this section we detail our experiments and highlight the results produced by the models we proposed.

### 5.1 Evaluation Datasets

For intrinsic evaluation of traditional embedding models we used the Arabic word analogy benchmark created by Elrazzaz et al. (2017). This dataset consists of nine relations that each consist of over 100 word pairs. We use the following datasets to evaluate our models extrinsically:

1. **APMD**: The Arab poem meters dataset (Alyafeai, 2020) which consists of 55,440 poem verses with each verse classified into one of the fourteen Arabic poetry meters. The data is split into training and testing sets.

| Dimension | | 50 | 100 | 200 |
|---|---|---|---|---|
| Skipgram | Base model | 5.76% | 8.33% | 8.88% |
| | Our model ($\alpha$=0.3) | 5.36% | 8.15% | 9.40% |
| CBOW | Base model | 6.00% | 8.72% | 10.05% |
| | Our model ($\alpha$=0.3) | **6.31%** | **8.92%** | **10.10%** |

Table 2: Top-1 accuracy in the word analogies test.

2. **HARD**: The Hotel Arabic Reviews Dataset (Elnagar et al., 2018) consists of 93,700 hotel reviews that are classified into positive or negative according to their rating. Reviews with a rating of four or five were assigned positive, and those with a rating of one or two were labeled negative. Reviews with a rating of three were ignored. We split the data into 80% and 20% training and testing sets respectively using the script provided by Antoun et al. (2020).

3. **LABR**: The Large-scale Arabic Book Reviews dataset (Aly and Atiya, 2013) consists of 63,000 book reviews rated between one and five. We use the unbalanced two-class dataset, where reviews with a rating of one or two are labeled negative, and those with a rating on four or five are labeled positive. The data is split into training and testing sets.

### 5.2 Traditional Embedding Models

#### 5.2.1 Intrinsic evaluation

Word analogies, which consists of sets of pairs that share a common relationship, are often used to evaluate different embedding techniques. For example, let's say that we have the following pairs: (king, queen), and (male, female). Both of these pairs contain a word that indicates masculinity and a second word that indicates the feminine version of the first word. A perfect word embedding representation should be able to capture this relationship, and the way to mathematically measure it is by calculating the vector king$-$male+female. After that, we check to see whether the resulting vector is the closest to the vector queen or not. We use the Arabic word analogy benchmark created by Elrazzaz et al. (2017) to evaluate our approach. We used Gensim's (Řehůřek and Sojka, 2010) word analogy evaluate function to evaluate the models and set the 'dummy4unknown' flag on so that all tuples of pairs that contain a word (or more) that are not in our vocabulary will get zero accuracy (instead of being skipped), similar to the procedure adopted by Elrazzaz et al. (2017).

We train two models: a vanilla Word2Vec model (base model) and our proposed model on the Arabic Wikipedia dataset mentioned in Section 3. For the base model, we set the window size to be five. Since our model segments words before learning embeddings, we compute the average number of subwords per word in our corpus and adjust the window size by that number. The average number of components per word is around two (1.97); to account for that we set window size in our model to be be ten instead of five. For both, we set the number of epochs to be equal to ten. We experimented with multiple $\alpha$ values for our proposed model and found that setting it to 0.3 achieves the best results. Moreover, to avoid vocabulary size discrepancies, we standardize the vocabulary size before the evaluation by ensuring that our model has the same vocabulary as the base model. To do that, we create a new empty set and go through all vocabulary in the base model and if the word exists in our model (words with only one subword) then we add its representation to the set; otherwise, we decompose it and then add its representation according to equation 2. The results are summarized in Table 2. Our method performs as well, if not better, than the Word2Vec while being around $60\%$ smaller in size. The difference in size come from the vocabulary size which is 155K for our model compared to 383K for the base model. We also notice that CBOW performs better than Skip-gram which is consistent with previous research findings (Elrazzaz et al., 2017).

#### 5.2.2 OOV Handling

One important distinction that separates our model from the base model is its ability to accommodate OOV words. To test the quality of these generated OOV vectors, we go through all the OOV words in our analogy benchmark and generate vectors for the ones we can, i.e. the ones for which we have entries

|           | Accuracy (without OOV handling) | Accuracy (with OOV handling) |
|-----------|---------------------------------|------------------------------|
| FastText  | 8.05%                           | 6.44%                        |
| Our model | 10.10%                          | 13.32%                       |

Table 3: Performance of our model compared to fastText when generating vectors for OOV words.

|            | APMD    | LABR    | HARD    |
|------------|---------|---------|---------|
| Base model | 29.95%  | 86.18%  | 92.99%  |
| Our model  | **37.75%** | **86.21%** | **93.09%** |

Table 4: Performance (accuracy) of our model compared to the base model on the three datasets.

for all their respective subwords. The total number of OOV words is 127 and we are able to generate representations for 70 of them covering 55.12% of all the OOV words. After that we follow a similar procedure to the one we have done in the previous subsection and check how the accuracy has been affected. We evaluated the performance of our best performing model (CBOW, dim=200) and found that adding the OOV representations increased the accuracy from 10.10% to 13.32%. To compare our OOV representations, we trained a fastText (Bojanowski et al., 2016) model, a popular embedding approach that can handle OOV, and then calculated the accuracy before adding the OOV entities and after; keep in mind that the vocabulary size in both, fastText and our model, will be the same. FastText achieves 8.05% before adding the OOV entities and 6.44% after adding them as shown in Table 3. Not only did fastText achieve worse gains than our model, it actually performs worse than before which calls to question the accuracy of fastText's OOV embeddings for Arabic.

### 5.2.3 Extrinsic Evaluation

We evaluate our approach on the three datasets mentioned above. We feed the embeddings of the words to a bidirectional Gated Recurrent Units (GRU) (Cho et al., 2014) network to train it. After that, we evaluate the network on the test set. Table 4 shows the performance of our model compared to the base model. We can see that our model clearly outperforms the base model in one dataset (APMD) and performs slightly better on the two other datasets (LABR and HARD).

### 5.3 Contextual Embedding Models

We fine-tune the three models: the base cased multilingual BERT, MorphBERT, and CharBERT; and then compare their performances on the three datasets mentioned above. We follow the recommendations from BERT's paper (Devlin et al., 2018) in setting the fine-tuning hyperparameters. We run them all for four epochs in batches of 32 or 16 depending on the lengths of input sequences to avoid memory issues on the GPU. We optimize using the Adam algorithm with a learning rate of $2e^{-5}$, $\beta 1 = 0.9$, and $\beta 2 = 0.999$. We also compare our models to AraBERT (AraBERTv0.1 and AraBERTv1) which consists of two monolingual BERT models trained on Arabic that were proposed by Antoun et al. (2020) and use the results reported by them for LABR and HARD. For APMD, we downloaded their models and fine-tuned them on the task. We also evaluate our models on the cleaned ANERcorp (Benajiba and Rosso, 2007; Antoun et al., 2020) NER dataset. For ANERcorp, we used the script provided by Antoun et al. (2020) in fine-tuning our models. Table 5 shows the performance of the five models on the downstream tasks.

It is interesting that by just changing the tokenization method we can improve BERT's performance in Arabic without retraining. As we can see in Table 5, MorphBERT and CharBERT achieve state of the art performance on LABR and APMD respectively. The previous state of the art model for LABR is the MCE-CNN model proposed by Dahou et al. (2019) which achieves an accuracy of 87.48%. Our models perform better than AraBERT in two tasks even though AraBERT was: 1) trained specifically for Arabic, and 2) trained on a larger Arabic corpus: 24GB of data for AraBERT compared to 4.3GB for the multilingual BERT. Although MultiBERT was trained on over a hundred languages, simply replacing tokenizations allowed us to add language specific information without requiring any training. While normally byte pair encoding learns representations of subwords without paying attention to their

| | metric | MultiBERT | MorphBERT | CharBERT | AraBERTv0.1 | AraBERTv1 |
|---|---|---|---|---|---|---|
| APMD | accuracy | 70.65% | 71.03% | **84.09%** | 70.02% | 60.99% |
| LABR | accuracy | 85.85% | **89.87%** | 85.89% | 85.90% | 86.70% |
| HARD | accuracy | 95.96% | 95.86% | 95.67% | 96.20% | **96.20%** |
| ANERcorp | macro-F1 | 78.4% | 79.86% | 71.76% | **89.17%** | 88.67% |

Table 5: Performance of MorphBERT and CharBERT compared to the multilingual BERT (MultiBERT), AraBERTv0.1, and AraBERTv1

meaning, we can utilize this procedure of breaking words into chunks that make more sense as we saw in the *mal'ab* example before. CharBERT in particular is interesting; one would expect that it will require more time to fine-tune since it only uses characters. Nevertheless, it achieves great performance without requiring more epochs than the other methods. One potential issue with CharBERT is that it results in very long sequences due to the character segmentation approach it follows which lead to more frequent truncations than other models. One potential way to mitigate this is by using new models such as Longformer (Beltagy et al., 2020) that allow longer sequences than BERT.

Previous research (Virtanen et al., 2019; Antoun et al., 2020; Vries et al., 2019; Martin et al., 2020) has shown that a language specific BERT model performs better than a multilingual one. This is the first work, according to our knowledge, that shows that by tweaking a multilingual BERT model one can beat a BERT model trained on a specific language. Natural language processing entered a new era with the advent of pretrained models that do not need to be trained from scratch for every task but can simply be tweaked/fine-tuned instead. Our results shows that it may be possible to only have one multilingual model that can be tweaked instead of learning a pretrained model for every language.

## 6 Related Work

Many works have noted how sensitivity to Arabic's morphological complexity can result in better performance in standard NLP tasks. However, we do not know of any previous work that has specifically focused on the effect of tokenization on different Arabic embedding models. Antoun et al. (2020) trained an Arabic specific BERT model. They also trained another Arabic BERT model in which they segment the text before training the model and showed that it usually improves performance. Taylor and Brychcín (2018) analyzed morphological relations in Arabic word embeddings. They noted that some morphological features are captured in embeddings representations. Shapiro and Duh (2018b) proposed utilizing subword information in training embeddings to enrich the representations and showed that it improves the performance on word similarity tasks. Salama et al. (2018) investigated morphological-based embeddings and lemma-based embeddings. They utilized part-of-speech information to train their embeddings, similar to Trask et al. (2015), and then build lemma-based embeddings from them by aggregating on different senses of each word first and them combining words that share the same lemma. El-Kishky et al. (2019) tackled the problem of extracting roots of words and proposed an extension to fastText (Bojanowski et al., 2016) that utilize morphemes.

## 7 Conclusion

We show that tokenization that pays attention to Arabic's morphology can create better traditional and contextual embedding models. Breaking words into subwords in Word2Vec not only leads to an increase in performance and reduction in the vocabulary size and hence the model size, but also provides a simple way to produce good out-of-vocabulary representations. We also show the importance of tokenization in BERT where we were able to achieve impressive performance without requiring any pretraining. One possible future work would be to investigate tokenization's effect in other morphologically rich languages such as Hebrew and Turkish and see if our results can be generalized to other highly inflected languages.

# References


Ahmed Abdelali, Kareem Darwish, Nadir Durrani, and Hamdy Mubarak. 2016. Farasa: A fast and furious segmenter for Arabic. In *Proceedings of the 2016 Conference of the North American Chapter of the Association for Computational Linguistics: Demonstrations*, pages 11–16, San Diego, California, June. Association for Computational Linguistics.

Mahmoud Al-Ayyoub, Aya Nuseir, Kholoud Alsmearat, Yaser Jararweh, and Brij Gupta. 2018. Deep learning for arabic nlp: A survey. *Journal of computational science*, 26:522–531.

Mohamed Aly and Amir Atiya. 2013. LABR: A large scale Arabic book reviews dataset. In *Proceedings of the 51st Annual Meeting of the Association for Computational Linguistics (Volume 2: Short Papers)*, pages 494–498, Sofia, Bulgaria, August. Association for Computational Linguistics.

Zaid Alyafeai. 2020. ARBML. https://github.com/zaidalyafeai/ARBML, January.

Wissam Antoun, Fady Baly, and Hazem Hajj. 2020. AraBERT: Transformer-based model for Arabic language understanding. In *Proceedings of the 4th Workshop on Open-Source Arabic Corpora and Processing Tools, with a Shared Task on Offensive Language Detection*, pages 9–15, Marseille, France, May. European Language Resource Association.

Iz Beltagy, Matthew E. Peters, and Arman Cohan. 2020. Longformer: The long-document transformer. *arXiv:2004.05150*.

Yassine Benajiba and Paolo Rosso. 2007. Anersys 2.0: Conquering the ner task for the arabic language by combining the maximum entropy with pos-tag information. In *IICAI*, pages 1814–1823.

Piotr Bojanowski, Edouard Grave, Armand Joulin, and Tomas Mikolov. 2016. Enriching word vectors with subword information. *arXiv preprint arXiv:1607.04606*.

Kyunghyun Cho, Bart van Merriënboer, Dzmitry Bahdanau, and Yoshua Bengio. 2014. On the properties of neural machine translation: Encoder–decoder approaches. In *Proceedings of SSST-8, Eighth Workshop on Syntax, Semantics and Structure in Statistical Translation*, pages 103–111, Doha, Qatar, October. Association for Computational Linguistics.

Abdelghani Dahou, Shengwu Xiong, Junwei Zhou, and Mohamed Abd Elaziz. 2019. Multi-channel embedding convolutional neural network model for arabic sentiment classification. *ACM Trans. Asian Low-Resour. Lang. Inf. Process.*, 18(4), May.

Jacob Devlin, Ming-Wei Chang, Kenton Lee, and Kristina Toutanova. 2018. Bert: Pre-training of deep bidirectional transformers for language understanding. *arXiv preprint arXiv:1810.04805*.

Ahmed El-Kishky, Xingyu Fu, Aseel Addawood, Nahil Sobh, Clare Voss, and Jiawei Han. 2019. Constrained sequence-to-sequence Semitic root extraction for enriching word embeddings. In *Proceedings of the Fourth Arabic Natural Language Processing Workshop*, pages 88–96, Florence, Italy, August. Association for Computational Linguistics.

Ashraf Elnagar, Yasmin S. Khalifa, and Anas Einea, 2018. *Hotel Arabic-Reviews Dataset Construction for Sentiment Analysis Applications*, pages 35–52. Springer International Publishing, Cham.

Mohammed Elrazzaz, Shady Elbassuoni, Khaled Shaban, and Chadi Helwe. 2017. Methodical evaluation of Arabic word embeddings. In *Proceedings of the 55th Annual Meeting of the Association for Computational Linguistics (Volume 2: Short Papers)*, pages 454–458, Vancouver, Canada, July. Association for Computational Linguistics.

Ali Farghaly and Khaled Shaalan. 2009. Arabic natural language processing: Challenges and solutions. *ACM Transactions on Asian Language Information Processing (TALIP)*, 8(4):1–22.

Philip Gage. 1994. A new algorithm for data compression. *C Users Journal*, 12(2):23–38.

Edouard Grave, Piotr Bojanowski, Prakhar Gupta, Armand Joulin, and Tomas Mikolov. 2018. Learning word vectors for 157 languages. In *Proceedings of the International Conference on Language Resources and Evaluation (LREC 2018)*.

Zellig S Harris. 1954. Distributional structure. *Word*, 10(2-3):146–162.

Armand Joulin, Edouard Grave, Piotr Bojanowski, and Tomas Mikolov. 2016. Bag of tricks for efficient text classification. *arXiv preprint arXiv:1607.01759*.

Yinhan Liu, Myle Ott, Naman Goyal, Jingfei Du, Mandar Joshi, Danqi Chen, Omer Levy, Mike Lewis, Luke Zettlemoyer, and Veselin Stoyanov. 2019. Roberta: A robustly optimized bert pretraining approach. *arXiv preprint arXiv:1907.11692*.

Louis Martin, Benjamin Muller, Pedro Javier Ortiz Suárez, Yoann Dupont, Laurent Romary, Éric Villemonte de la Clergerie, Djamé Seddah, and Benoît Sagot. 2020. Camembert: a tasty french language model. In *Proceedings of the 58th Annual Meeting of the Association for Computational Linguistics*.

Tomas Mikolov, Kai Chen, Greg Corrado, and Jeffrey Dean. 2013a. Efficient estimation of word representations in vector space. *arXiv preprint arXiv:1301.3781*.

Tomas Mikolov, Ilya Sutskever, Kai Chen, Greg S Corrado, and Jeff Dean. 2013b. Distributed representations of words and phrases and their compositionality. In *Advances in neural information processing systems*, pages 3111–3119.

Jeffrey Pennington, Richard Socher, and Christopher Manning. 2014. Glove: Global vectors for word representation. In *Proceedings of the 2014 conference on empirical methods in natural language processing (EMNLP)*, pages 1532–1543.

Matthew Peters, Mark Neumann, Mohit Iyyer, Matt Gardner, Christopher Clark, Kenton Lee, and Luke Zettlemoyer. 2018. Deep contextualized word representations. In *Proceedings of the 2018 Conference of the North American Chapter of the Association for Computational Linguistics: Human Language Technologies, Volume 1 (Long Papers)*, pages 2227–2237, New Orleans, Louisiana, June. Association for Computational Linguistics.

Radim Řehůřek and Petr Sojka. 2010. Software Framework for Topic Modelling with Large Corpora. In *Proceedings of the LREC 2010 Workshop on New Challenges for NLP Frameworks*, pages 45–50, Valletta, Malta, May. ELRA. http://is.muni.cz/publication/884893/en.

Rana Aref Salama, Abdou Youssef, and Aly Fahmy. 2018. Morphological word embedding for arabic. *Procedia computer science*, 142:83 93.

Rico Sennrich, Barry Haddow, and Alexandra Birch. 2015. Neural machine translation of rare words with subword units. *arXiv preprint arXiv:1508.07909*.

Pamela Shapiro and Kevin Duh. 2018a. Bpe and charcnns for translation of morphology: A cross-lingual comparison and analysis. *arXiv preprint arXiv:1809.01301*.

Pamela Shapiro and Kevin Duh. 2018b. Morphological word embeddings for Arabic neural machine translation in low-resource settings. In *Proceedings of the Second Workshop on Subword/Character LEvel Models*, pages 1–11, New Orleans, June. Association for Computational Linguistics.

Abu Bakr Soliman, Kareem Eissa, and Samhaa R El-Beltagy. 2017. Aravec: A set of arabic word embedding models for use in arabic nlp. *Procedia Computer Science*, 117:256–265.

Emma Strubell, Ananya Ganesh, and Andrew McCallum. 2019. Energy and policy considerations for deep learning in NLP. In *Proceedings of the 57th Annual Meeting of the Association for Computational Linguistics*, pages 3645–3650, Florence, Italy, July. Association for Computational Linguistics.

Stephen Taylor and Tomáš Brychcín. 2018. The representation of some phrases in arabic word semantic vector spaces. *Open Computer Science*, 8(1):182–193.

Andrew Trask, Phil Michalak, and John Liu. 2015. sense2vec-a fast and accurate method for word sense disambiguation in neural word embeddings. *arXiv preprint arXiv:1511.06388*.

Ashish Vaswani, Noam Shazeer, Niki Parmar, Jakob Uszkoreit, Llion Jones, Aidan N Gomez, ukasz Kaiser, and Illia Polosukhin. 2017. Attention is all you need. In *Advances in neural information processing systems*, pages 5998–6008.

Antti Virtanen, Jenna Kanerva, Rami Ilo, Jouni Luoma, Juhani Luotolahti, Tapio Salakoski, Filip Ginter, and Sampo Pyysalo. 2019. Multilingual is not enough: Bert for finnish.

Wietse de Vries, Andreas van Cranenburgh, Arianna Bisazza, Tommaso Caselli, Gertjan van Noord, and Malvina Nissim. 2019. BERTje: A Dutch BERT Model. *arXiv:1912.09582 [cs]*, December.

# Tracing Traditions: Automatic Extraction of Isnads from Classical Arabic Texts

**Ryan Muther and David Smith**
Northeastern University
Boston, MA
{muther.r, davi.smith}@northeastern.edu

## Abstract

We present our work on automatically detecting *isnads*, the chains of authorities for a report that serve as citations in hadith and other classical Arabic texts. We experiment with both sequence labeling methods for identifying isnads in a single pass and a hybrid "retrieve-and-tag" approach, in which a retrieval model first identifies portions of the text that are likely to contain start points for *isnads*, then a sequence labeling model identifies the exact starting locations within these much smaller retrieved text chunks. We find that the usefulness of full-document sequence to sequence models is limited due to memory limitations and the ineffectiveness of such models at modeling very long documents. We conclude by sketching future improvements on the tagging task and more in-depth analysis of the people and relationships involved in the social network that influenced the evolution of the written tradition over time.

## 1 Introduction

In classical Arabic texts, lists of the names of authorities that transmitted a piece of information (*isnads*) are often attached to a statement or report (the *matn)* to confirm its reliability. The study of *isnads* is an integral part of the study of *hadith* and the history of the Arabic written tradition in general. With the increasing availability of digitized texts, new methods are required to automatically locate and analyze *isnads* at scale in a wider variety of text than the canonical *hadith* collections used in smaller-scale studies (Harrag et al, 2014; Maraoui et al, 2019, Altammami et al, 2019). *Isnads* are often seamlessly integrated into running text, and are therefore difficult to distinguish from the surrounding text based on visual layout or punctuation information alone. The textual content of the *isnad* itself must therefore be used to determine its location. For instance, in the example *hadith* below, the names and transmissive terms indicate that the underlined section in the beginning of the text is the *isnad*, while the remainder is the *matn*.

حدثنا أبو داود قال: حدثنا هشام، عن قتادة، عن الحسن عن سمرة، أن النبي صلى الله عليه وسلم: قال

من قتل عبده قتلناه ومن جدعه جدعناه ومن خصاه خصيناه

"Abū Dāwūd transmitted to us, he said, 'Hishām transmitted to us, from Qatādah, from al-Ḥasan, from Samurah that the Prophet, may the peace and blessing of God be on him, said, 'Whoever kills his slave, we will kill; and whoever mutilates, we will mutilate him; and whoever emasculates, we will emasculate him.'" (Sulaymān, 204AH)

In theory, one could also extract the body of the *hadith*, but there are fewer significant linguistic cues that set a *matn* apart from the background text than there are for its corresponding *isnad*. Once one has





*Proceedings of the Fifth Arabic Natural Language Processing Workshop*, pages 130–138
Barcelona, Spain (Online), December 12, 2020

amassed a large collection of *isnads*, one could begin to extract the relationships between individual transmitters, as well as infer the exact identities of transmitters given the relationship network's structure and the variety of names used for the same individual. This would allow humanists to draw a larger scale picture of the evolution of the Arabic written tradition than has previously been possible by analyzing the social network involved in both the creation of individual texts and the corpus as a whole.

Long documents often contain passages in an *embedded genre*, distinct from the surrounding text. We can locate certain kinds of embedded texts using visual layout information to segment the text into smaller units, like articles in a newspaper, which could then be classified using any number of text classification methods (Lee et al, 2020), or using formatting and punctuation cues to locate poetic passages embedded in prose works (Lorang et al., 2015; Foley, 2019). If one does not have the ability to divide the text up into sufficiently granular units, or the embedded genre of interest is not easily separable from the surrounding background text using layout cues alone (e.g., indented lines of poetry), these approaches are not possible. However, *isnads* tend to have linguistic cues that indicate their presence, like the presence of a large number of names or particular transmissive terms in a small region of the text. In this paper we will follow a two-step approach to solving the problem of identifying *isnads* in long documents by first applying a retrieval model to find sections of a document likely to contain start points of *isnads*, then training a sequence tagging model on the retrieved sections to identify where within those spans the *isnads* begin. Upcoming work will involve inferring the endpoints of the *isnads* given the start points identified by the tagging model using a span prediction model.

This paper is organized as follows; in section 2 we present an overview of related work. Section 3 provides a deeper discussion of the data sources we use for our experiments. In section 4, we present the results of an inter-annotator agreement study done as part of the process of creating training data as a benchmark for human performance on the task. Section 5 discusses the models used in our experiments, as well as hyperparameters and training processes. Section 6 presents the results of our evaluation. Section 7 presents possible avenues of future work.

## 2   Related Work

This work is closely related to the problem of named entity recognition. Most named entity recognition models are evaluated using datasets like the CoNLL 2003 dataset (Tjong and de Meulder, 2003). In contrast to our data, the target entities in such datasets are at most a few words long, the training and test documents are much smaller than the whole texts we are working with, and almost all documents contain named entities. Neural models such as the BiLSTM and BiLSTM-CRF, as used by (Lample et al, 2016) have been shown to perform well on a performing named entity recognition in multiple languages. Additionally, a great deal of effort has been expended to improve the performance of named entity recognition on short documents like those found on social media sites like Twitter (e.g., Ritter, 2011). We seek to do the opposite, and explore performance on longer documents. While we could have approached the tasks described above as named entity recognition tasks, looking for names in *isnads* in particular, downstream tasks like information extraction or network inference would likely benefit from the additional structure present in the text around the names.

Unlike prior work on automatic *hadith* tagging, we focus exclusively on trying to identify *isnads*, rather than also trying to simultaneously extract the corresponding *matn* for each chain (Harrag et al, 2014; Maraoui et al, 2019, Altammami et al, 2019) or extract information from the identified isnads (Siddiqui et al, 2014), as others have done. We are working with a much larger and correspondingly more diverse collection of texts, rather than limiting our analysis to *hadith* collections. Finally, much of the existing work, like that cited above, focuses on using rule-based systems to identify isnads and the individual transmitters within them which limits the generalizability of these models to previously unseen texts.

## 3   Data and Preprocessing

The data for these experiments comes the Open Islamicate Texts Initiative (OpenITI) corpus (Romanov and Seydi, 2019,) a collection of 4,285 transcribed texts in classical Arabic collected from digital libraries by scholars from the University of Vienna and University of Leipzig totaling 1.5 billion words. The individual documents in the OpenITI corpus are complete texts and are often quite long, with the longest single text containing over 112 million words. The texts in the corpus are largely unpunctuated, and what punctuation there is is a modern editorial intervention, so we have removed punctuation from the texts when it exists.[2] Additionally, training any models on punctuated text would harm the performance on the model on the unpunctuated texts that make up the majority of the corpus. Since most of the corpus is unpunctuated, it is difficult to break the texts down into smaller units than complete texts. We have also performed orthographic normalization to remove different variants of the same character so that the model is not influenced by the orthographic choices of any particular author.

The training dataset we have created consist of data from fifty labeled texts, with 163 distinct tagged regions of text. While *isnads* are most common in *hadith* collections, they are also commonly used in historical writing, exegesis (*tafsir*), geographies, and literature. The specific texts were chosen over the course of several rounds of annotation, in which a CRF was trained and tested on existing training data, then the resultant tags in were analyzed by scholars to see where the model tended to fail to properly label *isnads*. When a weakness was found, new texts were selected that, in the experts' opinion, contain examples that could be used to give the model an understanding of how to avoid such failures in the future. In total, the tagged text consists of 907,110 tokens containing 3,071 *isnads*. The average length of the isnads in the tagged data is 31.9 tokens.

## 4   Inter-Annotator Agreement Study

To create training data for this task, we have used an iterative process of human-in-the-loop model training. Working in conjunction with experts in the fields of Islamic history and religious studies with a strong command of classical Arabic, we began by annotating a single text. Using these initial annotations, a CRF with token features (see section 5) was trained and used to automatically annotate other texts, which were then corrected by the annotators, creating additional training data while being able to use the automatic tags as a starting point. This not only makes annotation easier, as it presents the annotators with the task of modifying pre-existing tags created by the model rather than inserting tags from scratch, but also can be used to create training data that specifically addresses failures by the previous version of the model. As an illustrative example, one version of the model would often mislabel lists of students in a scholar's biography as chains of transmission, likely due to the presence of a high number of names in those regions of the text and a lack of examples to the contrary which would encourage the model not to label such sections as chains of transmission. This annotation process allowed the annotators to recognize that particular kind of language as a failure point of the model and create new training data which the model can use as evidence that those sorts of linguistic constructs are not chains of transmission. If the human annotators did not perform this process with the initial output from the model, it is possible that their annotations would not catch these sorts of cases, resulting in a less useful training dataset. By specifically providing examples of the kinds of data that confuse the model, we end up with a model whose judgements more closely resemble those of humans over several iterations, both as a result of the increased training data and the careful selection of the new text to annotate.

To get some understanding of how difficult the task of labeling *isnads* actually is for humans, we performed an inter-annotator agreement study using data from five of the annotators involved, each of whom annotated the same text, totaling 2000 lines of text across different sections of one work. Token level agreement between individual annotators is reported in Figure 1a, while the variance in the locations of start and end points of overlapping labeled spans is shown in Figure 1b. Overall, we see high agreement at the token level, which indicates that the task is not overly difficult for expert annotators, with Krippendorf's α of 0.84 indicating very strong agreement across all raters. Additionally, when multiple annotators marked overlapping spans, they all agreed on the starting point of the span seventy percent of the time, while the location of the endpoints varied more often, with complete agreement among the annotators occurring only fifty-three percent of the time. However, the vast majority of the disagreements were very small. The outliers in figure 1b were found to be mostly cases where annotators merged two adjacent *isnads*. This is a rare occurrence in the training data, with around three percent of identified *isnads* beginning right after the end of an *isnad*. There are two main points to take from this annotation when evaluating the results of any model attempting to solve this task. First,

---



[2] Similar to how Latin was largely unpunctuated prior to the introduction of printing, with verbs acting as sentence end markers, in classical Arabic certain words or phrases indicate transitions between sentences and clauses in lieu of punctuation. For more information, see https://www.britannica.com/topic/punctuation/Punctuation-in-Asian-and-African-languages

that identifying the end points is more difficult then identifying the start points for this particular task, and second, that properly segmenting adjacent spans is difficult even for human annotators.

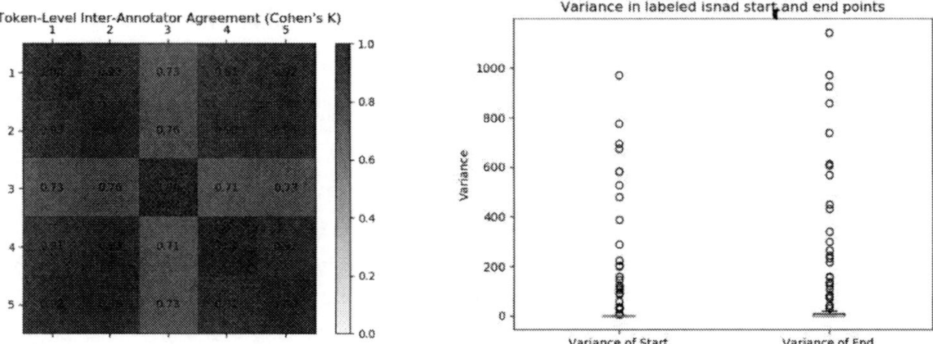

Figure 1. Inter-annotator agreement (1a, at left) and variance (1b, at right, in tokens) statistics

## 5 Experiments

### 5.1 Sequence Tagging Models

We initially experimented with solving this task by sequence labeling alone. These models tag every token in an input document as either the beginning of an *isnad* ("B"), inside an *isnad* ("I") or outside an *isnad* ("O"), as would be done for tasks like named entity recognition. As a baseline for comparison, we train CRF models (Lafferty et al., 2001) using counts within a fixed-size window on either side of the word to be tagged as well as the token to be tagged itself as features for the model. Thus, if the word "the" occurred twice before the token being tagged, the feature "the_before" would be created with the value 2. We also investigated using unsupported features (features for words that do not occur), but this created a large number of features that made model training too memory-intensive. The intuition behind these features is that the spans of text we seek to identify share common language that these features will enable the model to learn. Additionally, this form of model is able to use negative examples provided by the annotation to learn how the context of a word affects its likelihood of membership in a target span. Using information about the words around the word it is trying to tag, the model is able to learn how the context of a word affects its meaning, and not naively assume that all instances of the same word should be treated equally. One might try to solve this problem by training a pair of language models using example isnads to train an *isnad*-specific model and a general background model. Using these two models, one could attempt to label entire spans using the ratio of log odds between the two models to decide how to segment a text into *isnad* and background sections using a Viterbi-like inference method rather than making decisions at the level of individual tokens. However, such a model's inability to understand context would result in a model with no ability to determine when common words in the embedded genre should and should not be treated as part of one, giving many false positives as single words common in the embedded genre would often be labeled as part of one, regardless of their context.

We also train CRFs using 200-dimensional GloVe embeddings trained on the complete OpenITI corpus using the default parameters (Pennington et al, 2014) as features, concatenating the embeddings of the words within a window around the token to be tagged and using that as input to the model. Since different authors have different styles of citation, using different terms to indicate transmission, and draw from different sources, thus including different names in their chains, the unseen texts in the test set will contain chains that have a distinct vocabulary from those seen by the model in training. For the surface level token features described above, such mismatches in vocabulary are tokens that the model has no ability to understand the meaning of, as it never encountered them in training. Using the distributed representation provided by the GloVe embeddings, the model can leverage information about tokens with similar distributional semantics (i.e. other names or transmissive terms with similar embeddings) and gain some understanding of the meaning of an unknown token through its similarity to previously-seen ones, improving the generalizability of the model to previously unseen texts.

Additionally, we train a BiLSTM (Hochreiter and Schmidhuber, 1997; Graves, 2005) with a hidden layer size of 100 using 200-dimensional word embeddings fitted to each of the corpora, as discussed above. To speed up training, make processing long documents feasible, and avoid the known issues LSTMs have when modeling long documents, we split the documents in the OpenITI corpus into chunks of no more than 1000 words which are then used to train the model. After training, the results for the chunks are then concatenated to get results for the complete document. While this may cause issues when the chunking process splits the target spans into two pieces, the length of the chunks can be chosen such that the risk of that occurring is minimized. Furthermore, the chunks from within a document are padded with special symbols distinct from those used at the beginning and end of a document, allowing the model to learn that certain chunk beginnings are more likely to be part of the embedded genre, despite the lack of starting context provided by the beginning of the span. Although such splits are not impossible to recover from with sufficient training, they still present a nontrivial issue. This issue, in conjunction with memory limitations related to tagging very long texts in caused us to shift focus and move from trying to detect the spans with a single model to a two-step retrieve-and-tag approach to only detect start points, eliminating both the computational expense of modeling very long texts using these sequence to sequence models and the possibility of missing an isnad due to splitting it across chunks.

## 5.2 Retrieval-Tagging Models

If we are going to split the documents into chunks, it is worth noting that only 30% of the 100-token chunks contain starting points of *isnads*. Consequently, it may be beneficial to first filter out chunks that are unlikely to contain *isnad* starting points. The first step in the process of finding the starting points of is that of document retrieval. The two-stage retrieval-tagging models are trained as follows. First, the corpus is divided into training, validation, and test sets, where the retrieved test documents will ultimately be used to evaluate performance on the start point labeling task. In order to train the retrieval model, for which we use a bag-of-words logistic regression model, the test documents are divided into two halves at random and each document in both halves is divided into chunks of at most some fixed size, we experiment with the sizes {25, 50, 75, 100}. The chunks in each half of the training set are used to train a retrieval model to retrieve documents containing *isnad* start points which is used to retrieve documents in the other half of the training set. The union of these two sets of retrieved documents are used as training data for the tagging model. The whole training dataset is then used to train a retrieval model to retrieve chunks from the test data. Using the complete set of retrieved chunks from the training data and the retrieved chunks from the test data, we then train a single layer LSTM with hidden layer size of 100 to tag tokens as beginning an *isnad* or not using 200-dimensional GloVe embeddings as our starting token representations.

For the retrieval model, we experiment with a variety of different parameter settings to obtain a high upper bound on the recall of the overall model, which we measure through an oracle experiment in which all retrieved chunks are tagged perfectly. Table 1 below presents an overview of the different feature sets and chunk sizes used. We experiment with unigram, bigram, and trigram features, as well as choosing to weight the features by TFIDF scores or not. As we can see, longer documents tend to be easier to retrieve, while bigrams tend to give the best performance, and TFIDF scoring significantly improves performance. It is possible that informative trigram features generalize less well across texts and between authors due to variations in the sources, and thus in the names that occur in *isnads*, resulting in lower retrieval performance.

| Features | Chunk Size | Recall | Features | Chunk Size | Recall |
|---|---|---|---|---|---|
| Unigram | 25 | .767 | Unigram, TFIDF | 25 | .854 |
| Unigram | 50 | .848 | Unigram, TFIDF | 50 | .886 |
| Unigram | 75 | .872 | Unigram, TFIDF | 75 | .896 |
| Unigram | 100 | .860 | Unigram, TFIDF | 100 | .941 |
| Bigram | 25 | .802 | Bigram, TFIDF | 25 | .913 |
| Bigram | 50 | .857 | Bigram, TFIDF | 50 | .915 |
| Bigram | 75 | .887 | Bigram, TFIDF | 75 | .959 |
| Bigram | 100 | .849 | Bigram, TFIDF | 100 | .935 |
| Trigram | 25 | .784 | Trigram, TFIDF | 25 | .896 |
| Trigram | 50 | .802 | Trigram, TFIDF | 50 | .943 |
| Trigram | 75 | .864 | Trigram, TFIDF | 75 | .954 |
| Trigram | 100 | .874 | Trigram, TFIDF | 100 | .939 |

Table 1. Recall scores for retrieval models using various feature sets and chunk sizes with an oracle tagger.

Additionally, for each model, we select a retrieval threshold which optimizes the F2 (recall-weighted F-score) of the resultant model. The default threshold of 0.5 tended to have comparatively low recall at the chunk level, as can be seen in Figure 2, which presents an example precision-recall curve for a retrieval model with 2-gram, TFIDF-weighted features and a chunk size of 75. Note that chunk level recall (the fraction of chunks that contain *isnad* beginnings that are retrieved, rather than the fraction of *isnad* beginnings that are retrieved) is only around 0.2 with the default retrieval threshold of 0.5, while if a threshold around 0.15 were used, recall would be around 0.95 at the cost of only a small drop in precision. This has the added advantage of adding the "attractive distractors" that were mislabeled by the retrieval model to the training and test set for the tagging model, while those chunks that, from the retrieval model's perspective, clearly do not contain the starting point of an isnad are excluded. This results in training and test sets that do not contain the very easy examples that the retrieval model can dismiss, focusing the training data on the more informative examples. Other parameter settings exhibit this same trend, albeit with different optimal operating points and upper bounds on recall. For the later experiments with *isnad* start labeling, we will use a bigram retrieval model with TFIDF scores and a chunk size of 75, as it gives the highest upper bound on recall in this corpus, with an optimal threshold of 0.14.

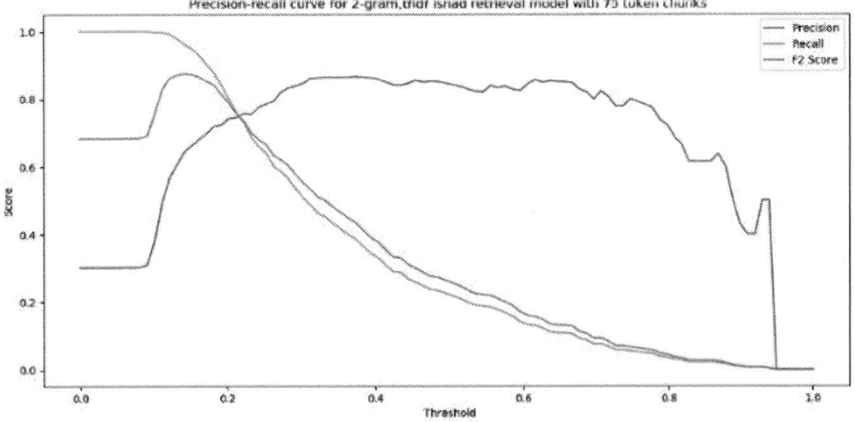


Figure 2: Example precision-recall curve for an *isnad* beginning retrieval model

# 6 Evaluation

## 6.1 Tagging Results

The token-based CRF, in addition to detecting start points, also labels tokens as part of an *isnad* using the "I" tag, as noted above. As such, we can evaluate not just the ability of the model the find starting point, but at identifying entire isnads. It should be noted that all results are given for models using eighty percent of the data for training, and ten percent each as validation and test data. The results for this task can be seen in Table 2 below.

| Exact Precision | Exact Recall | Exact F1 | Partial Precision | Partial Recall | Partial F1 |
|---|---|---|---|---|---|
| .270 | .241 | .254 | .873 | .804 | .835 |

Table 2: Span Level Results for the Token-Based CRF Sequence Labeling Model

The exact metrics report the precision, recall, and F1 when spans are considered correct if the model correctly identifies both the start and endpoints of an *isnad*, while the partial metrics give credit for an *isnad* if the model labels part of it as an *isnad*, even if the start and endpoints are incorrect.

## 6.2 Retrieval Results

We will focus on the results for the retrieve-and-tag approach to solving the problem of locating *isnad* start points, as seen in Table 3 below. As a baseline for comparison, we will compare our model to a naïve model which assumes that all instances of common *isnad* beginning terms, begin *isnads*.[3] We also compare the hybrid retrieval-tagging model to a CRF with local token features (as described in section 5.1) We report only the token level scores for the "Begin" tag, even though the model does solve the full problem of determining both where isnads begin and end. The retrieval portion of the combined model is, as stated above, a bigram bag of ngrams model trained on documents of 75 tokens in length using TFIDF scores as feature weights. All results shown are micro-averages across ten training/test splits at the document level (i.e. all the chunks of a tagged section of text are either all in the training set or all in the test set.)

| Model | Precision | Recall | F1 |
|---|---|---|---|
| Naïve | .188 | .378 | .219 |
| CRF (Tokens) | .475 | .422 | .432 |
| Retrieval-LSTM | .571 | .442 | .476 |

Table 3: Results for Isnad Beginning Labeling

While this model clearly outperforms both the naïve baseline and the CRF with token features at detecting isnad starting points, more will need to be done to improve its performance before moving on to the problem of finding the endpoint associated with a given starting point in the retrieve-and-tag framework.

# 7 Future Work

As noted above, the most immediate direction for future research is finishing the process of locating complete *isnads* in the hybrid model regime. Additional work will also be done to improve the performance of the *isnad* start point tagging model. It may be that additional features such as a gazetteer of common transmissive terms or the output of a named entity recognition system may improve the model's ability to detect isnads. It might also be worthwhile to look into modifying the retrieval model used in the above experiments to use more generalizable document representations than simple bag of ngram representations, which may generalize better to unseen texts.

---

[3] This list of common starting terms was created in collaboration with a domain expert in the field of Islamic religious studies. Common beginning terms include حدثنيه, حدثنا, سئل, and قال.

Additionally, once we can reliably identify *isnads* in text at scale, several new research questions about the social networks these chains represent become feasible, since *isnads* can be thought of as textual descriptions of a social network of individuals involved in the dissemination of a given piece of information. A reasonable first step would be to take a single *isnad* and extract the names of the individuals involved and the relationship between them. With that accomplished, we could then attempt to infer the social network in which the information is spread by linking names to the individuals they represent using the evidence provided by multiple *isnads* to differentiate between individuals when, for instance, one name is shared by multiple people or different names are used to refer to the same individual, essentially creating a social map of the written tradition's evolution over time. To this end, it will be useful to leverage information from biographical dictionaries and other sources of data about the relationships between individuals involved in transmitting the knowledge present in the corpus.

## Acknowledgements

This research was completed with funding from firstly the Qatar National Library, Digital Sira Project, and also from the European Research Council under the European Union's Horizon 2020 research and innovation programme (Grant agreement no. 772989, KITAB). Additionally, the authors would like to thank Sarah Savant, Abdul Rahman Azzam, Hamid Reza Hakimi, Kevin Jaques, Lorenz Nigst, Mathew Barber, and Simon Loynes for providing their expertise and time for data annotation, as well as the anonymous reviewers for their insightful comments.

## Reference

Abū Dāwūd Sulaymān b. Dāwūd al-Ṭayālisī (d. 204AH/819CE), *Musnad Abī Dāwūd al-Ṭayālisī*, Muḥammad b. ʿAbd al-Muḥasin al-Turkī ed., (Cairo: Dār al-Hijr, 1999), vol. 2, 223-4.

Altammami, Shatha, Atwell, Eric, and Alsalka, Ammar. 2019. Text Segmentation Using N-grams to Annotate Hadith Corpus. In *Proceedings of the 3rd Workshop on Arabic Corpus Linguistics*, 31-39. ACL.

Harrag, Fouzi. 2014. Text mining approach for knowledge extraction in Sahıh al-Bukhari. *Computers in Human Behavior*, 30:558–566.

Foley, John. 2018. Poetry: Identification, Entity Recognition, and Retrieval. Doctoral dissertation. University of Massachusetts Amherst, Amherst, USA.

Graves, Alex and Schmidhuber, Jurgen. 2005. "Framewise phoneme classification with bidirectional LSTM networks." In *Proc. IJCNN*.

Hochreiter, Sepp and Schmidhuber, Jürgen 1997. "Long short-term memory". *Neural Computation*. 9 (8): 1735–1780. doi:10.1162/neco.1997.9.8.1735.

Lafferty, John, A. McCallum, and F. Pereira. 2001. "Conditional Random Field: Probabilistic Models for Segmenting and Labeling Sequence Data." In *ICML 18*.

Lample, Guillaume, Ballesteros, Miguel, Subramanian, Sandeep, Kawakami, Kazuya, and Dyer, Chris. 2016. "Neural Architectures for Named Entity Recognition." In *Proceedings of NAACL 2016*.

Lorang, Elizabeth, Soh, Leen-Kiat, Datla, Maanas Varma, and Kulwicki, Spencer. 2015. "Developing an Image-Based Classifier for Detecting Poetic Content in Historic Newspaper Collections." In *The Magazine of Digital Library Research* 15(7). DOI: 10.1045/july2015-lorang.

Maraoui, Hajer, Haddar, Kais, and Romary, Laurent. 2018. "Segmentation tool for hadith corpus to generate TEI encoding." In *International Conference on Advanced Intelligent Systems and Informatics*, 252–260. Springer.

Pennington, Jeffrey, Socher, Richard and Manning, Christopher D. 2014. "GloVe: Global Vectors for Word Representation." In *Proceedings of the 2014 Conference on Empirical Methods in Natural Language Processing (EMNLP)*.

Ritter, Alan, Clark, Sam, Mausam and Etzioni, Oren. 2011. "Named Entity Recognition in Tweets: An Experimental Study."

Romanov, Maxim & Seydi, Masoumeh. (2019). OpenITI: A Machine-Readable Corpus of Islamicate Texts (Version 2019.1.1) [Data set].

Siddiqui, Muazzam, Saleh, Mostafa, and Bagais, Ahmed. 2014. Extraction and visualization of the chain of narrators from hadiths using named entity recognition and classification. *Int. J. Comput. Linguist. Res,* 5(1):14–25.

Tjong Kim Sang, Erik F.  and De Meulder, Fien. (2003) "Introduction to the CoNLL-2003 Shared Task: Language-Independent Named Entity Recognition." In *Proceedings of CoNLL-2003.*

# Embed More Ignore Less (EMIL):
## Exploiting Enriched Representations for Arabic NLP


**Ahmed Younes and Julie Weeds**
Department of Informatics, University of Sussex
Brighton, BN1 9RH, United Kingdom
`{ay227, juliewe}@sussex.ac.uk`


## Abstract


Our research focuses on the potential improvements of exploiting language specific characteristics in the form of embeddings by neural networks. More specifically, we investigate the capability of neural techniques and embeddings to represent language specific characteristics in two sequence labeling tasks: named entity recognition (NER) and part of speech (POS) tagging. In both tasks, our preprocessing is designed to use enriched Arabic representation by adding diacritics to undiacritized text. In POS tagging, we test the ability of a neural model to capture syntactic characteristics encoded within these diacritics by incorporating an embedding layer for diacritics alongside embedding layers for words and characters. In NER, our architecture incorporates diacritic and POS embeddings alongside word and character embeddings. Our experiments are conducted on 7 datasets (4 NER and 3 POS). We show that embedding the information that is encoded in automatically acquired Arabic diacritics improves the performance across all datasets on both tasks. Embedding the information in automatically assigned POS tags further improves performance on the NER task.


## 1 Introduction

Named Entity Recognition (NER) and Part-of-Speech (POS) tagging have traditionally been used as preprocessing steps in many Natural Language Processing (NLP) applications. For example, Yadav and Bethard (2018) discussed the use of NER across question answering, information retrieval, co-reference resolution, topic modeling, and machine translation. Similarly, POS tagging is often applied early in the NLP pipeline for many applications including information retrieval systems, syntax, and semantic analysis, speech recognition systems and machine translation (Abumalloh et al., 2016). In recent years, Arabic has been studied increasingly due to the explosion in the number of Arabic users on social media and the internet in general. Arabic is a morphologically rich language with complex grammatical structure (Shaalan et al., 2019). Arabic NLP researchers have used two types of approaches and sometimes a mixture of both to work with Arabic text. The first approach is the simplification approach where researchers tend to apply preprocessing (transformation) that simplify Arabic text such as letter normalization (Habash, 2010) and transliteration (Ameur et al., 2017). The second approach is the enrichment approach where researchers tend to apply minimum modification to the Arabic text and devise a way of incorporating the enriched features and potentially add more features to it.

We assume that the simplification approach may exclude some useful information, and hence take an enrichment approach. First, we add diacritics information inferred by automatic diacritization model called Shakkala, based on the assumption that the syntactic and semantic information encoded in diacritics might be useful in both the NER and the POS task. Once we have a diacritic-enhanced POS model, we use it to infer POS information for the NER corpora, based on the assumption that both diacritics and POS information can potentially improve the performance of the NER model. We are aware that this pipeline will raise the question of the quality of the inferred information and its effect on performance. Nevertheless, the experimental results shows that the addition of this automatically-inferred information enhances the performance.






*Proceedings of the Fifth Arabic Natural Language Processing Workshop*, pages 139–154
Barcelona, Spain (Online), December 12, 2020

Our specific contributions are that we propose a framework (EMIL) where we *Embed More and Ignore Less*. We show that applying minimal modification to the text and embedding more of the possible features into the model can outperform the standard sequence labeling models. We propose a diacritic-aware architecture for sequence labeling which extends and outperforms the current standard character-aware architecture of a Bi-directional long short-term memory network (Bi-LSTM) with a CRF. We also propose a combination architecture for NER that combines word, character, diacritic, and POS information and outperforms the standard character-aware architecture and our own diacritic-aware architecture.

## 2   Background and related work

We will now discuss the main characteristics of the Arabic language Section (2.1) and related work on Arabic NER and POS tagging Section (2.2).

### 2.1   The Arabic language

As discussed elsewhere, e.g., by Farghaly and Shaalan (2009), Arabic is rich morphology language with complex grammar structure which poses extra challenges to systems when considering Arabic text as input. Habash (2010) discussed the script differences such as letter shaping, script direction (right to left) and obligatory ligatures. Also Habash et al. (2013) discussed the lack of standard orthographies: e.g., غرام and جرام both mean (*gram*). One of the major challenges in Arabic NER is the lack of capitalization (Shaalan, 2014; Benajiba et al., 2008a). Shaalan (2014) also discussed the agglutinative nature of the Arabic language where new words and sometimes even sentences can be derived by adding affixes and clitics to Arabic words, making Arabic a morphologically rich language.

In our work, it is crucial to note that Arabic employs diacritics (short vowels) to encode phonetic, morphological, syntactic and semantic information. In traditional Arabic text, diacritics are symbols placed on top of Arabic letters. Figure (1) shows examples of three Arabic diacritic symbols. The choice of the diacritic on the last letter of the word describes the syntactic dependency of that word within the sentence. The choice of the diacritic on the first and the middle letters of the word disambiguates between different possible semantics of the word within the sentence. For example, the undiacritized word علم can be diacritized to become عَلِمَ (*knew*), عُلِمَ (*known*), or عَلَمْ (*flag*). However, due to the fact that most modern Arabic text is only partially diacritized or undiacritized, researchers often remove it for consistency (Habash, 2010). Thus one word in Arabic may be ambiguous and the reader must use the context to disambiguate.

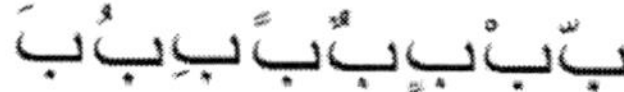

Figure 1: Arabic diacritics include: short vowels (first three letters), nunation (the second three letters), sukon (no vowel) and shadda (geminition) (the last two letters respectively).

### 2.2   Arabic Sequence Classification

Early work on the detection and classification of Named Entities in Arabic NER used a rule-based or grammar-based approach (Mesfar, 2007; Shaalan and Raza, 2007). Subsequently, the field shifted generally to a machine learning approach — thus avoiding the time-consuming and expensive maintenance of rule-sets. Within this general approach a wide variety of techniques have all been applied to the Arabic NER problem including Support Vector Machines (SVM) (Benajiba et al., 2008b), Conditional Random Fields (CRF) (Abdul-Hamid and Darwish, 2010; Benajiba et al., 2008a; AbdelRahman et al., 2010), Maximum Entropy (ME) (Benajiba et al., 2007), Hidden Markov Models (HMM) and Decision Trees (Nadeau and Sekine, 2007). Notably, Benajiba et al. (2007) developed an Arabic NER system, ANERsys 1.0, which employed maximum entropy and could recognize four types of Named Entities.

The authors also built their own linguistic resources, *ANERcorp* (an annotated corpus) and *ANERgazet* (a gazetteer), which have become benchmarks for evaluation. At this time, work was also done on incorporating POS information to improve NER. For example, Benajiba and Rosso (2007) proposed

ANERsys 2.0, where they used a POS tagger and a two step approach to enhance the performance of ANERsys 1.0.

More recently and following the general trend towards neural approaches, Gridach (2016) developed a character aware neural network model which attempts to capture contextual characteristics in Arabic by placing a CRF on top of a Bi-LSTM. This provided a hard state-of-the-art for other systems to beat and provides the foundation of our own approach. Very recently, Ali et al. (2019) applied a neural network model with a multi-attention layer to extract Arabic NEs. They used two attention units, the embedding attention layer, and the self-attention unit. They achieved an F1 score of 91.31 to achieve a new state-of-the-art on a large dataset proposed for evaluation in the same work. At the same time, Khalifa and Shaalan (2019) used character Convolutional Neural Networks (CNN) as a replacement for character-level bidirectional Long Short-Term Memory (LSTM) in Arabic NER. Their proposed system was able to outperform the state-of-art systems, including character-level Bi-LSTM on various standard Arabic NER corpora. Antoun et al. (2020) proposed AraBERTv0.1 which involves pretraining the BERT trans-former model for the Arabic language. They compared AraBERTv0.1 and the Bi-LSTM-CRF model on *ANERCorp*, the former achieved 84.2 F1 scores whereas the later achieved 81.7. Most recently, Sheng et al. (2020) proposed a transfer learning approach for Arabic NER with Deep Neural Networks where they showed that their model outperformed significantly the Bi-LSTM-CRF model. We have not con-sidered this approach here because our aim is not to create a new state of the art model but to show the effectiveness of incorporating language specific characteristics in the form of embeddings.

Turning our attention now to Arabic POS tagging, many approaches have also been adopted over the years including rule-based methods (Alqrainy, 2008; Zribi et al., 2016), statistical models (Al Shamsi and Guessoum, 2006; Kadim and Lazrek, 2018), hybrid models (Vashishtha and Susan, 2019; Forsati and Shamsfard, 2014) and neural networks (Yousif and Sembok, 2006; Yousif and Sembok, 2005). Performance is usually much higher for POS tagging than NER. Khoja (2001) introduced a hybrid POS tagger (with 33 tags) which combined HMM with a rule-based tagger. They used the Holy Quran Corpus and achieved an accuracy rate of 97.6% and 96.8% respectively. Yousif and Sembok (2008) used the SVM approach and a corpus of 177 tagged words. Zeroual and Abdelhak (2016) presented a probabilistic POS tagger for Arabic text based on HMM called Tree Tagger. The proposed tagger obtained accuracy rates of 99.4% using Al-Mus'haf corpus.

Similar to other NLP applications, the most recent attention in this area has been on neural approaches. Wang et al. (2015) demonstrated an effective way of applying a Bi-LSTM to the POS tagging task, achieving 97.4% on the English Penn Treebank. Darwish et al. (2017) used a Bi-LSTM in their work on Arabic POS tagging, achieving 95.50%. Alrajhi and ELAffendi (2019) used the LSTM-RNN model on the Quranic Arabic Corpus (QAC). They reported accuracy of 99.76% at the word level and 99.18% at the morpheme level. They also compared their system against the Word2Vec POS tagger, for which they reported accuracy levels of 97.33% and 99.55% for words and morphemes respectively.

Returning to the different approaches of handling Arabic text. As discussed in the previous sections letter normalization and transliteration are examples of the simplification approach. For example, letter normalization is commonly applied to reduce the noise and sparsity in the data (Habash, 2010). For transliteration, Ameur et al. (2017) applied a bidirectional attention-based encoder-decoder model for the task of machine transliteration between Arabic and English.

Since the removal of diacritics also clearly leads to a potential ambiguity as explained in Section (2.1) there has been some work on automatic diacritization of partially diacritized or undiacritized text (Mubarak et al., 2019a; Mubarak et al., 2019b; Abdelali et al., 2016).

Shakkala was built by Barqawi (2017) for Arabic text diacritization using Bi-LSTM networks com-bined with character embeddings. Fadel et al. (2019) demonstrated the superiority of the neural approach of Shakkala compared to other different automatic diacritization systems available online e.g., Ali-Soft, Farasa, Harakat, and MADAMIRA.

Some recent work in Arabic NLP has started to make use of such systems. For example, Al-Sallab et al. (2017) proposed AROMA, a recursive deep learning model for opinion mining in Arabic. Pre-processing in AROMA included morphological tokenization and automatic diacritization carried out by

MADAMIRA (Pasha et al., 2014). This resulted in improved performance in classifying opinion as positive or negative on a range of different Arabic corpora. Similarly, Baly et al. (2017) used a Recursive Neural Tensor Network (RNTN) for sentiment analysis and reported that adding orthographic features such as diacritics improved the performance. They incorporated orthographic features such as diacritics by enlarging the vocabulary to have distinct word forms for different versions of the word (diacritized/undiacritized) and then deriving embeddings by training a Continuous Bag of Words (CBOW) model (Mikolov et al., 2013). Similarly, Alqahtani et al. (2019) introduced automatic selective diacritization as a viable step in lexical disambiguation. They evaluated the system in downstream tasks including POS which improved from 97.99% by baseline to 98.70%. They trained word embeddings on selectively-diacritized dataset to enrich the vocabulary.

## 3  Hypothesis

The hypothesis of this research can be summarized thus:

1. Incorporating linguistic characteristics of Arabic text in the form of embeddings can be exploited by a neural network, thus improving performance in downstream tasks.

2. Inferring linguistic characteristics of Arabic text to use as embedded features in a downstream model can improve downstream performance.

We have already outlined in Section (1) that there are two approaches of handling Arabic text, the simplification approach which involves transforming the text into simplified representation and the enrichment approach which minimally modifies the text and potentially adds more exploitable features to the text. We have assumed that the simplification approach might exclude some useful information and hence have adopted an enrichment approach. More specifically, we have adopted a pipeline approach where we use one model to infer a particular linguistic characteristic and then use the inferred information as features further downstream. For example, we infer diacritic information, using existing models such as Shakkala. We then exploit these features of the text in the form of embeddings in order to enhance performance in POS-tagging. We then use diacritics inferred by Shakkala and POS information inferred by POS model to enhance performance in NER.

We reason that using minimally modified Arabic text as input to neural networks builds the potential for allowing the neural network to learn an enriched representation of the Arabic language. Further, a framework such as EMIL, which incorporates more language-specific characteristics of the text in the form of embeddings should result in improved performance. In particular, since Arabic syntax and word sense disambiguation relies heavily on diacritics, we reason that applying an automatic diacritization neural model to minimally transformed Arabic text can capture syntactic and semantic dependencies. Similarly, useful information for NER can also be derived via POS tagging. Finally, we hypothesize that incorporating embedding layers based on derived language characteristics such as diacritics and POS tags can improve the overall performance of a neural network in sequence labeling tasks.

## 4  Approach

We propose a three-step approach to Arabic sequence labeling. The first step is to automatically diacritize the text using the state-of-the-art automatic diacritization system Shakkala (Barqawi, 2017). The second step is the individual training of character and diacritic embeddings using the architecture proposed by Gridach (2016). The third step is to train all embedding layers together using a combination model (see section 4.3). There are two main advantages in adopting this architecture for EMIL. First, it is based on a standard approach in NER and sequence labeling in general, which remains very close to the state-of-the-art. Second, it is a relatively light-weight architecture requiring less computational resources than other alternatives (see section 5.3). We will discuss and justify our design choices and the computational aspects of the architecture further in Section (5.3) and Section (6). Figure (2) gives an overview of the overall training procedure for our EMIL framework, which we now explain in detail.

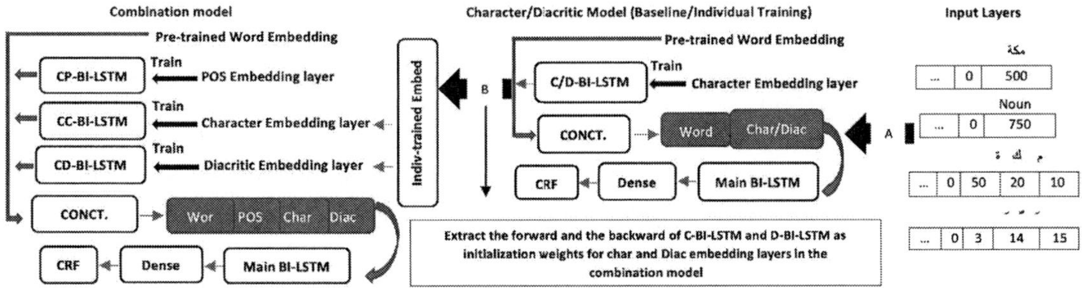

Figure 2: EMIL Training procedure.

## 4.1 Data Preparation

As shown in Figure (2), the *input layers* of our system are prepared with up to four types of input: word, POS, character and diacritic. The subset of input layers used depends on the task and setting. For example, when individually train the character model, we use the word and character input layers whereas when individually train the diacritic model, we use the word and diacritic input layers. For the final combination model for NER, we use all four input layers.

Since our data consists of variable length sentences, we use padding of 50 for the word and POS layers and 10 for the character and diacritic layers, which is consistent with the literature in this area. Thus, for each of the word and POS layers, the input has a shape of (50,). For each of the character and diacritic layers, the input has the shape (50,10) dimensions, which means for each word in the sentence there will be a 10 dimensional array representing the characters or diacritics respectively.

## 4.2 Individual-training: Character and Diacritic Models

Gridach (2016) proposed a character aware neural network model using a CRF on top of a Bi-LSTM. The aim of that model was to predict the NER tags by exploiting word and character embeddings. In our approach, we follow the same architecture. First, as shown in Figure (2) we use the *character model* directly to individually train character embeddings. The inputs to this model are word and character input layers as indicated by arrow (A). The word embedding layer takes as input pre-trained embedding matrix developed by Soliman et al. (2017), transforming the word input layer into word embeddings. The character embedding layer is randomly initialized and trained by the `C-Bi-LSTM`. The forward and the backward output from this `C-Bi-LSTM` is concatenated with the output from the word embedding layer and passed to the `main Bi-LSTM`. The output from this is passed to a `Dense` layer which maps the output of the `main Bi-LSTM` to the `CRF` layer, following Lample et al. (2016). After training the character model, we extract the forward and the backward output of the `C-Bi-LSTM` and use them to initialize the character embedding layer in the combination model.

The same approach is applied on *diacritic model* instead of using character information we use diacritics and instead of using `C-Bi-LSTM` we use `D-Bi-LSTM`. We extract the forward and backward outputs of the trained `D-Bi-LSTM` as individually-trained diacritic embeddings. It is worth noting that both of these models are trained on diacritized version of the datasets. Also it is important to mention that the output from this step are weights to initialize the character and diacritic embedding layers in the combination model and both of these sets of weights have been trained individually in separate models. The justification of this step can be found in Section (6) Table (2) where the experiments showed that training these embeddings separately and using them as individually-trained embedding in the final model improves the performance.

## 4.3 Combination model

As also shown in Figure (2), the final step in the EMIL training procedure is to combine all embedding layers and train them all together in a *combination model*. The first version of this model uses three input layers (word, character and diacritic) and is referred to as the *character-diacritic model*. The second version uses all four layers of input and is referred to as the *four-layer combination model*. We now discuss the embeddings corresponding to each input layer in turn. First, the word embedding layer is provided with pre-trained word embeddings. Second, the optional POS embedding layer is randomly initialized (as shown in Figure (2), there is no arrow coming from the individually-trained embedding) and trained using `CP-Bi-LSTM`. Third, the character embedding layer is initialized with the individually-trained character embedding and re-trained using `CC-Bi-LSTM`. Fourth, the diacritic embedding layer is initialized with individually-trained diacritic embedding and re-trained using `CD-Bi-LSTM`. The output from the pre-trained word embedding, POS embedding, and the forward and backward output from CC-Bi-LSTM and CD-Bi-LSTM layers are concatenated by stacking each level on top of the other. The `main Bi-LSTM` layer is then trained using the concatenated layer, and the output of that layer is passed to the `dense` layer and from there to the `CRF` layer.

## 5 Empirical Evaluation

The *character model* described previously is used both as a baseline and for training the individually-trained character embedding. We also empirically evaluate two versions of the *combination model*: the *character-diacritic model* which incorporates word, character, and diacritic embedding layers; and the *four-layer combination model* which has an additional POS layer. We evaluate our models on two sequence labeling tasks: NER and POS tagging. We now describe the datasets used Section (5.1), hyperparameter settings Section (5.2) and the experiments performed to test our hypotheses Section (5.3). We used $k$-fold cross validation in order to evaluate the statistical significance of our results. The value of $k$ used in $k$-fold cross validation varied according to the size of the dataset but was between 4 and 10 in all cases.

### 5.1 Datasets

We evaluate on 7 sequence labelling benchmarks: 4 of which are NER datasets and 3 of which are POS-tagging datasets[1]. In brief, each dataset consists of a sequence of sentences, where each sentence has a sequence of (word:tag) pairs. For NER we use the *BinAjeeba* (Darwish, 2013), the *ANERCorp* developed by Benajiba et al. (2007), and the *Wikipedia* and *Newswire* datasets which are mapped[2] versions of the fine-grained WikiFANE and NewsFANE datasets (Alotaibi and Lee, 2014) respectively. For POS-tagging we are evaluating on 3 standard datasets: *WikiNews* (Abdelali et al., 2019), *Al-Mushaf* (Zeroual and Abdelhak, 2016), *Prague Arabic Dependency Tree Bank (PADT)* (Hajic et al., 2004).

### 5.2 Hyper-parameters settings

Here, we are going to discuss the main hyper-parameters of the *combination model*. We did not tune these hyper-parameters — instead selecting values for computational efficiency (see section 5.3) and based on best practice from the literature. The `CP-Bi-LSTM`, `CC-Bi-LSTM` and `CD-Bi-LSTM` have 10 units each and the `main Bi-LSTM` has 20 units. Before we feed the output to the `CRF` layer, we use a `dense` layer with 20 units and tanh activation function to map the output of the `main Bi-LSTM` to the `CRF` layer. We use Keras which is an open source python library based on tensorflow. For optimization we used adam optimization technique [3].

Regarding the embeddings themselves, we used pre-trained word embeddings developed by Soliman et al. (2017) with 100 dimensions. The POS, character and diacritic embeddings have 10 dimensions each. The reason behind choosing 10 as the size of these embedding is that the size of the associated type vocabulary for each is small. For example, the Arabic alphabet contains 28 characters. We argue that 10 dimensional embedding will be enough to encode the information provided by the 28 character Arabic alphabet[4]. The word embedding is pre-trained, character and diacritic embeddings are individually-trained whereas the POS layer is randomly initialized. We set all of these embeddings to be

---

[1]For more details about the data sets, see Appendix A

[2]For the mapping, see Appendix A.1

[3]For more details about parameter settings, see Appendix B

[4]We also experimented with 25 dimensional embeddings as used by Gridach (2016) and found no further improvement

| Corpus | Character model | | | Character-Diacritic model | | | Four-layer Combination model | | |
|---|---|---|---|---|---|---|---|---|---|
| | F1 | Recall | Precision | F1 | Recall | Precision | F1 | Recall | Precision |
| ANERCorp (NER) | 0.708 | 0.762 | 0.662 | 0.818* | 0.833 | 0.803 | **0.929**** | 0.938 | 0.920 |
| BinAjeeba (NER) | 0.720 | 0.763 | 0.681 | 0.840* | 0.854 | 0.826 | **0.930**** | 0.936 | 0.924 |
| NewsWire (NER) | 0.612 | 0.718 | 0.534 | **0.751*** | 0.803 | 0.706 | - | - | - |
| Wikipedia (NER) | 0.758 | 0.794 | 0.726 | **0.834*** | 0.851 | 0.819 | - | - | - |
| Al Mushaf (POS) | 0.941 | 0.940 | 0.942 | **0.980*** | 0.9808 | 0.9806 | - | - | - |
| PADT (POS) | 0.94 | 0.941 | 0.939 | **0.954*** | 0.955 | 0.953 | - | - | - |
| WikiNews (POS) | 0.949 | 0.951 | 0.948 | **0.958*** | 0.960 | 0.956 | - | - | - |

Table 1: Summary of performance by each model on each dataset in the tasks. Best results are highlighted in bold. * indicates statistical significance at the 5% level in a paired sample comparison with the character model; ** with the character-diacritic model

trainable so they are trained together. We experimented with variations (randomly initialised character and diacritic embeddings (no individual-training), randomly initialised word embeddings, individually-trained POS embeddings and frozen embedding layers) during our ablation studies Section (6) and found this configuration of embeddings to be optimal.

## 5.3 Experiment

We conducted our experiments in five steps. First, as a baseline, we constructed a character aware model similar to the one in Figure (2) (*character model/baseline*) and trained it on the undiacritized version of the 7 datasets. It is worth noting that the dataset used to evaluate the baseline and the one used to evaluate the combination model are identical — the only difference between them is that the latter has been automatically diacritized using the Shakkala model.

Second, we used the diacritized version of the 7 datasets to extract the individually-trained character and diacritic embedding as described in Section (4.2) and passed it to the combination model. Third, we used the same diacritized version of the 7 datasets to train the *character-diacritic model* where we combine word, character and diacritic layers. The output from this sub-step is a diacritic-aware NER tagger for each of the 4 NER datasets and a diacritic-aware POS tagger for each of the 3 POS datasets. Fourth, we used our enhanced diacritic-aware POS tagger to tag 2 standard NER dataset (*BinAjeeba* and *ANERCorp*). Finally, we used these datasets to evaluate the *four-layer combination model* where we combine all four layers. It is worth noting that the amount of time required to cross-validate our models varied between 21 minutes and 387 minutes and the number of epochs required varied between 90 epochs and 340 epochs across all datasets. For example, cross-validating *ANERCorp* across the three models explained earlier took 77 minutes and 169 epochs for the *character model*, 85 minutes and 164 epochs for the *character-diacritic model* and 88 minutes and 240 epochs for the *four-layer combination model* which makes our architecture light-weight compared to BERT or other architectures which employ attention mechanisms[5].

## 6 Results

Table 1 summarises our results. For each model and dataset, we give the average precision, recall and F1-score calculated over the $k$ folds of cross-validation. The *character model* is our baseline and is evaluated on the undiacritized version of the 7 datasets. We also give results for the *character-diacritic model* evaluated on the diacriticized versions of all 7 datasets and results for the *four-layer combination model* evaluated on automatically diacritized and automatically POS-tagged versions of 2 datasets.

First, we compare results for the *character model* and the *character-diacritic model* to see the impact of adding diacritics. We observe that the proposed *character-diacritic model* outperforms the *character model* on all of the datasets for both NER and POS-tagging. Automatically diacritizing the text and adding the diacritic embedding layer boosts both precision and recall of the system. We used $k$-fold cross-validation and all of the differences observed are statistically significant at the 5% level using a

---

[5]For more details about the computational aspects, see Appendix C

paired sample test. Our best absolute performance in NER was on the *BinAjeeba* dataset where we achieved an F1-score of 0.84, substantially outperforming the *character model* which achieved 0.72. Our best absolute and relative gain in performance on POS-tagging was on the *Al Mushaf* dataset where F1 performance rose from 0.941 to 0.980.

Second, we compare the *character-diacritic model* with the *four-layer combination model* to evaluate the impact of adding POS information as well as diacritics. We note that automatically POS tagging the diacritized NER datasets and adding this information via a POS embedding layer leads to a substantial gain in performance on both datasets. The performance on the *BinAjeeba* dataset improved form 0.84 to 0.93 using the *four-layer combination model*. Similarly, F1-score performance on the *ANERCorp* dataset rose from 0.82 to 0.92.

We also performed a number of ablation experiments on one of the benchmark datasets (*ANERCorp*) which are summarised in Table (2). It is worth noting that all the embedding layers in the ablation experiments are trainable apart from A5. In our ablations, we consider the effect of randomly initialising or training the different embedding layers for the combination model as follows: (A1) all embeddings randomly initialised, this ablation shows the importance of the pre-trained and the individual-trained components of the combination model. As shown in the table the performance drops substantially when we remove these components; (A2) word embeddings and POS randomly initialised, individually-trained character and diacritic embeddings, this ablation shows the significance of the pre-trained word embeddings and evidently proves its impact on the model. When we use randomly initialized word embeddings the performance drop from 0.929 to 0.611; (A3) pre-trained word embeddings, randomly initialized character, diacritics and POS embeddings, this ablation shows the impact of removing the individual training step from the combination model. The result shows that without the individual training of character and diacritic embedding the model achieves 0.747 however, when initializing character and diacritic embeddings of the combination model with individually-trained weights which are trained separately the performance is boosted to 0.929; and (A4) pre-trained word embeddings and the rest are individually trained, this ablation is to test the effectiveness of individually training POS embeddings and the results shows that this approach still outperformed by the original approach where we use randomly initialized POS embedding. We also considered (A5) freezing the embeddings rather than allowing them to be trainable in the final model but our results show the massive benefit of trainable embeddings. The previous ablation experiments supports the choice of our architecture where we use pre-trained word embedding along with randomly initialized pos embedding and individually trained character and diacritic embeddings.

| EMIL | A1 | A2 | A3 | A4 | A5 |
|---|---|---|---|---|---|
| 0.929 | 0.617* | 0.611* | 0.747* | 0.927 | 0.591* |

Table 2: Summary of ablation results (F1-score); * indicates statistical significance at the 5% level in a paired sample comparison with EMIL

## 7   Error Analysis and Discussion

We now present a detailed analysis of the errors committed by each model on the *ANERCorp* dataset for the NER task. In our analysis, we identified 4 types of errors. **Type-one:** Boundary errors e.g., the word ديترويت (*Detroit*) appears once in the dataset tagged as B-ORG and is classified as I-ORG. **Type-two:** Low frequency words e.g., the word إسحق (*Isaac*) appears twice in the dataset tagged as B-PERS and is classified as O. We note that a lot of words in this type of error are foreign names. **Type-three:** Dominant tags e.g., the word السفير (*the ambassador*) is tagged twice as B-ORG and 12 times as O, and when this word appears as B-ORG a model classifies it as O. **Type-four:** Counter dominant tags e.g., the word مشهد (*Mashhad*) is labeled 17 times as B-LOC and once as O, and when it appears as B-LOC a model misclassifies it as O. We note that a lot of type-four errors appear to be gold standard errors where the word is tagged incorrectly and classified correctly by the model. For example, the word الضفة (*AL*

*Daffa (The bank, like in riverbank)*) is incorrectly tagged 4 times as O in the gold standard and our model classified it as B-LOC, which is in fact the correct label.

| Model | Type 1 | Type 2 | Type 3 | Type 4 |
|---|---|---|---|---|
| (Baseline) | 1540 | 2406 | 701 | 635 |
| (Character-Diacritic) | 889 | 1249 | 558 | 443 |
| (Four-layer Combination) | 214 | 683 | 117 | 60 |

Table 3: Summary of the errors committed by each model.

Table (3) shows a summary of the errors. We observe that the addition of diacritics reduced the number of errors in each type. Further, each error type was reduced again by the addition of POS information.

However, the largest reductions were for type-three and type-four errors which are both due to tag ambiguity. For example, the word السعودية (*Al Saudia*) can be tagged either as I-LOC or B-LOC depending on the context. Adding diacritics to this word will help disambiguate its sense. For example instances which should be tagged as B-LOC are adverbs and will be diacritized as السُّعُودِيَّة (*Al Saudiate*) whereas instances which should be tagged as I-LOC are adjectives and will be diacritized as السُّعُودِيَّة (*Al Saudiato*). It is worth noting that both words have the same meaning but each one plays a different syntactic and semantic role which can be encoded by the diacritics. This can be used as evidence to support our claim in Section (3) that neural network can learn syntactic and semantic information from the embeddings. In a perfect world, automatic diacritization will be optimal but we also note that Shakkala has some limitations. For example, foreign names written in Arabic, such as جينيرال موتور (*General Motors*), tend to produce errors, which is probably due to the sparsity of these types of names in Arabic corpora. Further, any errors committed by the automatic diacritization module tend to propagate through the sentence. Less frequently occurring diacritics such as gemination and nunation may also be misplaced. In some cases, the POS layer improved the performance as it was able to mitigate the errors produced by automatic diacritization. For example, if the word *Al Saudia* was incorrectly diacritized in the text, the POS tagger could mitigate this error by tagging it correctly as Adj or Adv based on its context. Of course, errors produced by the POS tagger will similarly affect the performance of the four-layer combination model As discussed in Section (3).

## 8   Conclusions and Future Work

In summary, we have shown that inferring and incorporating linguistic features of Arabic text in the form of embeddings can improve the performance of downstream tasks. Further, the pipeline approach that we are using may not be ideal regarding the quality of the inferred information but it still produces excellent results overall.

Focussing on diacritic information, we have shown that it is possible for a neural network to learn from the information encoded in the diacritics of the Arabic text and for this information to be used successfully in POS tagging and NER. By automatically diacriticising text and adding a diacritic-aware layer to existing neural architecture, performance (F1) was increased. We have also shown that adding POS information on top of diacritics in a similar way further improves performance at NER.

There are a number of directions for further work. First, further work on automatic diacritization, potentially directly including the diacritic inference model into the NER/POS training mode to reduce the effect of error propagation cause by the pipeline. Second, there is work to be done investigating the impact of embedding diacritic and POS information in attention-based architectures (Ali et al., 2019; Khalifa and Shaalan, 2019; Devlin et al., 2018).

Second, we believe that our approach of diacritic sensitive tagging will be useful in other areas of analysis including segmentation and deeper syntactic analysis. Further, embedding information from other analyses, including grammatical dependencies, might further improve performance in downstream tasks such as NER. Consequently, this is clearly only the beginning of investigating how the EMIL approach, where we *Embed More and Ignore Less*, can be applied to different sources of information, in different languages and to different downstream tasks.

## References

Ahmed Abdelali, Kareem Darwish, Nadir Durrani, and Hamdy Mubarak. 2016. Farasa: A fast and furious segmenter for arabic. In *Proceedings of the 2016 conference of the North American chapter of the association for computational linguistics: Demonstrations*, pages 11–16.

Ahmed Abdelali, Ali Elkahky, Hamdy Mubarak, Kareem Darwish, Mohammed Attia, and Younes Samih. 2019. Pos tagging for improving code-switching identification in arabic.

Samir AbdelRahman, Mohamed Elarnaoty, Marwa Magdy, and Aly Fahmy. 2010. Integrated machine learning techniques for arabic named entity recognition. *IJCSI*, 7:27–36.

Ahmed Abdul-Hamid and Kareem Darwish. 2010. Simplified feature set for arabic named entity recognition. In *Proceedings of the 2010 Named Entities Workshop*, pages 110–115. Association for Computational Linguistics.

Rabab Ali Abumalloh, Hassan Maudi Al-Sarhan, Othman Ibrahim, and Waheeb Abu-Ulbeh. 2016. Arabic part-of-speech tagging. *Journal of Soft Computing and Decision Support Systems*, 3(2):45–52.

Ahmad Al-Sallab, Ramy Baly, Hazem Hajj, Khaled Bashir Shaban, Wassim El-Hajj, and Gilbert Badaro. 2017. Aroma: A recursive deep learning model for opinion mining in arabic as a low resource language. *ACM Transactions on Asian and Low-Resource Language Information Processing (TALLIP)*, 16(4):1–20.

Fatma Al Shamsi and Ahmed Guessoum. 2006. A hidden markov model-based pos tagger for arabic. In *Proceeding of the 8th International Conference on the Statistical Analysis of Textual Data, France*, pages 31–42.

Mohammed Nadher Abdo Ali, Guanzheng Tan, and Aamir Hussain. 2019. Boosting arabic named-entity recognition with multi-attention layer. *IEEE Access*, 7:46575–46582.

Fahd Alotaibi and Mark Lee. 2014. A hybrid approach to features representation for fine-grained arabic named entity recognition. In *Proceedings of COLING 2014, the 25th International Conference on Computational Linguistics: Technical Papers*, pages 984–995.

Sawsan Alqahtani, Hanan Aldarmaki, and Mona Diab. 2019. Homograph disambiguation through selective diacritic restoration. In *Proceedings of the Fourth Arabic Natural Language Processing Workshop*, pages 49–59, Florence, Italy, August. Association for Computational Linguistics.

Shihadeh Alqrainy. 2008. A morphological-syntactical analysis approach for arabic textual tagging.

Khwlah Alrajhi and Mohammed A ELAffendi. 2019. Automatic arabic part-of-speech tagging: Deep learning neural lstm versus word2vec. *International Journal of Computing and Digital Systems*, 8(03):307–315.

Mohamed Seghir Hadj Ameur, Farid Meziane, and Ahmed Guessoum. 2017. Arabic machine transliteration using an attention-based encoder-decoder model. *Procedia Computer Science*, 117:287–297.

Wissam Antoun, Fady Baly, and Hazem Hajj. 2020. Arabert: Transformer-based model for arabic language understanding. *arXiv preprint arXiv:2003.00104*.

Ramy Baly, Hazem Hajj, Nizar Habash, Khaled Bashir Shaban, and Wassim El-Hajj. 2017. A sentiment treebank and morphologically enriched recursive deep models for effective sentiment analysis in arabic. *ACM Transactions on Asian and Low-Resource Language Information Processing (TALLIP)*, 16(4):1–21.

Zerrouki Barqawi. 2017. Shakkala, arabic text vocalization.

Yassine Benajiba and Paolo Rosso. 2007. Anersys 2.0: Conquering the ner task for the arabic language by combining the maximum entropy with pos-tag information. In *IICAI*.

Yassine Benajiba, Paolo Rosso, and José Miguel Benedíruiz. 2007. Anersys: An arabic named entity recognition system based on maximum entropy. In *International Conference on Intelligent Text Processing and Computational Linguistics*, pages 143–153. Springer.

Yassine Benajiba, Mona Diab, Paolo Rosso, et al. 2008a. Arabic named entity recognition: An svm-based approach. In *Proceedings of 2008 Arab International Conference on Information Technology (ACIT)*, pages 16–18. Association of Arab Universities Amman, Jordan.

Yassine Benajiba, Mona Diab, Paolo Rosso, et al. 2008b. Arabic named entity recognition: An svm-based approach. In *Proceedings of 2008 Arab International Conference on Information Technology (ACIT)*, pages 16–18. Association of Arab Universities Amman, Jordan.

Kareem Darwish, Hamdy Mubarak, Ahmed Abdelali, and Mohamed Eldesouki. 2017. Arabic pos tagging: Don't abandon feature engineering just yet. In *Proceedings of the Third Arabic Natural Language Processing Workshop*, pages 130–137.

Kareem Darwish. 2013. Named entity recognition using cross-lingual resources: Arabic as an example. In *Proceedings of the 51st Annual Meeting of the Association for Computational Linguistics (Volume 1: Long Papers)*, pages 1558–1567.

Jacob Devlin, Ming-Wei Chang, Kenton Lee, and Kristina Toutanova. 2018. Bert: Pre-training of deep bidirectional transformers for language understanding. *arXiv preprint arXiv:1810.04805*.

Ali Fadel, Ibraheem Tuffaha, Bara' Al-Jawarneh, and Mahmoud Al-Ayyoub. 2019. Arabic text diacritization using deep neural networks. *arXiv preprint arXiv:1905.01965*.

Ali Farghaly and Khaled Shaalan. 2009. Arabic natural language processing: Challenges and solutions. *ACM Transactions on Asian Language Information Processing (TALIP)*, 8(4):1–22.

Rana Forsati and Mehrnoush Shamsfard. 2014. Hybrid pos-tagging: A cooperation of evolutionary and statistical approaches. *Applied Mathematical Modelling*, 38(13):3193–3211.

Mourad Gridach. 2016. Character-aware neural networks for arabic named entity recognition for social media. In *Proceedings of the 6th workshop on South and Southeast Asian natural language processing (WSSANLP2016)*, pages 23–32.

Nizar Habash, Ryan Roth, Owen Rambow, Ramy Eskander, and Nadi Tomeh. 2013. Morphological analysis and disambiguation for dialectal arabic. In *Proceedings of the 2013 Conference of the North American Chapter of the Association for Computational Linguistics: Human Language Technologies*, pages 426–432.

Nizar Y Habash. 2010. Introduction to arabic natural language processing. *Synthesis Lectures on Human Language Technologies*, 3(1):1–187.

Jan Hajic, Otakar Smrz, Petr Zemánek, Jan Šnaidauf, and Emanuel Beška. 2004. Prague arabic dependency treebank: Development in data and tools. In *Proc. of the NEMLAR Intern. Conf. on Arabic Language Resources and Tools*, pages 110–117.

Ayoub Kadim and Azzeddine Lazrek. 2018. Parallel hmm-based approach for arabic part of speech tagging. *Int. Arab J. Inf. Technol.*, 15(2):341–351.

Muhammad Khalifa and Khaled Shaalan. 2019. Character convolutions for arabic named entity recognition with long short-term memory networks. *Computer Speech & Language*, 58:335–346.

Shereen Khoja. 2001. Apt: Arabic part-of-speech tagger. In *Proceedings of the Student Workshop at NAACL*, pages 20–25.

Guillaume Lample, Miguel Ballesteros, Sandeep Subramanian, Kazuya Kawakami, and Chris Dyer. 2016. Neural architectures for named entity recognition. *arXiv preprint arXiv:1603.01360*.

Slim Mesfar. 2007. Named entity recognition for arabic using syntactic grammars. In *International Conference on Application of Natural Language to Information Systems*, pages 305–316. Springer.

Tomas Mikolov, Ilya Sutskever, Kai Chen, Greg S Corrado, and Jeff Dean. 2013. Distributed representations of words and phrases and their compositionality. In *Advances in neural information processing systems*, pages 3111–3119.

Hamdy Mubarak, Ahmed Abdelali, Kareem Darwish, Mohamed Eldesouki, Younes Samih, and Hassan Sajjad. 2019a. A system for diacritizing four varieties of arabic. In *Proceedings of the 2019 Conference on Empirical Methods in Natural Language Processing and the 9th International Joint Conference on Natural Language Processing (EMNLP-IJCNLP): System Demonstrations*, pages 217–222.

Hamdy Mubarak, Ahmed Abdelali, Hassan Sajjad, Younes Samih, and Kareem Darwish. 2019b. Highly effective arabic diacritization using sequence to sequence modeling. In *Proceedings of the 2019 Conference of the North American Chapter of the Association for Computational Linguistics: Human Language Technologies, Volume 1 (Long and Short Papers)*, pages 2390–2395.

David Nadeau and Satoshi Sekine. 2007. A survey of named entity recognition and classification. *Lingvisticae Investigationes*, 30(1):3–26.

Arfath Pasha, Mohamed Al-Badrashiny, Mona Diab, Ahmed El Kholy, Ramy Eskander, Nizar Habash, Manoj Pooleery, Owen Rambow, and Ryan Roth. 2014. MADAMIRA: A fast, comprehensive tool for morphological analysis and disambiguation of Arabic. In *Proceedings of the Ninth International Conference on Language Resources and Evaluation (LREC'14)*, pages 1094–1101, Reykjavik, Iceland, May. European Language Resources Association (ELRA).

Khaled Shaalan and Hafsa Raza. 2007. Person name entity recognition for arabic. In *Proceedings of the 2007 Workshop on Computational Approaches to Semitic Languages: Common Issues and Resources*, pages 17–24. Association for Computational Linguistics.

Khaled Shaalan, Sanjeera Siddiqui, Manar Alkhatib, and Azza Abdel Monem. 2019. Challenges in arabic natural language processing. *Computational Linguistics*.

Khaled Shaalan. 2014. A survey of arabic named entity recognition and classification. *Computational Linguistics*, 40(2):469–510.

Jiabao Sheng, Aishan Wumaier, and Zhe Li. 2020. Poise: Efficient cross-domain chinese named entity recognization via transfer learning. *Symmetry*, 12(10):1673.

Abu Bakr Soliman, Kareem Eissa, and Samhaa R El-Beltagy. 2017. Aravec: A set of arabic word embedding models for use in arabic nlp. *Procedia Computer Science*, 117:256–265.

Srishti Vashishtha and Seba Susan. 2019. Fuzzy rule based unsupervised sentiment analysis from social media posts. *Expert Systems with Applications*, 138:112834.

Peilu Wang, Yao Qian, Frank K Soong, Lei He, and Hai Zhao. 2015. Part-of-speech tagging with bidirectional long short-term memory recurrent neural network. *arXiv preprint arXiv:1510.06168*.

Vikas Yadav and Steven Bethard. 2018. A survey on recent advances in named entity recognition from deep learning models. In *Proceedings of the 27th International Conference on Computational Linguistics*, pages 2145–2158, Santa Fe, New Mexico, USA, August. Association for Computational Linguistics.

Jabar H Yousif and T Sembok. 2005. Arabic part-of-speech tagger based neural networks. In *proceedings of International Arab Conference on Information Technology ACIT2005, ISSN*, volume 857.

Jabar H Yousif and T Sembok. 2006. Design and implement an automatic neural tagger based arabic language for nlp applications. *Asian Journal of Information Technology*, 5(7):784–789.

Jabar Hassan Yousif and Tengku Mohd Tengku Sembok. 2008. Arabic part-of-speech tagger based support vectors machines. In *2008 International Symposium on Information Technology*, volume 3, pages 1–7. IEEE.

Imad Zeroual and Lakhouaja Abdelhak. 2016. Adapting a decision tree based tagger for arabic. In *2016 International Conference on Information Technology for Organizations Development (IT4OD)*, pages 1–6. IEEE.

Inès Zribi, Inès Kammoun, Mariem Ellouze, L Belguith, and Philippe Blache. 2016. Sentence boundary detection for transcribed tunisian arabic. *Bochumer Linguistische Arbeitsberichte*, 323.

## 9 Appendix

## A Dataset

In this section we are going to present some statistics about the 7 datasets used in this paper. The data in this section is divided based on the tags that the datasets contain. For example, BinAjeeba and Wikipedia are gathered together because they have the same tags, and similarly, ANERCorp and NewsWire are gathered together. For POS, each corpus has its own POS tags so each data will be discussed separately.

| Corpus | B-LOC | I-LOC | B-PERS | O | I-ORG | B-ORG | I-PERS |
|---|---|---|---|---|---|---|---|
| BinAjeeba | 3553 | 1647 | 2910 | 501 | 1119 | 2342 | 98660 |
| Wikipedia | 46232 | 8615 | 22715 | 14732 | 9962 | 29895 | 881913 |

Table 4: Summary statistics of BinAjeeba and Wikipedia.

Table (4) shows the summary statistics of BinAjeeba and Wikipedia datasets. The *BinAjeeba* dataset contains 3889 sentences and 110732 tokens written in Modern Standard Arabic (MSA). The *Wikipedia* contains 31397 sentences, 1014064 tokens written in MSA and are the mapped versions of the fine-grained WikiFANE. We mapped the fine grained tags present in these datasets onto the 3 broad-grained tags similar to the ones in the table. Both of these datasets are following Automatic Content Extraction (ACE) tagging guidelines with three types of named entities: location, person and organisation.

| Corpus | B-LOC | I-LOC | B-PERS | O | B-MISC | I-ORG | I-MISC | B-ORG | I-PERS |
|---|---|---|---|---|---|---|---|---|---|
| ANERCorp | 4269 | 1070 | 1914 | 3440 | 586 | 468 | 1298 | 2702 | 117822 |
| NewsWire | 4631 | 906 | 2325 | 3521 | 1220 | 279 | 2127 | 2939 | 139537 |

Table 5: Summary statistics of ANERCorp and NewsWire.

Table (5) shows the summary statistics of ANERCorp and NewsWire datasets. The *ANERCorp* contains 3889 sentences and 133569 tokens written in MSA. The *Newswire* contains 4886 sentences, 157485 tokens and are mapped versions of the fine-grained NewsFANE datasets. We mapped the fine grained tags present in this dataset onto the 4 broad-grained tags similar to the ones in the table. Both of these datasets have three standard tags: person, location, organization and also a fourth miscellaneous tag and follows ACE tagging guidelines.

For POS-tagging we are evaluating on 3 standard datasets: *WikiNews* has 571 sentences, 29992 tokens and 27 POS tags see Table (6); *Al-Mushaf* has 6347 sentences, 84593 tokens and 9 POS tags see Table (7); *Prague Arabic Dependency Tree Bank (PADT)* has 7609 sentences, 282384 tokens and 16 POS tags see Table (8).

| Tag | Number of instances |
|---|---|
| NSUFF | 17 |
| FOREIGN | 2077 |
| FUT_PART | 1 |
| NOUN | 2 |
| ADJ | 5 |
| PART | 45 |
| NSUFF/ADJ | 339 |
| CASE | 1323 |
| ADV | 4317 |
| PRON | 45 |
| CONJ | 63 |
| PART/CONJ | 8840 |
| NSUFF/DET | 2 |
| PREP | 3367 |
| NOUN/DET | 16 |
| DET | 3 |
| NUM | 3 |
| ABBREV | 425 |
| NSUFF/NOUN | 974 |
| V | 48 |
| ADJ/NUM | 25 |
| ADJ/CONJ | 3 |
| PART/PREP+PART | 8 |
| PUNC | 2920 |
| PART/PART | 1512 |
| ADJ/DET | 1754 |
| PART/NOUN | 1858 |

Table 6: Summary statistics of WikiNews dataset.

| PRT | VERB | PUNC | DSIL | ADV | PN | NOUN | PRON | ADJ |
|---|---|---|---|---|---|---|---|---|
| 978 | 1730 | 30 | 39113 | 948 | 1380 | 15455 | 6346 | 18613 |

Table 7: Summary statistics of AlMushaf dataset.

| Tag | Number of instances |
|---|---|
| VERB | 29351 |
| SYM | 42555 |
| INTJ | 1071 |
| CCONJ | 2165 |
| DET | 25241 |
| NUM | 5896 |
| AUX | 8 |
| PART | 93705 |
| ADV | 7758 |
| ADP | 2190 |
| PROPN | 10877 |
| X | 245 |
| PUNCT | 22445 |
| NOUN | 388 |
| PRON | 21300 |
| ADJ | 17189 |

Table 8: Summary statistics of PADT dataset.

## A.1 Wikipedia and NewsWire Mapping

As mentioned in the previous section, both Wikipedia and NewsWire are mapped versions of the fine-grained WikiFANE and NewsFANE datasets. Both of WikiFANE and NewsFANE are following the (inside-outside-beginning) IOB format. WikiFANE has 103 tag in IOB format and 53 distinct tag trained on Wikipedia text. NewsFANE has 88 tags in IOB format and 46 distinct tags trained on NewsWire. We manually mapped each dataset by looking at the original tag and what it represents in order to map it to the equivalent tag. For example, FAC_Airport tag represents a location in the original dataset, hence it is mapped to location in the mapped dataset. For WikiFANE, we mapped each tag to the equivalent tags of BinAjeeba tagset which uses: Person, Location and Organization NEs, for NewsFANE we mapped each tag to the equivalent tags of ANERCorp tagset which uses: Person, Location, Organization and Miscellaneous NEs to create balance between datasets. It is worth noting that both WikiFANE and NewsFANE share the same level of granularity with different naming conventions and some extra tags. Table (9) shows a subset of the mapping in both Wikipedia and NewsWire.

| WikiFANE Tag | Wikipedia Map | NewsFANE Tag | NewsWire Map |
|---|---|---|---|
| FAC_Airport | LOC | Airport | LOC |
| FAC_Building-Grounds | LOC | Building-Grounds | LOC |
| FAC_Path | LOC | Continent | LOC |
| FAC_Subarea-Facility | LOC | County-or-District | LOC |
| ORG_Commercial | ORG | Commercial | ORG |
| ORG_Educational | ORG | Educational | ORG |
| ORG_Entertainment | ORG | Entertainment | ORG |
| ORG_Government | ORG | Government | ORG |
| PER_Artist | PERS | Artist | PERS |
| PER_Athlete | PERS | Athlete | PERS |
| PER_Businessperson | PERS | Businessperson | PERS |
| PER_Engineer | PERS | Engineer | PERS |
| PRO_Drug | O | Drug | MISC |
| PRO_Food | O | Food | MISC |
| PRO_Hardware | O | Hardware | MISC |
| PRO_Movie | O | Movie | MISC |

Table 9: Subset of the mapping of WikiFANE to Wikipedia and NewsFANE to NewsWire.

## B    Hyper-parameters Settings

In this section, we discuss the hyper-parameter settings in more detail. We used Keras which is an open-source neural-network library written in Python in the implementation of these models. For optimization, we used the adam optimization technique with a batch size of 32 batch, early stopping criteria based on the validation accuracy and validation split of 0.2 for all models. The models in our research can be divided in three types: baseline, individual-training models and combination model. In the following subsections we are going to discuss it in details.

## B.1 Baseline

In this section, we discuss the main hyper-parameters of the *baseline model*. We used pre-trained word embeddings with 100 dimensions and we set this layer to be trainable. The character embedding has 10 dimensions and we also set this layer to be trainable. The `C-Bi-LSTM` has 10 units wrapped with the `time distributed` Keras layer and 0.6 recurrent dropout. We concatenate the embeddings using Keras concatenation layer which stack each embedding on top of the other. The concatenated embedding here is the word embedding and the forward and the backward output of the `C-Bi-LSTM`. We also apply spatial dropout of 0.6 between the concatenation layer and the `main Bi-LSTM`. The `main Bi-LSTM` has 100 units with recurrent sequence sat to true and recurrent dropout of 0.6. We also placed a Keras dropout between the `main Bi-LSTM` and the `dense` layer. Before we feed the output to the `CRF` layer, we use a `dense` layer with 100 units, wrapped with `time distributed` Keras layer and tanh activation function to map the output of the `main Bi-LSTM` to the `CRF` layer. The size of the `CRF` layer is equal to the number of distinct tags.

## B.2 Individual-Training Models for training character embedding

In this section we discuss the *character model* and the *diacritic model* that are used to individual-train character and diacritic embedding layers. These two models are similar to the baseline and following exactly the same architecture. The only difference between these two models and the baseline is that after we train these models we extract the forward and the backward output of the `C-Bi-LSTM` and `D-Bi-LSTM` to use it as initialization weights for character and diacritic embedding respectively for the *combination model*.

## B.3 Combination Model

Here, we discuss the hyper-parameters of the *combination model*. This model has two versions *character-diacritic model* and the *four-layer combination model*. They both share the same parameters except two cases they are different, so we will mention the parameters all together and highlight the distinct parameters as we proceed. We used pre-trained word embeddings similar to the one mentioned earlier with 100 dimensions. The POS, character and diacritic embeddings have 10 dimensions each. The word embeddings are pre-trained, character and diacritic embeddings are individually-trained whereas the POS layer is randomly initialized. We set all of these embeddings to be trainable so they are trained together. In the *character-diacritic model* the `CC-Bi-LSTM` and `CD-Bi-LSTM` have 10 units with recurrent dropout of 0.6 each. In the *four-layer combination model* `CP-Bi-LSTM`, `CC-Bi-LSTM` and `CD-Bi-LSTM` have 10 units with recurrent dropout of 0.5 each. The `CC-Bi-LSTM` and `CD-Bi-LSTM` layers are wrapped with the `time distributed` Keras layer and the `CP-Bi-LSTM` is not. We concatenate the embeddings using Keras concatenation layer which stack each embedding on top of the other. In the *character-diacritic model* the concatenated embedding is the word embeddings and the forward and the backward output of the `CC-Bi-LSTM` and the `CD-Bi-LSTM` layers. In the *four-layer combination model*, the concatenated embedding is the word, POS embeddings and the forward and the backward output of the `CC-Bi-LSTM` and the `CD-Bi-LSTM` layers. We also apply spatial dropout of 0.6 between the concatenation layer and the `main Bi-LSTM` similar to the previous models. The `main Bi-LSTM` has 20 units with recurrent sequence set to true. We also placed a Keras dropout between the `main Bi-LSTM` and the `dense` layer. Before we feed the output to the `CRF` layer, we use a `dense` layer with 100 units, wrapped with a `time distributed` Keras layer and tanh activation function to map the output of the `main Bi-LSTM` to the `CRF` layer. The size of the `CRF` layer is equal to the number of distinct tags.

## C  Computational Aspects

In this section, we present the computational time and the number of epochs that each model took to train across all datasets. It is worth noting that we didn't compute the time and number of epochs of the individual-training models since it is a one time cost. Table (10) shows the time and number of epochs needed for each model on each dataset, where time is in minutes. This table shows that our proposed model is light weight which is an advantage over the other heavy weights models such as BERT or attention.

| Corpus | Character model | | Character-Diacritic model | | Four-layer Combination model | |
|---|---|---|---|---|---|---|
| | Time | Epochs | Time | Epochs | Time | Epochs |
| ANERCorp | 77 | 169 | 85 | 164 | 88 | 240 |
| BinAjeeba | 69 | 176 | 65 | 224 | 21 | 194 |
| NewsWire | 143 | 261 | 67 | 276 | - | - |
| Wikipedia | 350 | 90 | 387 | 104 | - | - |
| AlMushaf | 154 | 318 | 122 | 306 | - | - |
| PADT | 145 | 229 | 101 | 136 | - | - |
| WikiSeg | 20 | 282 | 16 | 340 | - | - |

Table 10: The time in minutes and the number of epochs taken to train each model for each dataset.

# MANorm: A Normalization Dictionary for Moroccan Arabic Dialect Written in Latin Script


**Randa Zarnoufi**
FST, Department of Computer Science
University Mohammed V in Rabat
randa_zarnoufi@um5.ac.ma

**Hamid Jaafar**
ENS, Department of Languages and Educational Sciences
University Hassan II
Jaafarhamid1973@gmail.com

**Walid Bachri**
ENSIAS
University Mohammed V in Rabat
bachriwalid@gmail.com

**Mounia Abik**
ENSIAS
University Mohammed V in Rabat
mounia.abik@um5.ac.ma



## Abstract

Social media user generated text is actually the main resource for many NLP tasks. This text however, does not follow the standard rules of writing. Moreover, the use of dialect such as Moroccan Arabic in written communications increases further NLP tasks complexity. A dialect is a verbal language that does not have a standard orthography, which leads users to improvise spelling while writing. Thus, for the same word we can find multiple forms of transliterations. Subsequently, it is mandatory to normalize these different transliterations to one canonical word form. To reach this goal, we have exploited the powerfulness of word embedding models generated with a corpus of YouTube comments. Besides, using a Moroccan Arabic dialect dictionary that provides the canonical forms, we have built a normalization dictionary that we refer to as *MANorm[1]*. We have conducted several experiments to demonstrate the efficiency of MANorm, which have shown its usefulness in dialect normalization.


## 1 Introduction

The large part of the world's population is daily connected and very active in Social Media (SM). This community produces a huge amount of data. This latter, especially textual one is actually very useful for the development of many NLP or text-based applications in general (Farzindar and Inkpen, 2018). However, these texts generated by SM users are of a noisy nature or in other words do not follow the rules of standard communications. Another phenomenon, which adds more complexity to this type of content, is the use of dialects, which are non-standard languages used mainly in verbal communication.

Since the advent of Short Messaging Service (SMS), Moroccan Arabic (MA) dialect has been introduced into users written communications[2] and today, in social media, this phenomenon is becoming widespread (Caubet, 2017). MA dialect is the mother tongue of most Moroccan people, it has been used in SM to freely and spontaneously express emotions and thoughts with other peers (Hall, 2015). This language does not have a standard spelling since it is not used as formal language. Therefore, each social media user writes according to his own. The writing variability is due to the diversity of individual's pronunciation related to their different regional and cultural backgrounds (Boukous, 1995). Thus, for the same word, we find different spellings. For instance, the word 'chkoun' (who) has other five different transliterations ('chkoune', 'chkon,' chkone', 'chkou', 'chkoon'). This problem constitutes a major handicap for many NLP tasks (Han and Baldwin, 2011). To overcome this problem, normalization can

---

[1] MANorm is available at: //github.com/MAProcessing/MANorm

[2] Until 1998, writing in MA was not yet recognized, with the exception of a few essays from literacy classes and some songs such as "Melhoun" and some linguistic resources (Jaafar, 2012).






*Proceedings of the Fifth Arabic Natural Language Processing Workshop*, pages 155–166
Barcelona, Spain (Online), December 12, 2020

be used as a preprocessing in front of the main NLP task. This preprocessing has proved his efficiency in sentiment analysis (Htait et al., 2018), dependency parsing (Van Der Goot et al., 2020) and also in POS tagging (Bhat et al., 2018). In a previous work (Zarnoufi et al., 2020), we have introduced Machine Normalization system for social media text standardization, that can be used as a preprocessing. The current work will be part of this system which will allow us to improve its performance.

For standard language, in general the task of normalization aims at mapping each out of vocabulary word to one correct form or standard form among a set of standard words candidates (n→1). On the contrary, for dialect, which is a non-standard language. Since there is no standard form for dialect words, this task starts from considering a transliteration of word phonemes (the words are written as spoken) as the canonical form. Then, we try to capture all its possible transliteration forms (1→n). In this work, we follow this approach for MA dialect normalization. First, we build a MA words dictionary that we consider as the lexicon of canonical word form. We then exploit distributed word representations models trained on a YouTube comments corpus to extract the most similar (semantically) words of each dictionary entry, and lexical similarity measures to select all the nearest word forms. The result is a normalization dictionary mapping between each MA word transliteration and its canonical form. We refer to the constructed normalization dictionary for Moroccan Arabic as MANorm.

In the next section, we discuss related works particularly closely related ones on standard languages. Then, we present the detailed solution with the used resources followed by the evaluation and the discussion of the resulted dictionary and we conclude with future directions and further challenges.

## 2  Related Works

Text normalization can be seen as the successor of spelling correction, with the difference that in the first case, the noisy writing style is often intentional (Han and Baldwin, 2011), for example when using abbreviations (e.g. use of 'u' instead of 'you'). Whereas in the second case, misspellings are unintentional and are mainly related to cognitive processes (J.Steffler, 2001). The first approaches for text normalization were based on rules and the noisy channel model (Shannon, 1948) mainly related to spelling correction techniques. They were used jointly for automatic normalization. Among these rules, we find lexical rules using edit distance[3] (Sidarenka et al., 2013) that can detect misspellings and regular expression patterns used for removing or replacing unnecessary character repetitions or URLs, hashtags and logograms[4]. They can also be used for the detection of SM special words (Cotelo et al., 2015). In addition, phonetic rules using Soundex algorithm variants, can serve to normalize noisy word related to pronunciation differences (Eryigit and Torunoglu-Selamet, 2017). The noisy channel model normalizes words by selecting the most probable formal ones using probabilities ranking from language model. It was used with supervised and unsupervised training (Cook and Stevenson, 2009). In general, these approaches capture the differences of the word's surface forms by detecting the similarity in the lexical level between informal and formal word forms. However, the semantic level remains inaccessible because these techniques are not able to capture the words' context. The problem here is that an informal word can be assigned to a formal one, only based on its lexical form without considering its meaning, which can constitute a source of ambiguity.

To mitigate this drawback, supervised learning, machine translation and other techniques were used. For supervised learning, features such as character N-grams, word embedding, POS tag, edit-distances, lookup lists and others are used with labeled data as in MoNoise (Van Der Goot and Van Noord, 2017), which is the current state-of-the-art model for most languages. In addition, different architectures of neural networks were adopted such as LSTM (long short-term memory) model to predict the word canonical form, using the word itself and its surrounding words as in (Min and Mott, 2015). In a very recent work, Muller et al. (2019) have tried to use contextualized embedding with BERT (Bidirectional Encoder Representations from Transformers) to learn lexical normalization for English. This task has also been approached as statistical machine translation SMT-like task (Kaufmann and Kalita, 2010) as a

---

[3] Edit distance is the number of applied operations to transform one string into another. It allows measuring the lexical similarity between strings. Levenshtein distance (Levenshtein, 1966) is the most used measure that includes insertion, deletion and substitution operations.

[4] Using a single letter or number to represent a word or word part.

means of context-sensitive technique, where the goal has been to translate noisy text into standard one using parallel corpora. CSMT or character level SMT has also been used for normalization and performed better results than word level SMT (Scherrer and Ljubeši´c, 2016). Neural machine translation (NMT) was also used, in Lusetti et al. (2018) a neural encoder-decoder with word and character level language model surpassed CSMT performance. Nevertheless, these techniques require a large scale of labeled data, which is in itself a complex and costly task.

To address these problems, Sridhar (2015) was the first to introduce the contextualized normalization with a fully unsupervised manner. He has employed the distributed representation of words or word embedding to capture contextual similarity that can match the noisy word to its canonical form if they share the same vector representation. In other words, their vectors are the closest to each other among all the vocabulary. He has used finite state machines (FSM) to represent the resulting lexicon, and the normalization process is carried out by transducing the noisy words from the FSM. The main advantages of this technique are, first, the needless of labeled corpus, he has used Twitter and customer care notes as training data therefore it is scalable and adaptive to any language. Second, the presence of the contextual dimension, which has been a key factor of its high performance in this task that surpassed Microsoft Word and Aspell accuracies.

These positive qualities have inspired other works on normalization. Bertaglia and Nunes (2016) have performed Portuguese normalization using word embedding model trained on products reviews and tweets. They have built a dictionary mapping between noisy and canonical words to represent the lexicon. They have conduct experiments on both internet slang and orthographic error correction. The obtained results outperformed existing tools. Htait and Bellot (2018) have employed the same approach to build normalization dictionaries for English, French and Arabic using Twitter corpora to overcome the lack of normalization resources available for these languages. They have also reached high performance in the three languages.

All these mentioned works have been done for standard languages normalization. For dialects that suffer from resources scarceness, the related works are very limited. Among them we find Conventional Orthography for Dialectal Arabic or CODA, first proposed in (Habash et al., 2012) for the Egyptian dialect. It was later improved to CODA* in (Habash et al., 2018) and extended to include new dialects. Al-badrashiny et al. (2014), have introduced a system that generates a list of all possible transliterations for each word in an input sentence using a finite-state transducer trained on character-level alignment from Egyptian dialect written in Arabizi (Latin script) to Arabic script. They have learned the transducer on parallel corpus of Egyptian Arabizi-Arabic words. Partanen et al. (2019) have used character level NMT to translate dialectal Finnish to standard one. They used LSTM and transformer models that has been trained on a hand-annotated corpus of transcriptions of different speech records starting from 1950. Word embedding has also been used in dialect processing for the construction of a comparable corpus and a lexicon of Algerian dialect (Abidi and Smaili, 2018) by alignment of a corpus extracted from YouTube. The built lexicon associates the different transliterations forms of dialect words written in Arabic and Latin scripts.

As a dialect, Moroccan Arabic is an under-resourced language. There is no available resource or tool for its normalization. The only work done for this purpose was (Tachicart and Bouzoubaa, 2019) where the authors have used a corpus from Facebook and YouTube to analyze spelling inconsistency of MA dialect used in SM text written in Arabic and Latin scripts. They have compared their corpus with a reference dictionary that has been previously built by the authors and they have found that 35% of this text is noisy. They have concluded that a spell-correction tool is essential to clean up and convert dialectal words into a single standard form of writing.

In line with previous works, namely Sridhar and Htait, we will employ distributed representation for our MA normalization for multiple reasons. First, we only need a corpus of unlabeled data and a dictionary of dialect words to serve as a lexicon for normalized word forms. Second, word embedding is able to identify semantically similar words because it constructs word vectors based on the assumption that semantically similar words are surrounded by the same context. Therefore, the semantic aspect of each reference word and its associated words is guaranteed. In other words, the reference word and these extracted synonyms have the same meaning in the context in use. The remaining task is then to measure the lexical similarity between these words to identify the different lexical forms of the same canonical word. Finally, a normalized form is provided to these words.

## 3   Moroccan Arabic Dialect words forms

The MA dialect is mostly derived from Arabic[5] about 86% and a mixture of other languages namely, French 11.72%, Tamazight 0.39% and Spanish 0.06% according to (Tachicart et al., 2016). As previously mentioned, we are interested in MA dialect normalization, specially the dialect written in Latin script (also called Arabizi). The first time this script appeared goes back to the beginning of SMS in early 2000's where mobile phones did not yet have an Arabic keypad and some phones cannot display messages written in Arabic script, whereas Latin script was accessible in all phones. However, until today, there are still people who are keeping this type of writing even if Arabic keypads are widely available. The MA dialect written in Latin script is the transliteration of phonemes mainly of Arabic origin, thus it is more speech like than writing like. This script uses Latin consonants that mimic Arabic ones and vowels as the equivalent of diacritics.

To identify the different phenomena that dialect normalization needs to address. We selected some comments from our collected corpus composed of YouTube comments (see Sec. 4). Then we analyzed the words forms to determine the sources of lexical variation. We identified five categories as listed below:

- *Vowels variants for the same phoneme*: this is mainly due to pronunciation differences between regions. For example, 'a' and 'e' may be used interchangeably as in 'bayan' and 'bayen' (clear). We have also observed that vowels may be omitted in some cases like in 'm3alqa' and 'm3lqa' (spoon).

- *Letter substitution by number*: some number are used instead of letter to represent Arabic grapheme, if their graphical form is close to a letter in Arabic script. For example, the use of '9' rather than 'ق' [q] and '7' instead of 'ح' [ḥ]. The detailed cases are presented in Table 1.

- *Gemination*[6]: is frequent in Arabic, and it is represented by double consonants that are mentioned by some users and overlooked by others. For example, 'm3allam' (skillful) may be written 'm3alam'.

- *Words combination*: the words in some specific phrases are combined to form one word. For example, "hamdo li allah" (thanks god) may be written for example as 'hamdoulillah' or 'hamdollah' or 'hamdouallah'.

- *Word agglutination*: MA is mostly derived from Arabic, which is highly inflectional or agglutinative language where affixes are combined with the main word. For example, the expression 'wlidatou' (his children) is the concatenation of 'wlidat' (children) + 'ou' (suffix used to mark possession equivalent to his). Moreover, in MA dialect the agglutination is used also to combine particles with the main word, like in 'fl7ayat' (in the life) the letter 'f' (in) is a preposition concatenated with 'l' (the) a definite article and '7ayat' (life) a noun.

These linguistic features of written dialect are the main source of variations and non-uniformity of MA text in SM. In the next sections, we will present our solution to normalize dialect word forms and hence increase this text uniformity.

## 4   Data extraction

The used data was gathered from YouTube video comments extracted using YouTube API. YouTube is the most popular SM platform in Morocco, used by 44.48% of the population[7]. These videos have been

---

[5] Both Classical Arabic and Standard Arabic.
[6] *Gemination* or consonant lengthening is an articulation of a consonant for a longer period of time than that of a singleton consonant (from Wikipedia).
[7] https://gs.statcounter.com/social-media-stats/all/morocco

selected using keywords related to various topics such as politics, sport, art, cooking, comedy, and others. For instance, for cooking we use key words like 'شهيوات مغربية', 'بسطيلة', 'حليمة الفيلالي'. The goal is to capture a wide range of words from different domains and thus ensure a large coverage of MA vocabulary. The collected corpus contains about 500K sentences.

## 5  Data preprocessing

Before starting the normalization steps, we conduct a set of pre-processing to prepare our corpus for word embedding. The first one is the selection of Latin script comments because the raw corpus contains also Arabic script comments, then duplicated comments or containing only numbers or just one word are removed and any repetitions of more than three letters are reduced back to two letters. In addition, we removed all punctuations, hashtags, URLs, at mentions, emoticons, symbols, and full number strings. Finally, we have substituted the numbers within words by their equivalent letters to meet those used in the dialect dictionary (see Table 1). Except for '7' (equivalent of 'ح') and '3' (equivalent of 'ع') because we do not have their correspondent letters in Latin script, and we lowercased the overall text. After these pre-processing, the resulted corpus consists of 160 651 sentences and 242 277 unique words.

| Numbers/Letters | Equivalent letters |
|:---:|:---:|
| 2 | a |
| 6 | t |
| 4 / 8 | gh |
| 5 / x | kh |
| 9 | q |

Table 1. Conversion rules from numbers to letters as observed in our YouTube corpus

## 6  Dialect Normalization

Our system for dialect normalization is based on two steps. Namely, transliterations extraction and transliterations selection. Starting from three word embedding models and a MA dialect dictionary that will serve as the lexicon of canonical word form. For each canonical word in this dialect dictionary, we first extract the most semantically similar words from the vocabulary produced by the word-embedding models. Semantic similarity aims to select the nearest neighbors to each canonical word based on their context. Then, from these selected words, we select the most lexically similar ones to the canonical word. The lexical similarity aims to select the most similar transliterations to the canonical word in terms of surface form. We will describe these processing steps in detail in the following sections.

### 6.1  Dialect dictionary

The canonical form considered for our normalization task was first based on a collection of MA dialect dictionaries of nouns, verbs and adjectives (Jaafar, 2012). This dictionary consists of 14548 entries that we have converted from an adapted IPA (International Phonetic Alphabet) transcription to match the Latin script employed by Social Media users. the different adopted conventions are listed in Table 2. Then, we have extended this dictionary to include some special words to social media (e.g. 'tagini' (tag me)). However, by checking the collected dictionary, we found that, only 16% of dictionary words are present in the word embedding models vocabulary. In fact, today, the use of most of these dictionary words are not common in youth-run SM. To overcome this problem, we have semi-automatically collected a set of words from the models vocabulary while focusing on useful words that can capture other transliterations. We mention that we consider borrowed word from other languages as neology and we include them as new entries in MA dictionary. For instance, the word 'stationi' (to park) is borrowed from French 'stationner'. The final dictionary is of size 2502 canonical words.

| Adapted API script | Latin script | MA phoneme | API symbol |
| --- | --- | --- | --- |
| ḥ | 7 | ح | ħ |
| ḍ/ đ | d | ض | dˤ |
| ε / Ɛ | 3 | ع | ʕ |
| ġ | gh | غ | ɣ |
| ħ | h | ه | h |
| ḫ / x | kh | خ | x |
| ḷ | l | ل (geminated) | l |
| r̲ / ṛ / ř | r | ر | r |
| ṣ | s | ص | sˤ |
| š / ṣ̌ | ch | ش | š |
| ṭ / ṭ | t | ط | tˤ |
| ž | j | ج | ʒ |
| ẓ / ż | z | ز | z |
| â | a | ا | ʔ / a |
| ə | e | - | - |
| î | i | ي | i |
| û | ou | و | u |

Table 2. Conversion rules from adapted API to Latin script used for MA dialect in SM and its equivalent in MA phoneme with the associated API symbol

## 6.2    Word Embedding model generation

We use three word-embedding models, namely, word2vec CBOW (continuous bag of words) and Skip-gram (Mikolov et al., 2013) and the third one is FastText (Bojanowski et al., 2017). According to Mikolov et al. both architectures CBOW and Skip-gram work well in semantic tasks. In addition, Skip-gram is efficient in presenting infrequent words, unlike CBOW that has better representations for more frequent words. FastText is also able to better model infrequent words. Therefore, these models can complement each other and if we combine their outputs, we can expand the coverage of the detected transliterations for each canonical word form. For the configuration of these models, we use two as minimum count for each word occurrences in the corpus to capture rare words forms with a context window of seven words from the left and right sides.

## 6.3    Normalization and transliteration word forms Association

The normalization starts with the extraction of the nearest neighbors of each word in the MA dictionary (normalization word form) based on the semantic similarity score using the cosine distance between the dimensional vector of each word in the model and each canonical word. We have used the class most_similar of Gensim framework and we have fixed the list size parameter to twenty. Because we found that lower values capture few words and higher values capture a lot of noise. The same finding has been noted by Htait and Bellot (2018).

The second stage in this process is lexical similarity where we extract the nearest words to the canonical one (from MA dictionary) according to its surface form. We do so by measuring the similarity between each canonical word and the set of extracted words in the previous stage. Then, we select the words that have a similarity score higher than a threshold value. This value has been defined empirically and we have fixed it at 70%. After several experiments (more details will be given in Sec. 7), we have observed that the smaller is the threshold, the larger is the coverage but many undesirable words are selected. However, higher threshold values eliminate a considerable part of word transliterations certainly in the case of word agglutination. For example, we cannot capture and normalize 'lmagrib' (Morocco) to 'maghrib' if the threshold is up to 70%.

To compute the lexical similarity score, we have used different measures. The first one is based on sequence matching with vowels and double consonants removing. We removed vowels from words because as we have mentioned, most of writing variations are related to the use of different vowels. For example, the word 'ya3tek' (give you) can be written in 13 different manners: ya3tek, ye3tek, yaatik, ya3tik, yatek, yaatek, yaetik, y3atik, ya3tike, ytik, yi3tik, ya3atik, ye3tik. Therefore, by suppressing vowels and keeping consonants we can catch a large part of word transliterations. Moreover, we reduced back all consecutive double consonants that are used to mention gemination because it is not respected by all SM users. For instance, the word 'allah' (god) can be written 'alah' by some users.

The second measure used for lexical similarity is sequence matching with Soundex adapted to MA dialect phonetic rules as shown in Table 3.

Finally, we have used the other lexical similarity measures employed in related works. Our goal is to show the effectiveness of each measure in capturing different word' transliterations. In Table 4, we list the different formula used for scoring functions in each study. The performance of these measures will be given in the evaluation section.

| MA Soundex phonetic rules | Conversion |
|---|---|
| b, f, m, p, v, w | 1 |
| d, t, l, n | 2 |
| s, z | 3 |
| j, y, ch | 4 |
| r, kh, gh | 5 |

Table 3. MA phonetic rules used for Soundex

| Approaches | Semantic similarity | Lexical similarity |
|---|---|---|
| Sridhar (Sridhar, 2015) | Cosine similarity $$= \frac{\sum_{i=0}^{D} u_i \times v_i}{\sqrt{\sum_{i=0}^{D}(u_i)^2 \times \sum_{i=0}^{D}(v_i)^2}}$$ | $$\text{lexical similarity}(s_1, s_2) = \frac{\text{LCSR}(s_1, s_2)}{ED(s_1, s_2)}$$ $$\text{LCSR}(s_1, s_2) = \frac{\text{LCS}(s_1, s_2)}{Max\ Lenght(s_1, s_2)}$$ LCSR = Longest Common Subsequence Ratio (Melamed, 1995) <br> LCS = Longest Common Subsequence <br> ED8 = Edit distance between the two strings. |
| Bertaglia (Bertaglia and Nunes, 2016) | Cosine similarity (same formula) | $$\text{lexical similarity}(s_1, s_2)$$ $$= \begin{cases} \frac{\text{LCSR}(s_1, s_2)}{MED(s_1, s_2)}, & if\ MED(s_1, s_2) > 0 \\ \text{LCSR}(s_1, s_2), & \text{otherwise} \end{cases}$$ $$\text{LCSR}(s_1, s_2) = \frac{\text{LCS}(s_1, s_2) + \text{DS}(s_1, s_2)}{Max\ Lenght(s_1, s_2)}$$ MED($s_1$,$s_2$) = ED($s_1$,$s_2$) - DS($s_1$,$s_2$) <br> MED = Modified edit distance <br> DS = Diacritical symmetry between s1 and s2 <br> N.B: As diacritics does not exist in our case, so DS = 0 and the lexical similarity formula will be the same as Sridhar one. |
| Htait [9] (Htait et al., 2018) | Cosine similarity (same formula) | Sequence Matching with a score of 50% |

Table 4. Scoring functions for both semantic and lexical similarities used in normalization approaches based on word embedding

---

[8] For English, the edit distance computation was modified to find the distance between the consonant skeleton of the two strings $s_1$ and $s_2$.

[9] Our implementation was initially based on the open code provided by Htait: https://github.com/OpenEdition/NormAFE

We have executed the same normalization process for the three generated word-embedding models. We have observed that each model can capture a set of different transliterations. Therefore, we have decided to merge the produced lexicon in each case. The resulting combinations (transliteration, normalization form) are then grouped together to form a single MANorm normalization dictionary.

## 7  Evaluation

The goal of the evaluation of MANorm dictionary is to test the quality of the normalization lexicon. Since this is the first work on MA dialect normalization, we do not have a gold standard or a reference to evaluate the performance of the produced lexicon. Therefore, it is impossible to proceed to an automatic evaluation, thus we have created our own reference. We first combined the outputs dictionaries of the three models, which produced a normalization dictionary of 3057 entries (transliteration, normalization form). We have then, validated each entry based on a human judgment by checking manually the correct association between each word transliteration and its canonical form. This operation resulted in a normalization reference dictionary of 2225 correct entries. Examples of result are given in Table 5.

| Canonical word form (MA dialect dictionary) | Transliterations (corpus) |
| --- | --- |
| awel (the first) | awl, awwal, awle, aaal, awale |
| choukran (thank you) | chokran, chokrane, chkran, khokran, chokrn |

Table 5. Normalization result examples

We have used precision and coverage as evaluation metrics rather than the common information retrieval ones (precision, recall and F-score). Because we are not able to measure the recall, which is the ratio between the number of the provided relevant results, and the total of relevant results that we have to provide. Since we do not know exactly how many transliterations, we can normalize by each given canonical word form, we cannot define the total value of relevant results. Therefore, instead of recall, we measure the coverage of the MA dictionary words. The coverage represents the ratio of useful canonical words or the words that were able to catch some other transliterations over the total of MA dictionary words.

To gain more insight into the performance differences of the three word embedding models individually, we calculate their coverages, and we measure their precisions by comparing each model with the created reference normalization dictionary. The results are shown in Table 6.

By looking at Table 6, we first observe that CBOW model achieved the best precision followed by Skip-gram, but their coverage is still very low. Second, FastText performance was the worst. Finally, it can be seen that after combining the three models' outputs we achieved the best coverage with a huge margin while keeping a good precision. From these results, we can conclude that models' combination allows to counter the imbalance between the high precision and low coverage of separated models.

We also evaluate the different scoring functions of lexical similarity used in other related works (with a threshold of 70%) and we report the results in Table 7. These results are related to the three merged models.

Table 7 shows that Lexim (used in Sridhar and Bertaglia) outperforms all the other scoring functions in term of precision but its coverage was the worst. In term of coverage, sequence matching with Soundex achieved the best coverage among all the other scoring functions. However, sequence matching with vowels and double consonants removing have balanced the precision and coverage scores. For this reason, we consider this last lexical similarity scoring function in MANorm dictionary generation.

To prove our choice of the threshold value for lexical similarity scoring we conduct a series of experiments. The obtained results are reported in Table 8. The main conclusion we can draw from this table is that higher threshold values give better precision but lower coverage. By raising the threshold from 60% to 80%, the precision improves considerably but the coverage decreases drastically. Thereby, in MANorm, we used the medium threshold 70% that balances between precision and dictionary coverage.

| Models | Precision | Coverage |
|---|---|---|
| Wrod2vec CBOW | 0.815 | 0.300 |
| Word2vec Skip-Gram | 0.775 | 0.280 |
| FastText | 0.414 | 0.163 |
| Merged dictionary (CBOW + Skip-gram + FastText) | 0.704 | 0.463 |

Table 6. Word embedding models performance

| Lexical similarity scoring function | Precision | Coverage |
|---|---|---|
| Lexim (used in Sridhar and Bertaglia) | **0.785** | 0.300 |
| Sequence matching (used in Htait) | 0.671 | 0.427 |
| Sequence matching + Soundex | 0.486 | **0.578** |
| Sequence matching + vowels and double consonants removing | 0.704 | 0.463 |

Table 7. Lexical similarity scoring functions comparison

| Threshold value | Precision | Coverage |
|---|---|---|
| 60% | 0.414 | 0.706 |
| 65% | 0.428 | 0.697 |
| **70%** | **0.704** | **0.463** |
| 75% | 0.703 | 0.462 |
| 80% | 0.744 | 0.424 |

Table 8. Threshold value influence on merged models precision and coverage

While validating MANorm, we have observed that agglutination which is mainly related to word inflection, is a real source of ambiguity because it opens the door for a high number of possible transliterations. As our main concern is to reduce spelling variation, in case of inflected word forms (e.g. conjugated verbs, nouns and adjectives plural and feminine forms), we consider word lemma or the nearest inflection form as the correct normalization. In MA dialect, the lemma of verbs is the past tense of the third person singular and for nouns and adjectives, the lemma is the masculine singular form. For instance, as shown in Table 9, the normalized form of the adjectives 'saknin' and 'sakna' is the lemma form 'saken'. Other examples are presented in Table 9.

Regarding normalization errors, they are related to different reasons. In some cases, we have observed, that one transliteration (input) can be assigned to several canonical forms. In such a case, throughout validation, we consider correct the canonical form that is closest in meaning according to the transliteration context that we find in the corpus. For example, the transliteration '7amad' has been assigned to '7amd' (praise) and '7amed' (sour) but according to their context the correct form is the second one.

We have encountered another issue related to agglutination, for example, the transliteration 'wqaaf' was affected to two canonical forms 'wqef' (hold on) and 'awqaf' (Islamic endowments). However, the word 'awqaf' used in the corpus is a concatenation of 'a' and 'wqaf' that means hold on (in a strong way). By checking their contexts in the corpus, we found that 'wqaaf' has the same meaning as 'wqef' that we therefore consider as correct.

Other errors are due to the fact that the phonemes transliteration conventions adopted in our dictionary do not always meet those used in the corpus. For instance, the noun '7aj' (pilgrimage) was assigned to the verb 'haj' (to rave) where 'h' was used as [ḥ] by some users. However, in MA dictionary we use '7' for this phoneme and 'h' to represent [ħ]. This problem is partly due to that during lexical similarity we do not differentiate between '7' and 'h', because doing so we can gather a large number of different transliterations.

There are cases where a transliteration can be given an inappropriate canonical form because both are used in the same context, and are lexically close to each other (similarity > 70%), although, they belong to different words. For example, '3id' (Eid/religious celebration) was assigned to 'sa3id' (happy) as canonical form.

| Word POS tag | Inflected form | Lemma/Nearest inflection |
|---|---|---|
| Adjective | saknin (they are living)<br>sakna (she is living) | Lem. masculine singular:<br>saken (he is living) |
| Noun | klamo (his words)<br>klamek (your words) | Lem. masculine singular:<br>klam (words) |
| Verb | 3aqo (they realized)<br>3aqna (we realized) | Lem. past tense, third person singular:<br>3aq (he realized) |
| | bakatni (she made me cry)<br>bakitini (you (singular) made me cry)<br>bakitona (you (plural) made me cry) | Lem. past tense, first person singular:<br>bkite (I cried) |
| | 3ajbatni (I liked it)<br>3jbatni (I liked it)<br>3jebni (I liked it)<br>kat3jabni (I like)<br>kay3jabni (I like) | Nearest inflection:<br>3jabni (I liked it) |

Table 9. Inflected word normalization

Finally, even if errors are quite common in MaNorm, it is still an interesting attempt to normalize dialect spelling variation. We are confident that with larger corpus and dictionary we can further more improve its performance.

## 8 Conclusion

Written dialect is a phonetic transliteration of spoken words that does not follow any standard orthography. It is mostly used in SM where each user improvises his own spelling. As a result, for each single word we find a mixture of spellings. Before performing any NLP task, it is mandatory to transform these dialect words written differently to one normalized form. In this work, we present our solution for MA dialect normalization based on semantic similarity using word-embedding and lexical similarity. We use three word-embedding models that we combine their outputs to form one normalization dictionary MANorm. In the resulting dictionary, we find the matching between each word from the corpus and the most similar word form from the MA dictionary. The merge allows us to make a compromise between precision and coverage. The evaluation of the normalization dictionary shows the good performance of this solution. However, other improvements can be done with a larger corpus, especially to increase MA dictionary coverage. As next direction, we will employ the same technique to normalize MA words written in Arabic script after building the appropriate dictionary for canonical forms.

## Reference


Abidi, K., Smaili, K., 2018. An Automatic Learning of an Algerian Dialect Lexicon by using Multilingual Word Embeddings, in: 11th Edition of the Language Resources and Evaluation Conference, LREC. pp. 832–838.

Al-badrashiny, M., Eskander, R., Habash, N., Rambow, O., 2014. Automatic Transliteration of Romanized Dialectal Arabic 30–38.

Bertaglia, T.F.C., Nunes, M. das G.V., 2016. Exploring Word Embeddings for Unsupervised Textual User-Generated Content Normalization, in: Proceedings of the 2nd Workshop on Noisy User-Generated Text. pp. 112–120.

Bhat, I.A., Bhat, R.A., Shrivastava, M., Sharma, M.D., 2018. Universal Dependency Parsing for Hindi-English Code-switching, in: Proceedings OfNAACL-HLT 2018. pp. 987–998.

Bojanowski, P., Grave, E., Joulin, A., Mikolov, T., 2017. Enriching Word Vectors with Subword Information. Trans. Assoc. Comput. Linguist. 5, 135–146.

Boukous, A., 1995. Société, langues et cultures au Maroc. Enjeux symboliques. Rabat, Publications de la Faculté des Lettres et des Sciences Humaines.

Caubet, D., 2017. Vers une littératie numérique pour la darija au Maroc , une démarche collective, in: Studies on Arabic Dialectology and Sociolinguistics. Proceedings of the 12th International Conference of AIDA.

Cook, P., Stevenson, S., 2009. An Unsupervised Model for Text Message Normalization, in: Proceedings Ofthe NAACL HLTWorkshop on Computational Approaches to Linguistic Creativity. pp. 71–78.

Cotelo, J.M., Cruz, F.L., Troyano, J.A., Ortega, F.J., 2015. Expert Systems with Applications A modular approach for lexical normalization applied to Spanish tweets. Expert Syst. Appl. 42, 4743–4754. doi:10.1016/j.eswa.2015.02.003

Eryigit, G., Torunoglu-Selamet, D., 2017. Social media text normalization for Turkish. Nat. Lang. Eng. 1–41. doi:10.1017/S1351324917000134

Farzindar, A., Inkpen, D., 2018. Natural Language Processing for Social Media Second Edition, 2nd ed.

Habash, N., Diab, M., Rambow, O., 2012. Conventional Orthography for Dialectal Arabic, in: In Proceedings of LREC, Istanbul, Turkey. pp. 711–718.

Habash, N., Eryani, F., Khalifa, S., Rambow, O., Abdulrahim, D., Erdmann, A., Faraj, R., Zaghouani, W., Bouamor, H., Zalmout, N., Hassan, S., Al-shargi, F., Alkhereyf, S., Abdulkareem, B., Eskander, R., Salameh, M., Saddiki, H., 2018. Unified Guidelines and Resources for Arabic Dialect Orthography, in: The International Conference on Language Resources and Evaluation (LREC 2018), Miyazaki, Japan. pp. 3628–3637.

Hall, J.L., 2015. DEBATING DARIJA : LANGUAGE IDEOLOGY AND THE WRITTEN REPRESENTATION OF MOROCCAN ARABIC IN MOROCCO.

Han, B., Baldwin, T., 2011. Lexical Normalisation of Short Text Messages : Makn Sens a # twitter, in: Proceedings of the 49th Annual Meeting of the Association for Computational Linguistics. pp. 368–378.

Htait, A., Fournier, S., Bellot, P., 2018. Unsupervised Creation of Normalisation Dictionaries for Micro-Blogs in Arabic , French and English, in: International Conference on Computational Linguistics and Intelligent Text Processing.

J.Steffler, D., 2001. Implicit Cognition and Spelling Development. Dev. Rev. 21, 168–204.

Jaafar, H., 2012. PhD Thesis: Le Nom et l'Adjectif dans l'Arabe Marocain: Etude Lexicologique. University Sidi Mohammed Ben Abbdellah.

Kaufmann, M., Kalita, J., 2010. Syntactic Normalization of Twitter Messages, in: International Confer- Ence on Natural Language Processing, Kharagpur, India. pp. 1–7.

Levenshtein, V.I., 1966. Binary codes capable of correcting deletions, insertions, and reversals. Sov. Phys. Dokl. 10.

Lusetti, M., Ruzsics, T., Göhring, A., Samardži´c, T.S., Stark, E., 2018. Encoder-Decoder Methods for Text Normalization, in: Proceedings of the Fifth Workshop on NLP for Similar Languages, Varieties and Dialects. pp. 18–28.

Mikolov, T., Corrado, G., Chen, K., Dean, J., 2013. Efficient Estimation of Word Representations in Vector Space, in: In Proceedings of Workshop at ICLR.

Min, W., Mott, B.W., 2015. NCSU _ SAS _ WOOKHEE : A Deep Contextual Long-Short Term Memory Model for Text Normalization, in: Proceedings of the ACL 2015 Workshop on Noisy User-Generated Text. pp. 111–119.

Muller, B., Sagot, B., Seddah, D., 2019. Enhancing BERT for Lexical Normalization, in: Proceedings Ofthe 2019 EMNLP Workshop W-NUT: The 5th Workshop on Noisy User-Generated Text. pp. 297–306.

Partanen, N., Hamalainen, M., Alnajjar, K., 2019. Dialect Text Normalization to Normative Standard Finnish, in: Proceedings Ofthe 2019 EMNLP Workshop W-NUT: The 5th Workshop on Noisy User-Generated Text. pp. 141–146.

Scherrer, Y., Ljubeši´c, N.L., 2016. Automatic normalisation of the Swiss German ArchiMob corpus using character-level machine translation, in: Proceedings of the 13th Conference on Natural Language Processing (KONVENS 2016). pp. 248–255.

Shannon, C.E., 1948. A Mathematical Theory of Communication. Bell Syst. Tech. J. 27, 379–423, 623–656.

Sidarenka, U., Scheffler, T., Stede, M., 2013. Rule-Based Normalization of German Twitter Messages, in: In

Proc. of the GSCL Workshop Verarbeitung Und Annotation von Sprachdaten Aus Genres Internetbasierter Kommunikation.

Sridhar, V.K.R., 2015. Unsupervised Text Normalization Using Distributed Representations of Words and Phrases, in: Proceedings of NAACL-HLT. pp. 8–16.

Tachicart, R., Bouzoubaa, K., 2019. Towards Automatic Normalization of the Moroccan Dialectal Arabic User Generated Text, in: Smaïli K. (Eds) Arabic Language Processing: From Theory to Practice. ICALP 2019. Communications in Computer and Information Science, Vol 1108. Springer, Cham. pp. 264–275.

Tachicart, R., Bouzoubaa, K., Jaafar, H., 2016. Lexical Differences and Similarities between Moroccan Dialect and Arabic, in: 2016 4th IEEE International Colloquium on Information Science and Technology (CiSt). pp. 331–337.

Van Der Goot, R., Ramponi, A., Caselli, T., Cafagna, M., Mattei, L. De, 2020. Norm It ! Lexical Normalization for Italian and Its Downstream Effects for Dependency Parsing, in: Proceedings Ofthe 12th Conference on Language Resources and Evaluation (LREC 2020). pp. 6272–6278.

Van Der Goot, R., Van Noord, G., 2017. MoNoise: Modeling Noise Using a Modular Normalization System. Comput. Linguist. Netherlands J. 7, 129–144.

Zarnoufi, R., Jaafar, H., Abik, M., 2020. Machine Normalization : Bringing Social Media Text from Non-Standard to Standard Form. ACMTrans. Asian Low-Resour. Lang. Inf. Process. 19, 30.

# A Unified Model for Arabizi Detection and Transliteration using Sequence-to-Sequence Models


**Ali Shazal, Aiza Usman, Nizar Habash**
Computational Approaches to Modeling Language (CAMeL) Lab
New York University Abu Dhabi, UAE
`{ali.shazal,aiza.usman,nizar.habash}@nyu.edu`



## Abstract

While online Arabic is primarily written using the Arabic script, a Roman-script variety called Arabizi is often seen on social media. Although this representation captures the phonology of the language, it is not a one-to-one mapping with the Arabic script version. This issue is exacerbated by the fact that Arabizi on social media is Dialectal Arabic which does not have a standard orthography. Furthermore, Arabizi tends to include a lot of code mixing between Arabic and English (or French). To map Arabizi text to Arabic script in the context of complete utterances, previously published efforts have split Arabizi detection and Arabic script target in two separate tasks. In this paper, we present the first effort on a unified model for Arabizi detection and transliteration into a code-mixed output with consistent Arabic spelling conventions, using a sequence-to-sequence deep learning model. Our best system achieves 80.6% word accuracy and 58.7% BLEU on a blind test set.


## 1 Introduction

The term *Transliteration* generally refers to the process of mapping the orthographic symbols used in one script into another. The types of mapping schemes can range from strict one-to-one transliterations (Beesley, 1997), to named-entity transliteration which can be partially constrained by spelling conventions of the target language (Al-Onaizan and Knight, 2002; Rosca and Breuel, 2016), and all the way to the spontaneous romanizations used in many places around the world, in competition with local languages and spelling traditions. In the Arab world, the latter of these phenomena is often called Arabizi,[1] Since it is used primarily in social media (SMS and chat), it's notoriously noisy and inconsistent although there are some common conventions. And because it is written in the Roman script, it encourages written linguistic code mixing between Arabic and English (or French). Furthermore, since it is not an official orthography, Arabizi is a resource poor language form compared to Modern Standard Arabic and some of its dialects, where there are more resources written in Arabic script. As such, many researchers work on mapping Arabizi to Arabic script as part of general text normalization. This task includes two components: identifying the language, and mapping it to the target script accordingly. For example, the code-mixed sequence *w aletli Tuesday* 'and she-said-to-me Tuesday' would be mapped to *Tuesday* وقالت لي

*wqAlt ly Tuesday*[2] 'and-she-said to-me Tuesday'. While the input and output here have the same number of words, they are not aligned one-to-one as Arabic spelling rules define words boundaries differently, an additional complexity of the task.

There have been a number of efforts in natural language processing (NLP) that worked on this interesting phenomenon using a range of techniques from classical machine learning and n-gram language models (Darwish, 2014; Al-Badrashiny et al., 2014; Eskander et al., 2014) to sequence-to-sequence

---

[1]**Arabizi** is a cross-lingual portmanteau of the English name of the **Arab**ic language and the Arabic name of the English language, إنجليزي *Ainjliyziy* 'Ingl**izi**'.

[2]All Arabic script examples are paired with a strict 1-to-1 transliteration in the HSB scheme (Habash et al., 2007).






*Proceedings of the Fifth Arabic Natural Language Processing Workshop*, pages 167–177
Barcelona, Spain (Online), December 12, 2020

neural models (Guellil et al., 2017; Younes et al., 2018; Younes et al., 2020). The various previous solutions differ in (a) whether and how they modeled the subtask of Arabizi detection (*which words are Arabic written in Roman script, and which are English/French*), (b) what amount of context they use, and (c) how they define the Arabic script target (*whether to allow token merges and splits or follow Arabizi word boundaries*). In this paper we present the first effort on a unified model of Arabizi detection and transliteration into a code-mixed output with consistent Arabic spelling conventions, using neural sequence-to-sequence models. Our best system achieves 80.6% word accuracy and 58.7% BLEU score on a blind test set — 9.9%, and 15.9% absolute improvements, respectively, over a simple but robust baseline. Our system's code is public.[3] But the data must be acquired from the LDC (see Section 5).

We discuss related work in Sections 2, and Arabizi challenges and task definition in Section 3. We present our system architecture and approach in Section 4, and our experiments and results in Section 5.

## 2   Related Work

### 2.1   Arabizi Data Collection and Annotation

The various efforts working on Arabizi collected, tagged and mapped different sizes of corpora for different Arabic varieties including Egyptian (Bies et al., 2014; Tobaili, 2016; Chen et al., 2017), Lebanese (Tobaili, 2016), Tunisian (Younes et al., 2015; Masmoudi et al., 2019), and Algerian (Guellil et al., 2017). We focus here on the work of Bies et al. (2014) since it is the largest by far, and because it targets a well-formed conventional orthography for dialectal Arabic, henceforth ARABIZICORPUS. Their data includes over 287K Egyptian Arabizi SMS and chat words that are automatically transliterated and manually validated. The corpus words are tagged for being Foreign, Name, Punctuation, sound, emoji/emoticon or the default Arabic. The Arabic text written in Arabizi is mapped to Arabic script using the conventional orthography for Dialectal Arabic (CODA) (Habash et al., 2012; Eskander et al., 2013; Habash et al., 2018). The CODA convention is close to Standard Arabic orthography while maintaining some of the unique morphological and lexical features of Dialectal Arabic. In addition to using different characters, CODA and Arabizi often use different word boundaries. Moreover, Arabizi is noisy and spontaneous while CODA is intended to be conservative and systematic. In addition to the parallel component, the ARABIZICORPUS includes about 1M Arabizi words that are not tagged or transliterated. An earlier version of this data set was used by Al-Badrashiny et al. (2014) and Eskander et al. (2014). Unfortunately, since the versions used by these earlier efforts do not correspond to the public version of the data set, and are not determinable from it, we cannot compare to them directly. We report in this paper on the latest public version of the data (Chen et al., 2017), and we describe in detail the splits we follow to enable future comparisons with our results (see Section 5.1).

### 2.2   Pre-neural Models for Arabizi Processing

Chalabi and Gerges (2012) presented a hybrid approach for Arabizi transliteration using manual and learned character mapping rules with a language model for ranking hypotheses. Their work does not address the detection of English words, punctuation, emoticons, and so on. Voss et al. (2014) focus on classifying tokens in Arabizi as Arabic or not. They work on a three-way classification of Moroccan Arabic, French and English. Darwish (2014) was the first effort to model the detection of Arabizi and non-Arabizi words before transliterating the Arabizi text. He employed a two-step system for identification and then conversion. For identification, he used word and sequence-level features with CRF modeling to identify three tags: Arabic, foreign and others. For transliteration, he learned character level mappings from a small parallel corpus and used them to generate alternative mappings, which are filtered using a word trigram language model.

Al-Badrashiny et al. (2014) extended the work of Darwish (2014) on transliteration. They trained a finite state transducer at the character level to generate all possible transliterations for the input Arabizi words to output Arabic words. They then filtered the generated list using a dialectal Arabic morphological analyzer. They picked the best choice for each input word using a word 5-gram language model. Eskander et al. (2014) presented a system that built on top of Al-Badrashiny et al. (2014)'s transliteration

---

[3]`https://github.com/CAMeL-Lab/seq2seq-transliteration-tool`

| | [1] | [2] | [3] | [4] | [5] | [6] | [7] | [8] | [9] | [10] |
|---|---|---|---|---|---|---|---|---|---|---|
| **Arabizi Input** | Okayyyy | I | confess! | 3aiza<br>'I want' | ageblk<br>'I bring to you' | el<br>'the' | swr<br>'pictures' | 3shan<br>'so as to' | ashoooooofk<br>'see you' | ☺ |
| **Token Type** | *For* | *For* | *For* | *Ar* | *Ar* | *Ar* | *Ar* | *Ar* | *Ar* | *Em* |
| **ML Input** | okayy | i | confess! | 3aiza | ageblk | el | swr | 3shan | ashoofk | # |
| **ML Output** | # | # | # | عايزة | أجيب[-]-لك | [+]ال | صور | عشان | أشوفك | # |
| **Postprocessed** | Okayyyy | I | confess! | عايزة<br>*ςAyzħ* | أجيب *Ajyb* / لك *lk* | الصور<br>*AlSwr* | | عشان<br>*ςšAn* | أشوفك<br>*Ašwfk* | ☺ |
| **Output** | عايزة اجيب لك الصور عشان اشوفك ☺ okayyyy i confess! <br>Okayyyy I confess! *ςAyzħ Ajyb lk AlSwr ςšAn Ašwfk* ☺ <br>'Okayyyy I confess! I want to bring you the pictures so I can seen ☺' | | | | | | | | | |

Figure 1: An example of Arabizi input and target output including the different representations for preprocessing, machine learning input and output, and postprocessing. The token types are Ar (Arabic), For (Foreign) and Em (Emoji).

pipeline. They investigated the issue of processing Arabizi input with code switching using the data from ARABIZICORPUS. They used SVMs and decision trees to identify a larger tag set than Darwish (2014): Arabic, foreign, names, sounds, punctuation and emoticons. For transliteration, they used the Al-Badrashiny et al. (2014) model with more training data.

## 2.3 Neural Model for Arabizi Processing

Deep learning models, specifically sequence-to-sequence (Seq2Seq) RNN models have shown a lot of success in the task of character-based transliteration for a number of languages (Rosca and Breuel, 2016; Kundu et al., 2018; Dershowitz and Terner, 2020).

In the context of Arabizi, three efforts are particularly notable (Guellil et al., 2017; Younes et al., 2018; Younes et al., 2020). Guellil et al. (2017) and Younes et al. (2018) worked on mapping Algerian Arabizi and Tunisian Arabizi, respectively, to Arabic script. Both used Seq2Seq models at the character level. Younes et al. (2020) redefined the problem as a sequence labeling task using BiLSTM with CRF decoding. All of these approaches were focused on word-level transliteration and did not address issues of code-mixing and Arabizi identification automatically, although they acknowledge these issues. In this paper we present a single unified model that addresses the issues of Arabizi identification and conversion together using a Seq2Seq model.

Although not Arabizi, a recent effort on automatic conversion of Judeo-Arabic text written in Hebrew script to Arabic script is relevant; Dershowitz and Terner (2020) also used a Seq2Seq RNN model and described a number of interesting tricks for addressing length mismatches and forgetfulness in the network. We refer to specific insights from their work in the paper.

Also not Arabizi, but relevant, is the work of Watson et al. (2018), who achieved the current state-of-the-art on Arabic spelling correction against a standard set using Seq2Seq models. Our baseline Seq2Seq set up is inspired by their work.

## 3 Arabizi Challenges and Task Definition

Our task of mapping code-mixed Egyptian Arabizi and English input into code-mixed Egyptian Arabic and English poses a number of challenges.

**Arabizi Noise and Ambiguity** While there are some common conventions for Arabizi-to-Arabic mapping, they are not strictly followed by far. This is further exacerbated by typical noisy spelling in spontaneous social media text. As a result, we have many-to-many mappings at the word level. For example, the Arabic word حبيبي *Hbyby* 'my beloved' appears in the ARABIZICORPUS paired with 24 different Arabizi spellings: (in order of frequency) *habibii, hbebe, habibi, 7abiby, 7abibi, hbebee, 7abeby, 7biby, habbii, 7bibi, 7abibii, hbybyy, hbbee, hbbebe, habiibii, habbyy, bbe, 7apipy, 7abiibii, 7abibyy, 7abebe,*

*7abby*, *3abiibii*, and *3abibi*. Similarly, the Arabizi word *arfo* is paired with three different Arabic words: عارفه *ςArfh* 'I know it', قرفوا *qrfwA* 'they made me loathe [something]' and قرفه *qrfh* 'its nastiness'.

We mitigate the noise and variability in modeling the Arabizi-to-Arabic transliteration as a character level sequence-to-sequence process. We also make use of word-level embeddings using FastText (Bojanowski et al., 2017) which models subword units within a bigger word-based context. Additionally, we handle common variations in social media text such as inconsistent capitalization and emphatic repetitions through global lower casing and repetition elision to two characters, e.g., Arabizi *Habiiiiiibiiiiii* is preprocessed to *habiibii*.

**Arabizi-Arabic Mis-alignment** The CODA convention we target for Egyptian Arabic does not align word-to-word with Arabizi as explained above. There are both splits and merges of words. In Figure 1, word [5] *ageblk* 'I bring to you' is split into اجيب لك *Ajyb lk*, and words [6] and [7] *el* 'the' *swr* 'pictures' are merged into one: الصور *AlSwr* 'the pictures'. We model these two issues in our work by learning to explicitly map the merge ([+]) and split ([-]) special characters used in the ARABIZICORPUS annotations.

**Code-switching and Emoji** Within our task, English (or other foreign words) are simply to be mapped to the output, without any attempt to normalize or modify their spelling. As such the task is more oriented towards modeling identification of foreign words – or from a different perspective, detection of Arabizi words. This is not always simple given that some Arabizi words are ambiguous with English words, e.g. the Arabizi word *men* can be the English word 'men' or the Arabic words من *mn* 'from' or مين *myn* 'who'. We model this subtask as mapping to a special symbol (#) used to identify which input words to copy to the output in a postprocessing step.

We handle emojis (e.g., 😊) and emoticons (e.g., :-P) in a comparable way to foreign words. Although for a small set of commonly used emoticons, we use a dictionary and preprocess them into the (#) symbol.

**Defining the Task Target** The ARABIZICORPUS provides a set of manually assigned tags per each Arabizi word specifying if it is Arabic, Foreign, Name, Sound or Punctuation. In the corpus, all of the words are automatically transliterated and manually validated except for the Foreign word transliterations into Arabic which are not manually validated. This is why Eskander et al. (2014) did not do a joint final evaluation but rather evaluated only on the manually validated words and treated identification of foreign words as a separate problem. In our work, we take a different approach where we define the task target to be a code-mix of Arabic (transliterated from Arabizi) and Foreign words in Roman script. We construct this target reference using the Arabizi word tags and the validated transliterations, by reinserting the foreign input word in place of its automatic non-validated transliteration. We also reinsert Emojis which are mapped to a special token (#) in the target side in the ARABIZICORPUS.

## 4 System Design

### 4.1 Approach

Due to the aforementioned complexities and a high number of out-of-vocabulary words, a word-level neural model cannot be used as an end-to-end solution. So, we opt for a character-level approach using sequence-to-sequence models to capture the complexity of the noise, variations and mistakes.

### 4.2 Data Preprocessing and Postprocessing

**Input-side Preprocessing** Each Arabizi input utterance goes through the following preprocessing steps: all letters are lowercased, repetition of more than two characters in a word are reduced to two, accented charactes are converted to their unaccented versions in the standard 7-bit ASCII, and all freestanding emojis, emoticons and punctuation are converted to hashtags. These steps can be seen in Figure 1 (ML Input row).

**ML Output-side Preprocessing** During training only, we convert all the foreign-tagged words to hashtags on the machine learning output side. Since our training input and output are aligned, the conversion ensures that the model learns to identify foreign words and convert them to hashtags. Identical to the

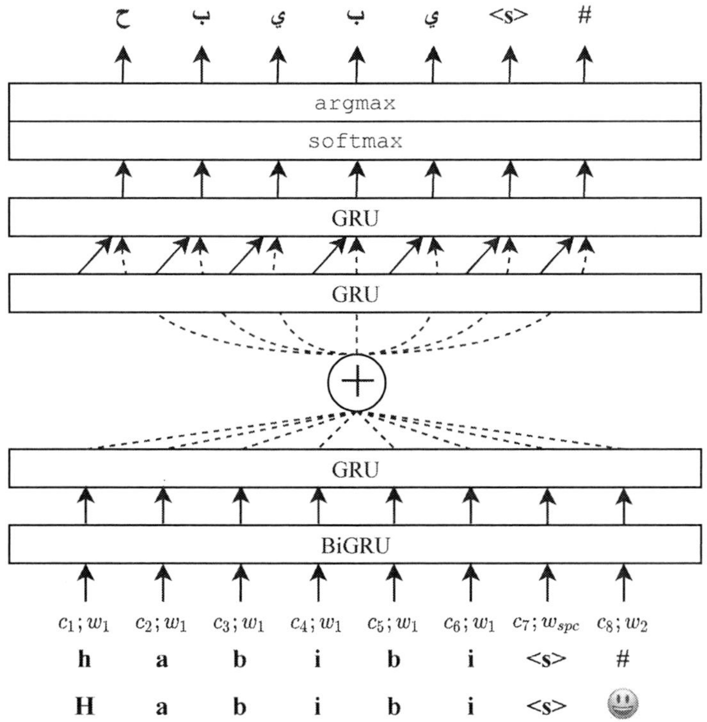


Figure 2: Illustration of the overall Sequence-to-Sequence architecture. The Arabizi (bottom of the figure) is preprocessed before being input into the network. $c_i$ is the character embedding, and $w_j$ is the word embedding.

input-side preprocessing, the ML output-side free-standing emojis, emoticons and punctuation are converted to hashtags during both training and prediction. We illustrate these steps in Figure 1 (ML Output row).

We do not apply AY normalization, i.e., the conversion of different versions of *Alif* and *Ya* to simple *Alif* and *Ya*, respectively (Habash, 2010; El Kholy and Habash, 2012), because it lowered the normalized accuracy by 0.1% absolute on average when we used it.

**ML Output-side Postprocessing** On the ML output side, we add a postprocessing step that converts hashtags back to the words that were in the source Arabizi. This is only possible if the input and output are aligned, so this step is applied before removing the [+] and [-] tokens. Moreover, to go to the final output, words with the [+] token are merged to the next word and [-] tokens are replaced with white space to split a word into multiple words. These steps can be seen in Figure 1.

### 4.3 System Architecture

**Encoder-Decoder Model** We use a character-level sequence-to-sequence architecture following Watson et al. (2018) to model $P(y|x)$ given an input $x$ and a target $y$. See Figure 2. The encoder consists of two gated recurrent unit (GRU) layers (Cho et al., 2014) with only the first layer being bidirectional following Wu et al. (2016). The decoder also has two GRUs along with the attention mechanism proposed by Luong et al. (2015). The initial states for the decoder layers are learned with a fully-connected `tanh` layer from the first encoder output.

The model uses scheduled sampling (Bengio et al., 2015) with a constant sampling probability, feeding character embeddings concatenated with embeddings of the words the characters appear in at every time step. The model uses dropout (Srivastava et al., 2014) for both encoder and decoder recurrent neural networks on the non-recurrent connections during training. A final `softmax` layer receives the decoder

| | CHT | | | SMS | | | CHT+SMS | |
|---|---|---|---|---|---|---|---|---|---|
| | Lines | Words | | Lines | Words | | Lines | Words | |
| **Train** | 45,794 | 185,275 | (80.0%) | 9,065 | 45,079 | (81.3%) | 54,859 | 230,354 | (80.3%) |
| **Dev** | 4,923 | 23,302 | (10.1%) | 485 | 5,559 | (10.0%) | 5,408 | 28,861 | (10.1%) |
| **Test** | 5,583 | 22,969 | (9.9%) | 1,070 | 4,831 | (8.7%) | 6,653 | 27,800 | (9.7%) |

Table 1: Data splits of the corpus into training, development and test sets

output to give the final output sequence $y$. The loss function is the cross-entropy loss per time step averaged over $y_i$.

We use beam search during inference with a fixed beam width to predict candidates with the highest log-likelihood at each step. We pick the individual beam with the highest overall log-likelihood as our prediction. As a final step in inference, we reduce repetitions of six or more text sequences to five repetitions. This addresses rare cases where the decoder misbehaves and produces non-stop repetitions of text.

**Model Settings**   We used a learning rate of 0.0001, batch size of 1024 and 2048 for different settings (see LINE2LINE vs WORD2WORD below), batch and character embedding sizes of 256, hidden layer size of 256, two RNN layers, dropout probability of 0.1, decoder sampling probability of 0.35, and gradient clipping with a maximum norm of 11.5. We used the Adam optimizer (Kingma and Ba, 2015) with a learning rate of 0.0005, $\epsilon = 1 * 10^{-8}$, $\beta_1$=0.9, and $\beta_2$=0.999, and trained the model for 40 epochs. When running all the trained models during inference, we used a beam width of 5.

All the word embeddings were trained using Fasttext and had dimension 300. They were trained on the unannotated Arabizi text that was part of the ARABIZICORPUS. In the experiments that included preprocessing, we also preprocessed the input-side Arabizi before training Fasttext. All Fasttext hyperparameters were kept to the default except the context window and minimum n-gram size which were both kept to two.

The network hyperparameters above were empirically identified in a series of ∼80 experiments starting with the hyperparamters of Watson et al. (2018) and tuning to achieve the best accuracy and BLEU score on the dev set.

**Line2Line vs Word2Word**   During initial experiments, we observed that the model was rather forgetful and not well performing when fed complete Arabizi input utterances (henceforth, we will refer to this Seq2Seq setting as the LINE2LINE setting). So, we considered the option of working at a WORD2WORD level similar to Younes et al. (2018) and Guellil et al. (2017), with the exception of adding a small context window similar to Mubarak et al. (2019), which is not itself mapped, but only provides contextual information. Contextual tokens such as beginning of sentence <bos>, end of sentence <eos>, beginning of word (under focus) <bow>, and end of word (under focus) <eow> were added to aid the model in this setting. We experimented with context windows of size three, two, and one words, and found +/- one word to be the best.

For example, the three-word Arabizi input *Alf salama hahaha* 'A thousand times safe haha', which is paired with the Arabic الف سلامة هيه *Alf slAmħ hhh*, is turned into the following three separate training input-output pairs:

```
<bos>    <bow>  Alf     <eow>  salama  →      الف    Alf
Alf      <bow>  salama  <eow>  haha    →     سلامة   slAmħ
salama   <bow>  haha    <eow>  <eos>   →      هيه     hhh
```

For WORD2WORD experiments, we use batch size of 2048 because the input sequences are shorter than the LINE2LINE setup for which we used batch size 1024. For both settings, we use the same character-based Seq2Seq architecture discussed above. The only difference is the size of the input in terms of words and whether context is used.

| System | Context | Prep | Accuracy | | BLEU | | Time (s) | |
|---|---|---|---|---|---|---|---|---|
| | | | Exact | Norm | Exact | Norm | Training | Prediction |
| **MLE** | No Context | No | 74.7 | 76.4 | 46.5 | 49.6 | 2 | 0.1 |
| **MLE** | No Context | Yes | 76.7 | 78.5 | 50.0 | 53.0 | 2 | 0.1 |
| **Seq2Seq** | LINE2LINE | No | 70.5 | 72.4 | 47.0 | 50.8 | 7,837 | 735 |
| **Seq2Seq** | LINE2LINE | Yes | 74.8 | 76.9 | 55.4 | 59.5 | 7,800 | 705 |
| **Seq2Seq** | WORD2WORD +/-1 Context | No | 83.5 | 85.8 | 63.5 | 68.0 | 30,492 | 1,893 |
| **Seq2Seq** | WORD2WORD +/-1 Context | Yes | **84.2** | **86.5** | **64.5** | **69.3** | 30,151 | 1,884 |

Table 2: Results on the development set with different setups

| System | Context | Prep | Accuracy | | BLEU | | Time (s) |
|---|---|---|---|---|---|---|---|
| | | | Exact | Norm | Exact | Norm | Prediction |
| **MLE** | No Context | Yes | 70.7 | 71.8 | 42.8 | 44.6 | 0.1 |
| **Seq2Seq** | WORD2WORD +/-1 Context | Yes | **80.6** | **82.5** | **58.7** | **62.6** | 1824 |

Table 3: Results on the test set with different setups

| Setup | Handled By | | Accuracy | | BLEU | | Prediction |
|---|---|---|---|---|---|---|---|
| | MLE | Seq2Seq | Exact | Norm | Exact | Norm | Time (s) |
| **MLE Only** | 85% | 0% | 76.7 | 78.5 | 50.0 | 53.0 | 0.1 |
| **MLE + Seq2Seq** | 85% | 15% | 82.9 | 85.1 | 61.9 | 66.3 | 270 |
| **Seq2Seq Only** | 0% | 100% | 84.2 | 86.5 | 64.5 | 69.3 | 1884 |

Table 4: Performance comparison of the hybrid, MLE, and Seq2Seq systems on the development set.

## 5 Evaluation

### 5.1 Experimental Settings

**Data**  We use the *BOLT Egyptian Arabic SMS/Chat and Transliteration* corpus (ARABIZICORPUS) (Chen et al., 2017; Bies et al., 2014).[4] We split the corpus following the suggestions given by Diab et al. (2013) for Arabic corpora. The documents were first sorted by filename alphabetically. Then, the divisions were applied on the file level, with the divisions being ∼80% training, ∼10% development and ∼10% test, from both chat and SMS subsets of the corpus. The details of the divisions can be seen in Table 1.[5]

**Metrics**  We use two metrics to evaluate our setup. The first, harsher metric, measures word-level accuracy of our Seq2Seq model. It compares the source aligned output of the system, which contains the [+] and [-] separation tokens, to the source aligned gold. In this regard, we measure both the exact-matching accuracy and the AY-normalized accuracy. After we remove the separation tokens, the number of words in the output may differ from the input; this is why we use BLEU (Papineni et al., 2002), which is generally used for translation evaluation, to measure the quality of the transliteration at the end. We measure the BLEU score for both the exact final output and the AY-normalized final output.

**Baseline**  For a baseline, we use Maximum Likelihood Estimate (MLE) to predict the most likely output (Arabic word or hashtag) as seen in training given an input word. This simple baseline experiment is conducted with and without preprocessing.

---

[4] https://catalog.ldc.upenn.edu/LDC2017T07
[5] Train: CHT_ARZ_{20121228.0001-20150101.0002} and SMS_ARZ_{20120223.0001-20130902.0002}.
Dev: CHT_ARZ_{20120130.0000-20121226.0003} and SMS_ARZ_{20110705.0000-20120220.0000}.
Test: CHT_ARZ_{20150101.0008-20160201.0001} and SMS_ARZ_{20130904.0001-20130929.0000}.

|  | MLE | | Seq2Seq | | Input | Reference | Output | English |
|---|---|---|---|---|---|---|---|---|
| **Acceptable** | 166 | (81%) | 195 | (95%) | | | | |
| *Correct* | 155 | (76%) | 175 | (85%) | share3 | شارع *šAr$ʕ$* | شارع *šAr$ʕ$* | street |
| *CODA Error* | 6 | (3%) | 11 | (5%) | 3ayznko | عايزينكو *$ʕ$Ayznkw* | عايزنكو *$ʕ$Ayznkw* | we want you |
| *Valid Variant* | 5 | (2%) | 9 | (4%) | Ok | Ok | أوكيه *Âwkyh* | Ok |
| **Unacceptable** | 39 | (19%) | 10 | (5%) | | | | |
| *Arabizi* | 37 | (18%) | 0 | (0%) | fat7na | فتحنا *ftHnA* | fat7na | we opened |
| *Wrong* | 2 | (1%) | 10 | (5%) | menu:) | menu:) | منه :) *mnh:)* | menu:) |
| **Word Total** | 205 | (100%) | 205 | (100%) | | | | |

Table 5: Error analysis summary comparing the MLE baseline and best Seq2Seq model with examples.

## 5.2 Experimental Results

**Development Results**   Results for the development set are shown in Table 2.   We see that the WORD2WORD setup with a context window of +/- one word outperformed the LINE2LINE setup and the baseline MLE. In all setups, preprocessing always helped the model. The best setting (WORD2WORD +/-1 Context + Preprocessing) improves over the strong MLE baseline (with Preprocessing) by 7.5% absolute accuracy and 14.5 BLEU points (in exact matching space).

**Blind Test Results**   For the blind test set, Table 3 presents the results on our best model determined above as and the MLE baseline. The results are consistent with the observations seen in development. The best model improves over the strong MLE baseline by 9.9% absolute accuracy and 15.9 BLEU points (in exact matching space).

**Speed vs Quality**   We would also like to comment on the trade off between speed and quality.   In our experiments, we saw that the faster systems had lower quality and vice versa. The MLE system was extremely fast but had much lower quality compared to the WORD2WORD system which was quite slow. Upon a closer look at the results, we saw that the best MLE setup did almost as well on words seen in training as the best Seq2Seq setup, and Seq2Seq easily outperformed MLE on unseen words. This led us to the idea of combining the two systems to create a hybrid system where the MLE model would predict words seen in training and the Seq2Seq model would predict unseen words. This did not affect training time because we used the pre-trained models; however, it decreased prediction time from 31 minutes to 4.5 minutes on the development set. The accuracy and BLEU score of this hybrid system was lower than the WORD2WORD model but higher than the baseline MLE model (See Table 4).

## 5.3 Error Analysis

We manually classified a sample of 50 development set utterances (50 lines, 205 Arabizi words) from the best MLE model and from the best Seq2Seq model. We grouped the output words into Acceptable and Unacceptable sets. The Acceptable set includes correct matches, as well as acceptable transliteration variants and minor CODA errors; while the Unacceptable set includes Arabizi, and wrong implausible outputs. Table 5 summarizes the results and includes examples for the different categories. Overall, our best Seq2Seq model produced acceptable transliterations for 95% of the Arabizi words, compared with 81% in the MLE model. The largest type of error for MLE was passing the input Arabizi to the output untouched. At the utterance level, 46% of the MLE outputs, and 82% of the Seq2Seq outputs were composed completely of acceptable word outputs. The error analysis demonstrates the power of the Seq2Seq model and its general quality.

For 11 words (5% of total words), the gold reference gave us pause. In almost three-quarters of the cases, there were CODA non-compliant, although plausible, variants, e.g., the word تبقي *tbqy* 'you [f.s.] remain' was rendered as تبقى *tbqý*. The most significant gold reference error was transliterating the English word *invite* to the nonsensical Arabic عنفيت *$ʕ$nfyt*.

### 5.4 Negative Result Experiments

We report next on three different streams of experiments that gave us negative results.

**Synthetic Data**  Inspired by successful results in machine translation, we considered the use of additional synthetic data to mitigate the lack of parallel training data (Sennrich et al., 2016). We initially considered a reverse transliteration model that would allow us to take large amounts of Egyptian Arabic text and map it to Arabizi space. However this was not simple and we quickly noticed a number of issues: (a) most of the available data is not in the chat and SMS genre, and (b) working from Arabic text eliminates examples of Arabizi style code-switching and tokenization. Instead, we opted to use the additional unannotated data we have from the ARABIZICORPUS ($\sim$242K Arabizi utterances containing $\sim$1M words). We used our best model to generate a synthetic Arabizi-Arabic parallel training set, and add it to our initial corpus. The results were negative on all used metrics. We hypothesize that the high degree of noise in the input may have resulted in weak or worse, very noisy, models. This may be consistent with the limited benefits of using the additional corpus as part of FastText pre-trained word embeddings.

**Foreign Language Embeddings**  Intuiting that the quality of Arabizi vs Foreign detection can be improved using additional models of English text as was successfully shown by (Eskander et al., 2014) in their non-neural models. We first took about 1M words (to match the size of data we have for Arabizi) from an English chat and SMS corpus (Chen et al., 2018) and trained another set of word embeddings using FastText; these word embeddings were concatenated to the already existing character embeddings and Arabizi word embeddings in the WORD2WORD setup. This did not show an improvement in terms of the used metrics. In a different experiment, we inserted a random sample of 21K words (or about 10% of training data, to avoid biasing the model too much) into random locations throughout the existing training data and paired those additions with the proper # symbol on the target side. This resulted in a slight decrease in scores, so we did not use it.

**Modeling Different Input Sizes and Context Windows**  Since sequence-to-sequence models are known to struggle with very long input sequences, we considered a solution similar to Dershowitz and Terner (2020), where we break the input and target into smaller sequences of size $N$ words during training. During inference, we do the same for the input, then concatenate the predicted output before evaluation. We considered different sizes of $N$ and found the minimal limit of $N = 1$ words to be the best performing system.

## 6 Conclusion and Future Work

We presented a character-level Seq2Seq model for Arabizi detection and transliteration together into a code-mixed output with a consistent Arabic spelling convention. Our best system improves over the baseline by 9.9% in word accuracy and 15.9 BLEU points on a blind test set. We report on a number of experiments including some negative results.

In the future, we plan to integrate our best model in an open source toolkit for supporting Arabic NLP. Furthermore, we want to work on Arabizi text from a range of Arabic dialects. Finally, we want to integrate our system into other Arabic NLP applications, such as machine translation from Arabizi to demonstrate the relevance of Arabizi-to-Arabic transliteration.

## Acknowledgements

This research was carried out on the High Performance Computing resources at New York University Abu Dhabi (NYUAD). We would like to thank Daniel Watson, Ossama Obeid, Nasser Zalmout and Salam Khalifa from the Computational Approaches to Modeling Language Lab at NYUAD for their help and suggestions throughout this project. We thank Owen Rambow, and the paper reviewers for helpful suggestions.

## References

Mohamed Al-Badrashiny, Ramy Eskander, Nizar Habash, and Owen Rambow. 2014. Automatic transliteration of romanized Dialectal Arabic. In *Proceedings of the Conference on Computational Natural Language Learning (CoNLL)*, pages 30–38, Ann Arbor, Michigan.

Yaser Al-Onaizan and Kevin Knight. 2002. Machine Transliteration of Names in Arabic Text. In *Proceedings of the Workshop on Computational Approaches to Semitic Languages (CASL)*.

Kenneth R. Beesley. 1997. Romanization, Transcription and Transliteration. http://www.xrce.xerox.com/.

Samy Bengio, Oriol Vinyals, Navdeep Jaitly, and Noam Shazeer. 2015. Scheduled sampling for sequence prediction with recurrent neural networks. *CoRR*, abs/1506.03099.

Ann Bies, Zhiyi Song, Mohamed Maamouri, Stephen Grimes, Haejoong Lee, Jonathan Wright, Stephanie Strassel, Nizar Habash, Ramy Eskander, and Owen Rambow. 2014. Transliteration of Arabizi into Arabic Orthography: Developing a Parallel Annotated Arabizi-Arabic Script SMS/Chat Corpus. In *Proceedings of the Workshop for Arabic Natural Language Processing (WANLP)*, Doha, Qatar.

Piotr Bojanowski, Edouard Grave, Armand Joulin, and Tomas Mikolov. 2017. Enriching word vectors with subword information. *Transactions of the Association for Computational Linguistics (TACL)*, 5:135–146.

Achraf Chalabi and Hany Gerges. 2012. Romanized Arabic transliteration. In *Proceedings of the Second Workshop on Advances in Text Input Methods*, pages 89–96, Mumbai, India, December. The COLING 2012 Organizing Committee.

Song Chen, Dana Fore, Stephanie Strassel, Haejoong Lee, and Jonathan Wright. 2017. BOLT Egyptian Arabic SMS/Chat and Transliteration LDC2017T07.

Song Chen, Dana Fore, Stephanie Strassel, Haejoong Lee, and Jonathan Wright. 2018. BOLT English SMS/Chat LDC2018T19.

Kyunghyun Cho, Bart van Merriënboer, Çağlar Gülçehre, Dzmitry Bahdanau, Fethi Bougares, Holger Schwenk, and Yoshua Bengio. 2014. Learning phrase representations using rnn encoder–decoder for statistical machine translation. In *Proceedings of the Conference on Empirical Methods in Natural Language Processing (EMNLP)*, pages 1724–1734, Doha, Qatar.

Kareem Darwish. 2014. Arabizi Detection and Conversion to Arabic. In *Proceedings of the Workshop for Arabic Natural Language Processing (WANLP)*, pages 217–224, Doha, Qatar.

Nachum Dershowitz and Ori Terner. 2020. Transliteration of Judeo-Arabic texts into Arabic script using recurrent neural networks. *ArXiv*, abs/2004.11405.

Mona Diab, Nizar Habash, Owen Rambow, and Ryan Roth. 2013. LDC Arabic treebanks and associated corpora: Data divisions manual. *arXiv preprint arXiv:1309.5652*.

Ahmed El Kholy and Nizar Habash. 2012. Orthographic and morphological processing for English–Arabic statistical machine translation. *Machine Translation*, 26(1-2):25–45.

Ramy Eskander, Nizar Habash, Owen Rambow, and Nadi Tomeh. 2013. Processing spontaneous orthography. In *Proceedings of the Conference of the North American Chapter of the Association for Computational Linguistics (NAACL)*, pages 585–595, Atlanta, Georgia.

Ramy Eskander, Mohamed Al-Badrashiny, Nizar Habash, and Owen Rambow. 2014. Foreign words and the automatic processing of Arabic social media text written in Roman script. In *Proceedings of the First Workshop on Computational Approaches to Code Switching*, pages 1–12, Doha, Qatar, oct. Association for Computational Linguistics.

Imane Guellil, cal Azouaou Fai Mourad Abbas, and Fatiha Sadat. 2017. Arabizi transliteration of Algerian Arabic dialect into Modern Standard Arabic. In *Social MT 2017/First workshop on social media and user generated content machine translation*.

Nizar Habash, Abdelhadi Soudi, and Tim Buckwalter. 2007. On Arabic Transliteration. In A. van den Bosch and A. Soudi, editors, *Arabic Computational Morphology: Knowledge-based and Empirical Methods*, pages 15–22. Springer, Netherlands.

Nizar Habash, Mona Diab, and Owen Rambow. 2012. Conventional Orthography for Dialectal Arabic. In *Proceedings of the Language Resources and Evaluation Conference (LREC)*, pages 711–718, Istanbul, Turkey.

Nizar Habash, Fadhl Eryani, Salam Khalifa, Owen Rambow, Dana Abdulrahim, Alexander Erdmann, Reem Faraj, Wajdi Zaghouani, Houda Bouamor, Nasser Zalmout, Sara Hassan, Faisal Al shargi, Sakhar Alkhereyf, Basma Abdulkareem, Ramy Eskander, Mohammad Salameh, and Hind Saddiki. 2018. Unified guidelines and resources for Arabic dialect orthography. In *Proceedings of the Language Resources and Evaluation Conference (LREC)*, Miyazaki, Japan.

Nizar Y Habash. 2010. *Introduction to Arabic natural language processing*, volume 3. Morgan & Claypool Publishers.

Diederik P. Kingma and Jimmy Ba. 2015. Adam: A method for stochastic optimization. *CoRR*, abs/1412.6980.

Soumyadeep Kundu, Sayantan Paul, and Santanu Pal. 2018. A deep learning based approach to transliteration. In *Proceedings of the Seventh Named Entities Workshop*, pages 79–83, Melbourne, Australia, jul. Association for Computational Linguistics.

Thang Luong, Hieu Pham, and Christopher Manning. 2015. Effective approaches to attention-based neural machine translation. In *Proceedings of the Conference on Empirical Methods in Natural Language Processing (EMNLP)*, pages 1412–1421, Lisbon, Portugal.

Abir Masmoudi, Mariem Ellouze Khmekhem, Mourad Khrouf, and Lamia Hadrich Belguith. 2019. Transliteration of Arabizi into Arabic script for Tunisian dialect. *ACM Transactions on Asian and Low-Resource Language Information Processing*, 19:1–21.

Hamdy Mubarak, Ahmed Abdelali, Kareem Darwish, Mohamed Eldesouki, Younes Samih, and Hassan Sajjad. 2019. A system for diacritizing four varieties of Arabic. In *Proceedings of the 2019 Conference on Empirical Methods in Natural Language Processing and the 9th International Joint Conference on Natural Language Processing (EMNLP-IJCNLP): System Demonstrations*, pages 217–222, Hong Kong, China, November. Association for Computational Linguistics.

Kishore Papineni, Salim Roukos, Todd Ward, and Wei-Jing Zhu. 2002. BLEU: a Method for Automatic Evaluation of Machine Translation. In *Proceedings of the Conference of the Association for Computational Linguistics (ACL)*, pages 311–318, Philadelphia, Pennsylvania, USA.

Mihaela Rosca and Thomas Breuel. 2016. Sequence-to-sequence neural network models for transliteration. *arXiv*, 1610.09565.

Rico Sennrich, Barry Haddow, and Alexandra Birch. 2016. Improving neural machine translation models with monolingual data. In *Proceedings of the 54th Annual Meeting of the Association for Computational Linguistics (Volume 1: Long Papers)*, pages 86–96, Berlin, Germany, August. Association for Computational Linguistics.

Nitish Srivastava, Geoffrey Hinton, Alex Krizhevsky, Ilya Sutskever, and Ruslan Salakhutdinov. 2014. Dropout: A simple way to prevent neural networks from overfitting. *The Journal of Machine Learning Research*, 15(1).1929–1958.

Taha Tobaili. 2016. Arabizi identification in Twitter data. In *Proceedings of the ACL 2016 Student Research Workshop*, pages 51–57, Berlin, Germany, August. Association for Computational Linguistics.

Clare Voss, Stephen Tratz, Jamal Laoudi, and Douglas Briesch. 2014. Finding romanized Arabic dialect in code-mixed tweets. In *Proceedings of the Language Resources and Evaluation Conference (LREC)*, pages 2249–2253, Reykjavik, Iceland.

Daniel Watson, Nasser Zalmout, and Nizar Habash. 2018. Utilizing character and word embeddings for text normalization with sequence-to-sequence models. In *Proceedings of the 2018 Conference on Empirical Methods in Natural Language Processing*, pages 837–843, Brussels, Belgium. Association for Computational Linguistics.

Yonghui Wu, Mike Schuster, Zhifeng Chen, Quoc V. Le, Mohammad Norouzi, Wolfgang Macherey, Maxim Krikun, Yuan Cao, Qin Gao, Klaus Macherey, Jeff Klingner, Apurva Shah, Melvin Johnson, Xiaobing Liu, Łukasz Kaiser, Stephan Gouws, Yoshikiyo Kato, Taku Kudo, Hideto Kazawa, Keith Stevens, George Kurian, Nishant Patil, Wei Wang, Cliff Young, Jason Smith, Jason Riesa, Alex Rudnick, Oriol Vinyals, Greg Corrado, Macduff Hughes, and Jeffrey Dean. 2016. Google's neural machine translation system: Bridging the gap between human and machine translation. *CoRR*, abs/1609.08144.

Jihen Younes, Hadhemi Achour, and Emna Souissi. 2015. Constructing linguistic resources for the Tunisian dialect using textual user-generated contents on the social web. In *International Conference on Web Engineering*, pages 3–14. Springer.

Jihene Younes, Emna Souissi, Hadhemi Achour, and Ahmed Ferchichi. 2018. A sequence-to-sequence based approach for the double transliteration of Tunisian dialect. *Procedia Computer Science*, 142:238 – 245. Arabic Computational Linguistics.

Jihene Younes, Hadhemi Achour, Emna Souissi, and Ahmed Ferchichi. 2020. Romanized Tunisian dialect transliteration using sequence labelling techniques. *Journal of King Saud University-Computer and Information Sciences*.

# Multi-Task Sequence Prediction For Tunisian Arabizi Multi-Level Annotation

**Elisa Gugliotta**[1,2,3]**, Marco Dinarelli**[1]**, Olivier Kraif**[2]

1. Université Grenoble Alpes - Laboratoire LIG, Getalp group.
2. Université Grenoble Alpes - Laboratoire LIDILEM.
3. Sapienza University of Rome.
`elisa.gugliotta@uniroma1.it`
`{marco.dinarelli,olivier.kraif}@univ-grenoble-alpes.fr`



## Abstract

In this paper we propose a multi-task sequence prediction system, based on recurrent neural networks and used to annotate on multiple levels an Arabizi Tunisian corpus. The annotation performed are text classification, tokenization, PoS tagging and encoding of Tunisian Arabizi into CODA* Arabic orthography. The system is learned to predict all the annotation levels in cascade, starting from Arabizi input. We evaluate the system on the TIGER German corpus, suitably converting data to have a multi-task problem, in order to show the effectiveness of our neural architecture. We show also how we used the system in order to annotate a Tunisian Arabizi corpus, which has been afterwards manually corrected and used to further evaluate sequence models on Tunisian data. Our system is developed for the Fairseq framework, which allows for a fast and easy use for any other sequence prediction problem.


## 1 Introduction

In the last decade neural networks became the state-of-the-art models in most NLP problems. Sequence-to-sequence models (Sutskever et al., 2014; Vaswani et al., 2017), built on top of recurrent (Hochreiter and Schmidhuber, 1997; Cho et al., 2014), convolutional (Gehring et al., 2017; Wu et al., 2019) or attentional (Bahdanau et al., 2014; Vaswani et al., 2017) modules, and structured in encoder-decoder architectures, are currently the most effective models for NLP problems. Neural networks have been used also for multi-task learning since early in their diffusion (Collobert and Weston, 2007; Collobert and Weston, 2008; Collobert et al., 2011).

As a semitic language, Arabic has a highly inflectional and derivational morphology, which makes Arabic processing an engaging challenge. This morphological complexity has traditionally been handled through morphological analysers, such as BAMA (Buckwalter, 2004), which has been used by the Linguistic Data Consortium (LDC) to develop the Penn Arabic Treebank (PATB) (Maamouri et al., 2004). Recently, the number of NLP contributions to morphological analysis, disambiguation, Part-of-Speech (PoS) tagging and lemmatization has increased substantially, for both Modern Standard and Dialectal Arabic (MSA and DA, respectively). Multitask learning was proved to be an effective way to process Arabic morphology for MSA fine-grained PoS tagging (Inoue et al., 2017), as well as for DA (Zalmout and Habash, 2019). Concerning NLP applied to DA, it is possible to observe two main macro-strategies aimed at remedying the lack of data for DA: **1.** *MSA systems adaptation to DA processing*, like (David et al., 2006) who exploited the Penn Arabic Treebank (PATB) (Maamouri et al., 2004) and used explicit knowledge about the relation between MSA and Levantine Arabic. Instead, (Duh and Kirchhoff, 2005) built a PoS tagger for Egyptian through a minimally supervised approach by leveraging the CallHome Egyptian Colloquial Arabic corpus (ECA). **2.** *The constitution of new resources not based on MSA-DA relations*, in particular dialectal corpora, such as the Fisher Levantine Arabic Conversational Telephone Speech (Maamouri et al., 2007).[1] This second strategy has been followed also collecting more *ad-hoc* resources. (Bouamor et al., 2018) presented the first parallel DA corpus, collecting the dialects of 25

---

[1]These resources are not freely available.






*Proceedings of the Fifth Arabic Natural Language Processing Workshop*, pages 178–191
Barcelona, Spain (Online), December 12, 2020

Arab cities, including the Tunisian dialects of Tunis and Sfax. The MADAR corpus has been created by translating selected sentences from the Basic Traveling Expression Corpus (BTEC) (Takezawa et al., 2007). Regarding Tunisian Dialect (TD), the resource constitution strategy has been instantiated as MSA resource adaptation to the DA, e.g. building lexicons (Boujelbane et al., 2013), PoS-taggers (Boujelbane et al., 2014; Hamdi et al., 2015), morphological analysers (Zribi et al., 2013) or morphological systems to disambiguate annotated transcriptions (Zribi et al., 2017). Considering the lack of freely available resources, we opted for an approach similar to the one used in *Curras* Palestinian corpus collection (Jarrar et al., 2017), which exploits MADAMIRA tools (Pasha et al., 2014), (cf. section 4.1).

The development of informal online communication provided a solution to most of the data availability problems, making accessible to the scientific community a large amount of texts, both written and oral. Concerning texts written in DA, it is possible to find two main writing systems: Arabic and Latin scripts. With regard to the second one, letters are used together with digits for the encoding of those Arabic letters without correspondence in the Roman alphabet. This system is already well known as *Arabizi*, or *Arabish* for non-Arabic speakers. Most of the work developed on Arabish focus on language identification (Darwish, 2014) and sentiment analysis (Duwairi et al., 2016; Fourati et al., 2020). Several works are focused on the conversion of Arabish into Arabic script, as the Parallel Annotated Egyptian Arabish-Arabic Script SMS/Chat Corpus (Bies et al., 2014). Transliteration has also been addressed for Tunisian Arabish (Masmoudi et al., 2015; Masmoudi et al., 2019; Younes et al., 2020).

In this paper we propose a multi-task sequence prediction system based on recurrent neural networks, that we used to annotate at multiple levels the Tunisian Arabish Corpus (TArC) (Gugliotta and Dinarelli, 2020). The annotation levels include tokenization, Part-of-Speech (PoS) tagging and Tunisian Arabish encoding into Arabic script. The system is learned to predict all the annotation levels in cascade, starting from Arabish input. We evaluate the system on the TIGER German corpus (Brants et al., 2004) in order to show the effectiveness of our neural architecture. While the purpose of this evaluation is not to improve state-of-the-art on this task, our results are comparable and sometimes better than the best published models. We show also how we used the system in order to annotate TArC, which has been afterwards manually corrected and used to further evaluate sequence models on Tunisian data. Our system is developped for *Fairseq*[2] (Ott et al., 2019), it can therefore be used for any problem involving sequence prediction.[3]

In the remainder of the paper we describe the TArC corpus, that we annotated with multi-level information, and we used to evaluate our neural system (in section 2). In section 3 we describe our multi-task neural architecture for multi-level annotation, in section 4 we describe the TIGER corpus, the experimental settings, and all the results obtained with our system, on both TIGER and TArC corpora. We conclude the paper in section 5.

## 2 Tunisian Arabish Multi-Level Annotated Corpus

The corpus used in this paper is the Tunisian Arabish Corpus (TArC) (Gugliotta and Dinarelli, 2020), the result of a multidisciplinary work with a hybrid approach based on: 1. dialectological research questions; 2. corpus linguistics standards and 3. deep learning techniques. TArC has been conceived with the aim to extend the dialectological investigation to the web, not only considering it as a new resource for linguistic analyses, but mainly because the object of TArC is a Computer Mediated Communication (CMC) writing system.

The gathering of CMC corpora for linguistic study purposes is a long-standing practice: as early as the 1990s, in order to study linguistic and communicational aspects, researchers began to collect corpora from mailing lists, newsgroups, electronic conferences or chat rooms (Yates, 1996; Todla, 1999; Berjaoui, 2001; Feldweg et al., 1995). Nowadays, the study of CMCs is a research domain it-self, crossing various disciplines such as sociology and linguistics. The linguistic questions related to CMC-corpora may for example concern paraverbal phenomena and the expression of emotions (Riordan and

---

[2]https://github.com/pytorch/fairseq

[3]Our system, with data used in this paper, is available at https://gricad-gitlab.univ-grenoble-alpes.fr/dinarelm/tarc-multi-task-system.

The last updated version of TArC is available at https://github.com/eligugliotta/tarc.

Kreuz, 2010; Tantawi and Rosson, 2019), politeness formulas and the degree of message formality (Brysbaert and Lahousse, 2019), the effects of orality in written communication (Soffer, 2010), the role of code-mixing and code-switching in mediated discourse (Morel and Doehler, 2013; Mave et al., 2018), their graphic and orthographic characteristics (Sullivan, 2017) (concerning Arabic). Lastly, a lot of research deals currently with the automatic processing of such corpora (Lopez et al., 2018; Panckhurst, 2017).

Among the purposes of dialectology there is the dialect collection and description with traditional approaches: fieldwork, oral text collection and transcription, glossary building. We observed that in the case of Arabic varieties the descriptive landscape is made of multiple studies on single phenomena. For this reason, we developed a resource inspired by dialectological investigation, which borrows the principles of corpus linguistics in order to guarantee representativeness, accessibility, balance and authenticity of the linguistic data (Szmrecsanyi and Anderwald, 2018; Wynne, 2005). The data gathered in TArC, together with various metadata, takes a snapshot of Tunisian Arabish writing and its evolution over the last ten years. TArC is built selecting data with the following criteria: 1. *text mode*: informal writing; 2. *text genres*: forum, blog, social networks, rap lyrics; 3. *domain*: CMC; 4. *language*: Tunisian; 5. *location*; 6. *publication date*. The last two items were registered via metadata extraction (publication date, user's age, gender and provenience).

The building process automation overcomes the *observer's paradox* problem (Labov, 1972), an issue much discussed in dialectology (Boberg et al., 2018). It also allows the reproducibility of the work, as well as the quantitative extension of an open corpus (such as TArC), which is normally difficult to ensure by dialectological research. TArC collection has therefore been enhanced thanks to the multi-task architecture, used for a semi-automatic annotation (cf. section 3) to get as close as possible to a consistent linguistic annotation (Wynne, 2005). The automatically generated annotations were post-edited by a linguist qualified in Arabic language and Tunisian variety, whose work was occasionally verified by native speakers.[4] Such annotation work complies with both the *applicative* and the *analytical* purposes of a corpus. The former concerns the generation of NLP tools for the Tunisian Arabish processing. The latter is realised through the multi-functional annotation levels of TArC, which allow global and systematic studies of Tunisian variety and its Arabish encoding. This way, TArC usefulness returns to the dialectological area, the field in which the preliminary research questions were addressed.

TArC has been annotated with four information levels. **1) Classification** of words in three classes: *arabizi*, *foreign* and *emotag*. The first class is for Tunisian and MSA words, the second one is to classify non-Arabic code-mixing; the third is used for elements as smileys or emoticons. **2) Encoding in Arabic script** in Conventional Orthography for Dialectal Arabic (CODA*) (Habash et al., 2018). **3) Tokenization**, Tunisian words encoded in CODA* have been tokenized following the *D3_BWFORM* configuration scheme where basically all clitics are tokenized, including the article (Pasha et al., 2014). **4) Part-of-Speech** according to the *PATB* guidelines (Maamouri et al., 2009). All levels have been developed following the same incremental and semi-automatic procedure described in (Gugliotta and Dinarelli, 2020) for the CODAfying stage.

## 3 Multi-Task Sequence Prediction System

There are several works about multi-task learning with neural networks for NLP problems (Wu and Huang, 2015; Luong et al., 2016), *inter alia*. Most of the time the neural architecture factorises some parameters for information that can be shared among tasks, and then uses different modules (e.g. decoders) for each task, which are learned independently.

As described in section 2, our goal for Tunisian Arabish data is a multi-level annotation scheme, where the different levels are potentially related. From an NLP point of view, this relations imply that some levels of annotation may help disambiguation when annotating other levels. For instance the classification information can disambiguate annotation into CODA*, tokenization and PoS tagging. Intuitively we expected that learning tasks in chain, organised in a cascade manner in a neural network, would benefit to each other, in contrast to learning tasks individually.

---

[4]Due to COVID-19 lockdown it was not possible to conduct the field research scheduled for March 2020.

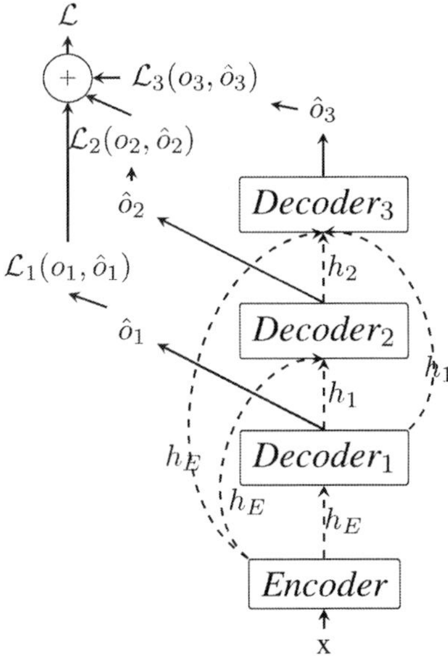

Figure 1: A high-level schema of our multi-task neural system

## 3.1 Multi-Task Neural Architecture

We follow the intuition above and we propose a multi-task neural architecture where the different learned tasks are organised in a cascade. The input is the Arabish text. The outputs, corresponding to the tasks to be learned, are, in this order, the classification information, the conversion into CODA* orthography, the tokenization of the *CODAfied* tokens and the PoS tags. Outputs from previous tasks are reused by the following tasks, they are thus learned jointly and interdependently. The input is transformed into hidden context-aware representations with an encoder based on recurrent layers. The outputs are processed by different decoders, each of them taking as input the hidden state of the encoder, and the hidden state of each of the previous decoders. The output of each decoder is used to learn each task.

More formally, let the task $i$ be represented by the model $M_i(x, H_i)$, with $x$ the input (Arabish text representations), and $H_i$ the list of hidden states from the previous models, plus the current model's hidden state $h_i$. Each model $i$ generates an output $\hat{o}_i$ and a hidden state $h_i$. $\hat{o}_i$ is the predicted output, which is used to learn the task $i$ by computing a loss $\mathcal{L}_i(o_i, \hat{o}_i)$ comparing $\hat{o}_i$ to the expected output $o_i$. Internally the global model $M$ is made of an *Encoder* and $I$ decoders *Decoder$_i$*, with $i = 1 \ldots I$. The list $H_i$ includes both the encoder hidden state $h_E$ and the decoders hidden states $h_1...h_i$. An high-level schema of this architecture, with the flow of information for three tasks ($I = 3$), is presented in figure 1. All the tasks are learned jointly by minimising the global loss $\mathcal{L} = \sum_i \mathcal{L}_i(o_i, \hat{o}_i)$, on top of the circled + in the schema (Figure 1).

Like in the original sequence-to-sequence model based on an attention mechanism (Bahdanau et al., 2014), each decoder attends to encoder and decoder's hidden state information with an attention mechanism. The decoder *Decoder$_i$* has therefore $i$ different attention mechanisms, one for attending encoder's information, and one for each previous decoder's hidden state. The queries for the attention mechanisms are always the *Decoder$_i$*'s hidden states, while keys and values are the encoder and previous decoder hidden states. The attention vectors computed by the attention mechanisms are *simply* summed together to generate the final state, used to predict the next output.[5]

---

[5]We note that we have been testing also gating mechanisms to *blend* the outputs of the attention mechanisms like in (Miculicich et al., 2018), but this always gave worse results than the sum.

| | Training | | Dev | | Test | |
|---|---|---|---|---|---|---|
| # sentences | 40 472 | | 5 000 | | 5 000 | |
| | Words | Labels | Words | Labels | Words | Labels |
| # tokens | 719 530 | – | 76 704 | – | 92 004 | – |
| dictionary | 77 220 | 681 | 15 852 | 501 | 20 149 | 537 |
| OOV% | – | – | 30,90 | 0,01 | 37,18 | 0,015 |

Table 1: Statistics of the German corpus TIGER

| | Sentences | Words | | |
|---|---|---|---|---|
| Total | 4121 | 32 062 | | |
| | | *arabizi* | *foreign* | *emotag* |
| forum | 756 | 6039 | 5856 | 14 |
| social | 3146 | 11 843 | 3614 | 587 |
| blog | 219 | 3763 | 343 | 3 |

Table 2: Statistics of the already annotated part of TArC

## 4 Evaluation

### 4.1 Data

In order to evaluate our multi-task system, we used two different corpora. One is TArC, described in section 2, the other is the German TIGER corpus (Brants et al., 2004).

**TArC corpus** has been initially collected from forums, social media and blogs, for a total of 32 062 words, and recently extended to 43 313 words by adding the text type of rap lyrics. In order to better organise the automatic annotation and the manual-correction stages, we split the initial corpus into blocks of roughly 6 500 tokens. Statistics of TArC are presented in table 2. The initial model, used to bootstrap the corpus annotation, has been trained using 2000 sentences from the Tunisian MADAR corpus. MADAR data are well-formed texts encoded in Arabic script, this avoid any code-switching and spelling inconsistency. We processed MADAR data using the MADAMIRA tool (Pasha et al., 2014).[6], producing tokenization and PoS tags. After a manual correction, we obtained the first TArC training block for starting the annotation procedure.

**The German corpus TIGER** (Brants et al., 2004) is annotated with rich morpho-syntactic information. These include PoS tags, but also gender, number, cases, and other inflection information, as well as conjugation information for verbs. The combination of all these components constitutes the output labels. We used the same data split used in (Lavergne and Yvon, 2017). Statistics of this corpus are given in table 1.

### 4.2 Settings

#### 4.2.1 Data Pre-processing

We first describe some data pre-processing performed on both corpora, in order to better exploit the small amount of data in TArC, on one side; on the other side, we performed a similar pre-processing on the TIGER corpus, in order to have similar experimental settings and therefore be able to validate the multi-task model with results comparable with the literature.

The TIGER corpus has been used as a benchmark for our multi-task system, before applying it to TArC. Since TIGER data are not natively multi-task, we re-organised TIGER labels in two parts: the first consisting of the PoS core-tag only, the second consisting of the whole label. For example, given the label *ADJA.PoS.Nom.Sg.Masc*[7], we take the PoS tag *ADJA* as a first level of information, and the whole label as a second level. This simple pre-processing allows to have two tasks to learn with our

---

[6]Version used: MADAMIRA 2.0. D3_BW* schemes (Habash, 2010).

[7]The different pieces stand for adjective, possessive, nominative, singular and male, respectively.

system: a coarse and a fine-grained morpho-syntactic tagging, where the second task, more complex, can be learned using also the information of the first, which is simpler.

In order to reduce data sparsity in TArC, we performed sequence prediction at each annotation level using sub-token units, except for the classification level. Sub-token units are characters for Arabish, *CODAfied* tokens and tokenization levels. For the PoS tags we performed an *ad-hoc* split into coarser units. The PoS tags annotated in TArC follow the LDC guidelines described in (Maamouri et al., 2009).[8] The tags contain rich information, like for the TIGER labels, describing the morphological structure of tokens. For instance the tag *PV-PVSUFF_SUBJ:3MS+[PREP+PRON_2S]PVSUFF_IO:2S*, contains information about a verb with inflectional morphology (*PV-PVSUFF_SUBJ:3MS*), plus information on a pre-pronominal enclitic group attached to the verb (*PREP+PRON_2S*). This group contains also an indirect object in suffix form (*PVSUFF_IO:2S*). Each of these 3 macro components contains person features, *3MS* for the verb, *2S* for the enclitic pronoun, and *2S* for the indirect object suffix.

Quite intuitively, such complex tags, taken as a whole, are very rare in the data. Indeed more than half of them occur only once in our data.[9] However their components are quite common (e.g. *PV, PVSUFF, SUBJ, 3, M, S* and so on). For this reason we split the tag above into a sequence of components like: *PV, PVSUFF, _SUBJ, :3, @M, @S, +, [, PREP, +, PRON, _2, @S, ], PVSUFF, _IO, :2, @S.* Symbols like @ are added for the post-processing phase to correctly reconstruct the whole tag. For the same reason, each time a tag is split in this way, the components are wrapped with start and end markers *¡SOT¿*, *¡EOT¿* (for Start and End Of Token). A whole tag sequence, associated to an input sentence, is made by concatenating the sequences resulting from the split of each tag. The same start and end markers are used also for the other annotation levels, which are split into single characters, so that the model can learn itself that each token in the input sequence corresponds to one token in all the annotation levels.

In order to have the same settings for TArC and TIGER data, we split the input tokens in the TIGER data into characters, adding the start and end markers. The labels are left unchanged, beyond artificially creating 2 label levels to test our multi-task system (we actually performed experiments also splitting TIGER labels into components, cf. table 3 and 4).

The TArC classification level was added first. This was done using a character-level model pre-trained exploiting: i) the Hussem Ben Belgacem's French dictionary, consisting of 336,531 tokens.[10], and ii) a Tunisian Arabish dictionary of 100,936 tokens, resulting from the merge of the TUNIZI Sentiment Analysis Tunisian Arabic Dataset (Fourati et al., 2020)[11] and the TLD dataset (Younes et al., 2015).

In order to obtain an *emotag* dictonary, we extracted all the smileys and emoticons from the Arabish dictionary above. Once the model was pre-trained on the above data, it was possible to apply also to this annotation level the semi-automatic and incremental annotation procedure used in (Gugliotta and Dinarelli, 2020). At the end of the procedure, the model reached 97% of accuracy. All data were manually checked and corrected.

### 4.2.2 Model Settings

Concerning model settings, we note that encoder and decoders in our multi-task neural models are all LSTM (Hochreiter and Schmidhuber, 1997).[12]

An optimisation of hyper-parameters like learning rate, dropout ratio (Srivastava et al., 2014), layer size, etc. has been performed on development data of TArC. For experiments on TIGER the same hyper-parameters have been used. The goal here is not to obtain the best absolute results on this task, it is to show that our system is competitive enough to be used safely on unpublished data. Such hyper-parameter optimal values resulted in: $5E^{-4}$ for learning rate, 0.5 for dropout ratio (at all layers, including embeddings), 5.0 for gradient clipping (Pascanu et al., 2012), 256 for both embeddings and hidden layer size (for all layers). We share all embeddings, at input and output layers, and in encoder and decoders.

---

[8] In the concatenation style we used "-" and the square brackets, to better manage the information through our model.

[9] More precisely, 423 PoS tags out of 776 in the dictionary, that is 54.9%, occur only once.

[10] https://github.com/hbenbel/French-Dictionary (last access on 15/09/2020).

[11] https://github.com/chaymafourati/TUNIZI-Sentiment-Analysis-Tunisian-Arabizi-Dataset (last access on 15/09/2020).

[12] The system is however generic, and potentially any kind of encoder and decoder available in Fairseq may be used. We are currently working on adding the use of Transformer encoder and decoders (Vaswani et al., 2017).

The loss functions used in all our experiments, for all the decoder outputs (see $\mathcal{L}$, $\mathcal{L}_1$, etc. in section 3.1), are the cross-entropy loss. All models are learned with an ADAM optimiser (Kingma and Ba, 2014) with default parameters. Model's outputs are evaluated with the accuracy, after applying post-processing to reconstruct original tokens. This means that if a single character or component in a token is wrong, the token is considered wrong in the accuracy.

### 4.3   Results

We present first results obtained on the corpus TIGER. We remind that we artificially performed multi-tasking on TIGER by isolating the core-tag from its features for each morpho-syntactic tag, and using the core-tag and the whole one as separated output to be predicted (see section 4.2).

The first set of experiments was performed to choose the optimal number of layers in each decoder of our multi-task system. Results are shown in table 3, the two tasks are **PoS**, for core-tags only, and **MORPHO** for core+feature tags. The results of both tasks show that the model performs at best with 3 layers in each decoder, though the gain with respect to the other choices is small. Despite the gain is small, we observed consistently the best results, both in terms of accuracy and loss values, and on both corpora, with 3 layers.

In the table 3 we show also the comparison of our results with the literature. To the best of our knwoledge the best results on the corpus TIGER have been published in (Dinarelli and Grobol, 2019), which improved previous state-of-the-art of (Lavergne and Yvon, 2017). Our results are comparable with the state-of-the-art, even slightly better on morpho-syntactic tagging, *Dev data*. We would like to insist on the fact that experiments on TIGER have been performed not with the goal to improve the state-of-the-art, but only for validating our multi-task system for performing multi-level annotation of TArC as multi-tasking. In this respect, the model used in (Dinarelli and Grobol, 2019) is quite sophisticated, it performs sequence labelling exploiting both token and character information on the input side, and performing bidirectional decoding on the output side. Our model performs decoding at character-level only, though using several layers over 2 tasks. Beyond this comparison, we consider our results on the TIGER corpus satisfactory for a multi-task setting.

The last 3 lines of table 3 and 4 show results on TIGER Dev and Test data, respectively. In these experiments we compare models learned for decoding label components, instead of whole labels, using character-level input (*Char decoding*), models learned with whole tokens on input and output side (*Token decoding*), and models combining both information, but learned from whole-token tag sequences (*Token+char decoding*). As we can see, *Char decoding* setting is by far the most effective. Combining token and character level information largely improves the *Token decoding* setting, but it is still much less effective than the *Char decoding* setting.

It could be interesting to observe which gain can be achieved with a multi-task model, e.g. on PoS tagging, with respect to a mono-task sequence-to-sequence model on the same task. In order to show such gain, we performed an experiment of PoS tagging with our multi-task system in a mono-task setting, with the same experimental settings. We compare this result with the multi-task counter-part in table 3. The two results are shown in table 5. As we can see, a substantial gain can be achieved performing PoS tagging as part of a multi-task setting. Even if, when learned for multi-tasking, PoS tagging is the first task and so it cannot exploit information coming from preceding tasks, the gain is given by the back-propagation of the morpho-syntactic tagging error through the whole network. Once again, results are obtained decoding at character level only for keeping the same experimental settings as for the TArC.

Experiments on TArC are divided in two phases, corresponding to two annotation phases: the first concerns the Arabish conversion into Arabic script. The second phase consists in classification of each token in *arabizi*, *foreign* or *emotag* classes, together with tokenization of Arabic-encoded tokens, and PoS tagging. Each phase was performed with a semi-automatic procedure, where a model was trained on a first block of data. Such model was used to annotate another block of data. This was then manually corrected and added to the training data. A new model was trained and used to annotate a new block. This procedure was iterated up to the annotation of the full corpus (32 062 tokens).

For the first phase of the annotation (Arabic script encoding only) we used the mono-task sequence-

| Corpus: TIGER Dev data | | |
| --- | --- | --- |
| **Best results** | | |
| | **PoS** | **MORPHO** |
| (Dinarelli and Grobol, 2019) | 98.37% | 93.94% |
| **Our results** | | |
| **Model** | | **LSTM** |
| **Task** | **PoS** | **Morpho** |
| 1 Enc + 1 Dec layers | 97.83% | 93.16% |
| 2 Enc + 2 Dec layers | 98.16% | 93.58% |
| 3 Enc + 3 Dec layers | 98.30% | 94.10% |
| Char decoding | 98.30% | 94.10% |
| Token decoding | 96.21% | 86.89% |
| Token+char decoding | 98.11% | 90.70% |

Table 3: Summary of results, in terms of accuracy, obtained on the TIGER development data set with the Tarc Multi-Task system.

| Corpus: TIGER Test data | | |
| --- | --- | --- |
| **Best results** | | |
| | **PoS** | **MORPHO** |
| (Dinarelli and Grobol, 2019) | 97.74% | 91.86% |
| **Our results** | | |
| **Model** | | **LSTM** |
| **Task** | **PoS** | **Morpho** |
| Char decoding | 97.44% | 91.81% |
| Token decoding | 94.44% | 83.37% |
| Token+char decoding | 97.25% | 87.87% |

Table 4: Summary of results, in terms of accuracy, obtained on the TIGER test data set with the Tarc Multi-Task system.

to-sequence model of (Dinarelli and Grobol, 2019). Indeed the Arabic script encoding of tokens is the most costly and difficult phase, so we thought it could be easier to have it first, annotating the other levels afterwards. The Arabic script encoding accuracy of the model was below 70% for the first block. This still allowed the annotator to correct the block 3 times faster than if the block was annotated from scratch. For the following data blocks, accuracy of the model increased progressively, up to roughly 76% for the fourth block. At this point we started the second phase, which included the annotation of the fifth and last block with encoding conversion.

In the second phase, we repeated the iterative semi-automatic annotation procedure of the first phase for the classification, tokenization and PoS tagging levels. These were performed with the multi-task system. The first model for bootstrapping the annotation procedure was trained on a part of the MADAR data (Bouamor et al., 2018) consisting of roughly 12,000 tokens ( 2,000 sentences). These data were annotated with tokenization and PoS information using MADAMIRA as explained in section 4.1, and then manually corrected. The classification information was added manually, which was trivial since all tokens belong to the *arabizi* class in this data. The model trained on MADAR data has been used to annotate the first block of TArC, which is the step 0 of the iterative procedure. In the following 3 iterations, the MADAR data were used together with the TArC blocks already manually corrected. The input for these 3 steps was thus the *CODAfied* Tunisian. Exploiting MADAR was only possible up to the 4th block, since the blocks after the fourth were not already provided with *CODAfied* tokens (see the 1st annotation phase above). However, we planned to add all the annotation levels to the 5th block, including

| Corpus: TIGER Dev data | |
| --- | --- |
| **PoS tagging results** | |
| **Model** | **LSTM** |
| Mono-task | 95.66% |
| Multi-task | 98.30% |

Table 5: Comparison of results of PoS tags decoding from source characters, on the TIGER development data with mono-task and multi-task models.

the encoding in Arabic script level, with the multi-task system. The 5th block was thus annotated using only TArC four blocks in Arabish as training data. At each iteration step, the Arabish data were split randomly into train and validation (dev) sets, so that the dev set is representative of the whole data at each iteration.[13]

We report the results on the 3 tasks of the first 4 steps, where the input was *CODAfied* Tunisian, and the results on the 4 tasks of the following steps, where the input was Arabish, in table 6. The tasks are indicated in the table with **Class** for classification, **Arabic** for Arabic script encoding, **Token** for tokenization, and **PoS** for PoS tagging, respectively. In the column **"Train. tokens"** of the table we report the number of training tokens for each step. Between parenthesis, when this is meaningful, we also report the number of training tokens coming from TArC (the remainder is from the MADAR corpus).

In table 6, *Step0* is the bootstrapping step, where the model is trained on MADAR data only. Results are on a randomly chosen dev data set consisting of 15% of the whole data set. Starting from *Step1*, the dev data set is a 15% random split of the TArC data only, as we are interested in the effectiveness of our multi-task system on spontaneous and informal writing data for annotation purposes.

Results in table 6 prove that the multi-task system is effective also on TArC, especially taking into account the small amount of data available for training the models. The classification task (**Class**) is quite well solved, as at best the model, when evaluated on TArC text, is over 97% of accuracy. Results for tokenization (**Token**) are also satisfactory, in particular at step 3, where the model is over 91% of accuracy. Results on PoS tagging (**PoS**) are quite lower with respect to the other tasks, but we note that this task is the most difficult, among the 3 of the first 4 steps. Indeed, classification only consists in associating to each token one of the 3 classes *arabizi, foreign* or *emotag*. The tokenization task consists in splitting a *CODAfied* token into its components with some orthographical transformations, input and output script is thus the same, the model needs to learn the splitting. In contrast, PoS tagging is a conversion from Arabic characters into PoS components.

As we have explained in section 4.2, PoS tags are quite complex, and splitting them into components allows to mitigate the problem of data sparsity. Moreover, accuracy is computed after post-processing, that is after PoS tags have been reconstructed from components. A single mistake on a component results in a wrong tag, affecting the accuracy. Taking all of that into account, we consider the best PoS tagging result of 76.38% of accuracy as an acceptable result.

In table 6 we observe a substantial drop of results from step 0 (where the model is evaluated on the MADAR dev set) to step 1 (where the model is evaluated on the Arabish dev set only).[14] This is not surprising, as MADAR is made of morphosyntactically well-formed text, while TArC is made of CMC spontaneous texts. This behaviour is useful to explain the difference of results between step 3 and step 4 and 5. Beyond that, the increased amount of TArC data with respect to MADAR data through steps 1 to 3, allows to improve results obtained on the MADAR data (*Step0*).

Results in table 6 drop again between steps 3 and 4. We remind that at step 3, data blocks from 1 to 3, plus the MADAR data, are used for training the model, a 15% split of the TArC data are used for validation, and the model is used to annotate the fourth data block. At step 4 only TArC data are used for training, again a 15% split is used for validation, and the fifth block is annotated. At this step an

---

[13] In this respect, we note that data in different blocks are heterogeneous, as they are not all from the same source. Hence keeping the same dev data set for all the iterations would not be representative.

[14] All MADAR tokens are classified as *arabizi*, it is thus normal that the model gets almost perfect result in classifying it.

| Task | Train. tokens | LSTM | | | |
|---|---|---|---|---|---|
| | | Class | Arabic | Token | PoS |
| Corpus: MADAR | | | | | |
| Step0 | 12 391 | 99.83% | - | 88.83% | 72.71% |
| Corpus: MADAR+TArC | | | | | |
| Step1 | 17 261 (4 870) | 92.69% | - | 77.66% | 59.56% |
| Step2 | 22 173 (9 780) | 97.21% | - | 87.53% | 74.30% |
| Step3 | 27 270 (14 870) | 96.69% | - | 91.47% | 76.38% |
| Corpus: TArC | | | | | |
| Step4 | 22 150 | 96.83% | 75.30% | 73.38% | 69.76% |
| Step5 | 27 435 | 97.17% | 75.08% | 73.07% | 66.24% |
| Step4$_{smart-init}$ | 22 150 | 95.91% | 76.55% | 74.96% | 72.57% |
| Step5$_{smart-init}$ | 27 435 | 97.08% | 77.83% | 75.69% | 69.76% |

Table 6: Summary of results, in terms of accuracy, obtained on the TArC data at the different steps of the iterative procedure for semi-automatic annotation of the corpus. The tasks are indicated with **Class** for classification, **Arabic** for Arabic script encoding, **Token** for tokenization, and **PoS** for PoS tagging.

additional task is performed: encoding of Arabish into CODA*.

As we can see in table 6, all results except for classification, substantially dropped. This is due to having an additional task with respect to the previous steps, and thus an additional decoder in the system, and to the use of a smaller training set. We note however this drop is similar to the one between steps 0 and 1. We conclude thus that MADAR well-formed texts have a positive effect on learning spontaneous Arabish text. It is interesting to observe that the drop in PoS tagging results with respect to tokenization, at steps 4 and 5, is much smaller than the drop at steps 1 and 3. This suggests to improve Arabish *CODAfication* results, which may be achieved by adding Arabish encoding to MADAR. Results on the step 5 are similar to step 4. This is not surprising as well, since data in the block 5 have a different style, coming from a different source (blogs). This balances the increased amount of data for training the model.

In order to exploit the MADAR data also at steps 4 and 5, we designed an *ad-hoc* parameter initialisation using the model trained at step 0. Note that such model has a different architecture as MADAR is in Arabic script, it doesn't contain Arabish.[15] Results obtained with this initialisation are reported in the last lines of table 6 marked as *smart-init*. As we can see, except for the classification task which is biased by the fact that in MADAR all tokens are in the *arabizi* class, all other task results improved with respect to step 4 and 5 without pre-initialisation.

## 5 Conclusions

We presented a multi-task sequence labeling system based on recurrent neural networks, developed for the Fairseq framework and used to annotate TArC on multiple levels. The annotation levels provided are: classification, tokenization, PoS tagging and encoding of Tunisian Arabish into Arabic script, according to CODA*. We described the annotation procedure, after showing the effectiveness of our neural architecture with an evaluation on the TIGER German corpus. As a next stage we plan to expand TArC quantitatively to improve the results and its usability in linguistics and NLP fields. Future work includes qualitative extension through the addition of further annotation levels, such as lemmatization.

## References

Dzmitry Bahdanau, Kyunghyun Cho, and Yoshua Bengio. 2014. Neural machine translation by jointly learning to align and translate. *CoRR*, abs/1409.0473.

---

[15]This resulted in a quite task-specific parameter initialisation.

Nasser Berjaoui. 2001. *Aspects of the Moroccan Arabic orthography with preliminary insights from the Moroccan computer-mediated communication*. na.

Ann Bies, Zhiyi Song, Mohamed Maamouri, Stephen Grimes, Haejoong Lee, Jonathan Wright, Stephanie Strassel, Nizar Habash, Ramy Eskander, and Owen Rambow. 2014. Transliteration of arabizi into arabic orthography: Developing a parallel annotated arabizi-arabic script sms/chat corpus. In *Proceedings of the EMNLP 2014 workshop on Arabic natural language processing (ANLP)*, pages 93–103.

Charles Boberg, John A Nerbonne, and Dominic James Landon Watt. 2018. *The handbook of dialectology*. Wiley Online Library.

Houda Bouamor, Nizar Habash, Mohammad Salameh, Wajdi Zaghouani, Owen Rambow, Dana Abdulrahim, Ossama Obeid, Salam Khalifa, Fadhl Eryani, Alexander Erdmann, et al. 2018. The madar arabic dialect corpus and lexicon. In *Proceedings of the Eleventh International Conference on Language Resources and Evaluation (LREC 2018)*.

Rahma Boujelbane, Mariem Ellouze Khemekhem, Siwar BenAyed, and Lamia Hadrich Belguith. 2013. Building bilingual lexicon to create dialect tunisian corpora and adapt language model. In *Proceedings of the Second Workshop on Hybrid Approaches to Translation*, pages 88–93.

Rahma Boujelbane, Mariem Mallek, Mariem Ellouze, and Lamia Hadrich Belguith. 2014. Fine-grained pos tagging of spoken tunisian dialect corpora. In *International Conference on Applications of Natural Language to Data Bases/Information Systems*, pages 59–62. Springer.

Sabine Brants, Stefanie Dipper, Peter Eisenberg, Silvia Hansen-Schirra, Esther Konig, Wolfgang Lezius, Christian Rohrer, George Smith, and Hans Uszkoreit. 2004. TIGER: Linguistic interpretation of a german corpus. *Research on Language and Computation*, 2(4):597–620, dec.

Jorina Brysbaert and Karen Lahousse. 2019. Computer-mediated versus non-computer-mediated corpora of informal french: Differences in politeness and intensification in the expression of contrast by au contraire. *Social Media Corpora for the Humanities (CMC-Corpora2019)*, page 48.

Tim Buckwalter. 2004. Buckwalter arabic morphological analyzer (bama) version 2.0. *Linguistic Data Consortium (LDC), University of Pennsylvania, Philadelphia, PA, USA*.

Kyunghyun Cho, Bart van Merrienboer, Çaglar Gülçehre, Fethi Bougares, Holger Schwenk, and Yoshua Bengio. 2014. Learning phrase representations using RNN encoder-decoder for statistical machine translation. *CoRR*, abs/1406.1078.

Ronan Collobert and Jason Weston. 2007. Fast Semantic Extraction Using a Novel Neural Network Architecture. In *Proceedings of the 45th Annual Meeting of the Association of Computational Linguistics*, pages 560–567, Prague, Czech Republic, June. Association for Computational Linguistics.

Ronan Collobert and Jason Weston. 2008. A unified architecture for natural language processing: Deep neural networks with multitask learning. In *Proceedings of the 25th International Conference on Machine Learning*, ICML '08, pages 160–167, New York, NY, USA. ACM.

Ronan Collobert, Jason Weston, Léon Bottou, Michael Karlen, Koray Kavukcuoglu, and Pavel Kuksa. 2011. Natural language processing (almost) from scratch. *J. Mach. Learn. Res.*, 12, November.

Kareem Darwish. 2014. Arabizi detection and conversion to arabic. In *In the Arabic Natural Language Processing Workshop, EMNLP*.

Chiang David, Mona Diab, Nizar Habash, Owen Rambow, and Safiullah Shareef. 2006. Parsing arabic dialects. In *Proceedings of EACL*, pages 369–376.

Marco Dinarelli and Loïc Grobol. 2019. Hybrid neural models for sequence modelling: The best of three worlds. *CoRR*. arXiv preprint 1909.07102.

Kevin Duh and Katrin Kirchhoff. 2005. Pos tagging of dialectal arabic: a minimally supervised approach. In *Proceedings of the acl workshop on computational approaches to semitic languages*, pages 55–62.

Rehab M Duwairi, Mosab Alfaqeh, Mohammad Wardat, and Areen Alrabadi. 2016. Sentiment analysis for arabizi text. In *2016 7th International Conference on Information and Communication Systems (ICICS)*, pages 127–132. IEEE.

Helmut Feldweg, Ralf Kibiger, and Christine Thielen. 1995. Zum sprachgebrauch in deutschen newsgruppen. *Osnabrücker Beiträge zur Sprachtheorie*, 50:143–154.

Chayma Fourati, Abir Messaoudi, and Hatem Haddad. 2020. Tunizi: a tunisian arabizi sentiment analysis dataset. *arXiv preprint arXiv:2004.14303*.

Jonas Gehring, Michael Auli, David Grangier, Denis Yarats, and Yann N Dauphin. 2017. Convolutional sequence to sequence learning. In *Proc. of ICML*.

Elisa Gugliotta and Marco Dinarelli. 2020. Tarc: Incrementally and semi-automatically collecting a tunisian arabish corpus. In *Proceedings of The 12th Language Resources and Evaluation Conference*, pages 6279–6286.

Nizar Habash, Fadhl Eryani, Salam Khalifa, Owen Rambow, Dana Abdulrahim, Alexander Erdmann, Reem Faraj, Wajdi Zaghouani, Houda Bouamor, Nasser Zalmout, et al. 2018. Unified guidelines and resources for arabic dialect orthography. In *Proceedings of the Eleventh International Conference on Language Resources and Evaluation (LREC 2018)*.

Nizar Habash. 2010. Introduction to arabic natural language processing. *Synthesis Lectures on Human Language Technologies*, 3(1):1–187.

Ahmed Hamdi, Alexis Nasr, Nizar Habash, and Núria Gala. 2015. Pos-tagging of tunisian dialect using standard arabic resources and tools. In *Proceedings of the Second Workshop on Arabic Natural Language Processing*, pages 59–68. Association for Computational Linguistics (ACL), July.

Sepp Hochreiter and Jürgen Schmidhuber. 1997. Long short-term memory. *Neural Comput.*, 9(8):1735–1780, November.

Go Inoue, Hiroyuki Shindo, and Yuji Matsumoto. 2017. Joint prediction of morphosyntactic categories for fine-grained arabic part-of-speech tagging exploiting tag dictionary information. In *Proceedings of the 21st Conference on Computational Natural Language Learning (CoNLL 2017)*, pages 421–431.

Mustafa Jarrar, Nizar Habash, Faeq Alrimawi, Diyam Akra, and Nasser Zalmout. 2017. Curras: an annotated corpus for the palestinian arabic dialect. *Language Resources and Evaluation*, 51(3).745–775.

Diederik P. Kingma and Jimmy Ba. 2014. Adam: A method for stochastic optimization. cite arxiv:1412.6980Comment: Published as a conference paper at the 3rd International Conference for Learning Representations, San Diego, 2015.

William Labov. 1972. *Sociolinguistic Patterns*. Conduct and Communication. University of Pennsylvania Press, Incorporated.

Thomas Lavergne and FranÃ§ois Yvon. 2017. Learning the structure of variable-order crfs: a finite-state perspective. In *Proceedings of the 2017 Conference on Empirical Methods in Natural Language Processing*, pages 433–439. Association for Computational Linguistics.

Cédric Lopez, Sarah Zenasni, Eric Kergosien, Ioannis Partalas, Mathieu Roche, Maguelonne Teisseire, and Rachel Panckhurst. 2018. Extracting absolute spatial entities from sms: comparing a supervised and an unsupervised approach. *Language and the new (instant) media*.

Thang Luong, Quoc V. Le, Ilya Sutskever, Oriol Vinyals, and Lukasz Kaiser. 2016. Multi-task sequence to sequence learning. In *International Conference on Learning Representations*.

Mohamed Maamouri, Ann Bies, Tim Buckwalter, and Wigdan Mekki. 2004. The penn arabic treebank: Building a large-scale annotated arabic corpus. In *NEMLAR conference on Arabic language resources and tools*, volume 27, pages 466–467. Cairo.

Mohamed Maamouri, Tim Buckwalter, Dave Graff, and Hubert Jin. 2007. Fisher levantine arabic conversational telephone speech. *Linguistic Data Consortium, University of Pennsylvania, LDC Catalog No.: LDC2007S02*.

Mohamed Maamouri, Ann Bies, Sondos Krouna, Fatma Gaddeche, and Basma Bouziri. 2009. Penn arabic treebank guidelines. *Linguistic Data Consortium*.

Abir Masmoudi, Nizar Habash, Mariem Ellouze, Yannick Estève, and Lamia Hadrich Belguith. 2015. Arabic transliteration of romanized tunisian dialect text: A preliminary investigation. In *International Conference on Intelligent Text Processing and Computational Linguistics*, pages 608–619. Springer.

Abir Masmoudi, Mariem Ellouze Khmekhem, Mourad Khrouf, and Lamia Hadrich Belguith. 2019. Transliteration of arabizi into arabic script for tunisian dialect. *ACM Transactions on Asian and Low-Resource Language Information Processing (TALLIP)*, 19(2):1–21.

Deepthi Mave, Suraj Maharjan, and Thamar Solorio. 2018. Language identification and analysis of code-switched social media text. In *Proceedings of the Third Workshop on Computational Approaches to Linguistic Code-Switching*, pages 51–61.

Lesly Miculicich, Dhananjay Ram, Nikolaos Pappas, and James Henderson. 2018. Document-level neural machine translation with hierarchical attention networks. In *Proceedings of the 2018 Conference on Empirical Methods in Natural Language Processing*, pages 2947–2954, Brussels, Belgium, October-November. Association for Computational Linguistics.

Etienne Morel and Simona Pekarek Doehler. 2013. Les 'textos' plurilingues: l'alternance codique comme ressource d'affiliation à une communauté globalisée. *Revue française de linguistique appliquée*, 18(2):29–43.

Myle Ott, Sergey Edunov, Alexei Baevski, Angela Fan, Sam Gross, Nathan Ng, David Grangier, and Michael Auli. 2019. fairseq: A fast, extensible toolkit for sequence modeling. In *Proceedings of NAACL-HLT 2019: Demonstrations*.

Rachel Panckhurst. 2017. *Entre linguistique et informatique. Des outils de traitement automatique du langage naturel écrit (TALNE) à l'analyse du discours numérique médié (DNM)*. Ph.D. thesis, Université Paris-Est, Paris, France.

Razvan Pascanu, Tomas Mikolov, and Yoshua Bengio. 2012. Understanding the exploding gradient problem. *CoRR*, abs/1211.5063.

Arfath Pasha, Mohamed Al-Badrashiny, Mona Diab, Ahmed El Kholy, Ramy Eskander, Nizar Habash, Manoj Pooleery, Owen Rambow, and Ryan Roth. 2014. MADAMIRA: A fast, comprehensive tool for morphological analysis and disambiguation of Arabic. In *Proceedings of the Ninth International Conference on Language Resources and Evaluation (LREC'14)*, pages 1094–1101, Reykjavik, Iceland, May. European Language Resources Association (ELRA).

Monica A Riordan and Roger J Kreuz. 2010. Emotion encoding and interpretation in computer-mediated communication: Reasons for use. *Computers in human behavior*, 26(6):1667–1673.

Oren Soffer. 2010. "silent orality": toward a conceptualization of the digital oral features in cmc and sms texts. *Communication Theory*, 20(4):387–404.

Nitish Srivastava, Geoffrey Hinton, Alex Krizhevsky, Ilya Sutskever, and Ruslan Salakhutdinov. 2014. Dropout: A simple way to prevent neural networks from overfitting. *Journal of Machine Learning Research*, 15:1929–1958.

Natalie Sullivan. 2017. *Writing Arabizi: Orthographic Variation in Romanized Lebanese Arabic on Twitter*. Ph.D. thesis, The University of Texas at Austin, USA.

Ilya Sutskever, Oriol Vinyals, and Quoc V. Le. 2014. Sequence to sequence learning with neural networks. In *Proceedings of NIPS*, Cambridge, MA, USA. MIT Press.

Benedikt Szmrecsanyi and Lieselotte Anderwald. 2018. Corpus-Based Approaches to Dialect Study. In *The Handbook of Dialectology*, pages 300–313. John Wiley & Sons, Ltd. Section: 17 _eprint: https://onlinelibrary.wiley.com/doi/pdf/10.1002/9781118827628.ch17.

Toshiyuki Takezawa, Genichiro Kikui, Masahide Mizushima, and Eiichiro Sumita. 2007. Multilingual spoken language corpus development for communication research. In *International Journal of Computational Linguistics & Chinese Language Processing, Volume 12, Number 3, September 2007: Special Issue on Invited Papers from ISCSLP 2006*, pages 303–324.

Yasmin Tantawi and Mary Beth Rosson. 2019. The paralinguistic function of emojis in twitter communication. *Social Media Corpora for the Humanities (CMC-Corpora2019)*, page 68.

Sunisa Todla. 1999. Patterns of communicative behaviour in internet chatrooms. *Unpublished master's thesis, Chulalongkorn University*.

Ashish Vaswani, Noam Shazeer, Niki Parmar, Jakob Uszkoreit, Llion Jones, Aidan N. Gomez, Lukasz Kaiser, and Illia Polosukhin. 2017. Attention is all you need. In *Advances in neural information processing systems*.

Fangzhao Wu and Yongfeng Huang. 2015. Collaborative multi-domain sentiment classification. In *2015 IEEE International Conference on Data Mining*, pages 459–468.

Felix Wu, Angela Fan, Alexei Baevski, Yann Dauphin, and Michael Auli. 2019. Pay less attention with lightweight and dynamic convolutions. In *International Conference on Learning Representations*.

Martin Wynne. 2005. *Developing linguistic corpora: A guide to good practice*. Oxbow Books Limited.

Simeon J. Yates. 1996. Oral and written linguistic aspects of computer conferencing. *Pragmatics and beyond New Series*, pages 29–46.

Jihen Younes, Hadhemi Achour, and Emna Souissi. 2015. Constructing linguistic resources for the tunisian dialect using textual user-generated contents on the social web. In *International Conference on Web Engineering*, pages 3–14. Springer.

Jihene Younes, Hadhemi Achour, Emna Souissi, and Ahmed Ferchichi. 2020. Romanized tunisian dialect transliteration using sequence labelling techniques. *Journal of King Saud University-Computer and Information Sciences*.

Nasser Zalmout and Nizar Habash. 2019. Joint diacritization, lemmatization, normalization, and fine-grained morphological tagging. *arXiv preprint arXiv:1910.02267*.

Inès Zribi, Mariem Ellouze Khemekhem, and Lamia Hadrich Belguith. 2013. Morphological analysis of tunisian dialect. In *Proceedings of the Sixth International Joint Conference on Natural Language Processing*, pages 992–996.

Inès Zribi, Mariem Ellouze, Lamia Hadrich Belguith, and Philippe Blache. 2017. Morphological disambiguation of tunisian dialect. *Journal of king Saud University-computer and information sciences*, 29(2):147–155.

# AraWEAT: Multidimensional Analysis of Biases in Arabic Word Embeddings


**Anne Lauscher,**[1] **Rafik Takieddin,**[2] **Simone Paolo Ponzetto,**[1] **and Goran Glavaš**[1]
Data and Web Science Research Group
University of Mannheim
[1]{anne, simone, goran}@informatik.uni-mannheim.de
[2] rafik.takieddin@gmail.com



## Abstract

Recent work has shown that distributional word vector spaces often encode human biases like sexism or racism. In this work, we conduct an extensive analysis of biases in Arabic word embeddings by applying a range of recently introduced bias tests on a variety of embedding spaces induced from corpora in Arabic. We measure the presence of biases across several dimensions, namely: embedding models (SKIP-GRAM, CBOW, and FASTTEXT) and vector sizes, types of text (encyclopedic text, and news vs. user-generated content), dialects (Egyptian Arabic vs. Modern Standard Arabic), and time (diachronic analyses over corpora from different time periods). Our analysis yields several interesting findings, e.g., that implicit gender bias in embeddings trained on Arabic news corpora steadily increases over time (between 2007 and 2017). We make the Arabic bias specifications (AraWEAT) publicly available.


## 1 Introduction

Recent research offered evidence that distributional word representations (i.e., word embeddings) induced from human-created text corpora exhibit a range of human biases, such as racism and sexism (Bolukbasi et al., 2016; Caliskan et al., 2017). With word embeddings ubiquitously used as input for (neural) natural language processing (NLP) models, this brings about the jeopardy of introducing stereotypical unfairness into NLP models, which can reinforce existing social hierarchies, and therefore be harmful in practical applications. For instance, consider the seminal gender bias example *"Man is to computer programmer as woman is to homemaker"*, which is algebraically encoded in the embedding space with the analogical relation $\vec{man} - computer\ \vec{programmer} \approx \vec{woman} - \vec{homemaker}$ (Bolukbasi et al., 2016). The existence of such biases in word embeddings stems from the combination of (1) human biases manifesting themselves in terms of word co-occurrences (e.g., the word *woman* appearing in a training corpus much more often in the context of *homemaker* than together with *computer programmer*) and (2) the distributional nature of the word embedding models (Mikolov et al., 2013; Pennington et al., 2014; Bojanowski et al., 2017), which induce word vectors precisely by exploiting word co-occurrences, i.e., thus also encoding the human biases as a (negative) side-effect, which represents, expressed according to the taxnomy of harms proposed by Blodgett et al. (2020), a *representational harm*, more specifically, *stereotyping*. In order to quantify the amount of bias in word embeddings, Caliskan et al. (2017) proposed the Word Embedding Association Test (WEAT), which is based on the associative difference in terms of semantic similarity between two sets of target terms, e.g., *male* and *female* terms, towards two sets of attribute terms, e.g., *career* and *family* terms. Most recently, the WEAT test, measuring the degree of explicit bias in the distributional space, has been coupled with other tests, aiming to measure other aspects of bias, such as the amount of implicit bias (Gonen and Goldberg, 2019) or the presence of the analogical bias (Lauscher et al., 2020).

While there is evidence that distributional vectors often encode human biases, the amount of biases does not seem to be universal across different languages and corpora, as recently shown by Lauscher and Glavaš (2019) in the analysis of distributional biases across seven different languages. In this work, we






*Proceedings of the Fifth Arabic Natural Language Processing Workshop*, pages 192–199
Barcelona, Spain (Online), December 12, 2020

focus on the multi-dimensional analysis of biases in Arabic word embeddings. The motivation for this work is twofold: (1) Arabic is one of the most widely spoken languages in the world:[1] this means that the biases encoded in language technology for Arabic have the potential for affecting more people than for most other languages; (2) language resources for Arabic – large corpora (Goldhahn et al., 2012), pre-trained word embeddings (Mohammad et al., 2017; Bojanowski et al., 2017), and datasets for measuring semantic quality of Arabic embeddings (Elrazzaz et al., 2017; Cer et al., 2017) – are publicly available, allowing for the analyses of biases that these resources potentially hide.

As a first step in the analysis of language technology biases for Arabic, we present ARAWEAT, an Arabic extension to the multilingual XWEAT framework (Lauscher and Glavaš, 2019). Because the WEAT test (Caliskan et al., 2017), though it has the notable advantage of drawing inspiration from psychology literature, has recently been shown to systematically overestimate the bias present in an embedding space (Ethayarajh et al., 2019), in this work, we couple it with several other bias tests, designed to capture and quantify other aspects of human biases: Embedding Coherence Test (Dev and Phillips, 2019), Bias Analogy Test (Lauscher et al., 2020) and Implicit Bias Tests (Gonen and Goldberg, 2019).

Our work, which is to the best of our knowledge the first study on quantifying biases in Arabic distributional word vector spaces, yields some interesting findings: biases seem more prominent in vectors trained on texts written in Egyptian Arabic than those written in Modern Standard Arabic (MSA). Also, the implicit gender bias in Arabic news corpora seems to be steadily on the rise over the ten year period between 2007 and 2017. Finally, we find evidence that the explicit bias effects, as measured by the WEAT test, in embeddings trained on the entire Arabic news corpus roughly correspond to averaging the biases measured across embeddings trained on temporally disjunct subsets of the corpus.

## 2 AraWEAT

We present ARAWEAT, our framework allowing for multi-dimensional analysis of bias in Arabic distributional word vector spaces.

### 2.1 Data for Measuring Bias

At the core of our extension are the Arabic bias test specifications, which are based on the original English WEAT test data. WEAT is an adaptation of the Implicit Association Test (Nosek et al., 2002), which quantifies biases as association differences measured in terms of response times of human subjects when exposed to different sets of *stimuli*. WEAT, in turn, measures the association differences in terms of the difference in semantic similarity between two sets of *target* terms towards two sets of *attribute* terms.

Our creation of WEAT tests for Arabic starts with automatically translating, using Google Translate, the term sets (i.e., the terms from each of two target and two attribute lists) from the English WEAT tests. We then hired a native speaker of modern standard Arabic (MSA), who manually verified and, when needed, corrected the translations. As Arabic is a language with grammatical genders, we made sure to account for both genders when translating the terms so that we do not artificially introduce a bias in our test specifications (e.g., we translated the genderless English word engineer as both مهندس (*engineer* m.) and مهندسة (*engineer* f.). While initially considered, we did not translate WEAT test specifications to the different Arabic dialects, as the differences between the MSA translations and dialectal translations for the terms from the WEAT test were observed only in a negligible fraction of

| T1 | *math algebra geometry calculus equations computation numbers addition* |
| T2 | *poetry art dance literature novel symphony drama sculpture* |
| A1 | *male man boy brother he him his son* |
| A2 | *female woman girl sister she her hers daughter* |
| T1 | معادلات الرياضيات الجبر الهندسة تحليل إضافة أعداد حساب |
| T2 | الشعر رقص فن الأدب رواية سمفونية تحت دراما |
| A1 | له ابن صبي الذكر شقيق رجل هو |
| A2 | ابنة أخت نساء أنثى فتاة هي لها |

Table 1: Original English version and MSA translation of the WEAT Test 7 specification.

---

[1] According to Mikael (2007), Arabic is the fifth most spoken language in the world with close to 300 million native speakers.

| Test | Bias Type | Target Set #1 | Target Set #2 | Attribute Set #1 | Attribute Set #2 |
|---|---|---|---|---|---|
| 1 | Universal | Flowers (e.g., *aster*) | Insects (e.g., *ant, flea*) | Pleasant (e.g., *health*) | Unpleasant (e.g., *abuse*) |
| 2 | Militant | Instruments (e.g., *cello*) | Weapons (e.g., *gun*) | Pleasant | Unpleasant |
| 7 | Gender | Math (e.g., *algebra, geometry*) | Arts (e.g., *poetry*) | Male (e.g., *brother, son*) | Female (e.g., *woman, sister*) |
| 8 | Gender | Science (e.g., *experiment*) | Arts | Male | Female |
| 9 | Disease | Physical (e.g., *virus*) | Mental (e.g., *sad*) | Long-term (e.g., *always*) | Short-term (e.g., *occasional*) |

Table 2: WEAT bias tests.

cases; and even in those cases the MSA translation is also in usage in other Arabic dialects.[2] We further omitted WEAT tests 3–6 and 10 as they are based on proper names. While it has been shown that names are a good proxy for identifying and removing bias towards specific groups of people (Hall Maudslay et al., 2019), it is difficult to "translate" them.[3] As an example of the resulting AraWEAT test, Table 1 list the Arabic translation of WEAT test $T7$. An overview on the remaining tests with their respective target and attribute term sets is provided in Table 2.

| Model | Lang | T1 | | | | T2 | | | | T7 | | | | T8 | | | |
|---|---|---|---|---|---|---|---|---|---|---|---|---|---|---|---|---|---|
| | | W | ECT | BAT | KM | W | ECT | BAT | KM | W | ECT | BAT | KM | W | ECT | BAT | KM |
| FT ARABIC | MSA | 0.85 | 0.69 | 0.47 | 0.71 | 0.51* | 0.62 | 0.43 | 0.63 | -0.15* | 0.17* | 0.5 | 0.56 | 0.05* | 0.02* | 0.44 | 0.56 |
| FT EGYPT | Egyptian | 1.17 | 0.45 | 0.49 | 0.95 | 0.97 | 0.56 | 0.51 | 0.65 | 0.65* | 0.54 | 0.51 | 0.6 | 0.09* | 0.63 | 0.47 | 0.6 |
| AV SG WIKI | MSA | 0.27* | 0.82 | 0.49 | 0.62 | 0.98 | 0.61 | 0.43 | 0.92 | 0.22* | -0.6 | 0.57 | 0.88 | 0.13* | -0.53* | 0.64 | 0.72 |
| AV SG TWITTER | Mixed | 1.21 | 0.27* | 0.50 | 0.63 | 0.87 | 0.33 | 0.41 | 0.75 | 0.38* | 0.05* | 0.46 | 0.70 | -0.98* | 0.50* | 0.42 | 0.60 |
| AV CB WIKI | MSA | 0.43* | 0.91 | 0.45 | 0.67 | 1.21 | 0.53 | 0.45 | 0.52 | 0.57* | -0.35* | 0.57 | 0.75 | -0.38* | 0.26* | 0.53 | 0.58 |
| AV CB TWITTER | Mixed | 1.00 | 0.53 | 0.39 | 0.78 | 0.92 | 0.54 | 0.43 | 0.71 | 0.41* | 0.48* | 0.31 | 0.72 | -0.49* | 0.83 | 0.40 | 0.76 |

Table 3: Bias scores for 300-dimensional pretrained FastText (FT) and AraVec (AV) n-gram distributional word vector spaces. We omitted test 9 as less than 20% of the test vocabulary was found in the FT and AV embedding spaces. We report explicit bias scores in terms of WEAT (W), ECT, and BAT, and implicit bias in terms of KMeans++ accuracy (KM). For AV, we report results for the Skip-gram (SG) and CBOW (CB) models. Asterisks indicate WEAT bias effects or pearson correlation scores that are insignificant at $\alpha < 0.05$.

## 2.2 Bias Evaluation Methodology

Aiming towards a holistic picture of biases encoded in Arabic word vectors, we put together several bias tests that quantify both implicit and explicit biases: (1) WEAT (Caliskan et al., 2017), (2) Embedding Coherence Test (ECT) (Dev and Phillips, 2019), (3) Bias Analogy Test (BAT) (Lauscher et al., 2020), and (4) Implicit Bias Test with K-Means++ (KM) (Gonen and Goldberg, 2019). For all bias tests, we adopt the notion of *implicit* and *explicit* bias specifications as proposed by Lauscher et al. (2020): an explicit bias specification consists here of two sets of target terms and two sets of attribute terms $B_E(T_1, T_2, A_1, A_2)$. The idea is to measure the bias between the target sets, e.g., *science* and *art*, *towards* the attribute sets, e.g., *male* vs. *female* terms, or vice versa. In contrast, an implicit bias specification consists of target terms only, i.e., $B_E(T_1, T_2)$. Accordingly, the intuition is to measure bias between the target term representations only, and not its explicit manifestation with regard to other concepts. Furthermore, we report the semantic quality for all word embedding spaces we induced ourselves: to this end, we report the scores on predicting sentence-level semantic similarity for Arabic (SemEval 2017 Task 1; we obtain sentence embeddings as averages of word embeddings) (Cer et al., 2017).

**Word Embedding Association Test (WEAT).** Let $B_E(T_1, T_2, A_1, A_2)$ be an explicit bias specification consisting of two sets of *target* terms $T_1$ and $T_2$, and two sets of *attribute* terms, $A_1$ and $A_2$. Caliskan

---

[2] Albeit possibly less frequently than the dialectal translation.

[3] Furthermore, WEAT tests 3–5 are tailored to test racial biases towards African-Americans, which is arguably much less prominent in the Arabic cultural area.

| # Sent | 2007 W | KM | STS | 2008 W | KM | STS | 2009 W | KM | STS | 2010 W | KM | STS | 2011 W | KM | STS | 2015 W | KM | STS | 2016 W | KM | STS | 2017 W | KM | STS |
|---|---|---|---|---|---|---|---|---|---|---|---|---|---|---|---|---|---|---|---|---|---|---|---|---|
| 300K | -.35* | .75 | .38 | -.33* | .76 | .38 | -.52* | .53 | .33 | -.45* | .50 | .34 | .06* | .64 | .35 | -.02* | .75 | .38 | .30* | .80 | .37 | .16* | .75 | .36 |
| 1M | – | – | – | .08* | .53 | .44 | .92 | .55 | .40 | .32* | .58 | .38 | .50* | .65 | .37 | .97 | .71 | .42 | .72* | .71 | .43 | .95 | .72 | .42 |

Table 4: Gender bias over time: WEAT test 7 bias effects and KMeans++ accuracy scores for 300-dimensional distributional word vector spaces induced using CBOW on Leipzig news corpora of size consisting of 300k and 1M sentences between 2007 and 2017. Asterisks indicate bias effects that are insignificant at $\alpha < 0.05$.

| Model | Dim. | T1 | T2 | T7 | T8 |
|---|---|---|---|---|---|
| ARAVEC SG UNIGRAM | 100 | 0.04* | 0.91 | 0.66* | -0.50* |
| ARAVEC SG UNIGRAM | 300 | 0.18* | 0.66 | 0.13* | -0.19* |
| ARAVEC SG N-GRAM | 100 | 0.49* | 1.19 | 0.54* | -0.49* |
| ARAVEC SG N-GRAM | 300 | 0.27* | 0.98 | 0.22* | 0.13* |

Table 5: WEAT bias effect sizes for ARAVEC SKIP-GRAM pretrained distributional word vector spaces trained on Wikipedia with embedding dimensionality 100 vs. 300 and unigram vs. n-gram preprocessing. Asterisks indicate the bias effects which are insignificant at $\alpha < 0.05$.

| | T1 W | KM | T2 W | KM | T7 W | KM | T8 W | KM | STS |
|---|---|---|---|---|---|---|---|---|---|
| AVG | 0.68 | 0.91 | 1.03 | 0.79 | 0.69 | 0.63 | -0.47 | 0.71 | 0.41 |
| CONC | 0.65 | 0.75 | 1.28 | 0.68 | 0.56* | 0.72 | -0.73 | 0.77 | 0.52 |

Table 6: Explicit (WEAT, W) and implicit (K-Means++, KM) bias scores for 300-dim. embedding spaces induced using CBOW on the Arabic portions of the Leipzig News Corpora of 1M sentences between 2007 and 2017; comparison of averaged biases over temporally non-overlapping portions (AVG) with those in embeddings induced on the whole corpus (CONC). Asterisks: insignificant bias effects ($\alpha < 0.05$).

et al. (2017) define the WEAT test statistic $s(T_1, T_2, A_1, A_2)$ as the association difference that $T_1$ and $T_2$ exhibit w.r.t. $A_1$ and $A_2$ – the association is measured as the average semantic similarity of $T_1/T_2$ terms with terms from $A_1$ and $A_2$:

$$s(T_1, T_2, A_1, A_2) = \sum_{t_1 \in T_1} s(t_1, A_1, A_2) - \sum_{t_2 \in T_2} s(t_2, A_1, A_2), \tag{1}$$

with associative difference for a term $t$ computed as:

$$s(t, A_1, A_2) = \frac{1}{|A_1|} \sum_{a_1 \in A_1} \cos(\mathbf{t}, \mathbf{a_1}) - \frac{1}{|A_2|} \sum_{a_2 \in A_2} \cos(\mathbf{t}, \mathbf{a_2}), \tag{2}$$

with $\mathbf{t}$ as the distributional vector of term $t$ and cos as the cosine of the angle between two vectors. The significance of the test statistic is measured by the non-parametric permutation test in which the $s(T_1, T_2, A_1, A_2)$ is compared to $s(X_1, X_2, A_1, A_2)$, where $(X_1, X_2)$ denotes a random, equally-sized split of the terms in $T_1 \cup T_2$. A larger WEAT effect size indicates a larger bias.

**Embedding Coherence Test (ECT).** Given an ARAWEAT explicit bias specification $B_E(T_1, T_2, A_1, A_2)$, ECT operates on the bias specification which "collapses" the two AraWEAT attribute sets into a single set: $B_E(T_1, T_2, A = A_1 \cup A_2)$. Next, as proposed by Dev and Phillips (2019), we compute the vectors $\mathbf{t_1}$ and $\mathbf{t_2}$ as averages of the word vectors of terms in $T_1$ and $T_2$, respectively. Then, we obtain two vectors of similarities by computing the *cosine similarity* between the vector of each term in $A$ and the mean vectors $\mathbf{t_1}$ and $\mathbf{t_2}$. The ECT score is finally the Spearman correlation between the two obtained similarity vectors. The intuition is to assess, whether the similarities of the average vectors $\mathbf{t_1}$ and $\mathbf{t_2}$, which represent the two target term sets, with the attribute terms are correlating. The larger the ECT correlation, the lower the bias.

**Bias Analogy Test (BAT).** Inspired by Bolukbasi et al. (2016)'s famous anology, the idea behind BAT is to quantify the fraction of biased analogies that result from querying the embedding space. Given an AraWEAT test $B_E(T_1, T_2, A_1, A_2)$, following Lauscher et al. (2020), we create all possible biased analogies $\mathbf{t_1} - \mathbf{t_2} \approx \mathbf{a_1} - \mathbf{a_2}$ for $(t_1, t_2, a_1, a_2) \in T_1 \times T_2 \times A_1 \times A_2$. Next we create two query vectors –

$\mathbf{q}_1 = \mathbf{t}_1 - \mathbf{t}_2 + \mathbf{a}_2$ and $\mathbf{q}_2 = \mathbf{a}_1 - \mathbf{t}_1 + \mathbf{t}_2$ – for each tuple $(t_1, t_2, a_1, a_2)$. We then rank the vectors in the vector space according to the Euclidean distance with $q_1$ and $q_2$, respectively, and report the percentage of cases where: $a_1$ is ranked higher than a term $a_2' \in A_2 \setminus \{a_2\}$ for $\mathbf{q}_1$ and $a_2$ is ranked higher than a term $a_1' \in A_1 \setminus \{a_1\}$ for $\mathbf{q}_2$. The higher the BAT score, the higher the bias.

**Implicit Bias Test: K-Means++ (KM).**  Sometimes, bias is not expressed explicitely, i.e., as bias between two target term sets in explicit relation towards certain attribute sets, but manifests implicitely. To also reflect this type of bias in our study, We follow Gonen and Goldberg (2019) and test the Arabic word vector spaces for the amount of implicit bias by clustering terms from $T_1$ and $T_2$ with KMeans++ (Arthur and Vassilvitskii, 2007). The higher the clustering accuracy, the higher the bias. We report the averaged accuracy over 20 independent runs.

**Semantic Quality (SQ).**  For the embedding models we train ourselves, we additionally report the semantic quality of the space by predicting sentence-level semantic similarity on the SemEval 2017 Task 1 for Arabic (ar-ar) (Cer et al., 2017). Let $\mathbf{s_a} = e_{a1}, ..., e_{an}$ be the set of embeddings of words in sentence $a$ and let $\mathbf{s_b} = e_{b1}, ..., e_{am}$ be the sequence of embedding representations for individual words in sentence $b$. We obtain aggregated sentence representations, by averaging the embeddings of words in the sentence: $\mathbf{s} = \frac{1}{l} \sum_{i=1}^{l} e_i$ and finally predict the similarity score as $cos(\mathbf{s}_a, \mathbf{s}_b)$.[4] We report Pearson correlation between our predicitions and the gold similarity annotations.

**Dimensions of Bias Analysis.**  We run our tests along 5 different dimensions: (1) embedding methods: we compare embeddings induced using SKIP-GRAM, CBOW and FASTTEXT embedding models; (2) source text types: we analyze vector spaces induced from corpora originating from different sources (Wikipedia, news, Twitter);[5] (3) vector sizes and preprocessing: we hypothesize that biases might be more prominent in higher-dimensional vectors. To this end, we compare 100- vs. 300-dimensional embeddings. Furthermore, we analyze the effect of unigram vs. n-gram preprocessing of Arabic text, as offered by pretrained vectors AraVec (Mohammad et al., 2017); (4) corpus size: Lauscher and Glavaš (2019) hypothesize that biases might be more expressed in bigger corpora. To further investigate this, we run several experiments controlling for corpus size; (5) temporal intervals: lastly, we conduct a diachronic bias analysis by training embeddings on corpora from different time periods.

**Distributional Word Vector Spaces.**  We conduct our analysis on (a) pretrained distributional word vector spaces from AraVec[6] (Mohammad et al., 2017) and FastText[7] (Bojanowski et al., 2017) and (b) embedding spaces we trained in order to be able to control for corpora size and preprocessing. In (b), we use Arabic corpora from the Leipzig Corpora Collection[8] (Goldhahn et al., 2012).

## 3   Findings

We present and discuss the findings of our analysis employing ARAWEAT.

**Embedding Methods, Text Sources, and Dialects.**  Bias scores for 300-dimensional pretrained Fasttext (FT) and AraVec (AV) embedding spaces are shown in Table 3. For both (FT) and (AV), we evaluated all available spaces, pretrained on different corpora. For FT, we investigate two models, one trained on the portions of Wikipedia and CommonCrawl corpora written in Modern Standard Arabic (MS) and the other on portions written in *Egyptian Arabic*.[9] We evaluate the four variants of ARAVEC vectors: (a) trained using either Skip-Gram (SG) or CBOW (CB) on (b) either Wikipedia (WIKI) or Twitter (TWITTER) text. Interestingly, most of these embedding spaces fail to exhibit significant explicit gender biases according to WEAT tests $T7$ and $T8$. However, the gender biases seem to be rather present

---

[4]This method was used as the simple aggregation baseline in the corresponding SemEval shared task.

[5]While Arabic Wikipedia is dominantly written in MSA, TWITTER is likely to exhibit non-negligible amounts of dialectical and colloquial Arabic.

[6]https://github.com/bakrianoo/aravec

[7]https://fasttext.cc/docs/en/crawl-vectors.html

[8]http://wortschatz.uni-leipzig.de/en/download/

[9]The language identification was performed automatically using the FT Language Detector

implicitly (KM) in most spaces. Comparing FT ARABIC versus FT EGYPTIAN, both implicit and explicit bias seems to be slightly more pronounced in the Egyptian than in the MSA corpus. Results of comparison over text types support the unexpected finding for other languages (Lauscher and Glavaš, 2019): embeddings built from user-generated content on average do not encode more bias than their counterparts trained on Wikipedia.

**Embedding dimensionality and preprocessing.** Next, we evaluate the effects of specific hyperparameter settings using the ARAVEC pretrained vector spaces. ARAWEAT bias effect sizes for different embedding dimensionalities and model types are listed in Table 5. For the ARAWEAT test specifications $T1$, $T7$, and $T8$, we did not observe prominent variance in the amount of explicit bias w.r.t. the vector dimensionality or pre-processing type. For the remaining test – $T2$ – the explicit bias (according to the WEAT test) is somewhat more pronounced in the lower-dimensional embeddings and in the n-gram versions of the AraVec embeddings.

**Diachronic Analysis and Corpora Sizes.** Table 4 displays WEAT effect sizes for test $T7$ (*gender bias*) in MSA 300-dimensional distributional word vector spaces we trained on the (temporally) disjunctive Arabic portions of the Leipzig News Corpora of sizes 300K and 1M sentences, respectively.

The smaller corpus, consisting of 300K sentences, exhibits no significant bias effect sizes across all years. This finding is in line with previous observations Lauscher and Glavaš (2019) that biases might be more expressed in embedding spaces obtained on bigger corpora. This could be a reflection of the overall quality of distributional vectors, which is lower when vectors are trained on smaller corpora (as supported by the corresponding STS scores). In the spaces obtained on the larger corpora segments, consisting of 1M-sentences, significant explicit (W) gender biases are present in years 2009, 2015, and 2017, with very similar effect sizes (between .92 and .97). The implicit gender bias (KM), on the other hand, steadily rises over the entire period under investigation (2007-2017).

Finally, we investigate how the biases in the embedding space induced on the whole Arabic Leipzig News corpus (2007–2017, CONC) relates to the biases detected in embedding spaces induced from its different, temporally non-overlapping subportions. To this end, we average the biases measured on embeddings trained on its yearly subsets (AVG). The correlation results, over all four tests and two measures (W, KM), are shown in Table 6. Indeed, the biases of the whole corpus (CONC) seem to be highly correlated with the averages of biases of subcorpora (AVG). In fact, we measure a substantial Pearson correlation of 66% between the two sets of scores (AVG and CONC). This suggests that one can roughly predict the biases of (embeddings trained on) a large corpus by aggregating the biases of (embeddings trained on) its (non-overlapping) subsets.

## 4 Related Work

Bolukbasi et al. (2016) were the first to study bias in distributional word vector spaces. Using an analogy test, they demonstrate gender stereotypes manifesting in word embeddings and propose the notion of the bias direction, upon which they base a debiasing method called hard-debiasing. Caliskan et al. (2017) adapt the Implicit Association Test (IAT) (Nosek et al., 2002) from psychology for studying biases in distributional word vector spaces. The test, dubbed Word Embedding Association Test (WEAT), measures associations between words in an embedding space in terms of cosine similarity between the vectors. They propose 10 stimuli sets, which we adapt in our work. Later, McCurdy and Serbetci (2017) extend the analysis to three more languages, Dutch, German, and Spanish, but only focus on gender bias. XWEAT, the cross-lingual and multilingual WEAT framework (Lauscher and Glavaš, 2019), covers German, Spanish, Italian, Russian, Croatian, and Turkish. XWEAT analyses also focused on other relevant dimensions such as embedding method and similarity measures. Zhou et al. (2019) focus on measuring bias in languages with grammatical gender. Several research efforts produced new bias tests: Dev and Phillips (2019) propose the Embedding Coherence Test (ECT) with the intuition of capturing whether two sets of target terms are coherently distant from a set of attribute terms. They also propose several debiasing methods. Gonen and Goldberg (2019) show that many debiasing methods only mask but do not fully remove biases present in the embedding spaces. They propose to additionally test for implicit biases, by trying to classify or cluster the sets of target terms. Lauscher et al. (2020) unify the different notions of biases into explicit and implicit bias specifications, based on which they propose methods for quantifying and removing biases. While their is some effort to account for gender-awareness in Arabic machine translation (Habash et al., 2019), we are, to the best of our knowledge, the first to measure bias in Arabic Language Technology.

## 5   Conclusion

Language technologies aim to avoid reflecting negative human biases such as racism and sexism. Yet, the ubiquitous word embeddings, used as input for many NLP models, seem to encode many such biases. In this work, we extensively quantify and analyze the biases in different vector spaces built from text in Arabic, a major world language with close to 300M native speakers. To this effect, we translate existing bias specifications from English to Arabic and investigate biases in embedding spaces that differ over several dimensions of analysis: embedding models, corpora sizes, type of text, dialectal vs. standard Arabic, and time periods. Our analysis yields interesting results. First, we confirm some of the previous findings for other languages, e.g., that biases are generally not more pronounced in user-generated text and that embeddings trained on larger corpora lead to more prominent biases. Secondly, our results suggest more bias is present in dialectal (Egyptian) Arabic corpora than in Modern Standard Arabic corpora. Next, our diachronic analysis suggests that the implicit gender bias of Arabic news text steadily increases over time. Finally, we show that the bias effects of the whole corpus can be predicted from bias effects of its subcorpora. We hope that ARAWEAT, our framework for multidimensional analysis of stereotypical bias in Arabic text representations, fuels more research on bias in Arabic language technology.

## Acknowledgments

Anne Lauscher and Goran Glavaš are supported by the Eliteprogramm of the Baden-Württemberg Stiftung (AGREE grant). We would like to thank the anonymous reviewers for their helpful comments.

## References

David Arthur and Sergei Vassilvitskii. 2007. K-means++: The advantages of careful seeding. In *Proceedings of SODA*, pages 1027–1035.

Su Lin Blodgett, Solon Barocas, Hal Daumé III, and Hanna Wallach. 2020. Language (technology) is power: A critical survey of" bias" in nlp. In *Proceedings of the 58th Meeting of the Association for Computational Linguistics*, pages 5454–5476, Online, July. Association for Computational Linguistics.

Piotr Bojanowski, Edouard Grave, Armand Joulin, and Tomas Mikolov. 2017. Enriching word vectors with subword information. *Transactions of the ACL*, 5:135–146.

Tolga Bolukbasi, Kai-Wei Chang, James Zou, Venkatesh Saligrama, and Adam Kalai. 2016. Man is to computer programmer as woman is to homemaker? debiasing word embeddings. In *Proceedings of NIPS*, pages 4356–4364.

Aylin Caliskan, Joanna J. Bryson, and Arvind Narayanan. 2017. Semantics derived automatically from language corpora contain human-like biases. *Science*, 356(6334):183–186.

Daniel Cer, Mona Diab, Eneko Agirre, Iñigo Lopez-Gazpio, and Lucia Specia. 2017. SemEval-2017 task 1: Semantic textual similarity multilingual and crosslingual focused evaluation. In *Proceedings of the 11th International Workshop on Semantic Evaluation (SemEval-2017)*, pages 1–14, August.

Sunipa Dev and Jeff Phillips. 2019. Attenuating bias in word vectors. In *Proceedings of AISTATS*.

Mohammed Elrazzaz, Shady Elbassuoni, Khaled Shaban, and Chadi Helwe. 2017. Methodical evaluation of Arabic word embeddings. In *Proceedings of the 55th Annual Meeting of the Association for Computational Linguistics (Volume 2: Short Papers)*, pages 454–458, Vancouver, Canada, July. Association for Computational Linguistics.

Kawin Ethayarajh, David Duvenaud, and Graeme Hirst. 2019. Understanding undesirable word embedding associations. In *Proceedings of the 57th Annual Meeting of the Association for Computational Linguistics*. Association for Computational Linguistics.

Dirk Goldhahn, Thomas Eckart, and Uwe Quasthoff. 2012. Building large monolingual dictionaries at the leipzig corpora collection: From 100 to 200 languages. In *In Proceedings of the Eight International Conference on Language Resources and Evaluation (LREC '12)*.

Hila Gonen and Yoav Goldberg. 2019. Lipstick on a pig: Debiasing methods cover up systematic gender biases in word embeddings but do not remove them. In *Proceedings of NAACL-HLT*, pages 609–614.

Nizar Habash, Houda Bouamor, and Christine Chung. 2019. Automatic gender identification and reinflection in Arabic. In *Proceedings of the First Workshop on Gender Bias in Natural Language Processing*, pages 155–165, Florence, Italy, August. Association for Computational Linguistics.

Rowan Hall Maudslay, Hila Gonen, Ryan Cotterell, and Simone Teufel. 2019. It's all in the name: Mitigating gender bias with name-based counterfactual data substitution. In *Proceedings of the 2019 Conference on Empirical Methods in Natural Language Processing and the 9th International Joint Conference on Natural Language Processing (EMNLP-IJCNLP)*, pages 5270–5278.

Anne Lauscher and Goran Glavaš. 2019. Are we consistently biased? multidimensional analysis of biases in distributional word vectors. In *Proceedings of the Eighth Joint Conference on Lexical and Computational Semantics (* SEM 2019)*, pages 85–91.

Anne Lauscher, Goran Glavaš, Simone Paolo Ponzetto, and Ivan Vulić. 2020. A general framework for implicit and explicit debiasing of distributional word vector spaces. In *Proceesings of AAAI*, pages 8131–8138.

Katherine McCurdy and Oguz Serbetci. 2017. Grammatical gender associations outweigh topical gender bias in crosslinguistic word embeddings. In *Proceedings of WiNLP*.

Parkvall Mikael. 2007. Världens 100 största språk 2007 (the world's 100 largest languages in 2007). *National Encylkopedin*.

Tomas Mikolov, Ilya Sutskever, Kai Chen, Greg S Corrado, and Jeff Dean. 2013. Distributed representations of words and phrases and their compositionality. In *Proceesings of NIPS*, pages 3111–3119.

Abu Bakr Mohammad, Kareem Eissa, and Samhaa El-Beltagy. 2017. Aravec: A set of arabic word embedding models for use in arabic nlp. *Procedia Computer Science*, 117:256–265, 11.

Brian A. Nosek, Anthony G. Greenwald, and Mahzarin R. Banaji. 2002. Harvesting implicit group attitudes and beliefs from a demonstration web site. *Group Dynamics*, 6:101–115.

Jeffrey Pennington, Richard Socher, and Christopher Manning. 2014. Glove: Global vectors for word representation. In *Proceedings of EMNLP*, pages 1532–1543.

Pei Zhou, Weijia Shi, Jieyu Zhao, Kuan-Hao Huang, Muhao Chen, Ryan Cotterell, and Kai-Wei Chang. 2019. Examining gender bias in languages with grammatical gender. In *Proceedings of the 2019 Conference on Empirical Methods in Natural Language Processing and the 9th International Joint Conference on Natural Language Processing (EMNLP-IJCNLP)*, pages 5279–5287.

# Parallel resources for Tunisian Arabic dialect translation


**Saméh Kchaou**
University of Sfax, Tunisia
samehkchaou4@gmail.com

**Rahma Boujelbane**
University of Sfax, Tunisia
rahmaboujelban@gmail.com

**Lamia Hadrich Belguith**
University of Sfax, Tunisia
Lamia.belguith@gmail.com


## Abstract


The difficulty of processing dialects is clearly observed in the high cost of building representative corpus, in particular for machine translation. Indeed, all machine translation systems require a huge amount and good management of training data, which represents a challenge in a low-resource setting such as the Tunisian Arabic dialect. In this paper, we present a data augmentation technique to create a parallel corpus for Tunisian Arabic dialect written in social media and standard Arabic in order to build a **Machine Translation (MT)** model. The created corpus was used to build a sentence-based translation model. This model reached a BLEU score of 15.03% on a test set, while it was limited to 13.27% utilizing the corpus without augmentation.


## 1 Introduction

Nowadays, the use of the dialect in social networks is becoming more and more important. Besides dialects emerge as the language of informal communication on the web (forums, blogs, emails and social media). Thus, there is a shift from a purely oral language to a written language, without established standardization or standard spelling. It is also obvious that the dialect becomes intensively employed by internet users in social networks to share their thoughts and opinions. This kind of writing is sometimes incompressible even by persons speaking the same dialect, especially Arabic written using the latin script. Consequently, it is necessary to transform the text from its informal type to a formal type in order to be understandable and suitable for **Natural Language Processing (NLP)** tools. In this work, we create parallel resources in order to build a MT model able to transform the **Tunisian Dialect (TD)**, written in social networks, into the **Modern Standard Arabic (MSA)**. This represents a motivating task for both academic and industrial fields. Indeed, switching to a standard language facilitates communication between people overall the word. It also makes automatic opinion analysis easier using well-equipped language tools. For instance, businesses operating on the global market rely on social media campaigns to promote their brand and products, creating engaging and catchy content that can be exploited by users. However, to our knowledge, until now there is no works that have dealt with the translation of TD, especially the one that exists in social networks.

We introduce, in this study, an augmentation technique in order to build useful resources to train an efficient TD-MSA MT model. For this, we collected a significant number of parallel written resources to start with a total word count of about 75k. Then, we segmented the MSA sentences and we generated partial parallel sentences using back translation based on a bilingual dictionary created from the collected corpus. Finally, in order to trained the efficiency of the proposed resources, we test a statistical MT model on different configurations of the created corpus. Obviously, the translation performance is improved by augmenting the size of TD-MSA parallel data sets. The remainder of this paper is structured as follows: In section 2, we review related work on data augmentation. In section 3, we describe the process of building parallel resources. Section 4 depict the different steps of building a statistical translation model. We discuss in section 5 the performance of the resulting model.






*Proceedings of the Fifth Arabic Natural Language Processing Workshop*, pages 200–206
Barcelona, Spain (Online), December 12, 2020

## 2   Related Work

Machine translation for low-resource language is a well-known task in the NLP community. Several works focused on it to form efficient MT models. In order to train these models, different configurations of parallel resources have been proposed. There are those who have proven that sentence segmentation associated with the technique of back translation is a very suitable method for constructing parallel resources for low resourced languages. For example, (Jinyi and Tadahiro, 2019) applied this technique to generate pseudo-parallel pairs of Japanese-Chinese sentences by dividing the long parallel sentence pair of the corpus into parallel partial sentences pairs and using back-translation from the target partial sentence. The pair of long parallel sentences was divided into segments at the level of punctuation marks such as ",", ";", ":". This method improved the performance of translation. (Alina et al., 2018) proposed also a back translation method for low resource languages. The authors used an iterative back-translation of monolingual low resource data with the models trained on the transliterated high-resource data and utilized the resulting parallel corpus to train the final models. Similarly, another method was suggested by (Rico et al., 2015) to generate an English-German and Turkish-English parallel corpus using the back-translating of monolingual target data into the source language in order to obtain pseudo-source sentences. The back-translation was based on a statistical translation model. The size of the corpus was increased by the pairs of pseudo-source sentences and the original target sentences. Otherwise, (Guillaume et al., 2018) proposed two models : a neural model and a sentence-based model in order to generate automatically a parallel data using the iterative back-translation and denoising the effect of the language models formed on the target side. (Marzieh et al., 2017) generated new pairs of sentences containing rare words in new synthetically-created contexts. Researchers used language models trained on a large amount of German monolingual data to produce new English-German and German-English sentence pairs. (Fei et al., 2019) presented a soft contextual data augmentation method in order to build neural machine translation. The method consists in replacing a randomly-chosen word in a sentence with a soft distributional representation provided by a language model. The translation results proved the effectiveness of this method. A new efficient data augmentation approach to improve German-English translation performance was presented in (Li et al., 2020). Authors proposed a diversified data augmentation strategy that does not use extra monolingual data. They trained a forward and backward model to translate the training data.

## 3   TD-MSA parallel resources

Parallel corpus aligned at the sentence level are essential resources to build MT systems. One of our goals is to collect the largest possible set of parallel TD-MSA sentences. We collected in the first step, the existing free parallel corpus used in the state of the art. Secondly, we translated manually a corpus scraped from social networks.

### 3.1   Existing resources

**Parallel Arabic DIalectal Corpus (PADIC) :** It is a parallel corpus combining Maghreb dialects (Algerian, Tunisian and Moroccan), Levant dialects (Palestinian and Syrian) and the MSA (Karima et al., 2015). It was built from two sub-corpora : the first was created by recording different conversions from everyday life of the Annaba dialect, and the second sub-corpora was formed by the recordings which correspond to films and television programs expressed in the dialect of Algeria [1]. Then, the transcribed data was translated into the Moroccan dialect. Afterwards, these two corpora of the Annaba dialect and the Algeria dialect were translated into MSA. MSA was subsequently used as a pivot language to obtain the other Tunisia, Syrian and Palestinian dialects. This corpus was utilized to develop several statistical translation systems between these dialects and the MSA. We extracted a sub-corpus containing 6.4K TD/MSA sentences per language. Sentence length varied between 1 and 29 words on the MSA side, and between 1 and 27 on the TD side.

---

[1] https://sites.google.com/site/torjmanepnr/6-corpus

**Multi Arabic Dialect Applications and Resources (MADAR)** : It is the second TD-MSA parallel free available corpus (Bouamor et al., 2018) built within the framework of the MADAR project [2]. This fine-grained corpus consists of several English sentences selected from the **Corpus Basic Traveling Expression (BTEC)** (Takezawa et al., 2006) and translated by native speakers into 25 different Arabic dialects plus MSA. It contains 1.8k sentences per language. In this study, we use only the pair of languages (TD-MSA). The long MSA sentences include 31 words inside MSA and 28 inside TD.

**Tunisian CONSTitution (TD-CONST)** : After the Tunisian revolution, the constitution written in MSA was translated into Tunisian Arabic dialect to be more understandable by the Tunisian community. We aligned the TD version with that of the MSA. This gave us a corpus containing about 500 parallel laws, in which the length of MSA sentences is between 3 and 37 words, and that of Tunisian sentences is between 3 and 27 words. This corpus was not used in previous researches dealing with machine translation.

## 3.2 Social media corpus

In order to adapt the existing corpus to the textual content of the social networks, we scraped 900 Tunisian **COM**ments (TD-COM) ) from Facebook. This corpus was then translated into MSA by a native speaker. We got TD-MSA parallel sentences composed of 31 MSA words as maximum words per sentence, and 30 words in TD side.

Thus, through the different sources, we collected 9.7K parallel sentences. Table 1 shows more statistics on this corpus.

| Corpus | #Lines | #TD words | #MSA words | #Distinct TD Words | #Distinct MSA Words |
|---|---|---|---|---|---|
| PADIC | 6.4k | 38.6k | 43.6k | 10k | 9.64k |
| MADAR | 1.8k | 9.8k | 11.8k | 3.8k | 4.1k |
| TD-CONST | 600 | 8.3k | 7.7k | 2.6k | 2.4k |
| TD-COM | 900 | 11.4k | 11.1k | 5.8k | 5.3k |
| All corpus | 9.7k | 68k | 74k | 18.17k | 17.53k |

Table 1: Statistics of the collected corpus

## 3.3 TD-MSA dictionary

We created a bilingual TD-MSA dictionary from the alignment of the collected parallel corpus. Indeed, we employed the statistical machine translation toolkit GIZA ++[3] (Och and Hermann, 2003) to form a HMM word alignment model with which an automatically align words was generated between the source and target sides of the dataset. Then, we checked manually the obtained lexicon in order to remove errors. The resulting lexicon contains 44k TD-MSA entries.

## 3.4 TD – MSA lexical differences

The dialect language, by virtue of its utilitarian nature, evolves much more rapidly than the standard language. We can now consider these two forms of a single language as two distinct languages although they are clearly related. According to (Boukadida, 2008), Arabic dialect differs from MSA on all levels of linguistic representation. We distinguished through the collected corpus, the lexical difference that exist between TD and MSA. Indeed, there are sentences that do not change when migrating to the MSA. For instance, this sentence : صباح الخير. *spA.h Alxyr "Good morning"* is used in both TD and MSA. Other ones change partially lexicons when migrating to MSA. For example, the TD sentence *'ndy* عندي اختبار يوم الخميس *'ndy dfwAr nhAr Alxmys* becomes in MSA عندي دفوار نهار الخميس

[2]https://sites.google.com/view/madar-shared-task/home
[3]https://github.com/moses-smt/giza-pp

*axtbAr ywm Alxmys "I have a test on Thursday".*

There is also sentences that change totally the lexicon. For example, the MSA sentence المَكَان جَمِيل جدًا

*mkAn jamyl jdA "The place is very nice"* becomes in TD مَحَلَّاه البَلَاصة تَبَيِل *ma.hlAh AlblA.sT thabel.*
Thus in order to explore the degree of similarity between the TD and MSA in the collected corpus, we generated the intersection set between the two vocabularies. Figure 2 shows the lexical similarity between these two languages in the different corpora. There is on average 30% of common words between TD and MSA, which proves the hypothesis that, although TD and MSA are clearly related, they can be considered as two different languages; hence the need for a translation process.

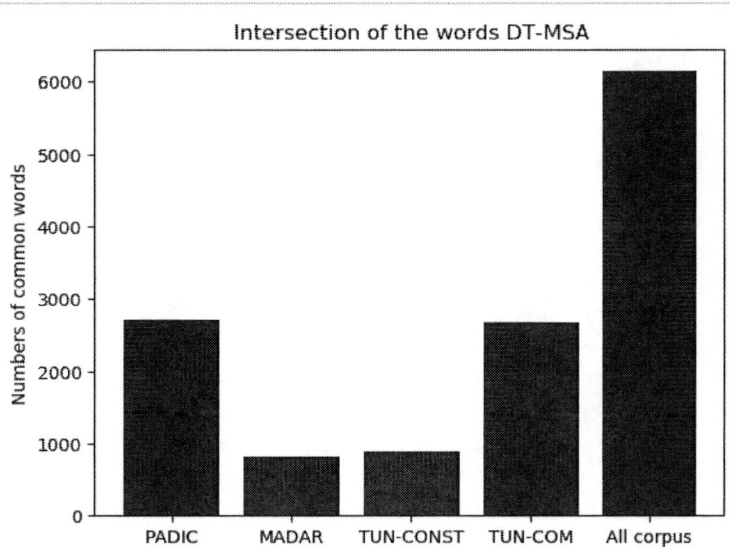


Figure 1: Intersection of the TD-MSA words.

## 3.5 Corpus pretreatment

**Text segmentation :** A part of the TD-CONST corpus contains a parallel text without any punctuation mark to delimit the sentences. So, based on the meaning of the sentence and referring to a native speaker, we proposed a segmentation to this corpus. This treatment allowed obtaining a set of 600 sentences while it was 500 parallels texts before the segmentation.
We then proposed a segmentation for all the MSA sentences of the corpus. In fact, as there is no TD segmentation tools or standard syntax rules, we segmented MSA sentences based on Arabic stop words and punctuation marks.
**Back translation :** The segmentation process resulted in a loss of pairwise alignment in many sentences. Figure 2 shows an example of misalignment of partial sentences after the segmentation of the MSA sentence. To remedy this problem, we opted for the back translation using the created MSA-DT dictionary in order to re-translate each MSA target partial sentences into corresponding TD sentences.

## 4 Statistical machine translation model

In order to test the efficiency of the resource-created method in the context of machine translation, we adapted a simple traditional sentence-based **Statistical Machine Translation (SMT)** model. Indeed, deep learning-based methods have made significant progress in recent years in the context of machine translation. We opted for the same methodology of (Och and Hermann, 2003). The latter has shown its effectiveness in several similar works as it is the case in (Guillaume et al., 2018).

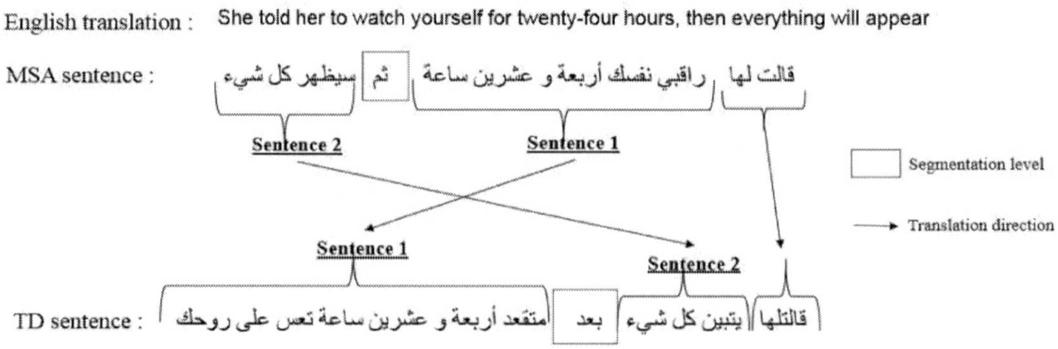

Figure 2: Example of TD-MSA sentence pair alignment.

## 4.1  Word alignment

The basic step of applying the proposed model is word-to-word translations. For this reason, we started with word alignment using the TD-MSA bi-text corpus. We applied GIZA ++ defined in the previous section in order to align the source and target sentence. Giza ++ takes a pair of sentences as input: source sentence matches its target sentence and returns the word alignment of the target sentence for the given source language. Then, sentence tables are created to store the probability that a certain n-gram in the source language is mapped to another n-gram in the target language. This step returns all possible sentences associated with a source sentence.

## 4.2  Comments translation probabilities

Sentence transition probabilities consists in assigning a probability for each sentence in the training corpus obtained in the previous phase by calculating the relative occurrences of the target sentence c for a given source sentence s for both directions. The sentence translation probability is given by the following equation.

$$\phi(\tilde{s}|\tilde{c}) = \frac{count(\tilde{s}|\tilde{s})}{\sum_{\tilde{c}_i} count(\tilde{s}|\tilde{c}_i)} \tag{1}$$

In addition to translation probabilities, we trained language models on source and target languages. The language model allowed improving the translation quality by sampling the structure and reorganization of words. We used the IRSTLM [4] toolkit to train the language models. IRSTLM: the IRST Language Modeling Toolkit is utilized to calculate statistical n-gram language models. It is integrated into the moses SMT decoder.
The final probabilities of the sentence were computed by combining the translation probability from the language model with the probability of translating the sentence from the source-target alignment matrix.

## 4.3  Phrase translation

In order to generate a sentence translation, the model used stack-based decoding to obtain the best translation from the sentence translation probabilities provided by training and to from the language model. The experiment was performed to translate TD sentences into MSA sentences.

## 5  Experimental results & discussion

In this section, we present an analysis of the SMT model applied on the created resources. We divided these resources into two sets: train set and test set. As we want to build a translation model for TD comments in social networks, we considered 500 parallel sentences among the 900 sentences of the TD-COM corpus as a test set. The remaining 400 sentences of the TD-COM corpus were used in the

---

[4]https://sourceforge.net/projects/irstlm/

train set. We carried out three experiments to analyze the utilized data. We increased the train corpus gradually in order to test the effect of the data augmentation on the applied model, as shown in Table 2.

**Experiment 1 :** We started by training the model with the available parallel data. We employed firstly TD-MSA data from the MADAR and PADIC corpus. We got a BLEU score of 13.07% on the test set. Then, we added the TD-CONST data set collected from the Tunisian constitution. This enrichment by the constitution data degraded the result of translation to 12%. This score can be explained by the nature of vocabulary utilized in the Tunisian constitution corpus which is different from that of social networks. Afterwards, we integrated the data into 400 sentences from the TD-COM corpus. The BLEU score was improved to 13.27% on the same Test set. Following this extension, we trained a model on the following configuration of corpus : MADAR, PADIC and TD-COM. The resulting model achieved an improvement in the BLEU score that rose to 13.67%. We can conclude, from this experiment, that the increase in corpus is preferably done with a corpus of the same domain or close domain.

**Experiment 2 :** Based on the results of experiment 1, we considered the corpus composed by the sub-corpora of MADAR, PADIC and TD-COM. We segmented all long sentences of this corpus. The aim of this experiment is to test the influence of the sentence size on the quality of translation. On the segmented corpus version, resulting from the back translation, we have learned again the SMT model. By this textual representation, the performance of the model has degraded. The model achieved a BLUE score of 11.58%. The dictionary-based translation led to the loss of meaning of some sentences and, consequently, reduced the score obtained in this experiment.

**Experiment 3 :** In this experiment, we combined, in the training set, the pairs of the segmented sentences with the pairs of the original sentences in the corpus. This improved the performance of the model which achieved a BLUE score of 15.03%.
Table 2 summarizes the variation of the BLUE score of the different models learned in the three experiments. All models were tested on the same test set. Thus, we can conclude from these different experiments that the injection of a parallel corpus of the target domain is very beneficial to improve translation. Besides, augmenting the corpus by a segmented version can further enhance the obtained results.

| Training set | #Lines | BLEU (%) |
|---|---|---|
| PADIC + MADAR | 8.2k | 13.07 |
| PADIC + MADAR + TD-CONST | 8.8k | 12 |
| PADIC + MADAR + TD-COM | 8.6k | 13.67 |
| PADIC + MADAR + TD-COM + TD-CONST | 9.2k | 13.27 |
| (PADIC + MADAR + TD-COM) segmented | 32K | 11.58 |
| (PADIC + MADAR + TD-COM) augmented | 41k | **15.03** |

Table 2: TD-MSA translation BLEU score.

## 6   Conclusion

We presented, in this paper, a process of creating parallel TD-MSA resources by exploiting firstly the available resources. Then, we enriched the data by building a parallel corpus scraped from social media. Afterwards, we proposed a corpus augmentation technique based on segmenting the well-endowed language and back translation. In order to test the effectiveness of the constructed resources, we trained a SMT model using different configurations of collected corpus and we tested it on a test corpus taken from social media. Experimental results show that the "augmented" configuration achieved better result of translation with a BLEU score of 15.03%.
We aim in future work, to further increase the size of the corpus and include other types of comments

like those that contain code switching. We also aim to test the efficiency of the neuronal approach to translate the written comments in social networks.

## References


Karakanta Alina, Dehdari Jon, and van Genabith Josef. 2018. Neural machine translation for low-resource languages without parallel corpora. In *Machine Translation 2018, 32*, page 167–189.

Houda Bouamor, Nizar Habash, Mohammad Salameh, Wajdi Zaghouani, Owen Rambow, Dana Abdulrahim, Ossama Obeid, Salam Khalifa, Fadhl Eryani, Alexander Erdmann, and Kemal Oflazer. 2018. The MADAR Arabic dialect corpus and lexicon. In *Proceedings of the 11th Language Resources and Evaluation Conference*, Miyazaki, Japan, may.

Nahed Boukadida. 2008. Connaissances phonologiques et morphologiques dérivationnelles et apprentissage de la lecture en arabe (etude longitudinale).

Gao Fei, Zhu Jinhua, Wu Lijun, Xia Yingce, Qin Tao, Cheng Xueqi, Zhou Wengang, and Liu Tie-Yan. 2019. Soft contextual data augmentation for neural machine translation. In *Association for Computational Linguistics*, Florence, Italy.

Lample Guillaume, Ott Myle, Conneau Alexis, and Denoyer Ludovic. 2018. Phrase-based neural unsupervised machine translation. In *Proceedings of the 2018 Conference on Empirical Methods in Natural Language Processing*, page 5039–5049.

Zhang Jinyi and Matsumoto Tadahiro. 2019. Corpus augmentation by sentence segmentation for low-resource neural machine translation. *CoRR*, abs/1905.08945.

Meftouh Karima, Harrat Salima, Jamoussi S, Abbas M, and Smaïli Kamel. 2015. Machine translation experiments on padic: A parallel arabic dialect corpus. In *Proceedings of 29th Paclic Asia Conference on Language, Information and Computation.*, pages 26–34.

Y Li, X. Li, Y. Yang, and R. Dong. 2020. A diverse data augmentation strategy for low-resource neural machine translation. In *Information 2020, 11, 255.*, pages 2078–2489.

Fadaee Marzieh, Bisazza Arianna, and Monz Christof. 2017. Data augmentation for low-resource neural machine translation. In *Proc. 55th Annual Meeting of the Assoc. for Computational Linguistics.*, page 567–573, Vancouver, Canada.

Franz Josef Och and Ney Hermann. 2003. A systematic comparison of various statistical alignment models. In *Computational Linguistics*, page 19–51.

Sennrich Rico, Haddow Barry, and Birch Alexandra. 2015. Improving neural machine translation models with monolingual data. In *Actes de la 54e réunion annuelle de l'Association for Computational Linguistics.*, page 86–96, Berlin, Allemagne.

Toshiyuki Takezawa, Kikui Genichiro, Mizushima Masahide, and Sumita Eiichiro. 2006. Multilingual spoken language corpus development for communication research. In *Chinese Spoken Language Processing*, pages 781–791.

# BERT Transformer model for Detecting Arabic GPT2 Auto-Generated Tweets


**Fouzi Harrag, Maria Debbah**
Computer Sciences Department
Ferhat Abbas University, Setif 1
Setif, Algeria
{fouzi.harrag,maria.debbah}@univ-setif.dz


**Kareem Darwish, Ahmed Abdelali**
Qatar Computing Research Institute
Hamad Bin Khalifa University (HBKU)
Doha, Qatar
{kdarwish,aabdelali}@hbku.edu.qa


## Abstract


During the last two decades, we have progressively turned to the Internet and social media to find news, entertain conversations and share opinion. Recently, OpenAI has developed a machine learning system called GPT-2 for Generative Pre-trained Transformer-2, which can produce deepfake texts. It can generate blocks of text based on brief writing prompts that look like they were written by humans, facilitating the spread false or auto-generated text. In line with this progress, and in order to counteract potential dangers, several methods have been proposed for detecting text written by these language models. In this paper, we propose a transfer learning based model that will be able to detect if an Arabic sentence is written by humans or automatically generated by bots. Our dataset is based on tweets from a previous work, which we have crawled and extended using the Twitter API. We used GPT2-Small-Arabic to generate fake Arabic Sentences. For evaluation, we compared different recurrent neural network (RNN) word embeddings based baseline models, namely: LSTM, BI-LSTM, GRU and BI-GRU, with a transformer-based model. Our new transfer-learning model has obtained an accuracy up to 98%. To the best of our knowledge, this work is the first study where ARABERT and GPT2 were combined to detect and classify the Arabic auto-generated texts.


## 1 Introduction

In recent years, social media has become an important source of news and information for users in the Arab world, with approximately 63% of Arab youth indicating that they turn to social media first for news (Radcliffe and Bruni, 2019). Due to the lack of editorial checks, fabricated content and misinformation are abundant on different social media platform. For example, recent advances in image and video processing have given rise to so called "deepfakes". Similarly, large generative language models, such as GPT-2 and GPT-3, have been used to generate increasingly human-like natural text. Such "deepfake" texts can be used by bots, such as Twitter bots, to generate sufficiently diverse content in their timelines to evade detection on social media platforms. We define deepfake texts as "automatically generated string sequences, with or without human seed input, that could fool a human into thinking that was generated by another human [1]." In this paper, we focus on the problem of detecting such deepfake texts. Specifically, we employ contextual embeddings, which have led to large improvements for a variety of NLP tasks such as part-of-speech tagging, question answering, and text classification (Torfi et al., 2020) without the explicit need for feature engineering. These advances in combination with Deep Learning (DL) enabled the effective detection of auto-generated texts. The trend now is to use deep learning models to solve old machine learning problems including text classification without the need for feature extraction. Deep learning approaches such as Convolutional Neural Networks (CNNs) and Recurrent

---

[1] https://www.wired.com/story/ai-generated-text-is-the-scariest-deepfake-of-all/






*Proceedings of the Fifth Arabic Natural Language Processing Workshop*, pages 207–214
Barcelona, Spain (Online), December 12, 2020

Neural Netowrks (RNNs) are now applied to enhance the performance of auto-generated text detection models(Iqbal and Qureshi, 2020). Despite theirs success, they still suffer from the lack of annotated data for training. GPT-2 (Radford et al., 2019), and BERT (Devlin et al., 2019a) are among new approaches recently considered for overcoming this issue. A language understanding model learns contextual and task-independent representations of terms. A huge amount of texts obtained from large corpora is used to build generic (multilingual multi-application) models. Numerous deep learning text detection methods have been proposed to help readers determine if a piece of text has been authored by machine or human. The results of employing such language models are very effective in the detection of misinformation and propaganda by providing mechanisms to reveal the nature of news articles and to ensure the authenticity of its source (Dhamani et al., 2019). In this paper, we propose a method for generating deepfake text using GPT2 and to consequently identify such texts using a pre-trained BERT model. As far as we know, it is the first time that such combined approach is proposed for Arabic Language. The outputs of the generative pre-trained language model will be used as inputs for the transfer-learning model that will detect if the input text is coming from human or machine. Our experiment results show that using the pre-trained BERT model outperforms RNN models in detecting Arabic deepfake texts.

The contributions of this work are:

- Generating a new Arabic dataset using GPT2-Small-Arabic .

- Proposing an efficient model to detect and identify auto-generated text using AraBERT.

- Comparing with different RNN-based baseline models.

## 2   Related Work

Several studies have been carried out on the classification and detection of social bots. In this section, we will provide an overview of relevant related works. This can provide a basic understanding on the state-of-the-art of social bot detection methods and approaches. Almerekhi and Elsayed (2015) proposed a system for the detection of automatically generated Arabic tweets. They evaluated their system using 3.5k labelled tweets randomly sampled and labeled by Crowd Flower. A set of features including formality, structural, tweet-specific, and temporal features has been extracted from Arabic tweets to train three classification algorithms, namely: Support Vector Machines (SVM), Naive Bayes, and Decision Trees. Their results show that classification based on individual categories of features outperform the baseline unigram-based classifier in terms of classification accuracy.

Varol et al. (2017) proposed a framework for bot detection on Twitter. They presented a machine learning based system used for the extraction of a collection of features from six different classes. The features were used in training robust models to identify bots. They evaluated the performance of their detection system using two different datasets: manually-annotated Twitter accounts dataset and a public honeypot dataset. Their analysis on the contributions of different feature classes suggests that user metadata and content features are the two most valuable sources of data to detect simple bots.

Darwish et al. (2017) looked at the problem of detecting propaganda accounts on Twitter. They crafted three different kinds of features, namely interaction features (ex. retweets and mentions), lexical diversity, and stylistic features (ex. offensiveness and sentiment). Using an SVM classifier, they found that interaction features where the most effective features for detecting propaganda accounts, and stylistic features benefited overall classification.

Akyon and Kalfaoglu (2019) presented a system for the detection of fake and automated accounts. Their system is tackling the problem of using a binary classification model. They constructed a dataset of 1,400 accounts from different countries. There were an equal number of real and automated accounts in their dataset. They proposed a set of derived features and the most effective features from this set were selected to develop a cost-sensitive genetic feature selection algorithm. Their results showed that neural network methods and SVM achieved the best F1 scores for the detection of automated accounts.

Santia et al. (2019) presented a simple model based on capturing regions to detect bots on Facebook. Features were leveraged in experimentation as bot indicators to separate bots away from the central range of the full feature distributions. They noted that some features that appear to cluster bots tightly are collaborating with high priority in the identification of a user as a human. Their system has been developed and evaluated on public pages as bot detection software using standard evaluation metrics such as F1 score. They found that a small percentage of interacting user population were showing signs to be social bots.

In the work of Kudugunta and Ferrara (2018) work, a deep neural network based on contextual long short-term memory (LSTM) was proposed. The architecture of the system exploits content and metadata features to detect bots at the tweet level. They used the features extracted from user's profile metadata and tweet text as inputs to the LSTM. They also proposed a very useful data augmentation technique for generating large labeled datasets based on synthetic minority oversampling. They showed that their model could identify bots from humans with a high accuracy. They also achieved a perfect classification accuracy by applying the same architecture to account-level bot detection.

Wei and Nguyen (2019) developed an RNN (biLSTM) word embeddings based model to discriminate Twitter bots from human accounts without requiring any prior knowledge or handcrafted features. By comparison with similar bot detection systems, their experiments on the Cresci-2017 dataset showed that their proposed system achieved reasonable performances. They also confirmed the ability of using biLSTM with word embeddings in their model to detect phishing email, webpages or SMSs.

In the work of Cai et al. (2017), a behavior enhanced deep model for bot detection was proposed and applied to detect bots under two deep learning frameworks. By fusing content and behavior information, the aim of the proposed model is to capture the latent features. Using a honeypot method, they collected a public dataset for theirs experiments using a CNN network. Their model was investigated by varying the number of filters and the filter width and number of hidden units in the hidden layer. Their proposed system achieved the highest F1 score compared to other state of the art systems.

## 3 Data Preparation

### 3.1 Collecting the Dataset

In this section, we focus on creating a dataset for detecting deepfake text. To the best of our knowledge, no such dataset exists. The closest dataset to our needs is that of Almerekhi and Elsayed (2015), which includes 3,503 tweets that are manually labeled as "human content" (1,559 tweets) or "bot content" (1,944 tweets). Upon inspecting their dataset, much of the bot content includes verses from the Quran, the Muslim holy book, proverbs, and sexual content. Though such are being distributed by bots, they don't fit the definition of deepfake text, which entails human-like texts that were automatically generated by machines with or without seed input. Thus, we needed to create a new dataset.

To prepare our dataset, we utilized the 1,559 tweets in the dataset of Almerekhi and Elsayed (2015) that were labeled as "human content", as we are sure are authored by humans. Due to the limited number of tweets in this set, we expanded the set by crawling the timeline tweets of the users in the set. This is based on the simplifying assumption that accounts that produced human content are unlikely to produce bot content or deepfake text. It is noteworthy that some of the accounts from which the tweets originated were in fact deleted or suspended or individual tweets themselves were deleted. Thus, we removed deleted tweets and we were not able to get the timelines of deleted or suspended accounts. After expansion, the number of tweets in our dataset increased to 4,196. We henceforth refer to this expanded set as the *human generated set*. We normalized the text of the tweets by removing URLs, splitting hashtags, replacing user mentions by USER, removing non-Arabic characters and punctuation marks, and removing diacritics, which are short vowels that are optionally written in Arabic text.

Given our human generated set, we needed a contrasting deepfake text set. To do so, we used the GPT2-Small-Arabic model[2] to auto-generate sentences based on our human generated set. Generally, GPT-2 is a pre-trained model that generates synthetic sentences by predicting the next word based on previous words (Radford et al., 2019). Similarly, GPT2-Small-Arabic was pre-trained on an Arabic Wikipedia dump (around 900MB of text) using the Fastai2 library (Abed, 2020). Unlike other transfer learning-based models that need 2 stages for training (pre-training and fine-tuning stages), GPT-2 like models do not require fine-tuning (Ma, 2019). We used GPT2-Small-Arabic to generate deepfake text that is seeded using the tweets in the *human generated set*. We generated a set of deepfake texts using

---

[2] https://huggingface.co/akhooli/gpt2-small-arabic

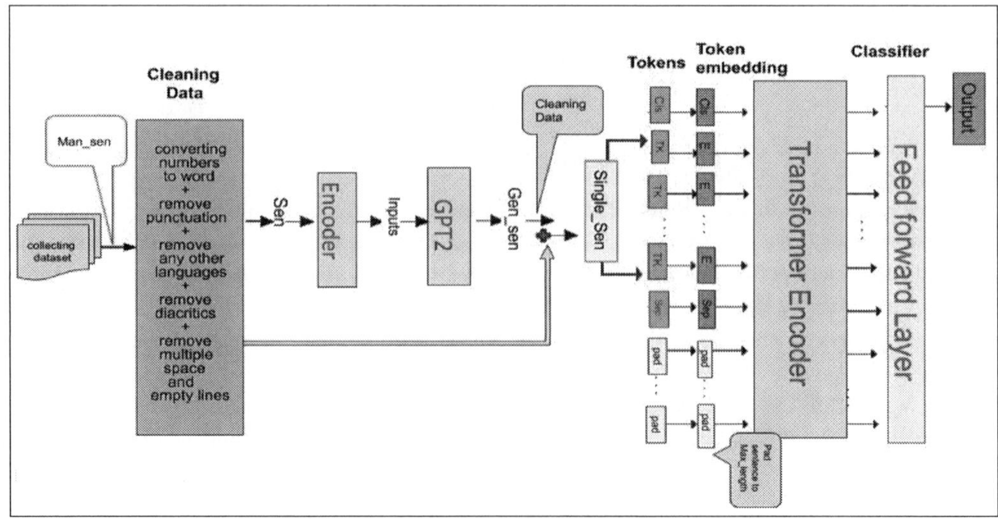



Figure 1: Overall architecture.

| Abbreviation | Meaning |
| --- | --- |
| Sen | Sentence |
| Man_Sen | Human generated sentences |
| Gen_Sen | Deepfake sentences |
| Pad | Padding |
| Tk | Tokens |
| E | Token embeddings |
| Max_length | Maximum length of all the sentences |
| ClS | For classification tasks, we must append the special [CLS] token to the beginning of every sentence |
| Sep | We need to append the special [SEP] token at the end of every sentence |

Table 1: Architectural elements

GPT2-Small-Arabic, where the generated texts ranged in length between 15 and 35 words. The set is composed of 3,512 deepfake texts. We henceforth refer to this set as the *deepfake set*. Table 3 shows an example of a tweet from the human generated set and the corresponding deepfake text that was generated from it.

## 4  Experimental Setup

We combined the human generated and deepfake sets, and we randomly divided the combined dataset into 80/20 training and test splits. We utilized 4 competitive deep learning Recurrent Neural Network (RNN) baselines to compare to our proposed transformer-based model. Figure 1 showcases the entire architecture of our proposed solution with the explanation of the elements therein in Table 1.

| parameter | LSTM | GRU | biLSTM | biGRU |
|---|---|---|---|---|
| Input layer size | 50 | | | |
| RNN layer size | 128 | | | |
| Dense layer size | 400 | | | |
| Learning rate | 0.001 | | | |
| Batch size | 100 | | | |
| Dropout (dense layer) | 0.4 | 0.5 | 0.3 | 0.5 |
| Epochs | early stopping with patience of 4 | | | |

Table 2: RNN model parameters.

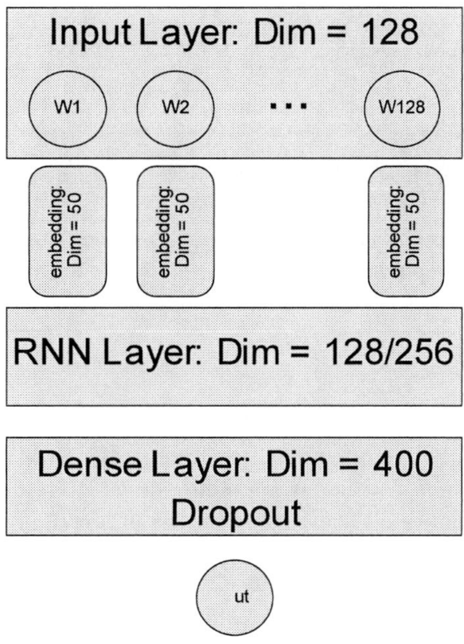


Figure 2: RNN baseline architecture.

## 4.1 Baseline

For the baselines, we used 4 different RNN models. As shown in Figure 2, all the models have a cascade of an input layer of size 128, randomly initialized word embeddings of size 50, an RNN layer of size 128 (or 256 for bidirectional), a dense layer of size 400, and an output layer with softmax activation. We used 4 different RNN layers, namely Long Short Term Memory (LSTM), Gated Recurrent Unit (GRU), bidirectional LSTM (biLSTM), and bidirectional GRU (biGRU). LSTMs have the advantage of effectively dealing with the vanishing gradients problem. Bidirectional GRUs and LSTMs make better use of the training data as the data is traversed twice, typically leading to improved performance (Siami-Namini et al., 2019). Table 2 lists the model parameters.

## 4.2 Our BERT-based Method

Recently, deep contextualized language models such as BERT (Bidirectional Encoder Representations from Transformers) (Devlin et al., 2019b) resulted in major improvements for many NLP classification and language understanding tasks. For our proposed method, we fine-tuned AraBERT (v 0.1) for the classification task (Antoun et al., 2020). AraBERT is pre-trained on an identical architecture to BERT, namely an encoder with 12 Transformer blocks, hidden size of 768, and 12 self-attention heads. It is trained on a large Arabic news corpus containing 8.5M articles composed of roughly 2.5B tokens, and it uses SentencePiece (BP) word segmentation. AraBERT has been shown to yield better results than multilingual BERT from Google, which is trained on Arabic Wikipedia only (Antoun et al., 2020). We

| Human generated | اليوم بعد الفجر رأيت رؤيا بمحمد إن شاء الله إنها خير |
| --- | --- |
| Deepfake | اليوم بعد الفجر. تم إطلاق على القوات الاسرائيلية على الفور، وتم إطلاق النار على طائرة إسرائيلية ثنائية الجنسية في ٢٦ مارس، مما أسفر عن مقتل أربعة وإصابة خمسة أشخاص. وقال |

Table 3: An example of GPT2-Small-Arabic generated text

|         | Accuracy | Precision | Recall | F1-Score |
| ------- | -------- | --------- | ------ | -------- |
| LSTM    | 95.0     | 92.8      | 96.8   | 94.8     |
| Bi-LSTM | 96.3     | 96.9      | 95.2   | 96.0     |
| GRU     | 94.7     | 91.2      | 98.2   | 94.6     |
| Bi-GRU  | 95.9     | 93.7      | 97.8   | 95.7     |

Table 4: Results for RNN based baseline models

used the PyTorch[3] implementation by HuggingFace[4] as it provides pre-trained weights and vocabularies, and we carried out 4 fine-tuning epochs.

## 5 Experimental Results

### 5.1 Baseline Results

Table 4 shows the results of dataset for our four RNN Baseline models, namely LSTM, biLSTM, GRU and biGRU. BiLSTM and biGRU were the best performers. BiLSTM has the highest balanced performance, compared to others models. Further, using bidirectional RNN, either biLSTM or biGRU, instead of unidirectional RNNs had a noticeable positive improvement on the results.

### 5.1.1 AraBERT Results

Table 5 shows the AraBERT results. The results clearly indicate the ability of transfer learning models to detect auto-generated texts with a high degree of accuracy. In addition, it is also clear through these experiments to what extent the hyperparameters impact the performance of these classifiers. Also, the AraBERT model significantly outperformed all baseline models. The improvements compared to the baseline results are +3.7% for LSTM, 4.0% for GRU, +2.4% for biLSTM, and +2.8% for biGRU. To better visualize the improvements, Figure 3 compares the results.

## 6 Conclusion

In this paper, we aimed to automatically detect deepfake text. We created a dataset of human generated tweets and deepfake tweets that we generated using GPT2-Small-Arabic. For classification, we experimented with different RNN models and compared them to AraBERT, a pre-trained BERT model for Arabic. The results show that we can effectively distinguish between human generated and machine generated tweets with high accuracy (98.7%) using a fine-tuned AraBERT model, which outperforms RNN models. For future work, we plan to use explainability tools to determine the reasons for the success of the AraBERT model. We suspect that the model is able to detect deepfakes due to repetitions in the text, which are a common artifact of automatically generated text, or the style of language of GPT2 generated text.

---

[3]`https://pytorch.org/`
[4]`https://github.com/huggingface/transformers`

| Accuracy | Precision | Recall | F1-Score |
| -------- | --------- | ------ | -------- |
| 98.7     | 98.9      | 98.5   | 98.7     |

Table 5: Results for AraBERT model

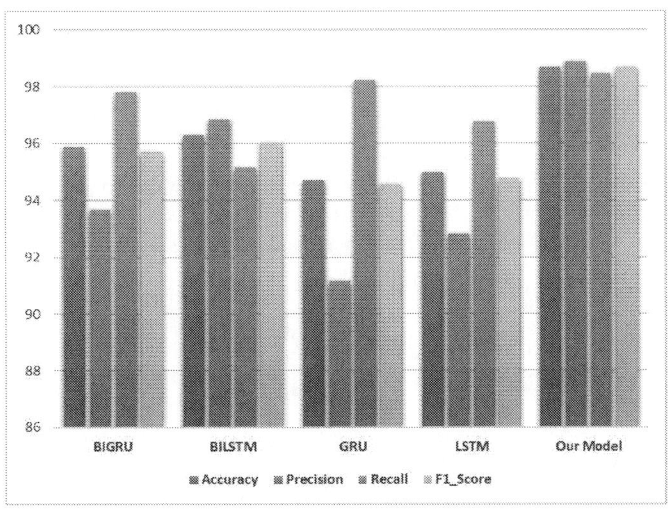


Figure 3: Improvement of our model compared to RNN baseline models

## References


Khooli Abed. 2020. huggingface , gpt2-small-arabic. `https://huggingface.co/akhooli/gpt2-small-arabic`. Available Online: 2019-01-15, Accessed: 2020-09-30.

Fatih Cagatay Akyon and M Esat Kalfaoglu. 2019. Instagram fake and automated account detection. In *2019 Innovations in Intelligent Systems and Applications Conference (ASYU)*, pages 1–7. IEEE.

Hind Almerekhi and Tamer Elsayed. 2015. Detecting automatically-generated arabic tweets. In *AIRS*, pages 123–134. Springer.

Wissam Antoun, Fady Baly, and Hazem Hajj. 2020. Arabert: Transformer-based model for arabic language understanding. *arXiv preprint arXiv:2003.00104*.

Chiyu Cai, Linjing Li, and Daniel Zengi. 2017. Behavior enhanced deep bot detection in social media. In *2017 IEEE International Conference on Intelligence and Security Informatics (ISI)*, pages 128–130. IEEE.

Kareem Darwish, Dimitar Alexandrov, Preslav Nakov, and Yelena Mejova. 2017. Seminar users in the arabic twitter sphere. In *International Conference on Social Informatics*, pages 91–108. Springer.

Jacob Devlin, Ming-Wei Chang, Kenton Lee, and Kristina Toutanova. 2019a. Bert: Pre-training of deep bidirectional transformers for language understanding.

Jacob Devlin, Ming-Wei Chang, Kenton Lee, and Kristina Toutanova. 2019b. BERT: Pre-training of deep bidirectional transformers for language understanding. In *Proceedings of the 2019 Conference of the North American Chapter of the Association for Computational Linguistics: Human Language Technologies, Volume 1 (Long and Short Papers)*, pages 4171–4186, Minneapolis, Minnesota, June. Association for Computational Linguistics.

Numa Dhamani, Paul Azunre, Jeffrey L. Gleason, Craig Corcoran, Garrett Honke, Steve Kramer, and Jonathon Morgan. 2019. Using deep networks and transfer learning to address disinformation.

Touseef Iqbal and Shaima Qureshi. 2020. The survey: Text generation models in deep learning. *Journal of King Saud University - Computer and Information Sciences*.

Sneha Kudugunta and Emilio Ferrara. 2018. Deep neural networks for bot detection. *Information Sciences*, 467:312–322.

Edward Ma. 2019. towards data science, too powerful nlp model (gpt-2), what is generative pre-training? `https://towardsdatascience.com/too-powerful-nlp-model-generative-pre-training-2-4cc6afb6655`. Available Online: 2019-02-21, Accessed: 2020-09-30.

Damian Radcliffe and Payton Bruni. 2019. *State of Social Media Middle East: 2018*. University of Oregon Libraries.

Alec Radford, Jeffrey Wu, Rewon Child, David Luan, Dario Amodei, and Ilya Sutskever. 2019. Language models are unsupervised multitask learners. *OpenAI blog*, 1(8):9.

Giovanni C Santia, Munif Ishad Mujib, and Jake Ryland Williams. 2019. Detecting social bots on facebook in an information veracity context. In *Proceedings of the International AAAI Conference on Web and Social Media*, volume 13, pages 463–472.

Sima Siami-Namini, Neda Tavakoli, and Akbar Siami Namin. 2019. The performance of lstm and bilstm in forecasting time series. In *2019 IEEE International Conference on Big Data (Big Data)*, pages 3285–3292. IEEE.

Amirsina Torfi, Rouzbeh A. Shirvani, Yaser Keneshloo, Nader Tavaf, and Edward A. Fox. 2020. Natural language processing advancements by deep learning: A survey.

Onur Varol, Emilio Ferrara, Clayton A Davis, Filippo Menczer, and Alessandro Flammini. 2017. Online human-bot interactions: Detection, estimation, and characterization. *arXiv preprint arXiv:1703.03107*.

Feng Wei and Uyen Trang Nguyen. 2019. Twitter bot detection using bidirectional long short-term memory neural networks and word embeddings. In *2019 First IEEE International Conference on Trust, Privacy and Security in Intelligent Systems and Applications (TPS-ISA)*, pages 101–109. IEEE.

# Contextual Embeddings for Arabic-English Code-Switched Data

**Caroline Sabty, Mohamed Islam, and Slim Abdennadher**
The German University in Cairo,
El Tagamoa El Khames, New Cairo, Cairo, Egypt
`caroline.samy,slim.abdennadher@guc.edu.eg`
`mohamed.islam@student.guc.edu.eg`

## Abstract

Globalization has caused the rise of the code-switching phenomenon among multilingual societies. In Arab countries, code-switching between Arabic and English has become frequent, especially through social media platforms. Consequently, research in Natural Language Processing (NLP) systems increased to tackle such a phenomenon. One of the significant challenges of developing code-switched NLP systems is the lack of data itself. In this paper, we propose an open source trained bilingual contextual word embedding models of FLAIR, BERT, and ELECTRA. We also propose a novel contextual word embedding model called KERMIT, which can efficiently map Arabic and English words inside one vector space in terms of data usage. We applied intrinsic and extrinsic evaluation methods to compare the performance of the models. Our results show that FLAIR and FastText achieve the highest results in the sentiment analysis task. However, KERMIT is the best-achieving model on the intrinsic evaluation and named entity recognition. Also, it outperforms the other transformer-based models on question answering task.

## 1 Introduction

Nowadays, due to globalization, bilingual communities tend to code-switch in everyday communication. Code-Switching (CS) is defined as the embedding of linguistic units such as phrases, words, and morphemes of one language into an utterance of another language (Myers-Scotton, 1997). This linguistic behavior occurs on both spoken and written scales. Primary language appears the most inside an utterance, while secondary language is the language of embedded words or phrases inside an utterance. The phenomenon of code-switching has been increasingly reported in linguistic studies in the past years as more people tend to code-switch. Furthermore, this phenomenon has become popular in Arab countries, where people code-switch between different dialects or their dialect and foreign languages. For instance, it is common to mix between Arabic and French in Tunisia and Egyptian Arabic and English in Egypt. CS behavior is common in online interaction, especially among social media users, generating vast amounts of CS data (Barman et al., 2014). For example, on Twitter, the multilingual users are more active than the monolingual ones (Hale, 2014). Thus, it is essential nowadays to process and understand the natural language of humans. This is performed by applying several Natural Language Processing (NLP) techniques while using different deep learning approaches. Lately, CS data started to gain attention in different NLP tasks (Hamed et al., 2017; Menacer et al., 2019; Sabty et al., 2019a).

One of the powerful developments in the NLP field is word embeddings; they represent words as vectors in a continuous space. This leads to having semantically similar words grouped near each other. It has been proven that adding word embedding instead of the traditional bag-of-words approach to different NLP tasks is very efficient (Soliman et al., 2017). Recently, bilingual word embeddings gained much attention to embedding in the same space words from two languages. Most of the standard bilingual word embedding techniques are intended to be trained and work on monolingual texts, not on a mix of





*Proceedings of the Fifth Arabic Natural Language Processing Workshop*, pages 215–225
Barcelona, Spain (Online), December 12, 2020

two languages. Thus, they are not the ideal option to learn embeddings for code-switched tasks (Pratapa et al., 2018b).

As our focus in this work is on the Arabic-English CS data, previously (Hamed et al., 2019) developed a classical word embedding model called Bi-CS. This model produced classical word embeddings by training on CS Arabic-English corpus. It was trained on monolingual data and a small amount of CS data, which acted as a gluing force bringing the monolingual embeddings closer in the vector space. However, classical word embeddings compute static vectors for each word. In polysemous words that depend on the context, classical word embeddings fail to model these words. Contextual embeddings, on the other hand, compute context-dependent nature vectors for words. This work aims to train bilingual contextual embedding models using state-of-the-art embedding types generated from our collected code-switched Arabic-English corpus. The models we created were using FLAIR, BERT, and ELECTRA. We also proposed a new contextual word embedding model called KERMIT based on the previous work (Devlin et al., 2018; Clark et al., 2020), capable of mapping both Arabic and English words inside one vector space efficiently in terms of data usage. All our trained and proposed models are available as an open source[1].

To compare our bilingual embedding models, we applied intrinsic and extrinsic evaluation methods. In the intrinsic evaluation, the models are tested on their ability to assign near-by vectors to similar tokens. This was achieved by calculating the cosine similarity between the tokens using $BERTS_{CORE}$ (Zhang et al., 2019). In the extrinsic evaluation, we evaluated our models on three downstream NLP tasks; Named Entity Recognition, Sentiment Analysis, and Question Answering on Arabic-English CS text. As a result of the intrinsic evaluation, the best model is KERMIT, which is capable of modeling higher cosine-similarity with similar code-switched words and lower for unrelated ones. In addition, the system we implemented using KERMIT is the best-achieving model for the NER task on Arabic-English data. Regarding the sentiment analysis, FLAIR and FastText achieved higher results compared to all other models. This shows that the character embedding outperformed the different types of embedding in some tasks on CS data. Results also show that the KERMIT model achieved the highest results on question answering task across the transformer-based models.

The paper is organized as follows. Section 2 presents some related work for word embedding models. In Section 3, the process of data collection and corpus creation is illustrated. Section 4 explains the different types of embedding models we trained. Section 5 discusses the different evaluation methods and their results. Finally, Section 7 concludes the paper and presents future work.

## 2   Related Work

Some studies implemented different word embedding models to deal with various Arabic NLP tasks. For example, Soliman et al. (2017) implemented Arabic pre-trained word embedding models. Their first version contained six distinct models built using either continuous Bag-of-Words (CBOW) or Skip-Gram (SG) techniques for the different text domains. They measured the similarity of word vectors of a subset of sentiment words and named entities to evaluate their models. Then they applied the clustering technique to see if, in each set, the words with the same polarity will be clustered together or no. They also used SemEval-2017 Semantic Textual Similarity to check how equivalent paired snippets of text. Another set of word embedding models for the Arabic language is presented in (Fouad et al., 2020). The models are implemented using CBOW, SG, and GloVe techniques, and they are generated from a set of Arabic tweets. They proposed a new way to measure the similarity of the Arabic words to evaluate the performance of their proposed models. Besides, they tested the performance in the multi-class sentiment analysis classification task.

Bilingual models have been explored as a link to bridge the gap between languages in CS word embedding and building models for low-resource languages. Several bilingual models have been proposed to align cross-lingual data, they used different alignment techniques such as word-level (Hermann and Blunsom, 2014; Faruqui and Dyer, 2014), sentence-level (Hermann and Blunsom, 2014; Gouws et al., 2015), both word and sentence level (Luong et al., 2015) and document-level alignments (Vulic and Moens,

---

[1]https://github.com/CSabty/Code-Switch-Arabic-English-Contextual-Embeddings

2015; Vulić and Moens, 2016). Besides Upadhyay et al. (2016) presented a comparison between four different cross-lingual embeddings models (Luong et al., 2015; Hermann and Blunsom, 2014; Faruqui and Dyer, 2014; Vulic and Moens, 2015), they vary in terms of the amount of supervision. Pratapa et al. (2018b) compared between the three bilingual models (Hermann and Blunsom, 2014; Faruqui and Dyer, 2014; Luong et al., 2015) for enhancing the downstream tasks of sentiment analysis and POS tagging on English-Spanish CS data. Moreover, they proposed an approach for training CS text generated by (Pratapa et al., 2018a) using skip-grams. In (Lachraf et al., 2019), they proposed several Arabic-English cross-lingual word embedding models trained on pairs of Arabic-English parallel sentences. It is essential to mention that training cross-lingual and multilingual embeddings require monolingual data. The set of syntactic structures and semantic associations of code-switched text are not shown in monolingual sentences. Thus, learning CS text analysis using cross-lingual and multilingual embeddings is not optimal. Code-switched embedding should be trained using CS text (Pratapa et al., 2018b).

Gao et al. (2019) proposed an approach to employ the BERT model and Generative Adversarial Net model for CS text generation. The developed system is capable of generating full CS sentences by training on low resourced CS data. Through this process, the BERT model learns contextual embedding representation. They evaluated their generated data in an ASR system on Mandarin-English CS data. A Multi-Encoder-Decoder Transformer model was proposed in (Zhou et al., 2020) for CS data. This model involves two language-specific encoder modules, each trained on monolingual data. These two modules are then integrated and trained on low resourced CS data. Eventually, this module is capable of representing contextual embedding.

Related to our work for Arabic-English CS data, Hamed et al. (2019) compared different bilingual embeddings (Hermann and Blunsom, 2014; Faruqui and Dyer, 2014; Luong et al., 2015) having different cross-lingual supervision. They also proposed two extensions, one of which depends on monolingual and small CS corpora, and another one combines the first two approaches. They evaluated the effect of using different embeddings in language modeling. However, the proposed embeddings are classical ones and do not consider the context of the words.

## 3   Data Collection

To train the word embedding models using Arabic-English code-switched text, we collected the data using three different techniques/sources and created two corpora. The first corpus *CS_TRAIN* is composed of 105 million tokens. The first source of data was using the CS corpus of (Hamed et al., 2019) collected from social media platforms. The second technique is generating 30 million Arabic-English CS tokens by translating monolingual Modern Standard Arabic corpus into Arabic-English CS data. We iterated automatically over the corpus and translated tokens according to a set of linguistic constraints using an open-sourced Neural Machine Translation API[2]. We followed the linguistic constraints inferred from evaluating real Arabic-English code-switched data in (Hamed et al., 2018). They defined trigger words such as (ال, the), (في, in) and (و, and), which are Arabic words preceding a CS point. The final part of the corpus is composed from the monolingual Arabic news-wire data. To augment the size of the training data, we created another corpus *CS_TRAIN++* by adding to the initial one *CS_TRAIN* 20 million tokens from the same Arabic monolingual news-wire data-set. Also, we translated them following the same linguistic constraints to form the other 19 million CS tokens. The corpus of *CS_TRAIN++* is composed of 144 million tokens. The corpora statistics are presented in Table 1.

| Data-set | English Tokens | Arabic Tokens | Sentences |
| --- | --- | --- | --- |
| *CS_TRAIN* | 10M | 95M | 7M |
| *CS_TRAIN++* | 17M | 127M | 9M |

Table 1: Detailed data statistics about the number of English tokens, Arabic tokens, the number of sentences

[2]https://rapidapi.com/gofitech/api/nlp-translation

## 4 Embedding Models

We trained several bilingual contextual embedding models to compare them and have an efficient model for Arabic-English CS data used in several NLP tasks. We used several state-of-the-art techniques and the type of contextual embeddings for building our models. We started by creating a baseline model using a stack of Arabic pre-trained Pooled FLAIR embedding and pre-trained FastText. The other models we built are using FLAIR, BERT, and ELECTRA. We also proposed a new model called the KERMIT.

### 4.1 Baseline

The baseline model used in our experiment is a stack of Arabic pre-trained Pooled FLAIR embedding (Akbik et al., 2019b) and pre-trained FastText. Pooled FLAIR embedding and FastText achieved the best results on NER downstream task for Arabic-English CS data in (Sabty et al., 2019b). It even out-performed the only available Arabic-English CS embedding of Bi-CS (Hamed et al., 2019). Pooling operation dynamically aggregates each unique word encountered, then retrieves previous embeddings produced from memory. Finally, the pool operation is performed, and all locally contextualized embeddings are concatenated to make the final embedding for the token. FastText can compute classical word embedding representation using the same methodology and architecture as the word2vec model (Mikolov et al., 2013) with an extension. FastText encodes character-level representations for a word, it breaks words into n-grams, and the word embedding is computed as the sum of all these n-grams. This capability helps FastText in outperforming word2vec in modeling word representations.

### 4.2 FLAIR

The first model trained is FLAIR (Akbik et al., 2018), a contextualized character-level language model. FLAIR model sentences as a sequence of characters and trains on the auto-regressive task. FLAIR can model sequence bidirectionally by stacking a forward and a backward character language model. Therefore, to get the whole context, we have pre-trained forward and backward FLAIR language models. FLAIR models can produce several embeddings for the same word based on its context and manage dealing with rare and misspelled words by modeling context as characters.

The pre-processing stage involved removing punctuation symbols and lower casing English characters in the corpus. In the tokenization phase, we have listed all the alphabetical English and Arabic characters. Hyper-parameters were configured following the original FLAIR parameters (Akbik et al., 2018). Forward and Backward language models were trained using the same vocabulary. We tracked the training performance on the validation set. Training took ten days for each of the backward and forward models on one GPU or halted when negligible gains were observed.

### 4.3 BERT

We have trained BERT (Bidirectional Encoder Representations from Transformers) (Devlin et al., 2018) on our CS corpora. BERT is a transformer-based language model. It is trained on the Masked Language Model (MLM) and Next Sentence Prediction (NSP) tasks. MLMs are trained on masking out random tokens by replacing them with special token [MASK] inside a sentence. The model then tries to predict the masked tokens using the whole context of a sequence. Also, NSP models are trained on distinguishing whether two input sentences are continuous segment or separate. Unlike FLAIR, BERT models sentences as a sequence of tokens. Each input token in a sequence flows through stacked encoders and outputs a hidden state representing the word embedding. This enables BERT to train in parallel.

We have implemented an additional pre-processing stage to our data set before proceeding to the training phase. This stage involves segmenting Arabic words using Farasa segmenter (Abdelali et al., 2016) to remove redundant forms of words. After segmenting the corpus, we produced a total of 64k tokens as a vocabulary for our model. We have trained BERT$_{\text{BASE}}$ sized model with 12 encoder layers, a hidden size of 768, and 12 attention heads. Training BERT is done by masking 15% of tokens in the input, of which 80% are replaced with a special token [MASK], 10% are replaced with random tokens, and 10% remains as an original token. This configuration helps to prevent pretrain-finetune-discrepancy. A learning rate of 2e-5 and Adam optimizer was used in the pre-training. We trained our model for a total of 1,000,000 steps with a batch size of 128. The next 250,000 steps were then trained with a batch size of 256 to speed up the training process. The training took three days to complete on eight cloud TPUs.

## 4.4 ELECTRA

We trained ELECTRA (Efficiently Learning an Encoder that Classifies Token Replacements Accurately) (Clark et al., 2020) on our CS corpora. ELECTRA is composed of two neural networks, a generator and a discriminator trained together on MLM and Replaced Token Detection (RTD) tasks. RTD is a special unsupervised task that trained discriminative models. The language model is given a sequence of tokens from a generator and tries to predict whether a generator or original token replaces a token. A full modeling context does this. The ELECTRA model is trained to minimize the combined losses of the generator and the discriminator. Compared with BERT, the ELECTRA training mechanism is considered more efficient because the task is defined over all input tokens rather than just the 15% tokens that were masked out.

The pre-training stage was similar to BERT, however, with different configurations. We used the same pre-processing and tokenization mechanism. We have trained ELECTRA$_{\text{BASE}}$ sized model. The discriminator of this model has the same size as BERT$_{\text{BASE}}$ model. It is composed of 12 encoder layers, a hidden size of 128, 12 attention heads, and outputs embedding of size 768. The generator component of the ELECTRA$_{\text{BASE}}$ model is 1/3 of the size of the discriminator model. This configuration makes it harder for the discriminator component to distinguish tokens and produces more robust representations. We have trained both the generator and discriminator jointly from scratch with a learning rate of 2e-4 and batch size of 256 for a total of 750,000 steps. This training took five days on eigh TPUs.

## 4.5 KERMIT

We proposed a novel model called KERMIT for producing word embeddings. The architecture of this model is an encoder variant of transformers. The pre-training of this model is divided into two stages, as shown in Figure 1. In the first stage, KERMIT is trained as a discriminator in ELECTRA architecture using RTD and MLM tasks. After pre-training, the generator is dropped, and the pre-trained discriminator weights are used for the next stage. In the second stage, we initialize the encoder and embedding layers of the BERT model with the trained discriminator model. Then, we further trained the model as a generator using the MLM task. This training mechanism helps avoid pretrain-finetune-discrepancy and allows the model to learn stronger representation through training on more than one task.

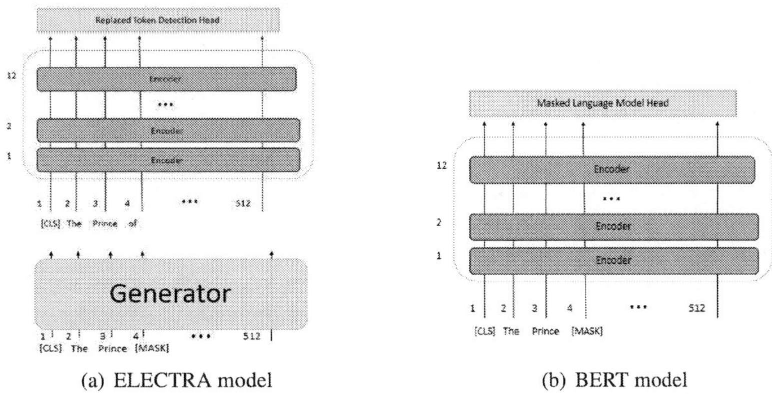


(a) ELECTRA model                    (b) BERT model

Figure 1: KERMIT encoder layers trained as discriminator in ELECTRA then as Generator in BERT

Furthermore, the model is trained on data with different augmentations. A generator replaced tokens at the first stage, and during the second stage, tokens were masked out. This helped to increase the diversity of data available for training. In the two stages of pre-training, we have used the same data pre-processing and tokenization vocabulary. We have trained the ELECTRA$_{\text{BASE}}$ model using the same hyper-parameters used for training the previous ELECTRA model. Using the same vocabulary, we transferred weights of the encoder and embedding layers and trained BERT$_{BASE}$ model using the same hyper-parameters used for training the previous BERT model. We have investigated different configurations for the transferred model. On the one hand, we trained the BERT model using trained generator prediction layers. On the other hand, we trained the model using randomly initialized generator prediction layers. Furthermore, we have changed the Adam optimizer variables so that loss affects only the encoder layers and applies less effect on the output layers. We have also tried to switch training stages through training BERT first then transferring weights to the ELECTRA model. The best configuration observed while training was using both randomly initialized generator prediction layers along with Adam optimizer variables.

## 5    Evaluation & Results

To evaluate our models, we have used intrinsic and extrinsic methods. We first trained the models using the *CS_TRAIN* and then using *CS_TRAIN*$_{++}$. For clarity, all models with a suffix ++ have been trained using *CS_TRAIN*$_{++}$.

### 5.1    Intrinsic Evaluation

The purpose of the intrinsic evaluation was to visualize and test how well the word embedding model can capture similarities in CS Arabic-English text. Thus, to evaluate our embedding models, we have leveraged cosine similarity between different tokens using BERTS$_{CORE}$ (Zhang et al., 2019). It is a new automatic evaluation metric for the generated text that computes token similarity using contextual embeddings. We evaluated the similarity between the tokens of several sentences, and the models performed the same in almost all of them. The following is an example of two CS sentences used to test the similarities stated by the models:

day كل news قراءه يحب احمد   (a)     أسبوع في كتاب ينهي Mohamed   (b)
'Ahmed loves reading news everyday'        'Mohamed finishes a book in a week'

Examining the results in Figure 2, we can see how word embeddings can help state the similarity between CS words. All the models trained with *CS_TRAIN*$_{++}$ performed better than those trained with the smaller data-set *CS_TRAIN*. We also noted that the baseline model did not get the similarities of the English words. It is an expected result as it was trained on monolingual Arabic data. On the one hand, the similarities of the FLAIR model between all words is low. On the other hand, the similarities obtained by the ELECTRA model is high. BERT$_{++}$ is capable of capturing small similarities between tokens, including cross-lingual. Moreover, KERMIT$_{++}$ is the best one; it was capable of modeling higher cosine-similarity with similar words and lower for unrelated ones.

### 5.2    Extrinsic Evaluation

The extrinsic evaluation is based on the possibility of using the word embeddings in downstream NLP tasks. We have evaluated the impact of our models in three tasks; Named Entity Recognition, Sentiment Analysis and Question Answering on Arabic-English CS text. As to the best of our knowledge there is no available contextual embeddings trained on Arabic-English CS data, we evaluated the recent Arabic model AraBERT (Antoun et al., 2020) in the three tasks to compare its performance with our models.

### 5.2.1    Named Entity Recognition

Named Entity Recognition (NER) is one of the essential tasks for NLP. It identifies named entities and classifies them into their types, e.g., person, location, and organization. We used two approaches to apply this task. The first one uses the deep learning NER model on Arabic-English CS data of (Sabty et al., 2019b), which is based on Bidirectional Long-Short-Term-Memory and Conditional Random Field along with the pre-trained word embedding layer. They compared the performance of their NER system using several types of embeddings. The best one was using Pooled FLAIR and FastText pre-trained Arabic

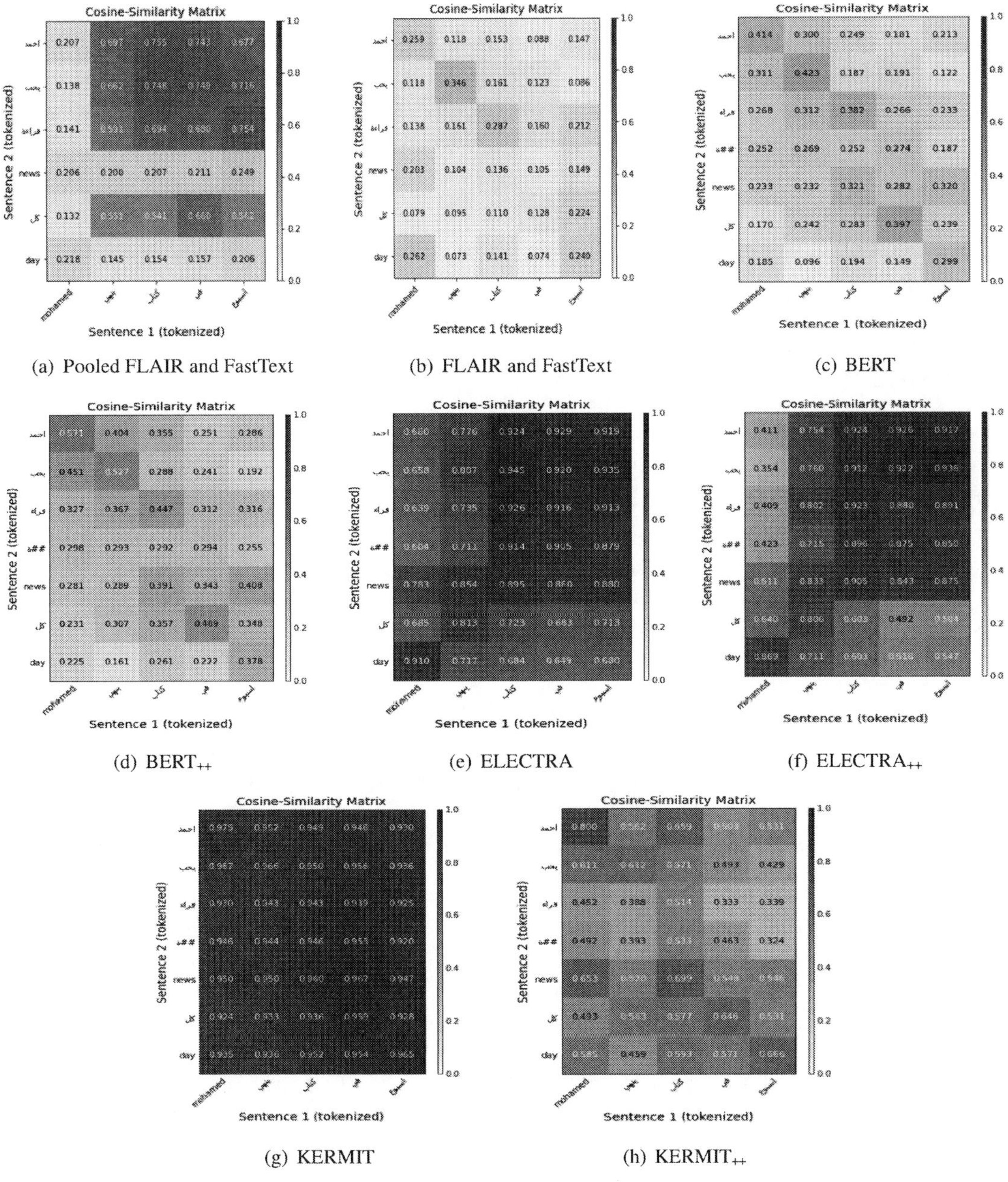

(a) Pooled FLAIR and FastText  (b) FLAIR and FastText  (c) BERT

(d) BERT$_{++}$  (e) ELECTRA  (f) ELECTRA$_{++}$

(g) KERMIT  (h) KERMIT$_{++}$

Figure 2: Results of comparing the tokens of two sentences using cosine-similarity of BERTS$_{CORE}$

embeddings, which we replicated in our baseline. Their best performance achieved an F-score equal to 77.69%. We used the same model and their training and testing data to compare the effect of using our different embeddings models on the performance. The second approach uses the NER system presented by the HuggingFace library that is based on fine-tuning (Wolf et al., 2019). We tested this system using the same training and testing of data of (Sabty et al., 2019b).

As shown in Table 2, we used all the models one by one as the embedding layer in the NER system, and we also combined some models. We combined FLAIR with Arabic FastText embedding, and it achieved the best results and enhanced the NER model by 0.51%. The results of using BERT$_{++}$, ELECTRA$_{++}$, and KERMIT$_{++}$ are all less than the baseline model, but the three are almost the same with minimal differences. We combined the highest one of them KERMIT$_{++}$ with the highest model of FLAIR and

| Embedding Model | NER Model (Sabty et al., 2019b) | NER HuggingFace (Wolf et al., 2019) |
| --- | --- | --- |
| Pooled FLAIR and FastText | 77.69 | - |
| FLAIR | 72.55 | - |
| FLAIR and FastText | **78.2** | - |
| KERMIT$_{++}$ and FLAIR and FastText | 76.6 | - |
| AraBERT(Antoun et al., 2020) | 58 | 66.7 |
| BERT | 64.5 | 76.5 |
| BERT$_{++}$ | 68.2 | 77.1 |
| ELECTRA | 67 | 75.4 |
| ELECTRA$_{++}$ | 68.3 | 76.29 |
| KERMIT | 65 | 78.7 |
| KERMIT$_{++}$ | 69 | **79.4** |

Table 2: The F1-score results (%) of using the different types of embeddings in the two NER systems

FastText, it improved the results but still less than the baseline. However, in the HuggingFace system it was hard to add the Pooled FLAIR and FLAIR embeddings to their fine-tuning model since the pooling is over past embeddings. Thus, it is hard to fine tune all of them due to memory limitations. As a result KERMIT$_{++}$ outperformed all other transformer-based models and even achieved higher results than the ones presented by the first NER approach by 1.2%.

### 5.2.2 Sentiment Analysis

We have also evaluated our models on sentiment analysis (SA) tasks using the methods proposed. It is a text classification task, where parts of the text are marked with binary labels to represent the sentiment type positive or negative in the text. We have created our data-set by translating a monolingual Arabic data-set of book reviews (Aly and Atiya, 2013) to have CS text using the same machine translation API and the linguistic constraints described previously in the data collection section. The results of experimenting sentiment analysis are stated in Table 3.

We used two approaches to apply this task. The first one uses the framework of FLAIR (Akbik et al., 2019a). It is based on the Recurrent Neural Network and linear classifier layers. While we added again to the FLAIR embedding the classical pre-trained FastText embedding, it improved the performance of the sentiment analysis model and scored the highest F1-score of 88.8%. The second uses the sentiment analysis system presented by HuggingFace based on fine-tuning (Linear Classifier) (Wolf et al., 2019); all transformer-based models are fine-tuned by adding a linear classifier layer. BERT model outperformed ELECTRA by about 1.6% and KERMIT by 0.9%. Furthermore BERT$_{++}$ scored higher than ELECTRA$_{++}$ by 0.4%. Finally, KERMIT$_{++}$ scored the highest in the second approach. However, using the first approach with FLAIR and FastText outperformed all models experimented.

### 5.2.3 Question Answering

Another important task that we tested the effect of using our embeddings models with it is the question-answering. It is finding the part of the text in a context that answers a given question. We have created our own data-set by translating text from the questions of the monolingual Arabic Question Answering (QA) corpus presented by (Mozannar et al., 2019) following the same approach stated in the sentiment analysis task. We could not translate words from the answers, as this would lead to changing their order, which could be misleading for the question-answering task.

We used only one approach for this task, which uses the question answering system of HuggingFace, which is based on fine-tuning (Linear Classifier) (Wolf et al., 2019). As shown in Table 4 KERMIT$_{++}$ achieved the highest score compared to all other fine-tuned models with an F1-score equal to 39.9%. It outperforms all models because, as state before training KERMIT as both generator and discriminator helps the model to compute better representation of the data. All the results of using the different embeddings are low as the answers in the training data did not contain CS behaviour, which could be enhanced

| Embedding Model | SA HuggingFace (Wolf et al., 2019) | SA FLAIR Framework (Akbik et al., 2019a) |
|---|---|---|
| Pooled FLAIR and FastText | - | 87.84 |
| FLAIR | - | 87.8 |
| FLAIR and FastText | - | **88.8** |
| AraBERT(Antoun et al., 2020) | 78.2 | - |
| BERT | 77.7 | - |
| BERT$_{++}$ | 77.38 | - |
| ELECTRA | 76.39 | - |
| ELECTRA$_{++}$ | 77.18 | - |
| KERMIT | 76.8 | - |
| KERMIT$_{++}$ | **79.9** | - |

Table 3: The F1-score results (%) of using the different types of embeddings in the two sentiment analysis systems

using a more accurate translation technique without affecting the order of words. As shown in the results our models achieved higher results than AraBERT embedding in all the three tasks. This is due to the fact that AraBert is trained on monolingual Arabic data.

| Embedding Model | QA HuggingFace (Wolf et al., 2019) |
|---|---|
| AraBERT(Antoun et al., 2020) | 30 |
| BERT | 37.8 |
| BERT$_{++}$ | 38.12 |
| ELECTRA | 34.1 |
| ELECTRA$_{++}$ | 37.2 |
| KERMIT | 32.8 |
| KERMIT$_{++}$ | **39.9** |

Table 4: The F1-score results (%) of using the different types of embeddings in the question answering system

## 6 Conclusion & Future Work

Word embedding is one of the cores of all NLP tasks. Pre-training word embeddings on extensive unlabelled data and using it on downstream tasks can save a lot of data annotation. However, it is a problem to find a large data-set when it comes to low resourced languages such as code-switched Arabic-English data. In this paper, we propose a solution to create a large corpus for pre-training word embeddings through several sources. We used this corpus for training different bilingual contextual embedding models: FLAIR, BERT, and ELECTRA. We also proposed a new model KERMIT. This model is trained as both a discriminator and a generator where each task has a different variant of the input. The different variants of the data helped the KERMIT model to train efficiently on the collected corpus. We have pre-trained and evaluated all the models on three downstream tasks. The character based-model FLAIR, along with FastText, outperformed all models in the task of sentiment analysis. However, KERMIT got better results in the NER task and outperformed the other transformer-based models in the question-answering task. Besides, we evaluated the performance of the models by calculating the cosine similarities between different tokens, and KERMIT captured the highest similarities.

In the future, more comparisons with available models could be done. We can pre-train variants of the model by keeping the monolingual data without CS text and compare the performance in different tasks. The models will be evaluated in different tasks using various annotated data-sets. An evaluation technique should be applied on the generated CS data to check how it simulates the CS behaviour.

# References


Ahmed Abdelali, Kareem Darwish, Nadir Durrani, and Hamdy Mubarak. 2016. Farasa: A fast and furious segmenter for arabic. In *Proceedings of the 2016 conference of the North American chapter of the association for computational linguistics: Demonstrations*, pages 11–16.

Alan Akbik, Duncan Blythe, and Roland Vollgraf. 2018. Contextual string embeddings for sequence labeling. In *Proceedings of the 27th International Conference on Computational Linguistics*, pages 1638–1649.

Alan Akbik, Tanja Bergmann, Duncan Blythe, Kashif Rasul, Stefan Schweter, and Roland Vollgraf. 2019a. Flair: An easy-to-use framework for state-of-the-art nlp. In *Proceedings of the 2019 Conference of the North American Chapter of the Association for Computational Linguistics (Demonstrations)*, pages 54–59.

Alan Akbik, Tanja Bergmann, and Roland Vollgraf. 2019b. Pooled contextualized embeddings for named entity recognition. In *NAACL 2019, 2019 Annual Conference of the North American Chapter of the Association for Computational Linguistics*, page 724–728.

Mohamed Aly and Amir Atiya. 2013. Labr: A large scale arabic book reviews dataset. In *Proceedings of the 51st Annual Meeting of the Association for Computational Linguistics (Volume 2: Short Papers)*, pages 494–498.

Wissam Antoun, Fady Baly, and Hazem Hajj. 2020. Arabert: Transformer-based model for arabic language understanding. In *LREC 2020 Workshop Language Resources and Evaluation Conference 11–16 May 2020*, page 9.

Utsab Barman, Amitava Das, Joachim Wagner, and Jennifer Foster. 2014. Code mixing: A challenge for language identification in the language of social media. In *Proceedings of the first workshop on computational approaches to code switching*, pages 13–23.

Kevin Clark, Minh-Thang Luong, Quoc V Le, and Christopher D Manning. 2020. Electra: Pre-training text encoders as discriminators rather than generators. *arXiv preprint arXiv:2003.10555*.

Jacob Devlin, Ming-Wei Chang, Kenton Lee, and Kristina Toutanova. 2018. Bert: Pre-training of deep bidirectional transformers for language understanding. *arXiv preprint arXiv:1810.04805*.

Manaal Faruqui and Chris Dyer. 2014. Improving vector space word representations using multilingual correlation. In *Proceedings of the 14th Conference of the European Chapter of the Association for Computational Linguistics*, pages 462–471.

Mohammed M Fouad, Ahmed Mahany, Naif Aljohani, Rabeeh Ayaz Abbasi, and Saeed-Ul Hassan. 2020. Arwordvec: efficient word embedding models for arabic tweets. *Soft Computing*, 24(11):8061–8068.

Yingying Gao, Junlan Feng, Ying Liu, Leijing Hou, Xin Pan, and Yong Ma. 2019. Code-switching sentence generation by bert and generative adversarial networks. In *INTERSPEECH*, pages 3525–3529.

Stephan Gouws, Yoshua Bengio, and Greg Corrado. 2015. Bilbowa: Fast bilingual distributed representations without word alignments. In *Proceedings of the 32nd International Conference on Machine Learning*, pages 748–756.

Scott A Hale. 2014. Global connectivity and multilinguals in the twitter network. In *Proceedings of the SIGCHI Conference on Human Factors in Computing Systems*, pages 833–842.

Injy Hamed, Mohamed Elmahdy, and Slim Abdennadher. 2017. Building a first language model for code-switch arabic-english. *Procedia Computer Science*, 117:208–216.

Injy Hamed, Mohamed Elmahdy, and Slim Abdennadher. 2018. Collection and analysis of code-switch egyptian arabic-english speech corpus. In *Proceedings of the Eleventh International Conference on Language Resources and Evaluation (LREC 2018)*.

Injy Hamed, Moritz Zhu, Mohamed Elmahdy, Slim Abdennadher, and Ngoc Thang Vu. 2019. Code-switching language modeling with bilingual word embeddings: A case study for egyptian arabic-english. In *International Conference on Speech and Computer*, pages 160–170. Springer.

Karl Moritz Hermann and Phil Blunsom. 2014. Multilingual models for compositional distributed semantics. *arXiv preprint arXiv:1404.4641*.

Raki Lachraf, Youcef Ayachi, Ahmed Abdelali, Didier Schwab, et al. 2019. Arbengvec: Arabic-english cross-lingual word embedding model. In *Proceedings of the Fourth Arabic Natural Language Processing Workshop*, pages 40–48.

Minh-Thang Luong, Hieu Pham, and Christopher D Manning. 2015. Bilingual word representations with monolingual quality in mind. In *Proceedings of the 1st Workshop on Vector Space Modeling for Natural Language Processing*, pages 151–159.

Mohamed Amine Menacer, David Langlois, Denis Jouvet, Dominique Fohr, Odile Mella, and Kamel Smaïli. 2019. Machine translation on a parallel code-switched corpus. In *Canadian Conference on Artificial Intelligence*, pages 426–432. Springer.

Tomas Mikolov, Ilya Sutskever, Kai Chen, Greg S Corrado, and Jeff Dean. 2013. Distributed representations of words and phrases and their compositionality. In *Advances in neural information processing systems*, pages 3111–3119.

Hussein Mozannar, Karl El Hajal, Elie Maamary, and Hazem Hajj. 2019. Neural arabic question answering. *arXiv preprint arXiv:1906.05394*.

Carol Myers-Scotton. 1997. *Duelling languages: Grammatical structure in codeswitching*. Oxford University Press.

Adithya Pratapa, Gayatri Bhat, Monojit Choudhury, Sunayana Sitaram, Sandipan Dandapat, and Kalika Bali. 2018a. Language modeling for code-mixing: The role of linguistic theory based synthetic data. In *Proceedings of the 56th Annual Meeting of the Association for Computational Linguistics (Volume 1: Long Papers)*, pages 1543–1553.

Adithya Pratapa, Monojit Choudhury, and Sunayana Sitaram. 2018b. Word embeddings for code-mixed language processing. In *Proceedings of the 2018 Conference on Empirical Methods in Natural Language Processing*, pages 3067–3072.

Caroline Sabty, Mohamed Elmahdy, and Slim Abdennadher. 2019a. Named entity recognition on arabic-english code-mixed data. In *2019 IEEE 13th International Conference on Semantic Computing (ICSC)*, pages 93–97. IEEE.

Caroline Sabty, Ahmed Sherif, Mohamed Elmahdy, and Slim Abdennadher. 2019b. Techniques for named entity recognition on arabic-english code-mixed data. *International Journal of Transdisciplinary AI*, 1(1):44–63.

Abu Bakr Soliman, Kareem Eissa, and Samhaa R El-Beltagy. 2017. Aravec: A set of arabic word embedding models for use in arabic nlp. *Procedia Computer Science*, 117:256–265.

Shyam Upadhyay, Manaal Faruqui, Chris Dyer, and Dan Roth. 2016. Cross-lingual models of word embeddings: An empirical comparison. *arXiv preprint arXiv:1604.00425*.

Ivan Vulic and Marie-Francine Moens. 2015. Bilingual word embeddings from non-parallel document-aligned data applied to bilingual lexicon induction. In *Proceedings of the 53rd Annual Meeting of the Association for Computational Linguistics (ACL 2015)*, volume 2, pages 719–725. ACL; East Stroudsburg, PA.

Ivan Vulić and Marie-Francine Moens. 2016. Bilingual distributed word representations from document-aligned comparable data. *Journal of Artificial Intelligence Research*, 55:953–994.

Thomas Wolf, Lysandre Debut, Victor Sanh, Julien Chaumond, Clement Delangue, Anthony Moi, Pierric Cistac, Tim Rault, Rémi Louf, Morgan Funtowicz, Joe Davison, Sam Shleifer, Patrick von Platen, Clara Ma, Yacine Jernite, Julien Plu, Canwen Xu, Teven Le Scao, Sylvain Gugger, Mariama Drame, Quentin Lhoest, and Alexander M. Rush. 2019. Huggingface's transformers: State-of-the-art natural language processing. *ArXiv*, abs/1910.03771.

Tianyi Zhang, Varsha Kishore, Felix Wu, Kilian Q Weinberger, and Yoav Artzi. 2019. Bertscore: Evaluating text generation with bert. *arXiv preprint arXiv:1904.09675*.

Xinyuan Zhou, Emre Yılmaz, Yanhua Long, Yijie Li, and Haizhou Li. 2020. Multi-encoder-decoder transformer for code-switching speech recognition. *arXiv preprint arXiv:2006.10414*.

# Improving Arabic Text Categorization Using Transformer Training Diversification


**Shammur A Chowdhury, Ahmed Abdelali, Kareem Darwish**
**Soon-gyo Jung, Joni Salminen, Bernard J Jansen**
Qatar Computing Research Institute
{shchowdhury, aabdelali, kdarwish, sjung, jsalminen, bjansen}@hbku.edu.qa



## Abstract

Automatic categorization of short texts, such as news headlines and social media posts, has many applications ranging from content analysis to recommendation systems. In this paper, we use such text categorization i.e., labeling the social media posts to categories like 'sports', 'politics', 'human-rights' among others, to showcase the efficacy of models across different sources and varieties of Arabic. In doing so, we show that diversifying the training data, whether by using diverse training data for the specific task (an increase of 21% macro F1) or using diverse data to pre-train a BERT model (26% macro F1), leads to overall improvements in classification effectiveness. In our work, we also introduce two new Arabic text categorization datasets, where the *first* is composed of social media posts from a popular Arabic news channel that cover Twitter, Facebook, and YouTube, and the *second* is composed of tweets from popular Arabic accounts. The posts in the former are nearly exclusively authored in modern standard Arabic (MSA), while the tweets in the latter contain both MSA and dialectal Arabic.


## 1 Introduction

Text classification, particularly of short texts, is an important problem in NLP and has been used in a variety of tasks in social media such as identifying people's sentiment (Mohammad et al., 2013), emotions (Abdullah and Shaikh, 2018), interests (Keneshloo et al., 2016), stance (Mohammad et al., 2016), offensive languages (Chowdhury et al., 2020; Hassan et al., 2020) and communication styles (Mubarak et al., 2020). Text classification requires the availability of manually tagged text to train effective classification models. Due to annotation costs, adapting labeled texts from one domain to tag texts in other domains is desirable, as it would avail the need to tag in-domain data.

With the recent success of pre-trained transformer-based models (e.g. BERT), various studies have adopted such models to generate contextualized embeddings for downstream tasks like text classification, using a small amount of in-domain data. To push the state-of-the-art performance, researchers have also experimented with variation in such model size (e.g. number of layers, attention head among others), architectures (BERT *vs* RoBERTa *vs* XLNet) and training data language (mono *vs* multilingual).

From the language perspective, many studies have reported that monolingual transformer models such as BERT performs significantly better than the multilingual BERT - mBERT (Polignano et al., 2019). However, very few studies have empirically shown the effect on the performance of diversifying a BERT pre-training data with formal and informal textual contents.

Therefore in this paper, we show the effectiveness of using a transformer model (named as QARiB),[1] which is trained on a *mixture of formal news* and *informal tweets* (i.e., written in dialectal Arabic). We compare the performance of QARiB with *(i)* multilingual BERT (mBERT), which is trained using multiple languages including Arabic, and *(ii)* AraBERT, which is trained on a large corpus of Arabic news (formal text only). For the evaluation, we employed these models and trained a multiclass short text classifier using *news headlines*, and then tested it on *tweets*.



[1] `https://github.com/qcri/QARIB`




*Proceedings of the Fifth Arabic Natural Language Processing Workshop*, pages 226–236
Barcelona, Spain (Online), December 12, 2020

As a byproduct of this work we annotate two new Arabic text categorization data sets. The *first* is a large set of social media posts collected from multiple platform – Twitter, Facebook, and YouTube – of a popular news site, where the posts are written in Modern Standard Arabic (MSA). The *second* is a set of mostly dialectal tweets that were authored by influential Arabic accounts. Details of the annotation guideline along with the annotated datasets are made publicly available.

Text categorization is complicated due to the fact that Arabic is the lingua franca for 22 countries with MSA being used as the formal language of communication while mutually unintelligible dialects are spoken in these countries and appear in social media posts. Further, social media posts, particularly tweets, are typically short and contain platform specific features such as hashtags and user mentions, further complicating the classification.

In summary, the contributions of this paper are as follows:

- We introduce two new Arabic text categorization datasets, which cover multiple social media platforms and different variations of Arabic including MSA and dialects. We publicly released the datasets along with annotation guidelines and examples.[2]

- We showcase the efficacy of using a transformer model that is trained on a mixture of formal and informal Arabic in providing effective domain adaptation for informal text categorization using formal Arabic training data.

## 2   Related Studies

The task of categorizing social media posts is challenging mainly due to the absence of largely annotated data. Most of the datasets that are currently available are based on news articles.

Some publicly available datasets are:

1. SANAD[3] (AlSaleh et al., 2020): This is one of the largest collection of news article for Arabic news text classification. This multi-class dataset includes news articles that are scraped from the AlKhaleej,[4] AlArabiya,[5] and Akhbarona[6] news portals. The dataset includes approximately 195k articles belonging to 6/7 categories.

2. NADiA[7] (Elnagar et al., 2020): This is a multi-label text dataset, collected by scraping SkyNewsArabia[8] and Masrawy[9] news sites. The released dataset include $486k$ articles with 52 categories.

3. Arabic News Text (ANT) Corpus[10] (Chouigui et al., 2017): This dataset was collected from RSS feeds and contains approximately 6k articles belonging to 9 categories

Other available datasets include: Khaleej-2004 (5k articles belonging to 4 categories) (Abbas and Smaili, 2005); Watan-2004 (20k articles belonging to 6 categories) (Abbas et al., 2011); and SL-RTANew[11] (20k articles belonging to 40 categories).

To capture syntactic and semantic information about words, pre-trained word static embeddings (Turian et al., 2010; Mikolov et al., 2013; Pennington et al., 2014) were widely used in many NLP tasks. Recent research advancements led to pre-trained contextual embeddings that capture much information about words in context, leading to significant improvements for many NLP tasks such as text classification and sequence labeling (Mikolov et al., 2017; Peters et al., 2018; Devlin et al., 2018; Howard and Ruder, 2018; Lan et al., 2019; Liu et al., 2019; Yang et al., 2019).

As for Arabic, various static and contextual embeddings representation have been trained. Some popular Arabic static embeddings include: Arabic word2vec (Soliman et al., 2017), a FastText model

---

[2]https://github.com/shammur/Arabic_news_text_classification_datasets

[3]https://data.mendeley.com/datasets/57zpx667y9/2

[4]http://www.alkhaleej.ae/portal

[5]https://www.alarabiya.net

[6]https://www.akhbarona.com

[7]https://data.mendeley.com/datasets/hhrb7phdyx/2

[8]https://www.skynewsarabia.com

[9]https://www.masrawy.com

[10]https://github.com/antcorpus/antcorpus.data

[11]https://data.mendeley.com/datasets/322pzsdxwy/1

that is trained on Wikipedia (Bojanowski et al., 2017), and dialectal word embeddings with small and noisy corpora (Erdmann et al., 2018) and with tweets (Abdul-Mageed et al., 2018; Farha and Magdy, 2019).

As for contextual embeddings, a handful of models are available (ElJundi et al., 2019; Antoun et al., 2020; Talafha et al., 2020). The first available BERT model for Arabic was multilingual BERT (mBERT), which was pre-trained on the Wikipedia dumps of 104 languages including Arabic. However, previous studies have shown that monolingual BERT models perform significantly better than the mBERT (Polignano et al., 2019). A recent Arabic BERT model (AraBERT) (Antoun et al., 2020) was trained on Wikipedia and a large collection of Arabic news articles, with the base configuration of the BERT model. The model showed success for many Arabic NLP downstream tasks. Recently, a Multi-dialect-Arabic-BERT (Talafha et al., 2020) model was released and entailed fine-tuning AraBERT on $10M$ tweets. The model was used to improve dialect identification.

Compared to the available datasets, which are mainly based on news articles, our introduced datasets are based on social media platforms. The datasets include posts written in standard and dialectal Arabic from multiple social media platforms, and labeled with 12 news categories. We publicly released the datasets for the research community.

Unlike most of the previous studies, we empirically show the effectiveness of monolingual BERT in compare to multilingual BERT for Arabic language processing and the importance of having diversely (pre-)trained BERT model for social media post classification task.

## 3 Datasets

In this paper, we used three different datasets. Two of them are written in MSA and contain short social media posts and news headlines, and the third is composed of tweets, many of which are authored in dialectal Arabic.

### 3.1 Arabic Social Media News Dataset (ASND)

To create this dataset, we collected the posts of the official Aljazeera news channel accounts on Twitter, Facebook, and YouTube from February, 2017 to September, 2019. We randomly selected 10k posts that included approximately 6k tweets, 2k Facebook posts, and 2k YouTube video titles. We annotated all the posts using Amazon Mechanical Turk (AMT).[12] We asked the turkers to assign a label to each post from one of twelve predefined categories. These categories include: *(i) art-and-entertainment, (ii) business-and-economy, (iii) crime-war-conflict, (iv) education, (v) environment, (vi) health, (vii) human-rights-press-freedom, (viii) politics, (ix) science-and-technology, (x) spiritual, (xi) sports,* and *(xii) others.* We provided the turkers with an elaborate and detailed description of each category along with example annotations. The provided annotation guideline and examples are publicly available.[13] Each turker was asked to annotated 25 different posts. We imposed three types of checks to ensure high quality annotations. These checks were as follows:

- We provided challenged questions to annotators to ensure their Arabic language proficiency. This entailed asking them 10 different multiple choice questions such as the one shown in *Example* 1. Turkers needed to answer at least 8 out of the 10 questions correctly to qualify.

- We embedded 5 posts, for which we had gold labels, within the 25 assigned to each turker. To accept the work of a turker, (s)he had to match the gold labels of at least 4 out the 5 posts. The gold labeled posts were drawn from a set of 5 thousand news headlines that were part of the SANAD dataset (AlSaleh et al., 2020).

- Each post was assigned to 3 turkers and at least 2 out of the 3 needed to agree on a label. If they did not agree, the annotations for the post were discarded. In doing so, we discarded roughly 1.7k posts. Overall, the inter-annotator agreement, as measure by Fleiss's kappa (Falotico and Quatto, 2015), was 0.69.

---

[12]https://www.mturk.com
[13]https://github.com/shammur/Arabic_news_text_classification_datasets

| Classes | ASND | | | SANAD | | AITD |
|---|---|---|---|---|---|---|
| | Train | Test | Dev | Train | Test | Test |
| art-and-entertainment | 345 | 57 | 29 | – | – | 6247 |
| business-and-economy | 161 | 27 | 14 | 9219 | 1024 | 12270 |
| crime-war-conflict | 889 | 147 | 76 | – | – | – |
| education | 65 | 11 | 5 | – | – | 498 |
| environment | 121 | 20 | 11 | – | – | 5010 |
| health | 157 | 26 | 13 | 9359 | 1040 | 9456 |
| human-rights-press-freedom | 337 | 56 | 28 | – | – | 19477 |
| others | 773 | 127 | 66 | – | – | – |
| politics | 3387 | 559 | 288 | 9352 | 1036 | 9369 |
| science-and-technology | 173 | 28 | 15 | 9353 | 1040 | 4936 |
| spiritual | 77 | 13 | 6 | 2571 | 276 | 29554 |
| sports | 191 | 32 | 16 | 9357 | 1039 | 18875 |
| Total | 6676 | 1103 | 567 | 49211 | 5455 | 115692 |
| # Labels | 12 | | | 6 | | 10 |

Table 1: Distribution of train and test labels for both ASND, SANAD and AITD datasets.

The final distribution of the dataset including the train/test/dev splits are listed in Table 1.

**Example 1** ماذا نسمي والد الأب؟

*What we call the father of the father?*
*Options are:*

   *1.* العم *(The uncle)*        *2.* الوالد *(The father)*

   *3.* الخال *(The maternal-uncle)*       *4.* الجد *(The grandfather)*

As a sanity check, we identified the most discriminating terms in the posts for each category. We compared the vocabularies of the twelve classes using the valence score (Conover et al., 2011; Mubarak and Darwish, 2019; Chowdhury et al., 2020) ($\vartheta$) for every token $x$ as follows:

$$\vartheta(x, L_i) = 2 * \frac{\frac{C(x|L_i)}{T_{L_i}}}{\sum_l^L C(x|L_l)} - 1 \tag{1}$$

where $C(.)$ is the frequency of the token $x$ for a given class $L_i$, and $T_{L_i}$ is the total number of tokens present in the class. The valence value $\vartheta(x)$ ranges between -1 and 1, with values closer to 1 indicating strong positive correlation and values closer to -1 indicating strong negative correlation. Table 2 lists the most frequent unigrams and bigrams with $\vartheta = 1.0$, and they seem to reflect the categories. For example, the tokens with high valence for *human-rights-press-freedom* include *justice* and *detainee*, and those for *art-and-entertainment* include *artist* and *theater*.

## 3.2 Single-Label Arabic News Articles Dataset (SANAD)

The SANAD dataset (AlSaleh et al., 2020) is a large collection of Arabic news articles that has been used for different Arabic NLP tasks. The collected articles were assigned one of seven categories, namely: *(i) culture, (ii) finance, (iii) medical, (iv) politics, (v) religion, (vi) sports,* and *(vii) technology*. As can be seen, the SANAD dataset has fewer categories than ASND dataset. This imposed some limitations on our experiments. Further, we aligned the SANAD categories to ASND categories by mapping *medical* to *health*, *religion* to *spiritual*, *technology* to *science-and-technology*, and *finance* to *business-and-economy*.[14] For our work, we only considered the headlines of the news articles, while maintaining the official train-test split. We used this dataset to: *(i)* validate the performance of the model trained using the news headlines and tested on social media data; and *(ii)* train models on both the SANAD and ASND data. Details of the dataset can be found in Table 1.

---

[14]For the task, we ignored the label culture from SANAD.

### 3.3 Arabic Influencer Twitter Dataset (AITD)

For the third dataset, a domain expert identified a list of 60 Arab influencers on Twitter, who predominantly tweet in specific categories. We performed weak annotation where we labeled all the tweets in an account by the most common tweet category therein. For example, the account "eToroAr" is the official Arabic account of a stocks trading company, and hence its tweets are assumed to belong to the *business-and-economy* category. We used the Twitter APIs to crawl the last 3,200 tweets per account.

To improve annotation, given our best classifier on the SANAD and ASND datasets, we filtered out noisy accounts where the classifier did not find at least 40% of the tweets to belong to one of the categories. As a result, for the final dataset, we retained 36 twitter accounts containing 115,692 Arabic tweets. More details of the dataset can be found in Table 1.

| art-and-entertainment | business-and-economy | crime-war-conflict | education |
| --- | --- | --- | --- |
| مسرحية (a show) | العربية عاجل (AlArabiya Breaking News) | المتحدث العسكري (Military Spokeman) | مقالات معنى (manaa articles) |
| الفنانة (artist) | عاجل https (Breaking News) | باسم الحوثيين (of Huthis) | manaa net |
| مسرح (theater) | alarabiya | الحزام (the belt) | ترجمات معنى (maana translations) |
| على مسرح (on theater) | الأسهم (Stocks) | الحزام الأمني (The security belt) | ترجمات (translations) |
| طارق العلي (Tariq Al Ali) | أوبك (OPEC) | تل أبيب (Tel Aviv) | https معنى (maana https) |
| الارشيف (archive) | كورونا https (Corona) | بطائرات (with airplanes) | الفلسفة (Philosophy) |
| من الارشيف (from the archive) | الربع الأول (First Quarter) | الحوثيون يعلنون (The Huthis annouced) | مقابلات (Interviews) |
| المسلسل (TV series) | أسعار النفط (Oil Prices) | الناطق (the spokmen) | مقابلات معنى (maana Interviews) |
| الفنان القدير (The great artist) | في الربع (In the Quarter) | قطاع غزة (Gaza strip) | مراجعات معنى (maana reviews) |
| سنة العرض (The year of performance) | برميل (Barrel) | قوات الاحتلال (Occupation forces) | مراجعات (reviews) |

| environment | health | human-rights-press-freedom | politics |
| --- | --- | --- | --- |
| ثادق (Thadiq) | أطعمة (Food) | المرصد (The Observartory) | حراك (movement) |
| الاشجار (trees) | القلب (heart) | المرصد السوري (The Syrian Observatory) | الداشر (Al Dasher) |
| وزارة البيئة (Environment ministry) | الصحة ارتفاع (heart elevation) | معتقلي (detainees) | ١ ٥ سبتمبر (05-Sep) |
| ثادق الوطني (Thadiq National) | مصابي (patiants) | السلطات السعودية (Saudi officials) | حراك ١ ٥ (movement 15) |
| منتزه (park) | وزيرة الصحة (Minister of health) | معتقلي الرأي (Opinion detainees) | غانم (Ghanem) |
| الغاف (Al Ghaf) | وخروجهم (with their exit) | التعسفي (arbitrary) | الدب (Bear) |
| عبيثران (Wormwood) | وخروجهم من (with their exit from) | المعتقل (detainnee) | الدب الداشر (The dasher bear) |
| الرعي (grazing) | كوفيد ١٩ (COVID-19) | القسط (justice) | أل سعود (Al Saud) |
| بثادق (in Thadiq) | المستجد كوفيد (novel COVID) | الاعتقال التعسفي (Arbitrary detention) | السناب (Snap) |
| استزراع (Farming) | حالات الشفاء (recovering cases) | تأكد لنا (was confirmed) | |

| science-and-technology | spiritual | sports | others |
| --- | --- | --- | --- |
| تي (T) | صل (PBUH) | الدوري (Championship) | شكراً على (Thanks for) |
| آي تي (IT) | تعالى (Almighty) | الدوري مع (Championship with) | عزيزي (Dear) |
| إم آي (MI) | القديس (Saint) | مع وليد (with Waleed) | صديقنا (Our friend) |
| ريفيو (Review) | قال الله (Allah said) | SBC | نشكرك (We thank you) |
| تكنولوجي (Technology) | بك من (from you with) | وليد (Waleed) | |
| تي تكنولوجي (T Technology) | الشعراوي (Shaarawi) | مع وليد (with Waleed) | تفاعلك (Your reaction) |
| تكنولوجي ريفيو (Technology review) | الله تعالى (Allah Almighty) | انفو جرافيك (Infographic) | :) |
| utm | إله (God) | انفو جرافيك الهلال (Hilal Infographic) | |
| هذا المقال (this article) | لا إله (No God) | كبير آسيا (Largest Asia) | على تفاعلك (for your reaction) |
| سامسونغ (Samsung) | سورة (Chapter) | وليد الفراج (Waleed Al Farraj) | طبعاً (of course) |

Table 2: List of most frequent uni- and bi-grams units per class with $\vartheta = 1.0$.

## 4 Experimental Setup

### 4.1 Experiments

We conducted a large battery of experiments where we trained our models on SANAD or ASND individually or in combination. We used the training/test splits of the datasets. Since there is a mismatch between the number of categories between both sets, when training or testing on *SANAD alone*, we restricted our evaluation to the *six categories*. When training using *ASND alone* or in *combination with SANAD*, we used all *12 categories*.

### 4.2 Models

As stated earlier, we wanted to see the effectiveness of using a transformer model that is trained on a mixture of formal and informal text in comparison to other models that are trained exclusively on formal text. We also compared the transformer models to a baseline that uses an SVM classifier that is trained on character and word n-grams.

### 4.2.1 Support Vector Machines (SVM)

SVM (Platt, 1998) has been shown to work well for a variety of text classification tasks (Lewis, 2001; Mubarak et al., 2020). To train the baseline classifiers, we used a combination of character n-grams and word n-grams. We used a bag-of-model tf-idf weighting. For character n-grams, we varied $n$ between 1 and 8, and we varied $n$ for words between 1 and 5.

### 4.2.2 Pre-trained Bidirectional Encoder Representations from Transformers (BERT) Models

We experimented with three different BERT models as follows:

**Multilingual BERT: mBERT (formal text):**  The model is pre-trained using a masked language modeling (MLM) objective using Wikipedia articles for 104 languages including Arabic. We used the case sensitive base model (Devlin et al., 2018).

**Arabic BERT: AraBERT (formal text):**  This model is pre-trained on a collection of publicly available corpora including Arabic Wikipedia, the $1.5B$ words Arabic Corpus (El-Khair, 2016), the OSIAN Corpus (Zeroual et al., 2019), Assafir news articles, and 4 other manually crawled news websites (Al-Akhbar, Annahar, AL-Ahram, AL-Wafd) from the Wayback Machine. The final model is trained on approximately 70M sentences containing roughly 3B Arabic tokens (Antoun et al., 2020).

**Arabic BERT: QARiB (mixed style text):**  This model is trained on the Arabic GigaWord corpus,[15] Abulkhair Arabic Corpus (El-Khair, 2016) , and OpenSubtitles (Lison and Tiedemann, 2016) in addition to 50 million tweets that were collected by issuing the query "lang:ar" against Twitter API. The final training corpus contains 120M sentences and tweets composed of 2.7B Arabic words.

**Downstream Task Design:**  For the downstream tasks, we fine-tuned the aforementioned BERT models for our classification task using a learning rate of $2e - 5$ with a batch size of 64 and 3 epochs. For the training, we restricted the maximum input length to 128 tokens, with no extra preprocessing of the data.

## 4.3 Evaluation

To asses the categorization effectiveness we used Macro F1, which is computed by average the F1 of all labels. We also report on precision $n$ with values of $n$ equal to 1, 2, and 3.

## 5 Results and Discussion

Table 3 summarizes the results of the experiments. Whenever SANAD is used alone for training or testing, the results are reported on 6 categories. When testing on SANAD while training on ASND or SANAD+ASND, we used the subset of ASND posts that contain the 6 categories. In all other cases, the training and testing were done on 12 categories. From looking at the results, we can observe the following:

**Mismatch in style leads to lower results.**  Though both SANAD and ASND use formal text, training on one and testing on the other produces significantly lower results compared to training and testing on SANAD alone. We suspect that this due to the difference in style between news headlines and social media posts, where the latter contain platform specific features such as hashtags and mentions. The drop in the effectiveness may indicate the inability of the models to generalize well when the style changes.

**Combining dataset of different styles helps.**  As the results show, training using ASND+SANAD performed on SANAD at par to training on SANAD. Further combining both training sets led to improved results for all models when testing on AITD. The results of training on both and testing on ASND yielded mixed results, where results of using BERT models improved significantly or matched the results of training on ASND alone. This was not the case for SVM, where the results dropped noticeably.

---

[15]https://catalog.ldc.upenn.edu/LDC2011T11

| Test Set | | Training Set | | |
| --- | --- | --- | --- | --- |
| | | SANAD | ASND | ASND+SANAD |
| SANAD | SVM | 93 | 55 | 93 |
| | mBERT | 93 | 55 | 93 |
| | AraBERT | 94 | 60 | 94 |
| | QARiB | 94 | 81 | 94 |
| ASND | SVM | 64 | 71 | 66 |
| | mBERT | 61 | 51 | 70 |
| | AraBERT | 68 | 51 | 72 |
| | QARiB | 67 | 77 | 76 |
| AITD | mBERT | – | 37 | 51 |
| | AraBERT | – | 38 | 54 |
| | QARiB | – | 57 | 60 |

Table 3: Results (Macro-F1) of training using SANAD, ASND, and ASND+SANAD and testing on SANAD, ASND, and AITD. When training or testing alone, only 6 categories are used (grey cells). For all other cases, 12 categories are used (white cells).

**A BERT model trained on a mixture of formal and informal data has much better generalization power compared to BERT models that are trained on formal text only.** This observation is apparent across all experiments where we conducted cross-dataset training and testing and there was a mismatch in style or language variety between them. For example, when training on ASND and testing on SANAD, QARiB results were 21 points better than using AraBERT (F1 of 81 compared to 60). A similar result is observed when training and testing on social media posts. When training on ASND or ASND+SANAD and testing on ASND, QARiB led to significant improvements over mBERT and AraBERT. Results of testing on AITD show the same trend. This indicates the importance of a trained BERT model with mixed style data for effective domain adaptation. To further understand the impact of having pre-existing style/domain knowledge, we analyzed the difference in per class predictions. From the Figure 1, we observe that QARiB performed significantly better for the majority of the classes. Table 4 reports on the precision $n$ when testing on the ASND and AITD datasets. The results show that using QARiB was far more likely, compared to AraBERT, to rank the proper category at the top. For example, when training and testing on ASND, P@2 was 90% when using QARiB compare to 69% when using AraBERT. The same was consistent regardless of which dataset is used for training (e.g., ASND+SANAD) or testing (e.g., ASND or AITD). This further reflects the efficacy of pre-training BERT on mixed data.

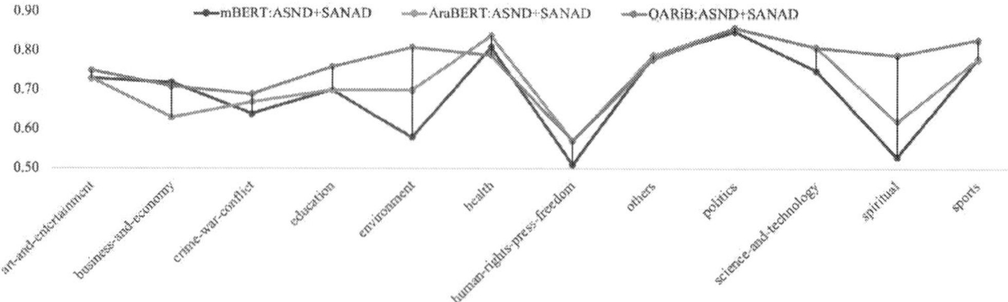


Figure 1: Class-wise F-measure performance on ASND test set using mBERT:ASND+SANAD, AraBERT:ASND+SANAD and QARiB:ASND+SANAD models.

**Discussion**

For error analysis we studied the confusion between categories by our best model, namely the QARiB:ASND+SANAD model. For the ASND test set, we noticed that the *politics* category is frequently confused with *crime-war-conflict* (28%) and *human-rights-press-freedom* (20%) – see Figure

|          |         | Training Sets | | | | | |
| Test Sets | Models | ASND | | | ASND+SANAD | | |
|          |         | P@1 | P@2 | P@3 | P@1 | P@2 | P@3 |
| --- | --- | --- | --- | --- | --- | --- | --- |
| ASND | mBERT | 62 | 77 | 83 | 73 | 85 | 90 |
| | AraBERT | 56 | 69 | 73 | 72 | 87 | 91 |
| | QARiB | 77 | 90 | 94 | 76 | 90 | 94 |
| AITD | mBERT | 46 | 57 | 73 | 59 | 70 | 77 |
| | AraBERT | 49 | 71 | 85 | 64 | 74 | 79 |
| | QARiB | 68 | 77 | 83 | 69 | 79 | 86 |

Table 4: Precision $n$ for models trained on ASND and ASND+SANAD and tested on ASND and AITD

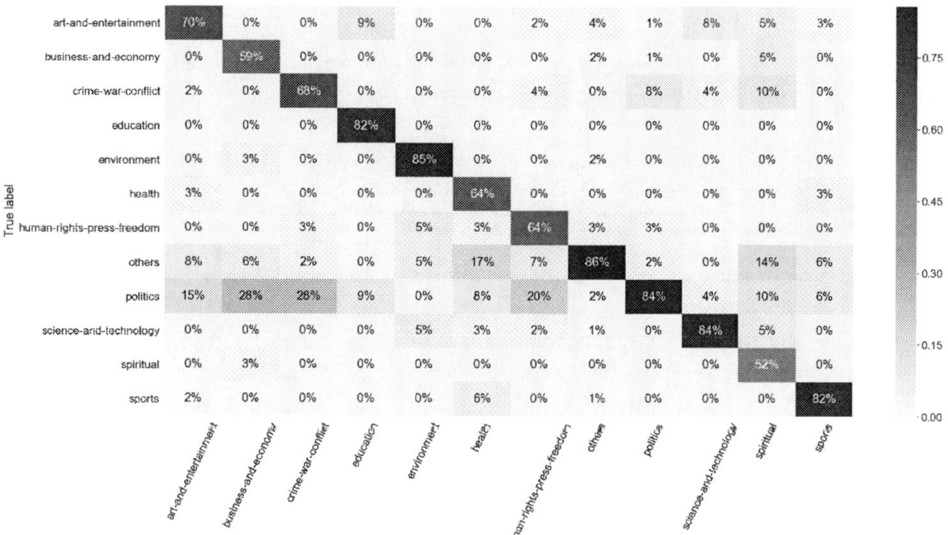

Figure 2: Confusion Matrix for the model QARiB:ASND+SANAD when tested on ASND test set.

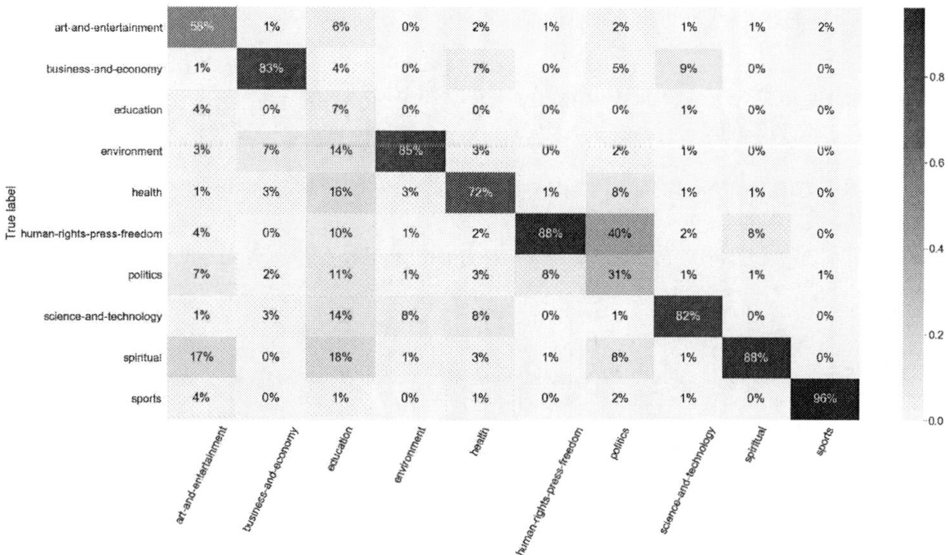

Figure 3: Confusion Matrix for the model QARiB:ASND+SANAD when tested on AITD test set. For AITD , we only considered 10 labels for our evaluation.

2. We observed a similar pattern when testing on AITD, where approximately 40% of *human-rights-press-freedom* tweets were misclassified as *politics* (see Figure 3). Further on AITD, approximately 14% and 8% of *science-and-technology* tweets were misclassified as *education* and *health* respectively. This reflects the contextual closeness of these categories and it might be beneficial to design a hierarchical ontology for such news categorization.

The key observation in this work is that diversifying the training set to cover different genres is important in improving the predictive power of models. Diversification can happen in two ways. One way is to diversify the training data for the specific task. For example, using models trained on SANAD, they were effective on the SANAD test set but yielded sub-optimal results on social media posts, though the posts were written in MSA. Training with both SANAD and ASND together significantly improved results. The second way is to diversify the training data for the pre-trained models such as BERT. As the results show, QARiB, which is trained on both formal text (news) and informal text (tweets) performed at par with AraBERT on the SANAD news headline dataset and significantly outperformed AraBERT on ASND and AITD. As evident by results on ASND, using mixed training data for BERT not only captures linguistic features (MSA vs. dialects) but also capture peculiarities of different platforms such as Twitter.

## 6 Conclusion

In this paper, we investigated the effect of pre-training a BERT model on a mixture of formal and informal text on text categorization compared to BERT models that were trained exclusively on formal text. We show that the former has greater generalization power, compared to the latter, and is able to significantly classify texts from different sources, such as news headlines and social media posts, and different varieties of Arabic, namely MSA and dialectal Arabic. We also introduced two new Arabic multi-class short text datasets. The first contains social media posts from the official Twitter, Facebook, and YouTube accounts for Aljazeera news channel. Though they are social media posts, they are written in MSA. The second dataset contains tweets from popular Twitter accounts, with large portion of their tweets being authored in dialectal Arabic. The key observation in our work is that diversifying the training data, whether by using diverse training data for a specific task or using diverse data to pre-train a BERT model, leads to overall improvements in classification effectiveness.

## References


Mourad Abbas and Kamel Smaili. 2005. Comparison of topic identification methods for arabic language. In *Proceedings of International Conference on Recent Advances in Natural Language Processing, RANLP*, pages 14–17.

Mourad Abbas, Kamel Smaïli, and Daoud Berkani. 2011. Evaluation of topic identification methods on arabic corpora. *J. Digit. Inf. Manag.*, 9(5):185–192.

Muhammad Abdul-Mageed, Hassan Alhuzali, and Mohamed Elaraby. 2018. You tweet what you speak: A city-level dataset of arabic dialects. In *Proceedings of the Eleventh International Conference on Language Resources and Evaluation (LREC 2018)*.

Malak Abdullah and Samira Shaikh. 2018. Teamuncc at semeval-2018 task 1: Emotion detection in english and arabic tweets using deep learning. In *Proceedings of the 12th international workshop on semantic evaluation*, pages 350–357.

Deem AlSaleh, Mashael Bin AlAmir, and Souad Larabi-Marie-Sainte. 2020. Snad arabic dataset for deep learning. In *Proceedings of SAI Intelligent Systems Conference*, pages 630–640. Springer.

Wissam Antoun, Fady Baly, and Hazem Hajj. 2020. Arabert: Transformer-based model for arabic language understanding. In *LREC 2020 Workshop Language Resources and Evaluation Conference 11–16 May 2020*, page 9.

Piotr Bojanowski, Edouard Grave, Armand Joulin, and Tomas Mikolov. 2017. Enriching word vectors with subword information. *Transactions of the Association for Computational Linguistics*, 5:135–146.

Amina Chouigui, Oussama Ben Khiroun, and Bilel Elayeb. 2017. Ant corpus: an arabic news text collection for textual classification. In *2017 IEEE/ACS 14th International Conference on Computer Systems and Applications (AICCSA)*, pages 135–142. IEEE.

Shammur Absar Chowdhury, Hamdy Mubarak, Ahmed Abdelali, Soon-gyo Jung, Bernard J Jansen, and Joni Salminen. 2020. A multi-platform arabic news comment dataset for offensive language detection. In *Proceedings of The 12th Language Resources and Evaluation Conference*, pages 6203–6212.

Michael D Conover, Jacob Ratkiewicz, Matthew Francisco, Bruno Gonçalves, Filippo Menczer, and Alessandro Flammini. 2011. Political polarization on twitter. In *Fifth international AAAI conference on weblogs and social media*.

Jacob Devlin, Ming-Wei Chang, Kenton Lee, and Kristina Toutanova. 2018. Bert: Pre-training of deep bidirectional transformers for language understanding. *arXiv preprint arXiv:1810.04805*.

Ibrahim Abu El-Khair. 2016. 1.5 billion words arabic corpus. *arXiv preprint arXiv:1611.04033*.

Obeida ElJundi, Wissam Antoun, Nour El Droubi, Hazem Hajj, Wassim El-Hajj, and Khaled Shaban. 2019. hulmona: The universal language model in arabic. In *Proceedings of the Fourth Arabic Natural Language Processing Workshop*, pages 68–77.

Ashraf Elnagar, Ridhwan Al-Debsi, and Omar Einea. 2020. Arabic text classification using deep learning models. *Information Processing & Management*, 57(1):102121.

Alexander Erdmann, Nasser Zalmout, and Nizar Habash. 2018. Addressing noise in multidialectal word embeddings. In *Proceedings of the 56th Annual Meeting of the Association for Computational Linguistics (Volume 2: Short Papers)*, pages 558–565.

Rosa Falotico and Piero Quatto. 2015. Fleiss' kappa statistic without paradoxes. *Quality & Quantity*, 49(2):463–470.

Ibrahim Abu Farha and Walid Magdy. 2019. Mazajak: An online arabic sentiment analyser. In *Proceedings of the Fourth Arabic Natural Language Processing Workshop*, pages 192–198.

Sabit Hassan, Younes Samih, Hamdy Mubarak, Ahmed Abdelali, Ammar Rashed, and Shammur Absar Chowdhury. 2020. Alt submission for osact shared task on offensive language detection. In *Proceedings of the 4th Workshop on Open-Source Arabic Corpora and Processing Tools, with a Shared Task on Offensive Language Detection*, pages 61–65.

Jeremy Howard and Sebastian Ruder. 2018. Universal language model fine-tuning for text classification. *arXiv preprint arXiv:1801.06146*.

Yaser Keneshloo, Shuguang Wang, Eui-Hong Han, and Naren Ramakrishnan. 2016. Predicting the popularity of news articles. In *Proceedings of the 2016 SIAM International Conference on Data Mining*, pages 441–449. SIAM.

Zhenzhong Lan, Mingda Chen, Sebastian Goodman, Kevin Gimpel, Piyush Sharma, and Radu Soricut. 2019. Albert: A lite bert for self-supervised learning of language representations. *arXiv preprint arXiv:1909.11942*.

David D Lewis. 2001. Applying support vector machines to the trec-2001 batch filtering and routing tasks. In *TREC*.

Pierre Lison and Jörg Tiedemann. 2016. Opensubtitles2016: Extracting large parallel corpora from movie and tv subtitles. In *Proceedings of the Tenth International Conference on Language Resources and Evaluation (LREC 2016)*, Paris, France, may. European Language Resources Association (ELRA).

Yinhan Liu, Myle Ott, Naman Goyal, Jingfei Du, Mandar Joshi, Danqi Chen, Omer Levy, Mike Lewis, Luke Zettlemoyer, and Veselin Stoyanov. 2019. Roberta: A robustly optimized bert pretraining approach. *arXiv preprint arXiv:1907.11692*.

Tomas Mikolov, Ilya Sutskever, Kai Chen, Greg S Corrado, and Jeff Dean. 2013. Distributed representations of words and phrases and their compositionality. In *Advances in neural information processing systems*, pages 3111–3119.

Tomas Mikolov, Edouard Grave, Piotr Bojanowski, Christian Puhrsch, and Armand Joulin. 2017. Advances in pre-training distributed word representations. *arXiv preprint arXiv:1712.09405*.

Saif M Mohammad, Svetlana Kiritchenko, and Xiaodan Zhu. 2013. Nrc-canada: Building the state-of-the-art in sentiment analysis of tweets. *arXiv preprint arXiv:1308.6242*.

Saif Mohammad, Svetlana Kiritchenko, Parinaz Sobhani, Xiaodan Zhu, and Colin Cherry. 2016. SemEval-2016 task 6: Detecting stance in tweets. In *Proceedings of the 10th International Workshop on Semantic Evaluation*, SemEval '16, pages 31–41, San Diego, California.

Hamdy Mubarak and Kareem Darwish. 2019. Arabic offensive language classification on twitter. In *International Conference on Social Informatics*, pages 269–276. Springer.

Hamdy Mubarak, Ammar Rashed, Kareem Darwish, Younes Samih, and Ahmed Abdelali. 2020. Arabic offensive language on twitter: Analysis and experiments. *arXiv preprint arXiv:2004.02192*.

Jeffrey Pennington, Richard Socher, and Christopher D Manning. 2014. Glove: Global vectors for word representation. In *Proceedings of the 2014 conference on empirical methods in natural language processing (EMNLP)*, pages 1532–1543.

Matthew E Peters, Mark Neumann, Mohit Iyyer, Matt Gardner, Christopher Clark, Kenton Lee, and Luke Zettlemoyer. 2018. Deep contextualized word representations. *arXiv preprint arXiv:1802.05365*.

John Platt. 1998. Sequential minimal optimization: A fast algorithm for training support vector machines.

Marco Polignano, Pierpaolo Basile, Marco de Gemmis, Giovanni Semeraro, and Valerio Basile. 2019. Alberto: Italian bert language understanding model for nlp challenging tasks based on tweets. In *CLiC-it*.

Abu Bakr Soliman, Kareem Eissa, and Samhaa R El-Beltagy. 2017. Aravec: A set of arabic word embedding models for use in arabic nlp. *Procedia Computer Science*, 117:256–265.

Bashar Talafha, Mohammad Ali, Muhy Eddin Za'ter, Haitham Seelawi, Ibraheem Tuffaha, Mostafa Samir, Wael Farhan, and Hussein T Al-Natsheh. 2020. Multi-dialect arabic bert for country-level dialect identification. *arXiv preprint arXiv:2007.05612*.

Joseph Turian, Lev Ratinov, and Yoshua Bengio. 2010. Word representations: a simple and general method for semi-supervised learning. In *Proceedings of the 48th annual meeting of the association for computational linguistics*, pages 384–394.

Zhilin Yang, Zihang Dai, Yiming Yang, Jaime Carbonell, Russ R Salakhutdinov, and Quoc V Le. 2019. Xlnet: Generalized autoregressive pretraining for language understanding. In *Advances in neural information processing systems*, pages 5753–5763.

Imad Zeroual, Dirk Goldhahn, Thomas Eckart, and Abdelhak Lakhouaja. 2019. Osian: Open source international arabic news corpus-preparation and integration into the clarin-infrastructure. In *Proceedings of the Fourth Arabic Natural Language Processing Workshop*, pages 175–182.

# Team Alexa at NADI Shared Task


**Mutaz Bni Younes**    **Nour Al-Khdour**    **Mohammad AL-Smadi**
mmbniyounes18 , naalkhdour17@cit.just.edu.jo    maalsmadi9@just.edu.jo

Department of Computer Science
Jordan University of Science and Technology
Irbid, Jordan


## Abstract


In this paper, we discuss our team's work on the NADI Shared Task. The task requires classifying Arabic tweets among 21 dialects. We tested out different approaches, and the best one was the simplest one. Our best submission was using Multinational Naive Bayes classifier with n-grams as features. Our best submitted score on the test phase was 17% F1-score and 35% accuracy. However, in the post-evaluation phase we used an ensemble model including BERT and Multinational Naive Bayes classifier and it outperformed the top submission on the task, this ensemble model achieved 27.73% F1-score and 40.90% accuracy.


## 1 Introduction

The interest of the research community concerning the Arabic natural language processing (NLP) currently is focused on dialect identification at several levels, region level, country level, and provinces. Most previous works focused on Modern Standard Arabic (MSA) (Elfardy and Diab, 2013) (Al-Sabbagh and Girju, 2012) because it is commonly used in formal writing between Arab countries. Many previous work on Arabic dialect classification used a combination of n-gram both on word and char level with Multinomial Naive Bayes such as (Salameh et al., 2018; Meftouh et al., 2019; Talafha et al., 2019). Eldesouki et al. (2016) successfully applied SVM. Zhang and Abdul-Mageed (2019) proposed a semi-supervised model with BERT and obtained the top rank for MADAR Twitter User Dialect Identification subtask in the MADAR Shared task (Bouamor et al., 2019). MADAR corpus was the first large-scale resource built for Arabic dialects (Bouamor et al., 2018).

The Nuanced Arabic Dialect Identification (NADI) (Abdul-Mageed et al., 2020) provided a labeled dataset consisting of Arabic tweets with two subtasks: the first subtask is based on country-level dialect identification and the second subtask is province-level dialect identification. The dataset was challenging and the same dataset was used for both subtasks, even the algorithms that achieved high results in similar tasks did not gain satisfying results. In this paper, we focused on the first subtask. Alexa model was built using a weighted ensemble model with n-grams features in the word and character levels. The ensemble model consists of the OneVsRest classifier with MNB, MNB, and Logistic Regression. Our model obtained a 17% F1-score and 35% accuracy; it ranks twelve based on F1 out of 18 participants.

The remainder of the paper is organized as follows: data analysis will be shown in section 2. Section 3 proposes a description of the Alexa model. The results for subtask 1 are discussed in Sections 4, and 5 respectively, followed by the conclusion in Section 6.

## 2 Data

The NADI shared task contains two subtasks; both use the same training and development data but differ in labels. The number of training, development, and testing datasets are shown in Table 1.






*Proceedings of the Fifth Arabic Natural Language Processing Workshop*, pages 237–242
Barcelona, Spain (Online), December 12, 2020

The first subtask contains country-level dialects as labels, where the second subtask contains province-level dialects as labels. The dataset has a total of 100 provinces, all of them are from 21 Arab countries.

The dataset is collected from tweets in different domains. It is highly imbalanced data; the number of classes for each country is shown in Table 2.

Table 2: Label Distribution

| Country | Number | Country | Number |
|---|---|---|---|
| Bahrain | 210 | Yemen | 851 |
| Djibouti | 210 | Syria | 1,070 |
| Sudan | 210 | Morocco | 1,070 |
| Mauritania | 210 | United_Arab_Emirates | 1,070 |
| Somalia | 210 | Libya | 1,070 |
| Qatar | 234 | Oman | 1,098 |
| Kuwait | 420 | Algeria | 1,491 |
| Palestine | 420 | Saudi_Arabia | 2,312 |
| Jordan | 426 | Iraq | 2,556 |
| Lebanon | 639 | Egypt | 4,473 |
| Tunisia | 750 | – | – |

## 2.1 Pre-processing

We experimented with different pre-processing settings, such as removing the links, @username, additional white spaces, punctuations, English alphabets, emojis, diacritics, repeated characters, and the non-Arabic tweets that use Arabic alphabets such as Pashto, Urdu, and Persian. However, preprocessing the data had a negative effect contrary to the expected; the results decreased, so we concluded that training the classifiers without preprocessing would be more effective.

## 2.2 Unlabeled Tweets

The organizers included 10 million unlabeled tweets. Some previous work used such data to generate more training samples. In Zhang and Abdul-Mageed (2019), the authors used self-learning method to augment the training dataset. This method increased their baseline's accuracy by 3% and their F1-score by 6%. However, we did not use this dataset since all our experiments exploiting it did not yield any improvements.

## 3 System

In this section, we propose our system (Alexa model) that consists of multiple steps. In feature extraction level, we extract features from the tweets such as language models (n-grams) (Brown et al., 1992) that assigns probabilities to a specific number of sequences of words or characters. There are many experiments done by combining different sets of language models on word level and character level (Talafha et al., 2019) and (Meftouh et al., 2019). On the word level, unigrams and bigrams (1,2) were the best, and on character level we end up with n_grams range from 1 to 5 character with two types of tfidf vectorizers as shown in the Figure 1 "char" and "char_wb." "char_wb" characters with the word boundaries. The features were weighted as follows: word-level unigram and bigram features weighted as 0.8, character-level Tfidf Vectorizer "char_wb" weighted as 1.1 and Tfidf Vectorizer "char" weighted as 1.0.

Then, the extracted features were concatenated to train the ensemble model; the ensemble model is composed of One Vs Rest strategy with MNB (Small and Hsiao, 1985), MNB, and Logistic regression (Kleinbaum et al., 2002). The prediction form the three classifiers are summed to produce the one label for each tweet. The parameters used to train each classifier:

1. One Vs Rest strategy with MNB parameters: alpha equal 0.05 and the default values for the rest parameters.

2. MNB parameters: alpha equal 0.02 and the default values for the rest parameters.

3. Logistic regression parameters: multi_class='ovr', and the default values for the rest parameters. When the assigned parameter in multi_class is 'ovr', then the algorithm uses one-vs-rest (OvR) scheme.

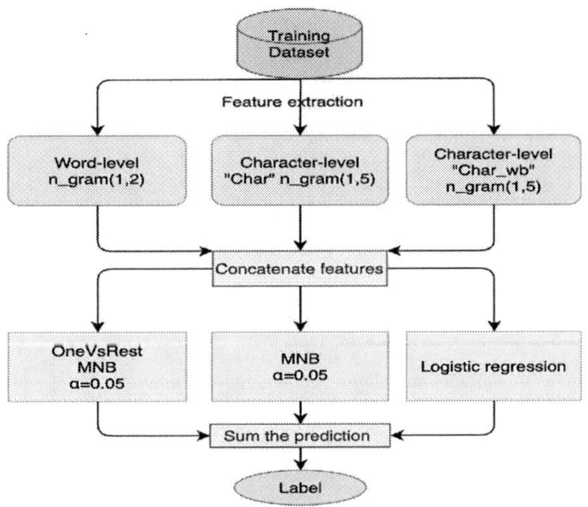


Figure 1: Alexa model architecture

## 4 Results

It is worth mentioning that using different pre-trained embedding models with this dataset did not perform well. We used BERT (Devlin et al., 2018) multilingual model and Aravec model (Soliman et al., 2017) to generate embeddings for the dataset. Both of them achieved low results when using them as main features or as extra features. On the other hand, using these models for training outperformed the best submission on the task. We will talk about the model and the results in the post-evaluation section.

### 4.1 Post-Evaluation

We tested out different ideas in the post-evaluation phase. We concatenated similar dialects into one label and used it to get extra features for the data we have. We ended up with four main dialects. "GULF", AFRICA", "LEVANT", and "MAGRIB". Stacking the probability of each dialect with the n-grams features did not boost the results by noticeable differences.

Another approach we tested is adding hand-written rules, adding a few rules boosted the F1-score by 2%. For example, we increase the probability of a tweet to be labeled as "Jordan" if we see the word "jordan" in it. However, some rules could lead to miss classifying some tweets.

### 4.1.1 Ensemble model

Figure 2 shows our ensemble model that concatenates weighted predicted probabilities from bert-large-arabic model (Safaya et al., 2020) and MNB classifier. BERT-large-arabic model is one of ArabicBERT models, ArabicBERT released on four different sizes (Large, Base, Medium, and Mini), as well it was trained on nearly 95 GB of Arabic text from Open Super-large Crawled and Wikipedia. Furthermore, training data was in Modern Standard Arabic and dialectical Arabic, in our opinion, this is the main reason to enhance the performance of dialect classification, as for this task because it produces a meaningful embedding representation.

The predicted probabilities were multiplied by weights in order to get the highest F1-score possible for the development dataset, the final weights were determined for both classifiers based on multiple experiments as follows: 0.35 for MNB probabilities and 1.4 for BERT probabilities. This model outperformed the best submission on the task. It achieved 27.73% F1-score and 40.90% accuracy. The parameters used to train each classifier:

1. One Vs Rest strategy with MNB parameters: alpha equal 0.01 and the default values for the rest of the parameters. The features were weighted as follows: word-level unigram and bigram features weighted as 0.8, character-level Tfidf Vectorizer "char_wb" weighted as 1.1 and Tfidf Vectorizer "char" weighted as 1.0.

2. BERT-large-arabic parameters: num_train_epochs equal 2, learning_rate equal 2e-5, and the default values for the rest of the parameters.

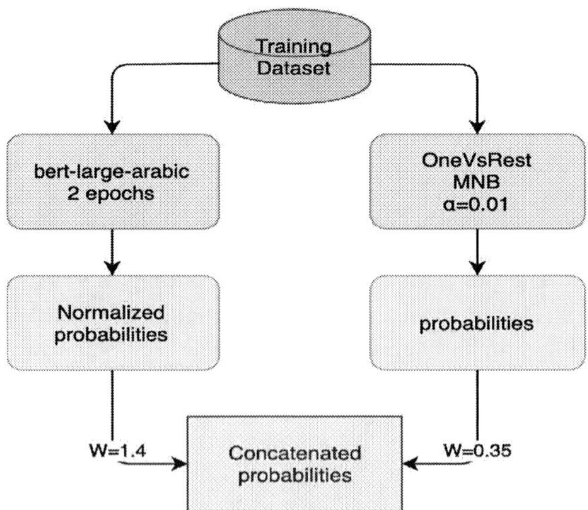


Figure 2: The ensemble model architecture

## 5   Discussion

The provided dataset did not include Modern Standard Arabic (MSA) label in the training and development dataset, see Figure 3 which contains wrongly classified tweets, the tweets in Figure 3 are written in MSA.

| Tweet | Label |
|---|---|
| اللهم طهر قلبي من النفاق ، وعملي من الرياء ، ولساني من الكذب ، وعيني من الخيانة<br>May Allah clean my heart and my work from hypocrisy, and my tongue from lying, and my eyes from betrayal | Egypt |
| انا لله و انا اليه راجعون الله يرحمه و يصبر ذويه<br>We belong to Allah and will return to him, may Allah have mercy on him and help his parents to be patient about their lost. | Morocco |
| ولن يخلف الله وعده<br>God will never renege his promise | Egypt |

Figure 3: examples of wrongly classified tweets

Our team investigated this problem; we used a model that was trained on detecting MSA text to extract the wrongly labeled tweets in our dataset. To train this model, we used MADAR corpus (Bouamor et al., 2018) because it contains MSA tweets and other dialects. Our used model achieves an accuracy score higher than the top submitted score on the MADAR Shared task. Such that, we assume that this model can accurately classify MSA tweets. We also used different Arabic datasets to see if our claim is true or not and we got similar results. Based on our system, more than 20% of the training and development tweets were MSA tweets. Table 3 shows our numbers.

Table 3: Number of MSA Tweets in Each Set

|  | Train | Dev | Test |
|---|---|---|---|
| Total | 21,000 | 4,957 | 5,000 |
| Estimated MSA | 4,930 | 1,074 | 1,074 |

To test our findings, we re-labeled MSA tweets to "MSA" and then applied multinomial naive bayes classifier on the development dataset, the results were as shown on table 4.

Table 4: Results after adding the MSA label

|  | F1-score | Accuracy |
|---|---|---|
| With MSA | 14.9 | 43.837 |
| Without MSA | 14.9 | 35.203 |

In Table 4, we noticed that the F1-score decreased when re-labeling the dataset, this because some tweets are written mostly in MSA but may contain some dialect words, so without having the MSA label, these tweets will be classified correctly to their labeled (provided label) class. But when adding the MSA label, such tweets will be classified as MSA tweets, which decreases the overall F1-score for many classes and increases it for the MSA class.

## 6 Conclusion

In this paper, we tested different approaches in an Arabic dialect classification task, NADI shared task. The best submitted score on the test phase was using an ensemble model that contains Multinational naive Bayes, OneVsRest MNB, and logistic regression. For features, we used both CountVectorizer and TfidfVectorizer features. Our best submission achieved 17% F1-score. However, in the post-evaluation phase, we used an ensemble model which outperformed the best submitted score on the task. Our ensemble model contained weighted concatenation between BERT's probabilities and MNB probabilities. This model achieved 27.73% F1-score and 40.90% accuracy. We also noticed that many tweets were wrongly labeled because there were tweets written in MSA, and there was no MSA label. Also, there are six countries with less than 240 tweets; this leads the model to never predict these dialects. For future work, we would like to overcome these issues by finding a way to deal with the imbalanced dataset and a way to overcome the MSA problem.

## References

Muhammad Abdul-Mageed, Chiyu Zhang, Houda Bouamor, and Nizar Habash. 2020. NADI 2020: The First Nuanced Arabic Dialect Identification Shared Task. In *Proceedings of the Fifth Arabic Natural Language Processing Workshop (WANLP 2020)*, Barcelona, Spain.

Rania Al-Sabbagh and Roxana Girju. 2012. Yadac: Yet another dialectal arabic corpus. In *LREC*, pages 2882–2889.

Houda Bouamor, Nizar Habash, Mohammad Salameh, Wajdi Zaghouani, Owen Rambow, Dana Abdulrahim, Ossama Obeid, Salam Khalifa, Fadhl Eryani, Alexander Erdmann, and Kemal Oflazer. 2018. The MADAR Arabic dialect corpus and lexicon. In *Proceedings of the Eleventh International Conference on Language Resources and Evaluation (LREC 2018)*, Miyazaki, Japan, May. European Language Resources Association (ELRA).

Houda Bouamor, Sabit Hassan, and Nizar Habash. 2019. The MADAR Shared Task on Arabic Fine-Grained Dialect Identification. In *Proceedings of the Fourth Arabic Natural Language Processing Workshop (WANLP19)*, Florence, Italy.

Peter F Brown, Vincent J Della Pietra, Peter V Desouza, Jennifer C Lai, and Robert L Mercer. 1992. Class-based n-gram models of natural language. *Computational linguistics*, 18(4):467–480.

Jacob Devlin, Ming-Wei Chang, Kenton Lee, and Kristina Toutanova. 2018. Bert: Pre-training of deep bidirectional transformers for language understanding. *arXiv preprint arXiv:1810.04805*.

Mohamed Eldesouki, Fahim Dalvi, Hassan Sajjad, and Kareem Darwish. 2016. Qcri@ dsl 2016: Spoken arabic dialect identification using textual features. In *Proceedings of the Third Workshop on NLP for Similar Languages, Varieties and Dialects (VarDial3)*, pages 221–226.

Heba Elfardy and Mona Diab. 2013. Sentence level dialect identification in arabic. In *Proceedings of the 51st Annual Meeting of the Association for Computational Linguistics (Volume 2: Short Papers)*, pages 456–461.

David G Kleinbaum, K Dietz, M Gail, Mitchel Klein, and Mitchell Klein. 2002. *Logistic regression.* Springer.

Karima Meftouh, Karima Abidi, Salima Harrat, and Kamel Smaili. 2019. The smart classifier for arabic fine-grained dialect identification.

Ali Safaya, Moutasem Abdullatif, and Deniz Yuret. 2020. Kuisail at semeval-2020 task 12: Bert-cnn for offensive speech identification in social media.

Mohammad Salameh, Houda Bouamor, and Nizar Habash. 2018. Fine-grained arabic dialect identification. In *Proceedings of the 27th International Conference on Computational Linguistics*, pages 1332–1344.

Kenneth A Small and Cheng Hsiao. 1985. Multinomial logit specification tests. *International economic review*, pages 619–627.

Abu Bakr Soliman, Kareem Eissa, and Samhaa R El-Beltagy. 2017. Aravec: A set of arabic word embedding models for use in arabic nlp. *Procedia Computer Science*, 117:256–265.

Bashar Talafha, Ali Fadel, Mahmoud Al-Ayyoub, Yaser Jararweh, AL-Smadi Mohammad, and Patrick Juola. 2019. Team just at the madar shared task on arabic fine-grained dialect identification. In *Proceedings of the Fourth Arabic Natural Language Processing Workshop*, pages 285–289.

Chiyu Zhang and Muhammad Abdul-Mageed. 2019. No army, no navy: Bert semi-supervised learning of arabic dialects. In *Proceedings of the Fourth Arabic Natural Language Processing Workshop*, pages 279–284.

# Voting Classifier vs Deep learning method in Arabic Dialect Identification


**Dhaou Ghoul**
STIH Lab, Sorbonne University
dhaou.ghoul@sorbonne-universite.fr

**Gael Lejeune**
STIH Lab, Sorbonne University
gael.lejeune@sorbonne-universite.fr


## Abstract


In this paper, we present three methods developed by the SORBONNE Team for the NADI shared task on Arabic Dialect Identification for tweets. The first and the second method use respectively a machine learning model based on a Voting Classifier with words and character level features and a deep learning model at the word level. The third method uses only character-level features. We explored different text representation such as TF-IDF (first model) and word embeddings (second model). The Voting Classifier was the most powerful prediction model, achieving the best macro-average F1 score of 18.8% and an accuracy of 36.54% on the official test. Our model ranked 9 on the challenge and in conclusion we propose some ideas to improve its results.


## 1 Introduction

The Arabic language is one of the most widely spoken language in the world, currently considered as the fifth language (Chung, 2008) with more than 330 million Arabic speakers. It is the official language of more than 22 countries. In its written form, commonly referred as Literary Arabic, it usually is divided into two categories: Classical Arabic and Modern Standard Arabic (MSA). However, in their daily life Arabic speakers mostly use dialects which are a linguistic variant of classical Arabic with their own features, varying with respect to the country or the region. One can say that MSA is only used for written and official communication while dialects are used for oral communication as well as for many device mediated communication forms: email, SMS, chat or blogs. Therefore, Arabic dialect identification (DID) has become a very important data preparation step that attracts many attention in NLP research. Indeed, the knowledge about the dialect of an input text is useful in several NLP tasks such as sentiment analysis (Al-Twairesh et al., 2016), machine translation or document classification. This paper describes our submission to the NADI shared task on Arabic fine-grained dialect identification cover a total of 100 provinces from all 21 Arab countries (Abdul-Mageed et al., 2020). Two subtasks were proposed:

- **Subtask 1:** Country-level dialect identification: 21,000 tweets covering 21 Arab countries.

- **Subtask 2:** Province-level dialect identification: the same tweets but with province label.

Our submission is dealing with the first subtask. In Section 2, we describe the dataset and in Section 3 we present our three methods. In Section 4, we detail our results and give future directions in Section 5.

## 2 Dataset

Arabic has a widely varying collection of dialects. Many of these dialects remain understudied due to rarity of resources. The dataset used in this work is made up of a collection of tweets shared by users in different Arab countries. This dataset is collected from 21 countries which are Algeria, Bahrain, Djibouti, Egypt, Iraq, Jordan, Kuwait, Lebanon, Libya, Mauritania, Morocco, Oman, Palestine, Qatar, Saudi-Arabia, Somalia, Sudan, Syria, Tunisia, United-Arab-Emirates, Yemen. The dataset for the shared task contains 25,957 tweets divided in training, development and test set as shown in Table 1.

The distribution of tweets among countries is very unbalanced. The Egyptian dialect is best represented in te dataset as shown in Figure 1. Around 21% (5543 tweets) of the tweets belong to Egypt while only 0.8% belong to Bahrain (218 tweets) and Djibouti (220 tweets).






*Proceedings of the Fifth Arabic Natural Language Processing Workshop*, pages 243–249
Barcelona, Spain (Online), December 12, 2020

| Datasets | Train | Dev | Test |
| --- | --- | --- | --- |
| # lines | 21,000 | 4,957 | 5,000 |
| # words | 269,644 | 60,467 | 64,211 |
| # characters | 2,798,691 | 633,134 | 667,597 |

Table 1: Size of the Train, Dev and Test sets

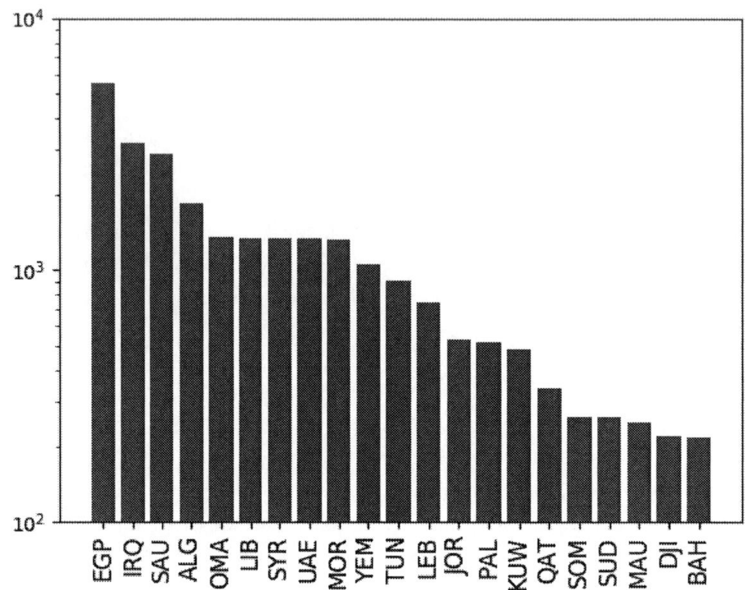


Figure 1: The distribution of the 21 Arabic dialects in NADI Twitter dataset (logarithmic scale)

## 3   Data Preparation and Classification Methods

### 3.1   Pre-processing

It is intended to help the classifiers to generalize and to remove potential biases. Our pre-processing is limited to a few steps of cleaning up, applied to each tweet. After several tests, we have kept this cleaning process in the following order: removing punctuation signs, digits, non Arabic words, repeated characters and finally emoticons.

Often, pre-processing also involves removing Arabic stop-words, diacritics and normalizing (Ayedh et al., 2016). It is known that for language identification tasks stop-words are very useful (McNamee, 2005) but we also noticed that removing diacritics and normalizing text reduces the identification as well.

### 3.2   Models

#### 3.2.1   Run1: Voting Classifier

Our first model is based on a traditional machine learning approach. To build and train the model, we use *FeatureUnion* in SCIKIT-LEARN (Pedregosa et al., 2011) which allows to combine easily different n-gram representations at the word level and the character level as shown in Figure 2. To train this model, we concatenate three vectors with the following features (weigthed with TF-IDF): word n-grams (1 to 5-grams), character n-grams (1 to 4-grams) and character n-grams (1 to 5-grams) with word boundaries explicitly marked with a space.

We use a set of classifiers based on a voting technique using the SCIKIT LEARN implementation of *VotingClassifier* in order to build an ensemble voting classifier with hard voting, where it uses predicted

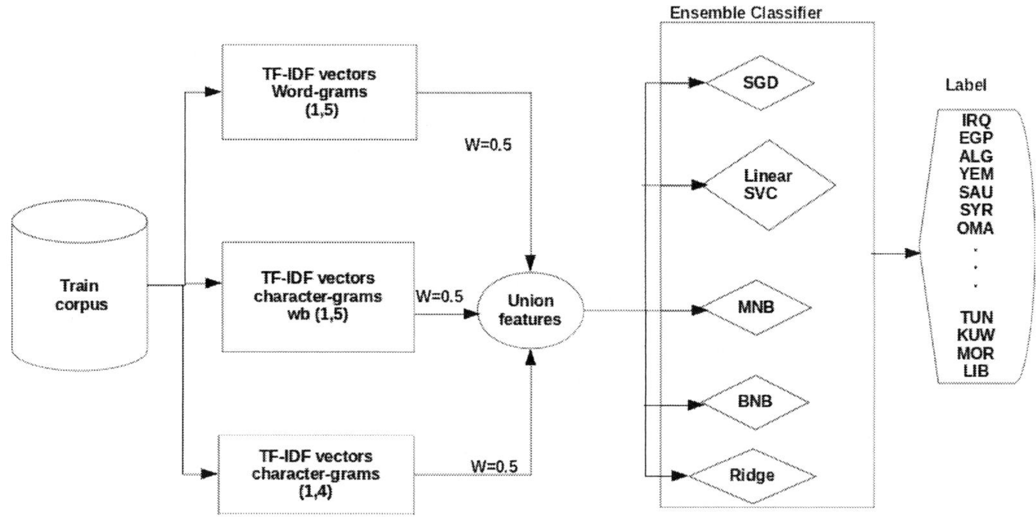


Figure 2: Model of Run1

class labels for majority rule voting. This ensemble is a combination of the following classfiers:

- SGDClassifier with `alpha` = 0.00001 and `penalty` = 'l2'
- LinearSVC with `penalty` = 'l2' and Tolerance for stopping set to 0.001
- Multinomial Naive Bayes with `alpha` = 0.01
- Bernoulli Naive Bayes with `alpha` = 0.01
- Ridge Classifier with `alpha` = 1

The results for the dev and test set with pre-processing are reported in Table 2.

| Trained on | Tested on | Precision | Recall | Accuracy | Macro avg F-score |
|---|---|---|---|---|---|
| Train Set | Dev Set | 22.82 | 17.02 | 36.33 | 17.69 |
| Train Set | Test Set | 22 | 15.9 | 31.9 | 16.06 |
| Train+Dev | Test Set | **24.87** | **18.05** | **36.54** | **18.8** |

Table 2: Results with pre-processing for Run1 with different training configurations

### 3.2.2 Run2: Deep Learning approach

To build the deep learning model for Run2, we used two pre-trained word embedding models:

- **Aravec:** proposed by *Soliman et al*, it is composed of three models trained trained with Word2Vec skip-gram and CBOW (Mikolov et al., 2013) on three datasets in Arabic: tweets, web pages and Wikipedia articles (Soliman et al., 2017). We used the 100-dimensional Twitter N-Grams model.

- **Unlabelled-tweetsVec:** Word2Vec skip-gram (300-dimensions) trained on NADI unlabelled tweets

In addition to this, we added features specific to tweets in the input layer of our neural network. When analyzing the train set, we found that there some features where useful to differentiate the dialects : user mentions and words specific to Twitter data. For instance, people tagging the user @*Mowafaglibya* mostly use Lybian dialect, so here the user mention is decisive. Some words as "شنو"(chnowa), "برشَا" (barcha) to identify the Tunisia dialect. These words are specific for the Tunisian dialect, they respectively mean 'what' and 'many'.

The deep neural network developed for this run is composed as follows: the input layer, an embedding layer, two LSTM layers and two Dense layers. To prevent over-fitting we add a dropout layer after each LSTM layer and the first dense layer. We use two word embeddings representation : AraVec and our own model trained on 10M unlabelled tweets. The final output is passed into one hidden layer and followed by a softmax output layer. To train these two models, we used the "NADI" train corpus with 10 epochs and evaluate it by "NADI" development corpus and. The results are reported in Table 3. We can see that, contrary to Run1, this model suffers from over-fitting when trained on both train and dev set.

| Word Embedding | Trained on | Tested on | Precision | Recall | Macro avg F-score | Accuracy |
|---|---|---|---|---|---|---|
| AraVec | Train Set | Dev Set | 21.99 | **16.24** | **16.68** | **35** |
|  | Train Set | Test Set | **22.54** | 16.13 | 16.18 | 32.56 |
|  | Train+Dev | Test Set | 20.4 | 15.03 | 14.94 | 33.7 |
| Unlabled-tweetsVec | Train Set | Dev Set | 14.92 | 14.26 | 14.2 | 29.03 |
|  | Train Set | Test Set | 13.98 | 14.76 | 13.96 | 27.98 |
|  | Train+Dev | Test Set | 17.22 | 15.28 | 15.06 | 29.94 |

Table 3: Results with pre-processing for Run2

### 3.2.3 Run3: character n-grams

This run uses MICHAEL the method developed for the 2019 MADAR challenge (Ghoul and Lejeune, 2019), this method does not use any pre-processing in order to act as a simple baseline. It is a character n-gram model with various range of n-gram size. The rationale behind this kind of model is to get a simplified representation without having to tackle the problem of tokenization, which is particularly difficult for languages like Arabic. The best configuration for this baseline was a Logistic Regression classifier with character 5-grams as features. For this baseline, the dataset has been used as it is without any pre-processing.

## 4   Results and Discussion

The results obtained by our different models for the test set with and without pre-processing are presented in table 4. In reality, there are similar dialects or with a minor difference. In other words, a short sentence can belong to several dialects because it is constructed with a reduced number of words. That is why, it is also impossible for Arabic speakers to detect the dialect from a very short sentence with 100% accuracy. Before analyzing our results, we wanted to briefly check for annotation errors. We focused on the 750 tweets annotated as Tunisian, divided into four provinces (Sousse: 212 tweets, Mahdia: 212 tweets, Ariana: 212 tweets and Kairaoun: 114 tweets). After this verification, we found out that the 212 tweets labeled as Mahdia are wrongly labelled. The majority of them belong to the Libyan dialect and the rest are Sudan tweets. For instance, this tweet (Train-4235): "تي متزعلش بكل تي نشريلك نيتفليكس" (Don't get angry, do you want me to buy you a netflix) is annotated as Tunisian (region of Mahdia) but is Libyan. Our verification was peformed by consulting the user profile in some cases and from the lexicon used in the tweets in other cases. The last example contains words from the Libyan lexicon like "بكل" and "تي". The imbalances in the dataset obviously makes the task harder. The imbalance ratio, defined as the ratio of the number of instances in the majority class to the number of examples in the minority class (ratio=0.047 and ratio=0.007). The Egyptian dialect is more represented with 5543 tweets (Train+Dev set). On the other hand, the Mauritania, Somalia, Sudan, Bahrain and Djibouti dialects are less represented with 210 tweets and the Qatari dialect with 234 tweets. All this shows that this shared task was very difficult.

There are dialects which are not easy to detect even by an Arabic speakers as they do not contain any clue words, like Mauritania and Djibouti. These tweets are often written in standard Arabic. Figure 3 shows that our models are not able to correctly classify these tweets. Bahrain, Djibouti dialects were the most difficult to detect : we had no True Positive (TP).

| Pre-processing | Features | Trained on | Precision | Recall | Accuracy | Macro avg F-score |
|---|---|---|---|---|---|---|
| With pre-processing | Union-features: TF-IDF | Train set | 22 | 15.9 | 31.9 | 16.06 |
| | Run1 | Train+Dev set | 24.87 | **18.05** | 36.54 | **18.8** |
| | Embedding: AraVec | Train set | 22.54 | 16.13 | 32.56 | 16.18 |
| | Run2 | Train+Dev set | 20.4 | 15.03 | 33.7 | 14.94 |
| Without pre-processing | Union-features: TF-IDF | Train set | 25.10 | 17.22 | 36.02 | 17.49 |
| | Run1 | Train+Dev set | **26.72** | 17.83 | **36.56** | 18.6 |
| | Embedding: AraVec | Train set | 18.78 | 14.69 | 32.6 | 14.89 |
| | Run2 | Train+Dev set | 19.38 | 14.28 | 33.8 | 14.28 |
| | Character 5-Grams | Train set | 19.13 | 14.24 | 32.38 | 14.2 |
| | Run3 | Train+Dev set | 18.56 | 14.81 | 32.7 | 14.59 |

Table 4: Results on the test set, models with and without pre-processing

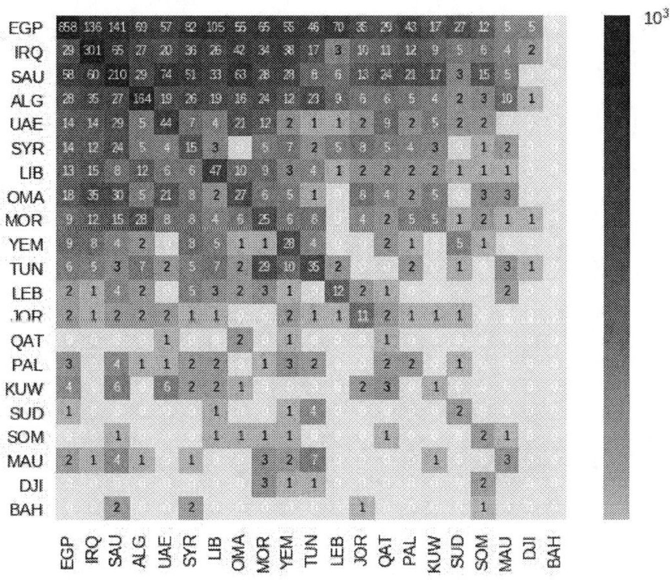

Figure 3: Confusion Matrix for Run1 (Voting Classifier) on the dev set

The confusion matrix in Figure 3 shows the numbers of actual and predicate labels for each dialect. There are some similar pairs of dialects for which the system made a lot of errors : (Iraq, Egypt) and (Saudi-Arabia,Egypt). We can also see on the confusion matrix that 70 tweets from Lebanon were classified as Egyptian. We manually checked the annotation of these 70 tweets: 63 of them are in fact from Egypt and as such are not classification errors. For exemple, "بس مش معَايَا انَا" (But, not with me) is annotated as Lebanon dialect but it is in reality Egypt dialect (after our verification). Our model predict this tweet as an Egypt dialect because it contains words belongs to the Egyptian lexicon. The table 5 presents some examples of tweets from the Train and Dev set and their transliteration. These examples shows the annoataion errors of the Train + Dev set.

For the evaluation purpose, we use the Macro averaged F-score which is retained as the official metric by the organizers of NADI shared task. In all the experiments, the best model is obtained for hard voting classifier with the previously mentioned algorithms (SGDClassifier, Linear SVC, MNB, BNB and RidgeClassifier) with Macro avg F-score of **18.8%** on the test set (line 3 in table 2). From the classification report which is produced from the dev set in Table 6, we find that some dialects were easier to detect than others, for example, the dialects Egypt, Algeria and Iraq with a lower score f respectively 0.58 , 0.41 and 0.46 compared to others such as: Bahrain (0.0), Djibouti (0.0), Kuwait (0.02) and Qatar (0.02).

| Id-tweet | Tweets | Label Before verification | Label After verification |
|---|---|---|---|
| Train-640 | مَاهي السنه فعلًا مفروض تختم بكدَا<br>mAhy Alsnh fElA mfrwD txtm bkdA | Lebanon | Egypt |
| Train-4280 | لولَا طولَي كنت لبسته ع طول<br>lwlA Twly knt lbsth E Twl | Lebanon | Egypt |
| Train-4842 | ليلة عمَانية حمرَاء بَأدن الَله<br>lylp EmAnyp HmrA' b¡*n Allh | Lebanon | Oman |
| Train-11283 | صديقي وزميلي ف الَأبتدَائي مش فَاضي بكل<br>Sdyqy w zmyly f Al¡btdAŷ m$ fADy bkl | Tunisia | Lybia |
| Dev-2672 | بعيد الشر ي ستي<br>bEyd Al$r y sty | Lebanon | Egypt |
| Dev-3290 | هَههههه اعمل ايه انتي الي مش فَاهمه<br>hhhhh AEml Ayh Anty Al y m$ fAhmh | Lebanon | Egypt |
| Dev-4046 | ذَا طلع ف نَاس معندهَاش دم فعلًا<br>dA TlE f nAs mEndhA$ dm fElAF | Lebanon | Egypt |

Table 5: Examples of annotation errors from Train and Dev Set

| | EGP | IRQ | SAU | ALG | UAE | SYR | LIB | OMA | MOR | YEM | TUN | LEB |
|---|---|---|---|---|---|---|---|---|---|---|---|---|
| Precision | 0.45 | 0.43 | 0.28 | 0.36 | 0.34 | 0.24 | 0.12 | 0.17 | 0.14 | 0.35 | 0.29 | 0.29 |
| Recall | 0.80 | 0.49 | 0.36 | 0.46 | 0.19 | 0.16 | 0.05 | 0.10 | 0.10 | 0.15 | 0.21 | 0.11 |
| F1-score | 0.58 | 0.46 | 0.32 | 0.41 | 0.24 | 0.19 | 0.07 | 0.12 | 0.12 | 0.21 | 0.24 | 0.16 |
| Support | 1070 | 636 | 579 | 359 | 265 | 265 | 265 | 249 | 249 | 206 | 164 | 110 |

| | JOR | QAT | PAL | KUW | SUD | SOM | MAU | DJI | BAH | Macro | Micro | Acc. |
|---|---|---|---|---|---|---|---|---|---|---|---|---|
| Precision | 0.35 | 0.14 | 0.08 | 0.03 | 0.22 | 0.29 | 0.12 | 0.00 | 0.00 | 0.22 | 0.31 | |
| Recall | 0.11 | 0.01 | 0.02 | 0.01 | 0.04 | 0.04 | 0.07 | 0.00 | 0.00 | 0.22 | 0.36 | 0.36 |
| F1-score | 0.16 | 0.02 | 0.03 | 0.02 | 0.07 | 0.07 | 0.09 | 0.00 | 0.00 | 0.17 | 0.32 | |
| Support | 104 | 104 | 102 | 70 | 51 | 51 | 40 | 10 | 8 | 4957 | 4957 | |

Table 6: Detailed classification report for the Voting Classifier on the Dev set

Finally, we think that the class imbalance in our data set had a direct influence on the prediction of the less presented class in train data with a TP rate close to zero and FN rate close to 100% as shown in the Figure 3 ("Sudan", "Somalia", "Qatar", etc).

## 5 Conclusion

In this paper, we described our system submitted to NADI shared task on country level dialect identification from Twitter data. We presented three methods for this shared task. Experimental results show that Voting Classifier was the most powerful prediction model, achieving the best macro-average F1 score than other machine learning and deep learning models. Despite the fact that there was a substantial amount of incorrectly annotated tweets in the dataset, we were still able to achieve an F1 score of 17.69% on the development set, 16.06% on the test set and 18.8% on the test set trained on the train and the development set. It would be interesting to correct the errors in training data in order to see the impact on the results. Another perspective would be to evaluate our model with other tokenizers like "MADAMIRA" (Pasha et al., 2014) and to perform a deeper analysis of classification errors.

## References

Muhammad Abdul-Mageed, Chiyu Zhang, Houda Bouamor, and Nizar Habash. 2020. NADI 2020: The First Nuanced Arabic Dialect Identification Shared Task. In *Proceedings of the Fifth Arabic Natural Language Processing Workshop (WANLP 2020)*, Barcelona, Spain.

Nora Al-Twairesh, Hend Al-Khalifa, and Abdulmalik AlSalman. 2016. AraSenTi: Large-scale twitter-specific Arabic sentiment lexicons. In *Proceedings of the 54th Annual Meeting of the Association for Computational Linguistics (Volume 1: Long Papers)*, pages 697–705, Berlin, Germany, August. Association for Computational Linguistics.

Abdullah Ayedh, Guanzheng TAN, Khaled Alwesabi, and Hamdi Rajeh. 2016. The effect of preprocessing on arabic document categorization. *Algorithms*, 9:27, 04.

Wingyan Chung. 2008. Web searching in a multilingual world. *Commun. ACM*, 51(5):32–40, May.

Dhaou Ghoul and Gaël Lejeune. 2019. MICHAEL: Mining character-level patterns for Arabic dialect identification (MADAR challenge). In *Proceedings of the Fourth Arabic Natural Language Processing Workshop*, pages 229–233, Florence, Italy, August. Association for Computational Linguistics.

Paul McNamee. 2005. Language identification: A solved problem suitable for undergraduate instruction. *J. Comput. Sci. Coll.*, 20(3):94–101, February.

Tomas Mikolov, Kai Chen, Greg Corrado, and Jeffrey Dean. 2013. Efficient estimation of word representations in vector space.

Arfath Pasha, Mohamed Al-Badrashiny, Mona Diab, Ahmed El Kholy, Ramy Eskander, Nizar Habash, Manoj Pooleery, Owen Rambow, and Ryan Roth. 2014. MADAMIRA: A fast, comprehensive tool for morphological analysis and disambiguation of Arabic. In *Proceedings of the Ninth International Conference on Language Resources and Evaluation (LREC'14)*, pages 1094–1101, Reykjavik, Iceland, May. European Language Resources Association (ELRA).

F. Pedregosa, G. Varoquaux, A. Gramfort, V. Michel, B. Thirion, O. Grisel, M. Blondel, P. Prettenhofer, R. Weiss, V. Dubourg, J. Vanderplas, A. Passos, D. Cournapeau, M. Brucher, M. Perrot, and E. Duchesnay. 2011. Scikit-learn: Machine learning in Python. *Journal of Machine Learning Research*, 12:2825–2830.

Abu Bakr Soliman, Kareem Eissa, and Samhaa R. El-Beltagy. 2017. Aravec: A set of arabic word embedding models for use in arabic nlp. *Procedia Computer Science*, 117:256 – 265. Arabic Computational Linguistics.

# Simple vs Oversampling-based Classification Methods for Fine Grained Arabic Dialect Identification in Twitter


**Mohamed Lichouri**
Computational Linguistics Department
CRSTDLA, Algiers, Algeria
m.lichouri@crstdla.dz

**Mourad Abbas**
Computational Linguistics Department
CRSTDLA, Algiers, Algeria
m.abbas@crstdla.dz


## Abstract


In this paper, we present a description of our experiments on country-level Arabic dialect identification. A comparison study between a set of classifiers has been carried out. The best results were achieved using the Linear Support Vector Classification (LSVC) model by applying a Random Over Sampling (ROS) process yielding an F1-score of 18.74% in the post-evaluation phase. In the evaluation phase, our best submitted system has achieved an F1-score of 18.27%, very close to the average F1-score (18.80%) obtained for all the submitted systems.


## 1 Introduction

Fine grained Arabic dialect identification is a very challenging topic due, in one hand, to the rarity of dialectal resources, and in the other hand, to the inter-closeness of Arabic dialects spoken by twenty two countries, as well as the intra-closeness of each sub-dialect spoken in many provinces of a country. One of the most recent scientific events dedicated to Arabic fine grained dialect identification was organized in the framework of the fourth workshop for Arabic natural language processing, MADAR'2019 (Bouamor et al., 2019), where a couple of works have been proposed. Indeed, in Abu Kwaik and Saad (2019), the authors proposed a system based on extracting and applying a feature union process on a set of features (TF-IDF word n-grams, TF-IDF character n-grams, TF-IDF character_with_boundary n-grams and TF-IDF skip n-grams) multiplied by a transformation weight. In fact, they applied empirical experiments to find the best values of "n" (n-grams) as well as the transformation weights. Other features have been added, like sentence length ratio for every sentence in the data. To classify these features, the authors used an ensemble hard voting classifier with three ML algorithms (Linear Support Vector Classifier "LSVC", Multinomial Naive Bayes "MNB" and Bernoulli Naive Bayes "BNB"). They obtained a macro F-score of 67.32%. Based on the work done by (Salameh et al., 2018), (Ragab et al., 2019) have suggested an ensemble of 5 classifiers (MNB, SVC, BNB, k-nearest-neighbours "KNN" and a weak dummy classifier based on prior probabilities of each dialect), in addition to 96 language models on word and char-level trained using KenLM (Heafield, 2011) from Moses, with default parameters. This setup has given an F1-score of 66.7%. In a more refined experiment, (Abdul-Mageed et al., 2019) presented a very large scale dataset covering 319 cities from all 21 Arab countries. They also introduced a hierarchical attention multi-task learning (HA-MTL) approach for dialect identification exploiting the data at the city, state, and country levels. They also evaluated the use of BERT on the three tasks, while comparing it to the MTL approach. More recently, (Abdelali et al., 2020) built a new corpus and called it QADI (18 countries). They experimented the AraBert model (Baly et al., 2020) on both QADI and MADAR corpus (25 cities + MSA). The score they achieved was 60.6% and 29% on QADI and MADAR, respectively.

In this paper, we present our contribution based on our system presented in (Lichouri et al., 2018) and (Abbas et al., 2019) to solve the challenge introduced in the first subtask, i.e. identifying 21 Arabic countries' dialects. In section 2, a description of the used dataset is presented. The applied cleaning steps and preprocessing are explained in section 3. In sections 4 and 5, we exposed the two adopted approaches (both simple and oversampling-based classification), respectively. Finally, the findings and discussion are presented in section 6.

---






*Proceedings of the Fifth Arabic Natural Language Processing Workshop*, pages 250–256
Barcelona, Spain (Online), December 12, 2020

## 2 Description of the Dataset

In this section, we describe the dataset used in our current (i.e., NADI) shared task (Abdul-Mageed et al., 2020). This dataset is collected from 21 Arab countries from the Twitter domain, covering a total of 100 provinces. The dataset is divided to three sets: train, dev and test, for which we addressed, in table 1, some statistics after applying a simple punctuation removal. As can be noticed from table 1,

|                        | Train   | Dev    | Test   | Total   |
| ---------------------- | ------- | ------ | ------ | ------- |
| # sentences            | 21,000  | 5,000  | 5,000  | 31,000  |
| # words                | 350,191 | 80,224 | 84,929 | 515,344 |
| Max # word per sentence | 228    | 248    | 249    | -       |
| Min # word per sentence | 1      | 1      | 1      | -       |
| Max # char per sentence | 488    | 673    | 535    | -       |
| Min # char per sentence | 3      | 3      | 1      | -       |

Table 1: NADI dataset statistics

the minimum number of words and characters per sentence in the training and development sets are 1 and 3, respectively. This information was useful to determine the number "n" of grams to be selected in the features extraction phase. In figure 1, we note that the numbers of words for the 21 dialects are differential in training dataset. As an example, we mention the case of Saudi Arabia versus Sudan or Iraq versus Libya. We also note that the ratio of the numbers of words to the number of sentences is more considerable for some dialects as Egyptian, Iraqi and Algeria.

## 3 Data Cleaning and Preprocessing

Dealing with texts collected from Twitter necessitates a cleaning process before doing analysis and processing. Hence we have applied two simple cleaning steps:

1. Emoji removal: We removed the emoticons, symbols & pictographs, transport & map symbols and flags (iOS).

2. Arabic and Latin punctuation removal: We removed a list of Arabic punctuation symbol that we prepared manually, whereas we used the Latin punctuation symbol list provided by the string library (string.punctuation).

For preprocessing, we explored the following steps: punctuation removal, normalization of Arabic letters, stop words removal, lemmatization, stemming, and part of speech tagging. For the lemmatization process we used Farasa[1] developed by (Abdelali et al., 2016), whereas for stemming and part of speech tagging, we used ISRI Arabic Stemmer and PosTagger of NLTK[2] (Bird et al., 2009). To investigate the impact of these six text functionalities, we combined them in different ways (see tables 2 and 3). We used different combinations of n-grams as features which resulted in 200 experiments. Nevertheless, we kept those which yielded the best performance, namely: 3-grams word, 5-grams word, 3-grams char, 5-grams char, 3-grams char_wb, 5-grams char_wb (see tables 2 and 3). These features have been transformed using the sklearn tfidf vectorizer (Pedregosa et al., 2011) as presented in (Abbas et al., 2019).

## 4 Simple Classification Model

This classification model is simply based on three linear classifiers, namely: Linear Support Vector Classification (LSVC), Ridge Classifier (RDG) and Stochastic Gradient Descent (SGD). The parameters we used for these classifiers are as follows: Linear SVC (C=0.01, penalty="l1", dual=False), Ridge Classifier (tol=1e-4, solver="sag") and SGD (alpha=.0001, max_iter=100, penalty='l2'). So as to avoid overfitting, we have applied a K-Fold Cross Validation (K=10) by using the Stratified K-Folds cross-validator (Pedregosa et al., 2011).

---

[1] http://alt.qcri.org/farasa/
[2] https://www.nltk.org/index.html

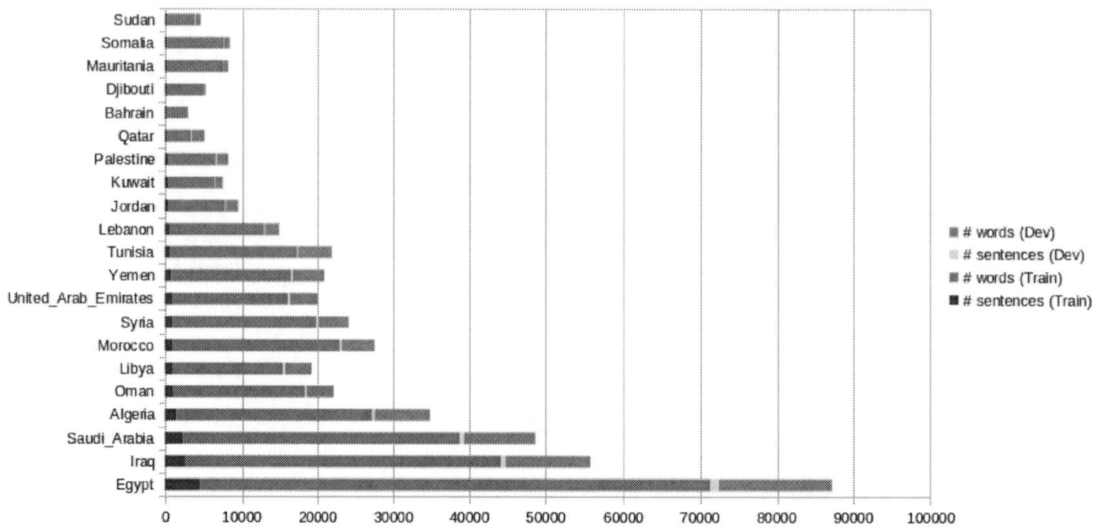

Figure 1: Dataset distribution: # sentences and words per country

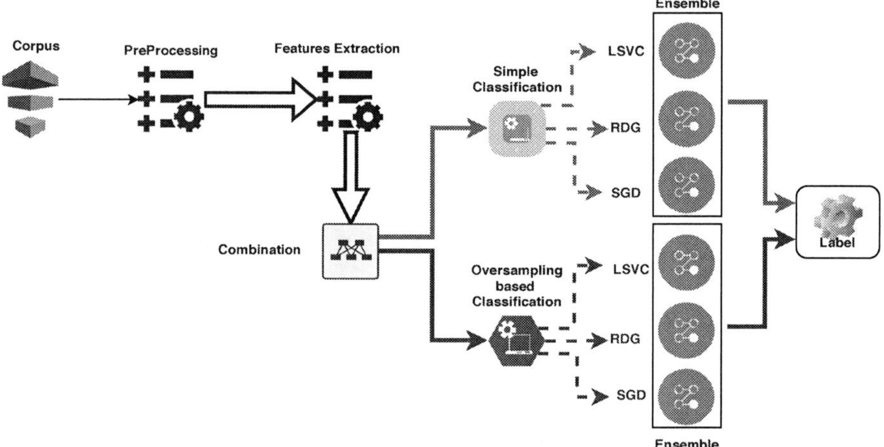


Figure 2: Classification system architecture of Arabic dialects.

## 5   Oversampling Based Classification

Since the dataset used in this task is imbalanced, as can be noticed clearly in figure 1, we used oversampling techniques to solve this problem (Lemaître et al., 2017). In the following, we briefly describe three different techniques that we used for oversampling:

**Random Over-Sampler (ROS):** This can be achieved by simply duplicating random examples from the minority class in the training dataset prior to fitting a model. This can balance the class distribution but does not provide any additional information to the model (Brownlee, 2020).

**Synthetic Minority Oversampling Technique (SMOTE):** It works by selecting examples that are close in the feature space, drawing a line between the examples in the feature space and drawing a new sample at a point along that line. Specifically, a random example from the minority class is first chosen. Then k of the nearest neighbors for that example are found (default k=5). A randomly selected neighbor is chosen and a synthetic example is created at a randomly selected point between the two examples in feature space (Brownlee, 2020).

**Adaptive Synthetic (ADASYN):** It is based on the idea of adaptively generating minority data samples according to their distributions using K nearest neighbors. The algorithm adaptively updates the distribution and there are no assumptions made for the underlying distribution of the data. The algorithm uses Euclidean distance for KNN Algorithm (Walimbe, 2017).

For these three models, we adopted the default configuration except two parameters which are: ratio='minority' and random_state=777. The full architecture of our system is presented in figure 2. It should be noted that we first combined all the six aforementioned preprocessing steps to generate all the possible textual presentations, after that we applied a second combination between n-grams (n=1,3,5) and tokenizer (word, char, char with boundary, union of the three) to generate all the possible vector features. Then we fed these features to our two proposed approaches: a simple classification model based on three classifiers (LSVC, RDG, SGD) and an oversampling-based classification approach based on the same three classifiers in addition to three oversampling procedures (ROS, SMOTE, ADASYN) which were applied before training. Finally we have used an ensemble classifier which will take as input the three predictions by the two approaches separately and apply a major voting rule to predict the dialect.

| Run | Model | Text PreProcessing | Morpho Features | Simple | | CV=10 | |
| --- | --- | --- | --- | --- | --- | --- | --- |
| | | | | Dev | Test | Dev | Test |
| 1 | LSVC | RP | - | 19.01 | 17.90 | 18.42 | **18.29** |
| | RDG | RP | - | 18.28 | 17.31 | 18.39 | **18.28** |
| | SGD | RP | - | 18.91 | 17.95 | 18.83 | 18.01 |
| | Ensemble | RP | - | 18.99 | 17.73 | **19.23** | **18.46** |
| 2 | LSVC | RP + Norm | - | 19.01 | 17.90 | 17.98 | 18.05 |
| | RDG | RP + Norm | - | 18.28 | 17.31 | 18.35 | 17.71 |
| | SGD | RP + Norm | - | **19.55** | **18.27** | 18.08 | 17.31 |
| | Ensemble | RP + Norm | - | 19.02 | 17.63 | 18.08 | 17.70 |
| 3 | LSVC | RP + Norm + RSW | - | 17.99 | 17.54 | 18.63 | **18.48** |
| | RDG | RP + Norm + RSW | - | 17.86 | 17.07 | 18.08 | 17.71 |
| | SGD | RP + Norm + RSW | - | 18.14 | 17.04 | 17.71 | 17.40 |
| | Ensemble | RP + Norm + RSW | - | 17.72 | 17.09 | 18.39 | 18.07 |
| 4 | LSVC | RP + Norm | Stem | 19.01 | 17.90 | 18.58 | 17.52 |
| | RDG | RP + Norm | Stem | 18.28 | 17.31 | 18.61 | 17.20 |
| | SGD | RP + Norm | Stem | 18.61 | 17.18 | 18.35 | 17.67 |
| | Ensemble | RP + Norm | Stem | 18.83 | 17.33 | 18.49 | 17.64 |
| 5 | LSVC | RP + Norm | Lem | 19.01 | 17.90 | 17.76 | 16.61 |
| | RDG | RP + Norm | Lem | 18.28 | 17.31 | 16.99 | 16.34 |
| | SGD | RP + Norm | Lem | **19.36** | **18.24** | 16.64 | 15.51 |
| | Ensemble | RP + Norm | Lem | 18.82 | 17.62 | 17.26 | 16.40 |
| 6 | LSVC | RP + Norm | PosTag | 19.01 | 17.90 | 15.62 | 15.47 |
| | RDG | RP + Norm | PosTag | 18.28 | 17.31 | 14.58 | 13.68 |
| | SGD | RP + Norm | PosTag | 18.20 | 17.39 | 13.90 | 13.80 |
| | Ensemble | RP + Norm | PosTag | 18.64 | 17.44 | 15.34 | 14.83 |
| 7 | LSVC | RP + Norm | Stem + Lem | 19.01 | 17.90 | - | - |
| | RDG | RP + Norm | Stem + Lem | 18.28 | 17.31 | - | - |
| | SGD | RP + Norm | Stem + Lem | **19.75** | **18.00** | - | - |
| | Ensemble | RP + Norm | Stem + Lem | 18.95 | 17.64 | - | - |
| 8 | LSVC | RP + Norm + RLL | Stem + Lem | 18.67 | 17.76 | - | - |
| | RDG | RP + Norm + RLL | Stem + Lem | 18.67 | 17.58 | - | - |
| | SGD | RP + Norm + RLL | Stem + Lem | 18.72 | 17.80 | - | - |
| | Ensemble | RP + Norm + RLL | Stem + Lem | 18.61 | 17.50 | - | - |

Table 2: The obtained results (macro average F1-score) in dev and test set for the simple classification model for the best 8 runs from the 200 run conducted.
**RP**: Removal of Punctuation, **Norm**: Arabic Letter Normalization, **RSW**: Removal of Stop Words, **RLL**: Removal of Latin Letters, **Stem**: Stemmer, **Lem**: Lemmatizer, **PosTag**: PosTagger.

## 6 Results and Discussion

After conducting more than 200 empirical experiments, in which we used different combinations of n-grams, we have reported the outputs of our 8 best configurations, as mentioned in tables 2 and 3, performed by the LSVC, RDG and SGD classifiers, in addition to the Ensemble classifier. Note that the oversampling-based method outperformed the simple classification model (F1-score = 18.74%). The impact of applying cross validation procedure k-CV (k=10) is also reported in tables 2 and 3. We should

| Run | Model | Text PreProcessing | Morpho Features | OverSamp Methods | CV=10 | |
|---|---|---|---|---|---|---|
| | | | | | Dev | Test |
| 1 | LSVC | RP | - | ROS | 18.26 | **18.74** |
| | RDG | RP | - | SMOTE | 18.47 | **18.27** |
| | SGD | RP | - | ADASYN | 17.28 | 17.66 |
| | Ensemble | RP | - | - | 18.30 | 18.23 |
| 2 | LSVC | RP + Norm | - | ROS | 18.00 | 18.04 |
| | RDG | RP + Norm | - | SMOTE | 18.61 | 17.65 |
| | SGD | RP + Norm | - | ADASYN | 17.36 | 16.94 |
| | Ensemble | RP + Norm | - | - | 18.24 | 17.48 |
| 3 | LSVC | RP + Norm + RSW | - | ROS | 18.32 | **18.60** |
| | RDG | RP + Norm + RSW | - | SMOTE | 18.06 | 17.77 |
| | SGD | RP + Norm + RSW | - | ADASYN | 16.91 | 17.23 |
| | Ensemble | RP + Norm + RSW | - | - | 18.12 | 18.25 |
| 4 | LSVC | RP + Norm | Stem | ROS | 18.56 | 17.80 |
| | RDG | RP + Norm | Stem | SMOTE | 18.59 | 17.33 |
| | SGD | RP + Norm | Stem | ADASYN | 17.33 | 16.84 |
| | Ensemble | RP + Norm | Stem | - | 18.76 | 17.37 |
| 5 | LSVC | RP + Norm | Stem | ROS | 17.84 | 16.58 |
| | RDG | RP + Norm | Stem | SMOTE | 17.01 | 16.02 |
| | SGD | RP + Norm | Stem | ADASYN | 16.40 | 15.80 |
| | Ensemble | RP + Norm | Stem | - | 17.21 | 16.62 |
| 6 | LSVC | RP + Norm | PosTag | ROS | 15.85 | 15.94 |
| | RDG | RP + Norm | PosTag | SMOTE | 14.55 | 13.94 |
| | SGD | RP + Norm | PosTag | ADASYN | 13.17 | 13.46 |
| | Ensemble | RP + Norm | PosTag | - | 14.82 | 14.97 |

Table 3: Macro average F1-score for the oversampling classification approach -best 6 runs-.
**RP**: Removal of Punctuation, **Norm**: Arabic Letters Normalization, **RSW**: Removal of Stop Words, **RLL**: Removal of Latin Letters, **Stem**: Stemmer, **Lem**: Lemmatizer, **PosTag**: PosTagger.

note that the TF-IDF features used in all the 8 experiments are the union of (5-grams word, 5-grams char and 5-grams char with boundary). We summarize the results describing the best performance achieved with the two proposed approaches " simple classification (Table 2) and oversampling-based classification (Table 3)" where the impact of preprocessing on the different experiments (runs) is clearly noticeable. Let us first introduce the positive impact of punctuation removal and Arabic letter normalization. Indeed, one can see the improvement achieved in the second run, with an F1-score of 19.55% in dev (18.27% in test), while the stop words removal yielded the worst performance (table 2). In the the following runs (4-8), we kept the stop words and we applied stemming, lemmatization and part of speech tagging separately. This didn't lead to an improvement compared to the first three runs. However, using stemming and lemmatization jointly, we obtained better results using the SGD classifier with an F1-score of 19.75% (dev) and 18% (test). Ironically, when we removed the Latin letters in the last run, performance decreased, which shows apparently that the Latin words are useful for identifying Arabic dialects. Furthermore, we mention herein the results reported using the test set that outperformed our best submission system. For the simple classification model, we recorded the following F1-socres: 18.28% (run 1-RDG), 18.29% (run 1-LSVC), 18.46% (run 1-Ensemble) and 18.48% (run 3-LSVC). In the case of oversampling-based approach, using 10-CV, we obtained the following results: 18.27% (run 1-Ensemble), 18.60% (run 3-LSVC) and 18.74% (run 1-LSVC). These results have shown that the 10-CV is practical in the presence of new data (test set).

## 7 Conclusion

In this paper, we presented a description of our system for identifying Arabic dialects from twitter collected from 21 Arabic countries. We have performed an empirical comparison study where we conducted 200 experiments in which we used several combinations of features and preprocessing steps, as stemming, lemmatization and part of speech tagging. We used a simple classification model comprising three classifiers: LSVC, RDG and SGD, while we tried to resolve the problem of imbalanced data using the oversampling methods. As expected, using a small and imbalanced dataset didn't help to get high scores, however, this task can be seen as the first try to identify high number of dialects with few resources.

## References


Mourad Abbas, Mohamed Lichouri, and Abed Alhakim Freihat. 2019. St madar 2019 shared task: Arabic fine-grained dialect identification. In *Proceedings of the Fourth Arabic Natural Language Processing Workshop*, pages 269–273.

Ahmed Abdelali, Kareem Darwish, Nadir Durrani, and Hamdy Mubarak. 2016. Farasa: A fast and furious segmenter for arabic. In *Proceedings of the 2016 conference of the North American chapter of the association for computational linguistics: Demonstrations*, pages 11–16.

Ahmed Abdelali, Hamdy Mubarak, Younes Samih, Sabit Hassan, and Kareem Darwish. 2020. Arabic dialect identification in the wild. *arXiv preprint arXiv:2005.06557*.

Muhammad Abdul-Mageed, Chiyu Zhang, AbdelRahim Elmadany, Arun Rajendran, and Lyle Ungar. 2019. Dianet: Bert and hierarchical attention multi-task learning of fine-grained dialect. *arXiv preprint arXiv:1910.14243*.

Muhammad Abdul-Mageed, Chiyu Zhang, Houda Bouamor, and Nizar Habash. 2020. The Shared Task on Nuanced Arabic Dialect Identification (NADI). In *Proceedings of the Fifth Arabic Natural Language Processing Workshop (WANLP2020)*, Barcelona, Spain.

Kathrein Abu Kwaik and Motaz K Saad. 2019. Arbdialectid at madar shared task 1: Language modelling and ensemble learning for fine grained arabic dialect identification. *ArbDialectID at MADAR Shared Task 1: Language Modelling and Ensemble Learning for Fine Grained Arabic Dialect Identification*, (Proceedings of the Fourth Arabic Natural Language Processing Workshop).

Fady Baly, Hazem Hajj, et al. 2020. Arabert: Transformer-based model for arabic language understanding. In *Proceedings of the 4th Workshop on Open-Source Arabic Corpora and Processing Tools, with a Shared Task on Offensive Language Detection*, pages 9–15.

Steven Bird, Ewan Klein, and Edward Loper. 2009. *Natural language processing with Python: analyzing text with the natural language toolkit.* " O'Reilly Media, Inc.".

Houda Bouamor, Sabit Hassan, and Nizar Habash. 2019. The madar shared task on arabic fine-grained dialect identification. In *Proceedings of the Fourth Arabic Natural Language Processing Workshop*, pages 199–207.

Jason Brownlee. 2020. Smote for imbalanced classification with python. `https://machinelearningmastery.com/smote-oversampling-for-imbalanced-classification/`. Accessed: 2020-06-23.

Kenneth Heafield. 2011. Kenlm: Faster and smaller language model queries. In *Proceedings of the sixth workshop on statistical machine translation*, pages 187–197. Association for Computational Linguistics.

Guillaume Lemaître, Fernando Nogueira, and Christos K. Aridas. 2017. Imbalanced-learn: A python toolbox to tackle the curse of imbalanced datasets in machine learning. *Journal of Machine Learning Research*, 18(17):1–5.

Mohamed Lichouri, Mourad Abbas, Abed Alhakim Freihat, and Dhiya El Hak Megtouf. 2018. Word-level vs sentence-level language identification: Application to algerian and arabic dialects. *Procedia Computer Science*, 142:246–253.

F. Pedregosa, G. Varoquaux, A. Gramfort, V. Michel, B. Thirion, O. Grisel, M. Blondel, P. Prettenhofer, R. Weiss, V. Dubourg, J. Vanderplas, A. Passos, D. Cournapeau, M. Brucher, M. Perrot, and E. Duchesnay. 2011. Scikit-learn: Machine learning in Python. *Journal of Machine Learning Research*, 12:2825–2830.

Ahmad Ragab, Haitham Seelawi, Mostafa Samir, Abdelrahman Mattar, Hesham Al-Bataineh, Mohammad Zaghloul, Ahmad Mustafa, Bashar Talafha, Abed Alhakim Freihat, and Hussein Al-Natsheh. 2019. Mawdoo3 ai at madar shared task: Arabic fine-grained dialect identification with ensemble learning. In *Proceedings of the Fourth Arabic Natural Language Processing Workshop*, pages 244–248.

Mohammad Salameh, Houda Bouamor, and Nizar Habash. 2018. Fine-grained arabic dialect identification. In *Proceedings of the 27th International Conference on Computational Linguistics*, pages 1332–1344.

Rohit Walimbe. 2017. Handling imbalanced dataset in supervised learning using family of smote algorithm. https://www.datasciencecentral.com/profiles/blogs/handling-imbalanced-data-sets-in-supervised-learning-using-family. Accessed: 2020-06-23.

# Semi-supervised Fine-grained Approach for Arabic Dialect Detection


**Nitin Nikamanth Appiah Balaji**
SSN College of Engineering
Kalavakkam, India
nitinnikamanthab17099@cse.ssn.edu.in

**B. Bharathi**
SSN College of Engineering
Kalavakkam, India
bharathib@ssn.edu.in


## Abstract


Arabic is a language with numerous dialects. It becomes extremely important to device a technique to distinguish each dialect efficiently. This paper focuses on the fine-grained country-level and province-level classification of Arabic dialects. The experiments described in this paper are submissions of team TRY_NLP for NADI SHARED TASK on Nuanced Arabic Dialect Identification. Various text feature extraction techniques such as TF-IDF, AraVec, multilingual BERT and FastText embedding models are studied. We thereby, propose an approach of text embedding based model with macro average F1 score of 22.32% for subtask 1 and 4.83% for subtask 2, with the help of semi-supervised learning approach.


## 1 Introduction

As Arabic has a diverse collection of dialects and as Dialect Arabic varies phonologically, lexically, and morphologically from Modern Standard Arabic (Bouamor et al., 2018), fine-grained dialect identification becomes an important task. The classification helps for studying various indigenous properties among different dialect speakers. Previously, work on fine-grained city-level classification has been done (Salameh et al., 2018), for MADAR tasks (Bouamor et al., 2018). NADI 2020 task consist of 21 class country-level dialect labels and 100 class province-level fine-grained dialect labels.

With recent development in text classification, from emerging techniques like embedding models, not only for English, but trained on multiple languages have opened opportunities for Arabic text classification. As models like Word2Vec, FastText and BERT perform excellent in text classification of English twitter data, these can be extended into the usage of Arabic languages. Features extracted from these models are then further fine tuned using neural network layers, to fit the required classification.

In this paper we propose a model giving extremely good scores, using a combination of labelled and unlabelled data, by semi-supervised learning technique. Unlabelled 10 million twitter data is collected with their ID provided for the challenge and the top confidence predictions are added to extend the main labelled data set to increase the training set. Repeated training with the added data in each step, increased the F1 score significantly.

The remainder of the paper is organized as follows. Section 2 discusses the description of the data set and preprocessing methods used. Section 3 outlines the features used for the experiments for both subtask 1 and subtask 2. Results are discussed in Section 4. Section 5 concludes the paper.

## 2 Data Description and Processing

The data provided in the NADI 2020 task consist of 21,000 labelled and 10 million unlabelled data set for training, 4,957 tweet dev set and 5,000 tweet test set. The data consist of 21 different country-level labels and 100 different province-level labels with unequal distribution of tweets in various classes. The details about the shared task is described in (Abdul-Mageed et al., 2020)






*Proceedings of the Fifth Arabic Natural Language Processing Workshop*, pages 257–261
Barcelona, Spain (Online), December 12, 2020

Additionally 10 million tweet IDs were given without labels. These unlabelled tweets were extracted by using the Twitter API. Out of the 10 million tweets approximately 92% of tweets are available and is considered for semi-supervised learning.

As the texts are direct tweet messages, it contains links, hashtags and numbers, which is against the context of our study. So tweets are cleaned by removing the unwanted links, English and special characters, considering just the Arabic text to maintain generality.

| Data type | # tweets |
| --- | --- |
| train-labelled | 21,000 |
| train-unlabelled | 10 million |
| dev | 4,957 |
| test | 5,000 |

Table 1: Dataset distribution.

## 3 Experimental Setup

For both subtask1 and subtask2, TF-IDF, AraVec, BERT and FastText features are extracted and these feature vectors are fine-tuned to classify dialect classes by appending an extra layer. By this method of transfer learning we have established an effective and faster way of training the model.

Due to the large number of classes and great class imbalance, macro average F1 score is suitable and is used in the NADI task. Also accuracy, precision and recall are observed.

### 3.1 TF-IDF Vectorization

TF-IDF abbreviated as term frequency-inverse domain frequency, which is a count based text-extraction model with inverse domain frequency term normalising the representation. This representation reduces the impact of the large repetition of one unimportant word in the sentence. This approach is better than just count vectorization of the sentences and works well for small train set (Mishra and Mujadia, 2019). Previously, TF-IDF model fusion models, presented to MADAR SHARED task (Bouamor et al., 2019) have shown good performance (Abu Kwaik and Saad, 2019; Mishra and Mujadia, 2019).

### 3.2 AraVec

As Arabic is a language with complex morphology and having different ways to express the same meaning, it becomes important to capture the syntactic and semantic relations among the words in the sentence.

Word2Vec models are shallow, two-layer neural networks, trained to reconstruct linguistic contexts of words (Mikolov et al., 2013). So it becomes a basic approach for understanding the semantics as well as run fast. Similar to word2vec trained on English corpus, AraVec (Soliman et al., 2017) is trained on Arabic corpus and becomes quicker and requires lesser data to fine tune the model. AraVec model, a n-gram model trained on Arabic twitter data and Wikipedia Arabic articles is considered suitable for this task.

### 3.3 Multilingual BERT

BERT is a Bidirectional Encoder Representations from Transformers architecture (Devlin et al., 2018). BERT is the state-of-the-art model available for twitter text classification, with transformer based unsupervised learning model. As the BERT model is pre-trained on a large corpus of data, to learn the context similarities of the sentences, it is easier to fine-tune and get good results. The multilingual cased BERT model which is trained on 104 different languages, including Arabic is used to generate the word vectors.

### 3.4 Arabic FastText

We use the FastText model trained on common crawl and Wikipedia data of Arabic sentences (Grave et al., 2018). It has been proven to give good results in (Samih et al., 2019). This produces a fixed embedding of length 300. The model is trained using CBOW (Continuous Bag of Words) with position-weights, with character n-grams of length 5, a window of size 5 and 10 negatives. The FastText model is fragment based, and gives good representation on even unseen words. The twitter dataset for the classification, mostly contains unknown words and so gives better representation with the implementation of FastText from magnitude (Patel et al., 2018).

Out of all the experiments conducted the Arabic FastText fine-tuned model produced great results on the development set with up-to 0.18% macro avg F1 score, out performing the multilingual BERT model. This is majorly because FastText Arabic specific pre-trained model is readily available, whereas BERT only has generalized multilingual variant and the limitation in the train data set size have made FastText shine.

### 3.5   Semi-supervised Learning

The limited labelled data constraints the model, to learn much and to overfit on the training corpus. To generate a generalized model, which could perform well on the test set, it is must to increase the data set to see any further improvements in the performance. So, by semi-supervised learning strategy (Zhang and Abdul-Mageed, 2019), we tried to get more labelled samples by pseudo labelling the unlabelled data with a previously trained model. The steps for semi-supervised learning used in the proposed approach is depicted in Figure 1.

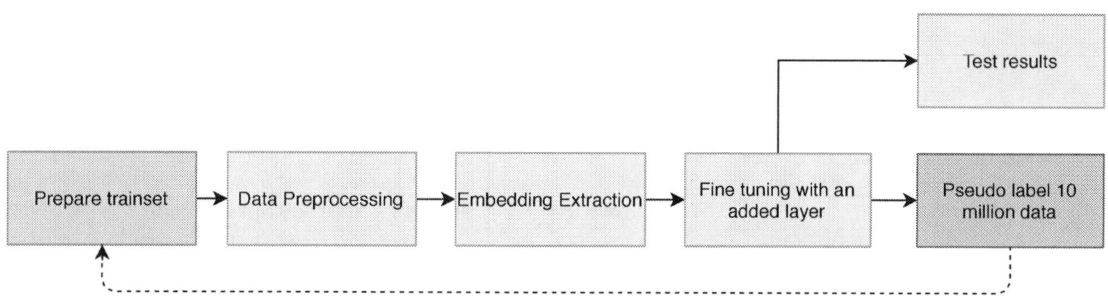


Figure 1: Semi-supervised learning pipeline

The FastText model, which has the best performance is considered and the unlabelled 10 million tweets are predicted along with their confidence scores. Then the top confidence score results are selected and added to the main training data. Then the training process is repeated again, and the addition of pseudo labelled data is repeated multiple times. The threshold of confidence score to be added to training set is experimented with different values as explained in (Zhang and Abdul-Mageed, 2019). This process of semi-supervised learning gave a significant improvement and reached 0.2232 macro avg F1 score.

## 4   Results

The pre-trained models for Arabic corpus is hard to find, making models like BERT perform slightly lesser than expected. Even though normalized count based model is basic, TF-IDF method showed relatively better results than the AraVec model, as TF-IDF transform is fitted on the training corpus, and not using different corpus.

Out of all models trained on only the labelled training data, the FastText model performs the best as its implementation with the magnitude library (Patel et al., 2018), as it assigns the same id for repeating words that doesn't exist in the pre-trained corpus. By this model we reach an excellent F1 score of 0.1890 for country-level classification and 0.0437 for province-level classification, on the dev set.

The results of each feature extraction technique are observed and tabulated in Table 2 and 3.

Then considering the unlabelled tweets, extracted using the tweeter API, the model is trained in a semi-supervised fashion. First the model already trained on the labelled data, is used to produce the labels for the 10 million tweets and out of which the top confidence results are selected and concatenated with the labelled data. To not induce excess error into the model, various thresholds of 1, 5, 10%

| Model | macro avg F1 | accuracy | precision | recall |
|---|---|---|---|---|
| TF-IDF | 0.1522 | 0.3099 | 0.1697 | 0.1487 |
| AraVec | 0.1159 | 0.3123 | 0.1321 | 0.1237 |
| multilingual BERT | 0.1175 | 0.2417 | 0.1294 | 0.1146 |
| FastText ar | 0.1890 | **0.3752** | 0.1939 | 0.1922 |
| Semi-supervised FastText | **0.2232** | 0.3674 | **0.2285** | **0.2404** |

Table 2: Subtask1 - Country-level classification report on dev set

is experimented. This addition of data to the train data, helped to increase the models performance significantly, approximately 20% increase compared to the supervised learning score.

| Model | macro avg F1 | accuracy | precision | recall |
|---|---|---|---|---|
| TF-IDF | 0.0442 | 0.0444 | 0.0476 | 0.0447 |
| AraVec | 0.0213 | 0.0268 | 0.0253 | 0.0271 |
| multilingual BERT | 0.0275 | 0.0313 | 0.0278 | 0.0331 |
| FastText ar | 0.0437 | 0.0516 | 0.0390 | 0.0560 |
| Semi-supervised FastText | **0.0483** | **0.0551** | **0.0451** | **0.0608** |

Table 3: Subtask2 - Province-level classification report on dev set

The FastText model was considered for submission in the NADI 2020 tasks and the results are as tabulated in Table 4 and 5.

| Model | macro avg F1 | accuracy | precision | recall |
|---|---|---|---|---|
| Semi-supervised FastText | 0.2004 | 0.3366 | 0.2070 | 0.2107 |

Table 4: Subtask1 - Country-level classification report on test set

| Model | macro avg F1 | accuracy | precision | recall |
|---|---|---|---|---|
| Semi-supervised FastText | 0.0403 | 0.0486 | 0.0374 | 0.0468 |

Table 5: Subtask2 - Province-level classification report on test set

## 5   Conclusion

coling.bst, line 1244 Fine-grained Arabic dialect classification is explored, with NADI challenge data set. The tasks of country-level and province-level dialect identification for 21 classes and 100 classes are studied. In this paper, we explore various models such as TF-IDF, AraVec, multi-BERT and ar-FastText. We could see that the FastText model performed relatively better than the other models for such small training set. And also we could see the improvement of performance, by semi-supervised learning technique using the unlabelled data. By this strategy we achieve 0.2232 and 0.0483 macro avg F1 for subtask 1 and subtask 2 respectively on dev data set. The model showed 0.2004 and 0.0403 macro avg F1 for subtask 1 and subtask 2 on test data set.

## References

Muhammad Abdul-Mageed, Chiyu Zhang, Houda Bouamor, and Nizar Habash. 2020. NADI 2020: The First Nuanced Arabic Dialect Identification Shared Task. In *Proceedings of the Fifth Arabic Natural Language Processing Workshop (WANLP 2020)*, Barcelona, Spain.

Kathrein Abu Kwaik and Motaz Saad. 2019. ArbDialectID at MADAR shared task 1: Language modelling and ensemble learning for fine grained Arabic dialect identification. In *Proceedings of the Fourth Arabic Natural Language Processing Workshop*, pages 254–258, Florence, Italy, August. Association for Computational Linguistics.

Houda Bouamor, Nizar Habash, Mohammad Salameh, Wajdi Zaghouani, Owen Rambow, Dana Abdulrahim, Ossama Obeid, Salam Khalifa, Fadhl Eryani, Alexander Erdmann, and Kemal Oflazer. 2018. The MADAR Arabic dialect corpus and lexicon. In *Proceedings of the Eleventh International Conference on Language Resources and Evaluation (LREC 2018)*, Miyazaki, Japan, May. European Language Resources Association (ELRA).

Houda Bouamor, Sabit Hassan, and Nizar Habash. 2019. The MADAR shared task on Arabic fine-grained dialect identification. In *Proceedings of the Fourth Arabic Natural Language Processing Workshop*, pages 199–207, Florence, Italy. Association for Computational Linguistics.

Jacob Devlin, Ming-Wei Chang, Kenton Lee, and Kristina Toutanova. 2018. Bert: Pre-training of deep bidirectional transformers for language understanding. *arXiv preprint arXiv:1810.04805*.

Edouard Grave, Piotr Bojanowski, Prakhar Gupta, Armand Joulin, and Tomas Mikolov. 2018. Learning word vectors for 157 languages. In *Proceedings of the International Conference on Language Resources and Evaluation (LREC 2018)*.

Tomas Mikolov, Kai Chen, Greg Corrado, and Jeffrey Dean. 2013. Efficient estimation of word representations in vector space.

Pruthwik Mishra and Vandan Mujadia. 2019. Arabic dialect identification for travel and twitter text. In *Proceedings of the Fourth Arabic Natural Language Processing Workshop*, pages 234–238.

Ajay Patel, Alexander Sands, Chris Callison-Burch, and Marianna Apidianaki. 2018. Magnitude: A fast, efficient universal vector embedding utility package. In *Proceedings of the 2018 Conference on Empirical Methods in Natural Language Processing: System Demonstrations*, pages 120–126.

Mohammad Salameh, Houda Bouamor, and Nizar Habash. 2018. Fine-grained arabic dialect identification. In *Proceedings of the 27th International Conference on Computational Linguistics*, pages 1332–1344.

Younes Samih, Hamdy Mubarak, Ahmed Abdelali, Mohammed Attia, Mohamed Eldesouki, and Kareem Darwish. 2019. QC-GO submission for MADAR shared task: Arabic fine-grained dialect identification. In *Proceedings of the Fourth Arabic Natural Language Processing Workshop*, pages 290–294, Florence, Italy, August. Association for Computational Linguistics.

Abu Bakr Soliman, Kareem Eissa, and Samhaa R El-Beltagy. 2017. Aravec: A set of arabic word embedding models for use in arabic nlp. *Procedia Computer Science*, 117:256–265.

Chiyu Zhang and Muhammad Abdul-Mageed. 2019. No army, no navy: Bert semi-supervised learning of arabic dialects. In *Proceedings of the Fourth Arabic Natural Language Processing Workshop*, pages 279–284.

# Arabic Dialect Identification Using BERT-Based Domain Adaptation


**Ahmad Beltagy**      **Abdelrahman Wael**      **Omar ElSherief**

Faculty of Engineering, Alexandria University
{a.beltagy97, abdelrahman.abouelenin}@gmail.com,
C.m_elshrief@hotmail.com



## Abstract

Arabic is one of the most important and growing languages in the world. With the rise of the social media platforms such as like Twitter, Arabic spoken dialects have become more in use. In this paper, we describe our our approach on the NADI Shared Task 1 that requires us to build a system to differentiate between different 21 Arabic dialects, we introduce a deep learning semi-supervised fashion approach along with pre-processing that was reported on NADI shared Task 1 Corpus. Our system ranks 4th in NADI's shared task competition achieving 23.09% F1 macro average score with a simple yet an efficient approach on differentiating between 21 Arabic Dialects given tweets.


## 1 Introduction

Arabic dialect classification is a task of identifying the dialect of the writer given an input text. This task has been an active field of research the past few years due to the rise of Arabic corpora which are made available  (Bouamor et al., 2018).  However, NADI's Arabic dialect corpus  (Abdul-Mageed et al., 2020) have been quite challenging and intriguing. NADI's corpora has 21 different country dialects from which some of them are quite similar to each other in terms of morphology.  Some of the data provided had some English words, others had Quran verses generated from third party apps which makes it extremely difficult for not just models, but also human cannot differentiate between the dialects if the tweet is a Quranic verse, since Quran compromises classical Arabic not dialectal Arabic. This is noise in the dataset that a model can not fix. Also, the imbalance of training data introduced other challenges and difficulties.

Previous work in this task involved the use of traditional ML algorithms, RNN with their variants, and hybrid approaches like in (Salameh et al., 2018).  However, we were inspired by self-attention technique (Vaswani et al., 2017). Due to the huge success of transformers in many classification tasks, we opted for approach of using pretrained BERT  (Devlin et al., 2018) in semi-supervised deep learning as it is proved by  Gururangan et al. (2020) that fine-tuning pretrained model to specific domain is an efficient solution. We fine-tuned pretrained BERT transformer on "AraBERT" (Antoun et al., 2020) Arabic text, which is trained on 23B GB of data, using masked language modelling with Huggingface interface (Wolf et al., 2019). This process was done after doing data pre-processing and data augmentation in order to alleviate the problems of having class imbalance and lack of training data.

Transfer learning has proven to be an efficient approach in classification tasks, especially when we do not have enough training data. We leveraged the unlabeled data provided by NADI (Abdul-Mageed et al., 2020) through twitter API's, for fine-tuning using language modelling to achieve domain adaptation. Where we adapt pretrained AraBERT to the domain of tweets. That is because of similarity of morphological and semantic features that both the unlabeled data and target data share. Pretrained BERT model "AraBERT" was fine-tuned on NADI's unlabeled corpus using masked language model to let it learn better features. These features are going to be used to classify target labeled training examples provided by






*Proceedings of the Fifth Arabic Natural Language Processing Workshop*, pages 262–267
Barcelona, Spain (Online), December 12, 2020

NADI, which have the same distribution as the unlabeled ones. Our results confirm that such a technique have improved our baseline performance significantly by 3% F1 macro average score.

The rest of the paper is organized as follows. Section 2 presents the data that were supplied for training our model. Section 3 is a description of our system in detail and what infrastructure we used to produce the results. In Section 4, we present our results using various techniques. Section 5 is a discussion about task and common errors that occured. Section 6 concludes the work we have done as well as suggested future work.

## 2   Data

The dataset was one of the factors that made this problem quite challenging. NADI shared task organizers (Abdul-Mageed et al., 2020) provided a corpus of Arabic tweets from Twitter platform having 21 class labels corresponding to countries {Egypt, Iraq, Saudi Arabia, Algeria, Oman, Emirates, Libya, Syria, Morocco, Yemen, Tunisia, Lebanon, Jordan, Kuwait, Palestine, Qatar, Bahrain, Djibouti, Mauritania, Somalia and Sudan}. The corpus is divided into training set, dev set and test set to report our final results on. The number of examples in the 3 sets is, 21,000 tweets, 4,957 tweets and 5,000 tweets respectively. To aid in the training and model building processes, the organizers also provided additional 10 million unlabeled tweets IDs from the same distribution of the labeled tweets, to be obtained using a provided python script.

In Figure 1, we show the distribution of each class in the training examples. The figure clearly shows the imbalance of training examples where a class like Egypt has 4,473 example and a class like Sudan has only 210 examples. It also shows that most of the classes had under 1,000 example, which was quite challenging to solve.

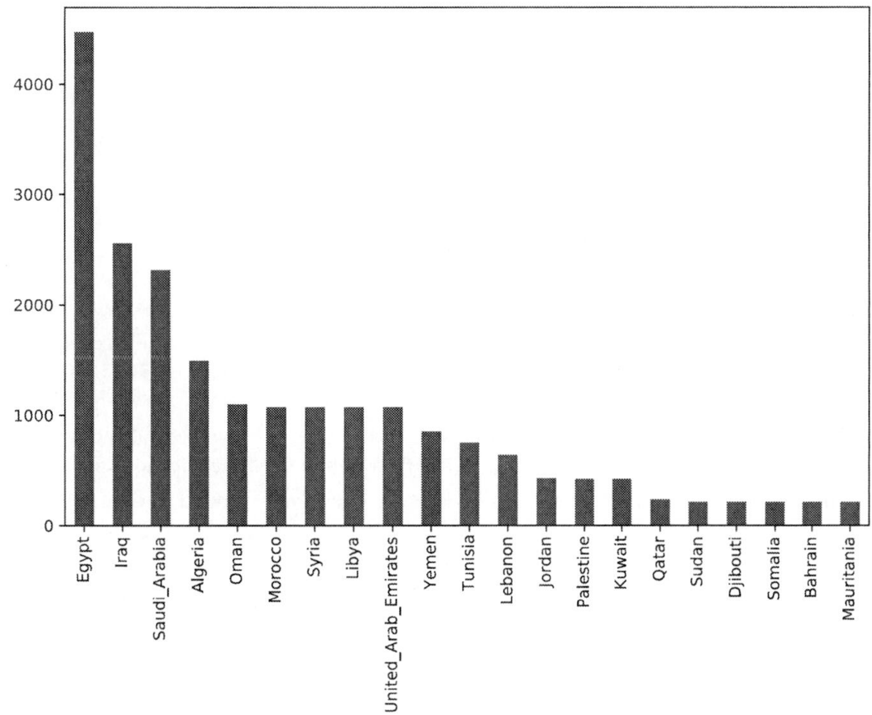

Figure 1: Distribution of 21 class labels across training data

### 2.1   Data Pre-processing

We start our pre-processing by cleaning the data and removing all the unnecessarily characters. We start the process of data cleaning by removing URLs, punctuation, mentions, email addresses, emojis and other unknown Unicode characters using regex patterns. Next step we removed all English characters as it won't help in differentiating between Arabic dialects. Moreover, we used PyArabic library (Zerrouki, 2010) to strip tashkil from Arabic sentences. We stripped tashkil because we observed the inconsistent use of it and even wrong usage, which it would be a burden rather than an advantage to keep it. At this point, we have a corpus of only Arabic characters. The next step of cleaning is to remove elongations ex: كملت لو اهخ متعععههههه والله . Here we won't need متعععههههه as it represents noise, we remove the repeated characters so the result متعه . Next we deal with the words that have same semantics but different syntax, those words differ not in the core of the word it self, but in the suffix and prefix, for example the word بعرفكيش, which means I don't know you, can be written in different forms with different dialects معرفكيش، ما بعرفك، لا أعرفك، مش هعرفك, so in order to provide more information to our model. We separate the suffix and prefix from the core of the word, for this step we use Farasa Segmenter (Abdelali et al., 2016), which is an Arabic NLP toolkit that serves as a sentence segmentation toolkit. Farasa takes a word and splits it into suffix and prefix, which completes our data processing step, example: امين يارب العالمين this is transformed to 'ين'+'عالم'+'ال'+'امين يارب'

## 2.2 Data Augmentation

Because of the imbalance of data as shown in figure 1, some minority classes like {Lebanon, Jordan, Kuwait, Palestine, Qatar, Bahrain, Djibouti, Mauritania, Somalia and Sudan} had less than 750 examples. Our proposed solution to this problem is to upsample the minority classes to 750 examples using scikit-learn library (Pedregosa et al., 2011). We chose this specific number after many trials with different numbers. We observed that above 750 examples we do not observe any increase in terms of accuracy. Other techniques for data augmentation were suggested in (Fares et al., 2019; Ibrahim et al., 2018; Ibrahim et al., 2020)

## 3 System

In this section, we describe our proposed approach used in NADI shared task 1 Corpus submission. All of our experiments were based on AraBERT (Antoun et al., 2020) which is an Arabic version BERT model trained on 23GB of Arabic text with 3B words having vocab size of 64,000. We present the building blocks of our system, then we go over to explain another experiment that we have tried.

## 3.1 Tokenization and Encoding

First, we used the tokenizer corresponding to the model which mainly is used to split the sentence to tokens, example: خلص يبقى بعرفكيش this is transformed to 'ش','كي','رف','بع','يبقى','خلص'. Then we proceed to convert each word to it's appropriate ID and if the tweet is smaller than the expected dimension (64 word), then it's padded with an appropriate token " [PAD] ". If it exceed it, then it's truncated and a binary vector, also known as a mask, is returned to emphasize if certain token correspond to a word or padding token. Then we feed AraBERT the sequence of IDs along with it's corresponding mask vector and it's label corresponding to which class of the 21 mentioned in data section.

## 3.2 Feature Extraction

AraBERT is originally a pre-trained BERT (Devlin et al., 2018) specifically for the Arabic language. It has a vocab size of 64,000 word, and uses the same small Bert-Base configuration that has 12 transformer encoders. These transformers encoders learn about features in the input text and outputs 768 hidden dimension at the end. After each sentence is fed to the model, it is converted to a vector representing it using vocab dictionary and then fed to encoder layers of the model to form an output of (768).

## 3.3 Domain Adaptation Using Fine Tuning

We were inspired by power of domain adaptation in various Natural Language Processing tasks. It was proven by Gururangan et al. (2020) that adapting a large pre-trained model to another domain would gain a lot in terms of accuracy. We started this task by crawling some of the 10M unlabeled tweets using Twitter API python script provided by NADI organizers (Abdul-Mageed et al., 2020). We only utilized

2M tweets, as we did not observe any gain in accuracy when going beyond 2M tweets. We trained a masked language model using HuggingFace interface (Wolf et al., 2019), to let the model learn about semantic features of the new domain 'tweets'. The masked language model was trained using an adaptive learning rate starting with 2e-5 was used, and with masking rate of 15% of input text. We trained with only 1 epoch, which took around 20 hours to complete training. The rest of the hyper-parameters were the default ones provided by HuggingFace.

## 3.4 Training Classifiers

We experimented with 2 different settings to classify tweets. First, which was the one we submitted. It relied only on AraBERT to classify the 21 labels, achieving F1 macro average score of 24.433% on dev set. Second Trial was a mix between AraBERT and Naive-bayes achieving 22.3% F1 macro average score.

### 3.4.1 AraBERT classification head

After each tweet was encoded into 768 features, a simple BERT classification layer was added after multiple experiments. The layer would take in the 768 features and using fully connected network it converts them to output a vector of 21 entries. Where each entry uniquely correspond to one of the 21 Arabic dialect classes.

### 3.4.2 AraBERT with naive-bayes

One of the promising models and inspired by (Kowsari et al., 2017) was a hierarchical classification model. Having observed that deep learning doesn't perform well with classes with small number of tweets, we also observed how well naive Bayes performed classifying these classes, so we were motivated to build a hybrid model using AraBERT and naive Bayes. We The idea was simple, we used AraBERT to classify majority classes {Egypt, Iraq, Saudi Arabia, Algeria, Oman, Emirates, Libya, Syria, Morocco, Yemen, Tunisia, Lebanon, Jordan, Kuwait, Palestine} normally and combining minority classes {Qatar, Bahrain, Djibouti, Mauritania, Somalia and Sudan} into one class {Not majority} labelled C16 as shown in figure 2. If AraBERT classified a certain tweet to belong to this special class then this tweet is passed to naive Bayes to more accurately classify which class from the minority classes does this tweet belongs to. This model proved capable of achieving f1 score of 22% but still falls a bit short than a pure AraBERT.

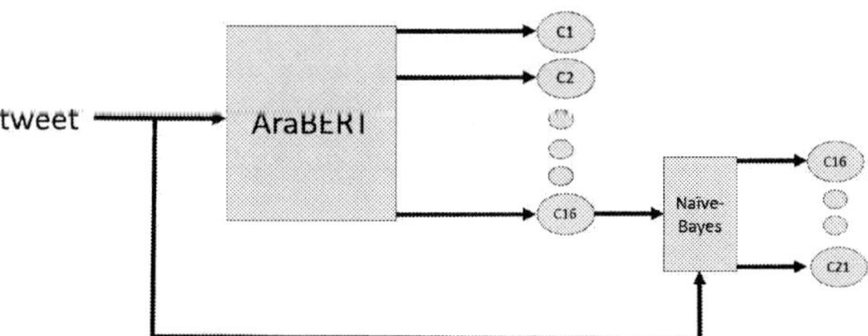


Figure 2: Visual of the classification head used in AraBERT with Naive Bayes. If AraBERT classifies a certain tweet to belong tominority class then it is passed to Naive-Bayes.

## 4 Results

We present our experiments results on the development set provided by organizers which consisted of 4,957 examples. In Table 1 we show our corresponding F1 macro average score on those models. We firstly show that our baseline model which consists of using AraBERT only resulted in 18.6% F1 macro average score. After cleaning process described in data section 2.1, we gained nearly 2% F1 macro average score which proved our pre-processing was efficient one. However, we noticed that our classifier

| Model | Dev-set F1-score |
|---|---|
| baseline (AraBERT without augementation and cleaning) | 18.6% |
| AraBERT with cleaning | 20.54% |
| AraBERT with cleaning + up sampling | 21.33% |
| AraBERT with cleaning + up sampling + MLM fine-tuning | 24.43% |
| AraBERT + Naive-Bayes with cleaning + up sampling | 22.3% |

Table 1: Our proposed models scores on dev-set.

is struggling with minority classes as described in data section 2.2, which gave us the idea of up sampling them. And that gained us a further 0.79% F1 macro average score. After further research we were fascinated by the power of fine-tuning approach of training a masked language model to improve classification task as described in system section 3.3 . This technique has given us the biggest improvement of 3.1% F1 macro average score. This was our submitted model in the task, which ranked 4th with 24.43% F1 macro average score in dev set and 23.09% on test set.

A second experiment which was not submitted was concluded based on hierarchical model of AraBERT with naive-bayes. However, this approach had an F1 macro average of 22.3%, which is still 2% F1 macro score less than a single transformer model.

## 5   Discussion

It was observed in our experiments, through analysis of data, that some of the tweets had noticeable noise that cannot be solved. Some users used to tweet through third party apps. We noticed that these tweets were mainly prayers or quran versus coming from various apps like {http://d3waapp.org, http://knzmuslim.com, http://Gharedly.com and http://du3a.org}. The main problem is that these tweets are given different labels according to the nationality of the user, and in fact they are not even differential by humans, which makes it very hard for a trained model. Another noticeable noise was that some tweets are actually a retweets. Where the retweeted content refers to a dialect, but it was given another label because the actual user retweeting is having a different dialect.

In future work, we plan on exploiting hierarchical models having transformer model, as it's backbone as we believe that regrouping our classes into different sets, would improve the results. Also another promising idea was to build a byte pair encoding tokenizer trained on extracting frequent sub words, which may prove to be helpful especially in dialect classification. We believe that the main differences between dialects are specific sub words that occurs in certain dialect more than others. We will also experiment ensemble techniques and how they can fit into our system.

## 6   Conclusion

We introduce a simple efficient single deep neural network model to classify 21 arabic dialects, which was based on the idea of fine-tuning approach using a pre-trained transformer model on similar domain after various cleaning and augmentation methods. We were able to achieve 4th best score in NADI shared task 1 competition with F1 macro average score of 22.03%.

## References


Ahmed Abdelali, Kareem Darwish, and Hamdy Durrani, Nadir andz Mubarak. 2016. Farasa: A fast and furious segmenter for Arabic. In *Proceedings of the 2016 Conference of the North American Chapter of the Association for Computational Linguistics: Demonstrations*, pages 11–16, San Diego, California, June. Association for Computational Linguistics.

Muhammad Abdul-Mageed, Chiyu Zhang, Houda Bouamor, and Nizar Habash. 2020. NADI 2020: The First Nuanced Arabic Dialect Identification Shared Task. In *Proceedings of the Fifth Arabic Natural Language Processing Workshop (WANLP 2020)*, Barcelona, Spain.

Wissam Antoun, Fady Baly, and Hazem Hajj. 2020. Arabert: Transformer-based model for arabic language understanding.

Houda Bouamor, Nizar Habash, Mohammad Salameh, Wajdi Zaghouani, Owen Rambow, Dana Abdulrahim, Ossama Obeid, Salam Khalifa, Fadhl Eryani, Alexander Erdmann, and Kemal Oflazer. 2018. The MADAR Arabic dialect corpus and lexicon. In *Proceedings of the Eleventh International Conference on Language Resources and Evaluation (LREC 2018)*, Miyazaki, Japan, May. European Language Resources Association (ELRA).

Jacob Devlin, Ming-Wei Chang, Kenton Lee, and Kristina Toutanova. 2018. Bert: Pre-training of deep bidirectional transformers for language understanding.

Youssef Fares, Zeyad El-Zanaty, Kareem Abdel-Salam, Muhammed Ezzeldin, Aliaa Mohamed, Karim El-Awaad, and Marwan Torki. 2019. Arabic dialect identification with deep learning and hybrid frequency based features. In *Proceedings of the Fourth Arabic Natural Language Processing Workshop*, pages 224–228, Florence, Italy, August. Association for Computational Linguistics.

Suchin Gururangan, Ana Marasović, Swabha Swayamdipta, Kyle Lo, Iz Beltagy, Doug Downey, and Noah A. Smith. 2020. Don't stop pretraining: Adapt language models to domains and tasks. In *ACL*.

Mai Ibrahim, Marwan Torki, and Nagwa El-Makky. 2018. Imbalanced toxic comments classification using data augmentation and deep learning. In *2018 17th IEEE International Conference on Machine Learning and Applications (ICMLA)*, pages 875–878, Dec.

Mai Ibrahim, Marwan Torki, and Nagwa El-Makky. 2020. Alexu-backtranslation-tl at semeval-2020 task [12]: Improving offensive language detection using data augmentation and transfer learning. In *Proceedings of the International Workshop on Semantic Evaluation (SemEval)*.

Kamran Kowsari, Donald E. Brown, Mojtaba Heidarysafa, Kiana Jafari Meimandi, Matthew S. Gerber, and Laura E. Barnes. 2017. Hdltex: Hierarchical deep learning for text classification. *2017 16th IEEE International Conference on Machine Learning and Applications (ICMLA)*, pages 364–371.

F. Pedregosa, G. Varoquaux, A. Gramfort, V. Michel, B. Thirion, O. Grisel, M. Blondel, P. Prettenhofer, R. Weiss, V. Dubourg, J. Vanderplas, A. Passos, D. Cournapeau, M. Brucher, M. Perrot, and E. Duchesnay. 2011. Scikit-learn: Machine learning in Python. *Journal of Machine Learning Research*, 12:2825–2830.

Mohammad Salameh, Houda Bouamor, and Nizar Habash. 2018. Fine-grained arabic dialect identification. In *Proceedings of the 27th International Conference on Computational Linguistics*, pages 1332–1344.

Ashish Vaswani, Noam Shazeer, Niki Parmar, Jakob Uszkoreit, Llion Jones, Aidan N. Gomez, Lukasz Kaiser, and Illia Polosukhin. 2017. Attention is all you need. *ArXiv*, abs/1706.03762.

Thomas Wolf, Lysandre Debut, Victor Sanh, Julien Chaumond, Clement Delangue, Anthony Moi, Pierric Cistac, Tim Rault, R'emi Louf, Morgan Funtowicz, and Jamie Brew. 2019. Huggingface's transformers: State-of-the-art natural language processing. *ArXiv*, abs/1910.03771.

Taha Zerrouki. 2010. pyarabic, an arabic language library for python.

# Weighted combination of BERT and N-GRAM features for Nuanced Arabic Dialect Identification

**Abdellah El Mekki**[1]*, **Ahmed Alami**[2], **Hamza Alami**[2]*, **Ahmed Khoumsi**[3], **Ismail Berrada**[1]

[1]School of Computer and Communication Sciences,
Mohammed VI Polytechnic University, Ben Guerir, Morocco
[2]Faculty of Sciences Dhar EL Mehraz,
Sidi Mohamed Ben Abdellah University, Fez, Morocco
[3]Department of Electrical and Computer Engineering, University of Sherbrooke, Canada
{abdellah.elmekki,ismail.berrada}@um6p.ma
ahmed.alami@usmba.ac.ma
hamza0alami@gmail.com ahmed.khoumsi@usherbrooke.ca


## Abstract


Around the Arab world, different Arabic dialects are spoken by more than 300M persons, and are increasingly popular in social media texts. However, Arabic dialects are considered to be low-resource languages, limiting the development of machine-learning based systems for these dialects. In this paper, we investigate the Arabic dialect identification task, from two perspectives: country-level dialect identification from 21 Arab countries, and province-level dialect identification from 100 provinces. We introduce an unified pipeline of state-of-the-art models, that can handle the two subtasks. Our experimental studies applied to the NADI shared task under the team name BERT-NGRAMS, show promising results both at the country-level (F1-score of 25.99%) and the province-level (F1-score of 6.39%), and thus allow us to be ranked 2nd for the country-level subtask, and 1st in the province-level subtask.


## 1 Introduction

Language identification is considered an important task in Natural Language Processing (NLP), as it helps personalizing applications, automatically detecting the source variety of a given text or speech segment, and collecting/tagging the data (Anshul and Arpit, 2012). In the case of Arabic language, the official language of over 20 countries, and with more than 360 million native speakers, this task becomes very challenging due to the different language variations (Dialectal Arabic), and the complex taxonomy of Arabic language (Zaidan and Callison-Burch, 2014).

In this paper, we consider the Arabic dialect identification task from two perspectives: country-level dialect identification and province-level dialect identification. In the case of the previous Multi Arabic Dialect Applications and Resources (MADAR) Shared Task (Bouamor et al., 2019) , several approaches have been proposed (Abbas et al., 2019). Zhang and Abdul-Mageed (2019) developed country-level identification models based on Bidirectional Encoder Representations from Transformers (BERT) (Devlin et al., 2018), and Gated Recurrent Units (Chung et al., 2014). They ranked 1st in the subtask aiming at classifying tweets with 71.70% macro F1-score and 77.40% accuracy. Talafha et al. (2019) investigated various feature extraction methods, such as term frequency–inverse document frequency (TF-IDF) and word embedding, in order to improve the model performances. The best results, 69.86% F1-score and 76.20% accuracy, were obtained using a simple Linear Support Vector Classification (LinearSVC) classifier with a user voting mechanism.

The main contribution of this paper is the introduction of a novel approach based on a pipeline of state-of-the-art models for both sub-tasks of NADI Shared Task (Abdul-Mageed et al., 2020). For country-level identification, we build a system based on raw tweets. The core of this system is an ensemble model that applies a weighted voting technique on two classifiers, namely *M_NGRAM* and *M_BERT* (will be used as labels for our models on the rest of this paper, the *M* stands for model). *M_NGRAM* uses TF-IDF

---

*equal contribution






*Proceedings of the Fifth Arabic Natural Language Processing Workshop*, pages 268–274
Barcelona, Spain (Online), December 12, 2020

with word and character n-grams to represent tweets. A stochastic gradient descent (SGD) classifier is then trained to optimize the Huber loss (Zhang, 2004). *M_BERT* fine-tunes AraBERT weights (Antoun et al., 2020) with a softmax classifier trained to optimize the multi-class entropy loss. For province-level identification, we build a hierarchical classification, by first performing the country-level identification, and then fine-tuning for each identified country a *M_BERT* model to predict its provinces. Figure 1 illustrates the overall architecture of the proposed solution. The proposed system generates F1-scores of 25.99% and 6.39% for the country-level identification and province-level identification, respectively.

The rest of this paper is organized as follows. Section 2 describes the Nadi Shared Task dataset. Section 3 describes the proposed approaches, models and our data preparation. Section 4 presents experimental results, error analysis and discussion. Finally, the conclusion is given in Section 5.

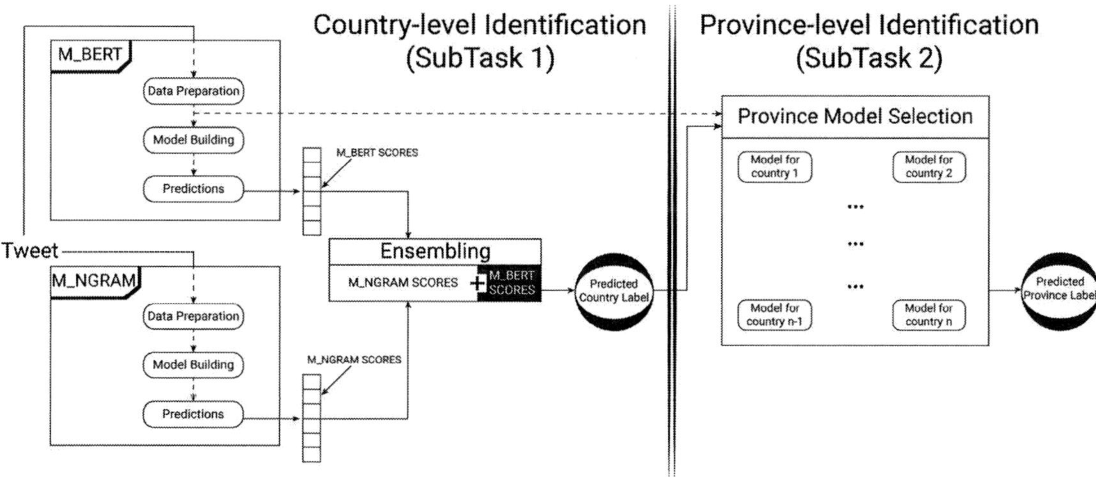


Figure 1: Global overview of the proposed system

## 2 Dataset presentation

The Nuanced Arabic Dialect Identification (NADI) shared task is the first task focusing on naturally-occurring fine-grained dialect. It has been divided into two subtasks: 1) the country-level identification subtask and 2) the province-level identification subtask. The organizers of the shared task provide four sets of collected tweets: the train set (21K), the development set (4,957), the test set (5,000), and the unlabeled tweets set (10M). As we can see in Figure 2, the NADI task is quite challenging due to the unbalanced distribution of tweets (as example a very low frequency of tweets for Djibouti (DJ) and Bahrain (BH) while the number of Egypt (EG) tweets is very high) and the nuance between Arabic dialects.

## 3 Methods

In this section, we review the data preparation pipeline and the proposed models, namely *M_NGRAM* and *M_BERT*, used to build our ensemble model.

### 3.1 Data preparation

As the final system is based on models that rely on different pre-processing steps, below we describe the data preparation pipeline for each model.

#### 3.1.1 *M_BERT* data preparation

For tweet preprocessing, we applied the approach of Hamza et al. (2020) to handle the pretrain-fine-tune discrepancy challenge. The latter can be explained by the fact that the special tokens such as *[MASK]*

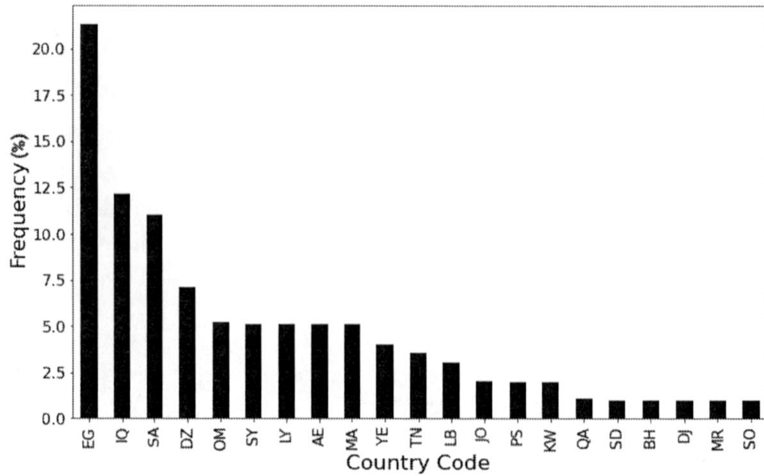

Figure 2: Label distribution of the training set. Country code following the ISO 3166-1 alpha-2 (Wikipedia, 2020)

used by *AraBERT* during pretraining are absent from specific datasets at fine-tuning step. As a tweet may contain words and emojis, the preprocessing pipeline is composed of the following steps:

1. Detecting emojis: the position and the meaning of each emoji is extracted within a tweet.

2. Substituting emojis: each emoji is replaced with the special token *[MASK]* and its meaning is translated from English to Arabic. This allows our model to overcome the pretrain-fine-tune discrepancy.

3. Concatenating emoji-free tweets with their respective emojis Arabic meanings: the special token *[CLS]* is added to the head of each sentence, while the special token *[SEP]* was added to delimit the tweet and the emojis Arabic meanings.

4. Tokenizing the output sentence: all words except special tokens are segmented by Farasa (Abdelali et al., 2016) and then tokenized with *AraBERT* tokenizer. The latter is based on WordPiece (Schuster and Nakajima, 2012) algorithm that is an unsupervised model and follows a sub-words units approach.

### 3.1.2 *M_NGRAM* data preparation

The data preparation for *M_NGRAM* model can be summarized as follows:

- **Data augmentation:** for subtask 1, we construct for each country a list of keywords used to extract tweets from the unlabeled 10 million tweets. The list contains flag emoji, country name, city names and jargon.

- **Data cleaning:** as Arabic dialects are not considered as official languages, it is hard to get rules and standards for each of them. This makes the pre-processing of the provided data for this task hard and limited. For the *M_NGRAM* model, the pre-processing of tweets is done by removing special characters, nomalizing some Arabic characters and words, nomalizing specific links using regular expressions, and removing Tatweel (characters elongation) and non-Arabic characters.

- **Feature extraction:** TF–IDF features are extracted from the pre-processed data in two levels:

  - *Word-level n-grams:* N-gram words are extracted, then vectorized using TF-IDF scores. Unigrams have been found to give the best performances.

    – *Character-level n-grams:* as the task is nuanced Arabic dialect identification, dialects of many countries cannot be differentiated based on words. Moreover, Arabic dialects have no standard writing. This raises the problem of Out-of-vocabulary (OOV) words in the validation phase. To tackle this problem, we use character-level n-grams that treat subwords as features. TD-IDF vectorization is then performed on character-level n-grams. After several experiments, (3,5) range shows the best performance on the character-level n-grams.

## 3.2 Country-level Identification

### 3.2.1 Building the *M_BERT* model

The *M_BERT* model aims to classify a tweet in a predefined country. Thus, the following steps are taken in order to build the model:

1. The tokens obtained from *M_BERT* data preparation step (section 3.1.1) are grouped into two segments. The first one contains tweet's tokens, while the second segment contains the tokens of the Arabic meanings of detected emojis.

2. The token embeddings or representations are computed by feeding their indices and segments to *AraBERT* model (Antoun et al., 2020).

3. The tweet representation is then the output of a global max pooling function applied on *AraBERT* token representation.

4. The probability that a tweet belongs to a country is computed by a softmax function that takes the tweet representation as input.

5. The model is trained to minimize the multi-class cross entropy loss.

We should mention that *AraBERT* model has the same configuration as *BERT-base* model (Devlin et al., 2019). It is composed of 12 encoder blocks, 768 hidden dimensions, 12 attention heads, 512 maximum sequence lengths, and a total of about 110M parameters. The model is trained on two objectives:

- Masked Language Model where the model is trained to predict a masked token.

- Next Sentence Prediction in which the model is optimized to predict if the second sentence follows the first one.

*AraBERT* is pre-trained on 70 million Arabic sentences, corresponding to ∼24GB of text. The authors consider a vocabulary that contains 64k tokens. Another key point to mention here is that during training, *AraBERT* parameters are fine-tuned on this specific task. Arabic Country-level Dialect Identification.

### 3.2.2 Building the *M_NGRAM* model

Since the training data is noisy and Arabic dialects are etymologically close with each other (Habash et al., 2012) , dialect identification gets harder for many tweets. Moreover, the followed data augmentation pipeline is not accurate since the augmentation criterion is chosen based on heuristics. Therefore, we decided to train our *M_NGRAM* model using stochastic gradient descent (SGD) with the following points:

- **Weighting of samples:** the size of the augmented data is 10 times larger than the original data. This makes the classification model more biased towards the augmented samples rather than the original ones. To address this issue, we weight respectively the original samples and the augmented samples with 1 and 0.25, respectively.

- **A loss function sensitive to outliers:** we use the Modified Huber Loss (Zhang, 2004) as a loss function for the SGD classifier. This loss showed to be less sensitive to outliers.

The SGD classifier is trained on the concatenation of TF-IDF vectors of the word-level n-grams and character-level n-grams extracted in section 3.1.2. We use Scikit-learn (Pedregosa et al., 2011) implementation for training our *M_NGRAM* model.

### 3.3 Province-level identification

We propose a hierarchical classifier to detect the province of a given tweet. We begin by grouping the dataset by countries. Then for each group (hence country), an AraBERT-based classifier is trained to predict the province label. All the province classifiers follow the same process described in section 3.2.1. To predict a tweet province, the tweet is first is prepossessed by the *M_BERT* data preparation step. Next, we identify the tweet's country with our Arabic country-level identifier. After that, the province-level classifier is chosen according to the identified country. Finally, the preprocessed tweet is fed to its province-level classifier to predict the province.

## 4 Experimental results, error analysis and discussion

In this section, we conduct experiments to evaluate the performance of the proposed models *M_BERT*, *M_NGRAM*, and *ensemble model* on the development set. Table 1 shows the obtained results in terms of macro precision, macro recall, macro F1-score, and accuracy. As we can see, for subtask 1 the ensemble model achieves the best results: 40.95% for the accuracy and 27.24% for the F1-score. We can notice that the *M_NGRAM* achieves 25.02% macro F1-score while the *M_BERT* scored only 22.42% macro F1-score. Thus, when applying weighted soft voting, the scores obtained by *M_NGRAM* must contribute more than M_BERT scores. Figure 3 confirms that 0.7 for *M_NGRAM* and 0.3 for *M_BERT* are the weights to reach the best F1-score. Our final models (the ensemble model and the hierarchical model) show to perform well on the test set too (Table 1). It is worth to be mentioned that our systems ranked 2nd and 1st for country-level identification and province-level identification, respectively.

| Subtask | DEV/TEST | Model | Precision | Recall | F1 | Accuracy |
|---|---|---|---|---|---|---|
| Subtask 1 | DEV Set | *M_NGRAM* | 31.85% | 24.03% | 25.02% | 37.72% |
| | | *M_BERT* | 28.11% | 21.86% | 22.42% | 37.32% |
| | | Ensemble Model | **33.75%** | **25.70%** | **27.24%** | **40.95%** |
| | TEST Set | Ensemble Model | **30.25%** | **24.85%** | **25.99%** | **39.66%** |
| Subtask 2 | DEV Set | Hierarchical classifier | **26.57%** | **26.02%** | **23.55%** | **26.24%** |
| | Test Set | | **7.84%** | **6.54%** | **6.39%** | **6.50%** |

Table 1: Subtask 1 and subtask 2 performances evaluation of used classifiers on dev and test sets.

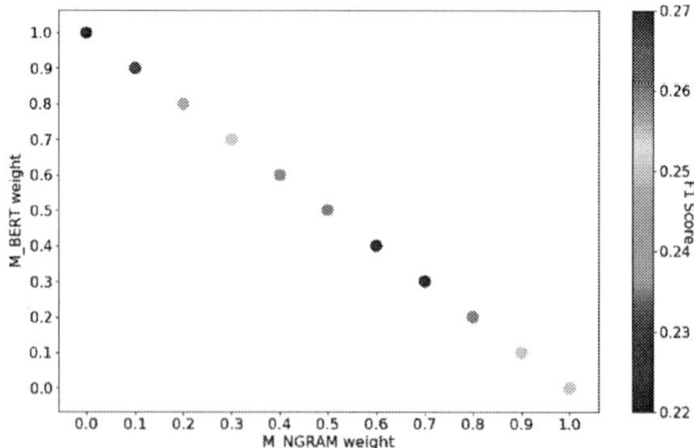


Figure 3: Performance of the weighted soft voting ensemble model with respect to the weights of M_NGRAM and M_BERT for the country-level identification.

In order to help future research in the field of automatic Arabic dialect identification, we discuss below some challenges that our ensemble model faced during the country-level identification:

1. Extremely imbalanced dataset challenge: Some countries like Egypt and Iraq present 21.30% and 12.17% of the training set (Figure 2) while other countries such as Djibouti or Bahrain present

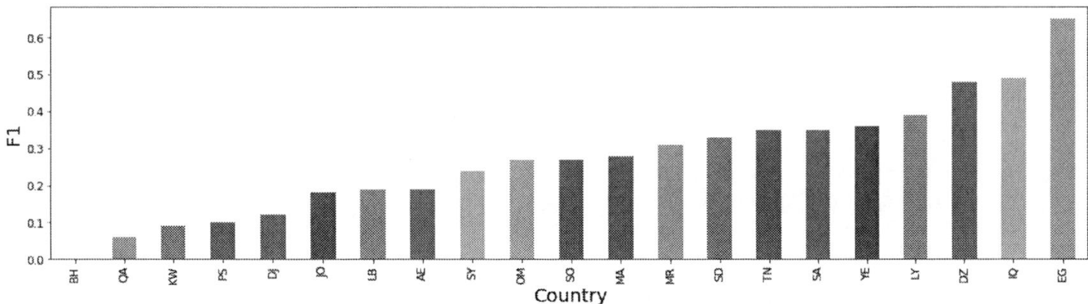

Figure 4: F1 scores of the ensemble model for the 21 countries dialects for the subtask 1. Country code following the ISO 3166-1 alpha-2 (Wikipedia, 2020)

only 1% of the training set. This led to a large gap between the F1-scores (Figure 4) of the well represented countries and the under represented countries, e.g., the F1-score of Egypt is about 68% compared to $\sim 8\%$ (respectively 0%) for Djibouti (respectively Bahrain).

2. Etymological challenge: All tweets within the dataset have Arabic as their root language. Thus, many expressions are shared between many dialects such as لا حول و لا قوة الا بالله ("There is no power but from God" /"lA Hwl w lA qw$h$ AlA bAllh"), إن شاء الله ("God willing" / "Ăn šA' Allh") or بسم الله الرحمن الرحيم ("In the name of Allah the Merciful" / "bsm Allh AlrHmn AlrHym"). One can notice that for each Arabic example we include its English translation and its Buckwalter-Habash-Soudi transliterations (Habash et al., 2007).

3. Unstructured and noisy nature of tweets challenge: Some model predictions are biased by the presence of some dialect-specific words or tokens within tweets. For instance, the expected label of the tweet هو مش كل حاجة بس بيعمل كل حاجة ("It is not everything, but does everything" / "hw mš kl HAj$h$ bs by$\zeta$ml kl HAj$h$") is United Arab Emirates, yet the model has predicted Egypt as the country label. The words الأهلي ("AlÂhly"), حاجه ("HAjh") and مش ("mš") exist more likely in tweets labeled as Egypt, therefore, the model will attribute the highest probability to Egypt label.

4. Topic-biased challenge: The predominance of one or more topics in a set of tweets that belong to the same country. Taking the class label Djibouti as example, we notice clearly that the majority of tweets are about soccer topic. As consequence, the model predict the majority of tweets related to the soccer topic as Djibouti tweets.

## 5 Conclusion

In this paper, we described our submission to the NADI Shared Task. We built a system composed of two classifiers: Ensemble model for country-level identification, and a Hierarchical classifier for province-level identification. The quote "alone we are strong, together we are stronger." has been verified: our ensemble model in subtask 1 increased significantly our F1-score to 27.24% on development set and 25.99% on the test set, allowing us to rank second in the competition. In subtask 2 the hierarchical classifier achieved 6.39% F1-score and ranked 1st. This work has shown that the combination of neural network-based features (BERT) with statistical features (TF-IDF) might increase the performance in other NLP tasks.

## References

Mourad Abbas, Mohamed Lichouri, and Abed Alhakim Freihat. 2019. ST MADAR 2019 shared task: Arabic fine-grained dialect identification. In *Proceedings of the Fourth Arabic Natural Language Processing Workshop*, pages 269–273, Florence, Italy, August. Association for Computational Linguistics.

Ahmed Abdelali, Kareem Darwish, Nadir Durrani, and Hamdy Mubarak. 2016. Farasa: A fast and furious segmenter for Arabic. In *Proceedings of the 2016 Conference of the North American Chapter of the Association for Computational Linguistics: Demonstrations*, pages 11–16, San Diego, California, June. Association for Computational Linguistics.

Muhammad Abdul-Mageed, Chiyu Zhang, Houda Bouamor, and Nizar Habash. 2020. NADI 2020: The First Nuanced Arabic Dialect Identification Shared Task. In *Proceedings of the Fifth Arabic Natural Language Processing Workshop (WANLP 2020)*, Barcelona, Spain.

Mittal Anshul and Goel Arpit. 2012. Stock prediction using twitter sentiment analysis.

Wissam Antoun, Fady Baly, and Hazem Hajj. 2020. Arabert: Transformer-based model for arabic language understanding. In *LREC 2020 Workshop Language Resources and Evaluation Conference 11–16 May 2020*, page 9.

Houda Bouamor, Sabit Hassan, and Nizar Habash. 2019. The MADAR shared task on Arabic fine-grained dialect identification. In *Proceedings of the Fourth Arabic Natural Language Processing Workshop*, pages 199–207, Florence, Italy. Association for Computational Linguistics.

Junyoung Chung, Çaglar Gülçehre, KyungHyun Cho, and Yoshua Bengio. 2014. Empirical evaluation of gated recurrent neural networks on sequence modeling. *CoRR*, abs/1412.3555.

Jacob Devlin, Ming-Wei Chang, Kenton Lee, and Kristina Toutanova. 2018. BERT: pre-training of deep bidirectional transformers for language understanding. *CoRR*, abs/1810.04805.

Jacob Devlin, Ming-Wei Chang, Kenton Lee, and Kristina Toutanova. 2019. BERT: pre-training of deep bidirectional transformers for language understanding. In Jill Burstein, Christy Doran, and Thamar Solorio, editors, *Proceedings of the 2019 Conference of the North American Chapter of the Association for Computational Linguistics: Human Language Technologies, NAACL-HLT 2019, Minneapolis, MN, USA, June 2-7, 2019, Volume 1 (Long and Short Papers)*, pages 4171–4186. Association for Computational Linguistics.

Nizar Habash, Abdelhadi Soudi, and Tim Buckwalter. 2007. On Arabic Transliteration. In A. van den Bosch and A. Soudi, editors, *Arabic Computational Morphology: Knowledge-based and Empirical Methods*, pages 15–22. Springer, Netherlands.

Nizar Habash, Mona Diab, and Owen Rambow. 2012. Conventional orthography for dialectal Arabic. In *Proceedings of the Eighth International Conference on Language Resources and Evaluation (LREC'12)*, pages 711–718, Istanbul, Turkey, May. European Language Resources Association (ELRA).

Alami Hamza, Ouatik El Alaoui Said, Benlahbib Abdessamad, and En-nahnahi Noureddine. 2020. Lisac fsdm-usmba team at semeval 2020 task 12: Overcoming arabert's pretrain-finetune discrepancy for arabic offensive language identification.

F. Pedregosa, G. Varoquaux, A. Gramfort, V. Michel, B. Thirion, O. Grisel, M. Blondel, P. Prettenhofer, R. Weiss, V. Dubourg, J. Vanderplas, A. Passos, D. Cournapeau, M. Brucher, M. Perrot, and E. Duchesnay. 2011. Scikit-learn: Machine learning in Python. *Journal of Machine Learning Research*, 12:2825–2830.

Mike Schuster and Kaisuke Nakajima. 2012. Japanese and korean voice search. In *2012 IEEE International Conference on Acoustics, Speech and Signal Processing, ICASSP 2012, Kyoto, Japan, March 25-30, 2012*, pages 5149–5152. IEEE.

Bashar Talafha, Wael Farhan, Ahmed Altakrouri, and Hussein Al-Natsheh. 2019. Mawdoo3 AI at MADAR shared task: Arabic tweet dialect identification. In *Proceedings of the Fourth Arabic Natural Language Processing Workshop*, pages 239–243, Florence, Italy, August. Association for Computational Linguistics.

Wikipedia. 2020. ISO 3166-1 alpha-2 — Wikipedia, the free encyclopedia. `http://en.wikipedia.org/w/index.php?title=ISO\%203166-1\%20alpha-2&oldid=972097545`. [Online; accessed 13-August-2020].

Omar Zaidan and Chris Callison-Burch. 2014. Arabic dialect identification. *Comput. Linguistics*, 40(1):171–202.

Chiyu Zhang and Muhammad Abdul-Mageed. 2019. No army, no navy: BERT semi-supervised learning of Arabic dialects. In *Proceedings of the Fourth Arabic Natural Language Processing Workshop*, pages 279–284, Florence, Italy, August. Association for Computational Linguistics.

Tong Zhang. 2004. Solving large scale linear prediction problems using stochastic gradient descent algorithms. In *Proceedings of the Twenty-First International Conference on Machine Learning*, ICML '04, page 116, New York, NY, USA. Association for Computing Machinery.

# Arabic dialect identification: An Arabic-BERT model with data augmentation and ensembling strategy


**Kamel Gaanoun[1]    Imade Benelallam[1,2]**

[1]SI2M Lab, National Institute of Statistics and Applied Economics, Morocco
[2]AIOX Labs, Morocco
kamel.gaanoun@gmail.com, i.benelallam@insea.ac.ma


## Abstract


This paper presents the ArabicProcessors team's deep learning system designed for the NADI 2020 Subtask 1 (country-level dialect identification) and Subtask 2 (province-level dialect identification). We used Arabic-Bert in combination with data augmentation and ensembling methods. Unlabeled data provided by task organizers (10 Million tweets) was split into multiple subparts, to which we applied semi-supervised learning method, and finally ran a specific ensembling process on the resulting models. This system ranked 3rd in Subtask 1 with 23.26% F1-score and 2nd in Subtask 2 with 5.75% F1-score.


## 1   Introduction

With the increasing internet access to Arab populations, their contributions to internet content are growing in a remarkable way. Indeed, the internet penetration rate increased from 30.3% to 51.6% between 2012 and 2019 in Arab countries (ITU 2019) . Additionally, there are multiple social networking platforms facilitating the sharing of content for all users. This has led to the appearance of Arabic dialect on internet platforms, which for a long time remained limited to oral conversations of everyday life, unlike Modern Standard Arabic (MSA), which is the only structured Arabic language that serves as the official language of writing and communication in all Arab countries. As a result, there is a growing interest in the treatment and exploitation of these dialects, which differ substantially from MSA and also differ between different countries (Zaidan & Callison-Burch 2013).

We can differentiate between two types of works related to Arabic dialects identification (DID): coarse-grained and fine-grained, where the former focuses on binary classifications (Aridhi et al. 2017, Elfardy & Diab 2013), or large groups of dialects such as Egyptian, Gulf, Iraqi, Maghrebi and Levantine (Habash 2010, Lulu & Elnagar 2018, Zampieri et al. 2017). Works for fine-grained identification has widened the field by incorporating a multitude of dialects reaching, among others, 17 Arab countries (Shon et al. 2020) and 25 different cities (Bouamor et al. 2019, Salameh et al. 2018).

The Nuanced Arabic Dialect Identification (NADI) shared task (Abdul-Mageed et al. 2020) reinforces this type of DID by offering two subtasks, namely Subtask 1 (country-level dialect identification) with 21 different countries dialects, and Subtask 2 (province-level dialect identification) with 100 different province dialects. In this paper, we present our contribution for both subtasks. Indeed, we confirm in our work the performance of the BERT models, which, contrary to traditional statistical methods or classical machine learning techniques, have not been often used for DID problems. In this paper, we expand upon the work of (Zhang & Abdul-Mageed 2019) with an Arabic specific BERT model and a new data augmentation approach concluded with an ensemble model. This approach allowed us to go from an F1-score=15.41% for the baseline model to an F1-score=25.01%; an improvement of 9.1 percentage points. The semi-supervised stage contributed with an improvement of 1.56 percentage points (from a score of 23.45%) scores obtained on the DEV dataset, see Results section.

In the next sections, we describe used data in Section 2, describe our system in Section 3, present our results in Section 4, discuss the data in Sections 5, and finally summarize our work in Section 6.






*Proceedings of the Fifth Arabic Natural Language Processing Workshop*, pages 275–281
Barcelona, Spain (Online), December 12, 2020

## 2 Data

### 2.1 Distribution

Datasets have been provided for the two subtasks: TRAIN for model training, DEV for evaluation and Unlabeled-10M, intended for the improvement of the systems. While the first two were made available to the participants, the third was to be crawled directly using the Twitter API. Indeed, the organizers provided us with the tweets IDs that we crawled up afterwards. This process allowed us to retrieve 9,999,978 tweets in total. By analyzing the content of these tweets, 3,184,508 tweets were unavailable, resulting in 6,815,470 tweets for this dataset.

As for the content of the TRAIN and DEV datasets, they contained the tweet IDs, their texts, the two variables to be predicted, namely country labels (Subtask 1) and province labels (Subtask 2), for respectively 21 countries and 100 provinces. Table 1 shows the statistics for the different datasets.

Finally, the organizers also provided us with the unlabeled TEST dataset, intended for the final evaluation of the system. The score obtained on this dataset was used for system ranking.

| Dataset | Number of tweets | Country labels | Provinces Labels |
|---|---|---|---|
| TRAIN | 21,000 | 21 | 100 |
| DEV | 4,957 | 21 | 100 |
| Unlabeled-10M | 9,999,978[1] | - | - |
| TEST | 5,000 | - | - |

Table 1. Distribution of NADI 2020 datasets

For both country and province labels, the distributions were unbalanced, with a dominance of the following countries: Egypt, Iraq, Saudi Arabia and Algeria with a combined proportion of 52% in TRAIN and 53% in DEV. This finding is reflected at the level of the provinces, since the latter countries are respectively represented by 21,12,10 and 7 provinces, while the rest contain 1 to 6 provinces. See Figure 1 for distribution:

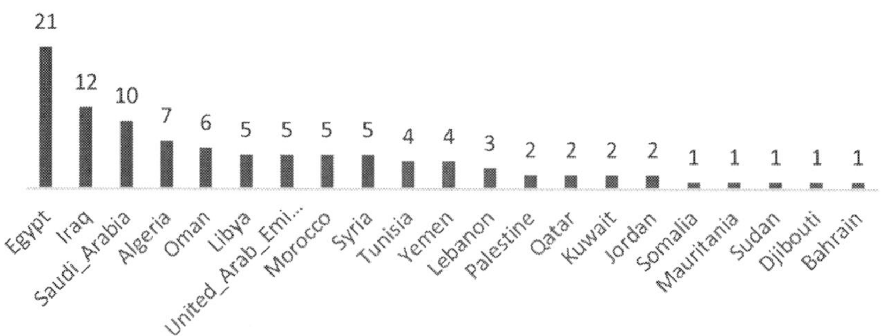


Figure 1. Provinces distribution per country

### 2.2 Preprocessing

We have defined different kinds of duplicate tweets, as follows:

- Islamic Duas (common Islamic invocations) duplicates, which are common to all countries, tweeted either directly by the user or via other platforms, like du3a.org, Gharedly.com, athkarapp.online, etc.

- MSA or classical Arabic text common for all Arabic countries like تصبحون على خير، بسم الله الرحمن الرحيم

- Common expressions in some dialects like,  الله يبارك فيك(Morocco, Saudi_Arabia, Libya...)

---

[1] 3,184,508 tweets were unavailable, thus only 6,815,470 unlabeled tweets were used for this dataset

- Real duplicates specific to some dialect for the same country like محدش استحمل الجزء السيء مني،
مرغوب فيا وانا لطيف بس.

We have therefore decided to delete (i) all tweets coming from other platforms, as they are not dialect specific, (ii) duplicate MSA tweets, (iii) real duplicates with same country. Hence, we removed tweets that could mislead the model's learning, since the same text is attributed to different entities (country or province). This step resulted in the deletion of 674 tweets from Train dataset.

The remaining preprocessing techniques consisted in removing usernames and hashtags, but keeping Arabic hashtags. We also removed words with the "Retweet" pattern, links, and numbers. Further, the Arabic text was standardized by removing diactrics, punctuation, and repeated characters. We also lowercased Latin characters and removed all other symbols.

## 3   System

The adopted system consists of three main steps, namely, (i) BERT-type model training, (ii) data augmentation with semi-supervised learning, and (iii) ensembling methods. These three steps will be described in this section.

### 3.1   BERT model

BERT (Bidirectional Encoder Representations from Transformers) is a language model that has proven its superiority in the field (Devlin et al. 2019). One of the strong points of this model is the possibility to fine-tune a pre-trained model on a new problem by simply adding a new output layer. This advantage was exploited in our system by adopting a pre-trained BERT model augmented by a multiple classification output layer.

The original BERT models named BERT-Base and BERT-Large were trained on a large English corpus, and since then several other language specific BERT models have been developed.

We chose to build our system using an Arabic-specific BERT model, i.e. a model that mimics the original BERT's architecture, but pre-trained on Arabic text. To this end, we compared two available models, namely AraBERT (Antoun et al. 2020) and Arabic-BERT (Safaya et al. 2020), and chose to use Arabic-BERT which obtained the best score on our problem. A brief comparison of the two models is given in Table 2

|  | **AraBERT** | **Arabic-BERT** |
|---|---|---|
| **Corpus size** | ~23GB of text with ~3B words | ~95GB of text with ~8.2B words |
| **Training corpora** | Arabic Wikidumps, The 1.5B words Arabic Corpus (El-Khair 2016) , The OSIAN Corpus, Assafir news articles, 4 other manually crawled news websites | Arabic version of OSCAR - filtered from Common Crawl, Recent dump of Arabic Wikipedia |

Table 2. Brief comparative descriptive of Arabic-BERT and AraBERT

Table 3 summarizes the details of the infrastructure and used hyperparameters.

| **GPU** | Tesla P100-PCIE-16GB |
|---|---|
| **Language** | Python 3.6.9 |
| **Main librairies** | Hugging Face Transformers 2.5.1, Torch 1.5.1, Sklearn 0.22.2, Pandas 1.0.5, Numpy 1.18.5, bayesian-optimization-1.2.0 |
| **Bert Hyperparameters** | Epochs: 3 , Batch size: 80 , Learning rate: 2e-5, Embedding maximum length: 128 |
| **Training average time** | Initial TRAIN data: 10 minutes unlabeled-10M subparts: 180 minutes |

Table 3. Used infrastructure and hyperparameters

### 3.2   Data Augmentation

Before the use of Unlabeled-10M, a first data augmentation was carried out starting with TRAIN. This operation consisted of taking all the tweets from the TRAIN, splitting them into three parts, then mixing them for each given country; this created new text while keeping the vocabulary of the dialect.

We called the model based on these data "Mix"; this model has proven to be efficient since it will appear in all the retained ensemble models, and more precisely, the model with the best score, as will be discussed in the results section.

We then used Unlabeled-10M to improve the predictive performance of our system using a semi-supervised method, defined by the following steps:

a. Unlabeled-10M was subdivided into 5 subparts

b. Label prediction for subpart 1 with our initial Arabic-BERT model based on TRAIN data.

c. Extraction of the tweets with the best softmax probabilities:

- For the majority countries (Egypt, Iraq, Saudi Arabia) we use the probabilities above the 99th percentile.

- For the other countries we use probabilities above the 80th percentile.

Indeed, we noticed that the model already scored well on the majority countries, but still needed improvement for the other countries, which is why it was decided to further augment the minority countries. This approach improved the minority countries' scores and thus the overall score of the model. That said, for subtask2, probabilities above the 90th percentile were taken for all provinces.

We point out that a total of 1,056,984 tweets were retained from Unlabeled-10M.

d. Concatenation of the predictions of the current subpart with the initial TRAIN data

e. Training a new model on this new data

For this step we train two models each time, namely a model based on the initial Arabic-BERT, and a model based on our initial model trained on the TRAIN data. The better of these two models will be compared to the model obtained for the previous sub-part (see step f, below).

f. Compare the obtained score with the last model's score and select the one that provided the best score for the prediction on the next subpart.

g. Repeat steps b,c,d,e,f for the following subparts with the selected model.

Our described model is a modified version of that done by (Zhang & Abdul-Mageed 2019), who used self-training to augment their model. By using self-training we risk falling into the problem of "catastrophic forgetting", i.e. our initial model may forget some of its original learning by forcing itself to learn the new data. Added to this, training and initial prediction errors may also become more pronounced. We also opted to subdivide the unlabeled-10M into several parts before applying our process to avoid a considerable amount of processing and resource use time in case of repetitive use of all the data, and also to be able to ensemble the different models obtained on each sub-part.

### 3.3   Ensemble methods

Once the data augmentation step is completed, we proceed to the ensembling of the different obtained models. In fact, we have a list of models containing data augmentation models in addition to our initial model Arabic-BERT and the MIX model. These different models will be ensembled according to the following methods:

- Hard majority voting
    - a    Original approach

The first method used is hard majority voting, which consists of taking for each tweet the label that was most often predicted by all the models. That's the statistical mode of predicted labels distribution.

b    Modified approach

The original mode-based approach poses a problem if there is an equal number of predictions for some labels. Indeed, if we take the example where labels 1,3 and 5 have all been predicted 3 times, the mode calculated in this case (with stats scipy's library on python) will be equal to 1, i.e. the smallest label.

We have modified the mode calculation to change this behavior by creating a modified version of the mode computation in scipy. This version consists of forcing the mode to be equal to the label corresponding to the majority country (Egypt, Iraq or Saudi Arabia) when it is predicted at the same frequency as other minority countries. For example:

On all the predictions, the most predicted countries were as follows: Djibouti (label 1), Egypt (label 3), and Jordan (label 5), the modified mode will be equal to the label 3 corresponding to the majority country (Egypt) instead of 1.

- Soft voting
  a    Unweighted approach

While hard voting is based on predicted labels, soft voting takes into account the softmax probabilities assigned to each label., The probabilities of each label are summed across the different models, then the label with the highest average probability will be assigned by the ensemble model.

b    Weighted approach

The unweighted method does not take into account the performance of the sub-models. We therefore proceeded to weight the models according to their score (larger weight for larger score). The choice of weights for this method was first done manually, followed by Bayesian optimization to maximize the F1-score.

We draw attention to the fact that these different methods were applied not only to all the models, but also to all their possible subsets. Indeed, we generate all possible combinations of the models before putting them together and retain the sub-set with the highest F1-score.

## 4    Results

We oriented the development of our system towards the use of the BERT model after performing a comparative study between the chosen BERT model and machine learning models; namely Naive-Bayes, Logistic Regression and XGBoost. These last three were all tested with a CountVectorizer (word counts) as an input, and TF-IDF (word and char levels with 2 and 3 ngrams). The best result was obtained with the XGBoost model with an F1-score=15.41%, but was still less performant than the chosen BERT. We consider XGBoost as the baseline model for our comparisons. Table 4 summarizes the results of the machine learning and BERT models on the DEV data for subtask 1.

| Model | F1-Score |
| --- | --- |
| Naive Bayes | 8.58% |
| Logistic Regression | 14.30% |
| XGBoost | 15.41% |
| Arabic-BERT | 23.45% |

Table 4. Arabic-BERT compared to other machine learning models (discarded TF-IDF based models results due to their low scores)

- **Subtask 1**

For subtask 1, four model variants were submitted for development data and three for test data. Once the prediction step on the subparts of the Unlabeled-10M was completed, we proceeded to try different ensemble methods and compared the results obtained on the development and test data.

Ensembling proved to be an improving element in the predictive power of the system, but the score varied depending on the method used. A first comparison between soft voting and hard majority voting lends an advantage to the latter, based on the mode (the label most often predicted by the ensemble models) with a score of 24.15% Vs 24.01% compared to the soft voting method. Modifying the hard voting by changing the mode's calculation increased the score to 24.32%. It is this method that recorded the best submitted score with an F1-Score=23.26%, we call it BestTest. However, it is by adopting the weighted version of the soft voting that we obtain the best score on the development data with respectively 25.006% with manually defined weights, and 25.01% using Bayesian optimization, this model will be called BestDev. (See Table 5)

| Model variant | DEV F1-Score | TEST F1-Score |
|---|---|---|
| Basic Hard Majority Voting | 24.15% | 22.52% |
| Modified Hard Majority Voting | 24.32% | 23.26% |
| Basic Soft Majority Voting | 24.01% | 23.21% |
| Manual Weighted Soft Majority Voting | 25.006% | 23.07% |
| Bayesian Weighted Majority Soft Voting | 25.01% | 23.03% |

Table 5. Subtask 1 scores

- **Subtask 2**

For subtask 2, we applied a similar process as for subtask 1, except that the ensembling did not result in an improvement. We have retained the subpart of the Unlabeled-10M that obtained the best score, namely an F1-score=4.72% for the development data corresponding to an F1-score = 5.75% on the test data.

## 5  Discussion

| | Majority countries | Minority countries |
|---|---|---|
| **BestTest** | 0.63 | 0.93 |
| **BestDev** | 1.10 | 1.67 |

Table 6. F1-score enhancements

One of the challenges we encountered during the creation of our system was the low quality of predictions of minority labels. As illustrated for subtask 1 (similar finding for the provinces) in Table 6, it appears that our semi-supervised method combined with the ensemble method had a higher impact on minority labels, with an improvement reaching +1.67 percentage points for minority labels compared to +1.10 percentage points for majority labels (Egypt, Iraq, Saudi Arabia, Algeria). However, the problem still persists since we note that our models are unable to predict certain dialects such as Bahrain, Qatar, Kuwait. It would therefore be judicious in future work to improve our data augmentation method by focusing even more on these minority labels. Additionally, our MIX model did not take this into consideration; the mixing of tweets did not favour the augmentation of minority labels, and should be explored in the future.

Our models also encountered the problem of tweets written in MSA, which makes their predictions confusing since these tweets are not specific to any dialect. It would be a good idea to have our models rerun after removing all MSA tweets. This would require the creation of a pre-model for the detection of MSA text.

Finally, we can still explore other ways to improve BERT-based models by using the embedding obtained with BERT as input for CNN networks, a method that has already proven its efficiency as at (Kim 2014, Zheng & Yang 2019).

## 6  Conclusion

In this paper, we have described our contribution to NADI shared task 2020 subtasks. Subtask 1 dealt with Arabic dialects identification (DID) at the country level (21 Arab countries) and subtask 2 focused on dialects by provinces (100 provinces). Our system is based on an Arabic-specific BERT model, a semi-supervised method for data augmentation and an ensembling of different models following the data augmentation. By recording an F1-score=23.26% at subtask 1 (ranked third) and 5.75% at subtask 2 (ranked second), this approach demonstrates the efficiency of our BERT models in the field of DID.

# References


Abdul-Mageed, M., Zhang, C., Bouamor, H. & Habash, N. (2020), NADI 2020: The First Nuanced Arabic Dialect Identification Shared Task, *in* 'Proceedings of the Fifth Arabic Natural Language Processing Workshop (WANLP2020)', Barcelona, Spain.

Antoun, W., Baly, F. & Hajj, H. (2020), Arabert: Transformer-based model for arabic language understanding, *in* 'LREC 2020 Workshop Language Resources and Evaluation Conference 11–16 May 2020', p. 9.

Aridhi, C., Hadhemi, A., Souissi, E. & Younes, J. (2017), Word-level identification of romanized tunisian dialect, pp. 170–175.

Bouamor, H., Hassan, S. & Habash, N. (2019), The MADAR shared task on Arabic fine-grained dialect identification, *in* 'Proceedings of the Fourth Arabic Natural Language Processing Workshop', Association for Computational Linguistics, Florence, Italy, pp. 199–207. https://www.aclweb.org/anthology/W19-4622

Devlin, J., Chang, M.-W., Lee, K. & Toutanova, K. (2019), BERT: Pre-training of deep bidirectional transformers for language understanding, *in* 'Proceedings of the 2019 Conference of the North American Chapter of the Association for Computational Linguistics: Human Language Technologies, Volume 1 (Long and Short Papers)', Association for Computational Linguistics, Minneapolis, Minnesota, pp. 4171–4186. https://www.aclweb.org/anthology/N19-1423

El-Khair, I. A. (2016), '1.5 billion words arabic corpus', *ArXiv* **abs/1611.04033**.

Elfardy, H. & Diab, M. (2013), Sentence level dialect identification in arabic, Vol. 2, pp. 456–461.

Habash, N. Y. (2010), *Introduction to Arabic Natural Language Processing*, Morgan & Claypool. https://ieeexplore.ieee.org/document/6813521

ITU (2019), Measuring digital development, facts and figures, Technical report, International Telecommunication Union.

Kim, Y. (2014), Convolutional neural networks for sentence classification, *in* 'Proceedings of the 2014 Conference on Empirical Methods in Natural Language Processing (EMNLP)', Association for Computational Linguistics, Doha, Qatar, pp. 1746–1751. https://www.aclweb.org/anthology/D14-1181

Lulu, L. & Elnagar, A. (2018), 'Automatic arabic dialect classification using deep learning models', *Procedia Computer Science* **142**, 262–269.

Safaya, A., Abdullatif, M. & Yuret, D. (2020), Kuisail at semeval-2020 task 12: Bert-cnn for offensive speech identification in social media, *in* 'Proceedings of the International Workshop on Semantic Evaluation (SemEval)'.

Salameh, M., Bouamor, H. & Habash, N. (2018), Fine-grained Arabic dialect identification, *in* 'Proceedings of the 27th International Conference on Computational Linguistics', Association for Computational Linguistics, Santa Fe, New Mexico, USA, pp. 1332–1344. https://www.aclweb.org/anthology/C18-1113

Shon, S., Ali, A., Samih, Y., Mubarak, H. & Glass, J. (2020), Adi17: A fine-grained arabic dialect identification dataset.

Zaidan, O. & Callison-Burch, C. (2013), 'Arabic dialect identification', *Computational Linguistics* .

Zampieri, M., Malmasi, S., Ljubešic, N., Nakov, P., Ali, A., Tiedemann, J., Scherrer, Y. & Aepli, N. (2017), Findings of the VárDial evaluation campaign 2017, *in* 'Proceedings of the Fourth Workshop on NLP for Similar Languages, Varieties and Dialects (VarDial)', Association for Computational Linguistics, Valencia, Spain, pp. 1–15. https://www.aclweb.org/anthology/W17-1201

Zhang, C. & Abdul-Mageed, M. (2019), No army, no navy: BERT semi-supervised learning of Arabic dialects, *in* 'Proceedings of the Fourth Arabic Natural Language Processing Workshop', Florence, Italy.

Zheng, S. & Yang, M. (2019), *A New Method of Improving BERT for Text Classification*, pp. 442–452.

# Faheem at NADI shared task: Identifying the dialect of Arabic tweet


**Nouf A. Al-Shenaifi**
Department of Computer Science,
College Comput. & Info. Sciences,
King Saud University,
Riyadh 11543, Saudi Arabia
noalshenaifi@ksu.edu.sa

**Aqil M. Azmi**
Department of Computer Science,
College Comput. & Info. Sciences,
King Saud University,
Riyadh 11543, Saudi Arabia
aqil@ksu.edu.sa



## Abstract

This paper describes *Faheem* (adj. of understand), our submission to NADI (Nuanced Arabic Dialect Identification) shared task. With so many Arabic dialects being understudied due to the scarcity of the resources, the objective is to identify the Arabic dialect used in the tweet, at the country-level. We propose a machine learning approach where we utilize word-level $n$-gram ($n = 1$ to 3) and *tf-idf* features and feed them to six different classifiers. We train the system using a data set of 21,000 tweets—provided by the organizers—covering twenty-one Arab countries. Our top performing classifiers are: Logistic Regression, Support Vector Machines, and Multinomial Naïve Bayes (MNB). We achieved our best result of macro-$F_1 = 0.151$ using the MNB classifier.


## 1 Introduction

Arabic language users constitute the fastest-growing language group when it comes to the number of Internet users. According to (www.internetworldstats.com/stats7.htm), Arabic language Internet users have grown by 9,348% followed by Russian with a growth of 3,653% during the last twenty years. There is a serious lack of Arabic contents in the Internet. As one author put it, searching for "How to make ice cream?" in Arabic yields 99,100 results, while the same search in English yields 37,600,000 hits. Contrast this with twenty-two Arab countries, holding 420M speakers, vs 260M native English speakers worldwide (Pangeanic.com, 2013).

The majority of the Arabic content in the web is in Modern Standard Arabic (MSA), and though it is understandable to most of the Arabs, the mass majority do not use it in their daily communication. Rather they switch to colloquial or informal Arabic, which was originally confined to the domain of verbal communication (Azmi and Aljafari, 2018). Social media gave masses the opportunity to write in whatever language suites them, and this led to a rise in writing informally. The dialectical Arabic differs from region to another, and the vocabulary of some dialects overlaps with MSA by as much as 90% (Cadora, 1976); however, differences include some very common words such as those meaning "see", "go", and "not", as well as phonology, syntax and morphology rules (Habash and Rambow, 2006).

Dialect identification is the task of automatically identifying the dialect of a particular part of text (Zaidan and Callison-Burch, 2014). Arabic dialects differ from one region to another, and there are no available dictionaries for their vocabulary nor written rules. The range of Arabic dialects is much more varied than the range of dialects that are typically considered to comprise European languages such as English and French (Azmi and Aljafari, 2018). Even with the lack of written rules there are common set of conventional orthography guidelines for Arabic dialect (Habash et al., 2018; Eryani et al., 2020). There guidelines may give clue to the dialect.

The Nuanced Arabic Dialect Identification (NADI) shared task is associated with the Fifth Arabic Natural Language Processing Workshop (WANLP 2020) (Abdul-Mageed et al., 2020). The shared task follows the efforts of Arabic Natural Language Processing (NLP) workshops and conferences that have taken place in the recent years (Bouamor et al., 2018; Bouamor et al., 2019). Bouamor et al. (2018)






*Proceedings of the Fifth Arabic Natural Language Processing Workshop*, pages 282–287
Barcelona, Spain (Online), December 12, 2020

describes the first effort to collect a large-scale corpus and lexicon for dialectal Arabic. The MADAR corpus is what was used to build the MADAR Shared task. Salameh et al. (2018) is another important work where the authors worked on city-level dialect identification. The NADI shared task consists of two subtasks. The goal of the first subtask is to identify the origin country of the tweet based on the dialect. While the second subtask focused on province-level dialect, where the goal is to predict the country province of the tweet. The organizers provided a data set of 21,000 labeled tweets covering 21 Arab countries with country and province labels. In addition, they provided 10M unlabeled tweets covering different Arab countries.

We briefly summarize the challenges as: (a) the maximum length of a tweet is 280 characters which includes hashtags, special characters, URLs, etc. This does not leave enough information—in term of words—to accurately predict the dialects; (b) some of the tweets are written in MSA rather than country dialect which complicates the classification task; (c) certain similarity between dialects and the mixing between MSA and dialect in a given text (Biadsy et al., 2009); and (d) some of the tweets are re-tweets possibly from another different country with a different country dialect.

In this paper, we develop a machine learning model to identify and predict the dialect of a tweet over 21 different Arabic dialects (NADI shared task subtask 1). Dialect identification can be seen as a multi-class text classification task, where we predict the probability of a dialect given a tweet (set of words) (Talafha et al., 2019). Our proposed system use word $n$-grams and *tf-idf* as features, and six different classifiers (e.g., Multinomial Naïve Bayes, Logistic Regression). In developing the system we relied solely on the data provided by the shared task organizers, no external data was involved. We assume the data is free of spelling error, and/or context-sensitive error. The latter error occurs when a user types a correctly spelled word when another is intended (Azmi et al., 2019), e.g. "I want a peace (piece) of cake".

The rest of the paper is organized as follows. In Section 2, we present the data set used in building our machine learning models. We describe the proposed system in Section 3. Section 4 discusses system performance and the results. We conclude with suggestions for future research in Section 5.

## 2 Dataset and evaluation

All the registered participants to the NADI shared task received the data set. The data set is divided into Train, Development (Dev), and Test sets (see Table 1). The Training set contains 21,000 Arabic tweets, with each tweet is associated with its dialect label. The labels mark the country the dialect is used in. Table 2 lists the 21 Arab countries which are covered by the Training set, along with their size. The Dev set contains 4,957 tweets with corresponding Arabic dialect labels, while the Test set contains unlabeled 5,000 tweets. This blind Test data set will be used to evaluate the output of the participating teams.

| Data set | No. of tweets |
|----------|---------------|
| Training | 21,000 |
| Dev | 4,957 |
| Testing | 5,000 |

Table 1: Details of the NADI shared task data set.

We have an imbalanced class distribution in the Training data set, tweets are not equally divided among the countries (see Table 2). Egypt has the highest number of tweets in the Training set ($\approx 21\%$), while only 1% of the tweets are labeled Sudan, Somalia, Mauritania, Bahrain, and Djibouti.

The evaluation metrics includes precision ($P$), recall ($R$), $F$-score, and accuracy. The official metric is the macro-averaged $F$-score, which computes the metric independently for each country and then take the average (hence treating all countries equally). Let $C = \{Egypt, Iraq, Saudi, \ldots\}$ be the list of countries. If we denote $F$-score of classifying the tweet into country $c$ by $F_1(c)$, then we can define the macro-average $F$-score as,

| Country | # tweets | % | Country | # tweets | % |
|---|---|---|---|---|---|
| Egypt | 4,473 | (21.30) | Lebanon | 639 | (3.04) |
| Iraq | 2,556 | (12.17) | Jordan | 426 | (2.03) |
| Saudi Arabia | 2,312 | (11.00) | Palestine | 420 | (2.00) |
| Algeria | 1,491 | (7.10) | Kuwait | 420 | (2.00) |
| Oman | 1,098 | (5.23) | Qatar | 234 | (1.11) |
| UAE | 1,070 | (5.10) | Sudan | 210 | (1.00) |
| Syria | 1,070 | (5.10) | Somalia | 210 | (1.00) |
| Morocco | 1,070 | (5.10) | Mauritania | 210 | (1.00) |
| Libya | 1,070 | (5.10) | Bahrain | 210 | (1.00) |
| Yemen | 851 | (4.05) | Djibouti | 210 | (1.00) |
| Tunisia | 750 | (3.57) | | | |

Table 2: Distribution statistics of the Training data set. Numbers inside bracket is the size as percentage.

$$\text{macro-}F_1 = \frac{1}{n} \sum_{c \in C} F_1(c).$$

## 3 System overview

Our goal is to accurately classify the tweets to one dialect out of 21 Arabic dialects (corresponding to twenty-one Arab countries). To develop our system, we used python, the machine learning library Scikit-learn[1] (Pedregosa et al., 2011), and NLTK (Natural Language Toolkit) library (Loper and Bird, 2002). There are three main stages in our system: pre-processing the data, feature extraction, and finally classification.

### 3.1 Data pre-processing

We pre-process all the data sets (i.e. Train, Dev, and Test). The pre-processing includes tokenizing over the white spaces, removing URLs and user mentions from tweets, removing punctuation and special characters, removing of non-Arabic words. No stemming was applied. Stemming is useful on MSA text but not for the dialect. There is no single stemmer that can be applied on all Arabic dialects, and so we need to apply a different stemmer for each dialect (e.g. stemmer for Arabian Gulf dialect, stemmer for Egyptian dialect, etc). As the dialect is not known beforehand, so it does not make sense to apply it. None of the participants in MADAR shared task 2019 (Bouamor et al., 2019) used stemming. Stopword removal is another task that is common in Arabic NLP applications. Again, we did not remove the stopwords. Simply, it is the same argument behind not using stemming.

### 3.2 Feature extraction

The *tf-idf* (short for Term Frequency-Inverse Document Frequency) is a weighting factor intended to reflect how important a word is to a document (tweet) in a corpus (Leskovec et al., 2014). The *tf-idf* value increases proportionally to the number of times a word appears in the document and is offset by the number of documents in the corpus that contain the word. In our system we build a model that depends on extracting a word-level $n$-grams *tf-idf* features for ($n = 1$ to 3), and character-level $n$-grams *tf-idf* features. According to Mishra and Mujadia (2019), combining word and character level $n$-gram *tf-idf* performs better than individual word or character *tf-idf* vectors. The word $n$-grams helps in differentiating between dialects as some words are confined to a single dialect. In contrast, the character-level $n$-grams help in finding morphological (prefixes and suffixes) characteristics of the dialects.

### 3.3 Training classifiers

After the features are extracted, we need to predict the tweets' dialect labels. We used six different classifiers. Based on the performance of different classifiers, we picked the following three classifiers to submit our official entry into the shared task:

---

[1]Available at `https://scikit-learn.org`.

- Multinomial Naïve Bayes (MNB) classifier with Laplace smoothing parameter alpha $= 0.5$.

- Support Vector Machines (SVM) classifier with a linear kernel, and cost $C = 1$. The multi-class is handled using one-vs-the-rest strategy.

- Logistic Regression (LR). For the multi-class training we used one-vs-the-rest scheme.

The other three classifiers which we experimented with but failed to yield satisfactory performance are: Gaussian Naïve Bayes (GNB), Decision Tree (DT), and Random Forest (RF).

Moreover, we also experimented with deep learning-based classifier using python Keras API (Géron, 2019). However, deep learning models did not perform well on this task. This is due to the nature of the data set itself. Deep learning models require huge training data set which is not the case here. There are twenty-one different dialects, and that leaves a relatively small number of tweets per dialect.

## 4 Results and discussion

### 4.1 Selecting language model

Our model uses word-level $n$-grams. We need to determine what is the appropriate range for $n$. We trained the system using Training data, and tested the system on Dev data (Table 1). Table 3 reports the performance measures for different values of $n \in [1, 4]$. For all the classifiers we do not observe any improvement in the performance for $n > 2$. So, it suffices we use language model $n$-grams for $n = 1$ and 2. However, we wanted to be extra cautious and went for $n = 1$ to 3.

| Classifier | $n = 1$ | | | $n = 1$–2 | | | $n = 1$–3 | | | $n = 1$–4 | | |
|---|---|---|---|---|---|---|---|---|---|---|---|---|
| | $P$ | $R$ | macro-$F_1$ | $P$ | $R$ | macro-$F_1$ | $P$ | $R$ | macro-$F_1$ | $P$ | $R$ | macro-$F_1$ |
| SVM | 0.84 | 0.83 | 0.82 | 0.85 | 0.84 | 0.83 | 0.85 | 0.84 | 0.83 | 0.83 | 0.82 | 0.80 |
| MNB | 0.79 | 0.77 | 0.76 | 0.81 | 0.79 | 0.78 | 0.78 | 0.76 | 0.74 | 0.78 | 0.76 | 0.74 |
| LR | 0.83 | 0.82 | 0.80 | 0.82 | 0.81 | 0.79 | 0.82 | 0.81 | 0.79 | 0.82 | 0.81 | 0.79 |
| RF | 0.71 | 0.70 | 0.69 | 0.71 | 0.70 | 0.69 | 0.71 | 0.69 | 0.67 | 0.70 | 0.68 | 0.66 |
| DT | 0.65 | 0.64 | 0.61 | 0.65 | 0.65 | 0.62 | 0.65 | 0.65 | 0.62 | 0.65 | 0.65 | 0.62 |
| GNB | 0.71 | 0.69 | 0.65 | 0.72 | 0.70 | 0.66 | 0.70 | 0.69 | 0.64 | 0.70 | 0.69 | 0.64 |

Table 3: Performance measurement on Dev data using different values of $n$ for word $n$-grams.

### 4.2 System performance

We tested our system on Dev data set as well as the Training data set (Table 1). For the latter, we used 10-fold cross-validation, where the 21,000 tweets were randomly divided into ten equal folds. In each iteration a different fold is used for testing, while the other nine folds are used for training. The whole process is repeated ten times. Cross-validation (CV) generally results in a less biased or less optimistic estimate of the model than other methods, such as a simple train/test split. Table 4 summarizes the results of testing on the Training data using 10-fold CV, and Dev data using different classifiers. In both cases, the top three classifiers are SVM, MNB, and LR, with a slight edge in favor of SVM. The SVM achieved macro-$F_1 = 0.42$ and 0.83 on the Training and the Dev data (respectively).

| Classifier | Training data (10-fold CV) | | | Dev data | | |
|---|---|---|---|---|---|---|
| | $P$ | $R$ | macro-$F_1$ | $P$ | $R$ | macro-$F_1$ |
| Support Vector Machine | 0.42 | 0.46 | 0.42 | 0.85 | 0.84 | 0.83 |
| Multinomial Naïve Bayes | 0.46 | 0.43 | 0.39 | 0.81 | 0.79 | 0.78 |
| Logistic Regression | 0.42 | 0.42 | 0.38 | 0.83 | 0.82 | 0.80 |
| Random Forest | 0.39 | 0.37 | 0.31 | 0.71 | 0.70 | 0.69 |
| Decision Tree | 0.31 | 0.33 | 0.31 | 0.65 | 0.65 | 0.62 |
| Gaussian Naïve Bayes | 0.33 | 0.36 | 0.33 | 0.72 | 0.70 | 0.66 |

Table 4: Summary of results using different classifiers on two data sets.

### 4.3 Official results

Based on our experiment, our best performing classifiers are SVM, MNB, and LR (Table 4). The organizers of NADI shared task (subtask 1) allow up to three submissions. Table 5 lists the official result of our submission on the Test data set as reported by the organizers. This time the Multinomial Naïve Bayes yield slightly better performance compared to SVM. However, the performance results of the three classifiers are close to each other.

| Classifier | $P$ | $R$ | macro-$F_1$ | Accuracy |
|---|---|---|---|---|
| Support Vector Machine | 0.17303 | 0.14810 | 0.14613 | 0.3224 |
| Multinomial Naïve Bayes | 0.22342 | 0.14714 | 0.15095 | 0.3402 |
| Logistic Regression | 0.25430 | 0.14305 | 0.14911 | 0.3280 |

Table 5: Official results of our submitted run on the Test data set.

### 4.4 Discussion

Of the six classifiers, SVM, MNB, and LR where the top three on two different data sets (Dev and Training using 10-fold CV). Surprisingly, none of the three classifiers did well in the official shared task. Our best performance on the Test data set was macro-$F_1 = 0.15095$ using the MNB classifier (Table 5), which is a far cry from its behavior in Table 4.

| | Actual judgment | |
|---|---|---|
| Classifier prediction | True | False |
| Positive | TP | FP |
| Negative | TN | FN |

Table 6: Confusion matrix.

Suppose we randomly assign the dialects to a tweet. As each tweet could belong to any of the 21 dialects, then the probability of correct assignment (assume equal likelihood) is $1/21 = 4.76\%$. The precision $P$ is defined as $TP/(TP + FP)$, while recall $R$ is given by $TP/(TP + FN)$, where TP, FP, and FN stands respectively for true positive, false positive, and false negative. The terms true and false refer to whether that prediction corresponds to the actual judgment and the terms positive and negative refer to the classifier's prediction (see Table 6). For example, we may interpret FP as the number of tweets $t$ that are falsely classified as belonging to dialect $d$; similarly, FN as the number of tweets $t$ that are falsely classified as *not* belonging to dialect $d$. We expect FN to be $1 - 1/21 \approx 0.95$ which is close to 1.

From the above argument, we can state that any value for $P$ and $R$ over 4.76% means the system is doing better than randomly assigning the dialects. Thus, $P = R = 0.476$ should be the baseline. From Table 5 the value of $R$ is almost the same for all three classifiers, while for $P$ there is a noticeable difference. If we take MNB classifier, $R = 0.147$, substituting 0.95 for FN and solving, we get $TP = 0.1637$. This means 16.37% of the time we are identifying the dialect correctly. Substituting into precision and solving, we get the value $FP = 0.57$. Which means over half of the time (57%) we are wrongly assigning the dialect. The F-measure $F_1 = 2/(1/P + 1/R) = 2TP/(TP + FP + TN + FN)$. This means if we want to improve macro-$F_1$ then we just need to boost TP.

## 5 Conclusion

In this paper we described our participation in the 2020 Nuanced Arabic Dialect Identification (NADI) shared task, where the goal is to build a system that can predict which of the 21 Arabic dialects the tweet is written in. We submitted the result of executing our system on a standard test data using three different classifiers: SVM, Multinomial Naïve Bayes, and Logistic Regression. Our official performance of macro-$F_1 \approx 0.151$ using the Multinomial Naïve Bayes classifier is not in par with our aspiration.

# References


Muhammad Abdul-Mageed, Chiyu Zhang, Houda Bouamor, and Nizar Habash. 2020. NADI 2020: The First Nuanced Arabic Dialect Identification Shared Task. In *Proceedings of the Fifth Arabic Natural Language Processing Workshop (WANLP 2020)*, Barcelona, Spain.

Aqil M Azmi and Eman A Aljafari. 2018. Universal web accessibility and the challenge to integrate informal Arabic users: a case study. *Universal Access in the Information Society*, 17(1):131–145.

Aqil M Azmi, Manal N Almutery, and Hatim A Aboalsamh. 2019. Real-word errors in Arabic texts: A better algorithm for detection and correction. *IEEE/ACM Transactions on Audio, Speech, and Language Processing*, 27(8):1308–1320.

Fadi Biadsy, Julia Hirschberg, and Nizar Habash. 2009. Spoken arabic dialect identification using phonotactic modeling. In *Proceedings of the EACL 2009 Workshop on Computational Approaches to Semitic Languages*, pages 53–61.

H Bouamor, N Habash, M Salameh, W Zaghouani, O Rambow, D Abdulrahim, O Obeid, S Khalifa, F Eryani, A Erdmann, and K Oflazer. 2018. The MADAR Arabic dialect corpus and lexicon. In *Proceedings of the 11th International Conference on Language Resources and Evaluation (LREC 2018)*, pages 3387–3396.

Houda Bouamor, Sabit Hassan, and Nizar Habash. 2019. The MADAR shared task on Arabic fine-grained dialect identification. In *Proceedings of the 4th Arabic Natural Language Processing Workshop*, pages 199–207, Florence, Italy. Association for Computational Linguistics.

Frederic J Cadora. 1976. Lexical relationships among Arabic dialects and the Swadesh list. *Anthropological linguistics*, 18(6):237–260.

Fadhl Eryani, Nizar Habash, Houda Bouamor, and Salam Khalifa. 2020. A spelling correction corpus for multiple Arabic dialects. In *Proceedings of the 12th Language Resources and Evaluation Conference*, pages 4130–4138.

Aurélien Géron. 2019. *Hands-on machine learning with Scikit-Learn, Keras, and TensorFlow: Concepts, tools, and techniques to build intelligent systems*. O'Reilly Media.

Nizar Habash and Owen Rambow. 2006. MAGEAD: a morphological analyzer and generator for the Arabic dialects. In *Proceedings of the 21st International Conference on Computational Linguistics and 44th Annual Meeting of the Association for Computational Linguistics*, pages 681–688.

N Habash, F Eryani, S Khalifa, O Rambow, D Abdulrahim, A Erdmann, R Faraj, W Zaghouani, H Bouamor, N Zalmout, S Hassan, F Al-Shargi, S Alkhereyf, B Abdulkareem, R Eskander, M Salameh, and H Saddiki. 2018. Unified guidelines and resources for Arabic dialect orthography. In *Proceedings of the 11th International Conference on Language Resources and Evaluation (LREC 2018)*, pages 3628–3637.

Jure Leskovec, Anand Rajaraman, and Jeffrey David Ullman. 2014. *Mining of massive datasets*. Cambridge University Press.

Edward Loper and Steven Bird. 2002. NLTK: the natural language toolkit. *arXiv preprint cs/0205028*.

Pruthwik Mishra and Vandan Mujadia. 2019. Arabic Dialect Identification for Travel and Twitter Text. In *Proceedings of the Fourth Arabic Natural Language Processing Workshop*, pages 234–238.

Pangeanic.com. 2013. Arabic content on the Internet: an unfilled gap. https://www.pangeanic.com/knowledge_center/arabic-content-internet-unfilled-gap/. Accessed: 2020-07-05.

F Pedregosa, G Varoquaux, A Gramfort, V Michel, B Thirion, O Grisel, M Blondel, P Prettenhofer, R Weiss, V Dubourg, J Vanderplas, A Passos, D Cournapeau, M Brucher, M Perrot, and E Duchesnay. 2011. Scikit-learn: Machine learning in Python. *Journal of Machine Learning Research*, 12:2825–2830.

Mohammad Salameh, Houda Bouamor, and Nizar Habash. 2018. Fine-grained Arabic dialect identification. In *Proceedings of the 27th International Conference on Computational Linguistics*, pages 1332–1344.

Bashar Talafha, Wael Farhan, Ahmed Altakrouri, and Hussein Al-Natsheh. 2019. Mawdoo3 AI at MADAR Shared Task: Arabic Tweet Dialect Identification. In *Proceedings of the Fourth Arabic Natural Language Processing Workshop*, pages 239–243.

Omar F Zaidan and Chris Callison-Burch. 2014. Arabic dialect identification. *Computational Linguistics*, 40(1):171–202.

# Identifying Nuanced Dialect for Arabic Tweets
## with Deep Learning and Reverse Translation Corpus Extension System


**Rawan Tahssin**  **Youssef Kishk**  **Marwan Torki**

Faculty of Engineering, Alexandria University
{eng-rowan.tarek1520, es-Youssef.Aly20}@alexu.edu.eg
mtorki@alexu.edu.eg



## Abstract

In this paper, we present our work for the NADI Shared Task (Abdul-Mageed et al., 2020): Nuanced Arabic Dialect Identification for Subtask-1: country-level dialect identification. We introduce a Reverse Translation Corpus Extension Systems (RTCES) to handle data imbalance along with reported results on several experimented approaches of word and document representations and different models architectures. The top scoring model was based on the Transformer-based Model for Arabic Language Understanding (AraBERT) (Antoun et al., 2020), with our modified extended corpus based on reverse translation of the given Arabic tweets. The selected system achieved a macro average F1 score of 20.34% on the test set, which places our team CodeLyoko as the 7th out of 18 teams in the final ranking Leaderboard.


## 1 Introduction

Arabic is one of the most complex languages, which presents significant challenges for natural language processing. Like other languages, Arabic has a number of dialectal varieties. Many of these varieties of Arabic have started being widely represented in the written form with the emergence of social media. Arabic language speakers use Modern Standard Arabic (MSA) as the official language in very formal situations , while they use an Arabic Dialect for everyday conversation. Dialect identification is the task of detecting the source variety of a given text or speech segment automatically. Previous work on Arabic dialect identification has focused on country-level varieties such as the Arabic Fine-Grained Dialect Identification task (MADAR) co-located with The Fourth Arabic Natural Language Processing Workshop (WANLP 2019) (Bouamor et al., 2019). The classification task remains challenging as it covers 21 different Arabic dialects with high similarities and common words. Throughout the paper, we propose an approach for data balancing and augmentation without using any external manually-labelled data sets. We also report the different systems that were experimented in feature extraction and word embedding such as Term Frequency-Inverse Document Frequency (TF-IDF) and fastText (Mikolov et al., 2018). For the tweets classification, Logistic Regression, Bi-directional Long Short Term Memory (LSTM) (Graves and Schmidhuber, 2005) and AraBERT were evaluated to reach the top score.

## 2 Data

### 2.1 Dataset Description

The data used in all of the proposed systems is based on the official available dataset for Subtask-1 with no external data sets used. Table 1 shows the distribution of available data across different sets.

|  | Train | Dev | Test |
|---|---|---|---|
| # Tweets | 21000 | 4957 | 5000 |

Table 1: Available dataset distribution






*Proceedings of the Fifth Arabic Natural Language Processing Workshop*, pages 288–294
Barcelona, Spain (Online), December 12, 2020

The available data is covering the dialects of 21 Arab countries with the distribution in Figure 1 for the training set.

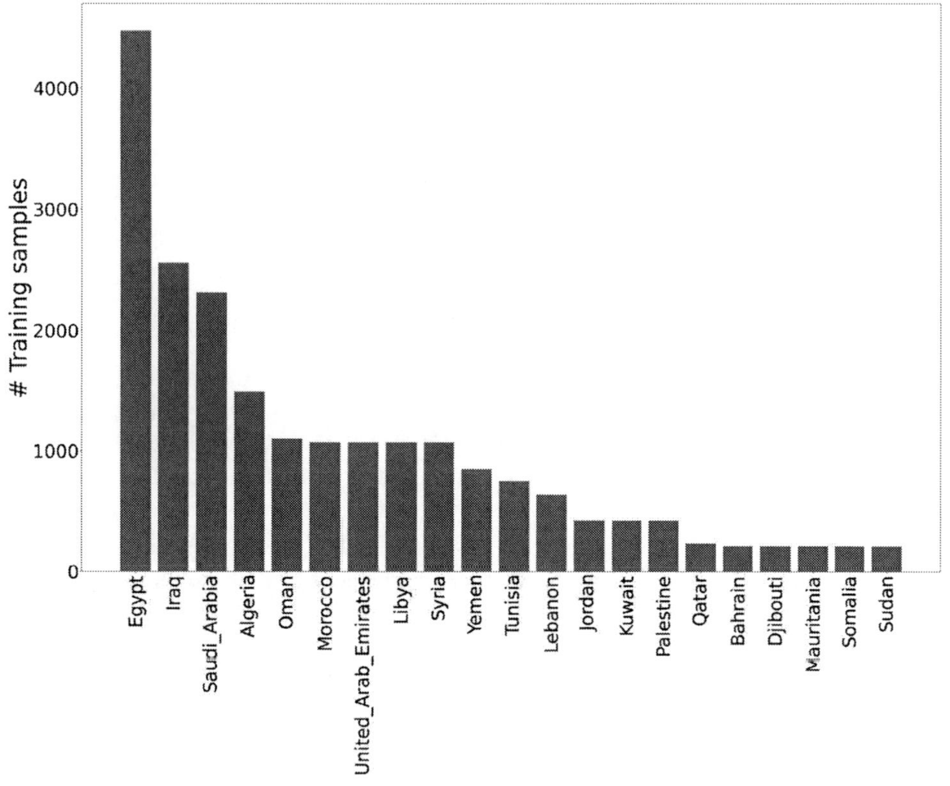

Figure 1: Training set classes distribution

## 2.2 Data Preprocessing

As the available dataset was collected from general tweets, thus, it required a generic transformation before its usage as an input to our systems. A pre-processing phase (Shoukry and Rafea, 2012) was implemented to remove punctuation, vowel elongation, URLs, mentions and diacritization. English and French words along with emojis were kept to be used as features.

## 2.3 Reverse Translation Corpus Extension System (RTCES)

The presence of class imbalance between countries labels within the training corpus was highly noticed as shown in Figure 1. Accordingly, a reverse translation approach was taken to handle this imbalance and augmentation. The approach consisted of a number of steps, starting from pre-processing module till the new generated sentence as shown in Figure 2.

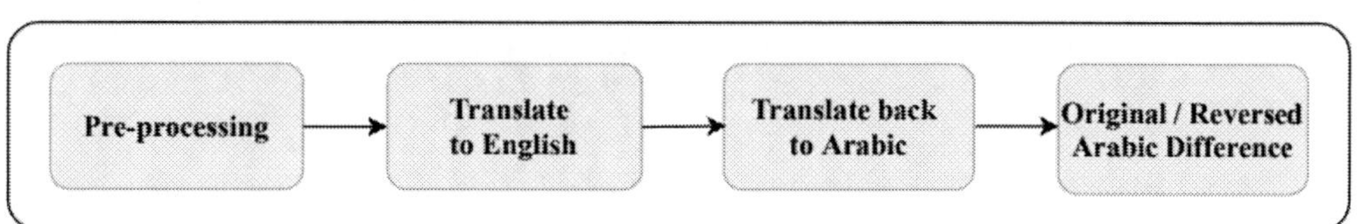


Figure 2: Reverse Translation Corpus Extension System

First, the entire pre-processed data is translated to English using Google's NMT API (Wu et al., 2016) to provide an equivalent corpus in English. The next step is the reverse translation of the newly created

English corpus to translate back the whole data to Arabic. As a final step, the extraction of the difference between the original Arabic tweet and the newly generated Arabic tweet from the reverse translation;to create a new sentence. An example of the steps applied on a tweet form the corpus is shown in Table 2.

| Steps | Output Sentence |
| --- | --- |
| Step 1 (Pre-processing) | فارقه كتير اوى راجع فرق الزمن وظروف الحياة وهتعرف |
| Step 2 (English translated) | Too much difference, review the difference in time and circumstances of life, and you will know |
| Step 3 (Reverse Translated) | الكثير الاختلاف راجع الفرق الوقت وظروف الحياه وستعرف |
| Step 4 (Sentence Difference) | فارقه كتير اوي فرق الزمن وهتعرف |

Table 2: RTCES applied on an Example from training set

One of the main observations that made this approach interesting, was the ability to filter out parts of the words based on Modern Standard Arabic (MSA) and keep the words reflecting the Arabic dialects of each country. This filtering served the purpose of our task and allowed the formation of new sentences for the classes with lower occurrences.

For our explored document and word representations as well as the classification model approaches, an extended corpus has been used. The new extended corpus consisted of the initial training set, added to it the new sentences generated from RTCES excluding the classes with higher occurrences (Egypt, Iraq and Saudi Arabia) to provide a more balanced distribution of classes. Figure 2 shows the complete system architecture. Finally, our extended training corpus is composed of 32,417 training sentences whose distribution is shown in Figure 3.

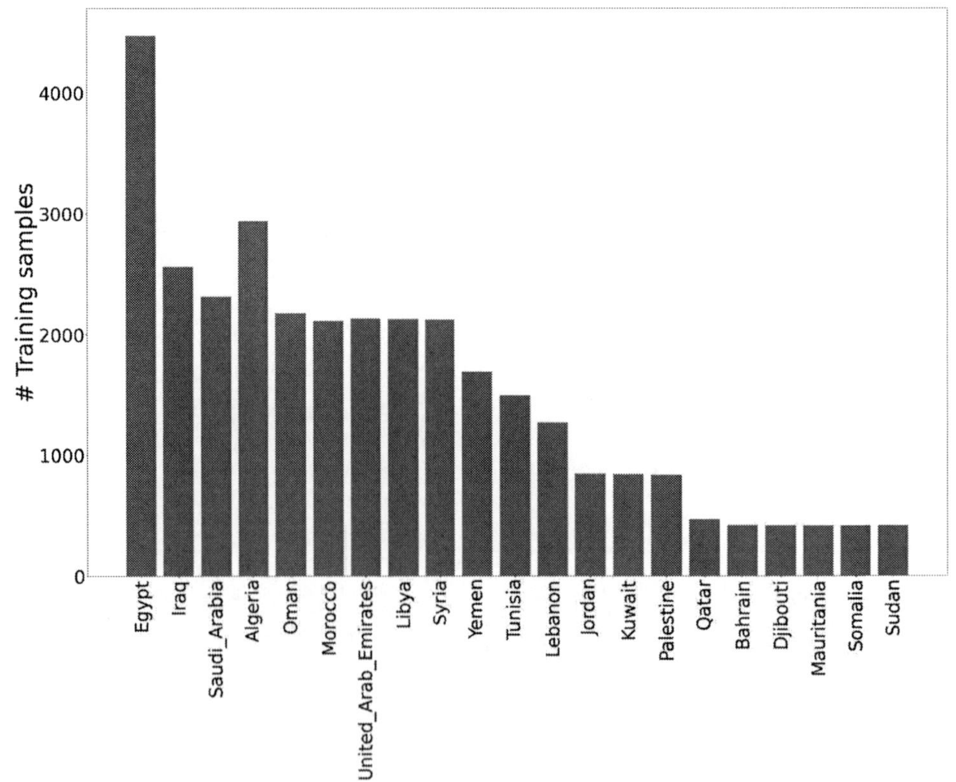


Figure 3: Modified corpus classes distribution

## 3  Systems

The aim of this work is to design a system that can classify 21 different Arabic dialects efficiently. In this section, we describe some selected experimented approaches and architectures out of various attempts to reach the goal of NADI Shared Task (Abdul-Mageed et al., 2020). All these approaches were applied to the output of the RTCES and their results were reported.

### 3.1  TF-IDF with Logistic Regression Model

Extracted features using TF-IDF and Logistic Regression Model from (Pedregosa et al., 2011) with the tuned parameters from k-fold cross validation as shown in Figure 4 (a).

### 3.2  FastText averaged word embeddings with Logistic Regression Model

fastText (Mikolov et al., 2018) is a deep learning-based approach for efficient learning of word representations. It was selected as it returns a vector representation to non-existing words in its vocabulary by computing the closest word based on the character level n-gram. The implementation of Gensim (Řehůřek and Sojka, 2010) was used. We trained fastText over the extra data corpus of 10M unlabelled tweets, after the pre-processing phase shown in section 2.1; to obtain efficient vector representations for each word. The returned vectors were averaged to obtain a representation suitable for the Logistic Regression input, the obtained result are shown in Figure 4(b).

### 3.3  FastText word embeddings with Bi-directional LSTM

The word vectors and labels were sequenced, padded and passed to a bi-directional LSTM (Graves and Schmidhuber, 2005) model which is able to exploit previous and future context of a given word and calculated the loss from the concatenation of the last hidden layer in both directions as shown in Figure 4 (b). The bi-directional LSTM model was built using Keras (Chollet, 2015).

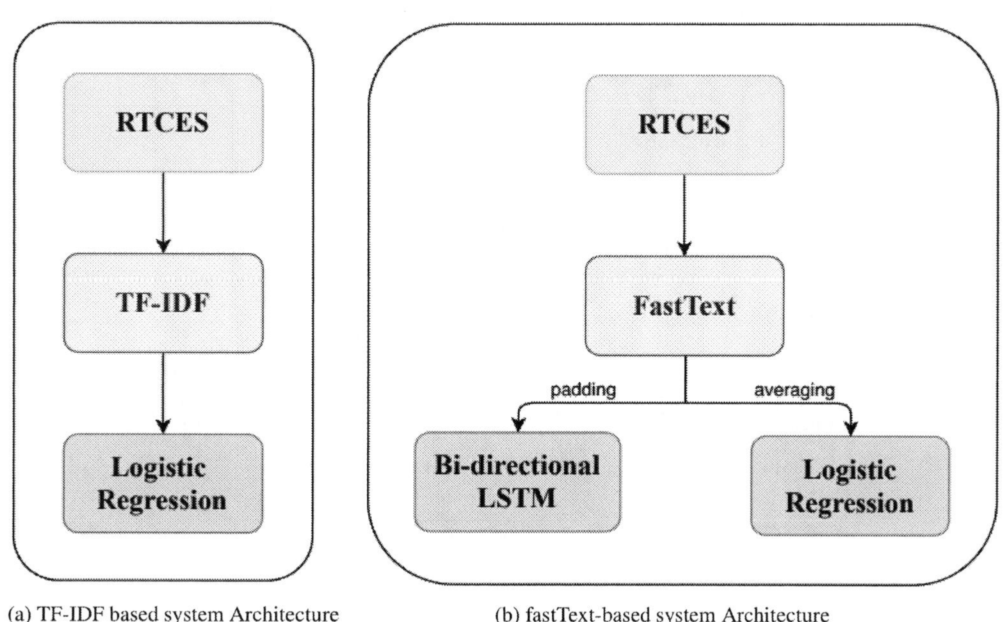


(a) TF-IDF based system Architecture

(b) fastText-based system Architecture

Figure 4: Implemented approaches Architectures

### 3.4  Fined tuned AraBERT

Our top submission model was based on AraBERT (Antoun et al., 2020), which is an Arabic language model based on Multilingual Bidirectional Encoder Representations from Transformers (BERT) trained on 70M sentences or 23GB of Arabic text with 3B words from a collection of publically available large scale raw Arabic text. We applied first a tokenization and segmentation phase using Fast and Accurate Arabic Word Segmenter (Farasa) (Abdelali et al., 2016) on the extended corpus described in section 2.3. The pre-trained AraBERT model is fine-tuned with one additional output layer of 21 classes, then the model is trained on our corpus which reaches a 20.34 test-set F1 score.

## 4   Results and Discussion

Interesting observations at the beginning of conducting our work showed that TF-IDF and a simple Logistic Regression model performed better than NN-based models. However, with more experiments, NN-based models outperformed it. The results of the approaches described in the previous section are shown in Table 3.

| Model | Macro Avg. F1 |
|---|---|
| TF-IDF + Logistic Regression | 17.34 |
| fastText + Logistic Regression | 14.24 |
| fastText + Bi-directional LSTM | 18.33 |
| Fine-tuned AraBERT | 20.73 |

Table 3: Results (in %) on Dev. set

The fine-tuned AraBERT score was the highest. Accordingly, its predictions were selected to be our final submission for the NADI Shared Task 2020 Subtask-1. Moreover, one of the observations of our approach was that our results on the development set are quite close to those on the test set. This indicates that no over-fitting took place as shown in Table 4. The final Macro average F1, accuracy, precision and recall scores for the best-performing model were addressed in section 3.4.

| Subtask # | Set | F1-score | Accuracy | Precision | Recall |
|---|---|---|---|---|---|
| 1 | Test | 20.34 | 36.26 | 27.83 | 20.56 |
| 1 | Dev | 20.73 | 36.59 | 29.29 | 19.97 |

Table 4: Final Submitted results (in %) of AraBERT on Test and Dev. sets

### 4.1   Two-level Hierarchical Prediction Structure

In an attempt to improve the reported results, the 21 countries were clustered to 5 super classes inspired by (Fares et al., 2019) according to the origin of the dialect labels as shown in Table 5.

| Maghreb | Egypt_Sudan | Gulf | Levant | Others |
|---|---|---|---|---|
| Morocco | Egypt | Iraq | Jordan | Somalia |
| Algeria | Sudan | UAE | Syria | Djibouti |
| Tunisia | | Saudi Arabia | Palestine | |
| Libya | | Qatar | Lebanon | |
| Mauritania | | Kuwait | | |
| | | Bahrain | | |
| | | Yemen | | |
| | | Oman | | |

Table 5: Two-level classes distribution

A two-level hierarchical prediction structure inspired by (de Francony et al., 2019) was implemented. The predicted labels from the first five super classes level are passed to the second level to output the prediction of the corresponding countries in each of the five origins. This is a general structure that can be used on different models. However, we reported its results on the first level classes using system explained in Section 3.1 using TF-IDF with Logistic Regression Model as shown in Figure 5. The result of the second level were close to that obtained from the system explained in Section 3.2 which is 14.241%. We aim to enhance this structure and report its results on other models as a future work.

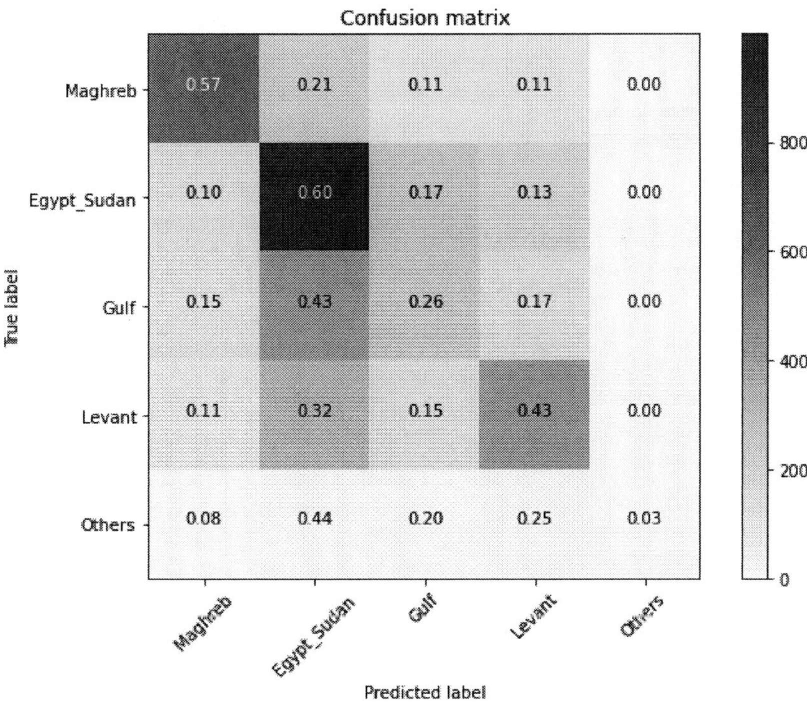


Figure 5: Confusion matrix for structure in 4.1 on first level classes

## 5   Conclusion

We introduced a reverse Arabic translation solution to handle unbalanced data and small data set, a hierarchical architecture to enhance the efficiency and deal with the 21 classes classification, several neural network based models built on different word and document representations. Future work will include trying to ensemble the mentioned models, enhance the two-level hierarchical prediction structure and exploring the effect of adding a named entity recognition system module for better focus on highly effective words that identifies each country such as places, food, public figures, etc. Moreover, we will examine more data augmentation methods such as suggested in (Fares et al., 2019; Ibrahim et al., 2018; Ibrahim et al., 2020).

### Acknowledgements

We would like to thank Ms. Samaa Abdelaal, our language editor for her dedicated work and efforts on this paper.

### References

Ahmed Abdelali, Kareem Darwish, Nadir Durrani, and H. Mubarak. 2016. Farasa: A fast and furious segmenter for arabic. In *HLT-NAACL Demos*.

Muhammad Abdul-Mageed, Chiyu Zhang, Houda Bouamor, and Nizar Habash. 2020. NADI 2020: The First Nuanced Arabic Dialect Identification Shared Task. In *Proceedings of the Fifth Arabic Natural Language Processing Workshop (WANLP 2020)*, Barcelona, Spain.

Wissam Antoun, Fady Baly, and Hazem Hajj. 2020. Arabert: Transformer-based model for arabic language understanding.

Houda Bouamor, Sabit Hassan, and Nizar Habash. 2019. The MADAR shared task on Arabic fine-grained dialect identification. In *Proceedings of the Fourth Arabic Natural Language Processing Workshop*, pages 199–207, Florence, Italy, August. Association for Computational Linguistics.

François Chollet. 2015. keras. `https://github.com/fchollet/keras`.

Gael de Francony, Victor Guichard, Praveen Joshi, Haithem Afli, and Abdessalam Bouchekif. 2019. Hierarchical deep learning for Arabic dialect identification. In *Proceedings of the Fourth Arabic Natural Language Processing Workshop*, pages 249–253, Florence, Italy, August. Association for Computational Linguistics.

Youssef Fares, Zeyad El-Zanaty, Kareem Abdel-Salam, Muhammed Ezzeldin, Aliaa Mohamed, Karim El-Awaad, and Marwan Torki. 2019. Arabic dialect identification with deep learning and hybrid frequency based features. In *Proceedings of the Fourth Arabic Natural Language Processing Workshop*, pages 224–228, Florence, Italy, August. Association for Computational Linguistics.

A. Graves and J. Schmidhuber. 2005. Framewise phoneme classification with bidirectional lstm networks. In *Proceedings. 2005 IEEE International Joint Conference on Neural Networks, 2005.*, volume 4, pages 2047–2052 vol. 4.

Mai Ibrahim, Marwan Torki, and Nagwa El-Makky. 2018. Imbalanced toxic comments classification using data augmentation and deep learning. In *2018 17th IEEE International Conference on Machine Learning and Applications (ICMLA)*, pages 875–878, Dec.

Mai Ibrahim, Marwan Torki, and Nagwa El-Makky. 2020. Alexu-backtranslation-tl at semeval-2020 task [12]: Improving offensive language detection using data augmentation and transfer learning. In *Proceedings of the International Workshop on Semantic Evaluation (SemEval)*.

Tomas Mikolov, Edouard Grave, Piotr Bojanowski, Christian Puhrsch, and Armand Joulin. 2018. Advances in pre-training distributed word representations. In *Proceedings of the Eleventh International Conference on Language Resources and Evaluation (LREC 2018)*, Miyazaki, Japan, May. European Language Resources Association (ELRA).

Fabian Pedregosa, Gaël Varoquaux, Alexandre Gramfort, Vincent Michel, Bertrand Thirion, Olivier Grisel, Mathieu Blondel, Peter Prettenhofer, Ron Weiss, Vincent Dubourg, Jake Vanderplas, Alexandre Passos, David Cournapeau, Matthieu Brucher, Matthieu Perrot, and Édouard Duchesnay. 2011. Scikit-learn: Machine learning in python. *J. Mach. Learn. Res.*, 12(null):2825–2830, November.

Radim Řehůřek and Petr Sojka. 2010. Software Framework for Topic Modelling with Large Corpora. In *Proceedings of the LREC 2010 Workshop on New Challenges for NLP Frameworks*, pages 45–50, Valletta, Malta, May. ELRA.

Amira Shoukry and Ahmed Rafea. 2012. Preprocessing egyptian dialect tweets for sentiment mining. 11.

Yonghui Wu, Mike Schuster, Zhifeng Chen, Quoc V. Le, Mohammad Norouzi, Wolfgang Macherey, Maxim Krikun, Yuan Cao, Qin Gao, Klaus Macherey, Jeff Klingner, Apurva Shah, Melvin Johnson, Xiaobing Liu, Łukasz Kaiser, Stephan Gouws, Yoshikiyo Kato, Taku Kudo, Hideto Kazawa, Keith Stevens, George Kurian, Nishant Patil, Wei Wang, Cliff Young, Jason Smith, Jason Riesa, Alex Rudnick, Oriol Vinyals, Greg Corrado, Macduff Hughes, and Jeffrey Dean. 2016. Google's neural machine translation system: Bridging the gap between human and machine translation. *CoRR*, abs/1609.08144.

# The QMUL/HRBDT contribution to the NADI Arabic Dialect Identification Shared Task


**Abdulrahman Aloraini**
Queen Mary University of London
United Kingdom

**Ayman Alhelbawy**
University of Essex
United Kingdom

**Massimo Poesio**
Queen Mary University of London
United Kingdom

{a.aloraini, m.poesio}@qmul.ac.uk
a.alhelbawy@essex.ac.uk



## Abstract

We present the Arabic dialect identification system that we used for the country-level subtask of the NADI challenge. Our model consists of three components: BiLSTM-CNN, character-level TF-IDF, and topic modeling features. We represent each tweet using these features and feed them into a deep neural network. We then add an effective heuristic that improves the overall performance. We achieved an F1-Macro score of 20.77% and an accuracy of 34.32% on the test set. The model was also evaluated on the Arabic Online Commentary dataset, achieving results better than the state-of-the-art.


## 1 Introduction

Arabic is widely spoken in the Middle East and certain parts of Africa–21 countries–and the total number of its speakers is approximately 420 million. It is also one of the six official languages of the United Nations. But Arabic is a general term that can refer to classical Arabic (CA), Modern Standard Arabic (MSA), or several Arabic dialects (ADs). Both classical Arabic and MSA are standardized, while Arabic dialects are not. So identifying different Arabic dialect varieties is quite a challenging task. Thus, many studies have been devoted to Arabic dialect identification, because it benefits automatic speech recognition, remote access, e-health, and other applications (Etman and Beex, 2015).

The main challenge for Arabic dialect identification is the lack of large dataset that can be exploited in computational models. Among the studies addressing this issue, Zaidan and Callison-Burch (2014) created a large dataset for this purpose, called Arabic Online Commentary (AOC). The data consists of texts in MSA and Arabic regional dialects collected from Arabic news sites. Zaghouani and Charfi (2018) collected and annotated Twitter data from 11 regions and 16 countries in the Arab world. Abdul-Mageed et al. (2018) also collected Twitter data and annotated them at the city-level i.e 29 cities of 11 countries. Bouamor et al. (2018) translated the Basic Traveling Expression Corpus (BTEC) (Takezawa et al., 2007) into 25 city dialects of Arab countries; this corpus is referred to as Corpus-25.

Among the models, some proposals only aim to separating one dialect (e.g., Egyptian) from MSA on the AOC dataset (Elfardy and Diab, 2013; Tillmann et al., 2014). Darwish et al. (2014) also distinguished between Egyptian and MSA, but focusing on twitter data. Zaidan and Callison-Burch (2014) proposed a model to identify MSA and regional dialects including Egyptian, Levantine, and Gulf. Huang (2015) applied a word-level n-gram model to identify MSA and regional dialects, and also considered Facebook posts . Elaraby and Abdul-Mageed (2018) used the AOC dataset to evaluate several machine learning and deep learning models. Salameh et al. (2018) proposed a fine-grained dialect identification module for Corpus-25 by applying a multinomial Naive Bayes classifier with a large set of features.

The Nuanced Arabic Dialect Identification (NADI) shared task aims to incentivise research on identifying different Arabic dialects in every Arab country (Abdul-Mageed et al., 2020). The NADI dataset was collected from Arabic twitter, and each tweet is labeled with two labels, country-label and province-label, for a total of 21 countries and 100 of their provinces. There are two subtasks in NADI: the first is targeting these country-level labels and the second one is targeting the provinces. In the rest of the paper,






*Proceedings of the Fifth Arabic Natural Language Processing Workshop*, pages 295–301
Barcelona, Spain (Online), December 12, 2020

| Country | Train | Dev | Country | Train | Dev | Country | Train | Dev |
|---|---|---|---|---|---|---|---|---|
| Egypt | 4,473 | 1,070 | UAE | 1,070 | 265 | Kuwait | 420 | 70 |
| Iraq | 2,556 | 636 | Syria | 1,070 | 265 | Qatar | 234 | 104 |
| Saudi Arabia | 2,312 | 579 | Yemen | 851 | 206 | Mauritania | 210 | 40 |
| Algeria | 1,491 | 359 | Tunisia | 750 | 164 | Bahrain | 210 | 8 |
| Oman | 1,098 | 249 | Lebanon | 639 | 110 | Djibouti | 210 | 10 |
| Morocco | 1,070 | 249 | Jordan | 429 | 104 | Somalia | 210 | 51 |
| Libya | 1,070 | 265 | Palestine | 420 | 102 | Sudan | 210 | 51 |

Table 1: Counts of country-level labels in the train and development (Dev) of NADI.

we firt introduce the datasets in Section 2. Our Arabic identification model is discussed in Section 3. We show the results on NADI subtask 1 and AOC in Section 4 and discuss them in Section 5. We conclude with Section 6.

## 2 Data

The NADI dataset was the main corpus used for training and testing the system. The dataset is partitioned into train, development, and test sets, containing 21,000, 4,957, and 5,000 tweets respectively. The test set was published unlabeled, and the system output was evaluated by the NADI shared task team. The training set was used to train our model while the development set was used to optimize model parameters. In addition, NADI also provided 10 million unlabeled tweets which we used to train a word embedding model for Arabic tweets. Table 1 shows the number of the annotated Arabic tweets for each country in training and development sets. The data samples distribution over the dialectal classes or countries is unbalanced.

Our model was also evaluated against another dataset, the Arabic Online Commentary (AOC). A subset of the data was annotated using crowd-sourcing and has been used in previous work (Zaidan and Callison-Burch, 2014; Cotterell and Callison-Burch, 2014). The AOC dataset classifies Arabic dialects into three dialects in addition to the MSA, so spoken dialects in different countries may be grouped together as one dialect. For example, the "Gulf" dialect label may includes all spoken dialects in Saudi Arabia, United Arab Emirates, Kuwait, Bahrain, Iraq, etc. (Elaraby and Abdul-Mageed, 2018) benchmarked a portion of AOC, and applied various machine learning algorithms to identify MSA and dialects based on three settings:

- Binary: where they classify the data to MSA and or not MSA.

- Three-way: where they classify three dialectal regions (Egyptian, Gulf, and Levantine).

- Four-way: where they classify between the three regional dialects and MSA.

The dataset statistics are shown in Table 2.

| | MSA | Egyptian | Gulf | Levantine | Total |
|---|---|---|---|---|---|
| Train | 50,845 | 10,022 | 16,593 | 9,081 | 86,541 |
| Dev | 6,357 | 1,253 | 2,075 | 1,136 | 10,821 |
| Test | 6,353 | 1,252 | 2,073 | 1,133 | 10,812 |

Table 2: AOC portions of MSA and region dialects from (Elaraby and Abdul-Mageed, 2018)

## 3 System

### 3.1 Tweet Text Prepossessing

Arabic tweets are very noisy, so we removed URLS, emojis, Latin-characters, numbers, mentions, and any non-Arabic characters. Arabic hashtags were kept as they are because they might contain important information such as (Lebanon revolts, لبنان ينتفض).

Text normalisation was carried out to normalise different forms of "Alif", "Yaa", removing punctuation, excessive character repetitions, Kashida "tatweel" and diacritics (Althobaiti et al., 2014). The class distribution is highly imbalanced, which could make a model biased towards certain classes. Therefore, random up-sampling for each data class was applied to match the size of the majority class, the Egyptian class.

## 3.2 Combined Features Model

Our approach to classifying tweets involves three components:

1. BiLSTM-CNN model: to extract word and character representations, we build a BiLSTM-CNN model following the same settings in (Ma and Hovy, 2016). We pre-trained FastText on the 10m unlabeled tweets to represent words. We randomly initialize character embeddings of size 30 and train them into a CNN neural network to learn morphological information, for example, the prefix or suffix of a word (Dos Santos and Zadrozny, 2014). We concatenate each word embedding with its character embedding and feed them into a BiLSTM network to learn the sentence information.

2. Character-level TF-IDF: we applied (1-5) character grams of TF-IDF on the train set. We tried to expand gram range, but that did not improve the performance. The TF-IDF component captures very common patterns of a dialect.

3. Topic modeling: is used to discover a set of topics from large documents where a topic is a distribution over words that are associated with a single subject. We used Latent Dirichlet Allocation (LDA) to learn topic modeling on the train set. We tried different number of topics {1, 10, ..,100 } and we empirically found 50 topics to yield the best results.

For each tweet, we concatenate its BiLSTM-CNN, character TF-IDF, and topic modeling features together and then feed them into a classifier made of two-layer neural network. There is a dropout layer between the two layers of the classifier. The overall model is in Figure 1. Also, we find training Fasttext on the 10 million unlabeled tweets to yield better results than using existing pretrained Arabic word embeddings. We train the model using the train set, and we optimize the hyperparameters based on the evaluation of the development set, the hyperparameter settings in Table 3. We applied the early stopping technique based on the F1-macro score.

In NADI shared task, we used the mentioned model for our first run.

## 3.3 Combined Features with Heuristic Model

Next, we augmented our model with a heuristic from Samih et al. (2019). The heuristic is based on a list of all Arabic speaking countries and their major cities. If a tweet mentions any country/city in the list, the tweet would be classified to the mentioned country/city. We excluded the cities because they did not boost the overall performance.

Our model combined with the heuristic was our second run to NADI challenge.

| Number of units in the first layer | 1200 |
|---|---|
| Number of units in the second layer | 800 |
| Cell size of BiLSTM | 500 |
| Learning rate | 1e-4 |
| Dropout rate | 0.5 |
| Optimizer | Adam |

Table 3: Hyperparameter settings.

We implemented the neural network using Tensorflow (Abadi et al., 2015), and we modelled the topics using Gensim (Řehůřek and Sojka, 2010).

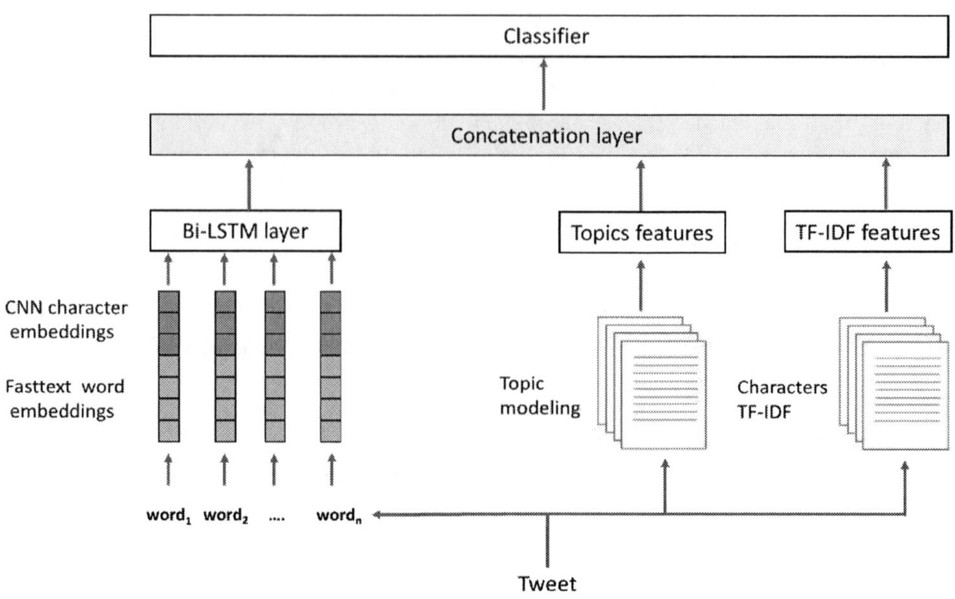


Figure 1: Our model

## 4   Results

As we can see in Table 4, the basic model achieved a recall, precision, macro-F1 scores of 0.231, 0.231, and 0.227 on the development set and 0.198, 0.203, 0.194 on the test set when we do not apply the heuristic (run 1). When we applied the heuristic (run 2), the scores increased to 0.244 (R), 0.250 (P), and 0.243 (F1) on the development set and .210 (R), 0.216 (P), and 0.207 (F1) on the test set. Investigating the system's outputs, we found the model successfully classified the three largest classes (Egypt, Iraq, and Saudi Arabia), but struggled to classify in particular the classes with fewer samples (Mauritania, Bahrain, Djibouti, Somalia, and Sudan). We also found that the model struggles with tweets containing words which are found in the dialectal varieties of different countries, such as the word *what* (وشو) which is common in Saudi Arabia, Oman, Kuwait and Qatar. In addition, we found that many NADI tweets are in classical Arabic or MSA and are difficult to classify even for native speakers; we discuss this issue more in Section 5.

| Run | Dataset | Recall | Precision | F1 | Accuracy |
|---|---|---|---|---|---|
| run 1 (without heuristic) | Development set | 0.231 | 0.231 | 0.227 | 0.387 |
|  | Test set | 0.198 | 0.203 | 0.194 | 0.337 |
| run 2 (with heuristic) | Development set | 0.244 | 0.250 | 0.243 | 0.392 |
|  | Test set | 0.210 | 0.216 | 0.207 | 0.343 |

Table 4: Evaluation on NADI country-level dataset on the development and test portions of two settings: run 1 (no heuristic) and run 2 (with heuristic).

The model has also been evaluated on the AOC benchmarks. We trained and optimized the model following the same splits as in (Elaraby and Abdul-Mageed, 2018). As we can see in Table 5, the model achieves the highest accuracy scores compared to previous approaches on all dataset settings, binary, three-way, and four-way.

## 5   Discussion

Our model was evaluated on two datasets: AOC and NADI. The results on AOC are very high compared to the results on NADI because NADI data contains many difficult cases. In NADI, there are many

| Model | Binary | | Three-way | | Four-way | |
|---|---|---|---|---|---|---|
| | Dev | Test | Dev | Test | Dev | Test |
| BiGRU    (Elaraby and Abdul-Mageed, 2018) | 87.65 | 87.23 | 87.11 | 86.18 | 83.25 | 82.21 |
| Att. BiLSTM (Elaraby and Abdul-Mageed, 2018) | 87.61 | 87.21 | 87.81 | 87.41 | 83.49 | 82.45 |
| Our model | 88.18 | 87.64 | 90.09 | 89.94 | 85.56 | 84.23 |

Table 5: The results of our experiments on the portion of benchmarked AOC compared with BiGRU and Attention BiLSTM of (Abdul-Mageed et al., 2018). Following prior works, we compare our experimental result in accuracy.

| Example | Sentence | Not MSA words | MSA ratio |
|---|---|---|---|
| 1 | انا عرفت انا هسقط ليه | هسقط | 4/5 |
| 2 | كلهم فتره ويذلفون | ويذلفون | 2/3 |
| 3 | بيخترعو قواعد من عندن | بيخترعو، عندن | 2/4 |

Table 6: The MSA ratio is the number of MSA words of a tweet divided by its total number of words. We consider a word in MSA if it is in AraVec dictionary.

tweets in classical Arabic and MSA, such as religious verses, popular poems, and others. Such cases are very hard to label even for native speakers because they are ubiquitous in all Arabic speaking countries. To gain more insights into the proportion of MSA tweets, we used AraVec dictionary (Soliman et al., 2017). AraVec is a distributed word representation model trained on Arabic Wikipedia articles which are mainly in MSA. Therefore, AraVec dictionary mostly contain MSA words. To know if a tweet is in MSA, we define the MSA ratio which is the number of tweet words in AraVec dictionary divided by the total number of words. We show a few examples in Table 6. The MSA ratio of all tweets in the training and development set is shown in Figure 2: as we can see, many tweets in the corpus have high MSA ratio. We found that 6291 of the 21,000 have an MSA ratio of 1.0 in the train set, and 1508 of the 4957 in the development. These cases can complicate the learning process and associate common MSA words/character-grams to a specific dialect. For example, our model classifies (السلام عليكم /Als~lAmu çalykum[1]) which is used in all dialects, as Somalian because many training instances with السلام عليكم are labeled as Somalian.

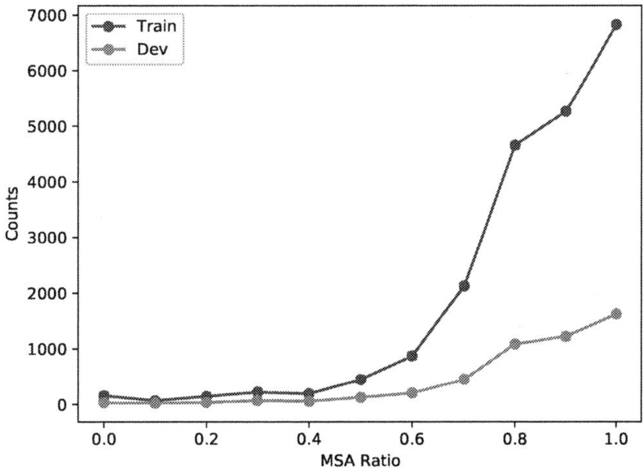


Figure 2: MSA ratios of train and development sets in NADI

---
[1]Following the Arabic transliteration scheme in (Habash et al., 2007)

## 6   Conclusion

We presented a model to identify Arabic dialects based on three components: BiLSTM-CNN, character-level TF-IDF, and topic modeling. We evaluated the model on the country-level subtask of NADI, and also on the AOC dataset. We showed their results and discussed the challenges of NADI dataset.

## Acknowledgements

The research was in part supported by the UK Economic and Social Research Council (ESRC) through the Big Data Human Rights and Technology project (grant number ES/M010236/1).

## References

Martín Abadi, Ashish Agarwal, Paul Barham, et al. 2015. TensorFlow: Large-scale machine learning on heterogeneous systems. Software available from tensorflow.org.

Muhammad Abdul-Mageed, Hassan Alhuzali, and Mohamed Elaraby. 2018. You tweet what you speak: A city-level dataset of arabic dialects. In *Proceedings of the Eleventh International Conference on Language Resources and Evaluation (LREC 2018)*.

Muhammad Abdul-Mageed, Chiyu Zhang, Houda Bouamor, and Nizar Habash. 2020. NADI 2020: The First Nuanced Arabic Dialect Identification Shared Task. In *Proceedings of the Fifth Arabic Natural Language Processing Workshop (WANLP2020)*, Barcelona, Spain.

Maha Althobaiti, Udo Kruschwitz, and Massimo Poesio. 2014. Aranlp: A java-based library for the processing of arabic text.

Houda Bouamor, Nizar Habash, Mohammad Salameh, Wajdi Zaghouani, Owen Rambow, Dana Abdulrahim, Ossama Obeid, Salam Khalifa, Fadhl Eryani, Alexander Erdmann, et al. 2018. The madar arabic dialect corpus and lexicon. In *Proceedings of the Eleventh International Conference on Language Resources and Evaluation (LREC 2018)*.

Ryan Cotterell and Chris Callison-Burch. 2014. A multi-dialect, multi-genre corpus of informal written arabic. In *LREC*, pages 241–245.

Kareem Darwish, Hassan Sajjad, and Hamdy Mubarak. 2014. Verifiably effective arabic dialect identification. In *Proceedings of the 2014 Conference on Empirical Methods in Natural Language Processing (EMNLP)*, pages 1465–1468.

Cicero Dos Santos and Bianca Zadrozny. 2014. Learning character-level representations for part-of-speech tagging. In *International Conference on Machine Learning*, pages 1818–1826.

Mohamed Elaraby and Muhammad Abdul-Mageed. 2018. Deep models for arabic dialect identification on benchmarked data. In *Proceedings of the Fifth Workshop on NLP for Similar Languages, Varieties and Dialects (VarDial 2018)*, pages 263–274.

Heba Elfardy and Mona Diab. 2013. Sentence level dialect identification in arabic. In *Proceedings of the 51st Annual Meeting of the Association for Computational Linguistics (Volume 2: Short Papers)*, pages 456–461.

Asmaa Etman and AA Louis Beex. 2015. Language and dialect identification: A survey. In *2015 SAI Intelligent Systems Conference (IntelliSys)*, pages 220–231. IEEE.

Nizar Habash, Abdelhadi Soudi, and Timothy Buckwalter. 2007. On arabic transliteration. In *Arabic computational morphology*, pages 15–22. Springer.

Fei Huang. 2015. Improved arabic dialect classification with social media data. In *Proceedings of the 2015 Conference on Empirical Methods in Natural Language Processing*, pages 2118–2126.

Xuezhe Ma and Eduard Hovy. 2016. End-to-end sequence labeling via bi-directional lstm-cnns-crf. *arXiv preprint arXiv:1603.01354*.

Radim Řehůřek and Petr Sojka. 2010. Software Framework for Topic Modelling with Large Corpora. In *Proceedings of the LREC 2010 Workshop on New Challenges for NLP Frameworks*, pages 45–50, Valletta, Malta, May. ELRA. http://is.muni.cz/publication/884893/en.

Mohammad Salameh, Houda Bouamor, and Nizar Habash. 2018. Fine-grained arabic dialect identification. In *Proceedings of the 27th International Conference on Computational Linguistics*, pages 1332–1344.

Younes Samih, Hamdy Mubarak, Ahmed Abdelali, Mohammed Attia, Mohamed Eldesouki, and Kareem Darwish. 2019. Qc-go submission for madar shared task: Arabic fine-grained dialect identification. In *Proceedings of the Fourth Arabic Natural Language Processing Workshop*, pages 290–294.

Abu Bakr Soliman, Kareem Eissa, and Samhaa R El-Beltagy. 2017. Aravec: A set of arabic word embedding models for use in arabic nlp. *Procedia Computer Science*, 117:256–265.

Toshiyuki Takezawa, Genichiro Kikui, Masahide Mizushima, and Eiichiro Sumita. 2007. Multilingual spoken language corpus development for communication research. In *International Journal of Computational Linguistics & Chinese Language Processing, Volume 12, Number 3, September 2007: Special Issue on Invited Papers from ISCSLP 2006*, pages 303–324.

Christoph Tillmann, Saab Mansour, and Yaser Al-Onaizan. 2014. Improved sentence-level arabic dialect classification. In *Proceedings of the First Workshop on Applying NLP Tools to Similar Languages, Varieties and Dialects*, pages 110–119.

Wajdi Zaghouani and Anis Charfi. 2018. Arap-tweet: A large multi-dialect twitter corpus for gender, age and language variety identification. *arXiv preprint arXiv:1808.07674*.

Omar F Zaidan and Chris Callison-Burch. 2014. Arabic dialect identification. *Computational Linguistics*, 40(1):171–202.

# Arabic Dialects Identification for All Arabic countries


**Ahmed Hussein Aliwy**
Faculty of CS and math
University of Kufa
Iraq

**Hawraa Ali Taher**
Faculty of education for girls
University of Kufa
Iraq

**Zena A. Abutiheen**
Dep. of CS
University of Kerbala
Iraq

{ahmed.almajidy,hawraaa.alshimirty}@uokufa.edu.iq,     z.aboaltaheen@uokerbala.edu.iq


## Abstract


Arabic dialects are among of three main variant of Arabic language (Classical Arabic, modern standard Arabic and dialectal Arabic). It has many variants according to the country, city (provinces) or town. In this paper, several techniques with multiple algorithms are applied for Arabic dialects identification starting from removing noise till classification task using all Arabic countries as 21 classes. Three types of classifiers (Naïve Bayes, Logistic Regression, and Decision Tree) are combined using voting with two different methodologies. Also clustering technique is used for decreasing the noise that result from the existing of MSA tweets in the data set for training phase. The results of f-measure were 27.17, 41.34 and 52.38 for first methodology without clustering, second methodology without clustering, and second methodology with clustering, the used data set is NADI shared task data set.


## 1 Introduction

Arabic Dialects is one of three variations of Arabic language (Classical Arabic CA, Modern Standard Arabic MSA and dialectal Arabic DA). It is a native language of Arabic people used in the communication among them and in the social media (Itani, 2018). Each country of 21 countries, in the Arab world, has its own dialect, sometimes they are written in same script with different pronunciation. Recently, dialect identification (DI) is interesting field in Natural Language Processing (NLP) and conducted by number of researchers because it is increasing rapidly on the web and social media.

There are nine distinct dialectal categories in Arab world: Egyptian, Gulf, Iraqi, Levantine, Maghrebi (El-Haj et al., 2018), Yemeni, Somali, Sudanese and Mauritania. Each one of them has many varieties according to the city and town.

It is clear that there are four levels of Arabic dialectal identification (ADI): (1) identification of dialectal Arabic from MSA and CA, it is very easy task similar to identification of Arabic language among other languages, (2) identification of the main category of dialectal Arabic of( nine or five categories), it is more difficult than previous point, (3) identification of country level out of 21 countries, it more difficult than the previous two points, (4) identification of city level or town level which is subfield of country level, it is the most difficult among all these levels. Table 1 show dialects of the word "أريكة-Ârykħ"-(sofa) [1] in some Arabic countries*.

| Country | Native word | Country | Native word | Country | Native word |
|---|---|---|---|---|---|
| Iraq | كرويت- krwyt<br>قنفة- qnfħ | Kuwait | كنبه- knbh<br>قنفه- qnfħ | Saudi Arabia | باطرمه- bATrmh<br>كنبه- knbh |
| Bahrain | قنفة- qnfħ | Lebanon | كنبايه- knbAyh | Syria | كنبايه- knbAyh |
| Egypt | كنبه- knbh | Oman | قنفة- qnfħ | Morocco & Tunisia | فوطوي- fwTwy |
| Algeria | فوطوي- fwTwy | Palestine | كنبايه- knbAyh | Yemen | كنبه- knbh |
| Jordan | كنبايه- knbAyh | Qatar | كنبه- knbh | United Arab Emirates | انتريه- Antryh, قنفة- qnfħ<br>كنبه- knbh |

Table 1: dialects of the word "أريكة- Ârykħ" (sofa) in 16 Arabic countries.

---






*Proceedings of the Fifth Arabic Natural Language Processing Workshop*, pages 302–307
Barcelona, Spain (Online), December 12, 2020

There are many challenges in ADI over identification of other types of Arabic language such as:

1. In case of the levels 2,3 and 4, all the countries and cities use MSA for writing in some times, therefore these will be noise in the dialectal identification.
2. Existing of a city in a specific country use dialect that very close to other country more than its country such as Basrah in Iraq use dialect very close to Kuwait dialect.
3. Some countries are much similar in most words and different in little words therefore identification of their dialects are much difficult.

this paper is a part of NADI 2020 shared task (subtask1) where the tweets in Arabic dialect has been classified into the country belong it by voting among three classifiers (Naïve Bayes NB, Logistic Regression LR, and Decision Tree DT) in different methodologies to make final decision. Also a preprocessing phase is done, before implementation of the classifier, such as noisy redundant, removing stopwords, feature extraction and feature selection.

## 2    Related work

There are many works for identification of Arabic dialects in all the levels. We chose some of the close works to our work.

Belgacem et al. (2010) worked on nine dialects (Tunisia, Algeria, Syria, Lebanon, Yemen, Egypt, Golf's Countries, Morocco and Iraq) using the platform Alize and Gaussian Mixture Models (GMM). They showed the complexity of the automatic identification of Arabic dialects. Elfardy & Diab (2013) used a supervised approach for identification of Arabic dialects. They got an accuracy of 85.5% on an Arabic online-commentary. Cotterell et al. (2014) presented a multi-dialect, multi-genre, human annotated corpus of dialectal Arabic with data obtained from both online commentary on the newspaper and Twitter. They used five Arabic dialects ( Egyptian, Levantine, Gulf, Maghrebi and Iraqi). Sadat et al.(2014) presented a set of experiments of letter-based (n-gram) Markov language model and NB classifiers on social media. Experimental results showed that NB classifier using character-level bigram model can identify the 18 different Arabic dialects with a considerable accuracy. Malmasi & Zampieri (2016) described a system to identify of four regional Arabic dialects (Egyptian, Levantine, Gulf, North African) and Modern Standard Arabic (MSA) in a transcribed speech corpus as a DSL shared task. They used  ensemble classifier of set of linear models as base classifiers and they achieved a score of 0.51 in the closed training track. El-Haj et al. (2018) presented Subtractive Bivalency Profiling (SBP) for identification of four Arabic dialects( Egyptian, Levant , Gulf , and North African) as well as MSA where the accuracy were 76%. Mishra, & Mujadia (2019) explored the use of different features (char, word n-gram, language model probabilities, etc) on different classifiers for Arabic dialects identification. The work is part of Multi Arabic Dialect Applications and Resources (MADAR) Shared Task (Bouamor, et al.,2019) in WANLP 2019 on Arabic Fine-Grained Dialect Identification. They showed that traditional machine learning classifier tends to perform better when compared to neural network models in a low resource setting. Salameh et al. (2018) presented a fine-grained dialect classification task covering 25 specific cities from across the Arab World, in addition to Standard Arabic. They used several classification systems with large space of features. Their results show that the exact city of a speaker can be identified at an accuracy of 67.9%.

ADI, in our work, is achieved by (i) identifying Arabic language from other similar languages, (ii) identifying dialects from MSA & CA, and (iii) identifying dialects among 21 Arabic dialects. The final step is achieved by voting among three well-known and very different classifiers (NB, LR and DT) in two different methodologies. Also, because the used data is none golden standard, little steps of noisy removal are done.

## 3    Data set

The used data set is NADI Tweeter data set (Abdul-Mageed et al., 2020). It consists of three parts training part of 21,000 tweets, development part of 4957 Tweets and Test set of 5,000 tweets. It is not golden standard corpus and has different noise levels such as existing of 405 non-Arabic tweets (Kurdish and Persian). Also, this data set is mixed of DA, MSA and CA. therefore a noisy removal should be taken as preprocessing. The data sets are labeled in two levels; first level (country level) of 21 countries and second level (provinces level) of 100 provinces. Table 2 show the statistics of training data set **with /without** non-Arabic tweets.

## 4    Our system

Our system consist of five phases: (i) preprocessing, (ii) noisy tweets removal, (iii) formal clitics and stop words removal, (iv) features extraction and selection, and (v) the classification. Figure 1 explained the proposed method. They  will be explained in the next few sections.

| Country | # doc with non-Arabic | # doc without non-Arabic | Country | # doc with non-Arabic | # doc without non-Arabic |
|---|---|---|---|---|---|
| Algeria | 1491 | 1486 | Oman | 1098 | 1072 |
| Bahrain | 210 | 210 | Palestine | 420 | 420 |
| Djibouti | 210 | 210 | Qatar | 234 | 234 |
| Egypt | 4473 | 4471 | Saudi_Arabia | 2312 | 2306 |
| Iraq | 2556 | 2174 | Somalia | 210 | 210 |
| Jordan | 426 | 426 | Sudan | 210 | 210 |
| Kuwait | 420 | 420 | Syria | 1070 | 1067 |
| Lebanon | 639 | 639 | Tunisia | 750 | 748 |
| Libya | 1070 | 1070 | United_Arab_Emirates | 1070 | 1063 |
| Mauritania | 210 | 210 | Yemen | 851 | 781 |
| Morocco | 1070 | 1069 | **Totally** | 21,000 | 20,496 |

Table 2: statistics of training data set with and without non-Arabic tweets

### 4.1    Preprocessing

Preprocessing is a step used in almost all NLP applications. In this work, this stage consists of two main steps **noisy preprocessing**, and **non-Arabic letter removal**. The first step is done before **noisy tweets removal**, it is achieved by deleting English letters, special symbols, numbers, tweeter mark-up, Emoticons, repetition letters etc., and unification of letter variants (normalization). The second step of preprocessing is removing non-Arabic letters from Arabic tweets (only), it is applied after noisy tweets removal.

### 4.2    Noisy tweets removal

As was mentioned previously the data set has levels of errors such as foreign tweets and MSA. Approximately 504 tweets were recorded manually as non-Arabic tweets. These tweets and the others are used for learning the binary classifier in character-level and word-level for identifying the foreign languages such as Persian and Kurdish languages. From many tests, the best was unigram for word-level and bigram for character-level with Naïve Bayes classifier. In the classification step of development and test sets, we should see that all the classified tweets as foreign language will be classified as Iraq class because of the probability of being foreign as Iraq class is the highest (2556-2174)/504 ≈ 0.76, see table 2 for more details.

In case of dialects and non-dialects (CA & MSA), 2,000 tweets are classified manually from training set as DA or non-DA. Then these two types of tweets (2,000 tweets) are used as centers for two clusters. Kmean clustering was used for clustering the remaining tweets into the two clusters using Simisupervised clustering where the manually classified tweets will not be changed their clusters in the iterations of Kmean clustering but stay always in the specific cluster. The non-DA cluster is checked manually only because it was small and all the dialects tweets were removed. The final clusters, in our case are two classes, are used for leaning a binary classifier for using it in the identification of dialects from non-dialects. In the classification step of development and test sets, we should see that all the classified tweets as non-DA will be classified as Egypt dialects but it is bad selection therefore it will produce extra errors in the evaluation.

### 4.3    Formal clitics removal

The third phase is formal clitics removal such as "ال -Al"- (the), "وال-wAl"-(and the) and "ولل-wll"-(and for the) but not the letter "هـ" "h" in word "هألعب- hÂlҫb"-(I will play) because it is dialectal clitics in Egyptian dialects but not formal clitics (not in modern standard Arabic). Also, the stop words will be deleted in this stage but a very simple list of stop words is taken and they are tuned using the training set according to threshold. For example, the word "عننه- çnnh"-(about us) is dialect therefore it will be not deleted but the word "عنه- çnh"-(about us) will be deleted.

### 4.4  Feature selection

The fourth phase is feature selection which started by selecting the effective prefixes and suffixes of size of (1-4) letters according to their threshold and weights. Also, all the words (without formal clitics) are taken as features where their features are TF-IDF according to the equation below.

$$\text{IDF}_w = \log \left( \frac{\text{Number of classes}}{\textit{Number of classes that contain word } w} \right) \dots (11)$$

$$TFIDF_{w,i} = \text{TF}_{w,i} * \text{IDF}_w \dots (12)$$

Where $w$ represents the word and $i$ represents the class.

### 4.5  Classification

The last phase, the classification process, is achieved by voting among three well-known and very different classifiers (Naïve Bayes, Logistic Regression, and Decision Tree). The classification process is done using voting in two methodologies; the first is normal classification using 21 classes. The second methodology is done using binary classifiers where each one is learned from two classes, the first class represent one class of 21 classes and the second class represent the other 20 classes. For each tweet, there are 21 classification processes done for two classes ("specific country" or "others"). If all classifiers produce "others" class except one give country then this class (country) will be selected as the class for this tweets otherwise other classifier is will be used for classifying among the candidate countries only. For example suppose we try to classify tweet $t$, 18 classifiers gave[2] "others" and 3 classifiers gave Iraq, Kuwait and Qatar respectively then this tweet will be feed to other classifier that learned from training tweets of these 3 classes only and the output will be the final class. But if, in our example, 20 classifiers gave "others" and one gave "Iraq" then the class of the tweet $t$ will be Iraq directly without using extra classifier. If all the twenty one classifiers are classified the tweet $t$ as "other", then this tweet is unknown tweet and it will be classified as Egypt class because Egypt class has the highest probability among other classes. We should see that there is not any possibility for getting two appearance of one country from two classifiers because each classifier of 21 classifiers is used for one country.

## 5  Results

The system was implemented on NADI shared task data set (subtask 1). The results for identification of foreign tweets in development set were 0.985, 1 and 0.992 for precision, recall and f-measure respectively where the total foreign tweets were 132, as part of noisy tweets removal.
The classification results (official[3]) is 27.17 as f-measure for voting without using clustering. For voting with clustering (unofficial), the f-measure is 41.34. For voting (21 binary classifiers) with clustering, the f-measure is 52.38. all these percent's are for development data set. Table 3 shows the results for these three types of tests. Table 3 shows the summary of all tests results.
We should know that the foreign tweets are classified as Iraq and the MSA tweets are classified as Egypt for evaluation purpose which it in most cases cause dropdown in the scores. Aslo, unknown tweets in the last test are classified as Egypt class.

| Test type | Dev data set(F-measure) | Test Data set(F-measure) |
|---|---|---|
| voting without clustering | 27.17 | 12.45 |
| voting with clustering | 41.34 | 17.61 |
| voting (21 binary classifiers) with clustering | 52.38 | 20.05 |

Table 3: All classification tests results

---

[2] Each classifier is done using voting among three classifiers (NB, LR and DT)
[3] Official means that the results are sent to NADI shared task team before the deadline.

## 6    Discussion

In this paper, ADI is implemented and applied on NADI shared task dataset of very close 21 classes. The proposed system starts from removing noise till the classification process for 21 classes of all Arabic countries. Three classifiers were combined and used in two methodologies (one classifier for classification of 21 classes or using twenty one binary classifiers). Selecting the classes Iraq, Egypt and Egypt classes for Foreign, MSA and unknown tweets respectively dropped down the macro-average score but really foreign and MSA are noise. The results of classification were very low for many reasons: (i) existing of 504 non-Arabic tweets in training set, (ii) existing of MSA tweets which is used in all the Arabic countries result in high noise in learning phase, (iii) some dialects are close to each other's, (iv) existing of ambiguous tweets where it written as MSA but can be pronounced in many dialects, (v) existing of a city in a country that used dialect close to other country more than its country, (vi) the tweets were classified, in the data set, according to user location but not user dialect which produce errors in the classes of training set and hence the wrong learning.

The result of using twenty two binary classifiers with clustering (removing MSA from training data) gave us the best results because the system will focus on the dialect of each country in the training process without noise tweets.

## 7    Conclusions and future works

Arabic Dialects are native languages for each country or city in Arab world where sometimes the writing of dialects is same but the pronunciations are different.
We can see four levels of Arabic dialectal identification (ADI) from the easiest task to the most difficult task. The first level is identification of dialectal Arabic from the other two Arabic language varieties. The second level is identification of the main category of dialectal Arabic of (nine or five categories). The third level is identification of country level out of 21 countries. The fourth level is identification of city dialects or town dialects. There are many challenges in ADI according to the level number.
Simply we can conclude that ADI is a hard task for many reasons as was mentioned in discussion section. The task need to golden standard corpus and a dictionary for almost all words used in each dialect. The learning from low noise data set gives a good results but the task is still need to special learning techniques and huge dataset (golden standard).

## References


Itani. M. 2018 "*Sentiment analysis and resources for informal Arabic text on social media.*" PhD diss., Sheffield Hallam University.

El-Haj M., Ryson P., and Aboelezz M., 2018 "*Arabic Dialect Identification in the Context of Bivalency and Code-Switching,*" Eleventh international conference  on language Resources and Evaluation LREC 2018.

Belgacem, M., Antoniadis, G., & Besacier, L. 2010. *Automatic Identification of Arabic Dialects.* In LREC2010.

Darwish, K., Sajjad, H., & Mubarak, H., 2014. *Verifiably effective Arabic dialect identification.* In Proceedings of the 2014 Conference on Empirical Methods in Natural Language Processing (EMNLP) (pp. 1465-1468).

Elfardy, H., & Diab, M. (2013, August). *Sentence level dialect identification in Arabic.* In Proceedings of the 51st Annual Meeting of the Association for Computational Linguistics (Volume 2: Short Papers) (pp. 456-461).

Cotterell, R., & Callison-Burch, C. 2014. *A Multi-Dialect, Multi-Genre Corpus of Informal Written Arabic.* In LREC (pp. 241-245).

Sadat, F., Kazemi, F., & Farzindar, A. 2014. *Automatic identification of Arabic language varieties and dialects in social media.* In Proceedings of the Second Workshop on Natural Language Processing for Social Media (SocialNLP) (pp. 22-27).

Malmasi, S., & Zampieri, M. 2016. *Arabic dialect identification in speech transcripts.* In Proceedings of the Third Workshop on NLP for Similar Languages, Varieties and Dialects (VarDial3) (pp. 106-113).

Mishra, P., & Mujadia, V. 2019, *Arabic Dialect Identification for Travel and Twitter Text*. In Proceedings of the Fourth Arabic Natural Language Processing Workshop (pp. 234-238).

Bouamor, H., Hassan, S., & Habash, N. 2019. *"The MADAR shared task on Arabic fine-grained dialect identification*. In Proceedings of the Fourth Arabic Natural Language Processing Workshop (pp. 199-207).

Salameh, M., Bouamor, H., & Habash, N. 2018. *Fine-grained Arabic dialect identification*. In Proceedings of the 27th International Conference on Computational Linguistics (pp. 1332-1344).

Abdul-Mageed, Muhammad, Zhang, Chiyu, Bouamor, Houda and Habash, Nizar 2020 *"The Shared Task on Nuanced Arabic Dialect Identification (NADI)"*, Proceedings of the Fifth Arabic Natural Language Processing Workshop (WANLP2020), Barcelona, Spain

# Arabic Dialect Identification Using BERT Fine-Tuning


**Moataz Mansour**      **Moustafa Tohamy**      **Zeyad Ezzat**      **Marwan Torki**

Faculty of Engineering, Alexandria University
{moataz.mansour.07, moustafatohamy96, zeyad.3ezzat}@gmail.com,
mtorki@alexu.edu.eg


## Abstract


In the last few years, deep learning has proved to be a very effective paradigm to discover patterns in large data sets. Unfortunately, deep learning training on small data sets is not the best option because most of the time traditional machine learning algorithms could get better scores. Now, we can train the neural network on a large data set then fine-tune on a smaller data set using the transfer learning technique. In this paper, we present our system for NADI shared Task: Country-level Dialect Identification, Our system is based on fine-tuning of BERT and it achieves 22.85 F1-score on Test Set and our rank is 5th out of 18 teams.


## 1 Introduction

Arabic is a very complex language, a fast-growing one with more than 400 million speakers around the world. Online social media platforms (Twitter in our case) are a very good place where Arabic speakers can communicate, express, and share their thoughts. It will be very useful if we can study people's behavior so we can help them in various ways, and dialect identification is the first step to identify a given country to study the behavior of its people.

Text classification is considered an easy task, not because it is simple in general, but it is considered one of the oldest research areas in Natural Language Processing (NLP). If we have two classes separated with obvious features, it is a fairly simple process, but in our task, we have 21 classes with a lot of common features so it gets a lot more challenging. We will discuss that in the data section.

We have found that the MADAR Arabic Dialect Corpus and Lexicon (Bouamor et al., 2018) is a data set quite similar to the one provided in the task but instead of 21 labels for countries, there are 25 city labels. Top-ranked systems proposed by Abu Kwaik and Saad (2019) on the MADAR data set were built on traditional machine learning algorithms. In our first trial we have used n-gram TF-IDF characters and words features for train linear and nonlinear Support Vector Machine, Bernoulli Naive Bayes followed by ensembling all of the three aforementioned classifiers, we reached a score of 18.1 on the development set of NADI Shared Task (Abdul-Mageed et al., 2020). Our final model was built by fine-tuning a pre-trained Bidirectional Encoder Representations from Transformers (BERT) (Devlin et al., 2018). The original trained model provided from Safaya et al. (2020) and trained on around 95 gigabytes of Arabic text from different resources, all the parameters of training will be described in the system section.

## 2 Data

The data set was created for this shared task from organizers. The provided training data set consists of 21,000 tweets with 21 different labels representing 21 (Egypt, Bahrain, Iraq, Saudi_Arabia, Algeria, Oman, Syria, United_Arab_Emirates, Libya, Morocco, Yemen, Tunisia, Lebanon, Jordan, Kuwait, Palestine, Qatar, Mauritania, Djibouti, Somalia, Sudan).

For reporting results, there are 4,957 labeled tweets for development, 5,000 for testing, and an extra 10 million tweets for other purposes. We split training data into 19,950 tweets for training and 1,050 for validation so we can make use of most of the given data, for testing we have used development test.






*Proceedings of the Fifth Arabic Natural Language Processing Workshop*, pages 308–312
Barcelona, Spain (Online), December 12, 2020

A simple pre-processing function was used to remove links, punctuation, and repeated characters. We also tried removing directs but the performance was slightly better without removing them.

Looking into the data set distribution in Figure 1, we can notice that the data is totally imbalanced. For example, Egypt's tweets represent 21.3% of the data but Bahrain represents 0.01% of the data set. What makes the task even more challenging is the similarity between classes as the Gulf countries (Bahrain, Kuwait, Iraq, Oman, Qatar, Saudi Arabia, and the United Arab Emirates) have a very similar dialect. It is already hard for humans to differentiate between them and this data represents 37% of the data set.

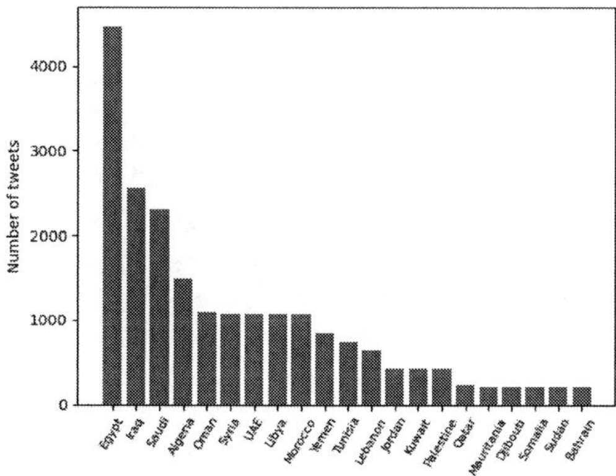

Figure 1: Training dataset labels distribution

## 3   Systems

In this section, we are going to introduce two systems with totally different approaches. The BERT system, which ranked as 5th in the leader board, and another system using feature extraction and ensemble of different Algorithms.

### 3.1   BERT System

BERT in its vanilla form is the English language model that can be used in different natural language processing tasks. It makes use of transformers which is an attention mechanism that tries to learn the contextual relations between words. We used a multilingual BERT (mBERT) base model with 12 hidden layers, 12 attention heads, 768 hidden layer size, and 110 million parameters. The Difference Between BERT and mBERT is that BERT is an English pre-trained language model but mBERT Provides pre-trained weights for Arabic and another 103 languages.

As mentioned earlier, we had used a pre-trained model and it was pre-trained on around 7.2 billion words from different resources such as the Arabic version of Oscar and recent Wikipedia Arabic articles. Our training process was divided into two phases: tuning the language model using 10 million tweets and then tuning using 19,950 tweets for the classification task.

**Language Model Training** : We have trained the model for one epoch on all unlabeled tweets, in the next section, we will provide more details about the training process. At first, we have truncated the long tweets and padded the shorter ones to get a 10-word length for all tweets. As described in Table 1, we had to add a drop out layer then linear layer mapping from the last hidden layer to vocabulary vectors After the BERT base model so we can do fine-tuning of it as a continuous bag of word model.

We have trained the model on 10 sessions and in each session, it was trained with 1 million tweets for one epoch. The training time for a session lasts around 12 hours as the optimizer used for training is Adam algorithm with weight decay (AdamW) with learning rate=2e-5, epsilon=1e-5, weight decay=0.001, and betas (0.9,0.999). All the training time was around 120 hours running on Azure virtual machine with a Tesla M60 GPU.

**Classification Training**: As described in table 1 We had to add a batch normalization, dropout, and linear layer mapping to classes. We had used the same optimizer, Adam, with decay with the same parameters as before. We used the weights after the language fine-tuning. We trained the model for 4 epochs, It takes around 1-hour training on GeForce RTX 2060 GPU.

| language model | classification |
|---|---|
| BERT Base model | BERT language model |
| Dropout layer with 0.1 drop_prop | Batch normalization with tanh activation function |
| linear layer | Dropout layer with 0.1 drop_prop |
| | Linear layer |

Table 1: Modified BERT Model architecture

### 3.2 Traditional Machine Learning

Deep learning consumes a lot of time in training, however, it saves a lot of time spent on feature extraction. Here we present our experiment of feature extraction and traditional models to solve the provided task.

**Feature Extraction**: we have used a combination of n-gram characters and unigram words of TF-IDF features.

- TF-IDF for unigram with max_df=0.05,min_df=0.0001 after removing stop words contained in natural language processing toolkit library in python(NLTK)

- (2, 9) character n-grams with respect to boundaries, using sublinear transformation and maximum number of feature =40,000 (twice)

  These features have been chosen empirically after a lot of different trials.

**Models**: These three models have been chosen and ensemble in a voting classifier with equal weights.

- One vs one linear Support Vector Machine and balanced class weights

- One vs one non-linear Support Vector Machine with RBF kernel function and balanced class weights

- Bernoulli Naive Bayes with alpha 0.1

## 4 Results and discussion

For the task, we have built several systems to achieve the models described above. A comparison between the results described in Table 2 illustrates different ways used that helped us find the best solution that suits the task. Non-deep learning models with different features have a very similar performance. We tried different character n-grams with and without respect to boundaries. TF-IDF word features are not the best for this task and increasing the n-grams most of the time decreases the performance. BERT model without fine-tuning of the language model is still very powerful just by adding a classification layer and after one hour of training, it reaches a 23.5 F1 score. The only way we found to increase the performance is by using the extra unlabeled tweets because it is closer to the tweets from Wikipedia articles which our pre-trained model provided from Safaya et al. (2020) originally trained on.

By looking at the confusion matrix for BERT with fine-tuning of language model in Figure 2, we can notice the consequences of class imbalance and overlapping of the features. The most obvious one is in the gulf countries mentioned before, we can observe that the model predicted most of them as Saudi Arabia and did not predict any of Bahrain correctly.

---

Source code: `https://github.com/zeyad3ezzat/Nadi-Shared-Task`.

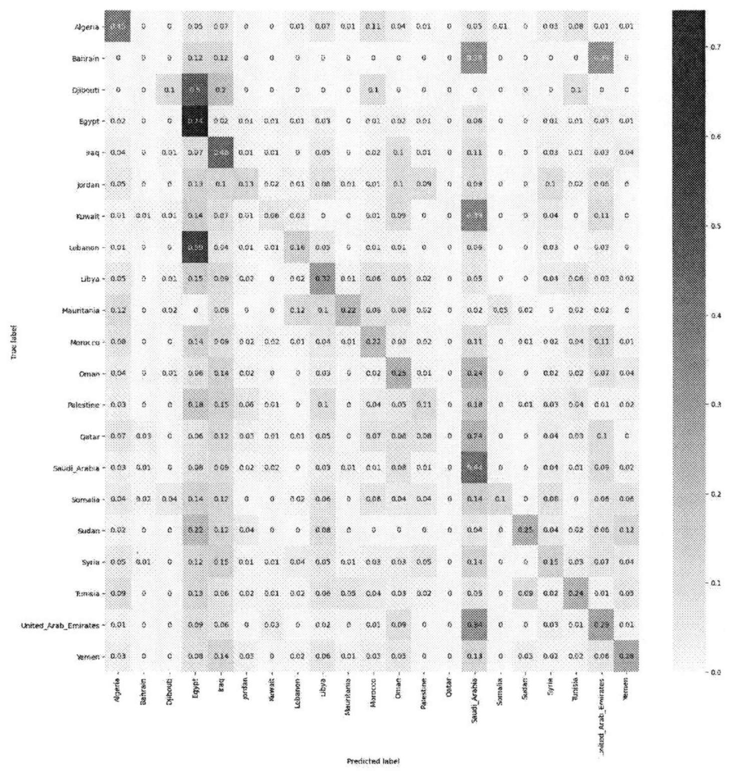

Figure 2: Confusion matrix of development set predictions

| Models | Features | | F1 score |
|---|---|---|---|
| | char_wb | word | |
| Non-linear SVM | (2,9) | | 17.1 |
| Non-linear SVM | | unigram | 13.1 |
| Non-linear SVM | (2,9) | unigram | 17.2 |
| Linear SVM | (2,9) | unigram | 16.3 |
| Bernolli NB | (2,9) | unigram | 16.0 |
| Voting classifier | (2,9) | unigram | **18.1** |
| | Deep Learning | | |
| BERT | Without fine-tuning of language model | | **23.5** |
| BERT | With fine-tuning of language model | | **24.05** |

Table 2: F1 Score of different models on development set

We could make use of the similarity between classes by combining similar dialects in a hierarchical classification approach. for example, a first classification level may be classified into(sham, gulf, Nile, others). The second level will be the normal 21 labels.

## 5   Conclusion

This paper described two methods applied to NADI shared sub-task 1 to predict an Arabic dialect from tweets. Our experiments show to show that the BERT model achieved the best F1 score betting other machine learning models. Using the unlabeled tweets to fine-tuning the language model is a great way to increase the performance but needs a lot of time and computation power. We had achieved a relatively high f1 score of 24.05 on the development set and 22.85 on the test set.

## References

Muhammad Abdul-Mageed, Chiyu Zhang, Houda Bouamor, and Nizar Habash. 2020. NADI 2020: The First Nuanced Arabic Dialect Identification Shared Task. In *Proceedings of the Fifth Arabic Natural Language Processing Workshop (WANLP 2020)*, Barcelona, Spain.

Kathrein Abu Kwaik and Motaz Saad. 2019. ArbDialectID at MADAR shared task 1: Language modelling and ensemble learning for fine grained Arabic dialect identification. In *Proceedings of the Fourth Arabic Natural Language Processing Workshop*, pages 254–258, Florence, Italy, August. Association for Computational Linguistics.

Houda Bouamor, Nizar Habash, Mohammad Salameh, Wajdi Zaghouani, Owen Rambow, Dana Abdulrahim, Ossama Obeid, Salam Khalifa, Fadhl Eryani, Alexander Erdmann, and Kemal Oflazer. 2018. The MADAR Arabic dialect corpus and lexicon. In *Proceedings of the Eleventh International Conference on Language Resources and Evaluation (LREC 2018)*, Miyazaki, Japan, May. European Language Resources Association (ELRA).

Jacob Devlin, Ming-Wei Chang, Kenton Lee, and Kristina Toutanova. 2018. BERT: pre-training of deep bidirectional transformers for language understanding. *CoRR*, abs/1810.04805.

Ali Safaya, Moutasem Abdullatif, and Deniz Yuret. 2020. Kuisail at semeval-2020 task 12: Bert-cnn for offensive speech identification in social media. In *Proceedings of the International Workshop on Semantic Evaluation (SemEval)*.

# LTG-ST at NADI Shared Task 1:
## Arabic Dialect Identification using a Stacking Classifier


**Samia Touileb**
Language Technology Group
University of Oslo
Norway
`samiat@ifi.uio.no`


## Abstract


This paper presents our results for the Nuanced Arabic Dialect Identification (NADI) shared task of the Fifth Workshop for Arabic Natural Language Processing (WANLP 2020). We participated in the first sub-task for country-level Arabic dialect identification covering 21 Arab countries. Our contribution is based on a stacking classifier using Multinomial Naive Bayes, Linear SVC, and Logistic Regression classifiers as estimators; followed by a Logistic Regression as final estimator. Despite the fact that the results on the test set were low, with a macro F1 of 17.71, we were able to show that a simple approach can achieve comparable results to more sophisticated solutions. Moreover, the insights of our error analysis, and of the corpus content in general, can be used to develop and improve future systems.


## 1 Introduction

Most resources for Arabic have been developed for Modern Standard Arabic (MSA) since it is the official language in most Arabic speaking countries. MSA is used in media coverage, politics, books, and even online. However, in each individual Arabic country, the predominant language used for everyday conversation (in real life and online) is a specific dialect for that region or country (Versteegh, 2014).

Arabic dialects are not standardized. There are no formal grammar rules nor formalism to guide the speakers (Zaidan and Callison-Burch, 2014). There are some efforts on creating standards for automatically processing such dialects (Habash et al., 2018), but the language use remains non-standardized. Within one same city, people can pronounce and write the same word differently. This aspect accentuates the difficulty of automatically processing such languages, and automatically distinguishing them from each other is as challenging, since no clear structure exists. Nevertheless, many attempts have been made for Arabic dialect identification. Despite the difficulty of the task, there are still syntactic and morphological aspects of the languages that can be exploited to differentiate them from each other.

Most works rely on machine learning approaches, and span various levels of accuracy depending on the dataset used and dialects being processed. The nearer (geographically) the countries are to each other, the more similar the spoken language, and therefore the more difficult it is to automatically distinguish the dialects (Bouamor et al., 2019).

The Multi Arabic Dialect Applications and Resources (MADAR) corpus (Bouamor et al., 2018) is an important resource for Arabic dialect identification. The corpus covers parallel sentences written in 25 Arabic city dialects from the travel domain. This corpus has been used in a shared task (Bouamor et al., 2019) for both fine-grained (26 dialects) and coarse-grained (6 dialects) Arabic dialect identification where various machine learning approaches have been used. A simple Mulitnomial Naive Bayes (MNB) has shown to be very powerful in the identification of the exact city of 26 dialects from the MADAR corpus with an accuracy of 67.9%, using as features character and word 5-grams language models and the output of the coarse-grained classifier (Salameh et al., 2018). Other approaches also focused on the use of machine learning and ensemble methods, using as features word counts, language models, and embeddings (Abu Kwaik and Saad, 2019; Meftouh et al., 2019; Ragab et al., 2019; Fares et al., 2019).






*Proceedings of the Fifth Arabic Natural Language Processing Workshop*, pages 313–319
Barcelona, Spain (Online), December 12, 2020

|       | # Tweets | # Tokens |
| ----- | -------- | -------- |
| train | 21,000   | 270,574  |
| dev   | 4,957    | 60,700   |
| test  | 5,000    | 64,458   |

Table 1: Number of tweets and total number of tokens excluding punctuation in the three splits.

In this paper, we present our participation in the Nuanced Arabic Dialect Identification (NADI) shared task (Abdul-Mageed et al., 2020). We participated in the first sub-task aiming at country-level Arabic dialect identification from tweets covering 21 Arab countries. Our contribution is based on a stacking classifier using Multinomial Naive Bayes, Linear SVC, and Logistic Regression classifiers as estimators; and Logistic Regression as final estimator.

We have experimented with various architectures, from traditional machine learning approaches as the approach presented in this paper and clustering, but also with more recent approaches as Bi-LSTMS and CNNs. We have also experimented using unlabeled tweets (provided by the shared task organizers) to train embeddings and language models. However, none of these architectures gave satisfying results.

In Section 2 we describe the NADI tweet corpus. We present our proposed model in Section 3, and describe our results and give an overall discussion of the results in Section 4. Finally, we conclude in Section 5 and discuss possible future work.

## 2   Data

We used the NADI corpus provided by the shared task organizers (Abdul-Mageed et al., 2020). The corpus comprises 21,000 tweets covering 21 Arab countries for the first sub-task, and 100 provinces from the same Arab countries (as sub-task 1) in the second sub-task. In the following, we will only focus on the data set for the country-level classification. Each tweet in the corpus is annotated with its associated country (i.e. dialect) label. Table 1 gives an overview of the size of the corpus in the three splits (train, dev, and test) in terms of number of tweets (size of data), and the total number of tokens excluding punctuation.

The dialects of the following countries are included in the NADI corpus: Algeria, Bahrain, Djibouti, Egypt, Iraq, Jordan, Kuwait, Lebanon, Libya, Mauritania, Morocco, Oman, Palestine, Qatar, Saudi Arabia, Somalia, Sudan, Syria, Tunisia, United Arab Emirates, and Yemen. Despite the relatively large amount of tweets used for training, the corpus is extremely unbalanced, which we believe has made this task even more difficult. As can be seen in Figure 1, the Egyptian dialect on it's own represents more than 21% of the training data, while the dialects from Djibouti, Bahrain, Sudan, Mauritania, and Somalia only represent 1% of the training data.

A further analysis of the corpus also showed that for all dialects except Egypt and Iraq, most of the word types were not representative of the language. Most vocabulary items are shared between dialects, which might confuse any classification system. In Figure 2 we show that the lightest (at the bottom) color represents the normalized number of unique words for each dialect. The color in the middle represents the normalized number of words shared between each dialect and up to four other dialects. The darkest color (at the top) represents the normalized number of words shared between each dialect with more than four other dialects.

From Figure 2 it is evident that 58% of the word types in the Egyptian and Iraqi tweets are unique to these dialects. However, for the remaining 19 dialects, over 50% of the word types were shared with other dialects. Our preliminary investigations have shown that many of these shared vocabulary items were actually MSA words. It is important to note that many dialectal words are shared with MSA.

For example the words شعور، أعتقد، مدريد، أجمل، النادي، عمرك، الفرح، يدخل respectively *enters, joy, your age, the club, more beautiful, Madrid, I believe, feelings* in English, were shared by more than 10 dialects. Another example is the word هُناك (*there*) which in the corpus is uniquely present in tweets labeled as Libyan, actually exists also in other forms in the corpus. When written هناكَ, it is only present

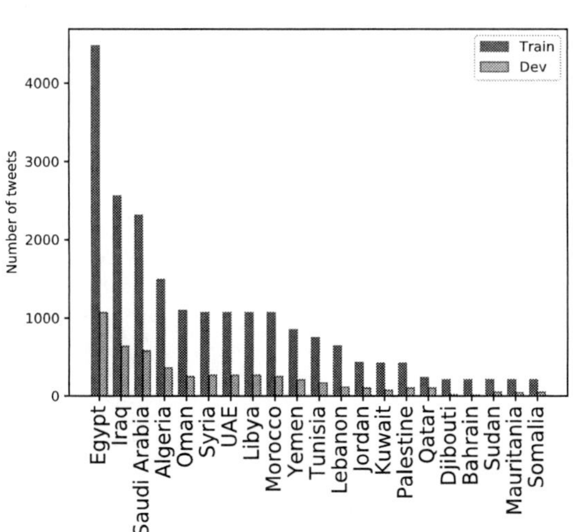

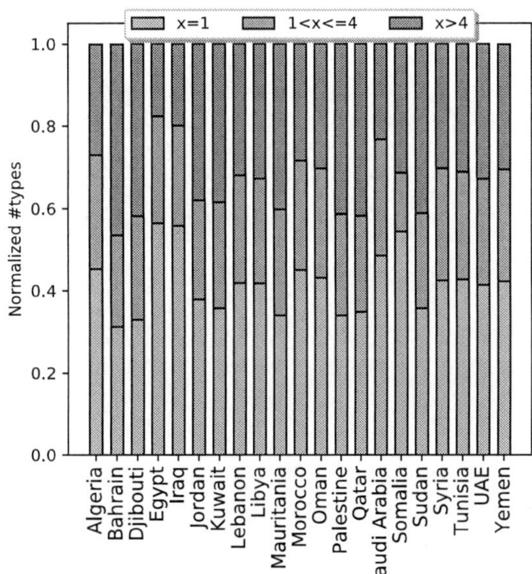

Figure 1: Number of tweets per dialect in both train and dev splits. This shows a very skewed distribution and the predominance of the Egyptian dialect in the data set.

Figure 2: Normalized number of word types in each dialect. The lightest color represents unique words to each vocabulary. The color in the middle represents words shared with one to four other dialects, and the darkest color represents words shared with more than four other dialects.

in tweets from Iraq and Morocco, while when written in its most basic form without vowels, هناك, it is present in tweets labeled with the 17 dialects from Algeria, Djibouti, Egypt, Iraq, Jordan, Lebanon, Libya, Morocco, Oman, Qatar, Saudi Arabia, Somalia, Sudan, Syria, Tunisia, United Arab Emirates, and Yemen. This also plays a role in the difficulty of the task. As most dialects share their vocabulary, the words distinguishing them from each others might actually not be that different from common shared words. Therefore distinguishing the dialects from each other gets more challenging.

## 3 System

Our model, as shown in Figure 3, is based on a stacking classifier. We first train three different models on the NADI train split, and use their respective predictions to train a final estimator to get our final predictions. Stacking allows us to use the strengths of each individual classifier by using their output as input of a final estimator. All of the experiments are implemented using Python and the `scikitlearn` library (Pedregosa et al., 2011).

Our model classifies tweets into the NADI 21 dialects. It uses a combination of word and character n-grams and skipgrams concatenated using Feature Union estimator in sklearn. We give different weights to each feature vector, which were selected after a thorough analysis by experimenting with various possible weights (and combination of weights) using grid search. We used the following features:

- TF-IDF vectors of word bi-grams, with a vector weight of 0.5.

- TF-IDF vectors of character n-grams in the range (2,5) when using word boundaries, with a vector weight of 0.5.

- TF-IDF vectors of character n-grams in the range (3,5), with a vector weight of 0.5.

- TF-IDF vectors of skip grams with both one word or one character skipping. The weight for the vector transformation for both these features was set to 0.3.

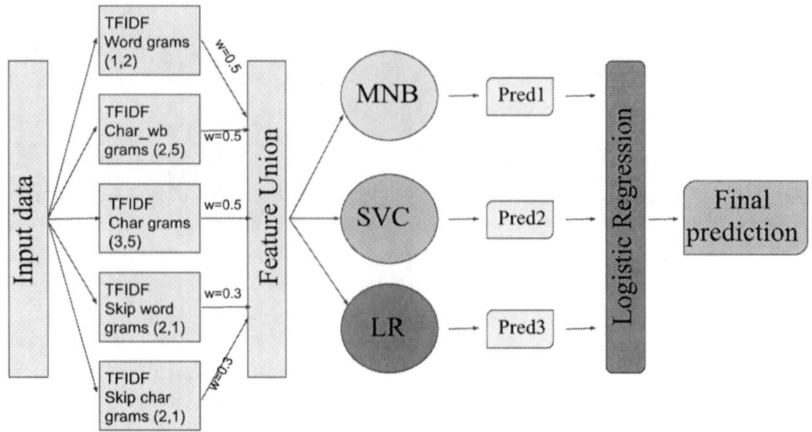


Figure 3: Model architecture. Our model is a stacking classifier. First, three different classifiers are trained on the NADI train split. Their respective predictions are thereafter used with a final estimator to get final predictions.

|  | dev | test |
|---|---|---|
| Macro average F1 | 17.87 | 17.71 |
| Overall accuracy | 37.26 | 36.22 |

Table 2: Accuracy and macro average F1 for both dev and test split.

Thereafter, we use these feature vectors to train three different classifiers:

- a Multinomial Naive Bayes (MNB) with alpha set to 0.004.

- a Support Vector Classification (SVC) using `hinge` loss with a tolerance for stopping criterion of 0.9.

- a Logistic Regressor (LR) with a `liblinear` solver.

The predictions of these classifiers are thereafter stacked and fed to a final classifier, in our case, a Logistic Regression using a tolerance for stopping criterion equal to 0.01 and `hinge` loss. As shown in Figure 3, the classifiers MNB, SVC, and LR are fitted on the full feature vector sets, while our final LR estimator is trained using cross-validated predictions of the three base estimators MNB, SVC, and LR.

## 4 Results and Discussion

We report in Table 2 our model's scores on both dev and test splits using the macro F1-score and accuracy metrics. Both metrics give very low scores, which reflect the difficulty of the task.

We believe that the main issue is the unbalanced nature of the dataset. We have experimented with various approaches to boost the performance. We used oversampling and under-sampling, as well as balanced sampling, but none of these gave satisfying results.

As can be seen in Figure 4 our model achieves high scores when predicting the Egyptian, Saudi Arabian, Algerian, and Iraqi dialects. From the confusion matrix it is also apparent that most dialects were miss-classified as these four dialects. We believe that these are partly due to the amount of tweets of each dialect present in the training set, as these represent the top four most frequent dialects in the train set (see Figure 1). To support this hypothesis, we trained our model only on tweets from these four dialects and achieved an F1-score of over 60%.

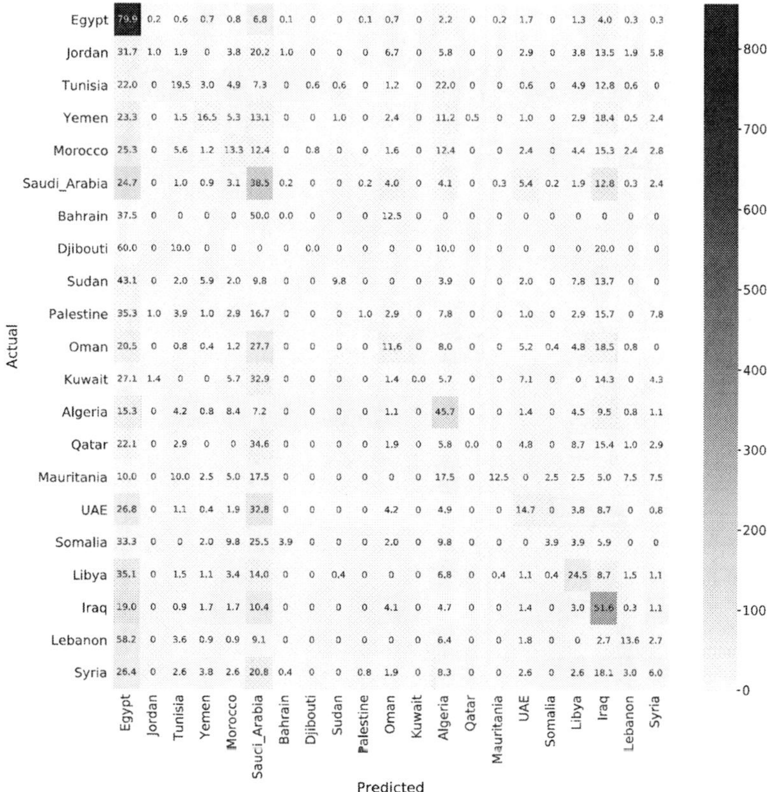

Figure 4: Confusion matrix of our model on the dev data set.

Further analysis of the output have shown that our model performs very poorly on the less frequent dialects. Our model is not able to correctly predict the dialects Qatar, Bahrain, Djibouti, and Kuwait. Once again, we believe that this is due to the skewed nature of the data. But also, the difficulty to differentiate between the dialects in general. The individual precision and recall scores (see Table 3) for each dialect also show that while our model performs poorly on these infrequent dialects, we achieve relatively high precision scores on them. This means that our model predicts very few examples of these dialects, but most of the predicted labels are correct.

A better performing system would have performed on the entire data set as our system performs on the Egyptian dialect: with high precision and high recall. A model that returns multiple predictions, with most predictions correctly labeled. We think that such a system might require a more diversified data set, with less overlap in the vocabulary.

Moreover, a close analysis of the tweets themselves revealed that many tweets labeled as dialects were actually written in (mostly) MSA, which we believe could have further skewed the classifications. As an example, consider the sentences (1) and (2). These are labelled as Algerian in the training data, despite being both written in MSA. We did not carry an exhaustive analysis on the amount of tweets that actually were written in MSA despite being labeled as Algerian, but from our preliminary analysis, it seems that many were either completely written in MSA, or mostly used MSA words. This might be partly due to which region the person tweeting is from, as people from different regions and backgrounds might prefer to write in MSA, or prefer to reach a broader international audience.

Admittedly, these sentences are generic and could in theory be present in all dialects. But it is exactly these type of sentences that can complicate the classification task. Social media platforms can be a gold mine for Arabic dialect identification, and having these type of sentences in a corpus is inevitable. We nevertheless believe that filtering these out, or even classifying them as MSA, might increase the performance of dialect identification systems.

| Label | Precision | Recall | F1 |
| --- | --- | --- | --- |
| Lebanon | 28.30% | 13.64% | 18.40% |
| Iraq | 41.57% | **51.57%** | **46.04%** |
| Sudan | **55.56%** | 9.80% | 16.67% |
| Yemen | 37.36% | 16.50% | 22.90% |
| Qatar | 0.00% | 0.00% | 0.00% |
| Saudi Arabia | 26.48% | 38.51% | 31.39% |
| Morocco | 20.12% | 13.25% | 15.98% |
| Kuwait | 0.00% | 0.00% | 0.00% |
| Mauritania | **50.00%** | 12.50% | 20.00% |
| Tunisia | 27.35% | 19.51% | 22.78% |
| Libya | 32.18% | 24.53% | 27.84% |
| Palestine | 20.00% | 0.98% | 1.87% |
| Syria | 18.39% | 6.04% | 9.09% |
| Djibouti | 0.00% | 0.00% | 0.00% |
| Somalia | 33.33% | 3.92% | 7.02% |
| United Arab Emirates | 25.83% | 14.72% | 18.75% |
| Bahrain | 0.00% | 0.00% | 0.00% |
| Algeria | 36.36% | **45.68%** | **40.49%** |
| Egypt | **46.64%** | 79.91% | **58.90%** |
| Oman | 21.97% | 11.65% | 15.22% |
| Jordan | 20.00% | 0.96% | 1.83% |

Table 3: Individual dialect precision, recall, and F1 scores. Values presented in bold are top three values for each measure.

(1)  a. مساء الخير والسرور والورود اختي الكريمة

b. Good evening, with pleasures and roses, my dear sister.

(2)  a. عيد ميلاد سعيد كل عام وانت بألف خير

b. Happy birthday, I hope that you will have a great and healthy year.

## 5 Conclusion

We proposed a model for automatically classifying 21 Arabic dialects using a corpus of tweets. Our system uses a stacking classifier relying on TF-IDF word and character features, and the three classifiers Multinomial Naive Bayes, Linear SVC, and Logistic Regression.

Our model did not achieve high scores on all dialects, but we believe that it shows that simple approaches can achieve satisfying results even when using heavily unbalanced data. We have experimented with more advanced deep learning approaches, but were not able to achieve satisfying results. We also believe that the poor results achieved reflect the data we have used. The heavy unbalance in the data has added an extra layer of difficulties to the task of dialect identification and we think that more balanced data can help us develop better models that can achieve higher accuracy.

However, the insights we have gained during the analysis of the train and dev data sets and our results, have enabled us to understand more what are the typical issues encountered during Arabic dialect identification, and we believe that these insights can be used to develop and improve future systems. We think that a more systematic approach based on contextualized word embeddings as BERT (Devlin et al., 2018) combined with sequence labeling approaches can give better results and achieve higher scores, and aim to go in this direction in future work.

## References

Muhammad Abdul-Mageed, Chiyu Zhang, Houda Bouamor, and Nizar Habash. 2020. NADI 2020: The First Nuanced Arabic Dialect Identification Shared Task. In *Proceedings of the Fifth Arabic Natural Language Processing Workshop (WANLP 2020)*, Barcelona, Spain.

Kathrein Abu Kwaik and Motaz K Saad. 2019. Arbdialectid at madar shared task 1: Language modelling and ensemble learning for fine grained arabic dialect identification. *ArbDialectID at MADAR Shared Task 1: Language Modelling and Ensemble Learning for Fine Grained Arabic Dialect Identification*, (Proceedings of the Fourth Arabic Natural Language Processing Workshop).

Houda Bouamor, Nizar Habash, Mohammad Salameh, Wajdi Zaghouani, Owen Rambow, Dana Abdulrahim, Ossama Obeid, Salam Khalifa, Fadhl Eryani, Alexander Erdmann, et al. 2018. The madar arabic dialect corpus and lexicon. In *Proceedings of the Eleventh International Conference on Language Resources and Evaluation (LREC 2018)*.

Houda Bouamor, Sabit Hassan, and Nizar Habash. 2019. The madar shared task on arabic fine-grained dialect identification. In *Proceedings of the Fourth Arabic Natural Language Processing Workshop*, pages 199–207.

Jacob Devlin, Ming-Wei Chang, Kenton Lee, and Kristina Toutanova. 2018. Bert: Pre-training of deep bidirectional transformers for language understanding. *arXiv preprint arXiv:1810.04805*.

Youssef Fares, Zeyad El-Zanaty, Kareem Abdel-Salam, Muhammed Ezzeldin, Aliaa Mohamed, Karim El-Awaad, and Marwan Torki. 2019. Arabic dialect identification with deep learning and hybrid frequency based features. In *Proceedings of the Fourth Arabic Natural Language Processing Workshop*, pages 224–228.

Nizar Habash, Fadhl Eryani, Salam Khalifa, Owen Rambow, Dana Abdulrahim, Alexander Erdmann, Reem Faraj, Wajdi Zaghouani, Houda Bouamor, Nasser Zalmout, et al. 2018. Unified guidelines and resources for arabic dialect orthography. In *Proceedings of the Eleventh International Conference on Language Resources and Evaluation (LREC 2018)*.

Karima Meftouh, Karima Abidi, Salima Harrat, and Kamel Smaili. 2019. The SMarT Classifier for Ara-bic Fine-Grained Dialect Identification. In *Proceedings of the Fourth Arabic Natural Language Processing Workshop (WANLP 2019)*, Florence, Italy.

F. Pedregosa, G. Varoquaux, A. Gramfort, V. Michel, B. Thirion, O. Grisel, M. Blondel, P. Prettenhofer, R. Weiss, V. Dubourg, J. Vanderplas, A. Passos, D. Cournapeau, M. Brucher, M. Perrot, and E. Duchesnay. 2011. Scikit-learn: Machine learning in Python. *Journal of Machine Learning Research*, 12:2825–2830.

Ahmad Ragab, Haitham Seelawi, Mostafa Samir, Abdelrahman Mattar, Hesham Al-Bataineh, Mohammad Zaghloul, Ahmad Mustafa, Bashar Talafha, Abed Alhakim Freihat, and Hussein Al-Natsheh. 2019. Mawdoo3 ai at madar shared task: Arabic fine-grained dialect identification with ensemble learning. In *Proceedings of the Fourth Arabic Natural Language Processing Workshop*, pages 244–248.

Mohammad Salameh, Houda Bouamor, and Nizar Habash. 2018. Fine-grained arabic dialect identification. In *Proceedings of the 27th International Conference on Computational Linguistics*, pages 1332–1344.

Kees Versteegh. 2014. *Arabic language*. Edinburgh University Press.

Omar F Zaidan and Chris Callison-Burch. 2014. Arabic dialect identification. *Computational Linguistics*, 40(1):171–202.

**Association for Computational Linguistics**
209 N. Eighth Street
Stroudsburg, Pennsylvania 18360

ISBN 978-1-7138-2843-3